I0800767

Czechoslovak Armored Fighting Vehicles 1918-1948

Czechoslovak Armored Fighting Vehicles 1918-1948

Charles K. Kliment & Vladimír Francev

Schiffer Military/Aviation History
Atglen, PA

ACKNOWLEDGEMENTS

The authors wish to thank Tom Jentz for providing the wartime unit assignment and manufacturing changes data for the Jagdpanzer 38(t), Charles Kliment Jr. for computer rendering of the camouflage schemes, and Jiří Tintěra (Prague Difrology Club) for his help with manuscript revision. Special thanks to Hilary Louis Doyle for his kind permission to use his excellent drawings of wartime and Hungarian vehicles.

Photographs, aside from the authors' collections, were provided by ČKD and Škoda archives, by Bundesarchiv, the former Slovak State News Agency, the Swedish Armour Association and by private collections of Ivan Bajtoš, Dénes Bernád (Romanian and Bulgarian armor), Jaroslav Janečka, Břetislav Nakládal and Terry Johns.

Book Design by Ian Robertson.

Copyright 1997 by Charles K. Kliment & Vladimir Francev.
Library of Congress Catalog Number: 96-

All rights reserved. No part of this work may be reproduced or used in any forms or by any means – graphic, electronic or mechanical, including photocopying or information storage and retrieval systems – without written permission from the copyright holder.

Printed in China.
ISBN: 0-7643-0141-1

We are interested in hearing from authors with book ideas on related topics.

Published by Schiffer Publishing Ltd.
77 Lower Valley Road
Atglen, PA 19310
Phone: (610) 593-1777
FAX: (610) 593-2002
Please write for a free catalog.
This book may be purchased from the publisher.
Please include $2.95 postage.
Try your bookstore first.

Contents

LIST OF TABLES

PREFACE

Considering the important part that Czech armor played in World War Two it is hard to understand why it took so long to finally publish a definitive work in English covering its history and development. As always, it was overshadowed by the innate interest shown in German armor, and its early adoption of Czech armor into their own Panzer divisions.

I first met Charles Kliment in Buffalo, New York in 1965, and even with the slight communication barriers at that time it was obvious that here was someone who was deadly serious about his research. Over the years we published numerous articles from him, each of which broke new and uncharted ground with respect to the development of Czechoslovak military vehicles and their deployment. All this has now come together as a magnificent history of their achievements.

Even the occupying German military acknowledged the high quality of the Czech armament industry when they immediately integrated much of the confiscated weaponry into their own forces. Throughout World War Two renowned companies like Škoda and ČKD were in full production supplying a full range of equipment, including new tanks, the famous "eighty-eight" multipurpose gun, and finally the unique Hetzer series.

Many of the photographs will speak for themselves, but the dedication by the authors devoted to unearthing them and finally presenting them in this work will never be fully appreciated. A lifetime of research in company files and private collections has all come together here. We have all had a glimpse of the more prominent Czech tanks and the popular 38(t) chassis adopted for so many of the German self-propelled gun carriages, but beyond that the real story of the Czech armaments industry has been largely neglected until now.

The authors have thoroughly researched even the most detailed aspects of vehicle production and proper designation of what seems to be every piece of Czech military equipment ever produced. Production quantities, serial numbers, allocation, service, camouflage, numbering, all have been documented in a concise and understandable way. Postwar coverage follows these designs into the cold war period under Soviet domination and their incorporation into the modern Czechoslovak army.

Finally, we all owe a debt of gratitude to the authors for such diligent work, and the mere fact that they were able to acquire and save for the future generations the full record of this important phase of military history.

George R. Bradford
Editor, AFV News

1

INTRODUCTION

Czechoslovakia and its neighbors, 1918-1938.

FORMATION OF THE CZECHOSLOVAK REPUBLIC

The Czechs, Moravians and the Slovaks are all western Slavs, like the Poles. The Czechs and the Moravians were living together in their own kingdom, which grew in power and importance. It reached its zenith in the fourteenth century under Charles IV, who was simultaneously the King of Bohemia and the Roman Emperor. The Slovaks were made part of the Hungarian kingdom in the tenth century.

The Bohemian kingdom practically ceased to exist after 1620, when the Habsburgs defeated the Czech armies and annexed the Czech lands to their empire. Thus, the Czechs were united with the Slovaks in one state, since Hungary was also a part of the Austrian Empire. Hungary, nevertheless, had a vastly different status in the empire than the Czech Lands, which were treated as mere colonies and were brutally Germanized and Catholicized. Hungary was treated more as a partner, and became a real one when the Austro-Hungarian Empire was proclaimed in 1867.

The European revolutionary upheavals in 1848 brought a new fervor to the oppressed nationalities of the Austro-Hungarian empire as well. In the Czech Lands, a nationalistic revival started with the purification and de-Germanization of the language, revival of Czech literature and later science, and gradual clamoring for more autonomy and political power. The Czech nationalists were also seeking contacts with their Slovak counterparts, who had a much harder task before them, as they were fewer in number and had to deal with a largely apathetic and subdued population.

At the beginning of the twentieth century, the situation in the two countries was quite different The Czech lands prospered economically and became the industrial center of the Empire. The revival of the Czech language and culture was complete, and the nation had again a strong sense of identity. Moreover, economic developments created a strong middle class and a wealthy class of industrialists, which acted as a counterbalance to the mostly German nobility. In the countryside, there was a strong and nationalistically inclined class of free, wealthy farmers. The political pressure for greater autonomy was intensifying both at home and in Vienna, though at this time the Czech politicians viewed themselves as a part of the Empire and had no plans to leave it.

The First World War changed quite a few things, including people's opinions. Neither nation accepted it as their war and the conscripts detested fighting for the Empire, which they at this time saw as a clear oppressor of their peoples and lands. The economic rape of the Czech Lands was also quite unacceptable, as raw materials and especially agricultural products were mercilessly plundered and shipped to Austria, while in the latter part of the war the Czech Lands experienced famine and severe shortages. These grievances contributed to the realization that continuing an existence within the Empire was politically and economically no longer acceptable or even feasible, and that in the end the Czech Lands and Slovakia had to work for their own independence.

They were helped in this quest by two lucky breaks. First, they had abroad a team of extremely capable and dedicated politicians in the persons of Tomáš Masaryk, Milan Štefánik and Eduard Beneš. Second, the general mood of the Allies was sympathetic to the various nations' aspirations to independence, and American President Woodrow Wilson's Fourteen Points gave these aspirations their final expression and seal of approval.

Tomáš Garrique Masaryk (he used Garrique to honor his American wife) was a philosopher, writer, university professor, journalist and politician of extraordinary vision, intelligence and integrity. He saw before all the other Czech politicians that a total break with the Austro-Hungarian Empire would be necessary, and worked to this end tirelessly during the whole war.

He was ably assisted by Eduard Beneš, who was a very skilled diplomat. While Masaryk was born in Moravia and Beneš was a Czech, the third member of this troika was a Slovak. Milan Rastislav Štefánik studied in France and became a French citizen. He was an astronomer and traveled widely before the war. During the war, he joined the French Air Force and distinguished himself as a pilot. His main asset was his extraordinary capability to reach all the influential circles of the French political and military establishment and to persuade them of the justness of the Czecho-Slovak aspirations. The French originally envisaged a formation of the "United States of Danube", but at a meeting between Masaryk, Štefánik, Dr. Blondel and the French President Deschanel in February 1916, the question of a free Czecho-Slovak state was raised for the first time.

Masaryk developed a good rapport with President Wilson, who was also an intellectual, a former university professor and an idealist, and secured his help. On January 22, 1917, President Wilson gave his historic speech before the joint houses of Congress about the right of every nation to form its own government. Thus, the Czecho-Slovaks had by the end of the war on their side both the French and the Americans. The English, though not exactly enthusiastic in their support, were at least not raising objections. Masaryk, Beneš and Štefánik formed the Czecho-Slovak Council, which was accepted by the Allies as a de facto government in exile. They were in contact with the leading politicians at home through various channels, and were coordinating their actions with them.

In late 1917 and early 1918, it was becoming increasingly clear to Emperor Charles of Austria and his government that the Empire was disintegrating and that the Allies, whose victory was no longer in any doubt, would help to bring this about. The Czech Lands now received from Vienna proposals for full autonomy in the framework of a federated Empire, something that they would have accepted eagerly a mere year earlier. Now it was too late, and the message from the Czecho-Slovak Council was loud and clear: do not accept any agreements with Vienna, as it will only complicate matters at the peace conference! Also, the proposal did not include the Slovaks, since the Hungarians were not as eager to grant them autonomy. It took them longer to realize that they also would be treated as a defeated nation and would be forced to grant many concessions.

There were several delicate points complicating matters even before the end of the war and the total disintegration of the Empire. One was the presence of a strong German minority in the Czech Lands, especially in Bohemia. The German colonists have been invited in by the Bohemian kings as early as in the twelfth century, but the Germanization and colonization really started in the seventeenth century and went on until the war. The result was a German minority of almost four million, living in a nearly continuous belt in the Western and Northern parts of Bohemia.

This minority now declared their right to autonomy, and proclaimed the formation of an independent state, carved out from the historical Czech lands. Luckily, the old Czech borders were well defined throughout history, and the claim of the defeated Germans was not accepted by the Allies. The Germans were forced to remain in the newly formed state, where they coexisted with the Czechs until 1938, when these lands were ceded to the German Reich as part of the infamous Munich Agreement.

In Slovakia, the problem was the lack of historical borders. Slovakia was never really a well-defined state, and its status as a part of Hungary for such a long time helped to confuse the issue. Moreover, there were large Hungarian minorities in the Southern part of the country (in some parts actually majorities), which allowed the Hungarians to claim these lands as their own and not as part of the newly-formed Czechoslovak Republic. The Czech and Slovak politicians did not press the issue at this time, but agreed to accept the decision of the peace conference in Paris, having every hope that the decision would be favorable for them. Such a decision was taken, and Hungary was forced to cede these lands. But it never relinquished them in spirit, got them back in 1938, and has its eye on them even today.

The Provisional Government (the former Czecho-Slovak Council) in Paris signed the text of the Declaration of Independence of the Czecho-Slovak Nation on October 19, 1918. The National Committee in Prague took over power in a bloodless uprising on October 28, 1918, and proclaimed the Czechoslovak Republic. Because it did not immediately have any army units at its disposal, it could not enforce its will in the German areas and in Slovakia, still occupied by the Hungarian army.

The German parts of the Czech lands were nonviolently "liberated" during the end of 1918, using Czechoslovak army units raised from Czech soldiers returning from the front, where they served in the Austro-Hungarian army. Simultaneously, the National Council in Prague nominated a first Slovak government, and sent it into Slovakia, backed by small military units. The Hungarians initially pulled back, but soon started offensive actions. Having pronounced superiority both in numbers and in heavy weapons, they had no problem in pushing the weak Czech units back across the border.

Following the signing of the agreement on the provisional borders between the National Council and Károlyi's government on December 6, 1918, Hungary pulled its army units out of Slovakia, but balked when ordered on December 24, 1918 by the Allied Mission in Budapest to evacuate all the area up to the new borders, agreed on in Paris. Finally, it had to comply, among other reasons because the Czech army, which had been reinforced by the Italian legion, started advancing into Slovakia. By January 20, 1919, all Slovakia was liberated.

POLITICAL SITUATION

Newly formed Czechoslovakia had a precarious outline, jutting across central Europe from the highly developed and industrialized Czech Lands in the West to the most primitive Transcarpathian

Czechoslovak General Šnejdáek, followed by a member of the French Military Mission in 1919 during the liberation of Lučenec in Slovakia.

Ruthenia in the East. For an area of 140,000 km^2, it had borders 4,114 km long. It bordered with Germany, Austria, Poland, Hungary and Romania. All of the above, except Romania, were not friendly to the new state, as all of them had some real or imagined grievances against it. The Germans viewed the Sudeten border areas, inhabited mostly by ethnic Germans, as their own. The Austrians grieved for their lost empire, while both the Hungarians and the Poles had territorial demands.

The new state was also a complex conglomerate of nationalities. The Czech were the predominant majority 7.5 millions strong, but there were also 2 millions Slovaks, 3.2 millions Germans, 750,000 Hungarians, 550,000 Ruthenes, 200,000 Jews and 100,000 Poles. Both the ethnic composition of the population and the attitudes of the neighbors came back to haunt the new state and finally led to its demise in 1939.

To counter the disadvantageous geographical and geopolitical situation, the new Minister of Foreign Affairs, Dr. Eduard Beneš, conducted, with the full approval of President Tomáš Masaryk and its government, foreign policy centered totally and exclusively on Czechoslovakia's mutual treaty with France. Later, he formed the "Little Entente" by forming a mutually supporting treaty of Czechoslovakia, Romania and Yugoslavia. It was designed to confine and isolate Hungary, which was perceived up to 1933 as the gravest threat to Czechoslovakia's safety.

The new state also had to organize and to strengthen its armed forces, as the situation in the neighboring states was far from placid. In Hungary, the communists formed a Soviet-style republic and invaded Southern Slovakia. The Poles backed their claims to Těšínsko by armed incursions, which had to be met by force.

In general, apprehension about the general political situation led Czechoslovakia to maintain an army larger than customary for a state of its size. In the twenties it was even larger than the German army, which was limited to 100,000 men by the treaty of Versailles. Czechoslovakia quickly built an army of 10,000 officers, 20,000 NCOs and 110,000 men. Military service was universal and obligatory. All men were to serve for 24 months and then pass into the first reserve, which contained men up to the age of forty. A second reserve included men between the ages of forty and fifty.

CZECHO-SLOVAK LEGIONS

The Czecho-Slovak legions, which fought on the side of the Allies against the Central Powers, were partly recruited from the emigrants living in United States and in France, but mostly from soldiers who had defected from the Austro-Hungarian armies and joined the Allies.

There were three such legions: the French, the Italian and the Russian. The French legion was the oldest (1916) and the smallest (one division) and was composed mainly of emigrants from the West, since the Austro-Hungarian army did not fight on the Western front. The Italian legion was second in size with its two divisions, and took part in some heavy fighting on the Italian front in the last stages of the war. At the end of the war, it was augmented with battalions formed from the Austrian POWs of Czech and German nationalities.

The Russian legion was the largest, over eighty thousand strong (three divisions with cavalry and artillery supporting units). It took part in prolonged fighting, initially against the Germans and Austro-Hungarians. Later, after the collapse of the Russian front in 1917, due to the Bolshevik Revolution, it fought against the Red Army and executed a fighting withdrawal along the Transsiberian Railway all the way to Vladivostok.

The new Czechoslovak army drew its men, and especially its officers and NCO's, from two sources: from the old Austro-Hungarian army's cadres, and from the ranks of the returning legionnaires. Though the army was originally organized following the Austro-Hungarian model, the French influence soon became paramount.

The legionnaire officers were preferred to the former imperial ones both in assignments and in pay. This naturally led to friction and bad feelings, especially as some of them lacked in experience. But this official policy remained in place, and the old imperial officers were gradually retired. By the late twenties, there was an influx of new graduates from the Military Academy in Hranice, and the situation stabilized. The Czechs formed the majority of the officers' corps up to 1939, as the Slovaks originally lacked basic education, and the Germans were not trusted.

The army inherited Austro-Hungarian equipment and armaments; the legions brought with them French, Italian and Russian equipment. During the first years, arms were purchased both from France and from old German and Austro-Hungarian stocks. The army started standardization and rearmament at an early stage, as it had at its disposal a large and modern armament industry.

FRENCH MILITARY MISSION

The new state had very strong ties to France diplomatically, and both President Masaryk and Dr. Beneš wanted to build the army on the French model. They also wanted to counter the influence of the former Austro-Hungarian officers of Czech origin, and to prevent the army from being based on a Swiss militia model, as was proposed in 1919.

Already in December 1918 an accord was reached between the French and the Czechoslovak governments to send to Czechoslovakia a French military mission, which was to command and organize the new Czechoslovak army. At the same time, Italy wanted to win influence in the new state, and sent a military mission under General Piccioni to Slovakia in November 1918. This naturally led to jealousy between France and Italy. Though the Italian legion was three times the size of the French, and though Italy was closer, the French influence finally prevailed. It was helped by the glory of French arms, which was greater than that of the Italians, but mostly by the influence of President Masaryk and Dr. Beneš. The head of the French military mission, General Pellé, arrived in Prague in February 1919, and was named a Chief of the General Staff and Commander-in-Chief of the armies in the field. He came into conflict immediately with General Piccioni, and General Štefánik had to negotiate a face-saving withdrawal of the Italians. This episode may have contributed to later Italian support for the Hungarians.

The original mission had over 100 officers, many of them generals. Its main function was to command and to organize the army. Even after the solving of many organizational problems in 1919 and 1920, the mission remained large and influential. In 1921 it still had 80 officers (six brigadier generals and seven colonels); in 1923 72 officers; in 1925, 43; and in 1929, 17. General Pellé was replaced as the head of the mission in 1920 by General Mittelhauser. He was replaced in 1926 by General Faucher, who remained up to 1938, though he no longer was a Chief of the General Staff.

The French not only organized the army and at the beginning commanded its staff and all the major units, but also set up all the military academies and schools according to French military doctrine, and commanded and taught in them for many years. Many promising Czech officers were also sent regularly to the most prestigious French military academies. This allowed for a gradual change in the command structure of the army, as the members of the French military mission were replaced by competent Czech officers in command positions. In 1926, General Syrový was made the first Czech Chief of the General Staff.

Though the mission was originally well accepted, in later years its influence and its cost were viewed with much less enthusiasm. The German and Hungarian political parties were especially eager to criticize the French at every opportunity. Nevertheless, the mission's political influence remained strong up to the thirties, due mainly to the unwavering support of the leading politicians.

THE ARMY AS A TOOL OF FOREIGN POLICY

In the first years of the new republic, the army was not a popular institution. Bad experiences from the war, combined with a lack of modern military traditions, caused the population to view the army as unnecessary and expensive. The social democratic party, which tended to view the army as a user of funds necessary for social programs, had won the first free elections.

This perception started to change when the people realized that the postwar world was not a safe place, and that small nations especially must have the means to defend themselves if they expect to survive. The invasion by communist Hungary of Béla Kun into southern Slovakia in July of 1919 provided a necessary awakening. This was followed by the attempt of Charles of Habsburg to reclaim his throne in Hungary, following the defeat of the communists. In response to his return to Hungary, the Czechoslovak government mobilized the army in October with great publicity.

Both these events persuaded the general population of the need to maintain a strong army, and aroused its nationalistic feelings. The Czechoslovak government in the following years used every opportunity to increase the popularity of the army as an indispensable part of the state.

As was already mentioned, the foreign policy of Czechoslovakia was subjugated to a close cooperation with France as its main theme. Dr. Beneš, who was responsible for Czechoslovakia's foreign policy for the whole 1918-1938 period, pursued this orientation to the exclusion of any possible rapprochement with his neighbors, especially with Germany and Austria in the twenties, and with Poland after 1933. Instead, in his obsession with Hungary, he formed the "Little Entente" treaty, which could not help Czechoslovakia's security vis-a-vis the aggressive Third Reich. The army thus had to be built up to compensate for Czechoslovakia's lack of friends, and maintained at this high level to provide a deterrent to a possible aggressor.

FORMATION OF ARMORED UNITS

The tank had shown its capabilities and had become an important weapon by the end of the first world war. The new state did not have any, because the Austro-Hungarian army has not developed this weapon during the war. But it inherited an armored train, with more built shortly after that, and acquired two Lancia armored cars of the Italian legion. Škoda built twelve armored cars on a Fiat-Torino truck chassis in 1920, and the French strongly advised the army to buy Renault FT light tanks from France. The army did not dispute the need of acquiring armored fighting vehicles, but was not eager to buy French equipment. It experienced the questionable quality of French weapons, when the supplied 7.5 cm field guns were found to be worn out to the point of not being usable. It wanted to spend its funds on domestic constructions and so only seven of the Renaults were ordered.

The first domestic vehicles were Škoda armored cars PA-I, PA-II and PA-III, followed by the Tatra OA vz.30 light armored car. These were followed in 1933 and 1934 by seventy tankettes and fifty light gun tanks from ČKD, and from 1936, by the Škoda LT vz.35 tanks. Simultaneously, the organization of the armored units was developed, schools for training both the commanders and mechanics were set up, and a doctrine for their proper use was promulgated.

The armament industries were also exporting hundreds of armored fighting vehicles (AFVs) and developing improved models for the planned upgrading and expanding of the army's armored formations. Though these plans were not realized, by 1938 the Czechoslovak armored formations had 348 tanks, 70 tankettes and over 80 armored cars.

THE MODERNIZATION PROGRAM AFTER 1933

By 1930, the army had a large pool of well-trained reservists, ample officers' corps, and a manufacturing base capable not only of supplying it with infantry and artillery weapons, but with armored vehicles and aircraft as well. Its funding increased dramatically after 1933, when Nazi Germany was viewed as more and more dangerous. Not only were new units raised and equipped, but new constructions of armored vehicles were ordered in large quantities for the planned armored "Mobile" divisions.

Starting in 1935, construction of a continuous belt of permanent fortifications was begun on the German borders. As these were envisaged to only slow the attacking army, additional funds were appropriated for accelerated motorization of the army formations, especially artillery, and for expanded production of AFVs, especially light and medium tanks. By 1938, the army had seventeen first line and seventeen reserve infantry divisions, four Mobile divisions, very strong artillery, and over 1.25 million men. Its weak points were its air force, antiaircraft defenses, extremely long borders and its ethnic composition.

THE END: MOBILIZATION, MUNICH AGREEMENT, GERMAN OCCUPATION

Hitler's Germany was actively supporting the separatist tendencies of the Sudeten Germans, who in the late thirties were brazenly asking for separation of the whole Sudeten area and its assimilation into the German Reich. They were actively demonstrating for their "rights". These demonstrations grew into sabotage and terrorist actions and oppression of the local Czech population. Simultaneously, German propaganda was skillfully painting the Sudeten Germans as brutally oppressed by the Czechoslovak state.

The situation came to boiling point in the summer of 1938. As the political solution seemed less and less possible, and as the terrorist actions of the Sudeten Freikorps became unbearable, the Czechoslovak government partially mobilized in May 1938 and sent the army into the border areas to restore order. This was speedily accomplished.

The Czechoslovak army was fully mobilized in September, when a German attack was feared, but such an attack did not materialize, because Adolf Hitler at this time still preferred a political solution. He persuaded the hesitant English and the weak French to grant his demands during the Munich conference in September 1938. The English and the French were not willing to risk war for a small nation, though France had a very strong mutual assistance treaty with Czechoslovakia. The Munich dictate forced Czechoslovakia to cede to Germany all the Sudeten regions with their fortifications and industry, and left the country crippled and incapable of further resistance. President Beneš abdicated and Dr. Hácha, a retired judge, got the unpleasant and unpopular task of becoming the new president.

The Czechoslovak government accepted the Žilina Agreement stipulating the formation of an autonomous Slovak government on October 6, 1938. Dr. Tiso was nominated as its head. The only common ministries remained Defense, Foreign Affairs and Finances. At the same time, a paramilitary Hlinka's Guard was formally founded with Karol Sidór as its supreme commander.

On October 17, representatives of the Slovak separatist People's Party (Ludová Strana) Ďurčanský, Karmazin and Šaňo Mach were received by Adolf Hitler. Several days later, Dr. Tiso met with Czechoslovak Generals Krejčí and Ingr and discussed the defense of Slovakia, as both the Poles and the Hungarians were threatening to take Slovak lands. On October 28, the first swearing-in of Hlinka's Guard officers took place. The Guard was almost 100,000 strong at this time.

On October 21, the Vienna Arbitration took place, where representatives of Germany and Italy decreed the size of the Slovak areas that would be ceded to Hungary. Though Tiso, Krno, Tuka, Ďurčanský, Teplanský and General Viest were all present, they could not influence the deliberations. Slovakia was forced to cede a large part of its southern lands to Hungary and certain areas in the north to Poland, which also claimed its pound of flesh from the disintegrating and helpless Czechoslovakia, whose name was changed to the Czecho-Slovak Republic on November 22, 1938.

On March 1, 1939 the Ministerial Committee of the Czecho-Slovak government met. The question of Slovak departure from the state had already been discussed during this meeting, though Dr.Tiso and some of his coworkers were against a total break with the Czechs. Karol Sidór led the Slovak delegation during these talks. He returned to Bratislava to discuss the situation with Dr.Tiso, and on March 6 the Slovak government proclaimed its loyalty to the Czecho-Slovak Republic and its wish to remain a part of the state. Meanwhile, on March 7, Ďurčanský and Tuka met with Hermann Göring, who pressed them to declare Slovakia's autonomy.

After their return to Slovakia on March 9, Hlinka's Guard was mobilized. The Czecho-Slovak President Hácha reacted strongly and declared martial law in Slovakia. He also sent in the army, which disarmed Hlinka's Guard, and removed Dr.Tiso as the prime minister of the Slovak government. Sidór returned to Bratislava on March 10 and was given the function of the prime minister. President Hácha accepted his nomination and rescinded the martial law.

On March 13, Dr. Tiso left for his meeting with Adolf Hitler, who offered him the option of proclaiming the Slovak State and ceding from Czechoslovakia. In such a case, Germany would be Slovakia's protector and would not allow the Hungarians to press on Slovakia any additional territorial demands. In case the Slovaks would not accept, Germany would occupy Bohemia and Moravia and leave Slovakia to the mercies of the Hungarians and the Poles.

Dr.Tiso returned to Bratislava and described the situation and his talks with Hitler to a joint session of the full Slovak assembly and the Slovak government. Those legislative bodies decided to proclaim the Slovak State on March 14, 1939, and thus allowed Hitler to occupy the Czech Lands on March 15, 1939 without fear of repercussions, because the guarantees France and England had given Czechoslovakia after the Munich agreement were now worthless, since Czechoslovakia ceased to exist.

2

THE MANUFACTURERS

Škoda

The Škoda works in Pilsen, by full name Škodovy závody, akciová společnost (Škoda Enterprises, Inc.), were founded in the late seventies of the nineteenth century. The small machinery manufacturer in Western Bohemia opened its first modern steel works in 1886. Its development was helped by two interconnected events. Around this time, bronze, which was the major material used for artillery barrels, was beginning to be replaced by steel. This work was pioneered mostly by Krupp in Germany. The Austro-Hungarian army was resisting this change, but the navy had a different view. Bronze was totally unsuitable for the large caliber naval guns, as it could not withstand the increased pressures. The Austro-Hungarian navy was buying its heavy guns from Krupp, but wanted to find a domestic producer, and their choice fell on Škoda. It is said that the navy's supreme commander, Admiral Sterneck, personally came to Pilsen to persuade Emil Škoda, the company's founder, to initiate gun manufacturing.

Škoda founded an armament department in 1890, which developed special steels with a high nickel content, and in 1894 started producing 4.7 cm naval guns. In 1897 the first 15 cm and 24 cm naval heavy guns and siege mortars were made. In 1900, the chrome-nickel steel was prepared for the first time for the 24 cm L/40 naval guns. Škoda at this time decided to go into production of field guns for the army, as these were needed in much larger volume. Škoda not only had the new special steel, but during the first decade of the twentieth century worked diligently on new types of breeches and on recoil mechanisms. The production was equipped with the most modern testing equipment and an artillery range for testing the guns was set up in Bolevec.

A group of Austro-Hungarian artillery officers with their Škoda 30.5 cm mortars on loan to the German army, Brussels, Belgium 1914.

The First World War saw a huge increase in field and siege gun manufacturing in Pilsen. Škoda specialized in the siege artillery and mortars and produced 21 and 30.5 cm mortars, 24 cm cannon and 38 and 42 cm howitzers. Even the German army had to borrow siege artillery from the Austro-Hungarians for its siege of the Belgian forts and of Verdun! The war also finally decided the fight between bronze and steel, with steel taking the whole field. And steel meant Škoda. During the war, Škoda added a munitions factory and expanded its production many fold.

After the war, the company was expropriated, as it was financially controlled by German and Austrian banks in Vienna. The Czechoslovak government needed capital to compensate the banks, and thus had to look for a foreign investor. An American consortium was interested in purchasing the company, but Škoda was finally sold to Schneider-Cruesot through the intermediary of L'Union Européenne Industrielle and Financiére. The French had several members on the board and a manager in the Prague Škoda headquarters, but otherwise did not interfere in business or technical matters.

Škoda also acquired a host of other companies, in the first place the former Laurin & Klement automobile manufacturer in Mladá Boleslav; Avia aircraft manufacturer; Kablo, a cable manufacturer; and Konstruktiva, builder of roads, tunnels and bridges. Škoda's main works were in Pilsen, but aside from there, it had eight other manufacturing companies all over Czechoslovakia. It did not manufacture guns only. The company was making complete electric generating stations, sugar mills, steel mills, locomotives and a host of other heavy machinery, and was exporting them all over the world. Its armaments works were second in size only to Krupp's. By the late thirties, they occupied 160 hectares and employed 15,000 employees. During the Second World War the factory employed 42,000 people and was supplying 5.5% of armaments of all German and European production combined.

Škoda was the sole manufacturer and supplier of artillery to the Czechoslovak army. It was also developing and manufacturing antitank and antiaircraft guns. Because of its experience with armor (Škoda was building whole armored turrets for the Austro-Hungarian navy), it was a logical choice for building armored trains and armored cars for the new army. The first armored cars were makeshift constructions on Fiat-Torino truck chassis, but already in 1923, Škoda developed a completely new model in its PA-I armored car. Its further development led to the famous PA-II Turtle in 1925, which was considered one of the best armored cars in its time. The last of its armored cars produced in quantity was the OA vz.27, of which the army ordered 15. Though Škoda's designers developed some very interesting and advanced prototypes in the thirties, none of them got into production.

The company concentrated its efforts on tank design. Since 1930, it developed several types of tankettes and a prototype of a light tank, the SU. The Czechoslovak army has already procured tankettes and one type of light tank from Škoda's competitor ČKD, and in 1934 was looking for its standard cavalry light tank. Škoda won the army competition with its LT vz.35 tank, which became the main tank of the army's armored formations, and was also exported and used by several countries.

Following the German occupation in March 1939, Škoda was integrated into the huge Hermann Göring Werke, and was fully occupied by turning out armaments for the Wehrmacht. Among other guns, it was a large producer of the famous "eighty-eights", various artillery tractors of its own and of German design, and a host of other armaments. It did not produce any tanks, though it proposed several interesting projects, and was mainly occupied with repairs of its old LT vz.35 for the German, Romanian, Bulgarian and Slovak armies. It managed to sell a license for its medium tank T-21 to the Hungarians, who manufactured it during the war years as the Turán. It started production of the Jagdpanzer 38(t) Hetzer simultaneously with ČKD in 1944, and produced it up to the end of the war and even afterwards as the G-13 for the Swiss army.

Škoda was unquestionably the most important arms manufacturer and supplier of the Czechoslovak army not only for its artillery and its armor, but also for passenger and command cars and for trucks and artillery tractors.

ČKD (Českomoravská-Kolben-Daněk)

The first part of ČKD, the "První Českomoravská továrna na stroje"(The First Czech-Moravian Machine Manufacturer), was founded in 1871 in Prague. The company was gradually enlarged (in 1886 a bridge manufacturing plant, in 1899 locomotive manufacturing) and in 1907 started car manufacturing in cooperation with Ringhoffer (later Tatra) under the name "Pražská továrna na automobily" (Prague Automobile Manufacturing). When Ringhoffer bowed out in 1908, the company under the new name PRAGA became part of Českomoravská.

Dipl. Ing. Kolben founded in 1896 a company manufacturing electrical installations and products under the name KOLBEN a spol. In 1921 his company was incorporated into Českomoravská under the new name - Českomoravská-Kolben a.s.

The last company added to ČK in 1927 was BREITFELD-DANĚK a spol., that was formed in the nineteenth century from various machinery companies: Daněk in 1854, Breitfeld & Evans in 1884, Machine Manufacturing in Blansko in 1897 and Bolzano-Tedesco in 1899.

ČKD a.s.(Inc.) in Prague was officially formed on January 1, 1927. The concern was a maker of various machinery (today they are world famous for their compressors), electrical installations, diesel locomotives and automobiles. For the army they manufactured searchlights (the license for one of their searchlight design was bought by the British Admiralty), aircraft engines and fully tracked artillery tractors, among other things. They were ideally suited for tank manufacture and were quick to seize the opportunity when the army was looking for a manufacturer of tankettes. ČKD bought a license for Carden-Loyd tankettes and several sample vehicles from Vickers, and developed one of their own, which was introduced as Tančík vz.33 by the army. Simultaneously, it developed a light tank, for which it acquired a license from Vickers for their 4.7 cm gun, but the army insisted on a Škoda gun. The tank was accepted as LT vz.34 with a 3.7 cm Škoda gun.

ČKD had new, much improved models on the drawing boards, but lost the light tank competition to Škoda. It participated on the production of the Škoda tank, due to a cartel agreement it had with Škoda since 1934, while it was also pursuing the development of its models. ČKD was very successful in exporting them in the years 1936-1939, the tankettes to Iran, Romania and Sweden, and its TNH light tanks to Iran, Peru and Switzerland.

It was an improved model of this light tank that won the army's competition in 1938 and was accepted and ordered as the LT vz.38

standard light tank. ČKD won also the competition with its medium tank V-8-H, but that one never got into production. The LT vz.38 was a different story, as it was accepted by the Germans, who maintained its production for the Wehrmacht, first as PzKpfw 38(t), later as a basis for various antitank, antiaircraft and howitzer carriers, and finally as the Jagdpanzer 38 Hetzer. Thus ČKD manufactured tanks for all the war years in large quantities, and repaired its own and other armored vehicles. Praga also supplied the army with command cars and trucks, and ČKD with fully tracked artillery tractors. All these were widely exported before the war as well.

During the war, the company was renamed "Českomoravské strojírny" (Czech-Moravian Machinery Manufacturing, or BMM - Böhmisch-Morawische Maschinenfabrik) to eliminate Kolben's name (he was Jewish). After the war the ČKD name was restored and it is proudly used up to this day.

TATRA (Závody Ringhoffer-Tatra a.s.)

Tatra had several manufacturing lines. Its factories in Prague produced railway rolling stock, streetcars, electric locomotives and some special rail cars. It had a factory manufacturing aircraft engines in Roudnice and a company making insulation materials in Beroun. Its main factory was in Kopřivnice in Moravia, manufacturing cars, trucks, tractors and automobile engines. It was supplying the army with specialized trucks and command cars in large quantities. Its only forays into the AFV realm was the light armored car OA vz.30, and an unsuccessful heavy tank T-III, built only in prototypes.

Tatra developed a radial air-cooled tank engine of 280 HP, but it was never adopted. During the war, it supplied Diesel engines for various German vehicles (Puma armored car, Luchs prototypes etc.) and manufactured half-track and regular trucks for the Wehrmacht.

ZB (Československá Zbrojovka a.s. Brno)

This company originated as an affiliate of the Austro-Hungarian arsenal, opened in 1916 in Brno in Moravia. From 1920 the company was called "Čs. státní zbrojovka" (Czechoslovak State Armament Company) and obtained its final name in 1924, when it went public. During the following years, it became the largest manufacturer of rifles and machine guns in Czechoslovakia, and one of the leading small arms manufacturers in the world.

At first, the company repaired various weapons for the army . Starting from 1919, it bought machines for the manufacture of rifles and pistols from Mauser, Löwe, Hahn & Kolb and Schutte in Germany. The army planned a complete rearming of its troops with domestic small arms during the years 1922 - 1924, and cooperated closely with ZB on the necessary types. By 1925 the army pistol, rifle, and light and heavy machine guns were all approved and their production set up. The rearming started in 1925 and was almost finished in 1939.

The most famous weapon developed and made in ZB was the light machine gun ZB vz.26. It became one of the best light machine guns in existence. Exported widely to almost thirty countries in large quantities, it is used up to this day by many smaller armies. A license sold in 1935 to the English Enfield arms manufacturing company led to the BREN (BRno ENfield) gun, which became the most widely used light machine gun not only during the Second World War, but in the following years as well.

Another fine product was the air-cooled heavy machine gun ZB-53. It was of a very modern construction, with a twin rate of fire (lower against infantry and higher against aircraft), and even today is considered one of the best in the world. It was manufactured for the infantry, but also for AFVs and fixed fortifications. Its license was also sold to the British company BSA, which supplied it under the name BESA for all English AFVs during the war.

Both the light and the heavy machine guns were used in all Czechoslovak AFVs, the light ones in the tankettes and light armored cars, the heavy ones in tanks.

Zbrojovka Ing. F. Janeček, Praha

F. Janeček was a very experienced inventor and executive. During the First World War he turned his talents to the design of hand grenades (one of his types was accepted by the Czechoslovak army after the war) and artillery munitions. After the war, he founded an armament factory in Mnichovo Hradiště, and moved it to Prague in 1922. He won the army contest for the adaptation of the Austro-Hungarian machine gun system Schwarzlose to Mauser 7.92 mm ammunition.

The Czechoslovak army inherited several types of machine guns after the war, and had to select one standard type. The Schwarzlose heavy machine guns were most common, but they were of 8 mm caliber, which was incompatible with the 7.92 mm caliber of the new army rifle and light machine gun. Aside from this, the Schwarzlose system used a closed breach, which required oiling of the cartridges during firing to ease their removal.

Janeček's factory submitted the lowest bid for the army adaptation and won the contract. The final machine gun was assigned the designation vz.24 (new manufacture) or vz.7/24 (old guns, adapted to the new standard). By the end of 1925 the army received 1,335 adapted vz.7/24 machine guns. In total, about 5,000 machine guns were adapted and about 2,250 manufactured as new vz.24.

The Schwarzlose machine guns were used in armored trains, in Škoda OA vz.27 armored cars and the MU-2 tankette. They were not very suitable for AFV use, as they were water cooled and a puncture of the water jacket disabled the gun. Also, they used cloth belts, which froze and broke easily during the winter months.

POLDI (Poldina huť, Kladno)

Poldi was founded in 1889 and from its beginning specialized in special steels for construction purposes, springs, later in steels for automobile and aircraft industries, and in armor plates. It supplied armor plate for most of the Czechoslovak army AFVs, and was very active during the war, when its special steels were in high demand.

Vítkovické Horní a Hutní Těžířstvo (VHHT)

This company was founded in 1829 and grew into a huge complex of steel mills, coal mines and armament factories over the years. It had ten steel mills in Vítkovice alone. It was supplying armor plate for the Austro-Hungarian navy and army in the form of ships' turrets, armor plate, coastal fortifications etc.

The company was also manufacturing munitions, supplying Škoda with steel ingots for gun barrels, and manufactured a host of other products.

VHHT supplied the armor for half the manufactured LT vz.35 tanks and for other AFVs, and armor cupolas for the fixed fortifications on the German borders.

3

DEVELOPMENT OF CZECH ARMORED FIGHTING VEHICLES

FIRST ARMORED CARS

The last transport of the Italian Legion brought with it two Lancia armored cars. These were built on a truck chassis and were armed with three Vickers-Terni heavy machine guns; two in a large circular turret and one in a small turret, sitting on top of the large one. Each car had a crew of five and maximum speed on the road of 50 km/hour. Both cars were sent immediately to Slovakia to fight against the communist attackers as part of the Italian Legion's 6. Division.

Their success led the French Mission to ask for additional armored cars to be bought as soon as possible. Klofáč, the Minister of National Defense, in his letter to General Pellé from October 25, 1919, gave his approval to order an additional twelve cars. The army contacted the manufacturers, but neither Škoda nor ČKD could provide the cars in the prescribed short time. Praga did make a small lot of ten armored cars, built on their R truck chassis in 1916, but neither company had a suitable truck chassis to use at this time.

In the end, Skoda got the order, because it promised to armor the army's Fiat-Torino trucks by the end of December 1919. It kept its promise and the prototype was ready at the beginning of January. It was first presented to an army commission, led by French Captain Didelet, on January 20.

The fairly high body had two small turrets, each with one Maxim 08 heavy machine gun. For each machine gun 9,000 rounds were carried. The car also carried 150 hand grenades, which could have been ejected from three throwers, called "tromblons".

The main drawbacks were the weak engine and narrow solid tires, which as a combination made cross-country movement practically impossible. The 5 mm armor withstood both rifle and machine gun fire, but was easily penetrated by the "S" armor-piercing machine gun rounds. The commission accepted the car nevertheless, and an additional eleven cars were ordered.

Škoda promised delivery at the end of July 1920. The total bill for the twelve cars was 2,882,000 Kč (Korun Československých = Czechoslovak Crowns) or $ 115,000, not a paltry sum in 1920! The cars were sent directly from the manufacturer to field units. Due to the weak engine, faulty brakes and a host of other problems, the

Praga R armored car from 1916 followed the usual design practice of its time: unimproved truck chassis, boxy superstructure from thin armor plate and heavy machine gun armament, in this case in an open-top revolving turret. Ten cars were delivered to the Austro-Hungarian army.

The Lancia and Škoda Fiat-Torino armored cars side-by-side. The two offset machine gun turrets of the Škoda vehicle are well visible. This arrangement was more practical than the turrets one on top of another in the Lancia design.

Praga L armored car in a factory photograph. The turret is turned machine gun-forward. The vehicle was lower than the Škoda design and had a better power to weight ratio and armament, but was not advanced enough to warrant production. Its construction and the light armor is visible in this "open" view.

cars were used mostly for drivers training. Eight cars were scrapped in 1925 and the remaining four in 1929.

Another armored car of purely domestic origin was not very successful either. Developed in 1921 on the chassis of the Praga truck L, it was armored by Škoda and armed with a short 3.7 cm gun and a machine gun on the opposite sides of a fully rotating turret. The army commission saw the unfinished car in December 1921 and raised many objections. In the end, the army bought the car for 539,000 Kč ($ 21,500). Škoda finished the car in 1922, and it was used for driver training till 1925, when it was converted to a command car by removing the armored box and installing a "break" body.

Praga L armored car between two Škoda Torino vehicles, showing the 3.7 cm gun in the turret.

Side view of the Praga L, showing the machine gun. Both weapons were mounted on opposite sides of the turret, making their simultaneous firing quite difficult. The hull had many large visors.

Wooden mock-up of Škoda PA-I armored car.

ŠKODA ARMORED CARS

Škoda promised in 1922 to develop a better armored car and kept its promise. In 1923, two prototypes of the PA-I (Pancéřový Automobil I) were ready. They were of a revolutionary construction, because Škoda did not use a standard truck chassis, as was customary in those times, but developed a special one for this purpose. It had four-wheel drive and four-wheel steering, and it could be driven in both directions with the same ease and at the same speed. This was important, as it was difficult to turn the cars around on the narrow roads of the twenties.

The two prototypes got numbers 16 and 17 on August 2, 1923. They were armed with two heavy machine guns in a fully rotating turret, and carried two drivers. Each of them could drive the car by using a "reverser" lever, which made his front wheel the steered ones and the rear ones the driven ones. The cars were also fast, having an engine of sufficient output. Though the cars were quite revolutionary and represented a huge improvement over existing models, they had some shortcomings and the army asked for further improvements.

The production PA-I, showing the boat-like hull, ventilation louvres above the engine and the turret with two heavy machine guns. This was the first Czechoslovak armored car with a specially developed chassis with four-wheel drive and four-wheel steering. The car could be driven in both directions. The two drivers sat in the opposite corners of the fighting compartment, leaving its center free for the gunners. This vehicle carries the civilian "dealer's plate", showing that it is still being evaluated by Škoda.

Front view of the PA-I. The headlights have been moved to the fenders as opposed to their original position on the center louvres. The vehicle carries already the army registration number. The PA-I cars were painted in a five-tone splinter camouflage, different from later camouflage schemes.

They saw them in the next model, PA-II, the famous "Želva" ("Turtle"). Twelve cars were ordered in 1923 and were delivered between December 1924 and January 1925. Škoda kept the chassis with its revolutionary drive, but completely rebuilt the body. By removing the turret, it lowered the silhouette and made the cars much more stable. All surfaces were fully rounded, which provided a ballistically excellent body, but expensive to manufacture (each car cost 627,159 Kč, or $ 25,000!). Four Maxim 08 heavy machine guns were placed in the four sides of the rounded body, allowing a 360° field of fire. The cars were also quite fast, 70 km/hour, though their cross-country performance was still lacking, due to their high weight of 7.36 tons. Another disadvantage was the size of the fighting compartment, where the two machine gunners did not have enough room to service their weapons simultaneously.

Though the PA-II armored cars were never officially accepted into the armed forces, and their planned designation OA vz.23 was not officially assigned, they were used extensively by the army and were shown on all the contemporary maneuvers and parades.

The only two PA-Is built lead PA-II Turtles during a parade in Milovice.

One of the two identical axle assemblies of the PA-II. All four wheels were steerable. Massive drum brakes carried ten wheel fastening screws each.

The PA-IIs proved their worth during several exercises. For example, in August 1925, a three-car company drove from Milovice to Žilina, Košice, Bratislava, Praha and back to Milovice, 1,600 km in all, maintaining a daily average between 381 and 412 km, an unbelievable achievement for that time.

The PA-II armored cars were used as late as in the spring of 1933, when a company of nine cars was sent to Opava to bolster the defenses of the Hlučín border area against an expected German annexation attempt.

When the PA-III cars became available, Škoda sold three of the PA-II cars to the Vienna police, with the stipulation that it would replace them free of charge with the new model. The army sold the remaining cars to the Czech riot police in 1937.

On the same chassis was also built one upgunned prototype. In a heightened superstructure, it carried a Škoda 7.5 cm gun in its frontal armor and one heavy machine gun in the rear plate. The

The chassis of PA-II armored car was almost identical to the PA-I chassis. The engine was in the front. Note the massive differential and scissors-type shock absorbers. The small size of the fighting compartment is apparent. This vehicle is the training PA-II, number NIX-70.

Driver's seat of the PA-II. It had a strap backrest which was removed when the door was opened, allowing access to the fighting compartment. The hanging leather straps in the middle are back supports for the machine gunners. Two of them plus the commander had to fit into the small central part of the fighting compartment.

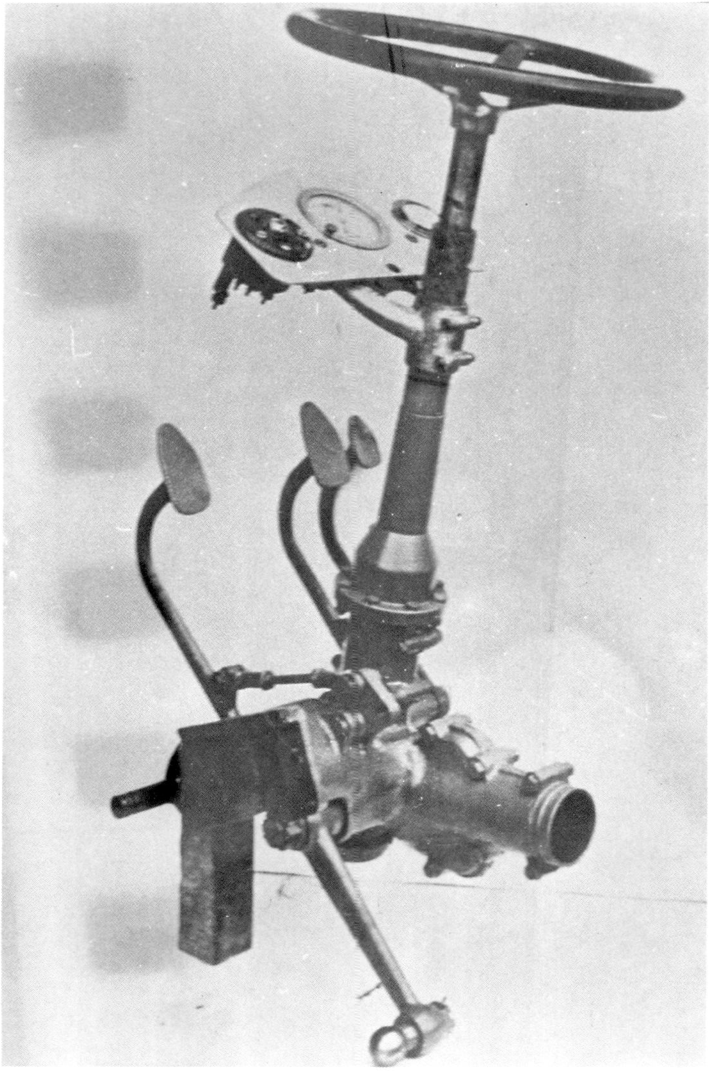

The compact driving assembly of the PA-II armored car.

Side view of the PA-II Turtle in the new five-tone camouflage and carrying the white number on its doors. The headlights are covered with armored flaps. Behind the front wheel is the engine's cooling fan.

The same car with headlights uncovered. The old registration number is painted directly on the front plate. The well-rounded hull was not only balistically advantageous, but the vehicle was very clean looking, when compared with contemporary armored cars.

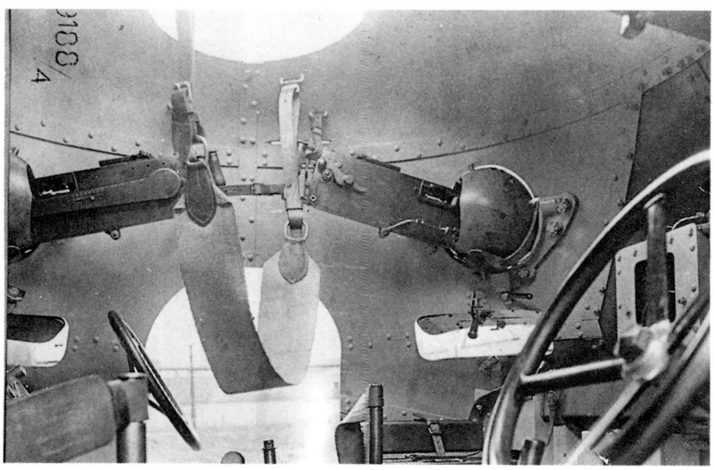

Two of the four machine guns in ball mounts and one of the two top hatches are visible, together with the two drivers' positions. Simultaneous firing of all four guns was not envisioned and would have been practically impossible, due to space constraints.

One of the PA-II armored cars with the new recognition number following its transfer to police units in 1937.

A company of PA-II cars during maneuvers. Note the open hatches above the engines and the top hatches. The driver's visor was placed well back on the right, which made it hard to observe the road left front when driving, a disadvantage even greater considering that in the prewar Czechoslovakia he had to drive on the left!

army accepted it, but at nine tons it was much heavier and less mobile than the standard PA-II. It was never put into production.

Instead, from the beginning of 1924, and in parallel with the manufacture of PA-II cars, the new PA-III car was taking shape. Škoda kept the main features of the chassis, but the new car was designed to be smaller, more mobile and especially less expensive. The army slowed the development by demanding constant changes. The originally rounded shape of the body was transformed into an array of angled straight plates. This arrangement was much less expensive to manufacture, while providing the same ballistic advantages as the rounded surfaces. Škoda made several variants of the body shapes in the form of wooden mock ups, and in August 1925 the final one was approved by the army commission. It was manufactured as an iron prototype and went through long and arduous tests both by the factory and by the army.

The army finally accepted the prototype on July 28, 1927. As it was not armored, it was used only for training and testing. But,

PA-II armored cars during a parade in Prague.

One of the three PA-IIs sold to Vienna police in 1927. The Austrians modified at least one of them by adding a small commander's cupola.

One of the unmodified PA-II of the Vienna police after suppression of the Nazi putch and the murder of Austria's Chancellor Dr. Dollfuss in July 1934; in front of the Chancellor's palace.

The front view of the PA-II-čěl, the upgunned prototype from 1927. In the front part of a heightened superstructure the 7.5 cm Škoda gun was mounted in a ball mount. Only one machine gun was carried, but there were three ball mounts installed.

Same vehicle from the ***rear****. The engine was moved to the back. The body is made from flat panels, not rounded as on PA-II vehicles. Small commander's cupola was also fitted.*

The chassis of PA-III. Note the gear-box in the middle, fuel tank and radiator with its fan in front of the engine, and double steering identical to PA-II. The tires mounted are the combat type with air compartments.

based on its performance, the army approved the car as the new OA vz.27 armored car on December 16, 1927.

At this time, the army had twelve complete chassis, manufactured by Škoda already in 1925, and thus needed to order only the armored bodies. Škoda delivered fifteen cars (twelve plus three as replacements for the three PA-IIs sold to Vienna) between May and October 1929. The armored regiment in Milovice was assigned six cars, while the remaining nine went to the cavalry-subordinated squadron. The army planned to acquire additional nine cars as a replacement of the PA-II cars, but never did.

The OA vz.27 was robust, easy to maintain and with much improved fire efficiency, due to the use of spotting scopes on the machine guns. Its drawbacks were a high weight of 6.5 tons, and a very high cost - 626,770 Kč ($ 25,000). The army simply could not afford to buy more cars at that time. The new cars took part in army maneuvers at the end of 1929. A three-car company drove from Prague to Košice in Slovakia, a distance of over 700 km, participated in the maneuvers and drove back in ten days. Some minor defects found during these long trips were quickly repaired by Škoda mechanics. The new car made a very good impression abroad, and Škoda got inquiries from Yugoslavia, Romania, Poland, Belgium, Holland, Sweden, Switzerland, Portugal, China and Japan. Though the Ministry of Defense did not raise any objections to export sales, Škoda in the end did not have sufficient capacity to manufacture the vehicles for export, being fully saturated by army orders.

Wooden mock-up of the PA-III armored car. It reverted to a fully rotating turret and its armor was of a simplified construction.

Rear view of the PA-III prototype. The turret machine gun's side ball mounts, driver's visor and the Scintilla searchlight under its armored cowl in the rear wall of the turret are clearly visible. The vehicle is carrying civilian registration number, as it is still being tested by Škoda. In the rear is Škoda Sentinel, steam-driven truck built under English license.

Front view of the same vehicle.

Nice detail shot showing the driver behind its opened visor, and the commander in the turret's hatch.

OA vz.27 armored cars during a parade held in Prague's Venceslaus Square.

During the reorganization of the armored units in the second half of the thirties, the armored cars were taken out of the cavalry units and were transferred to the armored regiments. PÚV-1 (PÚV=Pluk Útočné Vozby, or Armored Regiment) in Milovice fielded nine cars, while the PÚV-2 in Olomouc and PÚV-3 in Turčianský sv.Martin each got three cars. This assignment remained in effect till 1939.

In the thirties the OA vz.27 were already aging, but were used widely in all army maneuvers and parades. In late 1938 they were regularly used in the fighting in the Sudeten region with great success. In March 1939 three cars were in Transcarpathian Ruthenia; following its occupation by Hungary, they retreated into Romania. The Slovak State took over three cars, the Germans confiscated the rest. The Slovak cars were scrapped in February 1943, the German ones probably even sooner. The Romanians used theirs for guard duty and two vehicles were destroyed during the American air raid on Ploesti oil fields in 1944. One car was still in existence in Czechoslovakia in 1949, used as a tractor.

The construction of the PA-III was revolutionary for its time. The frame chassis had in its front part a four-cylinder gasoline en-

One of the three OA vz.27 of the Slovak army after March 1939. It still carries the gray one-tone camouflage. It's hull machine gun is missing, and the armored cowl of the searchlight is open. Note the placement of the registration number on the bottom part of the left fender. The crew's overalls are also ex-Czechoslovak army.

Two of the OA vz.27 during field maneuvers in Milovice. In front of them are the Tančík vz.33 tankettes and an OA vz.30 light armored car.

The Romanian army confiscated three OA vz.27 armored cars from units of the Czechoslovak army which retreated to Romania from Transcarpathian Ruthenia after March 15, 1939. Two of them were destroyed in the Škoda's truck repair shop in Ploesti during an American air-raid in 1944.

An OA vz.27 under way. Compare the placement of the registration number with the one in picture 3/29. The car in the background is Praga Picollo with military utility body.

gine, connected with a gearbox with four gears. Both axles were driven and steered, but only one at a time, depending on the direction the car was driven. It thus was not a full four-wheel drive. The vehicle used two types of tires: for training normal 38x7" tires and for combat 720x30 mm tires with air compartments.

The body consisted of 5.5 mm armor plates riveted to a frame, which was constructed from angled steel pieces. Each driver had two vision slits, protected by bulletproof glass blocks and armored flaps. The center part of the body carried a conical turret with a heavy machine gun vz.7/24 in a ball mount. Two additional ball mounts were on the sides of the turret, while on its rear was a searchlight under an armored protective cowl. Another heavy machine gun of the same type was fixed in the rear part of the body, with a 72° field of fire. Each car carried also a spare ZB vz.26 light machine gun inside. Though installation of a radio station vz.23/28 with a 40 km range had been tested, radios were not introduced, and the cars communicated with colored flags. Access to the fight-

A company of OA vz.27 armored cars during summer army maneuvers, being admired by the local population. The old style of their registration numbers places this photograph before December 1932.

Another view of one of the Romanian OA vz.27 destroyed at Ploesti. Note the shape of the commander's hatch and the engine hatch up front.

Pictures of a Škoda prototype armor treatment of their Rapid passenger car. They show armor protection for the two front passengers, with the light machine gun ZB vz.26 in the windshield.

The same car as in 3/36, but with a small turret fitted. All these were planned as light reconnaisance cars.

A much more modified car. The passenger compartment has been eliminated. Front plate has two visors and the machine gun mount.

ing compartment was through doors on each side and through a hatch on top of the turret.

The cars were painted matte gray, as this color was found to be less conspicuous on the roads than the normal three-tone camouflage. At first the cars carried black numbers 31 - 45 on their doors, but these were later discontinued. The cars originally carried numbers NIX-201 - 215 on black license plates front and rear, from December 1932 the new numbers 13338 - 13352 (the prototype had a number NIX-216 and later 13353 and carried the three-tone camouflage).

In later years, Škoda projected the PA-IV armored car, which was the PA-III with a 3.7 cm gun in the turret, but this car was never built. Similarly, plans to mount a large caliber machine gun in these vehicles were never realized.

ŠKODA ARMORED CAR PROTOTYPES

Škoda over the years submitted several interesting prototypes, some of them of very advanced design both mechanically and in their armament. One of these definitely was the project of a heavy armored car from 1931, Škoda model PAd, project number Zb 5554P. The car was an eight-wheeler. Both the front and the rear four wheels had their own six-cylinder gasoline engine with an output of 94 HP(69.5 kW). The car again had two drivers and could be driven in both directions at 80 km/hour. All four front wheels were steered, while all eight wheels were driven in either direction. Its most interesting feature was the proposed armament: twin 40 mm dual-purpose Škoda Z guns in a large turret, and four ZB vz.26 light machine guns. It is regrettable that this armored car was never built, as it was quite revolutionary for its time and even at the beginning of the war in 1939 there were not many armored cars with similar properties and armament available.

The next project, Zb 5560P from 1932, was its total opposite. It was a highly modified chassis of a Škoda passenger car, armored with a very low body for two men, carrying one ZB vz.26 machine gun. The engine was placed transversely behind the rear axle. The car was proposed as a light reconnaissance vehicle.

The Z-scout car of Zbrojovka Brno was another prototype for the light reconnaisance vehicle category. As the Škoda cars, it was built only as a prototype.

The two Tatra 26 prototypes after being fitted with armored bodies. In front is the open-top personnel carrier, in the rear the reconnaisance car. Taken during the June 1927 evaluation trials in Krkonoše Mountains.

Next in line was a project of another heavy armored car, Škoda 6-OAM-6, factory designation Zb 5253P. It carried a 4.7 cm antitank gun and a ZB vz.26 machine gun in a fully rotating turret, another ZB vz.26 machine gun in the front plate. This was a six-wheeler of an orthodox construction, with one driver only, and a six-cylinder 49 HP(36.2 kW) engine in the back. Even so, its maximum speed on the roads was 60 km/hour. Its cross-country performance was helped by a pair of spare wheels on the side of the body, mounted on stub axles, which could be lowered hydraulically so that the wheels touched the ground. This armored car had a better armament than most contemporary tanks, and could have been quite effective in an antitank role, despite its weak armor.

Next came PA 4/I from 1933, project number Zb 5564P. This was a light armored car with a rear-mounted six-cylinder engine of 50 HP(40 kW), armed with two vz.24 heavy machine guns, one in a fully rotating turret, one in the front plate. The car had a four-wheel drive and maximum speed on the road of 60 km/hour. With a crew of three men and 5.5 mm armor its weight was 4.5 tons.

The next project was in a way a step backwards, probably necessitated by the need to design a less expensive vehicle. Called 4LT-VI, project number Zb 5388P from 1934, it was built on a three-axle standard truck chassis, armed with two vz.24 heavy machine guns in the usual configuration, one in a fully rotating turret and one in the front plate.

Škoda also proposed armored additions to the army's standard passenger or command cars. One was designed for the command car type 903, factory number Zb 5598P. Conceived in 1936, it provided an armored superstructure with a small turret, carrying the ZB vz.26 light machine gun. The same year several proposals were made on how to armor standard Škoda Rapid passenger cars; either with an armored insert for the driver and the machine gunner, or even with a small turret on the roof of the vehicle. Škoda built some of these modifications as prototypes.

TATRA ARMORED CARS

Though the Škoda armored cars were satisfactory, they had one great disadvantage - their high price. The army, limited by its peacetime budget, could not afford procuring such expensive vehicles in the planned quantities.

The modernization and motorization of the artillery and cavalry units brought a need for command and reconnaissance vehicles with good cross-country capabilities. Between 1922 and 1925, the army bought from France two three-axle Renault command cars and four Citroen-Kegresse half-tracks. Because neither of these vehicles was entirely satisfactory, the army asked the domestic manufacturers to develop new models of their own. At the beginning, only ČKD was interested and submitted its six-wheeler command car, based on its civilian Praga-Grand chassis. As the company was not ready to accept the army's specifications, the army did not order the car.

Meanwhile the army was monitoring a new "peoples'" car from Tatra. It had an air-cooled two-cylinder 12 HP(9 kW) engine and an unusual chassis with a central tube and independently sprung

Two of the Tatra 26/30 personnel carriers during the 1929 maneuvers. These were provisional bodies fitted by the Milovice workshops.

The Tatra 26 NII-678 during the mountain trials.

The Tatra 26 (right front) NII-678 and two of the Tatra 26/30 with wooden bodies built by the Milovice workshops during a parade there.

rear half-axles, which allowed good cross-country performance. The army bought one chassis and tested it in the Krkonoše mountains in very difficult terrain. The car covered 10,000 km between December 1926 and March 1927, and at the end of the test showed minimum wear. The army bought a second chassis and Tatra equipped them with bodies from 5 mm iron plates. One car was built as an open-top personnel carrier, one with a fixed turret with the ZB vz.26 machine gun as a light reconnaissance armored car.

In June 1927 these two cars participated in additional trials side by side with the Renault and Citroen-Kegresse competitors in Krkonoše mountains. The two little Tatras reached the top with no problems, negotiating gradients up to 37%.

In December both cars were returned to Tatra. The personnel carrier was rebuilt into an armored car with a fully rotating turret, armed with a vz.7/24 heavy machine gun, while the reconnaissance car was left intact. The modified cars were shown in February 1928 to President Masaryk, among other vehicles of the armored battalion.

In March 1928 both cars performed successfully during their last mountain test. The army ordered nine more chassis of the Tatra 26/30, with 24 HP(18 kW) four-cylinder engines. The chassis were delivered to the workshops of the armored battalion in Milovice, which built on all nine chassis wooden mockups of armored car bodies with various turrets. Part of them was armed with vz.7/24 heavy machine guns, part with ZB vz.26 light machine guns. All eleven "armored cars" took part in the 1928 maneuvers, and during the next three years were widely used for drivers', machine gunners' and tactical training. They also participated in all parades.

In the spring of 1928 the army finalized the body and armament of the planned light armored car. It carried two ZB vz.26 light machine guns, one in a small cylindrical, fully rotating turret, one in its frontal plate. Tatra was asked to build a prototype, using one of the army's nine chassis and 5 mm armor plates supplied by Poldi. The finished car returned to Milovice in July 1930 and was extensively tested. The battalion obtained another Tatra armored car prototype in August 1929, built on the Tatra 17/34 chassis with a six-cylinder engine. This car had a mild steel body and was slated for testing and evaluation only.

On December 11, 1930 the armament commission of the Ministry of Defense decided, based on the good results of the testing of the prototype, to order the Tatra armored car as the OA vz.30 in larger quantities for the cavalry and infantry divisions' reconnaissance units. Simultaneously, command and telegraph cars vz.30 were ordered, based on the same Tatra 26/30 chassis.

The same car being shown after its modification to President Masaryk in February 1928.

Prototype of Tatra 17/34 light armored car with a six-cylinder engine. The army bought just one vehicle with a mild steel body for evaluation (NIX-257).

Various pictures of production OA vz.30 armored cars, showing their camouflage, exterior stowage, details of visors and the turret, and their small size.

Tatra submitted its bids on December 15, 1931 and the final order was placed by the army in early 1932. The order anticipated originally bringing the remaining eight chassis to the standard of the prototype, and building an additional 43 new cars of the same type. The eight chassis were sent to the factory in October 1932, and the final order was placed on March 6, 1933. The contract stipulated delivery time as December 1933. The army changed its order shortly after placing it, as it decided to have Tatra build all 51 armored cars as new constructions, and modify the eight chassis as command cars. The total order was for 8,314,960 Kč (over $ 332,000), and the delivery was postponed till April 9, 1934. Tatra started completing the chassis in August 1933 and in the second half of December began building the armored bodies. All the finished cars had their armor tested against rifle fire from 100 m; all the bodies passed. The first six cars (nos. 13376 to 13381) were accepted by the army on January 29, 1934. In the second half of February the army took over another sixteen cars, but the following

The prototype of the OA vz.30 (Tatra 72) already in the proper camouflage paint. Note the marks caused by test firing against its armor.

cars were not accepted until July 1934, because their garages in Milovice were not ready in time.

The OA vz.30s were made part of the 1st and 2nd training squadron of armored cars, but most of them were stored. Four combat squadrons, located in Přelouč, Brno, Bratislava and Košice, were assigned two cars each. The OA vz.30s were shown to the public for the first time in May 1934 in Český Brod.

Tatra was supposed to get an order for an additional 55 armored cars with gun armament, designed to fight enemy armored vehicles. The concept of such a car was discussed in army circles during the entire year of 1934, but the final decision was not to order such vehicles. The OA vz.30 was too lightly built to incorporate the 3.7 cm Škoda antitank gun, and the available large caliber machine guns did not have sufficient armor penetration to be really effective against tanks. It would have been feasible to armor chassis of larger automobiles (see Škoda projects), but the lack of financial means precluded such a solution.

OA vz.30 and OA vz.27 shown with the LT vz.35 tanks in Milovice.

Shortly after assigning the OA vz.30 cars to units, the initial enthusiasm for these vehicles somewhat waned. The construction of the car was undoubtedly very modern, but the vehicles had some important shortcomings. Their engines were weak, and did not allow the use of the cars in the terrain in a way their chassis would otherwise allow. The cars were not even able to cross the ditches at the edges of the roads. Only belatedly it was found that the fully armored and equipped vehicles were not so nimble as their light wooden-bodied predecessors. The armor was thin, and could be penetrated even by normal rifle rounds from short distances. Finally, the light ZB vz.26 machine guns could not provide sustained fire, as heavy machine guns would.

Though some proposals planned to use the vehicles as radio cars, or even as carriers and spreaders of chemical weapons, due to the lack of other options, they had to remain with the units as armored cars.

The new organization of the armored units, valid from October 1935, set up three armored regiments: PÚV-1 in Milovice and PÚV-2 in Olomouc had each one combined company of armored cars and tankettes, PÚV-3 in Turčianský sv.Martin had two such companies. Each company during the peacetime had six OA vz.30 cars, the others were stored. The School of Armored Vehicles in Milovice had three OA vz.30 cars (one of them the prototype) and two testbed Tatra's 26 nos.13322 and 13321 and the six-cylinder prototype 34. no.13354. The disposition of the OA vz.30 vehicles was thus as follows: PÚV-1 - 9 cars, PÚV-2 - 13 cars and PÚV-3 - 27 cars. The remaining three cars were with the school in Milovice. The next year, during the reorganization, nine cars were transferred from the 2. company of PÚV-3 to PÚV-1.

Further changes occurred in September 1937, when the School of Armored Vehicles was moved from Milovice to Vyškov. It left its three OA vz.30s to PÚV-1 and took only the three experimental vehicles. Thus PÚV-1 had 21 vehicles (20 regular OA vz.30s and the prototype), PÚV-2 still had its 13 cars and PÚV-3 was left with 18 cars.

In the case of mobilization, PÚV-1 was supposed to supply OA vz.30 cars for two reconnaissance companies of the 1st and 4th

Mobile divisions, i.e., 18 cars (2 x 3 three-cars platoons). Its remaining three vehicles were slated for an independent platoon of the 32nd Border Area. PÚV-2 supplied vehicles for the reconnaissance company of the 2nd Mobile division and an independent platoon for the 37th Border Area. Finally, PÚV-3 supplied vehicles for the reconnaissance company of the 3rd Mobile division and three independent platoons, one for the 39th Border area and two for the 42nd Border Area.

Most of the OA vz.30s were used during the 1938, but not according to the above plan. Their first "combat" use came during the securing of the borders in May. During the summer of 1938 various units were sent to the Sudeten area to help the police and army units in suppressing the German uprising. PÚV-1 sent a total of six platoons of armored cars, PÚV-2 two. By the end of August additional vehicles were assigned to border areas, mainly from PÚV-3. The OA vz.30 cars were quite successful in this role, and fought the Freikorps on many occasions. Following the general mobilization in September 1938, some platoons and even individual cars did reach their units, but mostly they remained in the border areas. Because of this, the reconnaissance platoons of the Mobile divisions never attained their planned strength. For example, the 1st and the 4th Mobile divisions had only three OA vz.30s each; 2nd Mobile division got seven, but only after it reached its combat position; and only the 3rd Mobile division in Slovakia had a complete company, though not until October 1938.

Most of the OA vz.30s did not reach their peacetime units even after demobilization, as companies of the armored cars were sent to Slovakia and Transcarpathian Ruthenia. During the winter of 1938-1939, nine OA vz.30s from PÚV-1 and nine from PÚV-2 were fighting in Transcarpathian Ruthenia.

The loss of the border areas following the Munich agreement eliminated the need to provide their headquarters with independent armored car platoons. The army decided to transfer ten of the OA vz.30s to the gendarmerie as support vehicles. In February 1939 PÚV-2 gave two of its cars, nos. 13324 and 13325, and PÚV-3 eight cars in March, nos.13404, 13408 and 13413-13418. The army lost one OA vz.30 in October 1938, because car no. 13381 was in the Tatra factory in Kopřivnice for repairs, and after the incorporation of the Sudeten region into Germany it was confiscated by the Wehrmacht.

Slovak OA vz.30 during upkeep and maintenance. They still carry the original Czechoslovak army camouflage scheme and registration numbers, but now with the Slovak cross on the turrets. The Slovak army used them until 1943, although after 1941 in anti-partisan duties only.

On March 15, 1939, the rest of the Czech Lands was occupied by the Germans, Slovakia declared its state and Hungary occupied Transcarpathian Ruthenia. The Hungarians captured one OA vz.30 (no.13326) in Transcarpathian Ruthenia in January 1939, but the rest were able to retreat. On March 17, one complete company with three OA vz.27s and nine OA vz.30s retreated to Romania, while eight cars of the PÚV-2 retreated to Slovakia and joined the ten OA vz.30s of the PÚV-3.

The Slovak army thus had eighteen OA vz.30s. It used five of them in combat against the attacking Hungarians on March 24, 1939, and lost one during a counterattack at Zavadka, where it was hit by a Hungarian antitank gun. In all, a total of nine of the armored cars participated in this short encounter.

During the Polish campaign, the Slovak army used thirteen of its OA vz.30s, but only four participated in combat, when they penetrated with a squadron of cavalry into Tylicz's main square. One car was hit by armor-piercing ammunition and two members of its crew were injured. All the cars pulled back safely. The other cars were used for patrol and reconnaissance duties.

For the invasion of the Soviet Union in July 1941, the Mobile brigade had five of the OA vz.30s and the Army corps an additional ten in the reconnaissance groups of its infantry divisions. The Mobile brigade's cars took part in the battle for Lipovec on July 22, 1941. One of its OA vz.30 cars was hit by an antitank gun and burned, two others were heavily damaged (nos. 13403, 13327 and 13328).

All the Slovak armored vehicles returned to Turčianský sv.Martin in August, but six OA vz.30s joined the Security division in the Ukraine between June 1942 and January 1943. The Se-

The Tatra 72 was also evaluated by the French army. Lorraine fitted its own body to the supplied chassis. The onset of hostilities prevented the possible licensing agreement.

Part of the seven-car order of the Praga TNSPE police riot armored cars, manufactured for Romania in 1936-1937, in the yard of the ČKD factory.

Front view of the TNSPE armored car shows its clean lines, small visors for the driver and the commander, and the supplementary light ZB vz.26 machine gun in the turret. The armor of the engine and the fighting compartment was 8 mm, with bottom and top plates being 4 mm thick. The body was riveted.

curity division fought against the partisans, and during one such fight, at Lojev, it lost two of its OA vz.30s (nos.13399 and 13411) which were hit repeatedly by antitank rifles. The remaining vehicles were pulled back and with the others were relegated to training. Some of them were used during the Slovak National Uprising in August 1944, but their final fate is not known.

The Germans confiscated only 24 of OA vz.30 cars after March 1939 (11 at PÚV-1, two at PÚV-2 and ten from the gendarmerie). Seven of them were used by the field propaganda units as radio-cars; it is quite improbable that any of the other cars were used in any combat capacity.

Closer view of the TNSPE car. Built on Praga TN truck chassis, it was equipped with a water cannon in a fully rotating turret. In the rear, unarmored part, were installed the pumps and a tank with 5,000 liters of water.

ČKD ARMORED CARS

Following the unsuccessful Praga L armored car from 1922, the next design from ČKD dates to 1936. In this year, it built seven Praga TNSPE riot armored cars for Romania. They were built on the Praga TN truck chassis, as they did not have to have any cross-country capability. Their armament was a mixture of riot-control and lethal. In the small fully revolving turret, they carried one ZB vz.26 light machine gun, and a water cannon for crowd control. The water tank and the pumps were in the rear part of the vehicle, while the driver and the commander sat in the cabin forward. Access to the cabin was through doors on both sides of the cabin, observation through visors, protected by armor flaps.

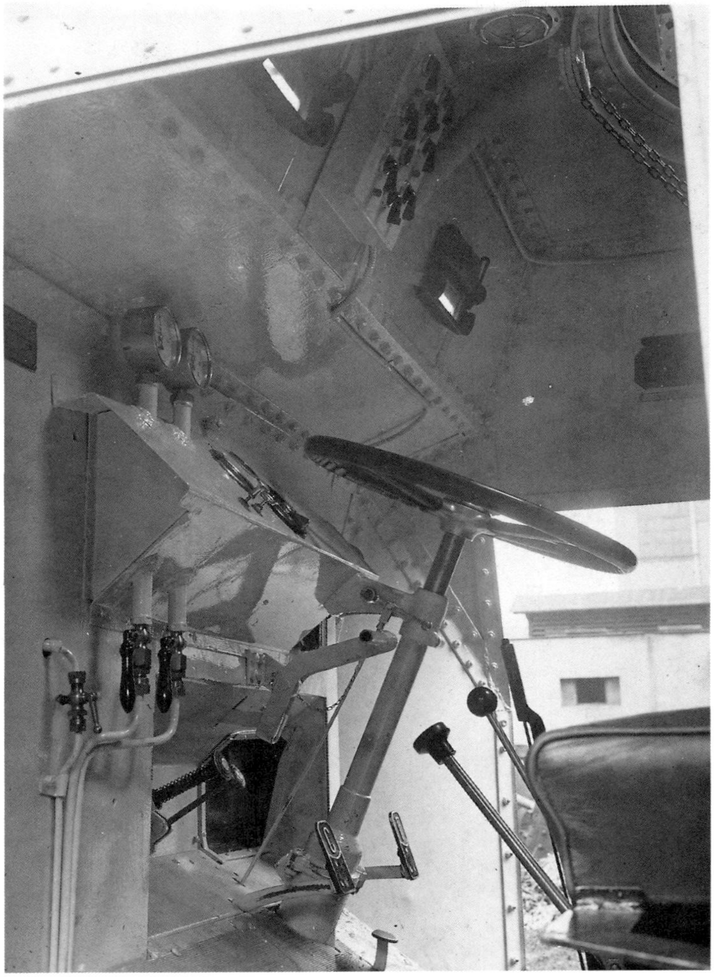

Driver's station inside the TNSPE car. Aside from the normal truck instruments, there are two manometers for monitoring the pumps' pressure and a panel with switches and control lights for the pumps and the tanks. The visors were protected by bulletproof glass blocks.

The inside of the turret with the machine gun and more ammunition boxes. Each held 200 rounds in ten magazines for a total of 1,000 rounds. The turret was not equipped with power traverse and had to be rotated by hand. It had one hatch in its top panel.

Rear view of the TNSPE riot police car.

Driver's and commander's seats and commander's turret seat. Behind it is a ready supply of machine gun ammunition and an exhaust fan.

All seven of the Renault FT tanks of the Czechoslovak army during a review in Milovice training grounds.

FIRST TANKS OF THE CZECHOSLOVAK ARMY

The French Renault FT light tank was tested as a prototype in 1917 and was immediately accepted as type M.17 FT. Built in large quantities (by the end of the fighting in 1918 the French army already had 3,177 of them), it was considered the best in its category. It was built under license by the United States and Italy, and without one by Poland and the Soviet Union. All the other states who wanted to build their armored formations were trying to buy these tanks.

The Renaults were expensive: while the prototype's cost was 43,430 French francs, the cost of production vehicles in 1918 was 51,890 French francs, in 1920 100,000 French francs and in 1922 a staggering 120,000 French francs. It was this high cost that limited the introduction of these tanks into the Czechoslovak army.

At the end of 1919, the commanders of the Czechoslovak army decided it would be advantageous to obtain at least some tanks, so that the fledgling armored units could gain some experience with this type of vehicle. Because the army expected from the start that the domestic armament industry could manufacture tanks in the future, it planned to order only six Renault FT tanks. The head of the French military mission, General Pellé, was of a different opinion. With the blessing of Klofáč, the Minister of National Defense, he ordered tanks for a whole battalion. The 75 tanks would have cost the army 40-50 million Kč. The Czech commanders with the cooperation of the Finance Ministry managed to stop such order. This angered the French to such an extent that they refused to sell even a single tank.

A nice view into the turret of a gun-armed Renault FT tank, showing detail of the open door, the observation cupola and the engine's cover. The crew is dressed in standard "working" uniforms and garrison caps, which were worn for daily servicing and upkeep.

The question of buying the tanks was raised again half a year later, but the army did not have the necessary three million Kč, as its budget has been meanwhile cut. Following difficult negotiations with the French, the first M.17 FT tank was finally ordered in 1921. The tank was delivered on January 14, 1922 to the training unit in Milovice. Additional four tanks (two armed with a gun, two with a machine gun) were ordered one year later, in January 1923, and were delivered in five months. The army now had a full platoon of tanks to show and to train with. The new head of the French military mission, General Mittelhauser, recommended buying an additional two tanks, one command and one radio equipped, but surprisingly did not recommend this type as a standard equipment for the army, as he deemed it to be already obsolete. The last two Renaults were ordered at the end of 1923 and in the Fall of 1924 the tank unit of the armored battalion had its seven tanks.

The Renault tanks remained the only tanks of the Czechoslovak army for a full ten years. Though they did not increase the fighting value of the army by much, they more than fulfilled their role as training vehicles, as hundreds of drivers and gunners were trained on them. Moreover, they participated in all maneuvers and field exercises, and afforded both the officers and the infantrymen the opportunity to train both in cooperation with and combat against the tanks.

As the tanks were heavily used, their condition deteriorated rapidly. During 1927-1928 they all underwent a complete repair and rebuilding. Even so, their technical condition deteriorated further and the first of them was scrapped in 1933 after covering a total of 2,249 km. To keep the number of combat tanks constant, its turret with the gun was transferred to the radio tank, whose fixed superstructure was removed. Further two cars were scrapped in 1935, when the LT vz.34 tanks were coming to the units, and another one in 1936. The remaining three tanks were used for drivers' training till 1939. The Germans understandably were not interested in them, and thus they lingered through the war in Milovice, where they still were in the early fifties.

The Renault FT light tanks at the time of their conception were truly revolutionary. They formed the backbone of many armies' armored units, and they played an important part in the Czechoslovak army, not as combat vehicles, but as trainers. The army's command resisted buying them in quantity; this decision helped and accelerated the development of domestic designs.

The Renault FT tanks had a body riveted from straight armor plates between 6 and 16 mm thick. The round turret had a 22 mm armor on the front part, 16 mm on its sides. The commander/gunner serviced either a 3.7 cm Puteaux SA gun or an 8 mm Hotchkiss

The Renault FT tanks company during a country exercise.

KH-50 fording a river during the mountain trials. The tractor was pulling a loaded trailer to simulate a gun.

machine gun (in 1929 all the machine-gun tanks were rearmed with the Schwarzlose vz.24 heavy machine guns). The driver sat in the front part of the body. In the rear part was a four-cylinder water-cooled Renault gasoline engine. The radio tank had in place of a turret a fixed box-like superstructure with an E 10ter radio set with a range of 8 km. Its crew consisted of three men: a driver, a radio operator and an observer. The tank had a maximum speed of 7.8 km/hour on the road and an action radius of 35 km. Its weight was 6.5 tons (MG) or 6.7 tons (gun).

The Czechoslovak army's Renaults were painted in olive drab overall, with brown snakelike spots. Their original numbers were 51 - 57; from 1932 the new numbers were 13006 -13012. In the second half of the thirties the remaining vehicles were painted in the typical three-tone camouflage of dark green, ochre and reddish brown.

The Renaults inspired the first tracked vehicle, built by ČKD in 1924, the Praga MT artillery tractor. Two prototypes were tested

The prototype KH-50 being tested as an artillery tractor in the Krkonoše mountains. The wheels of the undercarriage are in the raised position.

by the 51. Artillery Regiment and the Armored Battalion, but were not found acceptable. Though ČKD had plans to armor them, they were never realized and both tractors were scrapped in 1933.

WHEEL-CUM-TRACK

The concept of a combined chassis for tanks that would use wheels to move fast on roads and switch to tracks for cross-country running was popular in the twenties for two reasons: the contemporary tanks were slow, and their tracks and running gear were not very durable. One way to solve this problem was pioneered by the American designer Christie. His extremely fast cruiser tanks used their running wheels for driving on the roads after removal of their tracks. Though not a prophet in his own country, his designs won acceptance and wide use both in England and especially in the Soviet Union.

A second, more complicated design was bought by the Czechoslovak army from Dipl. Ing. Vollmer's company Ingemer for 1,300,000 Kč ($ 52,000). His design provided a retractable, four-wheel undercarriage on the Hanomag WD-50 fully tracked tractor. Two vehicles, designated KH-50 (Kolo-Housenka, or wheel-cum-track), were originally built as artillery tractors in 1924 in cooperation between the Ringhoffer factory in Kopřivnice (later Tatra), Laurin & Klement car manufacturer (later part of Škoda) and, as the final assembler, the company Breifeld-Daněk (later ČKD). While one prototype was scrapped, the other got a tank-like superstructure of mild iron plates, and a small turret with a 4.7 cm Vickers gun. The vehicles carried their own ramps for the wheel to track change, which took about 15 minutes.

The vehicles were extensively tested for several years by the Military Technical and Aeronautical Institute in Prague without much success. They were modified after Breifeld-Daněk became part of ČKD, and under the designation KH-60 one was finally accepted by the army (no. 13362) in 1930. Two additional KH-60s were built in 1927 and were sold to the Soviet Union the same year. One KH-70 was sold to Italy about the same time.

An improved version, the KH-60, still as an artillery tractor, during the mountain trials. Note the ramps being carried between the running wheels.

The KH-60 in its "tank" guise, armed with the 4.7 cm Vickers gun. This prototype was finally accepted by the army and was assigned registration number 13362 in 1930. It was used only for testing and in 1935 was assigned to the armor school in Milovice as a static training tool.

By that time it was clear that this design had no future, and ČKD turned their attention to normal tanks. Though the Czechoslovak army had only one KH-60 vehicle, it was widely published in foreign military press (Heigl, Zurkiewicz, Mostověnko), even after it was transferred in 1935 from the active list to the armor school as a training object. It was even listed in German recognition tables from 1939!

The failure of the combined chassis did not deter the army's command and the Military Technical and Aeronautical Institute from pursuing this idea further. In 1932 both Škoda and Tatra were asked to develop prototypes of heavy tanks with combined wheel-cum-track chassis. Each company was asked to build two prototypes and the army assigned 5.9 million Kč ($236,000) for this project.

The companies could not use any of the design features of the KH-50, as these were protected by Vollmer's patents. The specifications were also quite demanding: maximum speed of 40 km/hour, eight hours running time, and high engine output of 11 HP/ton. The specified 16 mm armor was light for a heavy tank. The proposed armament was originally a 7.5 cm gun and two heavy machine guns, all this in a vehicle not heavier than 12 tons (later increased to 15).

The vehicle had to use the special ramps for the change from wheels to track and vice versa. Each change took about ten minutes.

Škoda accepted the specification in May 1933, with the cost of the prototype contracted to be 1.8 million Kč ($ 72,000), but found out very soon that designing and building it would not be as easy as originally expected. Its "Medium combined attack vehicle", project number Zb 5553P, was interesting because it had the wheeled undercarriage inside the tracks, concealed in the tanks' body, two four-cylinder engines and complicated gearing. But its weight was 16.5 tons and it was plagued by constant problems with the chassis.

Škoda stopped all work on the prototype and asked the army for permission to build the vehicle as tracked only, with an increased armor thickness. The army declined, but gave Škoda permission to exceed the specified weight up to 16.5 tons. In March 1934, the army commission was meeting with Škoda in Pilsen to discuss the proposed armament of the new tank. Guns from 3.7 to 6.6 cm and various combinations of heavy machine guns were considered. In July 1934, the General Staff accepted a simplified specification for the vehicle, with tracked chassis only, with double the armor thickness, and a new weight limit of 15 tons. The proposed tank was planned as an infantry support and attack vehicle, usable for breaching prepared enemy positions and for fighting enemy tanks.

The Škoda vehicle, named Š-III, was equipped with frontal armor 32 mm thick and side armor between 24 and 30 mm thick. The final armament was one 4.7 cm gun and two heavy machine guns. Maximum weight was 15 tons, maximum speed 25 km/hour on the road and 12-15 km/hour cross-country.

Tatra simultaneously had developed a wheel-cum-track chassis, which it later used in its KTT artillery tractor, where the change from wheels to tracks and back was performed hydraulically from the driver's seat. Its tank got a designation T-III. It was powered by an air-cooled eleven-cylinder radial engine with an output of up to 280 HP(207.4 kW) and had hydraulic steering.

The only known photograph of the Škoda Š-III medium tank. Two prototypes were built and accepted by the army, but both were unsuccessful. With 32 mm frontal armor their weight was over 15 tons.

Both manufacturers accepted the new specifications, but their designs did not fare much better. Škoda's Š-III prototypes were plagued by many problems, especially the Š-III-8 with its new engine, and though they were finally bought by the army (nos. 13638, 13639), they never fulfilled their promise. Tatra built two prototypes (nos. 13640 and 13641), but they were even worse. The army had to return them to Tatra in 1936 as totally unacceptable, and Tatra spent the following two years trying to improve their shortcomings, especially engine's overheating and extremely high fuel consumption (300 liters/hour).

In general it can be said that the wheel-cum-track concept did not bring any progress and it slowed the design and procurement of real tanks.

Tankettes

ŠKODA TANKETTES 1930-1938

After the first World War, the trend in tank construction turned from heavy, slow and heavily armed tanks to much lighter, faster and lightly armed and armored tankettes. The English led the way again, both in Fuller's theories and in actual development. The most famous of their constructions was the Carden-Loyd Mk.VI, which became a standard of this class for many years to come. It was licensed by Italy, Poland, France, Soviet Union and Czechoslovakia and saw combat service in the initial stages of the Second World War.

In Czechoslovakia, the license was bought by ČKD, which developed its Tančík (tankette) vz.33, accepted by the Czechoslovak army as their first tracked armored vehicle of local manufacture. Though the fighting value of the tankettes was quite limited, they represented an affordable armored fighting vehicle for the cash-strapped armies of the thirties.

Škoda in the late twenties was developing and manufacturing armored cars for the army, and started with tankette development simultaneously with ČKD. Their first prototype was designated MU-2, built in one prototype in 1931. The chassis was based on the Carden-Loyd design, though Škoda did not buy its license. The vehicle was armed with one heavy machine gun, placed in a rotating turret with a 290^0 field of fire (full rotation was hampered by the driver's raised cupola).

The machine gun was the water-cooled 7.92 mm Schwarzlose vz.7/24. The armor was thin, from 4 to 5.5 mm, and was welded. The four-cylinder gasoline water-cooled engine had an output of 33 HP(24.4 kW). The MU-2 tankette was never accepted by the

First of the Škoda tankettes, the MU-2. It was armed with a heavy machine gun in a partially rotating turret, but was too small and cramped, its armor was thin and the riding qualities were poor.

The prototype of the MU-4 tankette as originally built, with individual crew's hatches, painted in an unorthodox camouflage scheme. In this front view, the ball mounts for the ZB vz.26 light machine guns are well visible.

A factory photograph of the MU-2 tankette, showing nice detail of the running gear and an angular body with the small turret.

army, as the two-men crew had very cramped quarters, the armor was too thin and the riding qualities were poor. It was used for several years as a test bed and was eventually scrapped.

Škoda's second tankette, the MU-4, returned to the typical tankette configuration, with its armament in the front plate of the crew's compartment. In its original version, it had an air-cooled flat-four engine and a similar chassis with four running wheels, paired in twos, sprung with leaf springs and carried on a common beam, which also supported the rear idler wheel.

It was shown to the army representatives in 1932 in Pilsen and in 1933 it was shown in Yugoslavia. After its return to Pilsen, it was equipped with a new, 40 HP (29.6 kW) air-cooled engine and the hull was improved. In 1934 it was shown again to the Czechoslovak army commission and in October of the same year it won the Yugoslav army competition against the ČKD's P-1 and the Polish TK-3. Nevertheless, it was not ordered by Yugoslavia nor by the Romanians. Afghanistan had shown some interest as late as 1939, and Hungary and Sweden as late as 1940, but no sales were ever consummated. MU-4 (later Š-1 and T-1) remained as one prototype. It survived the war and postwar scrapping frenzies, and was recently completely restored by the Prague Military Museum to running condition.

The MU-4 was armed with two ZB vz.26 light machine guns. Its armor was up to 10 mm thick and was welded. It carried a crew

Rear-side view of the original MU-4 prototype, showing the original engine cover of its first engine, the improved running gear and the rear visor. The vehicle was blind to the sides, though.

The MU-4 after the 1933 modifications. The two hatches were replaced by one large one, and a stronger engine was installed. This is the restored vehicle on the grounds of the Military Museum in Prague, Kbely.

The same vehicle with its armament installed. Note the interesting traveling locks for the machine gun barrels. In the background is the restored LT vz.38 light tank.

The second engine of the modified MU-4. In the rear corners are the two fuel tanks, while the oil tank sits in the ventilator's mounting. The carburetor is visible between the firewall and the engine.

of two. The vehicle was fast (41 km/hour on the road) and very agile, with good cross-country performance.

Škoda submitted for trials in 1933 an enlarged version, designated MU-6. It was actually a prototype of a light tank, carrying a 4.7 cm gun in a fully rotating turret. The vehicle was lengthened by 86 cm by adding another pair of running wheels per side. It got a larger, six-cylinder engine, developing 55 HP(40.7 kW). The crew of four had three ZB vz.26 light machine guns besides the main gun. The armor was again light, 5.5 mm, and the construction was welded.

The vehicle was for its time and type quite heavily armed, but its chassis construction was too light. Also, Škoda had at this time on the drawing board the SU and Š-II-a tanks, carrying much heavier armor, clearly more promising designs. The MU-6 was changed into the carrier of the new Škoda 4 cm Z1 dual purpose (antitank and antiaircraft) gun, but the Czechoslovak army was not inter-

New engine cover with a cooling ventilator of the modified prototype. Both engines were air-cooled, but in the original installation there were problems with engine overheating.

The ventilator cover is connected with the fighting compartment, exhausting thus the fumes caused by firing the guns. In the firewall are two openings with sliding doors; the right side one is open, showing the driver's seat.

Driver's position in the MU-4, showing his front and front-side visors, empty mounts for the machine guns, steering levers and gear lever, and the rudimentary instrumentation.

MU-4, MU-6, one of the STH artillery tractor prototypes and various trucks lined in the yard of the Škoda factory in Pilsen in 1933.

ested in such hybrid and the whole project was scrapped by the end of 1934. Škoda was nevertheless not ready to abandon the tankettes, especially when its main competitor ČKD was so successful with its AH-IV tankette, exporting it in quite large numbers to Iran (50 vehicles) and Romania (35 vehicles).

In 1935 an assault gun, according to Second World War nomenclature, was developed on a modified chassis. Its armor went up to a maximum of 20 mm and its weight to 4.55 tons It carried the 3.7 cm Škoda A3 antitank gun and the ZB vz.26 machine gun in the front plate. A crew of two was again carried, the driver being responsible for the machine gun and the commander serving also as the gunner. The vehicle was designated Š-I-d, -d- meaning "dělový" or "gun armed". With a six-cylinder air-cooled 60 HP(44.3 kW) engine, the vehicle's maximum speed was a respectable 41 km/hour. It had a range of 200 km, and was equipped with a cupola with an all-round view for the commander, an important improvement.

Škoda was finally successful with the Š-I-d. The Czechoslovak army still was not interested, but the Yugoslav army ordered eight vehicles of the modified Š-I-d type in 1937. It was designated T-32 in Yugoslav service. A Škoda 3.7 cm A3 gun was carried as the main armament, and one ZB vz.30J light machine gun was on the driver's side. The range remained at 200 km. A crew of two men was carried, which from the point of combat demands was clearly insufficient. However, it was probably impossible to fit another crew member into the small fighting compartment. The T-32s were used in battle against the Wehrmacht in 1941 at the approaches to Belgrade, but their small number and limited fighting qualities could not influence the outcome. Škoda's prototype of this vehicle was sold to the Waffen SS in 1940.

MU-6 prototype from 1933. Armed with 4.7 cm Škoda A2 gun in a fully rotating turret and two ZB vz.26 light machine guns in the front plate, it had nice, clean lines and heavy armament. But its armor was very light, only 5.5 mm, and its running gear was flimsy.

The final version of the MU-6 as a carrier of the dual-purpose 4 cm Škoda Z1 gun. This photograph shows it in the antitank configuration. One of the ZB vz.26 machine guns was retained in the front plate. The gun could penetrate a 32 mm thick armor plate at 1,500 m.

The rebuilt MU–6, but this time in antiaircraft role. The driver's compartment could be folded to provide the gun crew with an easy access for servicing the gun. The gun was effective against aircraft up to 6 km high.

In 1938 Škoda designed an improved prototype, designated Š-I-j (later T-3D). It had 30 mm armor, a 4.7 cm Škoda gun and a Diesel engine. The vehicle was developed for the Yugoslav army, which planned to order 108 of them. The prototype was shown to the Yugoslavs at the end of 1938 but, due to the changing war situation, the order was never placed. The Š-I-j prototype returned to Škoda. In 1943 the Waffen SS purchasing commission bought it; its further fate is not known.

The last of the tankettes was the Š-I-P (Přezvědný = reconnaissance) light tank, built by Škoda on their own initiative as a reconnaissance tank for the Czechoslovak army in 1937. It had a small turret with a wooden mockup of the VK ZB-60 15 mm machine gun, which was not available at that time, and one heavy ZB vz.37 machine gun. In 1939 it was renamed T-2, and was rebuilt according the wishes of a prospective customer - Afghanistan. The

The prototype of Škoda's Š-I-P reconnaisance tankette. In this original form it carried a wooden mock-up of the VK-ZB-60 15 mm heavy machine gun (which was not available at this time), and one ZB vz.35 heavy machine gun in a fully rotating turret.

All eight T-32s were used to defend the approaches to Belgrade during the German invasion of the Balkans in 1941, but did not last long. Here is one of the disabled ones being guarded by a German trooper.

Škoda Š-I-d tankette as T-32 in Yugoslav service. Armed with the 3.7 cm Škoda A3 gun and ZB vz.30J light machine gun, it had reasonable armor of 22 mm and commander's cupola with vastly improved observation.

The last of the Škoda gun tankettes, the Š-I-j, was developed in 1938 as an improved version of the Š-I-d. With a 4.7 cm Škoda A9J gun and 30 mm armor it would have been a more formidable opponent, especially with a new Diesel engine and an improved running gear. Only one prototype was built, as the war precluded any sales to Yugoslavia, who originally planned to acquire 108 vehicles of this type. The prototype was bought by the Waffen SS in 1943.

Š-I-P as it appeared after its rebuilding in 1939. The turret was removed, Škoda gave up on the 15 mm machine gun and placed the heavy ZB vz.37 and one light ZB vz.26 machine guns into the front plate.

armament of one heavy and one light MG was carried in the front plate. The crew was again two men. The bolted armor was 15 mm thick. It got also a new and stronger 6-cylinder air-cooled 60 HP(44.3 kW) engine. This gave the 4.6 ton vehicle a maximum speed of 45 km/hour. Finally, in 1943 it was tested with a center driving sprocket and lowered hull. This arrangement did not work, as the weak tracks suffered excessive damage. The vehicle was scrapped in January 1946.

The Škoda tankettes were of quite modern and interesting design, and gained the company the experience in tracked AFV construction, which came useful in the LT vz.35 and T-21 development.

Škoda tankettes were:

MU-2	1930-1931
MU-6	1932-1933
MU-4	1933
Š-I-d	1935
Š-I-d(T-32)	1937 (eight vehicles)
Š-I-P	1937-1943
Š-I-j	1938

The final version of the Š-I-P, as a testing vehicle for a middle driving sprocket. Once the test were discontinued, the vehicle was scrapped in 1946.

ČKD TANKETTES

As it was already mentioned, in 1927 the Carden-Loyd Mk.VI became the prototype of the tankette everybody was striving to copy or to license. With armor between 6 and 9 mm thick and 20 HP(15 kW) Ford T engine, it carried two men, a heavy machine gun and had a maximum speed of 45 km/hour. Manufactured by Vickers, these tankettes were exported to many countries, with quite a few of them signing licensing agreements. Between them Italy (CV.33 and CV.35) and especially the Soviet Union (T-27) built them in large quantities. The Polish version was called TK-3 and TKS, and the Poles built almost six hundred of them. During the Second World War the tankettes were shown to be totally worthless, but in the late twenties they seemed to be progressive and affordable armored vehicles.

The Czechoslovak army succumbed to the tankette's lure in 1930 and bought three Vickers vehicles and the license for their manufacture. This business was initiated by Lt. Colonel Albrecht, the head of the department for evaluating new constructions in the Military Technical and Aeronautical Testing Institute. He visited Vickers-Armstrong in 1929, and after his return enthusiastically recommended the tankettes as the ideal light armored vehicle for the infantry divisions. ČKD acted as a go-between and offered to manufacture 300 tankettes for the army, which from the beginning was not very enthusiastic. The first meeting was held on November 4, 1929, and already then the army representatives stated clearly that they did not believe the tankettes could be effective and that the army did not really need them. Due to strong behind-the-scenes pressures, it was nevertheless decided to order six test vehicles as a start, and only after their thorough testing to decide if any more would be needed.

In March 1930 three Mk.VI tankettes, one trailer and one transport flatbed arrived in Prague from England. The shipment's cost was 488,745 Kč ($ 20,000), but the army had to pay 1,150,000 Kč ($ 46,000). In this sum was already included the first third of the licensing royalties of Ł 12,000.

Inside of the Praga-Carden-Loyd tankette, showing the cramped fighting compartment, with the unprotected engine directly between the two crew members. This engine placement caused excessive heat and noise in the fighting compartment and led to the fast fatiguing of the crew. The rear open bins were used to store the ammunition for the machine gun.

ČKD has demonstrated the tankettes to the army's representatives in May 1930, but afterwards returned them to the factory for a closer study and the army got them only in July 1930. At this time, ČKD was busily building three domestic copies, designated Praga-Carden-Loyd, or Vehicle P. The vehicles were promised for August 1930 but, due to last minute breakdowns, the tankettes were delivered at the end of September. ČKD billed the army 221,325 Kč ($ 8,800) for each tankette, which was more than twice the originally estimated amount. Moreover, ČKD built four of the tankettes, one as "company" vehicle. It is quite probable that its cost was divided among the three army vehicles, and its final disposition (see Chapter 4) seems to corroborate this assumption.

During the Fall maneuvers in 1930 only the English tankettes participated. All the original misgivings of the army's experts were

The three Praga-Carden-Loyd tankettes during cross-country running in September 1930, when they were shown to the army representatives.

The prototype of the ČKD P-1 tankette during the ditch crossing test in the factory. As compared with the Mk.VI, the crew compartment was enlarged and was provided with observation slits on all sides. The engine was moved to a separate engine compartment in the rear.

This frontal view of the P-1 shows the armored cover of the front differential, the driver's visor on the right and the left ball mount for the ZB vz.26 light machine gun. The two top entry hatches are also visible.

fully corroborated: the crews had very poor vision through the narrow slits, the machine guns had a very narrow field of fire; not only the vehicles, but even the crew members in a single vehicle could not communicate properly; and the slow and underpowered vehicles had a high incidence of defects. In all instances, their role was better fulfilled by the OA vz.30 armored cars.

To be usable, the tankettes had to be radically reconstructed. ČKD rebuilt one of its prototypes for 115,363 Kč ($ 4,600) during 1931. The gunner now had the ZB vz.26 light machine gun with a 60° field of fire behind an armored shield and his ammunition was carried inside the vehicle, not in bins outside as it was with the original Carden-Loyd. Both the driver and the gunner got visors to the front, sides and the back, protected with armored flaps and bulletproof glass blocks. The track guiding was improved to prevent its shedding, which plagued the Mk.VI tankettes, and the radiator in the back was protected with armored slits instead of the impractical doors.

The modified tankette, called Praga P-1, covered 4,350 km during the 1931-1932 tests. The army representatives asked for an upgrading of the armor from 6 to 8 and from 9 to 12 mm, and for an addition of a second machine gun, this one fixed at the driver's side and fired by him via a Bowden cable. The other two prototypes were similarly rebuilt and the completed trio was accepted finally on October 17, 1933 by the armored regiment in Milovice.

Now came the question of a production order. The army staff was resisting, but Lt. Colonel Albrecht and ČKD found a strong ally in the Minister of Defense Bradáč, who finally ordered his experts to place an order for seventy vehicles, officially named "Tančík vz.33 (Tč.vz.33)". The final order was placed on April 19, 1933. The cost was 131,200 Kč ($ 5,250) plus Ł 32 of licensing royalty per vehicle.

ČKD promised to deliver forty of the tankettes by the end of the year and the rest before September 1934. Due to various delays, the assembly of the vehicles started as late as November 1933. The first ten vehicles were ready on January 9, 1934, but the army accepted them in February. Twenty more were delivered in March, another ten in April, twenty in August and the last ten in October 1934. The driving tests were performed on the road Praha - Milovice - Praha. During the armor tests the armor plates were penetrated several times by the test rounds, but the holes were simply filled with rivets and the cars were accepted.

The tankettes were armed by two light machine guns as originally planned. Heavier armament was evaluated, but unsuccessfully. The ČZ vz.30 aircraft machine gun overheated during sustained fire, and the new ZB-52 heavy machine gun was too large for the mounts. The light machine guns proved to be unsuitable. The driver had his hands full with driving the vehicle and could not fire his fixed machine gun. The gunner had trouble holding his weapon at speeds over 10 km/hour and could not lay it properly at all. Most of the tankettes took part in the final maneuvers in 1934. All the misgivings about their usefulness were fully validated. The vehicles had trouble negotiating the terrain, their firepower was abysmally low, and coordination among the five vehicles in a platoon was impossible to maintain with the provided flags and acoustical signals.

The tankettes were similarly unsuitable for reconnaissance, as the crew had trouble enough to observe the road and could not survey the terrain. Due to their low firepower they could not act as supporting vehicles for infantry, and combat with the enemy's armored vehicles was totally out of question. Finally, the army decided to use them in three-vehicle platoons as support vehicles in the border areas.

In the years 1934-1936 the tankettes had to be used for training as a replacement for the light tanks, which were not yet available. Heavy utilization caused continuous breakdowns, especially as the vehicles had many weak points due to insufficient design and/or faulty materials used during their manufacture. Many parts were substituted or reworked before the vehicles were brought to a partially acceptable standard. They were divided among the three armored regiments. PÚV-1 had 24 tankettes, PÚV-2 had 16 and PÚV-3 had 30.

Tančík vz.33 from the rear, already in the three-tone standard camouflage. Note the engine's cooling louvres on the back wall, observation slits above the engine compartment, the muffler and the placement of various tools and towing cable.

Tančík vz.33 of the Slovak army in 1944.The Slovaks inherited thirty of the tankettes, and though they planned to use them against the partisans first in the Ukraine and later at home, they used them only for training.

Some tankettes were used in the border areas during 1938. One three-car platoon supported the 2nd infantry division in Southern Bohemia, one platoon was with the 44th infantry regiment in Northern Bohemia and the last supported the 8th infantry division in Moravia. As the tankettes fought only against lightly armed Freikorps units, they were relatively successful, providing mostly moral support to own units and demoralizing the enemy. Luckily, no one fired on them, and so they did not come to any harm.

The tankettes were used again during the September 1938 mobilization, but again proved to be highly troublesome and unreliable. Some of them fought later that year in the Transcarpathian Ruthenia, but those were only isolated actions. After March 1939, forty of the tankettes were confiscated by the Germans, who probably stored them or used them for training. The Slovak state's thirty tankettes were kept in running condition, though the Slovak army did not use them operationally at all. In 1944 their use was envisaged as supporting vehicles for the anti-partisan units, and some were even used during the uprising in 1944, but on both occasions without much success.

These three photographs show the manning of the tankettes and their start from the garage area in Milovice during an exercise. Their crews wear the leather tanker's helmets and side arms. The vehicles have the registration numbers assigned and are in the three-tone camouflage. Note the padding on the inside of the hatches and the driver's machine gun on the right side of the hull.

Technical description:

The vz.33 tankette was a small (2.7 m long, 1.45 m high) vehicle for a two-man crew, armed with two ZB vz.26 light machine guns with 2,600 rounds. The frontal armor was 12 mm, sides 8 mm, top plates 6 mm and bottom 4 mm thick. The frontal armor withstood armor piercing 7.92 mm infantry rounds from over 125 m away, side armor from over 185 m away. Both were supposed to withstand standard infantry rounds from over 50 m away. The weight of the vehicle was 2.3 tons. The body was constructed from L-shaped steel profiles with flat armor plates riveted to them.

The driver's visor was 300 x 125 mm, protected by a 120 x 40 bulletproof 50 mm thick glass block and an armored flap with a 90 x 2 mm slot. The gunner had a similar visor, but only half the size. Similar visors were on the sides and one in the back plate. Access hatches on the roof were 646 x 400 mm, 4 mm thick and opened to the rear.

The gasoline engine employed was a four-cylinder, water cooled in line Praga AH of 1.95 liters displacement. Its maximum output was 30 HP(22.2 kW). The gearbox (4 + 1), reduction, differential, driving shafts and brakes were taken from the Praga AN truck. Maximum speed on the road was 35 km/hour, and the endurance with 50 liters of fuel was 4.5 hours in light terrain or 100 km on good roads.

Running gear consisted of two tracks, each assembled from 130 links, 170 x 90 mm. Their ground contact length was 1,300 mm. The tracks were stretched over the front driving and rear idler sprockets. Four rubber-tired running wheels on each side were paired into two frames, sprung by leaf spring clusters. The running wheels had a diameter of 340 mm and were 80 mm wide. The upper part of the tracks was supported in wooden grooves, inlaid with sheet metal.

The tankettes could cross a ditch 1.20 m wide, climb an obstacle 0.5 m high and wade up to 0.4 m deep. Both the theoretical gradient and side stability were 45°. Ground pressure was 0.5 kg/cm^2.

Standard equipment consisted of a pick, a shovel, a jack, a track tensioning spanner and a towing cable, all fastened to the outside of the body.

All Tančík vz.33s were painted in the standard three-tone camouflage scheme, and their only identification were the black plates with white numbers in the front and on the rear plate. The vehicles were assigned numbers 13420-13489, the three prototypes had numbers 13359-13361 (old numbers before December 1932 NIX-223 - NIX-225). The original Carden-Loyd Mk.VI tankettes were painted in one color, probably dark gray or khaki, and were assigned the numbers 13355-13357 (old numbers NIX-219 - NIX-221).

ČKD developed another, much more successful tankette slightly later. It was of a modern and progressive construction and its fighting properties were infinitely better than those of Tančík vz.33. It is regrettable that this vehicle came too late for the army contract, and had to prove its excellent qualities in other countries' armies. The ČKD AH-IV tankette is described in Chapter 4.

Domestic Tanks: Army Specifications and how they changed

The tank had clearly shown its possibilities in the last years of the First World War. The world's armies in the twenties had accepted it as part of their arsenals but did not have any clear ideas on how to use it to the best advantage, or even what technical and tactical properties it should have.

The concept of a "standard" tank did not emerge until the thirties. It was a fully tracked armored vehicle, which carried its main armament, a gun, in a fully revolving turret, and had a secondary armament of one or more machine guns. The tanks differed in their weight, armor thickness and gun caliber from country to country. These differences were conditioned by the various tactical doctrines. Any tank was a compromise between its armor protection, speed and its offensive power, i.e., its gun caliber.

States with an offensive doctrine, like Germany, designed their tanks with lighter armor but with higher speed, and planned to use them in cooperation with motorized infantry and artillery units in the Panzer Divisions for the breakthrough and deep penetration of enemy lines. States with a prevalently defensive doctrine, like France, saw the tanks as a support arm for the infantry, similar to artillery. Their tanks usually had heavier armor, low speed, and were tied to their infantry units.

The Czechoslovak army was led and trained by the French Military Mission, so it is only natural that it basically accepted the French view on the use of tanks and their organizational incorporation into army formations. But there was a difference. In several theoretical treatises, various Czechoslovak officers published their views on the use of tanks and armored vehicles in general. First was Lt.Colonel Veselý, the commander of the armored battalion. In 1923 he submitted to the army command a study on the use of tanks. He proposed to form strong units, combining tanks, motorized infantry and motorized artillery, as the main attack force of the army. At the same time, he stressed the need to build strong anti-tank defenses. Similarly progressive views were expressed by Captain Sovadina in 1930 in his booklet "Armored Formations". The last of the tank theoreticians was Major Papoušek, who in 1935 published a book titled "Tanks in Combat, Their Tactical Use in Examples".

The official view was published in a report describing the tasks of tanks, written by the 3. Department of the General Staff in 1932. The tanks were still not accepted as a full-fledged offensive weapon, but were viewed as an ideal tactical defensive mobile weapon for Czechoslovakia with its long borders. The lack of manpower and artillery could be offset by fast, powerful, mobile formations.

The army was in this laudable task slowed by concentrating its attention and budgetary means on the development of tankettes and wheel-cum-track vehicles. This similarly led to some confusion when the specifications for new models were issued. We have already seen how the specifications for the wheel-cum-track vehicles changed. The Czechoslovak army's first real tank, the LT vz.34, was a private venture of ČKD, and a specification covering this type was issued only after its acceptance by the army.

The ascension of the Nazis to power in neighboring Germany led to a reevaluation of the Czechoslovak army's rearmament plans. The "Report on Tank Situation" from August 1934 specified a need for a new category of light tanks, both for the cavalry units and for infantry support. The category II was a cavalry tank, with 15 mm armor (i.e., the LT vz.34). The II-a category was planned for combat in cooperation with cavalry, and with infantry only during attacks on unprepared defenses. These tanks carried a frontal armor of 25 mm and 15 mm on the sides and back. II-b category was an infantry-support vehicle, with 25 mm armor on all sides. All three light tanks were armed with one 3.7 cm gun and two heavy machine guns.

Tanks of the category III, the mediums, had 32 mm armor, 4.7 cm gun and were planned for infantry support in attacks on a prepared defense, and to fight armored vehicles of the enemy. Besides these main categories, prototypes of various special vehicles were also ordered and developed, as we will see later.

During the years 1920-1935, the tank development in the world was slow and sluggish. Only the emergence of various conflicts and the shadow of the approaching war fueled the development of this type of weapon. Czechoslovakia was a member of an exclusive club of states who designed and built their own tanks. Besides the Western democracies such as the United States, England, France, Sweden and Poland, there were totalitarian states like Germany, Italy, the Soviet Union and Japan building their own tanks. The Czechoslovak design school became quite famous between the wars, and the production capacity of Czechoslovak industry was also quite impressive. For comparison, the United States during the period 1920-1938 built a total of 300 tanks, while the diminutive Czechoslovakia built over 430 for its own army and 389 for export.

The first vehicles of the fifty tanks production lot, at this stage still without any armament, and before final painting.

THE DEVELOPMENT AND INTRODUCTION OF THE LT vz.34

Following the debacle of the Tančík vz.33, it became clear both to the army's command and to the manufacturers that the tankettes could not replace tanks, not even light tanks. Design projects for equipping the tankettes with a fully rotating turret had shown that the vehicle would have to be changed so radically that it would be easier to design a new one. This is what ČKD did in the end and submitted to the Military Technical and Aeronautical Testing Institute as project P-II. It was a light tank with 7.5 tons weight, 4.6 m long, and a crew of three. The planned armament was a 4.7 cm Vickers 44/60 gun, for which ČKD signed a licensing agreement, and two machine guns. Planned armor thickness was only 8 to15 mm . Designed maximum speed was 30 km/hour on the road, endurance was eight hours. ČKD asked 418,000 Kč ($ 16,700) for the prototype. The army's staff accepted the offer in 1931 and contracted ČKD to build one prototype. The first domestic construction of a light tank, the P-II, was slow in coming and only in November 1932 did the army accept the prototype. The tank was assigned number 13363 and was placed under the auspices of the Military Technical and Aeronautical Institute. Its testing was done by the armored battalion in Milovice. By February 1933 the prototype had already covered 3,400 km without any serious defects. The Minister of National Defense met with the director of the Military Technical and Aeronautical Institute on February 17, 1933 and was given a full report on the new tank's performance. Because the report was highly positive, the Minister decided to order not only the tankettes, but the light tanks as well. Already the next day the Chief of the General Staff instructed General Ne[illegible]ík, the head of the 2nd Division of MNO, to order from ČKD fifteen tankettes and ten light tanks.

The manufacturing line for the LT vz.34 tanks at ČKD factory in Prague Libeň. Note the two wooden rails between the return rollers, which carried the track; the cooling fan tunnel in the rear and the turret ring opening taking up the whole width of the hull.

The whole following month the army's representatives met with ČKD executives. The main topic of these meetings was the price of the ordered vehicles. The army wanted to keep the cost of its light tanks around 300,000 Kč, while ČKD calculated a price of 400,000 Kč. In the end, the manufacturer prevailed and the cost of each of the new tanks was finalized at 413,330 Kč ($ 16,500), this without armament, optics and a radio set. The total order was increased to seventy tankettes and fifty light tanks.

The order was placed on April 19, 1933. Six vehicles were to be delivered by September 30, 1933, the following 24 by September 30, 1934 and the last 20 by July 30, 1935. The first six vehicles represented an evaluation series, and the remaining tanks were supposed to be approved into production only after the acceptance of the first six tanks. Some defects found on the first prototype after its disassembly required changes in the gearbox and reduction, on the radiator and to the exhaust.

When the order was finally placed, the question of the armament was not decided, and ČKD thus could not complete the design of the turret. The army emphatically rejected the Vickers gun and the ZB vz.26 machine guns, proposed by ČKD. It specified a domestic (i.e., Škoda) gun and heavy machine guns, capable of sustained fire. ČKD got the final turret design with the Škoda 3.7 cm A3 gun as late as December 1933. One year later, the prototype was equipped with this gun and with two ZB-53 air-cooled machine guns.

The P-II prototype, army registration number 13363, during inspection by an army commission of the Military Technical and Aeronautical Institute in November 1932.

The second batch of production tanks, fully armed and with army registration numbers allotted, awaiting approval by the army's purchasing commission in 1935.

The production of the first six tanks started in ČKD's factory in Slaný in September 1933 with the understanding that they were to be provisionally armed with only two ZB vz.26 machine guns. Simultaneously, the first lots of armor plate from Poldi were found to be of very bad quality, as they were cracking when hit. This problem slowed the production, as acceptable armor plates were not ready until December 1933. Thus, the first six tanks were handed over to the armored battalion on April 23, 1934.

The new Praga P-II tanks were assigned to the 3. company of light tanks, which thus far had only the seven old Renault FTs. Following a short training of the crews, the new tanks (nos.13490-13495) immediately took part in the May maneuvers. They trained in cooperation with the tankettes. The P-II tanks showed good behavior in terrain and were easy to drive. Though still plagued by defects, they crossed trenches and crushed barbed wire obstacles with ease, and proved to be a good support vehicle for both infantry and cavalry. The only problem was their weak 15 mm armor, which was not strong enough to withstand antitank guns.

Because the tank did not carry guns, the battalion command asked for permission to install the 3.7 cm guns from the Renault tanks on three of them, so that the troops could train with gun-armed vehicles. This request was denied and it took 18 months before these first vehicles were fitted with the proper armament. The refitting took place in ČKD between January and August 1936 and the tanks returned to Milovice, where they remained on the roster of PÚV-1 even after September 1937, when the tank school moved to Vyškov.

The Czechoslovak army officially accepted the P-II tank on July 13, 1935 as the LT vz.34 (Lehký[light] tank vz.34). The first of the 44 production tanks were shipped to units at the end of 1935. Six vehicles, nos. 13496-13501, were obtained by PÚV-1 on December 18, 1935. The next batch of 14 tanks (nos.13520-13533)

A prototype turret armament mount of the P-II with Škoda A3 gun and ZB vz.35 machine gun. In the production vehicles the combined pivoting mount was abandoned and replaced with a separate gun mount and a ball mount for the machine gun. The prototype retained this mount, and it can be seen on the P-II-R reconstructed tank.

The first tanks of the production series of 44 tanks, assigned to PÚV-1.

Nice views of an LT vz.34 tank during cross-country tests. The three-tone paint scheme is well visible, as are various details of the vehicle and its exterior equipment. On the first picture the civilian boy below the tank and the farmer's wife in the background with her sheep provide a quaint contrast to the buttoned down vehicle.

went to PÚV-3, momentarily stationed also in Milovice. PÚV-2 in Moravia got its 18 LT vz.34 (nos. 13502-13519) on January 8, 1936 and the last six tanks (nos.13534-13539) went directly to the new station of PÚV-3 in Turčianský sv.Martin on January 14, 1936. Only after the delivery of these production tanks were the "prototype six" returned to ČKD for reconstruction, and their delivery on August 17, 1936 was considered the fulfilling of the original order.

The LT vz.34 tanks at the time of their conception in 1932 were comparable to the best tanks in the field, but the progress in tank design came quickly, and thus in 1935-1936 their armor and mobility were not up to par. The improved prototypes, P-II-a from 1935 and P-II-b from 1936, were not as successful as P-II and were not developed further. This was not true for the P-II prototype, which was later modified and improved.

By July 1934 it had already covered 6,329 km and even survived a collision with a train on an open crossing in March of the same year. The tank suffered only a torn mudguard and a broken driving pinion; it is not known what happened to the locomotive. The long-term tests ended in September 1935 and the vehicle was transferred from the roster of the Military Technical and Aeronautical Institute to the tank school in Milovice. In 1937 ČKD proposed to the army a modification of the LT vz.34, namely the installation of the Praga-Wilson gearbox and planetary steering used on its export models. The army accepted the offer and the reconstructed vehicle returned to Milovice in August 1937 as P-II-R (reconstructed).

The results of its testing were very encouraging: the cross-country riding properties were highly improved and the excessive wear of the steering clutches suffered by the production tanks was eliminated together with another unpleasant property: the shedding of the tracks. ČKD was encouraged by the results and proposed to enter the P-II-R into the forthcoming army trials for a new light tank after additional modifications.

These consisted of mounting the new Scania-Vabis six-cylinder engine, built under license by Praga, with an output of 125 HP(92.6 kW), versus the original engine's 62 HP(45.8 kW). Be-

LT vz.34 tanks as part of a military parade in Prague, saluting the reviewing stand of the President of the Republic and the visiting Romanian King Carol in 1936.

cause of this, the prototype with a factory number P-10 071 had a maximum speed of 50 km/hour (30 km/hour before reconstruction), excellent cross-country performance and even longer endurance. The only problems encountered were with the running gear, so the testing continued in 1938. Simultaneously, ČKD was testing the installation of the new Škoda A7 gun, intended for the new LT vz.38, into the turret of LT vz.34. Based on very favorable driving and firing tests, it was proposed to modify all the fifty LT vz.34 tanks at a modest expense, but historical events did not allow it.

Because the LT vz.34 was designed in the period of not fully crystallized design conceptions, its frontal armor of 15 mm was insufficient already at the time of its introduction, and it was quickly replaced with the LT vz.35 tank that had 25 mm frontal armor. The tanks were organized into three-vehicle sections and assigned to the companies of the armored regiments, to train as many crews as possible. Once the LT vz.35 tanks started arriving at the regiments, the LT vz.34s were delegated to less important units. Starting in 1937, according to the mobilization plans, the LT vz.34 tanks were assigned to reconnaissance mixed units of the infantry divisions. There they were supposed to act as reconnaissance vehicles but their low speed handicapped them severely in this task. The vehicles were reassigned in the following way: PÚV-1 had 17 of them, PÚV-2 obtained additional six for a total of 24 vehicles, and PÚV-3 was left with nine. In November 1938 the general staff decided to strengthen the PÚV-3 in Slovakia. From PÚV-1 nine tanks (nos.13492 and 13493-13500) were sent to PÚV-3, from PÚV-2 nine vehicles (nos.13504, 13506, 13507, 13511-13513, 13521, 13522 and 13524). The Martin regiment thus had (with its LT vz.34 nos.13531-13539) a total of 27 vehicles of this type.

Following the Munich agreement, the army offered to sell its fifty LT vz.34s, but did not find a buyer. It decided to concentrate all the vehicles in Slovakia with PÚV-3 to form one tank battalion. The German occupation in March 1939 ended all these plans. Slovakia kept its 27 tanks and the remaining 23 production vehicles with the P-II-R prototype were confiscated by the Wehrmacht. Due to their obsolescence and small number, they were probably scrapped quickly.

In the Slovak army, the LT vz.34s soldiered on as training vehicles till 1944. During the uprising, the insurgents left ten tanks in the Martin barracks during their retreat and the remaining ones were used in the role of fixed fortifications on the approaches to Zvolen. The Germans had the ten LT vz.34s transported to Škoda in Pilsen for repairs. Škoda obtained in October 1944 LT vz.34 nos. 13493, 13497, 13498, 13499, 13504, 13511, 13521, 13524, 13533 and 13536. The residing German military representative with Škoda had the vehicles scrapped because of their obsolescence and very poor condition. This led to a small upheaval, as the main armament office of the Waffen SS was interested in these vehicles. They planned to have them assigned to the army of the Croatian dictator Pavelič. But by this time, March 1945, all the turrets were shipped from Škoda to be mounted in fixed fortifications, rearmed with two machine guns; the bodies were converted into heaps of armor plate. Only two vehicles remained in their original state and survived the war, to be scrapped in the fifties with other historically irreplaceable equipment.

The reconstructed prototype P-II-R during his trials in Milovice in 1938. This tank is not fully modified, as it still carries the original A3 gun.

TECHNICAL DESCRIPTION

Construction of the tank:

The tank was small, only 4.6 m long, 2.1 m wide and 2.22 m high. Its fully loaded weight was 7.5 tons. It carried a crew of three: the commander/gunner, the driver and the radio operator.

The body of the tank was made from steel profiles. Flat armor plates were either bolted or riveted to the frame, using bolts and rivets from a special steel. Up to a height of 100 cm all the joints were waterproofed. The vertical frontal and side armor plates were 15 mm thick, the slanted plates were 12 mm thick, the engine's cover hatch was 10 mm thick and both the floor and the top plates were 8 mm thick. The armor was certified to withstand armor-piercing "S" rounds fired from either a rifle or a machine gun from distances over 75 m.

The crew compartment was separated from the engine compartment by 3 mm thick firewall. Access to the engine from the crew compartment was possible through a door in the firewall, which also had ventilation openings that closed. All inside fittings were finished in a way that prevented injury to the crew, or a possibility of any part of the crew's uniforms or equipment getting snagged. In the front part of the fighting compartment the driver and the radio operator sat on leather seats with padded leather strap backs. The driver sat on the right side. In front of him he had a 300 x 75 mm visor, protected by two flaps. In the inside flap was installed an episcope with a 25° field of view. The outside armor flap was connected with the inside flap, so that opening one closed the other. The outside flap in a closed position formed a vision slit 3 mm wide. In the right front wall, the driver had a vision slit 120 mm long, protected by a bulletproof glass block 50 mm thick. The position of both visors allowed the driver to observe the road from his normal sitting position. The front visor was provided with padding so that the driver could lean his head on the episcope when driving.

In the middle of the front wall was installed the ZB vz.35 machine gun in a ball mount, allowing a 30° field of fire, with an elevation of 25° and depression of 10°. The machine gun had a spotting telescope, or could be fired over open sights, built into the driver's visor. In case of need, the driver could lock it in a central position and fire it using a Bowden cable. In this case, the gun was set to hit the ground 250 m in front of the vehicle on a horizontal plane.

In front of the radio operator there was a 120 x 50 mm visor, protected by a bulletproof glass block 50 mm thick and by an armored flap from the outside. Spare glass blocks and two driver's episcopes were carried inside. Access to the fighting compartment was possible through the commander's cupola and through a 450 x 400 mm floor escape hatch.

The fully rotating turret sat in a ball-race ring of 1,265 mm diameter in the top plate of the fighting compartment. It was constructed the same way as the hull. The straight frontal 15 mm thick plate carried in its center the main gun, and on the right side the ball mount for the turret machine gun. The turret sides were made from 15 mm thick armor plates. Its upper armor plate was 8 mm thick. The turrets were freely interchangeable between vehicles.

In the upper plate was placed eccentically the commander's cupola with an inside diameter of 570 mm. Its sides were 15 mm thick and the dished hatch was 8 mm thick. The cupola was provided with four episcopes, oriented to front, rear and to both sides. The commander also had at his disposal a monocular mirror periscope 565 mm long, which he could extend through the hole in the cupola hatch. The periscope had a field of view of 35° and its enlargement power was 1.3x. The cupola's hatch had another 30 mm opening for using the signal flags during the day, and a special signal lamp during the night. The openings in the hatch were covered with armored flaps when not in use.

Drive train:

The tank was equipped with four cylinders, water cooled, in line engine with an SV valve-train. The engine was tuned to use an alcohol-gasoline mixture. It had a bore of 110 mm, stroke of 160 mm and a displacement of 6.08 liters. At 1,350 rpm its output was 62.5 HP(46 kW). It gave the vehicle a maximum speed of 30 km/hour on the road and about 15 km/hour in medium terrain.

The engine was pressure lubricated, with a dry sump, three gear pumps and an oil filter. Scintilla magnetos and all electrical installation were shielded to prevent interference with the radio set. Fuel to a Solex carburetor was supplied by an electric Autopulse pump and by an injector Espero. Two 64.5 liter fuel tanks were placed in the sides of the engine compartment. An oil tank was placed above the right-hand side fuel tank. Both gasoline and oil supply was assured up to a 50° gradient.

The water cooling system used a standard radiator and an exhaust fan. The cooling was sufficient up to 35°C outside temperature. The capacity of the radiator was 35 liters. Starting the engine was possible by an electric Scintilla starter motor and by hand, both from outside and from inside the vehicle.

Directly connected to the engine was the main clutch, equipped with a clutch brake. The engine's torque transferred from the clutch to the reduction in the front part of the fighting compartment via a drive shaft, running in the floor of the fighting compartment under a metal cover. The reduction had two steps, engaged by the driver with a mechanical lever on his left. In front of the reduction was the gearbox with four forward gears and one backward. The gear shifting lever was placed on the cover of the gearbox. The driving sprockets of the tracks were driven from the gearbox through beveled gears and directional clutches, equipped with brakes.

Chassis:

The driving sprockets each had 19 teeth 20 mm wide. The running gear had eight 340 x 80 mm rubber-tired running wheels. Two pairs of wheels fastened on a common shackle in their middle formed a frame. Two frames formed a wheel carrier, sprung with leaf spring clusters. There were two wheel carriers per side. The 395 x 40 mm bronze guiding wheels were sprung on a lever that also was used for tensioning the track.

Each track consisted of 107 links 272 mm wide and 90 mm long. The track was guided by two return rollers and by wooden, metal-lined grooves. The tank had a ground pressure of only 0.50 kg/cm^2.

The tank could cross a ditch 2 m wide, climbed an 0.8 m high obstacle and waded in water 0.8 m deep. It could uproot trees 0.18 m thick and breech a brick wall 0.5 m thick.

Steering:

The vehicle was steered by the directional clutches and their brakes. Steering was mechanical, by two horizontal levers in front of the driver. The foot brake acted on the gear mechanism, the driving brakes on the directional clutches. Each brake could keep the vehicle stationary on a 100% gradient.

Exterior and interior equipment:

On the left front wall of the fighting compartment was installed the radio set vz.35 with a range of 2 km. It worked in the telegraph mode: the operator sent messages with his Morse key and received them in his headphones. The aerial was on the left front fender. The signal lamp and the signal flags for exterior communication were stored in the turret. The tanks were also equipped with a four-tone siren for acoustical communications, driven by the exhaust gases.

The ammunition for the machine guns was carried in 100-round belts in ammunition boxes, the gun rounds were carried in six-round magazines in the turret overhang. A standard ammunition supply was 60 rounds for the gun and 2,000 rounds for the machine guns. Spare parts and tools for servicing both the gun and the machine guns were carried in leather bags in the turret.

The driver had in front of him the control panel with an oil pressure gauge, speedometer, and the starter and electric horn buttons. On the left side of his visor at eye level the driver had three signal lights - a red, a green and a blue bulb. By lighting them according to a prearranged code, the commander in the turret conveyed his orders to the driver. The controlling buttons for these lights were of different shapes and were in the turret.

The fighting compartment was illuminated by a ceiling lamp in the rear. Exterior lighting consisted of two contour 5 W lamps in metal casings, mounted on the front part of the fenders. The same type of lamp on the rear plate illuminated the number plate. The tank also carried a 50/35 W headlight with a diameter of 108 mm on the front plate between the visors. It could be used as a spotlight or a work light, as it was equipped with a long cable.

Larger tools were carried outside the hull. On the right fender were attached the shovel, the pick and an iron crowbar. A five-ton jack and the spanner for track tensioning were on the left fender. On the rear of the left fender were two spare track links and on the right fender the wooden block for jack support. On the upper hatches of the engine compartment a towing cable was carried. It was 12 m long, with eyelets, and had a towing capacity of 14 tons. The tank had four towing hooks, two on each corner of the hull. All were 600 mm above ground level, and all had the capacity of 3.5 tons.

Armament:

The LT vz.34 tank carried in the turret a 3.7 cm tank gun, coaxial with a 7.92 mm heavy machine gun, both having a full 360° field of fire. Elevation of both weapons was 25°, depression 10°. The gun penetrated a vertical cemented armor 45 mm thick at 500 m, and was capable of penetrating 25 mm armor at 30° angle at 1,000 m. The semiautomatic breech mechanism allowed a high rate of fire, up to 15 rounds/min., and the range was 4,000 m with a HE round and 1,500 m with an AP round. The 3.7 cm gun was officially designated in the Czechoslovak army vz.34ÚV (Škoda's designation A3). It was very effective for its time.

Beside the main gun, the tank carried two ZB vz.35 heavy machine guns, manufactured by Československa Zbrojovka Brno. Both were mounted in special ball mounts, one in the turret and one in the front plate of the hull. The turret machine gun could be fired coaxially with the main gun or separately.

All the weapons were aimed through spotting scopes with 1.25x enlargement and a 25° observation field. The turret scope had the distance scale for the main gun up to 1,500 m. The machine gun scopes were scaled up to 1,000 m.

In case of a damage to the turret scope, the gun could be aimed up to 600 m over an open sight by opening an armored cover in the front plate of the turret. The machine guns could use iron sights after removing steel plugs in the ball mounts.

The turret was rotated in two ways: by turning the wheel of the rotating mechanism (one revolution corresponded to 3° turn), or by moving the turret manually by pushing on the main gun's shoulder pad after disconnecting the turning mechanism. An arresting gear stopped the turret in any position.

Camouflage and markings:

The Czechoslovak LT vz.34 tanks carried the standard camouflage scheme, used in the thirties. All of their exterior surfaces were painted in three matte colors: dark green, ochre and dark brown. The inside of the engine hatches were camouflaged the same way, the interior of the cupola hatch was upholstered with dark brown leather. The whole interior of the fighting compartment was painted in an ivory color.

The white assigned police registration numbers were carried on black plates on both front and rear plates. The LT vz.34 tanks carried numbers 13490 to 13539, the prototype had the number 13363.

THE DEVELOPMENT AND INTRODUCTION OF THE LT VZ.35

The ascension of the Nazis to power in neighboring Germany led to a reevaluation of the Czechoslovak Army's rearmament plans. The "Report on the Tank Situation" from August 1934 specified the need for a new category of light tanks, both for cavalry units and for support of the infantry. At the same time, the army's budget between the years 1934 and 1937 included almost 240 million Kč (approximately $10 million) for a procurement of 279 light and 42 medium tanks.

The Škoda works in Pilsen, the leading armament manufacturer, was the sole supplier of guns, but beginning in the early thirties it tried to establish the monopoly for supplying fighting vehicles. It was frustrated by the success of its rival ČKD in supplying the army with first the tankettes and later with the light tanks. Škoda did not spare any effort (including alleged bribes) to make

The prototype of a light Škoda tank SU from 1934. It carried the 4.7 cm Škoda A2 gun and two Schwarzlose vz.24 water-cooled machine guns, but its armor was only 15 mm.

Frontal view of the SU tank. This vehicle had the pneumatic steering and gear changing used later on Š-II-a, and similar running gear, though the hanging of the front idler wheel was somewhat unorthodox and was changed for the LT vz.35.

sure it would obtain the next order for the new light tanks. Simultaneously, it consummated a cartel agreement with ČKD, according to which both companies would share in the production of whatever design won an Army contract.

Škoda had developed several prototypes of tankettes during the early thirties, but the army did not accept any of them. Its next prototype was the light tank SU (Střední Útočný vůz, or Medium Attack vehicle), presented to the army commission as a prototype. Its armor was too weak, only 15 mm, and it was not even seriously considered for the upcoming army trials. It did serve as a basis for the development of the Š-II-a prototype, though.

By the end of 1934 the Czechoslovak army formulated its tank specifications and asked the leading armament companies Škoda, ČKD and Tatra to submit prototypes for the various tank categories. The companies were most successful in the II-a category of cavalry tanks. ČKD used its experience with the P-II type, already bought by the army, but Škoda also gained experience with its Š-II (ex SU) prototype. Both prototypes were ready by the summer of 1935 and testing by the army commission began. The tank from Pilsen emerged victorious and the Czechoslovak army decided to accept it as its standard light tank under the designation LT vz.35.

The introduction of the LT vz.35 tank was widely discussed and critically judged during the following years in Czechoslovakia. These discussions were instigated in both army and government circles by ČKD, which considered itself injured by the introduction of the Škoda tank. It is true that both prototypes were not so different, while the P-II-a was undoubtedly simpler. But because it closely followed the P-II's construction, it was judged to be inca-

Finished R-2 tanks awaiting delivery, but still without machine guns. This is the last lot manufactured for Romania in February 1939.

pable of further improvements. The Š-II-a, on the other hand, was a brand new construction, which used from its predecessor only the engine and steering. It was thus expected that the prototype would be amenable to further improvements according to the army demands. This expectation actually was not realized in practice, but removal of its prototype from export offerings signified that ČKD did not consider it marketable.

Forgetting the circumstances of LT vz.35 introduction, it must be noted that the Czechoslovak army obtained in the second half of the thirties a tank that had no par in its category anywhere in the world. Its only competition was just beginning to grow in ČKD, but its TNHPS tank was ready to compete with the LT vz.35 tank only by the beginning of 1938. It is thus completely wrong to accuse the Czechoslovak army of making a faulty decision by introducing the Š-II-a in 1935.

The Škoda prototype (13620) had an interesting history. While the ČKD P-II-a prototype soon disappeared, the Škoda tank was transferred to the Armored Corps school in Milovice. It was modified often before becoming a full-fledged fighting vehicle. In September 1937 it was transferred to Vyškov and from there in August 1938 was shipped with one army LT vz.35 (13903) to Moscow. Both vehicles were shown to a commission of the Red Army in Kubinka. The Soviets proposed to buy one vehicle, but Škoda suspected they were planning an unlicensed production and refused. Romania interned both vehicles on their way back and released them only in time for them to arrive on Czechoslovak soil on March 14, 1939. On March 15 both vehicles fought against the attacking Hungarians. The army tank was destroyed by a Hungarian antitank gun, but the prototype retreated to Romania. Škoda managed to get it back after six months and, because its original owner, the Czechoslovak army, did not exist anymore, kept it under the designation T-11. It was constantly improved and modified, until it caught the attention of the Waffen SS purchasing commission in December 1942. The Germans bought the veteran tank with 22,000 km on its odometer and took delivery in September 1943. Thus, Škoda managed to sell it twice: to the Czechoslovak army for 783,550 Kč and to the Germans for 35,000 Deutschmarks.

The Ministry of Defense (MNO) ordered on October 30, 1935 a total of 160 LT vz.35 tanks, which it needed to equip the tank battalions of four cavalry brigades. The order was parceled equally between Škoda and ČKD. An additional 35 tanks were ordered on May 12, 1936, and one month later the army ordered another 106 tanks. Thus the total of the LT vz.35 tanks ordered by the army was 298, with their deliveries planned between September 30, 1936 and July 30, 1937.

At the end, neither company could honor its delivery dates, because the design of the tank was not completed and the production was slowed by frequent changes and high reject rates. ČKD participated in the production without any enthusiasm and used every occasion to accuse Škoda of technical incompetence or dirty dealings.

Doubts about the suitability of the LT vz.35 design led the army to order long-term tests, using chosen vehicles from the current production. The first test, running from January to March 1937, during which the tested vehicle covered more than 4,000 km, was

Three views of the only prototype of the ČKD's entry for the army's competition for a standard light cavalry tank - the P-II-a. Its close resemblance to the P-II type is obvious.

LT vz.35's cross-country performance being tested.

LT vz.35 breaching a brick wall and uprooting a tree. It could uproot a tree 35 cm in diameter and penetrate a brick wall 45 cm thick.

moderately successful. The second test had shown certain shortcomings of the design. From April 6 to the end of September 1937 tanks number 13683, 13696 and 13721 covered between 6,000 and 7,000 km each. Following their disassembly some excessive wear became evident, caused by faulty design, inferior assembly and poor materials.

Both these tests and a high rate of defects of the tanks already with the army units led to a certain lack of trust in the new tank. The Czechoslovak army was forced by the constantly deteriorating international situation to rearm as fast as possible, but suspected the quality of the delivered tanks. This led, combined with the unyielding position of both companies in financial matters, to a peculiar status of the third order for 106 LT vz.35 tanks. Though they were manufactured and already partially shipped to the army, the Ministry of Defense did not issue its official purchase order, backed by budgeted funds. Following tough negotiations between the representatives of both companies and the army, the latter yielded and issued the purchase order on November 9, 1937.

The army accepted its first LT vz.35 tanks from Škoda on December 21, 1936. Škoda fulfilled its obligations by delivering the last three vehicles as late as April 8, 1938. ČKD delivered their 149 vehicles already during 1937, but lost any interest in these tanks, as it had some promising export orders for its own designs. Both companies still had to perform warranty repairs on all their vehicles, their extent based on the experience gained by the armored units and by the long-term tests.

In December 1936 the first fifteen LT vz.35 tanks arrived at the 1st Armored Regiment in Milovice. The other two regiments started getting their vehicles shortly after that. Of the 298 new LT vz.35s, the PÚV-1 obtained 197 (Škoda made 13666-13720, 13864-

PzKpfw 35(t) in the Aberdeen Proving Grounds armor museum in the state of Maryland, USA.

One of the army's LT vz.35, resplended in its three-tone camouflage.

13893 and 13903-13914, ČKD made 13721-13784 and 13915-13950), PÚV-2 49 (ČKD made 13785-13817 and 13951-13966) and PÚV-3 52 (Škoda made 13818-13860 and 13894-13902). All regiments were supposed to fill the needs of the four Mobile divisions with men and material, as the planned strength of each Mobile division was 98 light tanks, three OA vz.27 and 9 OA vz.30 armored cars. Besides this, the regiments had to supply 34 independent three-vehicle tank platoons for infantry divisions and border areas, and 23 tankette and six armored car platoons for the border areas.

Based on the results of the meeting of VTLÚ (Military Technical and Aeronautical Institute) from May 30, 1938, a complete list of necessary design changes was prepared, together with a plan of tank shipments from the units to the factories. Each factory was supposed to modify twenty tanks monthly, besides normal repairs. At the same time, the ZB vz.35 machine guns in the tanks were

The crew of an LT vz.35 tank, dressed in tanker's exercise overalls and wearing leather helmets.

Crews of two LT vz.35 tanks during training. The leather flap on the mudguard was to prevent soil or mud being thrown forward by the tracks, thus obscuring the driver's vision. On this photograph, the military censor eliminated the hull machine guns.

On this highly retouched official photograph of the LT vz.35 tanks all details are clearly visible. Note the padding of the inside of the open hatches, coiled cable on the driving light and the drivers open visor and bead sight for the front machine gun.

The fronts of a series of brand new LT vz.35 tanks, showing the massive bolts on the front armor and the typical armored recoil brake cylinder above the gun barrel.

gradually exchanged for the ZB vz.37 type. For these reasons, the army in the critical days in May 1938 did not have its full complement of tanks. The ones it did have, did not have their full machine gun armament. Obviously this situation would have had an unfavorable impact on an armed conflict with Germany, the extent of which is difficult to evaluate today.

In the summer of 1938, the LT vz.35 tanks were widely used both in the most mobile units of the Czechoslovak army - the Mobile divisions, but also in support units, which were suppressing the insurgency of Henlein's followers in the Sudeten region. During repeated and long marches, the tanks covered thousands of miles. This intensive utilization did not cause an increased incidence of breakdowns, showing that the manufacturers had already eliminated the worst defects. The good familiarization of the crews with their vehicles after a year of training also helped. It is interesting that most of the defects were caused by the electrical system, not by the complicated pneumatic installation.

Right after the September general mobilization, the army placed an urgent order with Škoda for an additional 105 LT vz.35 tanks, because it feared that the already ordered LT vz.38 tanks of ČKD would not be available in the near future. This special order was in place for several days only, as immediately after the Munich agreement it was rescinded. Its realization in the case of conflict with Germany was dubious anyway, but the Czechoslovak army had an option to obtain several scores of new LT vz.35 tanks manufactured for Romania. The major part of the Romanian order of 126 R-2 tanks was in September 1938 in the Škoda factory in Pilsen in an almost finished state. Several of them, which were finished, were confiscated by the army.

Immediately following the Munich agreement, due to the changed international and domestic situation, the Czechoslovak army lost interest in further expansion of its armored units. It was even willing to sell some of its tanks, especially the older ones. During this period, several countries expressed interest in buying Czechoslovak tanks, both through Škoda and ČKD. The most important of these was England, once a tank superpower. The British

In May 1940, the original Š-II-a prototype, modified as T-12, was shown to the Hungarians. It had a modified turret with an overhang and a new commander's cupola.

T-12 during the tests. It carried the 4.7 cm A9 gun.

knew the LT vz.35 tank and, because at this time they did not have its equal in their armory, they wanted to buy them. They were interested in buying a hundred vehicles from the army's inventory and another hundred directly from Škoda.

Simultaneously, the English company Alvis Straussler asked for a manufacturing license for this type. Negotiations dragged from September 1938 till April 1939, but the political situation and finally the German occupation in March 1939 made any agreement impossible.

The Soviet Union also negotiated with Škoda in the second half of 1938 a license for manufacturing the Š-II-a. The Soviet experts knew this tank from their visits with Škoda and asked for its demonstration in USSR. Between September 14 and October 11 two of these tanks went through extremely difficult evaluation trials in the tank center at Kubinka under the auspices of a large group of Soviet tank experts and covered more than 1,000 km. Both the official protocols from these tests and personal comments by the Soviet experts have confirmed the good impression made by the Škoda tank.

The following negotiations had clearly shown that the Soviets were interested only in buying one tank. This was typical of how the Soviet tank corps operated: based on a foreign prototype they started full-scale manufacturing of vehicles, adapted for domestic conditions. Škoda naturally was not interested in such a deal and tied the sale of the prototype to the sale of a license. The Soviets declined and the whole matter thus died.

Nazi Germany was also very interested in the LT vz.35 as a potential adversary. First, the Germans tried to obtain information through bogus companies, but Škoda was not allowed to show the tank abroad and this approach was unsuccessful. Next, the Abwehr tried open spying, using Germans residing in Czechoslovakia. Several spies were apprehended, but some information probably leaked out anyhow. The Germans also tried to gain information from Romania, which was not careful enough in protecting their R-2 tanks.

Škoda also tried to sell the Š-II-a tanks to Yugoslavia. It designed them with a new turret with a 4.7 cm gun and a Diesel engine. Škoda put together one prototype with the new turret, but the contract was never consummated due to the international situation in 1940.

Even Poland became interested in the LT vz.35 tanks, but because of its strained relations with Czechoslovakia, it could not have hoped to close a regular contract. The Polish intelligence service managed to look over the R-2 tanks, as they were transported to Romania at the beginning of 1939 through Polish territory. A Polish military delegation visited Pilsen on March 9, 1939. They were interested in buying Škoda tanks, but this time the heavier Š-II-c type. The occupation of Czechoslovakia naturally stopped this sale also.

The last export order came in 1940, when Afghanistan ordered ten improved Š-II-a (T-11) vehicles with the A8 gun. The Germans originally allowed their production, but later changed their mind and the tanks were finally sold to Bulgaria under the new designation T-11.

TECHNICAL DESCRIPTION

Designation:

Š-II-a	factory designation (Škoda, category II-a)
T-11	factory designation from May 1939 (Tank, Light, 1 Cat.)
LT vz.35	designation of the Czechoslovak army
LT-35	designation of the Slovak army (Lahký Tank - 35)
L.T.M.35	Leichte Tank Muster 35, German designation used at the beginning of the war
PzKpfw 35(t)	Wehrmacht designation (Panzerkampfwagen 35 tschechisch) used from January 1940
R-2	Romanian army designation for both the tanks delivered originally by Škoda and the ones delivered by the Germans
JleK TahK	Škoda-Bulgarian army designation

According to the original categorization of the Czechoslovak army, the light tanks of II-a category were destined to serve in the ranks of cavalry, only exceptionally in cooperation with infantry. They were light tanks for maneuver combat, especially in terrain, in the ranks of tank units (similar to the British designation "Cruiser Tank").

Production:
Developed by the Škoda works in Pilsen and based on a prototype approved by the Czechoslovak army, which ordered 298 vehicles of this type. From this number, Škoda manufactured 149 and ČKD in Prague the other 149 according to a cartel agreement between these two companies. In 1942, two additional machines were assembled from parts of eleven scrapped tanks.

The final manufacturers completed the vehicles from parts of mostly their own manufacture. Lesser components were supplied by a host of suppliers in Czechoslovakia. Only in special cases foreign suppliers were used (for example Swedish SKF bearings). The main guns were supplied exclusively by Škoda and the machine guns by Zbrojovka Brno. The armor plate was manufactured by both the Poldi steel mill in Kladno and by "Vítkovické Horní a Hutní Těžířstvo" in Moravia, each supplying 149 sets.

Price:
When the first contract was signed, the price was set to be 524,640 Kč ($ 21,000) with the Poldi armor, and 527,840 Kč ($ 21,100) with the Vítkovice armor. This price did not include armament, optical equipment, radio and NIFE batteries, which were billed separately. The total amount the army paid for a complete vehicle was 741,868 or 745,068 Kč ($ 29,700 or 29,800). The manufacturing costs are impossible to find out today.

Construction of the Tank:
The hull and the turret of the tank were assembled from L-shaped steel profiles, to which were riveted flat armor plates. Both the rivets and the screws were made from special steel. Up to a height of 100 cm all the joints were waterproofed. The front plates of both the hull and the turret were 25 mm thick, side and angled plates were 16 mm thick and plates angled more than 30° were only 12 mm thick. Both the bottom of the hull and the top plates were 8 mm thick.

The front 25 mm plates were impenetrable to armor-piercing rounds of the 20 mm Oerlikon gun from 250 m and farther; the 25 and 16 mm plates could withstand vz.31 armor-piercing machine gun and rifle rounds at any distance. For the vz.31 rounds, the safe distance for the 12 mm plates was 100 m, for the 8 mm plates 125 m.

The hull was divided by a bulkhead 4 mm thick into fighting and engine compartments. In this firewall there were several openings, covered with a wire mesh, which allowed easy access to important engine parts from inside the fighting compartment. This construction of the firewall was required by the cooling design, where the cooling air was drawn in through the commander's cupola on the turret and was passed through the fighting compartment to the engine radiator. The disadvantage of such a design was the constant drought in the fighting compartment, danger of engine fire penetration through the firewall, and increased crew fatigue due to engine noise and heat. Its advantage was the excellent ventilation of the fighting compartment during firing of the weapons, lack of which caused great problems in other tanks.

The driver and the radio operator sat in the front part of the fighting compartment, the driver on the right side. He had in the front plate a 390 x 90 mm observation slot, covered with an ar-

Inside view of the front part of the fighting compartment. The driver's seat is on the right, with his driving levers, episcope and instrument panel. The radio station is on the left wall and the hull machine gun is partially concealed behind the signal lights panel hanging from the turret's ring. Behind the seats are two boxes of machine gun ammunition and a fire extinguisher.

The driver's visor in the open and closed positions.

Front view of the tank. Driver's visor is partially open. It has the fixed sight for the front hull machine gun. The front part of the sight was on the front edge of the hull, but on this vehicle it is missing and only its base is left. The hull machine gun's ball mount and the armored barrel protector are well visible. The plug in the middle of the ball mount was removable in case the iron sights had to be used. The holder in the middle of the front plate carried the spotlight. On the right is the cylindrical mount of the aerial. Note the many traces of machine gun fire. Though they did not penetrate, they left quite an impression on the front plate.

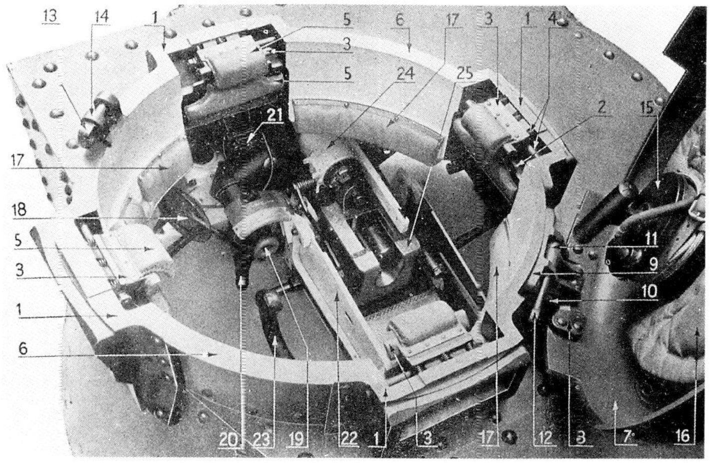

An inside view of the turret through commander's hatch. The gun breach (25), spotting scope (19) and padded episcopes (5) are well visible.

mored shutter 28 mm thick, and protected from inside with a bulletproof glass 50 mm thick. In the right side armor plate he had a smaller vision slit 120 x 3 mm, similarly protected with 50 mm thick bulletproof glass. The radio operator had a similar opening in the front plate, but smaller, 150 x 75 mm. The machine gun was in the center of the front hull plate in a ball mount, allowing a 30° field of fire, with an elevation of 25° and depression of 10°. The machine gun had a spotting telescope, or could be fired over open sights, built into the driver's visor. If necessary, the driver could lock it in central position and fire it using a Bowden cable.

Escape from the fighting compartment was possible though the driver's hatch, through the commander's cupola and, finally, through a floor escape hatch of 50 cm diameter.

The fully rotating turret sat in a ball-race ring of 1,267 mm diameter in the top plate of the fighting compartment. It was constructed the same way as the hull. The front straight 25 mm thick plate carried in its center the main gun, and on the right side the ball mount for the turret machine gun. The turret sides were made from 16 mm thick armor plates, which were slightly curved. Its upper armor plate was 8 mm thick. In the upper plate was eccentrically placed the commander's cupola with an inside diameter of 570 mm. Its sides were 16 mm thick and the dished hatch was 8 mm thick. The cupola was provided with four episcopes, situated front, rear and on both sides. The commander had for his disposal also a monocular mirror periscope 565 mm long, which he could extend through the hole in the cupola hatch. The periscope's field of view was 30° and the enlargement 1.3x.

Driver's hatch and his side visor. The hatch's front edge lies on top of the front plate and is not protected against bullet penetration, as the machine gun hit clearly shows. The turret was not provided with an anti-splash ring either.

Commander's cupola with its four episcopes, armored periscope and covers over the holes for signal flags and the signal lamp.

Detail of the hinge of the cupola and its stop that held it in the upright position when open.

The cupola's hatch had another opening for using the signal flags during the day, and a special signal lamp during the night. The openings in the hatch were covered with armored flaps when not in use.

Drive Train

The tank carried an internal combustion, four-stroke, water cooled, four cylinder engine with a rated output of 120 HP(88.7 kW) at 1,800 rpm. With bore and stroke of 140 x 140 mm, the engine's displacement was 8,620 cc. The cylinders were in one block, with a removable head made from aluminum alloy, and with SV valvetrain. The crankcase was made from cast steel alloy. The split crankshaft was carried in main cylinder bearings. The engine was pressure lubricated, with a dry sump. The oil was circulated by a gear pump through a filter and an oil cooler. The engine could use gasoline, alcohol-gasoline blends and Dynalcol. It was equipped with two Zenith Udd carburetors, accessible from the fighting compartment.

Fuel was supplied by two fuel pumps, a mechanical membrane one (AC pump) and an electrical one (Autopulse). The main fuel tank had a capacity of 124 liters and was placed on the left side of the engine. An auxiliary 29 liters tank was situated on the side of the fighting compartment.

The ignition was magneto-electric, doubled, with Scintilla 12 V magnetos. Each cylinder had two spark plugs, firing through two

Three views of the Škoda T-11/0 engine. It was in-line four cylinder gasoline engine, water cooled, with displacement of 8,620 cc and 120 HP(88.2 kW) output. The weight of the engine and its accessories was 900 kg. Its fuel consumption was 184 g/hour/kW.

An open engine compartment of the R-2 tank. The main engine (3) is in the center, with its valve covers (4), distributors (6), magnetos (7), coils (11,12), radiator (26), main (25) and auxiliary (24) fuel tanks, exhaust manifold (21) with heat exchanger (20) and intake air manifold (23).

Detail view of the muffler. Note the track pins and the mud scraper in front of the rear drive wheel.

Two views of the LT vz.35 transmission and its actuating pneumatic cylinders.

Detailed view of the rear, driving sprocket of the LT vz.35 tank, with its reduction and two19-teeth rings.

independent electrical circuits. The engine was started with a Scintilla starter that had an output of 2.94 kW at 24 V, but the tank also had a provision for hand cranking from inside the fighting compartment.

The cooling water was circulated by a water pump through a tunnel radiator on the right side of the engine compartment. It was equipped with a fan, powered by the engine. The cooling water capacity (including the equalizing tank) was 50 liters. Exhaust gases were led through an armored elbow into a muffler, situated on top of the right rear fender. Because the tank was pneumatically steered, it was equipped with two three-cylinder two-stage compressors, driven by the main engine. Their working pressure was 810.6 KPa, their output was 100 liters/min. and the necessary input 0.44 kW.

The crankshaft was connected to the transmission with three triple planetary cog wheels, which were constantly engaged with two cog wheels, connected via shafts to the clutches of the individual gears; and to one cog wheel, to whose hollow shaft the reduction was attached. The transmission had three gears. The first and the second gear were activated by belt brakes, pneumatically controlled; the third (direct) gear was activated through a dry multiple plate clutch, similarly pneumatically controlled. The first gear could in emergencies be engaged via a Bowden cable.

Behind the transmission was the reduction with two stages formed by cog wheels, engaged through a gear clutch, pneumatically actuated. In an emergency it was possible to use a mechanical lever. The total number of gears was six forward and six in reverse.

From the transmission the driving force transferred to the rear driving shafts via beveled cog wheels, while the pinion wheel engaged two dish beveled cog wheels, which were freely mounted. Through the gear clutch one or the other of those wheels was connected with the corresponding drive shafts, and that caused forward or reverse movement. The clutch was actuated by a lever pneumatically, and in an emergency mechanically.

Into the drive train was interposed a planetary gear for each track, which allowed their steering. Its outer ring engaged through a pinion gear the brake drum of the driving sprocket. When the brake was engaged by compressed air, or in an emergency hydraulically, the driving force was transferred from the planetary gear through a Cardan joint to the drive sprocket. By loosening the brake, a gradual or sudden disconnecting of the driving force from the track was achieved, and thus turning in a curve or on the spot.

Detail of the front sprocket and the lug for the unsprung front wheel.

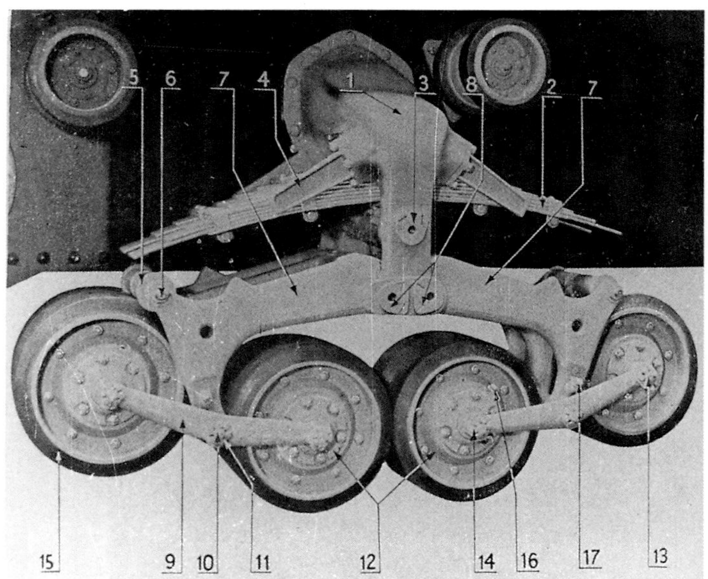

Detail of the LT vz.35 running gear; one of its four wheel carriers with four pairs of rubber-tired running wheels of 350 mm diameter.

Detail of the front idler sprocket and the box holding the track's grousers. The two toothed rings are clearly visible.

Chassis:

The running gear consisted of two tracks, stretched over rear driving and front idler toothed sprockets, running wheels and return rollers. The tracks consisted of 111 links each, 320 mm wide and 95 mm long. The links were manufactured from a hard manganese steel and had a life of 6,500 km in a period when a 1,600 km track life was considered outstanding.

The teeth of the driving and idler sprockets engaged into the slots in the track links. Both sprockets had the same diameter, 575 mm, and on their outer rims carried two rings, each with 19 teeth. Both sprockets were equipped with brakes. In the center of each track link was a guide lug, which centered the track between the paired running wheels and in the grooves in the drum of each sprocket.

The track links were connected with link pins, made from tough steel, which were loosely inserted into the links. This arrangement allowed for the fast exchange of damaged track links or pins. To prevent the pins from loosening during running, both driving and idler sprockets had from both sides mounted dish-like plates, which pushed the loose pins back into the links. For especially difficult terrain it was possible to mount grousers on some pins. These were normally stored in metal boxes behind the front sprockets.

The track was supported by running wheels, eight pairs on each side. Each wheel had a diameter of 350 mm and was 94 mm wide. They were rubber-tired and contacted the track on both sides of the guide lugs. Two pairs of wheels fastened on a common shackle in their middle formed a frame. Two frames formed a wheel carrier, sprung with 900 x 90 mm leaf spring clusters. There were two wheel carriers per side. This system provided a comfortable ride.

In the front, under the idler sprocket, there was an unsprung double wheel of the same size and design as the running wheels. These wheels were fixed on lugs on the sides of the body. They improved the centering of the track, but especially improved the obstacle crossing capability of the tank. The four pairs of return rollers on each side had dimensions of 200 x 60 mm and were similarly rubber-tired. Fixed blades mounted in front of the driving sprockets prevented their blocking by accumulated mud.

Though the running gear of the Š-II-a tank was complicated, it worked very well in cross-country driving and had shown great endurance. For example, the German commission, which was taking the tanks over following the German occupation in March 1939, tried purposefully to shed a track when running the tanks in terrain, but unsuccessfully. Only during a fast driving on hard, stony surfaces the rubber tires of the running wheels overheated and were easily damaged. This was due to their small size.

Steering:

Škoda introduced pneumatic steering on all its tanks, designed in the thirties. Compressed air as working medium eased the physical strain, caused by driving a contemporary tank with mechanical steering. The compressed air was easy to deliver to the various mechanisms, allowed fine regulation of the controlling tasks, acted fast and saved weight and room in the fighting compartment. On the other hand, pneumatic steering was complicated. This led to increased incidence of breakdowns, which were difficult to repair in field conditions.

In the LT vz.35 tank the compressed air, provided by the compressors, was stored in a 18-liter pressure flask, mounted on the side wall of the fighting compartment. Gear changing was performed using an air controller mounted in front of the driver. By placing the lever of the controller into the proper slot, the air was fed through

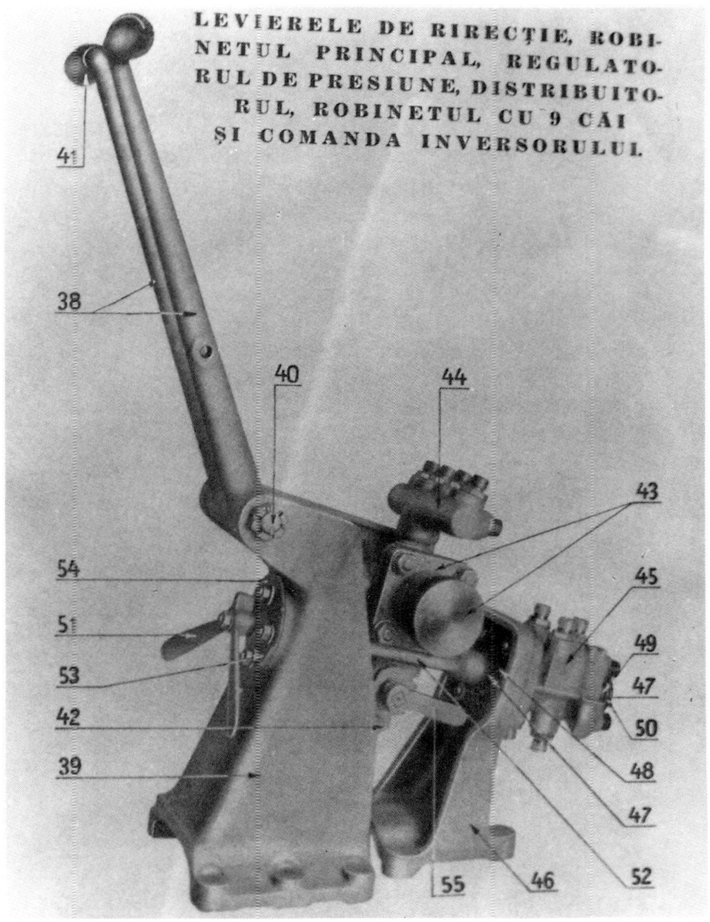

Main driving levers with their pneumatic valves.

a system of valves to the pneumatic cylinders of the controlling mechanisms of the clutches or the brakes.

The reduction was engaged by depressing the clutch pedal. A dedicated lever controlled the valve that fed the compressed air to the clutch actuating the forward or reverse running. In case of failure of the pneumatic system, it was possible to engage the first and fourth gears mechanically with the help of a hand wheel. With a mechanical lever it was possible to engage the reduction and the reverse.

Steering was controlled by the driver with two steering levers, connected to the distribution valves. By gradually pulling the steering lever toward himself, the driver loosened through the driving brake the planetary gear and thus disconnected the track from the driving force. By pulling the steering lever still further, he fed the compressed air into the main brake of the driving sprocket and thus braked the track already disconnected from the engine. This caused the tank to turn in a curve. By pulling the steering lever all the way back, the track was completely braked and the tank turned on the spot. In this instance, the track was braked by the brake in the idler sprocket. In reverse, it was braked by the brake in the driving sprocket.

By pulling both steering levers back together, the tank was braked in a straight line. Both sprocket brakes could be also controlled by the foot brake pneumatically. In an emergency it was possible to use the hand brake, which acted mechanically on the brakes of the front sprockets. The hand brake was also used for parking.

When the pneumatic steering was disabled, it was possible to steer the tank by steering levers, placed on both sides of the driver's seat. Their movement was transferred mechanically to a hydraulic cylinder, whose piston was connected with a lever actuating the brakes of the planetary gear. Naturally, steering this way asked for a much higher physical exertion than the pneumatic steering (65 kg versus 20 kg).

This description of the steering shows how complicated it was: yards of pressure lines all over the hull, eleven actuating cylinders, two compressors, many valves and stopcocks. All these were expensive to manufacture, used special materials and necessitated painstaking assembly and upkeep. To be fair to the manufacturers, it must be stressed that this system worked dependably in the field and had very few defects.

Exterior and Interior Equipment:

The inner space of the fighting compartment and of the turret was fairly cramped, due to the small dimensions of the tank. It had to be therefore used in the most practical manner to place all the necessary equipment and armaments without limiting the crew in their duties.

In the fighting compartment of the hull the driver and the radio operator sat next to each other on upholstered leather seats. Their seats' backs were formed by a wide leather strap, carrying a small cushion. On the left hull wall was mounted the vz.35 radio set with its accessories. The radio station had a range of 2 km and worked in the telegraphic mode: the operator used a Morse sending key and received into headphones in his helmet. The radio station sent through a rod aerial, mounted on the left front fender. The Wehrmacht introduced its standard phonic radio station, once it took these tanks over.

The driver was seated so that he had all its controlling levers in easy reach and did not have to strain to reach them. On the right side of the front visor he had the control panel with oil and air pressure, speedometer and electric horn button. The other switches of the electrical equipment and control lights were on a panel on the right-hand side of the hull. On the left side of its visor, the driver had at his eyes' level three signal lights - a red, a green and a blue bulb. By lighting them according to a prearranged code, the commander in the turret conveyed his orders to the driver. The controlling buttons for these lights were situated on three sites on the circumference of the turret. This primitive communication equipment did not pass the combat test, and thus the Wehrmacht installed an intercom in their PzKpfw 35(t). The crew members were connected via long cables to a central box, mounted next to the radio set. They communicated using a throat microphone and headphones.

For outside communication between the tanks besides the radio, signal flags (red and yellow) were used. The commander showed them through a hole in the cupola's hatch. During the night, he could use a special signal light with color filters.

The fighting compartment was illuminated by a ceiling lamp in its rear. Outside lighting consisted of two contour 5 W lamps in metal casings, mounted on the front part of the fenders. The same type of lamp on the rear plate illuminated the number plate. The tank also carried on the front plate between the visors a 50/35 W headlight of 108 mm diameter. As it was equipped with a long cable, it could be used as a spotlight or as a work light. Starting in 1940, the PzKpfw 35(t) tanks had additional lighting installed. On the front left fender was mounted the Notek light, which provided diffused light for night driving. The rear plate illumination was eliminated and was replaced on the left with the rear distance light (Abstand Rücklicht) and on the right with the accessory rear light (Zusatz Schlusslicht). This lighting was standard on all Wehrmacht vehicles and was manufactured by Nove-Technik in Munich. From October 1941 on the accessory rear light was replaced by a rear brake light (Bremseschlusslicht DIN 72624FL).

The tank carried two alkaline batteries NIFE 9AL/10 with 12 V and 100 Ah, stored in wooden compartments and charged by two dynamos from the engine.

The fighting compartment under the turret had enough room for the tank commander to service the tank's armaments. On the side wall were fastened four flat containers containing ammunition for the main gun (4 x 6 antitank rounds), a first aid kit and leather containers with tools. On the floor behind the driver's and radio operator's seats were two boxes with machine gun ammunition (2 x 300 rounds) and a fire extinguisher. Additional six boxes (6 x 300 rounds) were attached to the frame in front of the firewall. The last 300 rounds were in a ready box under the turret's ring.

The room under the turret was sufficient to allow the Wehrmacht to add the fourth crew member. In the original three-men crew, the commander had too many functions: commander, layer and loader of the main gun and turret machine gun operator. The role of the loader and machine gun operator was thus given to

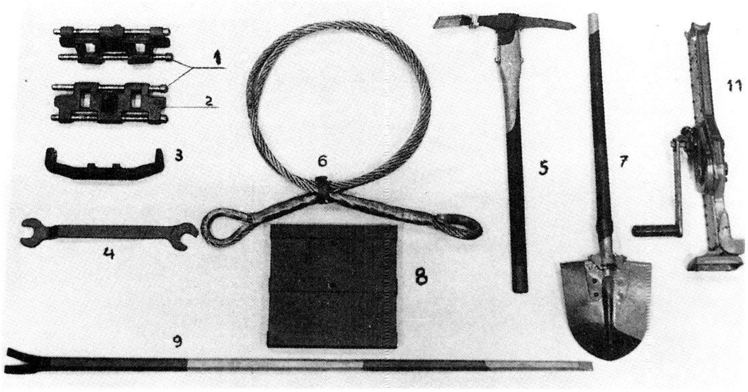

Outside equipment of the LT vz.35 tank: jack (11), shovel (7), pick (5), towing cable (6), jack's support block (8), crowbar (9), track tensioning spanner (4, and track links (1,2).

Front of the turret, showing the gun mount and its armored recoil cylinder. The turret machine gun was removed with its ball mount.

the new crew member. In the Czechoslovak service, the commander had a bicycle-type seat, hung on three chains in the turret. During the war round, tilting seats were attached to the turret's ring for both the commander and the loader.

Besides tools and spare parts for both the vehicle and for its weapons, carried mostly in wooden bins or leather bags in the fighting compartment, there were larger tools carried outside the hull. On the left hull side above the fender were attached the shovel and the pick, on right side an iron crowbar, an 8-ton jack and the spanner for track tensioning. On the rear of the left fender were two spare track links and on the right fender the wooden block for jack support. On the upper hatches of the engine compartment a towing cable was carried. It was 6 m long, with eyelets, and had a towing capacity of 10 tons. The tank carried four towing hooks, two on each corner of the hull. All were 60 cm above ground level, and all had the capacity of 5 tons.

Armament:

The LT vz.35 tank was very well armed for its time and class. In its turret it carried a 3.7 cm tank gun, coaxial with a 7.92 mm heavy

Top view of the engine's compartment. Note the hooks for fastening the towing cable on the slanted cover. The side plates are screwed on, not bolted, for easy removal in case of engine change or other extensive servicing.

machine gun, both having a full 360° field of fire. Elevation of both weapons was 25°, depression 10°. The gun penetrated a vertical cemented armor 45 mm thick at 500 m, and was capable of penetrating 25 mm armor at 30° angle at 1,000 m. The semiautomatic breech mechanism allowed a high rate of fire, up to 15 rounds/min., and the range was 4,000 m with a HE round and 1,500 m with an AP round. The ÚVvz.34 3.7 cm gun, as officially designated in the Czechoslovak army (Škoda's designation A3), made the LT vz.35 tank a dangerous adversary to any contemporary tank.

Beside the main gun, the tank carried two ZB vz.35 or ZB vz.37 heavy machine guns, manufactured by Československá Zbrojovka Brno. Both were mounted in special ball mounts in the turret and in the front plate of the hull. The turret machine gun could be fired coaxially with the main gun or separately.

All the weapons were aimed through spotting scopes with 2.6x enlargement and a 25° observation field. The turret scope had the distance scale for both the main gun and for the machine gun. The machine gun scopes were scaled up to 1,600 m. In case of damage to the turret scope, the gun could be aimed up to 600 m over an open sight by opening an armored cover in the front plate of the turret. The machine guns could use iron sights after removing steel plugs in the ball mounts.

The turret was rotated in two ways: by turning the wheel of the rotating mechanism (one revolution corresponded to a 3° turn), or by moving the turret manually by leaning on the main gun after disconnecting the turning mechanism. An arresting gear stopped the turret in any position. Most of the gun ammunition was stored in the turret overhang (eight magazines with six rounds each), which allowed fast loading. A ready magazine with six rounds was mounted directly above the gun on the turret's ceiling. It allowed the loader to fire the first six rounds almost immediately.

In the turret's overhang was also a box with tools for the main gun repair. Empty cartridge cases fell into a bag, fixed under the recoil frame. Similarly, the machine gun empty cartridge cases were collected into cloth bags.

In the Czechoslovak army service the LT vz.35 tanks carried 78 rounds for the main gun (24 AT and 54 HE rounds) and 2,700

Machine gun ammunition boxes, used in all Czechoslovak AFVs. The white band denoted vz.31 high-velocity armor-piercing rounds.

machine gun rounds (900 of which were vz.31 armor-piercing rounds) in 100-rounds belts, stored three to a box. Wehrmacht specified for its PzKpfw 35(t) 72 rounds for the main gun and 1,800 rounds for the machine guns. The command tanks carried even less ammunition due to the need to make room for additional equipment (a second radio station and a gyrocompass).

Camouflage and Markings:
The Czechoslovak LT vz.35 tanks carried the standard camouflage scheme, used in the thirties. All of their outside surfaces were painted in three matte colors: dark green, ochre and dark brown. The insides of engine hatches were camouflaged the same way, the interior of the crew hatches were upholstered with dark brown leather. The whole interior of the fighting compartment was painted in an ivory color. The assigned police registration numbers were carried on plates on both the front and the rear plates. The LT vz.35 tanks carried numbers 13666 to 13860 and 13864 to 13966.

The Mörserzugmittel on the chassis of PzKpfw 35(t). The turret was removed and the fighting compartment was covered by a tarpaulin on a simple frame. Additional jerrycan rack was added.

The long journey from the prototype to the ignominious end of the last production vehicles on scrap-heaps of several states took more than ten years. In its time, the LT vz.35 belonged undoubtedly to the world's best in its category. It had its shortcomings, but it soldiered well in even the worst conditions. A robust design and quality manufacture gave it endurance much higher than was the current wartime norm. It was designed to meet the specifications of the Czechoslovak army in the thirties, and therefore could not meet all wartime demands. Despite this, its contribution to the Wehrmacht's successes in Poland and France during 1939-1940 was quite important.

It was also the only captured tank that was incorporated into regular German tank formations. Thousands and thousands of French and Soviet captured tanks were used only in second line or police units, or were converted into weapons carriers.

In 1936 Škoda also built a 13 tons prototype Š-II-b, side-by-side with ČKD's prototype of P-II-b. Both tanks were ordered as prototypes in 1935 by VTLÚ. The tanks were delivered in January and in July 1936, and though they met the army's specifications, both were pronounced unusable. The army bought them from the manufacturers and assigned them the registration numbers (13637 and 13638), but they were used only as training aids.

The white chassis number was painted on the front inside fender. This vehicle carried a Notek light and had no hull machine gun and no radio.

In the rear, a massive tow-bar was welded to the hull. It had a towing capacity of 12 tons. The vehicle carried the rear distance light (Abstand Rücklicht), which was designed to show the following driver at right the correct following distance of 35 m. The light had four slots in two pairs. If the driver saw all four of them, he was too close. If he saw one rectangle, he was too far. Only when he saw two rectangles, was he at the right distance.

The two prototypes, the original Š-II-a and the Romanian prototype Š-II-aR were modified several times. In 1939 they were renamed T-11. After modifications, their names changed to T-12 (with the 4.7 cm gun), T-12D with the Diesel engine and T-13 with the increased armor. T-13M was a prototype with mechanical steering.

TABLE 1 lists all of the LT vz.35 tanks manufactured by Škoda and ČKD, their chassis and Czechoslovak army numbers, their assignment in the PÚVs and their final disposition.

TABLE 1
LT vz.35 PRODUCTION, NUMBERS AND FINAL DESTINATION

DATE	MANUFACTURER	CHASSIS NUMBER	CSA NUMBER	ASSIGNED TO PÚV	AFTER 1939	FURTHER ASSIGNMENT
1935	Škoda	prototype	13620	Škoda	Waffen SS	
21/12/36	Škoda	50130	13666	1	Heeres	Romania
21/12/36	Škoda	50131	13667	1	Heeres	
21/12/36	Škoda	50132	13668	1	Heeres	
21/12/36	Škoda	50133	13669	1	Heeres	
21/12/36	Škoda	50134	13670	1	Heeres	Romania
21/12/36	Škoda	50135	13671	1	Heeres	scrapped 40
21/12/36	Škoda	50136	13672	1	Heeres	
21/12/36	Škoda	50147	13673	1	Hungary	1E-406
21/12/36	Škoda	50139	13674	1	Heeres	
21/12/36	Škoda	50140	13675	1	Heeres	scrapped 43
21/12/36	Škoda	50144	13676	1	Heeres	
21/12/36	Škoda	50148	13677	1	Heeres	
21/12/36	Škoda	50142	13678	1	Heeres	
21/12/36	Škoda	50143	13679	1	Heeres	MZM 42
21/12/36	Škoda	50137	13680	1	Heeres	Romania
25/1/37	Škoda	50138	13681	1	Heeres	
25/1/37	Škoda	50141	13682	1	Heeres	
25/1/37	Škoda	50149	13683	1	Heeres	
25/1/37	Škoda	50151	13684	1	Heeres	MZM 43
25/1/37	Škoda	50152	13685	1	Heeres	MZM 43
25/1/37	Škoda	50153	13686	1	Heeres	
25/1/37	Škoda	50154	13687	1	Heeres	damaged 39
25/1/37	Škoda	50157	13688	1	Heeres	
25/1/37	Škoda	50158	13689	1	Heeres	MZM 43
25/1/37	Škoda	50161	13690	1	Heeres	
25/1/37	Škoda	50167	13691	1	Heeres	damaged 40
25/1/37	Škoda	50150	13692	1	Heeres	Bulgaria
25/1/37	Škoda	50162	13693	1	Heeres	
25/1/37	Škoda	50163	13694	1	Heeres	MZM 43
25/1/37	Škoda	50160	13695	1	Heeres	MZM 42
3/4/37	Škoda	50195	13696	1	Heeres	MZM 42
3/4/37	Škoda	50204	13697	1	Heeres	Romania
3/4/37	Škoda	50205	13698	1	Heeres	

DATE	MANUFACTURER	CHASSIS NUMBER	CSA NUMBER	ASSIGNED TO PÚV	AFTER 1939	FURTHER ASSIGNMENT
3/4/37	Škoda	50206	13699	1	Heeres	burned 39
3/4/37	Škoda	50207	13700	1	Heeres	Romania
3/4/37	Škoda	50194	13701	1	Heeres	
3/4/37	Škoda	50209	13702	1	Heeres	
19/7/37	Škoda	50186	13703	1	Heeres	
19/7/37	Škoda	50280	13704	1	Heeres	
19/7/37	Škoda	50279	13705	1	Heeres	
19/7/37	Škoda	50283	13706	1	Heeres	Romania
19/7/37	Škoda	50278	13707	1	Heeres	MZM 42
19/7/37	Škoda	50282	13708	1	Heeres	
19/7/37	Škoda	50272	13709	1	Heeres	
19/7/37	Škoda	50281	13710	1	Heeres	
19/7/37	Škoda	50285	13711	1	Heeres	Romania
31/7/37	Škoda	50284	13712	1	Heeres	MZM 42
31/7/37	Škoda	50289	13713	1	Heeres	
31/7/37	Škoda	50290	13714	1	Heeres	Romania
31/7/37	Škoda	50288	13715	1	Heeres	
31/7/37	Škoda	50277	13716	1	Heeres	
31/7/37	Škoda	50287	13717	1	Heeres	PzBef 35(t)
31/7/37	Škoda	50286	13718	1	Heeres	MZM 43
31/7/37	Škoda	50292	13719	1	Heeres	MZM 43
31/7/37	Škoda	50291	13720	1	Heeres	
1937	ČKD	1048	13721	1	Heeres	
1937	ČKD	1027	13722	1	Heeres	Bulgaria
1937	ČKD	1028	13723	1	Heeres	Bulgaria
1937	ČKD	1029	13724	1	Heeres	Bulgaria
1937	ČKD	1030	13725	1	Heeres	
1937	ČKD	1031	13726	1	Heeres	MZM 42
1937	ČKD	1032	13727	1	Heeres	
1937	ČKD	1033	13728	1	Heeres	Bulgaria
1937	ČKD	1034	13729	1	Heeres	
1937	ČKD	1035	13730	1	Heeres	
1937	ČKD	1036	13731	1	Heeres	Bulgaria
1937	ČKD	1037	13732	1	Heeres	
1937	ČKD	1046	13733	1	Heeres	
1937	ČKD	1047	13734	1	Heeres	MZM 42
1937	ČKD	1045	13735	1	Heeres	
1937	ČKD	1049	13736	1	Heeres	
1937	ČKD	1050	13737	1	Heeres	
1937	ČKD	1051	13738	1	Heeres	
1937	ČKD	1052	13739	1	Heeres	
1937	ČKD	1053	13740	1	Heeres	
1937	ČKD	1054	13741	1	Heeres	Bulgaria
1937	ČKD	1055	13742	1	Heeres	
1937	ČKD	1056	13743	1	Heeres	
1937	ČKD	1057	13744	1	Heeres	burned 39
1937	ČKD	1058	13745	1	Heeres	
1937	ČKD	1059	13746	1	Heeres	
1937	ČKD	1060	13747	1	Heeres	Bulgaria
1937	ČKD	1061	13748	1	Heeres	Romania
1937	ČKD	1062	13749	1	Heeres	scrapped 42
1937	ČKD	1063	13750	1	Heeres	PzBef 35(t)
1937	ČKD	1064	13751	1	Heeres	PzBef 35(t)
1937	ČKD	1065	13752	1	Heeres	MZM 42
1937	ČKD	1066	13753	1	Heeres	
1937	ČKD	1067	13754	1	Heeres	MZM 42
1937	ČKD	1068	13755	1	Heeres	Romania
1937	ČKD	1069	13756	1	Heeres	
1937	ČKD	1070	13757	1	Heeres	Bulgaria
1937	ČKD	1071	13758	1	Heeres	
1937	ČKD	1072	13759	1	Heeres	scrapped 42
1937	ČKD	1073	13760	1	Heeres	
1937	ČKD	1074	13761	1	Heeres	MZM 42

DATE	MANUFACTURER	CHASSIS NUMBER	CSA NUMBER	ASSIGNED TO PÚV	AFTER 1939	FURTHER ASSIGNMENT
1937	ČKD	1075	13762	1	Heeres	
1937	ČKD	1076	13763	1	Heeres	Romania
1937	ČKD	1077	13764	1	Heeres	scrapped 42
1937	ČKD	1078	13765	1	Heeres	
1937	ČKD	1079	13766	1	Heeres	
1937	ČKD	1080	13767	1	Heeres	
1937	ČKD	1081	13768	1	Heeres	Bulgaria
1937	ČKD	1082	13769	1	Heeres	
1937	ČKD	1083	13770	1	Heeres	Bulgaria
1937	ČKD	1084	13771	1	Heeres	
1937	ČKD	1085	13772	1	Heeres	Romania
1937	ČKD	1086	13773	1	Heeres	
1937	ČKD	1087	13774	1	Heeres	
1937	ČKD	1088	13775	1	Heeres	
1937	ČKD	1089	13776	1	Heeres	Bulgaria
1937	ČKD	1090	13777	1	Heeres	scrapped 41
1937	ČKD	1091	13778	1	Heeres	scrapped 42
1937	ČKD	1092	13779	1	Heeres	Bulgaria
1937	ČKD	1093	13780	1	Heeres	Romania
1937	ČKD	1094	13781	1	Heeres	
1937	ČKD	1095	13782	1	Heeres	scrapped 42
1937	ČKD	1096	13783	1	Heeres	Romania
1937	ČKD	1097	13784	1	Heeres	
13/2/37	ČKD	1001	13785	2	Heeres	MZM 42
13/2/37	ČKD	1002	13786	2	Heeres	MZM 43
13/2/37	ČKD	1003	13787	2	Heeres	Bulgaria
13/2/37	ČKD	1004	13788	2	Heeres	
13/2/37	ČKD	1005	13789	2	Heeres	Bulgaria
12/2/37	ČKD	1006	13790	2	Heeres	
13/2/37	ČKD	1007	13791	2	Heeres	scrapped 40
13/2/37	ČKD	1008	13792	2	Slovakia	
13/2/37	ČKD	1009	13793	2	Heeres	Waffen SS
13/2/37	ČKD	1010	13794	2	Heeres	Romania
5/3/37	ČKD	1011	13795	2	Heeres	
5/3/37	ČKD	1012	13796	2	Heeres	
5/3/37	ČKD	1013	13797	2	Heeres	
5/3/37	ČKD	1014	13798	2	Heeres	
5/3/37	ČKD	1015	13799	2	Heeres	Bulgaria
5/3/37	ČKD	1016	13800	2	Heeres	Bulgaria
5/3/37	ČKD	1017	13801	2	Heeres	
5/3/37	ČKD	1018	13802	2	Slovakia	
5/3/37	ČKD	1019	13803	2	Heeres	Bulgaria
5/3/37	ČKD	1020	13804	2	Heeres	
5/3/37	ČKD	1021	13805	2	Heeres	
5/3/37	ČKD	1022	13806	2	Slovakia	
5/3/37	ČKD	1023	13807	2	Heeres	Bulgaria
5/3/37	ČKD	1024	13808	2	Heeres	Romania
5/3/37	ČKD	1025	13809	2	Heeres	Bulgaria
1937	ČKD	1038	13810	2	Slovakia	
1937	ČKD	1039	13811	2	Heeres	
1937	ČKD	1040	13812	2	Heeres	
1937	ČKD	1041	13813	2	Heeres	Bulgaria
1937	ČKD	1042	13814	2	Heeres	Bulgaria
1937	ČKD	1043	13815	2	Heeres	
1937	ČKD	1044	13816	2	Heeres	MZM 42
1937	ČKD	1026	13817	2	Heeres	
10/4/37	Škoda	50155	13818	3	Slovakia	
10/4/37	Škoda	50156	13819	3	Slovakia	
10/4/37	Škoda	50168	13820	3	Slovakia	
22/2/37	Škoda	50164	13821	3	Slovakia	
22/2/37	Škoda	50165	13822	3	Slovakia	
22/2/37	Škoda	50166	13823	3	Slovakia	
10/4/37	Škoda	50169	13824	3	Slovakia	

DATE	MANUFACTURER	CHASSIS NUMBER	CSA NUMBER	ASSIGNED TO PÚV	AFTER 1939	FURTHER ASSIGNMENT
10/4/37	Škoda	50170	13825	3	Slovakia	
10/4/37	Škoda	50172	13826	3	Slovakia	
10/4/37	Škoda	50173	13827	3	Slovakia	
10/4/37	Škoda	50174	13828	3	Slovakia	
10/4/37	Škoda	50176	13829	3	Slovakia	
10/4/37	Škoda	50184	13830	3	Slovakia	
22/2/37	Škoda	50188	13831	3	Slovakia	
10/4/37	Škoda	50159	13832	3	Slovakia	
10/4/37	Škoda	50171	13833	3	Slovakia	
10/4/37	Škoda	50175	13834	3	Heeres	
10/4/37	Škoda	50177	13835	3	Slovakia	
10/4/37	Škoda	50179	13836	3	Slovakia	
10/4/37	Škoda	50181	13837	3	Heeres	
10/4/37	Škoda	50145	13838	3	Slovakia	
10/4/37	Škoda	50178	13839	3	Slovakia	
10/4/37	Škoda	50180	13840	3	Slovakia	
10/4/37	Škoda	50182	13841	3	Heeres	Romania
10/4/37	Škoda	50183	13842	3	Slovakia	
10/4/37	Škoda	50185	13843	3	Slovakia	
15/3/37	Škoda	50187	13844	3	Slovakia	
15/3/37	Škoda	50190	13845	3	Heeres	
15/3/37	Škoda	50192	13846	3	Slovakia	
15/3/37	Škoda	50200	13847	3	Slovakia	
15/3/37	Škoda	50189	13848	3	Slovakia	
15/3/37	Škoda	50191	13849	3	Slovakia	
15/3/37	Škoda	50193	13850	3	Slovakia	
15/3/37	Škoda	50196	13851	3	Slovakia	
15/3/37	Škoda	50198	13852	3	Slovakia	
15/3/37	Škoda	50199	13853	3	Heeres	
15/3/37	Škoda	50201	13854	3	Heeres	
15/3/37	Škoda	50203	13855	3	Slovakia	
15/3/37	Škoda	50208	13856	3	Slovakia	
15/3/37	Škoda	50202	13857	3	Slovakia	
3/4/37	Škoda	50210	13858	3	Slovakia	
3/4/37	Škoda	50270	13859	3	Slovakia	
3/4/37	Škoda	50271	13860	3	Slovakia	
2/10/37	Škoda	50300	13864	1	Heeres	
2/10/37	Škoda	50299	13865	1	Heeres	
2/10/37	Škoda	50301	13866	1	Heeres	
2/10/37	Škoda	50298	13867	1	Heeres	
2/10/37	Škoda	50297	13868	1	Heeres	
2/10/37	Škoda	50296	13869	1	Heeres	
2/10/37	Škoda	50294	13870	1	Heeres	
2/10/37	Škoda	50293	13871	1	Heeres	Romania
2/10/37	Škoda	50295	13872	1	Heeres	MZM 42
2/10/37	Škoda	50304	13873	1	Heeres	
2/10/37	Škoda	50302	13874	1	Heeres	
2/10/37	Škoda	50303	13875	1	Heeres	scrapped 40
12/11/37	Škoda	50306	13876	1	Heeres	MZM 42
12/11/37	Škoda	50313	13877	1	Heeres	scrapped 40
12/11/37	Škoda	50314	13878	1	Heeres	
12/11/37	Škoda	50308	13879	1	Heeres	MZM 43
12/11/37	Škoda	50309	13880	1	Heeres	MZM 42
12/11/37	Škoda	50310	13881	1	Heeres	scrapped 42
12/11/37	Škoda	50311	13882	1	Heeres	damaged 39
12/11/37	Škoda	50307	13883	1	Heeres	MZM 42
23/11/37	Škoda	50312	13884	1	Heeres	
23/11/37	Škoda	50315	13885	1	Heeres	
18/12/37	Škoda	50316	13886	1	Heeres	MZM 42
18/12/37	Škoda	50317	13887	1	Heeres	
18/12/37	Škoda	50320	13888	1	Heeres	MZM 43
18/12/37	Škoda	50323	13889	1	Heeres	scrapped 39
18/12/37	Škoda	50319	13890	1	Heeres	PzBef 35(t)

DATE	MANUFACTURER	CHASSIS NUMBER	CSA NUMBER	ASSIGNED TO PÚV	AFTER 1939	FURTHER ASSIGNMENT
18/12/37	Škoda	50322	13891	1	Heeres	
18/12/37	Škoda	50318	13892	1	Heeres	MZM 42
18/12/37	Škoda	50321	13893	1	Heeres	MZM 42
8/1/38	Škoda	50305	13894	3	Slovakia	
28/1/38	Škoda	50324	13895	3	Heeres	
28/1/38	Škoda	50325	13896	3	Slovakia	
28/1/38	Škoda	50326	13897	3	Slovakia	
28/1/38	Škoda	50316	13898	3	Slovakia	
28/1/38	Škoda	50327	13899	3	Slovakia	
28/1/38	Škoda	53914	13900	3	Heeres	
28/1/38	Škoda	53901	13901	3	Slovakia	
28/1/38	Škoda	53919	13902	3	Heeres	MZM 42
11/3/38	Škoda	53918	13903	1	Hungary	1H-407
11/3/38	Škoda	53921	13904	1	Heeres	MZM 42
11/3/38	Škoda	53917	13905	1	Heeres	
11/3/38	Škoda	53922	13906	1	Heeres	Romania
11/3/38	Škoda	53923	13907	1	Heeres	
11/3/38	Škoda	53924	13908	1	Heeres	
11/3/38	Škoda	53925	13909	1	Heeres	scrapped 42
11/3/38	Škoda	53926	13910	1	Heeres	Romania
11/3/38	Škoda	53920	13911	1	Heeres	burned 42
8/4/38	Škoda	50146	13912	1	Heeres	
8/4/38	Škoda	53928	13913	1	Heeres	
8/4/38	Škoda	53927	13914	1	Heeres	Romania
1937	ČKD	1098	13915	1	Heeres	Belgrade mus.
1937	ČKD	1099	13916	1	Heeres	MZM 43
1937	ČKD	10100	13917	1	Heeres	MZM 42
1937	ČKD	10117	13918	1	Heeres	Romania
1937	ČKD	10118	13919	1	Heeres	scrapped 42
1937	ČKD	10119	13920	1	Heeres	Bulgaria
1937	ČKD	10120	13921	1	Heeres	
1937	ČKD	10121	13922	1	Heeres	scrapped 40
1937	ČKD	10122	13923	1	Heeres	
1937	ČKD	10123	13924	1	Heeres	Bulgaria
1937	ČKD	10124	13925	1	Heeres	
1937	ČKD	10125	13926	1	Heeres	
1937	ČKD	10126	13927	1	Heeres	Bulgaria
1937	ČKD	10127	13928	1	Heeres	scrapped 42
1937	ČKD	10128	13929	1	Heeres	
1937	ČKD	10129	13930	1	Heeres	damaged 39
1937	ČKD	10130	13931	1	Heeres	Romania
1937	ČKD	10131	13932	1	Heeres	
1937	ČKD	10132	13933	1	Heeres	
1937	ČKD	10133	13934	1	Heeres	
1937	ČKD	10134	13935	1	Heeres	Romania
1937	ČKD	10135	13936	1	Heeres	MZM 43
1937	ČKD	10136	13937	1	Heeres	
1937	ČKD	10137	13938	1	Heeres	Bulgaria
1937	ČKD	10138	13939	1	Heeres	
1937	ČKD	10139	13940	1	Heeres	Romania
1937	ČKD	10140	13941	1	Heeres	
1937	ČKD	10141	13942	1	Heeres	
1937	ČKD	10142	13943	1	Heeres	
1937	ČKD	10143	13944	1	Heeres	MZM 42
1937	ČKD	10144	13945	1	Heeres	scrapped 40
1937	ČKD	10145	13946	1	Heeres	MZM 42
1937	ČKD	10146	13947	1	Heeres	
1937	ČKD	10147	13948	1	Heeres	scrapped 40
1937	ČKD	10148	13949	1	Heeres	
1937	ČKD	10149	13950	1	Heeres	MZM 42
1937	ČKD	10101	13951	2	Heeres	MZM 43
1937	ČKD	10102	13952	2	Heeres	
1937	ČKD	10103	13953	2	Heeres	

DATE	MANUFACTURER	CHASSIS NUMBER	CSA NUMBER	ASSIGNED TO PÚV	AFTER 1939	FURTHER ASSIGNMENT
1937	ČKD	10104	13954	2	Slovakia	
1937	ČKD	10105	13955	2	Slovakia	
1937	ČKD	10106	13956	2	Slovakia	
1937	ČKD	10107	13957	2	Heeres	
1937	ČKD	10108	13958	2	Heeres	
1937	ČKD	10109	13959	2	Slovakia	
1937	ČKD	10110	13960	2	Heeres	MZM 42
1937	ČKD	10111	13961	2	Heeres	MZM 42
1937	ČKD	10112	13962	2	Heeres	MZM 42
1937	ČKD	10113	13963	2	Heeres	
1937	ČKD	10114	13964	2	Slovakia	
1937	ČKD	10115	13965	2	Heeres	MZM 42
1937	ČKD	10116	13966	2	Heeres	
1937	Škoda	50197	prototype for Romania, in Pilsen till			1945
6/42	Škoda	50223	assembled from eleven			Romania
6/42	Škoda	50224	scrapped tanks			MZM
1937	Škoda	50255	these fifteen tanks were			Romania
1937	Škoda	50256	taken from the series made			Romania
1937	Škoda	50257	for the Czechoslovak Army			Romania
1937	Škoda	50258	and were sent to Romania.			Romania
1937	Škoda	50259	The Czechoslovak Army had			Romania
1937	Škoda	50260	them replaced by the series			Romania
1937	Škoda	50261	with chassis numbers begin-			Romania
1937	Škoda	50262	ning with 53 (53901-53928)			Romania
1937	Škoda	50263				Romania
1937	Škoda	50264				Romania
1937	Škoda	50265				Romania
1937	Škoda	50266				Romania
1937	Škoda	50267				Romania
1937	Škoda	50268				Romania
1937	Škoda	50269				Romania

1938 COMPETITION FOR NEW TYPES

On October 23, 1937, in the conference room of the II. Department of the Ministry of Defense, a meeting was held between the representatives of the II. Department, I. Department, the Military Technical and Aeronautical Institute, the General Staff and the commanders of the Armored regiments. The participants had to decide if the army would order additional LT vz.35 tanks, or choose a different type. While some officers supported the Škoda design, most of them, and especially the officers from the armored regiments, had a wide variety of critical observations and objections. They presented a long list of repeating defects, criticized the low cross-country mobility, short endurance, cramped crew conditions and a host of other problems. The discussion was spirited, but the final decision came from General Netík. He clearly favored testing all the available prototypes before ordering an additional 273 light tanks. His view was later confirmed by the Operational Department of the General Staff, which decided on November 20, 1937 not to order additional Škoda tanks. Instead, all the new designs and prototypes of both manufacturers would be exhaustively tested and the best of them would be chosen as the army's new light tank.

Though both Škoda and ČKD had consummated a cartel agreement for manufacturing tanks equally by both companies, the acceptance of their designs in the forthcoming competition was not only a matter of prestige, but also had important financial considerations. The winning design brought its company payment for the work performed on the prototypes and also licensing royalties from the other company. Thus, both manufacturers pulled all stops to win this competition.

Škoda reconstructed its Š-II-a into two prototypes, the LT vz.35 Rek.I with an improved running gear and the LT vz.35 Rek.II with a new five-speed gearbox. In addition, it promised to present its new design, Š-II-a-2. ČKD planned to send its reconstructed LT vz.34 with a new engine and the Praga-Wilson gearbox, and two new designs, the LTL, manufactured for the Latvian army, and a modified TNHPS tank, manufactured for the Iranian army. The testing of the supplied prototypes was entrusted to a new testing unit, formed at the beginning of 1938 at the Tank School in Vyškov. The actual testing was performed in Milovice under the auspices of PÚV-1.

The evaluation tests began on January 19, 1938, when ČKD supplied its TNHPS prototype. One week later came the reconstructed LT vz.34. The two reconstructed LT vz.35s were not delivered until in the second half of March 1938, while the LTL from ČKD and the Š-II-a-2 from Škoda were not ready in time to take part in those tests.

By April 28, the two Škoda tanks covered 2,814 and 3,419 km, respectively. They again experienced many defects and had to be repaired. The reconstructed LT vz.34 covered 5,118 km and had

ČKD's TNHPS prototype with the untypical baltic aerial on the left fender. This was the vehicle used or the army trials in 1938.

The Praga TNH-SI tank during factory trials. This was the first production tank manufactured against the Slovak state order. It carries the civilian "dealer's plates" and is painted in one color, probably olive drab. It also carries the prototype A7 gun, which in its final version had the recoil cylinder repositioned inside the turret.

shown excellent cross-country mobility and general improvement, but the running gear was still defect prone, and the armor was only 15 mm. The testing group did not consider it as a contender, but recommended strongly to modify all the fifty LT vz.34 tanks in this way, as it would considerably increase their combat value.

The clear winner of the competition was the TNHPS from ČKD. It covered a total of 5,584 km, 1,954 km in terrain and 3,630 km on roads. Its daily average was 160-210 km. During the three months of testing, the vehicle did not have one serious defect. Small defects were easily and speedily repaired. Based on these results, the testing unit unanimously recommended the TNHPS tank as the new light tank of the Czechoslovak army. Their evaluation was seconded by the Commanding officer of PÚV-1 and the head of the 7/I Department of the Ministry of Defense. Originally, the order for the new tanks was supposed to be placed only at the end of the evaluation of all submitted vehicles. The rapidly deteriorating international situation forced the army to change its original intent: 150 of the new tanks were ordered into production on April 20, 1938 under the designation LT vz.38. At the same time, the army planned to order a large amount of 3.7 cm gun ammunition. Because ČKD was not able to build the new tanks fast enough, the army proposed a wide cooperation, encompassing not only ČKD and Škoda, but also Walter, Tatra and other manufacturers.

Between May and June 1938, the army fought ČKD tenaciously over the cost of the new vehicles. While the cost per kg for a new LT vz.34 was 57 Kč and for the LT vz.35 51 Kč, ČKD asked 79 Kč/kg for the LT vz.38! The army finally was able to save some money by ordering the armor plate and some ancillary equipment directly from the manufacturers, but even so the new tanks were much more expensive than originally envisaged. The final order for 150 LT vz.38 tanks was signed on July 22, 1938. Its total value was 92,993,100 Kč ($3,700,000), about 13 million Kč more than the army had expected.

Side-by-side with the pricing discussions, the testing unit carried on with the evaluation tests. By June 11, the TNHPS tank covered a total of 7,185 km without any major problem. In 1937 Škoda had developed for the light tanks two guns: the A7 tank gun, similar to the army vz.37 antitank gun, and the A8 tank gun, similar to the vz 34 antitank gun. During the test firings the A7 gun gave better results and was accepted by the army as the ÚV vz.38 tank gun and was chosen as the gun for the new LT vz.38. The tests of the other prototypes were also duly performed, though then it was a mere formality, as the TNHPS was already chosen as the new standard tank.

The production of the first 150 vehicles started in ČKD on time, but the army never saw any of these tanks, because the German occupation in March 1939 interfered. The new tanks were taken over and used by the Wehrmacht under the designation PzKpfw 38(t), as we will see in Chapter 9.

Rear view of the TNH-SI tank with one of the engine's hatches open.

Obstacle climbing test. The tank carried a complete set of exterior fittings, on the right fender a storage box, the jack with its wooden block and spare track links.

V-8-H prototype during the trials in 1938. This is the original turret configuration with wide double hatches in its roof. The mufflers are mounted on the engine covers and open with them, an unusual arrangement.

Simultaneously, a second group of the testing unit was evaluating medium tanks. Both Škoda and ČKD submitted their prototypes. ČKD was developing its V-8-H since 1936. In early 1937 the design was finalized and the prototype was built during 1937. Its testing in Milovice started on December 21, 1937. Škoda sent its Š-II-c, which was an enlarged version of the LT vz.35, using the same gearbox and pneumatic steering.

By May 3, 1938, the V-8-H covered 4,555 km, 1,533 of those in cross-country running. The daily average was about 150 km. The tank was plagued by initial defects; the engine proved especially troublesome and had to be replaced and modified by ČKD. Initially, the rubber tires of the running wheels kept falling off and it took the rubber manufacturers several months to rectify the situation. At the end, the testing unit gave the vehicle a conditional approval. Because the testing program was not finished and because the Škoda prototype was not properly tested, it did not recommend its acceptance as a standard medium tank at that time.

Commander's hatch in the open position. Crowbar, pick and shovel and a towing cable were carried on the left fender.

By the spring of 1938 the Czechoslovak army could no longer wait. The political situation forced it to order its medium tanks at once, and the V-8-H was the only available prototype capable of immediate production. On April 20, 1938 the 1st Department of the General Staff asked the 2nd Department of the Ministry of Defense to order 300 medium tanks of the V-8-H type with the army's planned designation Medium Tank ST vz.39, but the actual order was never placed. The planned number to be ordered was increased to 450 during the September 1938 mobilization. The army had ample funds for procuring its tanks: it spent 450 million Kč ($ 18 million) for its armored vehicles between 1927 and 1937, but it planned to use 3.2 billion Kč ($ 128 million) between 1939 and 1942 for this purpose. It became obvious during the price litigation with ČKD that the army would need every penny of it, as the price ČKD asked for its medium tanks was much higher than the 997,600 Kč ($ 40,000) the army originally calculated.

In the case the contract was signed, ČKD promised to deliver the first ten vehicles by the end of April 1939, the rest of its 95 vehicles by September 1939. Škoda, who was supposed to manufacture 205 tanks out of the 300 ordered (ČKD was manufacturing the LT vz.38 at the same time), contracted to deliver the first tanks in July 1939 and the last ones by February 1940. Needless to say, the whole order was canceled immediately after the Munich agreement, and none of the V-8-H vehicles were manufactured. The Germans ordered one more prototype to be built in late 1939 and tested it in early 1940, but because the V-8-H was comparable to the PzKpfw III, they were not interested in its production.

The Škoda Š-II-c prototype was not seriously considered by the Czechoslovak army, but its improved version T-21 was successfully displayed to Hungarian Honvéd in June 1940. The Hungarians bought the manufacturing license from Škoda and manufactured the tank under the designation TURÁN in large quantities, as described later in this chapter.

LT VZ.38

ČKD's new light tank, the TNH, appeared for the first time at the end of 1935. At this time, the company has been designing and manufacturing tanks for over five years and was supplying the Czechoslovak army with tankettes and light tanks based on Vickers designs. As these were not entirely satisfactory, ČKD lost the competition for the new light tank of the Czechoslovak army to Škoda. ČKD was not successful with these types in export either and decided to concentrate on their own designs.

The TNH tank was the result of that decision. Its designer was Dipl.Ing. Alexander Surin, a Russian emigré, who worked for ČKD since the early twenties. In the new TNH tank he produced a masterpiece: a compact vehicle with an almost ideal balance between the main properties - armor, armament and speed. On top of that, the new vehicle was rugged and simple, needing minimum upkeep and maintenance. Its success can be judged by several facts. First, the basic design did not have to be changed during the ten-year period ČKD manufactured these vehicles and their modifications, based on the same chassis. Second, the Germans themselves decided in September 1944 to build all their new constructions on two chassis only: the light ones on the LT vz.38, the heavy ones on the Panther. Finally, by many experts the LT vz.38 is considered one of the two really outstanding tank designs of the Second World War, the other being the Soviet T-34 tank.

The tank had its engine in the rear. The gearbox, the clutches with their brakes and all steering mechanisms were concentrated in the front part of the hull, in front of the driver. This arrangement brought simplicity of installation and easy access to all the parts. The chassis used four large diameter wheels on each side, sprung with leaf springs clusters. With a new strong engine, the chassis gave the tank outstanding cross-country performance and high speed. The tank used the Praga-Wilson gearbox, licensed from the Rolls-Royce company. It allowed very smooth driving with a minimum of physical exertion by the driver. An excellent Škoda tank gun was in the fully rotating turret, with the standard ZB machine gun. The tank was small, but surprisingly roomy inside for its size. The engine was the Swedish Scania-Vabis 1664, built by ČKD under a licensing agreement. Thus, the best Czech tank had a Swedish engine, English gearbox and was designed by a Russian!

Praga TNHP engine, a license-built Scania-Vabis 1664 six cylinder, water cooled SV of 7,754 cc displacement and 126 HP at 2,200 rpm output.

During the army evaluation, the testing group proposed several improvements, which ČKD accepted and promptly realized, thus improving the combat value of the tank even further. The new tank was offered to thirty states, but due to the coming war no export sales were realized. The company's prototype was shown to the British army between March 16 and March 29, 1939 in their Mechanical Experimental Establishment. The British were not interested in this tank, which is surprising, as they did not have at that time any tanks that in performance came even close to the TNHPS.

The Germans were not as shortsighted as the British and recognized an outstanding design when they saw one. Following their occupation of Prague, the military commission, to its surprise, found in the ČKD factory an almost finished production run of 150 ve-

Front clutches and their brakes.

The TNHP engine installed in the prototype. This is the carburetor side with the air filter.

The TNHPS prototype in England, March 1939. It carried the A7 gun in its final configuration. The British tested it, but found it lacking in crew comfort and ride.

hicles. The Wehrmacht did not know about this type until now, but the German armor specialists recognized immediately the qualities of the produced tanks. Between May 2 and May 6, 1939 ČKD was visited by a commission from Heereswaffenamt, led by Lt. Colonel Olbrich, who was responsible for all new developments of armored vehicles. The commission immediately decided to buy all the 150 tanks and use them in arming the Panzer formations of the Wehrmacht. Ten days later, the quality control and acceptance department of the Wehrmacht started its work in ČKD, which delivered the last tank of this series by November 23, 1939.

Rear view of the TNHPS prototype in England.

TECHNICAL DESCRIPTION

Designation:

TNHPS	factory designation
LT vz.38	designation of the Czechoslovak army
LT-38	designation of the Slovak army (Lahký Tank - 38)
L.T.M.38	Leichte Tank Muster 38, German designation used at the beginning of the war
PzKpfw 38(t)	Wehrmacht designation (Panzerkampfwagen 38 tschechisch) used from January 1940
T-38	Romanian army designation
T-38 könnyü harckocsi	Hungarian army designation
JleK TaHK Praga	Bulgarian army designation

Several views of the Slovak LT-38, kept as a monument of the Slovak uprising against the Germans in August 1944 in Banská Bystrica. It is an Ausführung A, but its engine cover is from an Ausführung G, which seems to indicate this tank was one of the eight Ausf.A vehicles the Slovak army bought from the Wehrmacht in September 1943.

The completely restored PzKpfw 38(t), Ausführung A, chassis number 008, of the Military Museum in Prague, Kbely. It is painted in the three-tone pre-war camouflage of the Czechoslovak army.

The left side of the restored tank. It is in running condition. In the background is the Tatra 111 heavy truck, first manufactured in 1944 for the Wehrmacht.

According to the original categorization of the Czechoslovak army, the light tanks of II-a category were destined to serve in the ranks of cavalry, only exceptionally in cooperation with infantry. They were light tanks for maneuver combat, especially in terrain, in the ranks of tank units (similar to the English designation "Cruiser Tank").

Production:
Developed by the ČKD in Prague and based on export vehicles, it was accepted by the Czechoslovak army as its new light tank LT vz.38, 150 tanks of this type being ordered in 1938. First deliveries were to the Wehrmacht in 1939, which continued producing this type up to 1942, by which time a total of 1,396 vehicles had been produced. Another 37 tanks were manufactured for the Slovak state.

After 1942, the chassis was used for a large variety of tank hunters, self-propelled howitzers, antiaircraft tanks and reconnaisance vehicles. Its final development was the Jagdpanzer 38 Hetzer and its modifications.

The manufacturer completed the vehicles from parts of many suppliers. Škoda supplied the guns, while Zbrojovka Brno manufactured the machine guns. Spotting scopes were manufactured by Optikotechna Přerov and the armor plate by both Poldi in Kladno and VHHT in Moravia. All the other parts were made by ČKD and its affiliates. The radios and special lighting system were supplied by German companies.

For the Wehrmacht were manufactured not only the standard tanks with the Fu5 radio sets, but also command tanks Panzerbefehlswagen 38(t). The first model, SdKfz 266, was for company and battalion commanders, and carried both the Fu5 and Fu6 radio sets and two rod aerials. These tanks had the front machine gun deleted. The second modification was the SdKfz 267 for regimental and divisional headquarters, which had the Fu5 and Fu8 radio sets with the large frame antenna. This vehicle also had its main gun removed and replaced by a wooden mock up. All the command tanks carried a gyrocompass for navigation.

Price:
For the Czechoslovak army the price was set to be 620,146 Kč ($ 24,800) with the Poldi armor, and 619,570 Kč with the VHHT armor. This price did not include armament, optical equipment, radio set and the NIFE batteries, which were billed separately. For example, the cost of the Škoda A7 gun was 103,500 Kč, of each machine gun 13,540 Kč. The total amount the army paid for a complete vehicle was around 900,000 Kč ($ 36,000). To the Wehrmacht, ČKD sold each PzKpfw 38(t) for 56,000 Deutschmark, in comparison to the 100,000 DM charged for the PzKpfw III.

Construction of the Tank:
The tank was 4.60 m long, 2.12 m wide and 2.40 m high. Its fully loaded weight was 9.4 tons. Its ground pressure was low, only 0.5 kg/cm^2. Its crew consisted of four men: driver, radio operator, commander and gunner.

Front part of the 008. The machine guns are not fitted, and the lights are not authentic either for the Czechoslovak or the German version. Otherwise, the restoration is perfect.

Detail of the hull machine gun and radio operator's visor. The tank has the German aerial base.

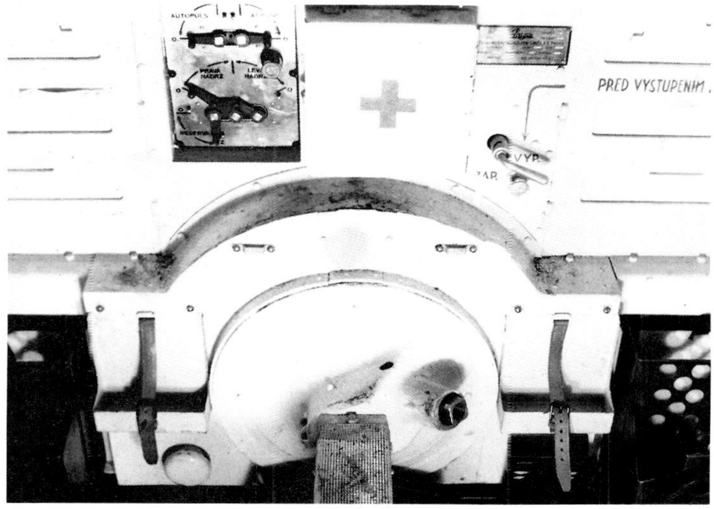

Detail of the firewall of a Slovak LT vz.38. On the left panel are the switches for the two fuel pumps above and valves for both fuel tanks below them.

The hull and the turret of the tank were assembled from L-shaped steel profiles, to which were riveted flat armor plates. Both the rivets and the screws were made from special steel. Up to a height of 100 cm all the joints were waterproofed. The front plates of both the hull and the turret were 25 mm thick, side and angled plates were 15 mm thick and plates angled more than 30o were only 12 mm thick. Both the bottom of the hull and the top plates were 8 mm thick. The running wheel covers were 6 mm thick. The front 25 mm plates were impenetrable to armor-piercing rounds of the 20 mm Oerlikon gun from 250 m and over; the 25 and 15 mm plates could withstand vz.31 armor-piercing machine gun and rifle rounds at any distance. For the vz.31 rounds, the safe distance for the 12 mm plates was 100 m, for the 8 mm plates 125 m.

The hull was divided by a firewall 5 mm thick into fighting and engine compartments. In this firewall there were two solid doors, which allowed easy access to important engine parts from inside the fighting compartment. The firewall was lined with asbestos on the engine's side.

The driver and the radio operator sat in the front part of the fighting compartment, the driver on the right side. He had in the front plate a 203 x 82 mm observation visor with a rotating episcope. The episcope could be fixed in any position. The observation visor was protected from outside by an armored shutter 28 mm thick with an 130 x 4 mm observation slot, protected from inside with bulletproof glass 50 mm thick. The visor was arranged in such a way that when the episcope was removed, the outer cover closed automatically; and when the bulletproof glass block was in place, the outer cover could not be opened. In the right side armor plate the driver had a smaller vision slit 120 x 3 mm, similarly protected with a 140 x 70 x 50 mm bulletproof glass. In the right front wall there was a fixed episcope of the same type as in the commander's cupola. Under the episcope there was a 180 x 25 mm vent, constructed in a way that precluded penetration of rounds or splinters inside the vehicle. A similar 220 x 25 mm vent was in the left front wall, behind the radio station.

Left wall of the fighting compartment. From the firewall forward: machine gun ammunition, gun ammunition, radio operator's seat. The commander's seat is in the forward position. The Bowden cable from the machine gun leads to the driver's trigger.

Right side of the fighting compartment, with machine gun and gun ammunition, fire extinguisher and driver's seat.

Driver's visor in the open position, with the bulletproof glass fitted.

The radio operator had his own observation visor in the front plate, but smaller, 130 x 60 mm. The armored cover in its closed position formed a 120 x 3 mm observation slit, again protected by a bulletproof glass block 50 mm thick. All the observation devices were equipped with upholstered leather headrests. Reserve episcopes and bulletproof glass blocks were carried in protected containers.

The machine gun was in the center of the front hull plate in a ball mount, allowing a 28° field of fire, with an elevation of 10° and a depression of 10°. The machine gun had a spotting telescope, or could be fired over open sights, built into the driver's visor and on the front plate in front of it. If need be, the driver could lock it in a central position and fire it using a Bowden cable. The gun in this case was sighted to hit the road in front of the vehicle at a distance of 300 m.

Escape from the fighting compartment was possible through the radio operator's hatch or through the commander's cupola. All the interior surfaces were smooth. The top plates of the fighting compartment and of the turret were upholstered and covered by leather; all protruding fixtures were either padded or leather covered, and were constructed in a way that precluded the clothing and/or equipment of the crew members snagging on them.

The fully rotating turret sat in a ball-race ring of 1,265 mm diameter in the top plate of the fighting compartment. It was constructed the same way as the hull. The straight 25 mm thick front plate carried in its center the main gun, and on the right side the ball mount for the turret machine gun. The turret sides were made from 15 mm thick armor plates that were slightly curved. Its upper armor plate was 8 mm thick.

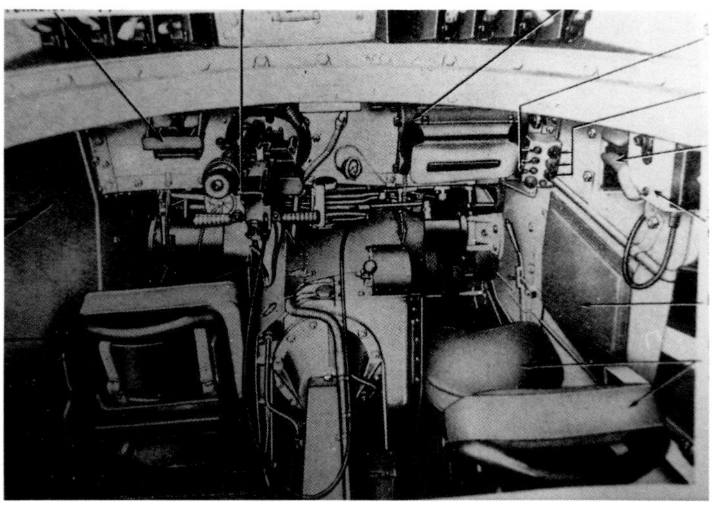

The front part of the hull with the driver's position on the right and the radio operator's on the left. In between them is the gearbox, in front of them the clutches and their brakes. The hull machine gun is off-center to the left.

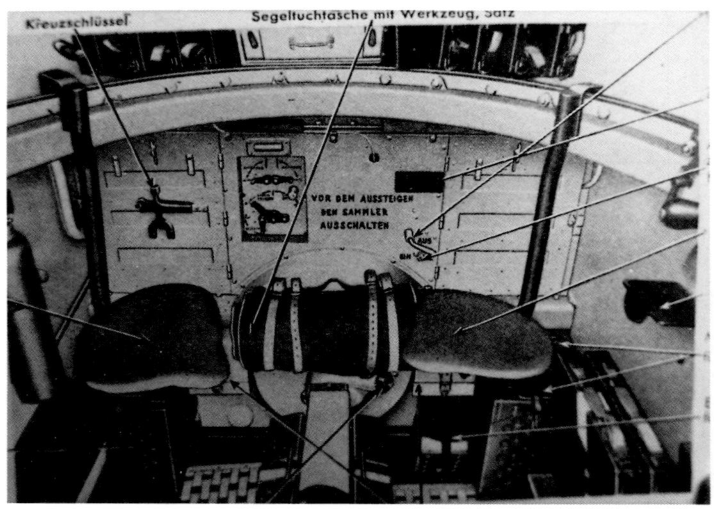

Rear interior of the fighting compartment with the commander's and gunner's seats. Between them was the bag with spare parts and tools. There were two doors in the firewall with ventilating slots. This photograph is of the PzKpfw 38(t) with the four-man crew.

The inside of the PzKpfw 38(t) turret, showing from top: the turret's rotating gear and wheel, spotting scopes for the commander and the gun, the gun, and the machine gun with its spotting scope.

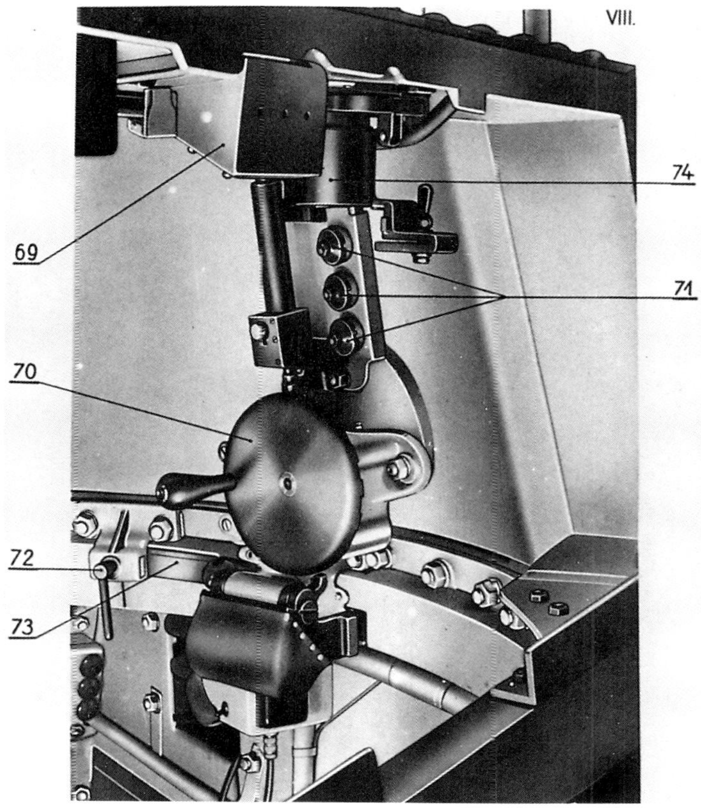

Detail of the turret rotating and arresting gear, and the panel with the switches for the three signal lights.

The commander's cupola with an inside diameter of 570 mm was eccentrically placed in the upper plate. Its sides were 15 mm thick and the hatch was 8 mm thick. The cupola was provided with four episcopes, situated on the front, rear and both sides. The front episcope could be rotated along its vertical axis. The commander also had at his disposal a rotating monocular mirror periscope in its own armored mount, placed on the top plate in front of the cupola. The periscope's field of view was 20° and the enlargement was 2.6x.

The cupola's top plate had two small openings for using the signal flags during the day, and a special signal lamp during the night. The openings were covered with armored flaps when not in use.

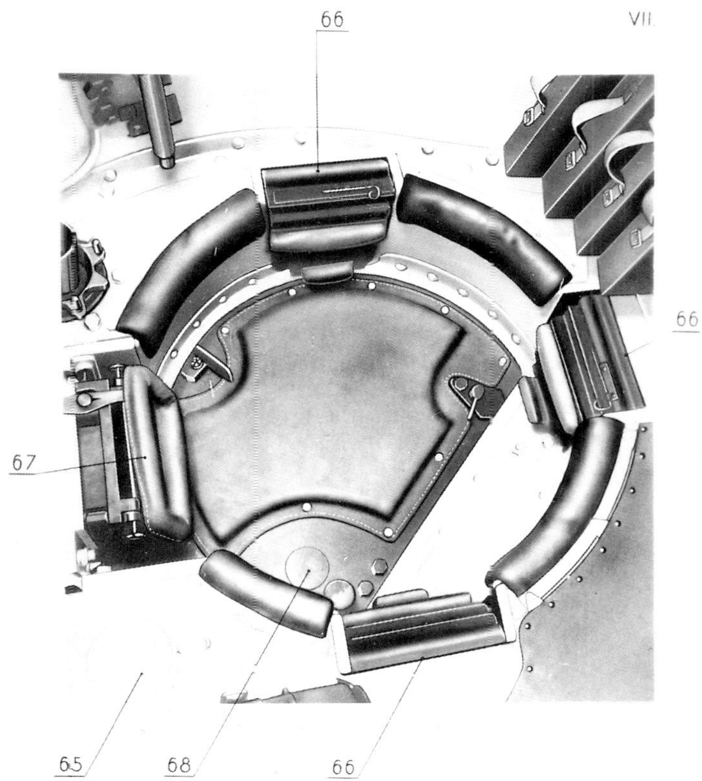

The overhang of the turret with gun ammunition storage. In the middle is a wooden box with spare parts and tools for repairing the gun.

Inside the commander's cupola, showing the episcopes, upholstered rim and inside of the hatch with the opening for the signal flags.

Commander's cupola and the separate periscope.

Commander's cupola and its hatch.

Drive Train:

The tank was powered by an internal combustion, four-stroke, water cooled, six cylinder engine with a rated output of 130 HP(95.5 kW) at 2,200 rpm. With a bore and stroke of 110 x 110 mm, the engine's displacement was 7,754 cc. The cylinders were in one block, with a removable head made from aluminum alloy, and with an SV valve-train. The crankcase was made from cast steel alloy. The crankshaft was carried in seven main cylinder bearings. The engine was pressure lubricated, with a dry sump. The oil was circulated by a gear pump from the oil tank through a filter and an oil cooler. The filter was of an ingenious design, which allowed the removal of the filtered impurities by turning the filter's lamellae from outside. The impurities fell to the bottom of the filter casing, from where they could be removed periodically. Cleaning the oil filter was possible even with the engine running. The engine could use gasoline, alcohol-gasoline blends and Dynalcol. It was equipped with a Solex "Tous Terraine" carburetor, accessible from the fighting compartment. Fuel was supplied by two fuel pumps, a mechanical membrane one (AC pump) and an electrical one (Autopulse). Two fuel tanks had a capacity of 110 liters each and were placed on both sides on the bottom of the engine's compartment. Their placement was designed to assure that in a case of a fuel explosion, the fuel tanks would blow outside the engine compartment and would not force the burning fuel into the fighting compartment.

The ignition was magneto-electric, with a Bosch Vertex 12 V magneto. The engine was started with a Bosch starter that had an output of 3 HP at 12 V, but the tank also had a provision for hand cranking both from inside the fighting compartment and from outside.

The completely rebuilt original engine with its carburetor, fuel pump and air filter.

Same side of the engine compartment, showing the exhaust pipe and the radiator being filled. The engine compartment is uncluttered and all the parts are easily accessible.

Detail of the running gear and the rear idler wheel.

The cooling water was circulated by a water pump through a radiator on the rear of the engine compartment. The cooling fan, powered by the engine, drew the cooling air through slits in the engine's covers, across the radiator and exhausted it to the rear. The slits were equipped with slots that allowed the regulation of the size of their openings, depending on the outside air temperature. The cooling system was designed to assure proper cooling of the engine up to an outside temperatures of 45°C. Exhaust gases were led into a muffler, situated on top of the engine compartment's back plate.

The engine was equipped with a massive flywheel and a spring-loaded sliding clutch that prevented the transfer of sudden engine surges to the gearbox. The Cardan shaft between the engine and the gearbox was interrupted by a special vibration dampening clutch. The Praga-Wilson gearbox was of a planetary type and had five gears forward (speeds ranging from 4.1 km/hour in first gear to 42 km/hour in fifth gear) and one backward (6.1 km/hour). It had a preselector of gears. The driver selected the next gear, which was engaged when he depressed the clutch pedal. The outer "crown" cog wheels were braked by belt brakes on their circumference. The brakes were equipped with automatic alignment, assuring constant pressure even with worn lining. The gearbox was lubricated by the engine oil, which was circulated by three pumps through a cooler, a special filter and back to the engine.

The rear plate with the proper covers fitted.

Detail of two of the main wheels with their spring cluster and a return roller.

Gear selection was extremely simple. Before starting the engine, the gear selector had to be in neutral, and the pedal had to be depressed once. This assured that no gears were engaged. Once the engine was running, the driver selected the first gear, depressed the pedal and the tank started moving. When stopping the vehicle, the selector was placed on neutral and by depressing the pedal, the gear was disengaged.

In front of the gearbox was a differential box with track clutches and brakes. The driving shafts ended in pinion wheels that engaged the teeth on the inside perimeter of the driving wheels (1:6.33 ratio). This arrangement eliminated the need for a reduction on the gearbox.

Chassis:

The running gear consisted of two tracks, stretched over front driving and rear idler sprockets, running wheels and return rollers. Each track was composed of 94 links, 293 mm wide and 104 mm long. The links were manufactured from hard manganese steel.

Driver's position. The fighting compartment is surprisingly roomy, considering the small size of the tank. The left opening in the machine gun mount is for the spotting scope, the smaller one above the gun is for the iron sights.

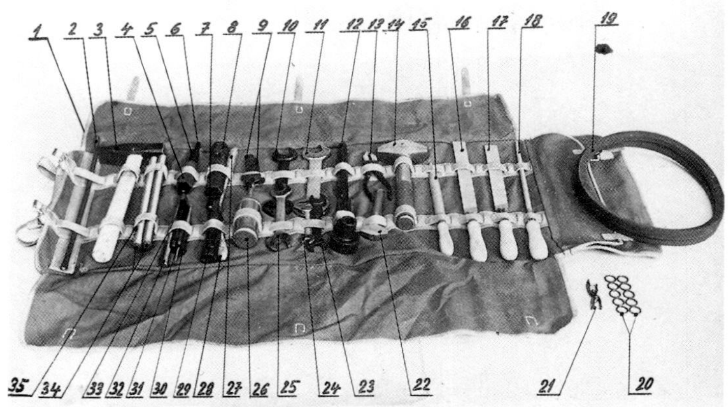

The bag with tools and some spare parts, carried at the rear firewall.

The teeth of the driving sprocket engaged into slots in the track links. The driving sprockets had a diameter of 637 mm, and on their outer rims carried two rings, each with 19 teeth. Each track link had two guide lugs, which centered the track on the outside of the running wheels. The track links were connected with link pins made from tough steel that were secured with spring clips in the links. This arrangement allowed faster change of damaged track links or pins. For especially difficult terrain it was possible to mount grousers on the track links.

The track was supported by running wheels, four on each side. Each wheel had a diameter of 775 mm and was 118 mm wide. They were rubber-tired and contacted the track between the guide lugs. Each wheel was covered with an armor dish, 6 mm thick and 662 mm in diameter. Two pairs of wheels were fastened on a common wheel carrier and were sprung with 1,040 x 90 mm leaf spring clusters. There were two wheel carriers per side. Two return rollers on each side were similarly rubber-tired. The rear idler wheel had a diameter of 535 mm and was 241 mm wide. This system provided excellent cross-country performance and a reasonably comfortable ride.

The tank could cross a ditch 2.10 m wide, climb a 0.8 m high obstacle, wade water 0.9 m deep and uproot trees of up to 0.3 m diameter.

Steering:

When driving in a straight line, the steering clutches were engaged and both driving shafts, and thus both tracks, were moving at the same speed. By pulling one steering lever, its clutch was disengaged and its brake was more or less engaged, depending on how far the lever was pulled back. The epicycloidal gears of the differential allowed the braked track to slow, while the other track accelerated. This system allowed very smooth driving in curves. For turning the vehicle on the spot, it was necessary to depress a button on the steering lever. This disengaged the epicycloidal gears and

Radio operator's position. The radio set is not installed.

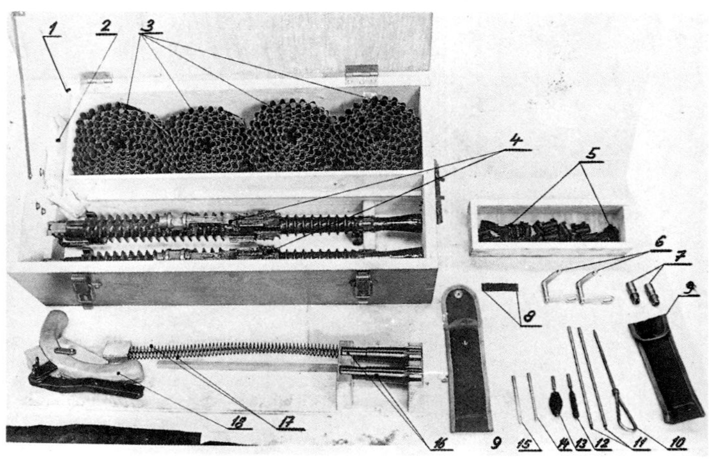

Box with spare parts for the machine guns contained two replacement barrels, four empty belts, springs and other spares. One such box was assigned to each platoon.

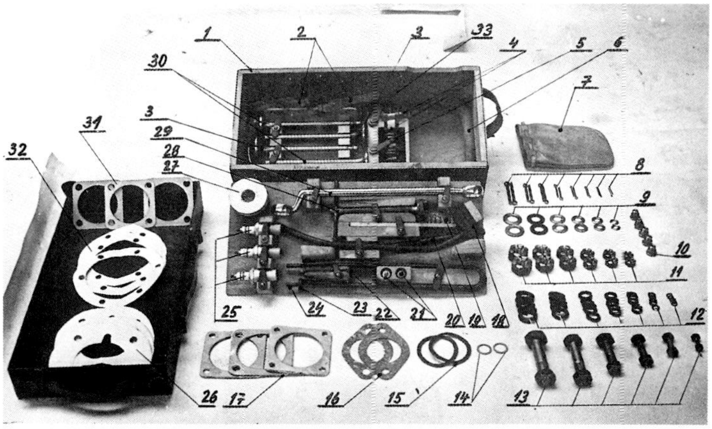

Box with spare parts for the engine, including valves, spark plugs, seals and other spare parts.

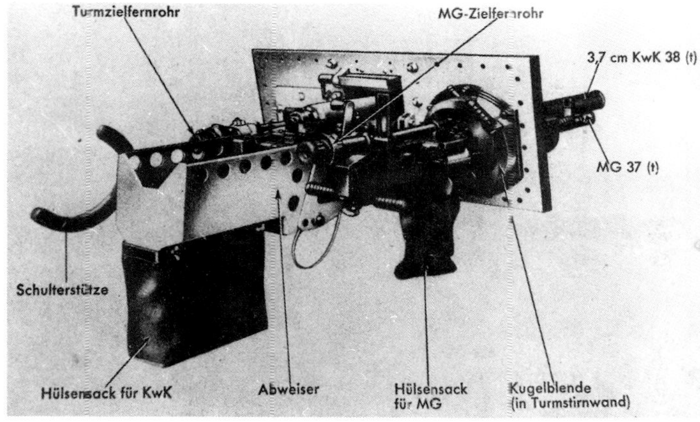

The front plate of the turret with the gun and the machine gun installed.

allowed to stop the inner track completely. Depressing the brake pedal, the vehicle was braked or stopped in a straight line.

Exterior and Interior Equipment:

In the fighting compartment of the hull the driver and the radio operator sat next to each other on upholstered leather seats. Both the position of the seats and the angle of the seats' backs could be easily changed. On the left hull wall was mounted the newly developed vz.37 radio set with its accessories. This radio set had a range of 4 km and worked in the telegraphic mode: the operator sent messages with his Morse key and received them into headphones in his helmet. The radio set transmitted through a rod aerial, mounted on the left front fender. The Wehrmacht introduced their standard phonic radio set Fu5.

The driver was seated so that he could reach all the controlling levers easily and did not have to strain to use them. On the left side of the front visor he had the control panel with the oil pressure gage, gearbox oil level warning light, speedometer and the electric horn button. On the right side of its visor, the driver had at eye level three signal lights - a red, a green and a blue bulb, and their buttons. By lighting them according to a prearranged code, the commander in the turret could communicate with the driver and vice versa. The commander's controlling buttons for these lights were situated on the circumference of the turret, and had different shapes. The Wehrmacht replaced this primitive system with an intercom in the PzKpfw 38(t)s. The crew members were connected via long cables to a central box, mounted next to the radio station. They communicated with a throat microphone and headphones.

For exterior communication between the tanks besides the radio, signal flags (red and yellow) were used. The commander showed them through a hole in the cupola's top plate. At night, he could use a special signal light with color filters.

The fighting compartment was illuminated by three lamps: one was above the driver's panel, one on the firewall and one in the turret. Outside lighting consisted of two contour 5 W lamps in metal casings, mounted on the front part of the fenders. The same type of lamp on the rear plate illuminated the number plate. The tank also carried a 50/35 W headlight of 108 mm diameter on the front plate between the visors. As it was equipped with a long cable, it could be used as a spotlight or as a work light. The PzKpfw 38(t) tanks had additional lighting installed. On the front left fender was mounted the Notek light. The rear plate illumination was eliminated and was replaced on the left with the rear distance light (Abstand Rücklicht) and on the right with the accessory rear light (Zusatz Schlusslicht). This lighting was standard on all Wehrmacht vehicles and was manufactured by Nove-Technik in Munich. From October 1941 on the accessory rear light was replaced by a rear brake light (Bremseschlusslicht DIN 72624FL). The tank carried an alkaline battery NIFE 9AL/10 with 12 V and 100 Ah, stored in a wooden compartment and charged by a dynamo from the engine.

The fighting compartment under the turret had enough room for the tank commander and the gunner to service the tank's armaments. Most of the 90 gun rounds carried were stored in the turret's rear part in eight six-round metal magazines. The magazines for the armor-piercing rounds (a total of 30 rounds) were marked with a 5 cm wide white band. The rest of the gun ammunition and most of the machine gun ammunition was stored on the sides and on the floor of the fighting compartment. Spare parts and tools for gun repair were in a wooden box in the turret's rear part, while a leather bag with tools was stored on the floor between the commander's and gunner's seats in the rear of the fighting compartment. The fire extinguisher was on the right-hand wall under the turret. On the floor behind the driver's and radio operator's seats were two boxes with machine gun ammunition (2 x 300 rounds). A total of 2,700 rounds for the machine guns were carried in nine boxes, three of them with armor-piercing rounds were again marked with a white band.

Larger tools were carried outside the hull. On the left hull side above the fender were attached the shovel, the pick and an iron crowbar. An 8-ton jack and the spanner for track tensioning were carried on the right side under the turret. On the rear of the right fender were two spare track links and on the left fender the wooden block for jack support. A towing cable was carried either on the left side, coiled on the shovel, or on the rear of the hull. The tank carried four towing hooks, two on each end of the hull. All were 600

Front of the turret, showing the machine gun in its ball mount, the main gun and the opening for the two spotting telescopes for the gunner and the commander.

The main gun with its spotting scope.

mm above ground level, and all had the capacity of 5 tons. A fifth towing hook with 2 ton capacity was in the middle of the rear plate.

Armament:
The LT vz.38 tank was well armed. In its turret it carried the new Škoda 3.7 cm gun ÚVvz.38, coaxial with a 7.92 mm heavy machine gun, both having a full 360° field of fire. Elevation of both weapons was 25°, depression 10°. The gun penetrated a vertical cemented armor 50 mm thick at 500 m, and could penetrate 30 mm armor at 30° at 900 m. The semiautomatic breech mechanism allowed a high rate of fire, up to 15 rounds/min. The range was 4,000 m with the HE round and 1,500 m with the AP round.

Besides the main gun, the tank carried two heavy machine guns ZB vz.37, manufactured by Československá Zbrojovka Brno. Both were mounted in special ball mounts in the turret and in the front plate of the hull. The turret machine gun could be fired coaxially with the main gun or separately.

All the weapons were aimed through spotting scopes with 2.6x enlargement and a 25° observation field. The turret scope had the distance scale for both the main gun and for the machine gun. The gun scope was scaled to 2,000 m, the machine gun scopes were scaled up to 1,500 m. In case of damage to the turret scope, the gun could be aimed up to 600 m over an open sight by opening an armored cover in the front plate of the turret. The machine guns could use iron sights after removing steel plugs in the ball mounts.

The turret was rotated in two ways: by turning the wheel of the rotating mechanism (one revolution corresponded to a 3° turn), or by moving the turret manually by pushing on the main gun's shoulder pad after disconnecting the turning mechanism. An arresting gear stopped the turret in any position. Empty cartridge cases fell into a bag, fixed under the recoil frame. Similarly, the machine gun empty cartridge cases were collected into cloth bags.

Camouflage and Markings:
The LT vz.38 tanks were supposed to carry the standard three-tone camouflage scheme. The first five tanks supplied to the Slovak state were finished in this scheme, although the following tanks were already painted olive drab.

For the Wehrmacht the PzKpfw 38(t)s were painted originally in the standard field gray, later in sand color. The insides were always ivory white. In the Wehrmacht's service, the tanks carried the large white crosses for the Polish campaign, normal Balkenkreuze from 1940 on, and the standard three-digits call numbers on the turret sides.

The ČKD prototype tested in 1938 carried a factory license plate, but because it was never bought by the Czechoslovak army, it was never assigned the army number.

The 37 Slovak tanks bought directly from ČKD carried Slovak army numbers V-3000 to V-3029 and V-3051 to V-3057. The additional 37 vehicles bought from the Germans carried numbers V-3063 to V-3083, V-3099 to V-3110 and V-3129 to V-3133. These numbers were carried in white on black plates, one each on the front and on the rear plate. From 1941 on, the Slovak cross in white was painted on the sides and the rear plate of the turret; from May 1942 these crosses were replaced by the Slovak blue-white-red tricolor shield.

The PzKpfw 38(t)s in Honvéd service were painted dark olive green with irregular patches of reddish brown and ochre. They carried numbers1H-725 to 1H-832 and 1H-876 to 1H-878. The tanks carried national insignia in the form of green crosses with a white border and a red triangle in the middle up to 1944, when the national insignia were changed to white crosses on a black square on the sides and on the rear of the hull and white call numbers on the sides of the turrets.

The Romanian PzKpfw 38(t)s were painted olive drab, carried Romanian crosses on the front sides of the hull and a large one on top of the engine cover, and white call signs on the turret.

Medium Tanks

The failure of the Š-II-b and P-II-b tanks led both Škoda and ČKD to a decision to jointly develop the infantry tank ŠP-II-b. The companies signed the agreement on July 30, 1936. The army concurred and ordered a prototype in September 1936. All three sides optimistically expected to have the prototype finished by May 1937 and large-scale production started two months later (!).

These plans were disrupted by gradual changes in the army's specifications, and by the infighting between the companies. Originally, ČKD was made responsible for the drive train and the hull, while Škoda was developing the running gear, pneumatic steering and the turret with the gun. Škoda was entrusted with the final assembly of the vehicle and its testing.

The original specifications for a 13-ton vehicle with 25 mm armor all around and a 3.7 cm gun gradually changed to 32 mm armor and a 4.7 cm gun, with a corresponding increase in the vehicle's weight to 16 tons. The army, disappointed by the failure of Š-III and T-III prototypes, was hoping to obtain this way the needed medium tank. In its final form the ŠP-II-b was a medium tank, though it was kept on the army's books as a light tank until April 1938.

The prototype was driven for the first time by the end of 1937. It covered 1,967 km on roads around Pilsen and finally on March 5, 1938 was transferred for official evaluation to Milovice. There it covered less than 700 km before its high incidence of defects forced Škoda to take it back for repairs. The tank remained in Pilsen for the next ten months, and only the army's threat to withhold payment caused Škoda to finish its repairs and ship it to the army on February 23, 1939.

Shortly after signing their agreement, both companies started to work on their own prototypes of medium tanks, each using the parts it contributed to the ŠP-II-b as a basis for a new construction. Škoda developed the Š-II-c medium tank with a new hull and drive train. The prototype left the factory already in May 1937, concur-

Two views of the first appearance of the V-8-H prototype, here without its armament and visors fitted.

ŠP-II-b with its armament removed in the yard of PÚV-2 in Vyškov in 1939. Started as a light infantry tank, its weight grew to 16.55 tons. Only one prototype was built, but it became the basis for both the Škoda T-21 and ČKD V-8-H mediums.

rently with the ŠP-II-b prototype, but was plagued by so many defects that Škoda was not able to submit it to the army's evaluation trial for new tanks in 1938.

ČKD started on its medium, V-8-H, at the same time. It tested the tank in the summer of 1937 and during 3,900 km covered did not find any serious problems with it. ČKD immediately asked for and obtained a release from MNO to sell its V-8-H abroad and included it in its tank offers. In the winter 1937-1938 ČKD offered this tank to England, China, Denmark, Egypt, Finnland, Iraq, Iran, Yugoslavia, Latvia, Norway, Romania, Sweden, Switzerland and Turkey, and one year later to USSR, Japan, Lithuania, Netherland and Siam. None of the export sales were realized, mostly because of the high cost of the vehicle. ČKD offered it for the army trials in 1938, as it was the only candidate sufficiently ready to be considered as the standard medium tank, as both the ŠP-II-b and Š-II-c were still suffering their teething troubles.

ST vz.39

The ČKD medium tank was designated V-8-H. Its designers were Dipl.Ing. Alexander Surin, who had previously developed the very successful TNH light tanks (later LT vz.38), and Karel Exner. The vehicle was built around the Škoda 4.7 cm gun with fairly heavy armor for its time. The suspension was similar to the system used by Škoda, with eight small running wheels in four carriages per side, sprung with leaf springs. A new V-8 ČKD Praga engine provided it with high speed and good mobility.

The prototype was built in 1937 and the army trials started on December 21, 1937. The supplied prototype at this time had only a mock-up turret without armament, lacked vision devices etc. During the trials several problems with the engine surfaced. It was returned to the factory for overhaul during February 1938 and reinstalled on March 8. Smaller problems were encountered with the clutches, though the gear box worked perfectly. The suspension proved to be rugged and well suited for the heavier vehicle; there was only the problem with shedding of the rubber tires on some wheels. This problem was solved by the rubber manufacturers.

The trials resumed in March 1938, and were accelerated due to the time lost during the engine overhaul. The test crews covered up to 250 km per day. They praised mostly the easy upkeep of the vehicle, which took no more than two hours per day, with eight-hours main upkeep every seven days. The tank covered between January 4 and November 17, 1938 a total of 12,735 km, 5,473 of this in rough terrain.

Once the trials ended in early May 1938, the Army Testing Center submitted a list of recommended improvements, including changes to the cooling system, carburetors, engine, fuel tanks, suspension and the turret. As all these changes were minor, the factory strived to incorporate them quickly, as it was expecting additional trials. The Škoda gun was installed and test fired in June 1938. The final appearance of the tank changed from the originally submitted prototype; quite a few inside installations were similarly changed and improved.

Factory drivers during the comparison trials with T-21 in Romania in 1939. This was the only ČKD tank with a rear drive (aside from the LTL prototype). The running gear was based on the LT vz.35 tank, but was scaled up. The turret was modified with the commander's cupola and gunner's hatch. The tank carried a massive "combat" frame antenna around the front part of the hull, in addition to the normal whip aerial.

V-8-H fording a stream during the trials. Details on the turret's top are well visible on this photograph.

Two more V-8-H photographs from the 1939 trials.

Various views of the V-8-H prototype in its final form during winter 1939 tests, showing details of the turret, aerial, running gear and exterior fittings.

Meanwhile, the political situation dictated fast action. The army planned to order 300 tanks and 270,000 rounds for the 4.7 cm guns (30% AP, 70% HE) on April 20, 1938, even before the trials were officially ended, though they were not very happy with the high cost of the vehicle. In September 1938, during the mobilization, the planned order was increased to 450 vehicles. The tank was supposed to be designated ST vz.39, and production was planned by both ČKD and Škoda.

Three views of the V-8-H II, built for the Germans in late 1939. It carries a concrete block in place of the turret and a makeshift driver's compartment. It also has the German lights (the Notek lamp and the rear Abstand Rücklicht) installed. The prototype was tested in 1940, but was not accepted for production.

The production never did start as, after the Munich dictate and the occupation of the Sudetenland by Germany, all the special budget appropriations for the army were canceled and so were any plans to order the tanks. Interestingly, the Czechoslovak army never bought the V-8-H prototype from the factory, and therefore never assigned it an army number.

Following the cancellation of the order, MNO gave ČKD permission to export the tank freely, and even proposed to assign to it formally the ST vz.39 designation to increase its appeal to foreign customers. For this, the army asked for 5% of the selling price as compensation of funds already spent for the tank's development. ČKD refused this offer.

The Germans occupied the rest of Czechoslovakia on March 15, 1939, and took over all its armament industries. They were not very much interested in the V-8-H, as it was comparable to the PzKpfw III, whose production was by that time gaining speed. Nevertheless, they had ordered a second prototype in late 1939 for 201,632 DM. The prototype was built and was tested under the designation V-8-H II in 1940 without a turret, just with a weight box, as the question of the main armament and thus of the turret design was not solved then. The tank was not accepted into production and both prototypes were scrapped after the war.

In November-December 1939 both the V-8-H and Škoda's T-21 were shown in Romania. The Romanian army ordered 216 T-21 tanks from Škoda, but at the end did not get any of them. ČKD tried to sell the V-8-H to Sweden and Italy in 1940-1942, but again unsuccessfully.

TECHNICAL DESCRIPTION

Designation:

V-8-H (V-8-He)	factory designation
ST vz.39	planned official designation of the Czechoslovak army

According to the categorization of the Czechoslovak army, the medium tanks were destined to support infantry, attacking prepared fortifications and to fight enemy armor. For these two tasks, they had to have heavier armor and armament and also high speed.

Production:
One prototype built by ČKD in 1937, tested by the army testing unit in 1938 and modified according to the army's wishes. A second prototype built for the Waffenprüfamt in 1939. Both scrapped after the war.

Price:
ČKD made their bid in cooperation with Škoda. Their price for one vehicle was 891,395 Kč ($ 33,250). With 240,000 Kč for the Škoda gun, 27,100 Kč for the two ZB machine guns and 10,500 Kč for their mounts, and the cost of the spotting scopes and the radio set, the cost for a complete vehicle climbed to over 1,250,000 Kč ($50,000). The price for the second prototype was 201,632 DM.

Construction of the tank:
The tank was 5.35 m long, 2.27 m wide and 2.34 m high; its fully loaded weight was 16.2 tons. Ground pressure was low, only 0.56 kg/cm^2. Its crew was four men: driver, radio operator, commander and gunner.

Construction of the tank's hull and turret followed the LT vz.35 and LT vz.38 tanks: it was constructed from steel L-profiles, on which the rolled homogenous armor plate was bolted. The frontal armor was 32 mm thick, the sides were 25 mm thick and top and bottom plates 12 mm. The crew compartment was pressurized and sealed against chemical agents. The fighting compartment was divided from the engine compartment by a 5 mm thick firewall.

The driver had in front of him a 300 x 60 mm visor, protected by a bulletproof glass block and shutter to close it to an observation slit. The same arrangement was provided also for the commander, whose visor (170 x 20 mm) was in the front of his cupola on the top of the turret. The cupola was also provided with two periscopes with 360° observation field. The gunner and the machine gunner in the hull observed through the gun spotting scopes.

The commander's seat was on the right-hand side of the turret, the gunner was on the left. Both had their own escape hatches in the roof of the turret (cupola). The driver sat on the right side of the vehicle, the hull machine gunner/radio operator on the left. The driver had his escape hatch above his position, the radio operator could use any one of the three escape hatches, or the access door to the clutches on the horizontal front plate.

The fully rotating turret sat in a ball-race ring on the top plate of the fighting compartment. The front plate had the main gun in the middle and one of the machine guns in a ball mount. The other machine gun was mounted between the driver and the radio operator in the front plate of the hull.

The original drawings provided for a full-width cupola on the roof of the turret, but the prototype as built had a round cupola for the commander and a circular escape hatch for the gunner. The cupola probably had the provisions for extending signal flags and/or signal lamp, similar to the other Czechoslovak tanks.

Drive train:
The tank had a new Praga V-8 gasoline, water cooled engine of 14,230 cc displacement. Each bank of cylinders had its own carburetor, fuel pump, radiator with fan and dynamo. Maximum output was 260 HP(192.2 kW) at 2,200 rpm. This gave the vehicle a maximum speed on the road of 44 km/hour, while the speed in medium terrain was 25-27 km/hour. The engine had oversize air filters and could run on several types of fuel used by the Czechoslovak army. It was equipped with electric and hand starters and also had a compressed air cylinder with a compressor for emergency starting.

The fuel capacity was 270 liters, which gave the tank approximately six hours endurance, about 150 km on the road.

The gear box was of the well-tested Praga-Wilson type with five speeds forward and one back. It had a pre-selector, gears were selected beforehand and were engaged by depressing the clutch pedal. Though the steering was only mechanical, with no power assist, it was reported to be very easy and not tiring for the driver. The design followed closely the well-tested construction of the LT vz.38. The only difference was in the placement of the driving sprockets, which were in the rear.

Chassis:
The chassis was very similar to the one used on Škoda's LT vz.35, only more robust, as was needed for the larger and heavier vehicle. The track was stretched over rear driving and front idler sprockets, eight running wheels and four return rollers. The running wheels were doubled and rubber tired. Two pairs were mounted on a frame; two frames formed a wheel carrier, sprung with leaf spring clusters. Like the LT vz.35, the V-8-H had an unsprung doubled wheel under the idler sprocket in the front of the vehicle. These wheels were fixed on lugs on the side of the body and were meant to improve centering of the track and obstacle crossing. The running gear provided a satisfactory ride both on roads and cross-country. The vehicle could cross ditches 2.3 m wide, climb obstacles 1 m high and ford the same depth. It could climb 40° slopes.

Exterior and interior equipment:
The tank supposedly would have contained all the standard equipment of the contemporary Czechoslovak tanks. There were some improvements, though: the commander was connected with the accompanying infantry by telephone in a box on the rear plate, the vehicle was equipped with a gyrocompass, was sealed against chemical agents, and a more powerful radio set and intercom for the crew were planned.

The original look of the medium tank Š-II-c in 1937. The resemblance to the ŠP-II-b is obvious. Only one prototype was built.

Š-II-c engine was a new Škoda V-eight of 13,800 cc displacement and 240 HP output. Here it is shown complete with the transmission and the steering unit.

Armament:
After some initial discussions, the army had decided in the spring of 1938 to arm the V-8-H with the new 4.7 cm Škoda A11 tank gun, army designation 4.7 cm tank gun ÚVvz.38. It could penetrate a 40 mm armor plate at a 30° angle up to 1,000 m. The gun was again semi-automatic, but during the firing trials in 1938 some defects of the automatic function of the breach were observed. Škoda strived to eliminate them, but the gun was never officially accepted by the army.

The machine guns were the standard ZB vz.37. Both gun and machine gun spotting scopes were also of the already described types. It was proposed to use a heavier caliber machine gun in the turret, but as such guns were not ready in 1938, they were never tried.

Conclusion:
The V-8-H was a promising vehicle. When compared with the PzKpfw III, Ausf.E, it had about the same armor protection, but was riveted, while the German tank was welded. It had a lower weight, and thus higher HP/ton ratio and higher speed. Its ground pressure was lower and its obstacle crossing capability was better. What is most important, it had a much more efficient gun of a higher caliber, and could have engaged the PzKpfw III at longer distances. On the other hand, PzKpfw III had a five-man crew, which was proven to be more efficient in combat situations.

ŠKODA T-21 MEDIUM TANK

After its unsuccessful medium tank Š-III, Škoda developed a new medium Š-II-c, based loosely on the design of the ŠP-II-b. The

The first model was modified several times until its final appearance as T-21.

The front view of the Š-II-c, showing the business end of the 4.7 cm Škoda A9 gun and the massive frames of the front visors. The front armor was 30 mm, comparable with PzKpfw III and IV tanks.

The rear-end view of the Š-II-c.

vehicle carried the new 4.7 cm Škoda A11 tank gun, had 16-30 mm armor and a more powerful eight-cylinder engine of 13,800 cc displacement and with an output of 240 HP(77.4 kW) at 2,200 rpm. This gave the 16.5 tons vehicle a speed of 50 km/hour on the road. The vehicle was also considerably larger, with a length of 5.56 m, a width of 2.45 m and a height of 2.37 m.

The layout of the four-men crew was standard: the driver on the right front side of the fighting compartment, the radio-operator on the left, with one ZB vz.37 machine gun between them in the front plate. The commander and the gunner were in the turret and had at their disposal the 4.7 cm gun and another ZB machine gun.

Side view of the Škoda Š-II-c (T-21) after reconstruction. It retained the same running gear and turret, the hull was modified only slightly.

Overhead view of the T-21, showing the new Škoda V-8 engine. Details of the rotating commander's cupola and the driver's hatch are well visible.

The chassis was of the same design as on the LT vz.35 tank, only more robust, as required by the greater weight. Škoda also kept the pneumatic steering and its planetary gear-box of the type used on the LT vz.35, but again beefed up.

This medium tank had the same improvements that were introduced in the ČKD's V-8-H, namely the improved radio set, gyrocompass and the fighting compartment sealed against chemical weapons.

Škoda planned to enlist the T-21 prototype in the army trials for the standard medium tank in 1938, but the vehicle was not ready in time and thus was not tested. The Wehrmacht ordered one prototype without a turret in 1940, this one designated T-22. Simultaneously, the company built on its own accord another prototype, T-23, this one with mechanical steering. All the prototypes were scrapped shortly after the end of the war.

TURÁN

Toward the end of the thirties it became obvious to the automotive department of the Honvéd that the tankettes and the light tanks used by the army were becoming quickly unsuitable as battle tanks. The only solution was to start a production of medium tanks as soon as possible. Because the medium Weiss Manfred V4 tank was found lacking, it was decided to license a suitable construction.

In 1939, Honvéd started negotiations with the Swedish company Landsverk AB, which had a medium tank LAGO under development for some time. The Hungarians wanted to buy a prototype for testing, but as the development lagged into 1940, Mavag and Ganz ended the Swedish contacts in August 1940. During the visit of the Hungarian Military delegation in Germany in April 1939, the question of a license for a German vehicle was raised, but the German reply was evasive. The Hungarians persisted and raised the question again in December 1939 in Budapest, where they proposed to buy 180 medium tanks for 27 million Deutschmarks. The Germans did not agree this time either, and even refused to sell the Hungarians a "sample" PzKfpw IV. The Italians were contacted next. They offered first the M 11/39. This the Hungarians refused as unsuitable, but they were interested in the M 13/40. The Italians promised to send a sample vehicle, but by the time it was ready in August 1940, the Hungarians had already bought a license for the Škoda tank.

Škoda T-23. Built as a company venture in 1941, it survived the war and was shown to the Ministry of Defense commission in July 1945. Note the prewar uniform of the officer on the right, and the British battle dresses of the two tank officers next to the tank.

Water trials.

A Honvéd officer in its turret, T-21 in Hungary.

During the fighting in Southern Slovakia and in Transcarpathian Ruthenia, the Hungarians had captured two LT vz.35 tanks of the Czechoslovak army in March 1939 (Czechoslovak numbers 13903 and 13673). Vehicle 13903 was hit and was burnt out. The tanks were totally disassembled in the Military Technical Institute of Honvéd (HTI). The Hungarians liked the construction of the vehicles and wanted to repair them, so that they would be usable for training and further study. Honvéd invited in October 1939 Dipl.Ing.Figl from Škoda to discuss with him the conditions under which Škoda would be willing to repair these two tanks. Škoda contracted to repair both vehicles for 645,000 Kč ($ 26,000), but later, after the license for the T-21 tank was signed, repaired them free of charge. Both tanks were returned to Hungary in March 1941 and were used by the tank school in Esztergome till 1943.

During his visit in Budapest in October 1939 Škoda's trade director Figl gave the Hungarians a list of Škoda military vehicles whose export the Germans had approved. On the list were both T-11 (LT vz.35) and T-21 tanks. The Hungarians got very interested in the T-21 as a vehicle suitable for their needs, and once Figl assured them that it will be possible to manufacture them under a license, they asked for its testing in Hungary.

Škoda promised to deliver a sample vehicle for testing by the beginning of 1940. In February 1940, the OKH approved its sale and its licensing to the Hungarians, and on February 20, 1940 Dipl.Ing. Figl reported to the president of Škoda that the Hungarians wanted to order 180 tanks, or to buy the licensing rights. HTI proposed to transfer the license to Weiss Manfred in Budapest, as it already had certain experience with tank manufacture with their V4 type. Besides Weiss, Mavag and Ganz in Budapest and Magyar Vagon (Raba) in Györ were to take part in the production. Mavag in Diosgyor was contracted to make the guns and Danuvia in Budapest the machine guns.

WM contacted Škoda, and one of its directors, János Korbuly, traveled as a member of the Honvéd delegation to Pilsen in April 1940 to close the deal. Škoda sent the technical description of the T-21 and a proposal of the license to Hungary in May 1939. The cost was 1,350,000 Pengö for the license, and 292,000 Pengö per vehicle in the case of a fifty-vehicle order. HTI planned the testing

Climbing trials.

Nice view of the inside of the cupola's hatch with the periscope.

Inside of the T-21 turret with the gun and gun ammunition storage.

T-21 during the demonstration in Hungary in June 1940. The engine deck was clean and uncluttered.

of the prototype (1,000 km on roads and 200 km in country) in May. Simultaneously, the four companies were consulted as to their manufacturing capabilities and delivery times. Weiss Manfred and Raba accepted eagerly, as their military programs were limited, while Mavag and Ganz were much less enthusiastic, as at that time they were still trying to get the license from Landsverk.

Škoda sent the prototype with its factory driver to Hungary on June 3, 1940. At this time, the Hungarians calculated the cost per vehicle in the case the production would be done in Hungary, and came with a lower cost per vehicle than Škoda quoted, 264,000 P. This already influenced them toward buying the license, and when Dipl.Ing. Figl reported to them that the Germans would not be willing to tie up Škoda's production capacity for export, it was decided on May 26, 1940 to buy the license.

The testing of the T-21 started on June 10, 1940 in Hajmaskeri. The Honvéd commission was headed by general János Vertesy. The tests were very successful, the first 400 km were covered without any mishaps. The tank was returned to Budapest on June 20, and the turret front plate with the 4.7 cm Škoda A11 gun was exchanged for a new plate with the Hungarian 4 cm M.37 gun, developed originally for the V4 tank. 8mm M.34/40 Gebauer machine guns and a Hungarian radio were also fitted. The testing commission recommended this tank as a medium tank of the Honvéd.

The military tests started at the beginning of July on the sandy puszta in Bugac, but on July 5 the tank returned to Hajmeskeri for further tests. On July 9 and 10 general Laszlo Horvath, the commander of the armor training center of Honvéd, witnessed the tests and highly praised the speed, agility and cross-country capabilities of the Škoda tank and judged it to be able to fulfill all the requirements for the medium tank. The testing was finished on July 10, in the presence of general Barthy, the minister of defense. The tank covered over 800 km in rough terrain with flying colors.

The Hungarian commission asked for minor changes, such as increasing the armor thickness from 30 to 35 mm, replacing the rotating commander's cupola with a fixed one and replacing the Scintilla electrical equipment by Bosch. During July 11, the tank was shown to the directors of Weiss Manfred (Korbuly), Magyar Vagon (Berza and Matray) and Ganz (Vamosy, Jendrasik).

On July 12, 1940, general Ruszkiczay-Rudiger gave the Škoda representatives a proposal for a license for the T-21 tank and at the same time asked for a speedy proposal for a license for a Škoda 4 cm gun. After some haggling about the price, Škoda gave the Hungarians its final proposal, and the licensing agreement was signed on August 6, 1940. Škoda sold the license for an unlimited production of the tank and the new A17 4 cm gun for 1,184,200 P, and also agreed to repair the two LT 35 tanks free of charge. Both sides agreed to exchange any improvements during the development, and Hungary agreed to manufacture the tanks only for its internal use and not for export.

TURÁN I (TURÁN 40)

The general staff of Honvéd ordered under the HUBA II plan 230 tanks, needed to equip the two planned armored divisions. On September 3, 1940 the vehicle was introduced as a standard medium tank, the **M.40 TURÁN közepes harckosci** (Turán was the mythological fatherland of the Hungarians in Asia). On September 19 the order was parceled out to the four manufacturers. Weiss Manfred and Raba got orders for 70 vehicles each, Mavag 40 and Ganz 50 vehicles. WM and Raba were supposed to start the deliveries in August 1941, while the other two manufacturers in April 1942, because of their active Toldi (light tank) program. But because of many technical changes and manufacturing delays, the first Turáns came out of the factories as late as in April 1942.

Škoda transferred to WM the first two sets of manufacturing drawings in October 1940, and the production started the same month. Both Škoda and WM further modified the design, which led to delays and even losses, as some engine parts (heads) had to be scrapped. The Hungarians increased the turret ring's diameter by 200 mm to accept the third crew member (the Turán was envis-

TURAN I shows the familiar lines of the T-21. Armed with a 4 cm Mavag 41.M gun and two 34/40 A.M. machine guns, it had a crew of five.

TURAN I of the 2nd Armored Division from the top. It shows the different commander's cupola, new access doors in the sides of the turret and large intake vent on the top of the engine's cover. The white cross on the engine cover is visible, but the call number on the turret was removed by the censor. This photograph was taken in Galicia in 1944.

aged from the beginning to have five crew members, while the original T-21 had a crew of four) and cut crew access doors into the sides of the turret.

The first iron prototype (H-801) was finished on July 1941 and its testing started on July 22. Škoda at this time had already proposed a new radiator, but even this had proved to be insufficient and the engine was overheating. Engineers from WM designed their own radiator that was fully successful, and all the Turáns were equipped with them. Some problems were also encountered with the chassis and the gear-box. The testing commission summarized all the problems into 17 points, and HTI stopped any further production until all these problems were solved.

Another set of problems appeared in connection with the armor plate. The Hungarian steel mills so far manufactured armor plate only up to13 mm thickness. Besides, Hungary had problems with obtaining certain additives, like vanadium and nickel. The steel mill in Diosgyori developed a new type MESTER, which did not contain any nickel. Its production started in May 1941. Its disadvantage was that it was very difficult to make in thicknesses below 20 mm.

To overcome this problem, Magyar Vagon developed an improved AJAX, which was comparable to the Mester plates, but could have been manufactured in any thickness. Ajax plate also contained titanium, which was imported from Switzerland and Belgium. Both plates were very resistant to penetration, but were somewhat brittle and once penetrated, spalled heavily. The Ajax plate was further developed, and in October 1943 became available in 75 mm thickness with 78-90 kg/mm² penetration resistance.

WM obtained Mester plates for the first 1 tanks on June 26, 1941, and began cutting them. In the beginning of September the manufacturers had armor plate for 119 tanks At this time it was decided to increase the frontal from 25 to 35 mm, and later even to 50 mm. The manufacturers, because of the lack of 50 mm plates, combined 25 and 35 mm plates routinely.

Many changes slowed the production. In February 1942, WM had only 12 complete bodies and turrets, 15 engines and 70 sets of interior equipment. Only 60% of the remaining materials were delivered. The first finished vehicles left the factories in April and May 1942 and were delivered to units in June. Badly trained drivers, insufficient upkeep and frantic training programs caused quite a high incidence of problems on this first Turán series. Besides, several changes on the gear-box necessitated recalls (the last in February 1943), during which 31 small changes were also made. Thus, the final version of the Turán was completed as late as 1943.

TURAN I during a training run. Open turret side door above the white cross in black rectangle.

TURANs I during a parade. The crew wears leather coats and leather helmets, similar to the Italian ones.

Field Marshal Model inspecting with Hungarian General Lakatos a unit of TURANs at Stanislav in April 1944.

The improvements in driver training and maintenance caused a marked increase in the vehicles' reliability, which was proven during the heavy fighting the Turáns underwent later.

The first TURÁN deliveries went to the tank school in Esztergom; in July 1942 the armored battalions 2/I and 3/I began receiving theirs, and in August battalions 1/I and 4/I. Most of the 230 vehicles ordered under HUBA II were delivered in 1942, with the balance in 1943. The TURÁN I was ordered also under the HUBA III program to keep the production running, so that the Honvéd had on October 30, 1943 already 242 TURÁNs available. The 3rd Armored Regiment attained full status in August 1943 with the 1st Armored Regiment being supplied concurrently. Once it attained its full status, the 1st Cavalry Division was supplied next.

The HUBA III order for 215 vehicles was placed on July 24, 1941. It was lowered to 207 in August (18 by Weiss Manfred, 95 by Magyar Vagon, 60 by Ganz and 34 by Mavag). The cost per vehicle had risen to 290,000 P and the final cost, due to inflation, was even higher, 393,254 P. The order was again lowered in May 1942 to 124 vehicles, but even this was not realistic and the number produced was only 55 vehicles (Magyar Vagon 12, Ganz 24 and Mavag 19).

Rear view of TURAN I with the turret's perforated skirting installed. This skirting was installed on all vehicles returning to the factories for repairs from February 1944 on.

The final production numbers by manufacturers were:

MANUFACTURER	HUBA II	HUBA III	TOTAL
WEISS MANFRED	70	-	70
MAGYAR VAGON (RABA)	70	12	82
GANZ	50	24	74
MAVAG	40	19	59
TOTAL	230	55	285

(Plus two iron prototypes from 1941)

Production was running smoothly up to middle 1943. Later that year, there were power outages, which slowed the production. In 1944, there were grave problems with deliveries of the armored plate. Combined with several heavy allied air attacks on the factories, and the desire of the German occupiers (after March 1944) to

Front view, showing the turret skirting.

Rear view of TURAN I, showing the installation of smoke candles on the rear plate.

use the Hungarian industry for their own use, all production practically ceased in the second half of 1944. In 1944, the factories used their remaining capacity for repairing existing vehicles, and for some improvements. One of them was the addition of perforated armored plates as an additional protection for the chassis and the turret, which was developed by HTI in 1943 and was tested on the H-830 TURÁN in February 1944. As it was highly successful, it was gradually introduced on the vehicles coming back to the factories for repairs.

TURÁN II

The battle experience from the Eastern front had shown decisively not only that the light tanks and the tankettes were useless as first-line fighting vehicles, but also that any tank with a gun smaller than 7.5 cm would be at a great disadvantage against the Soviet armor. The General Staff of the Honvéd decided even before October 1, 1941 to start planning for the increased gun caliber of the future TURÁN tanks.

Though these tanks were designated as "heavy" in the new organizational tables, they were in effect mediums, upgunned with the 7.5 cm gun. According to the specification, published on May 7, 1941, the basic TURÁN was supposed to get a new turret with the 7.5 cm short gun and a heavy 12.7 mm machine gun, being developed by Danuvia. The gun had a muzzle velocity of 500 m/sec, and was supposed to be effective against a 50 mm vertical armor plate at 500 m. The tanks' armor was to be increased by 30-40 mm, retaining the rest of the design.

According to the new organization, 143 heavy tanks were needed for the newly formed formations. The prototypes of both the tank and the new gun were ordered in June 1941 from HTI. Production was supposed to start in December 1942 and to run in parallel with the production of TURÁN I. The prototype of the new gun was planned to be finished in January 1942, in time for the gun factory in Diosgyor to start its production in March. HTI was commissioned to develop new piercing and high explosive ammunition for the gun.

In September 1941 the specification was changed, as Danuvia reported that the new heavy MG would not be ready in time. It was decided to use two 8 mm machine guns, like in the TURÁN I. The prototype of the new turret with the new gun was finished in January 1942. The turret was found acceptable, but the gun mantlet

Destroyed Hungarian armor in Bratislava, Slovakia in May 1945.

The prototype of TURAN II during acceptance trials in May 1942 in Hajmaskeri.

TURAN II with its short 7.5 cm Mavag 41.M gun. The changed shape of the turret's top is well apparent.

A new turret with the long 7.5 cm Mavag 43.M gun of the TURAN III (75 Hosszu). Only one prototype was built.

cracked, and so the first tests of the prototype with this new turret in February 19-22 in Esztergome were concerned only with the interior arrangement of the crew in the new turret, which was more cramped than that of the TURÁN I. The testing commission found that the rotating mechanism of the turret needed improvement, and proposed new placement of the ready rounds and of the radio inside the turret.

Based on the results of the final tests in May 1942 in Hajmaskeri, which included the firing of the main gun, the tank was accepted as the **41.M TURÁN nehéz harckosci** or **TURÁN 75 rövid csövü**. The first four tanks of this type were delivered to the army in May 1943, but without the main armament, because the ballistic tests of the gun were running late. The first 28 tanks finally obtained the main guns and their optics in July 1943. Also, in August began the production of the approved munitions. The heavy tank companies started their training with the new tanks in the fall of 1943.

The new order of the Defense Ministry from July 4, 1941 specified building 90 vehicles of the TURÁN II type in place of the 168 TOLDI II tanks, ordered from Ganz and Mavag. The production of the 90 TURÁN IIs was given totally to Weiss Manfred, and its part of the production of TURÁN I tanks was parceled out between Ganz and Mavag. The order was increased to 102 vehicles on July 24, 1941. The cost per vehicle was quoted by WM as 325,000 P, but the final cost in 1943 came to 428,254 P.

The order was increased again in May 1942 to 205 vehicles, 102 by Weiss Manfred, 76 by Magyar Vagon and 27 by Ganz. During further discussion in late 1942, the number was again increased to 382 vehicles. On February 24, 1943, the representatives of the army met with the manufacturers to finalize the production requirements. The army wanted WM to manufacture 147 tanks, Magyar Vagon 127, Ganz 48 and Mavag 60. The companies protested that they did not have the capacity for such production. The final arrangement was for Ganz to make 36 vehicles (because of its commitments in the TOLDI IIa 40mm program), Mavag was taken out completely, WM got 147 tanks and Magyar Vagon 127. With Ganz back to the 48 originally planned, the total came to 322, 127 in 1943 and 195 in 1944.

Even this plan was not final. In May 1943, the General Staff decided to end the production of all TURÁN models in the spring of 1944. The total need for the TURÁN II vehicles was specified as 143 vehicles for the battle formations and 79 for training and replacement. The new total was 222 vehicles, which were parceled to WM (62), Magyar Vagon (68) and Ganz (92).

The first four vehicles left the factory at Czepel on May 15, 1943, and were assigned to the 3rd Armored Regiment. Until the end of August, the army had taken over only 49 tanks, and in September, 14 additional vehicles were assigned to the assault gun batteries. By the end of September 1943, there were 74 vehicles delivered to the army, and in the middle of 1944, when the production ended, the total stood at 139 vehicles.

The final production numbers by manufacturers were:

A destroyed TURAN II. Ammunition explosion blew the side and rear armor plates off the turret.

Side view of the TURAN III prototype with the new raised turret and the long gun.

MANUFACTURER	MANUFACTURED	HONVED NUMBERS
Weiss Manfred	54	2H-000 - 2H-053
Magyar Vagon(Raba)	39	2H-077 - 2H-086,2H-213 - 2H-235
Ganz	36	2H-400 - 2H-435
Unknown	10	2H-054-2H-061,2H-436-2H-437
TOTAL	139	

TURÁN III

In February 1943, the General Staff of the Honvéd decided that it is necessary to modernize the existing TURÁN tanks by an incorporation of a new 7.5 cm gun with higher muzzle velocity, to make them sufficiently effective against Russian armor until the introduction of the planned TAS heavy tank. The modifications were supposed to start in the second half of 1944, using the newly developed 43.M tank gun. Simultaneously, the frontal armor protection would be upgraded to 80 mm.

Front view of the prototype TURAN III. The higher roof of the turret was necessary to allow sufficient depression of the gun.

As early as February 1943 HTI found that the new gun could not fit into the turret of the TURÁN II. They used a TURÁN II chassis (2H-012) to test a new turret with an iron mockup of the 43.M gun with a long barrel and a muzzle brake. On July 22, 1943, HTI placed an order with Weiss Manfred for the manufacturing of one iron turret with complete interior installations and electrical turning. In August 1943 WM obtained the iron mockup of the gun, and built the prototype on the chassis of a TURÁN I (H-830) with the new turret and 25 mm additional armor on the front and back. The vehicle and the turret sides were protected with spaced perforated armored plates. Its army designation was **43.M TURÁN nehéz harckcsci** or **TURÁN 75 hosscu scövü**.

It was planned to build the 43.M gun into the prototype in December 1943, but its development lagged and the prototype was not finished until June 1944. Though its testing in Hajmaskeri went very well, it never got into full scale production, due to disruptions and final cessation of all industrial production in Hungary in the second half of 1944.

The Turáns went to the two armored and one cavalry divisions, formed during the reorganization in 1942. They were also assigned to assault gun battalions 1. to 8. instead of proper assault guns. The tanks went to war for the first time in April 1944, when the 2nd Armored Division with its 3rd Armored Regiment left as part of

Rear view of the TURAN III, showing the large door in turret's rear wall and shape of the cupola.

A Zrinyi with the perforated side skirts fitted.

the 1st Hungarian army to defend Eastern Galicia. From then on, the Turans fought well in bitter defensive battles. Most of them ended their operational carrier North of Budapest on the Danube, though small units managed to retreat into Slovakia and Austria, where they surrendered.

The Hungarians were happy with the tanks, and considered their mobility and armor protection superior to the German PzKpfw IV, which they also used.

ZRÍNYI II ASSAULT GUN

The Turán chassis was also used for another vehicle, the Zrínyi assault gun. In 1942 Weiss Manfred proposed to build an assault gun, carrying the 40.M 10.5 cm howitzer, on a widened Turan chassis. The Honvéd general staff accepted this proposal eagerly, as the army was planning to raise assault gun battalions, but did not have a suitable assault gun.

The prototype was finished in December 1942 and its tests ran from December 12, 1942 to January 28, 1943 in Hajmaskeri. After proposing minor modifications, the Honvéd accepted the vehicle

Front detail of the 10.5 cm Mavag 40/43.M howitzer and its ball mount. Accepted into production in January 1943, the Zrinyis were supposed to fill the assault gun battalions. Though 140 were ordered, only 66 were delivered.

Side view of Zrinyi II assault gun. A low silhouette, good armor and an effective gun made the Zrinyi a very effective tank hunter.

A rear view of the Zrinyi, showing the extremely low fighting compartment.

Zrinyi at speed. Though weighing 21.5 tons, it still had a very respectable top speed of 40 km/hour. Crew is in summer uniforms.

Replenishing the Zrinyi with ammunition. One of the shortcomings of the Mavag howitzer was its two-part ammunition.

Two views of a destroyed Zrinyi II in Bratislava in May 1945, showing nice details of the periscopes and the gun mount.

on January 26, 1943 and ordered 40 of them for 440,000 P each under the designation **40/43.M ZRÍNYI rohamtarack or ZRÍNYI 105**. The vehicle's weight was 21.5 tons, due to its 75 mm frontal armor and the heavier gun, but it was still agile, with a ground pressure of 0.91 kg/cm^2. It carried four men and 52 rounds for the gun in a fully enclosed superstructure. The gun fired a 15 kg AP round, or a 17 kg HE round, this one at 10.5 km distance.

Though 100 additional Zrínyis were ordered, only 26 were made after the first order of 40 was delivered, due to the allied bombings and German takeover.

The success of the Zrínyi II led to the development of the **44.M ZRÍNYI I rohamágyú or ZRÍNYI 75** tank hunter in 1944. Its armament was the 7.5 cm 43.M Mavag antitank gun; its frontal armor was increased to 100 mm. The prototype was rebuilt from the mild steel Turán prototype (H-801), but only four production vehicles were made.

Several Zrínyi II vehicles were captured in the restored Czechoslovakia after the war and one of them (3H-C50) was repaired by Škoda in 1947. The Czechoslovak army assigned it its number 67495 and used it for training until the fifties.

Other Prototypes

F-IV-H II amphibious tank of ČKD. Ordered by the army in 1937, it was modified and tested for the Germans during the war.

Rear view of the F-IV-H II. It had a rear drive.

AMPHIBIOUS TANKS

In October 1936 the Czechoslovak army asked both Škoda and ČKD to design a light amphibious reconnaissance tank, armed only with machine gun(s). The required speed in water was 16 km/hour, which proved to be highly optimistic, as such speed cannot be reached by even the most modern amphibious vehicles today. Based on submitted projects, the Ministry of Defense ordered the prototypes in November 1937.

The ČKD prototype was named F-IV-H and the army paid 718,000 Kč for it. Its weight was 6.5 tons, armor from 6 to 14 mm, and its projected maximum speed was 45 km/hour on the road and 9 km/hour in the water. It had a flat-four gasoline engine with an120 HP(88.7 kW) output and in the water was powered by two propellers in the rear. Its armament was one heavy ZB vz.37 machine gun in a fully rotating turret. The vehicle was ready for testing as late as August 1939 and thus was evaluated by the Germans. An improved version was tested in 1942, but the tank was not accepted for production.

The Škoda design ŠOT (Škoda Obojživelný Tank, or Škoda Amphibious Tank) was more complicated. It used a scaled-down chassis of the LT vz.35, and was armed with two ZB vz.37, one of them in a fully rotating turret. What was unusual on this design was the drive train. Škoda first considered a 225 HP (166.3 kW) Armstrong-Siddeley twelve cylinder engine, coupled to a Praga-Wilson gearbox, but finally decided to use a modified Avia TR-12 radial aircraft engine. The engine was supposed to run an electrical generator, powering electromotors coupled to the driving sprockets and to the propellers. The propellers were placed in tunnels in

The small turret with one ZB vz.37 machine gun and the raised engine air intake and exhaust muffler are on the top deck. The two screws are angled inward.

The prototype F-IV-H before modifications. The pontoons were lengthened, the rear of the hull was modified and the muffler was repositioned to the rear. The turret's cupola was also modified.

F-IV-H at speed in water, winter 1939. It almost attained its projected speed of 9 km/hour, a good showing even by today's standard.

The engine compartment of the ŠOT amphibious tank, showing the COTAL electromagnetic clutches, gearbox and engine.

the hull. As this design was not fully satisfactory, Škoda designers in January 1937 opted to transfer the engine's power through Cotal electromagnetic gearboxes. These were duly ordered from France, but they did not arrive at Škoda until March 1939. The Germans allowed Škoda to work on the prototype, whose testing started also in the summer of 1939. The heavy vehicle (7.5 tons) was incapable of floating, and because the Wehrmacht was not interested in further redesign and testing, the project was abandoned. Škoda thus lost the 754,000 Kč from the Czechoslovak army, and at the end has spent 1,254,000 Kč of its own money on this unlucky design.

At the same time, Škoda was developing its ŠET (Škoda Elektrický Tank, or Electric Tank). This was a Škoda-financed project, meant to test the gasoline-electrical drive train. As the tank was not meant to be amphibious, its hull was roomier. The chassis was again based on the simplified LT vz.35 running gear. The body was built from 15 mm thick mild steel plates, and the envisaged turret was never fitted. The drive train consisted again from the radial Avia TR-12 engine of 155 HP (114 kW) output. It was coupled with a generator giving 108 kW at 675 V. The system had two traction electric motors wired in series, each of 48 kW and 337 V. The power from the electric motors was transferred by shafts to reductions and from those to rear driving sprockets. The vehicle was steered by a steering wheel like a car. The steering wheel was connected to a controller that switched the electric motors either in the same or in opposite directions. The tracks were thus continuously and smoothly braked or accelerated for turns. The speed was governed by a foot accelerator, and varied between 2.3 and 40.5 km/hour. Braking was done similarly by the electric motors. The electrical installation was developed by Škoda's electrotechnical department.

The work on ŠET was stopped in 1940, as it was becoming quite costly. The Germans became interested in the concept and

F-IV-H climbing out of the river. The driver's hatch is open, a wise precaution during such tests.

Škoda's ŠET during evaluation by the Wehrmacht. This vehicle was a test bed for an advanced gasoline-electric drive, developed by Škoda. The tank was never fitted with a turret.

The engine compartment of the ŠET (electric tank).

asked Škoda to finish the vehicle, which finally took its first ride on October 6, 1941. It was planned to send ŠET to the Kummersdorf Wehrmacht tank testing center for evaluation, but at the end it was tested in Pilsen. The sudden unexpected interest in this vehicle could be explained by Porsche's development of a similar drive train for the heavy assault gun Ferdinand in 1943. Škoda supplied running gear parts for the 90 Ferdinands produced, but it is difficult to judge today if its gasoline-electric drive train did influence Porsche's design in any way.

LKMVP

This complex acronym denoted "Lehký Kanonový Motorový Vůz Pásový" or "Light Cannon Motorized Tracked Vehicle". It was supposed to be a fully tracked carrier for the 3.7 cm Škoda vz.37KPÚV(M) antitank gun, its crew and ammunition. The army again asked both companies to design prototypes in 1936. The gun was either towed by the vehicle, or was carried on its rear platform, from which it could be fired, if necessary.

ČKD produced its prototype in time for the 1938 trials, where it covered over 5,000 km. Though the army had reservations, it did accept and buy the prototype under the number 14124 in August 1938 and assigned it to PÚV-1. The vehicle weighed 7.1 tons with armor up to 12 mm, was 4.28 m long, 2.15 m wide and 1.69 m high. Its engine had an output of 92 HP (68 kW), which gave it a maximum speed of 52 km/hour. Endurance was eight hours. Crew was two men plus four men of the gun's crew, all carried inside the hull. The obstacle crossing capacity was as good as any tank's: ditch 1.8 m, vertical obstacle 0.8 m, wading up to 0.5 m. 90 rounds for the gun were carried.

Škoda did not finish its vehicle in time. The army refused to accept it, and Škoda had to bear the development costs. Interestingly, this was the first tracked Škoda vehicle where they used the Praga-Wilson gearbox!

Driver's position inside the ŠET, showing the steering wheel and the accelerator. Those and the brake levers were the only controls needed to drive this revolutionary vehicle.

Škoda's LKMVP, or the carrier of the 3.7 cm Škoda vz.37M antitank gun. The gun could have been carried on the vehicle, or towed behind it. The vehicle carried also a crew of six (2 + 4) and 90 rounds for the gun.

4

EXPORT OF CZECH ARMORED FIGHTING VEHICLES

Prewar Export of Czech Armored Fighting Vehicles

ČKD

Though at the beginning of the thirties the Czechoslovak army orders kept the armament manufacturers busy, their capacity was still not fully utilized. The companies were actively pursuing export orders. In this role they were so successful that Czechoslovakia (according to the League of Nations statistical reports) became a member of the leading world armaments exporters, side by side with United States, England and France. In 1931, Czechoslovakia was the third largest arms exporter in the world, in 1934-1935 the first and in 1936-1937 the fourth.

AH-IV tankette prototype for the Iranian army being tested on ČKD's private testing track. In the rear is the TNH light tank prototype, tested at the same time.

Though the bulk of Czechoslovak arms exports consisted of Škoda guns and ZB small arms, Czechoslovak AFV manufacturers were able to disrupt the hegemony of Renault and Vickers and to take a lion's share of tank orders in the late thirties.

Iran was actively building up its army during the period between the two world wars. Between 1931 and 1941 it bought from the Czech manufacturers over 300,000 rifles, 6,000 light and several hundred heavy machine guns and about 350 antitank, field and heavy guns. It was thus natural that when the Iranian army wanted to acquire armored vehicles, it turned to the Czech manufacturers.

In January 1935 both Škoda and ČKD obtained identical letters from the Iranian purchasing commission in Paris. The Iranians planned to buy around a hundred light (2-3 tons) tanks, and to procure complete outfitting and organizing of their planned tank units. While Škoda offered its Š-I tankette for Ł 1,632 per piece, ČKD sent not only a proposal based on their new designs AH-IV and TNH, but shipped to the Persian Shah the fourth P-I prototype (built concurrently with the three prototypes for the Czechoslovak army) as a gift.

The gift clearly impressed the monarch and ČKD obtained a firm order as early as May 14, 1935. It was for 30 Praga AH-IV tankettes, armed with one heavy and one light machine gun, and 26 TNH light tanks, each with one gun and two heavy machine guns. The whole order had to be shipped in one year. Delivery was dependent on availability of armor plates from Poldi, machine guns from ZB and guns from the only domestic producer - Škoda.

The Iranians asked Škoda in April 1935 about the availability of tank guns in 3.7 or 4.7 cm caliber. Because Škoda did not get a reply for their original proposal, they believed that the Iranians bought their tanks from Vickers. Škoda's representatives were thus quite surprised when they met their colleagues from ČKD on May 10, 1935 during a conference with the Iranian officers in Prague. They had to overcome their antipathies, especially when the Iranians hinted that they are in contact with Vickers and with Bofors. Both Czech companies buried their hatchet for the time being and

Prototypes of the Iranian TNH light tank and the AH-IV tankette. The turrets are in their final shapes, but without openings for the armament.

Carrying already the Iranian crest on the turret, this vehicle shows the open side visor.

agreed to arm the ordered tanks completely with Czech guns and machine guns. Škoda gained from this meeting an order for 32 3.7 cm tank guns, 26 for the planned tanks and six reserve ones.

ČKD delivered both prototypes in September 1935. The vehicles were not yet armed, because while ZB delivered its machine guns in short order, the Škoda 3.7 cm gun A4 Beta became available as late as August 12, 1936. Even so, the demonstration of the prototypes to the Iranian purchasing commission, led by General Ismail Khan, was so successful that the Iranians increased their order on September 10, 1935. Their order stipulated delivery of 50 AH-IV tankettes for Ł 1,629 each and 50 TNH light tanks for Ł 3,570 each by October 1936. On the same day the Iranians ordered the guns (60 A4 Beta guns from Škoda), the machine guns and the optical equipment from the corresponding manufacturers.

ČKD began the manufacture of both vehicles in its satellite factory in Slaný. Meanwhile, both prototypes underwent rigorous testing of their engines, running gear and armaments. Iranian officers supervised the tests, but Czechoslovak officers from the armored units also took part. The design of the vehicles and their armament proved to be extremely advanced, and the tests went on without

AH-IV negotiating a vertical obstacle. When compared with the old P-I tankette, the AH-IV was much roomier with adequate vision devices, strong engine, excellent cross-country capability and good armament.

While negotiating a steep gradient, this AH-IV tests the depression of the main armament.

Iranian TNH tank in Iranian markings, ready for delivery. Ordered in May 1935, it was the first member of the eminently successful line of ČKD light tanks. It had a round turret with a small observation cupola. Side visors and the forward slot on the turret were the same as on the AH-IV tankettes.

TNH tank from the rear. With a 15 mm armor, its weight was 8.2 tons.

any mishaps. The production was thus not disturbed by enforced design changes and proceeded smoothly. The Iranians passed to ČKD's designers combat experiences gained by the Italian army during its invasion of Ethiopia. Some small changes and improvements were incorporated into the design of both tanks to improve their combat worthiness. First twelve AH-IV tankettes were shipped on August 17, 1936; following shipments of both types were approximately 20 vehicles per month. The tanks were shipped by rail to Bremen in Germany and from there by ship to the Iranian port of Saleabad. The last part of the shipment of 102 vehicles (50 AH-IVs, 50 TNHs and two prototypes) arrived in Teheran in May 1937. The delay was caused by the Iranian mission in Prague. Its members liked the life in Czechoslovakia and tried to prolong their stay there accordingly.

Because the armament was shipped separately from the vehicles, it took several more months before the vehicles were ready. Moreover, during the assembly several complications with the machine gun mounts, guns alignment and on the chassis caused the ČKD, Škoda and ZB technicians to sweat even more than was due to the local weather. Their work was finished in November 1937, when all the vehicles were combat ready.

The first eleven completed TNH tanks were shown to the public for the first time on February 22, 1937 in Teheran. Their appearance caused great ovations by the Shah's subjects and consternation on the faces of the various military attaches, who did not expect to see such modern armored vehicles in this backwater.

The Czechs then had to train the crews and organize the armored units. In this task they were hampered by the low technical

A detail of the mounting of the Škoda A4 Beta gun and the ZB vz.35 machine gun in the Iranian TNH tank.

The prototype TNH during cross-country testing. The observation slots in the cupola are well visible.

TNH in Iranian service. At the time of its introduction in February 1937, these tanks did not have a competitor in the Near East area.

The modified Romanian prototype of the R-1 tankette uprooting a tree during a demonstration. It could uproot trees up to 20 cm diameter.

level of the Iranian crews, and by some high placed conservative Iranian officers, who resented these "unwelcome novelties". It took some time before all the vehicles were maintained in running condition by their trained crews and before this new weapon was accepted by the conservatives, but finally twenty five tanks of each type were allocated to the First and Second divisions. The tanks were eventually so well accepted that the Iranian army was planning in 1938 to order between 100 and 300 additional vehicles of each type to strengthen its armored units. The Second World War prevented the realization of those plans.

TNH on parade in Teheran in 1950. Though the Iranian army planned to order up to 300 additional tanks of this type, it was left with the original fifty, due to the advent of the war.

Iran also bought a large number of aircraft machine guns, manufactured by Česká Zbrojovka (Strakonice). These were adapted for water cooling and were used in the Iranian Marmon-Harrington armored cars. Thus, all Iranian AFVs had Czech armament.

The Iranian army was left with the 100 ČKD tanks as their only armored tracked vehicles, and used them well into the fifties. In 1940 the tanks were equipped with Telefunken radios, but otherwise they were not modified.

The Iranian contract opened the world for ČKD and its tank designs. The next customer for ČKD tanks was **Romania**. The country was an ally of Czechoslovakia in the "Little Entente" and its army had been buying Czech arms since the twenties. ČKD asked the Ministry of Defense in 1933 for permission to export its P-II tanks to Romania. The permit was granted, but the sale was not realized. In November 1934, during the visit of staffs of the Romanian and Yugoslav armies, Škoda and ČKD showed their tanks Š-I, Š-II, P-I and P-II. Both companies obtained the necessary export permits in the spring of 1935.

In November 1935 the Romanian purchasing commission visited both Renault and Vickers, but finally decided to buy the tanks from Czechoslovakia. On January 8, 1936 both Škoda and ČKD were asked to submit bids for several types of tanks in lots of 50, 100, 200, 300, 400 and 500 vehicles. The executives of both companies met on January 22 and decided that each company would offer its own types, but they would consult about their bids before submitting them, so that no large price discrepancies would result. Škoda offered Š-I, Š-I-d, Š-II, Š-II-aj and Š-II-a. ČKD submitted AH-IV, P-II, P-IIa, P-II-aj, TNH and TNHb (Š-II-aj, P-II-j and

Romanian R-1 in Romanian service. The crew is wearing winter uniforms and leather helmets. The turret flap is in the open position. The driver could drive in a head-up position.

The Romanian company Malaxa built one prototype of the planned indigenous production of the R-1, but the production was never started. The prototype, chassis number 201, army number U058445, had a commander's cupola on top of the turret, similar to the Swedish version.

TNHb existed only as preliminary designs). Prices varied between 300,000 and 1,000,000 Kč per vehicle.

At first, it seemed that ČKD won the whole contract. On April 2, 1936 a contract for delivery of 100 P-II-aj tanks and 36 AH-IV tankettes was signed in Bucharest. This contract was changed in May 1936, when the Romanians decided to buy the "mediums" Š-II-a instead of the P-IIaj tanks. One of the stated reasons for this change of heart was the Czechoslovak army's decision to accept this tank as its main battle tank. ČKD was thus left with an order for 35 AH-IV tankettes, named R-1, signed on August 14, 1936. According to this contract, the company had to submit a prototype in two months. In the third month, thorough testing under the auspices of the Romanian commission would lead to the acceptance of the type; all the production vehicles would be delivered in seven months. In reality, the testing lasted much longer, as the Romanian experts demanded many changes on the prototype. The company simultaneously initiated manufacturing of the whole order, and the changes had to be introduced on all the vehicles on the production line.

ČKD sent the first ten production tankettes to Romania in October 1937, where they participated in the autumn army maneuvers. As they were driven by company drivers, they made a very good impression and returned on October 22. ČKD finished the 35 vehicles and started their trial runs in November 1937. Meanwhile, the Romanian commission refused to accept the first ten finished vehicles to the trials, because they did not conform to the specifica-

R-1 during a parade in Bucharest in Romania. Note the "peacetime" black on white registration number on the front plate.

R-1 tankette modified as the AH-IV Hb with a Tatra engine in 1948.

The prototype of the Swedish AH-IV Sv, designated Stvr m/37 in the Swedish army, was assembled in Sweden from parts supplied by ČKD. It was the heaviest of the series, with armor up to 12 mm. It carried both machine guns (Karlskrona Ksp m/39) in a new turret, had a Volvo 85 HP engine and a maximum speed of almost 60 km/hour. It was equipped with a radio set.

Stvr m/37 during a maneuvers in Sweden with unusual markings on the turret.

tions. All these delays kept the tankettes in the factory till April 1938. The order was shipped to Romania at the beginning of May and the acceptance protocol was signed in Sibio on May 19, 1938. This did not mean that the Romanian army officially accepted the vehicles, though. Such official acceptance was issued only on August 19, 1938, following a successful trial of two vehicles (Nos. 8 and 15) under summer conditions. All the tankettes were assigned to the reconnaissance units of the Cavalry Divisions and fought with them on the Eastern front. Several of them survived till 1945 and participated in the liberation of Slovakia.

The owner of the Romanian company Malaxa signed personally the licensing agreement for the R-1 tankette and the V-8-H tank in September 1938 in Prague. Because he made some unauthorized changes in the document, ČKD refused to honor it. After protracted negotiations, a new agreement was signed in February 1939. Following the signing, ČKD sent the drawings to Bucharest to its representative with the strict orders to release them to the customer only against full payment. Mr. Malaxa transferred the money and got the drawings in October 1939. The licensing agreement was worth 1,962,540 K (a new designation of the crown, as Czechoslovakia ceased to exist in March 1939), which sum included a prototype vehicle.

Malaxa never paid the whole sum and finally went into bankruptcy. His company was taken over by the state. BMM did not deliver the prototype, which the Malaxa company built mostly from available spare parts for the R-1 tankettes. The licensed production never started.

The original R-1 prototype remained the property of ČKD and in 1948 became a prototype for the Ethiopia order. It was equipped with the Tatra 114 air-cooled Diesel engine and remained with ČKD until the seventies, when it was scrapped.

ČKD also exported to Romania in 1936-1937 seven riot police armored cars Praga TNHSPE. These were built on the chassis of the Praga TN truck. The boxy armored superstructure carried a fully

Front view of the prototype AH-IV Sv. The driver had a new visor. Note the strange side lights on the front fender.

Stvr m/37 during the winter maneuvers in Sweden in an all white camouflage.

Stvr m/37 in the Military Museum in Sweden, showing the standard camouflage paint and markings. It has a different driver's visor than the original vehicles.

rotating turret with a light machine gun ZB vz.30 and a water cannon. The water tanks and the pumps were in the rear part of the vehicle.

While the Romanians were concerned with operating their tankettes under high heat conditions, the next ČKD's customer, **Sweden**, had totally opposing demands. Sweden in 1936 decided to build up its armored units by incorporating armored battalions in their Royal Skaraborg and Royal Soedermanland regiments. For this purpose the Swedish Parliament allocated 4.5 million Swedish Crowns. As this was not enough to obtain the needed number of light tanks, the army decided to buy the tankettes and only 16 Strv m/38 tanks from Landsverk. Though Sweden had its own tank manufacturing capability and indigenous designs, its army purchasing commission arrived in Prague in February 1937. It asked to see ČKD tanks under winter conditions. ČKD showed its vehicles in the Krkonoše mountains. Their performance in deep snow managed to convince the Swedes that the vehicles would work well in winter.

The Swedish army ordered 48 AH-IV Sv tankettes. The Stvr m/37, the AH-IV-Sv's designation in the Swedish army, was equipped with a more powerful Scania-Vabis engine. The armament, two Ksp m/39 machine guns was installed in the turret, which had a small observation cupola on top. The vehicle was the heaviest of the three AH-IV models manufactured so far, but with a more powerful engine had the same speed as the first two models.

ČKD manufactured one prototype for testing and for evaluation of the necessary modifications. The order was shipped in parts and the vehicles were assembled by Oskarshams. ČKD also supplied drilling masters and calibration sets. The total shipment filled 13 railway cars and was finished by September 13, 1938. The last missing parts, 38 gun mounts and 20 optical sets, were shipped in November.

Sweden was the last customer for the AH-IV tankettes. While of a very advanced design, and with technical parameters superior to the PzKpfw I, in 1938 the tankettes did not have enough fighting power to be employed as battle tanks.

TECHNICAL DESCRIPTION:

AH-IV was a small vehicle, 3.20 m long and 1.73 m wide. The weight of the three models increased from 3.5 tons for the Iranian AH-IV to 4.68 tons for the AH-IV-Sv. When compared with the Tančík vz.33, the AH-IV was much roomier, with better vision devices, protected with armored flaps and bulletproof glass blocks. Its armor ranged from 6 to 15 mm, which gave it enough protection for its class. Its main armament, one ZB vz.35 or vz.37 heavy machine gun, was in a fully rotating turret, allowing continuous fire in a field of 360°.

Its main advantage was the chassis and the drive train. The chassis used four main rubber-shod wheels on each side, protected by 6 mm armor discs. Each pair of wheels was sprung by leaf-spring clusters. The running gear was a scaled down version of the very successful running gear of the TNH tanks. Similarly, the tankette had the Praga-Wilson gearbox with a preselector of gears. Driving the vehicle was very easy (see the description for the LT vz38 tank in Chapter 3). Coupled with an adequate Praga six-cylinder water-cooled engine of 3.4 liters displacement and 55 HP(40.7 kW) output, the vehicle had a maximum speed of up to 45 km/hour and excellent cross-country riding qualities. ČKD literature claimed that due to its well-placed center of gravity, the vehicle did not oscillate when running cross-country and thus provided an excellent gun platform for firing on the move.

While the vehicle's speed on the road was comparable to the speed of contemporary armored cars, it had infinitely better capabilities in cross-country running. Its armor was also superior and it would have made an excellent reconnaissance vehicle, especially if equipped with a radio, as the Swedish Strv m/37 were.

FURTHER DEVELOPMENT OF THE TNH SERIES:

The next order for light tanks came from an unstable region - South America. There, the war in the Gran Chaco between Bolivia and Paraguay in 1934-1935 has shown the importance of aircraft and armored vehicles in combat. On the other hand, the combatants did

The same vehicle from the rear, showing the detail of the open turret hatch.

The LTP prototype for Peru. In contrast to the TNH, it had three return rollers instead of two, heavier armor of 25 mm and was the first to have the Scania-Vabis engine mounted.

The LTP obtained also a new turret, here still without armament. It had the shape used on all subsequent models. On LTP it retained the small observation cupola.

not have the financial means for procuring large numbers of such expensive vehicles. Thus, the order for 24 tanks from Peru was the most important tank acquisition in this region in the thirties.

Peru decided in 1935 to acquire tanks from Europe. Its original specifications were for seven five-tons vehicles with a gun and two machine guns. But there was an unusual specification: the vehicles had to be able to fight in the mountains up to an elevation of 4,000 m. The Peruvian army contacted the well-known manufacturers Vickers, Renault and Fiat, and simultaneously also Škoda and ČKD. Škoda at this time had its hands full with supplying the LT vz.35 tanks for the Czechoslovak army and the R-2 tanks for Romania and declined. ČKD on the other hand reacted quickly and offered both its AH-IV tankette and the TNH light tank.

The Peruvian army changed its final specifications to a weight between five and six tons and an armament of one 3.7 cm gun and one machine gun. The planned number increased to 36 vehicles. ČKD had to submit a new offer, because the AH-IV could not incorporate a gun and the TNH tank was heavier. But it had at this time on a drawing board a lighter model of the LTL tank designed for Latvia, which met the Peruvian specifications exactly.

The purchasing commission of the Peruvian army in Paris, led by General Tamayo, arrived in Prague in October 1936. It found the exhibited tank prototypes acceptable. The commission returned to ČKD in April 1937 and decided to order 24 vehicles of the LTP type. ČKD thus was successful even in competition with the best contemporary tank manufacturers in the world!

Ordering the guns for the LTP tanks presented a small problem. The only gun manufacturer was Škoda, which was bound by a distribution agreement with its parent company, Schneider-Creuzot. According to this agreement, Peru was in the French sphere and Škoda was not allowed to sell its guns there. Both companies at the end found a solution: the guns were "bought" from the stocks of the Czechoslovak army by ČKD, with the provision that Škoda would replace them. As the army had on hand at this time only ten spare guns, Škoda had to modify fourteen of its standard antitank guns.

In January 1938 ČKD proposed a change: to replace the promised LTL-based tank by an LTH tank, newly developed for Switzerland. Filling both orders by manufacturing the same type would lower the final cost of the vehicles. Moreover, the LTH was a better design, which in the end was accepted also by Latvia. The problem was that ČKD did not have a finished prototype of either vehicle and had to persuade the temperamental South Americans that the proposed change was in their best interest. ČKD sent to Paris its CEO, its export director and the chief designer Surin and after protracted meetings the final order was finally signed on February 15, 1938.

According to the contract, ČKD was to supply 24 light tanks with a weight of 6.3 tons, a 120 HP(88.7 kW) engine and armor 8-25 mm thick. The tanks were to be armed with a 3.7 cm Škoda vz.34 gun, one ZB vz.35 heavy machine gun and one ZB vz.30 light machine gun. Simultaneously, Peru ordered 8,000 HE and 5,334 AP rounds for the guns. The prototype tank had to be sent

Another LTP tank, with the gun's recoil cylinder fitted without the barrel. The LTP was almost identical to the LTH, built for Switzerland, though the LTH was better armored and was consequently slightly heavier.

Designed to be driveable in the mountains over 4,000 m high, the LTP was a very successful design, and served in the Peruvian army up to 1988!

immediately to Peru for additional trials in the mountains; the remaining vehicles were to be finished between September 15 and October 20, 1938. The Peruvian army had to pay a total of Ł 170,447, divided between ČKD (Ł 99,240), Škoda (Ł 31,200 for the guns and Ł 32,402 for the munitions) and ZB (Ł 5,479 for the machine guns).

As the Peruvian army planned to raise an armored battalion with two tank companies, ČKD proposed to equip the battalion with additional vehicles, a workshop and spare parts. On April 9, 1938 a supplemental contract was signed for Ł 13,225. For this amount ČKD contracted to supply the tracked tractor Praga T-6 with the workshop on a wheeled trailer, a supply of spare parts, one Praga AV command car and one Praga RV truck by March 31, 1939.

Immediately following the signing of the contracts, ČKD started the manufacturing of the tanks. The armor plate was ordered from Poldi. The engines were ordered from the Swedish manufacturer Scania-Vabis, and were specially modified for working in high mountain conditions. An aircraft carburetor was equipped with air bleeding from the float chamber, and in the inlet duct was a valve that opened above 2,000 m and increased the compression ratio from 1:5.7 to 1:7.2. The production of the first tank began on April 21, 1938 and the vehicle was finished on August 8. It was accepted by the Peruvian army commission - Captain Cornejo and two mechanics, who were present during the whole manufacturing cycle. The commission found that the contracted weight of 6.3 tons increased to 7.33 tons, but the tank exhibited such good properties during the first trials that this deviation from the specifications was tolerated. The tank was painted in the standard Czechoslovak army three-tone camouflage, and carried a white inscription "Lima" on the side of the hull. After a short trial, it was sent immediately to Peru. It arrived on September 13 on the ship Frida. ČKD sent its service group, consisting of Director Mladějovský, supervisor Ševčík and two factory drivers-mechanics.

The tank was loaded on a train in the port of Callao on September 17 and was taken to the railway station of Croya, 3,726 m high in the Andes. There, for five days the tank was driven in very difficult terrain to heights up to 4,500 m without any problems. During one trial the tank fell from 5 m high embankment, but was repaired during the night and the next day went on with the trials. The final trials in sandy terrain close to the capital of Lima were also very successful and the design was accepted without reservations.

LTP during an obstacle crossing test at ČKD.

The second part of the LTP production run in winter 1938 during their gun trials on the army's gun range in Brdy.

The Peruvian army used the three-tone camouflage, as seen here on two of their tanks during field trials in Peru.

Meanwhile, back in Czechoslovakia the army mobilized on September 23, 1938, and for a short time requisitioned the LTPs in ČKD. Once the mobilization was called off, ČKD got its tanks back and shipped the first six tanks on November 4. They reached Peru on December 7, 1938. One of the remaining 17 tanks had, according to the contract, to cover 1,000 km. One of the vehicles covered in one week 1,300 km across the whole of Czechoslovakia, most of it in mountainous terrain, without a single defect. The remaining tanks were tested only along a 150 km distance and all had to undergo armament and armor tests. Because all tanks passed, Captain Cornejo signed the acceptance protocols and the tanks were shipped accordingly. Nine vehicles arrived in Peru on February 14, 1939 and the rest thirteen days later. Immediately following the tanks, ČKD shipped the workshop, tractor, spare parts and the two vehicles, which completed the order. Though the original delivery term was not met, Peru did not insist on any deduction from the payment, because the mobilization was accepted as vis major.

Members of the Peruvian army were trained at the same time in using and maintaining the tanks by both ČKD experts and officers of the Czechoslovak army. The tanks, designated Tanque 38/39 in the Peruvian army, were used for the first time on February 19, 1939 against anti-government insurgents. The whole battalion was for the first time shown to the public during a parade in Lima on June 7, 1939. The tanks made quite an impression, as at this time no other state in South America had a comparable tank unit.

The success of the Peru contract opened the door for ČKD in the whole region. Already in 1938 Bolivia, Brasil, Columbia, Paraguay and Uruguay exhibited strong interest in acquiring ČKD tanks of their own, followed finally by Argentina. The first negotiations were promising, but the coming war ended all contacts.

Immediately after the war's end in 1946, Peru wanted to buy an additional 24 to 36 vehicles of the same type, as the ČKD tanks were extremely successful, much more than the American Stuarts. ČKD supplied only spare parts in 1950, which allowed the tanks to soldier on. Some of the tanks were reported combat ready as late as 1988, when two of them were seen in a fortress near Callao. A fifty-year lifetime is something unheard of for a tank, and thus the LTPs can be rightly counted among the AFV legends.

On April 17, 1936 ČKD obtained another order for their TNH tank, this time from **Switzerland**. The Swiss ordered 24 tanks on December 16, 1937. They differed from the Peruvian model by heavier armor, up to 30 mm, and also in engine and armament. The Swiss specified their Saurer-Arbon diesel engine of 125 HP(92.4 kW), which gave the 7.5 ton vehicle a maximum speed of 45 km/hour. The first twelve tanks were shipped complete, i.e., with the Scania-Vabis 1664 engines, but without armament. The next twelve tanks were supplied disassembled and the Swiss installed their engines, the 24 mm Oerlikon antitank gun (muzzle velocity of 930 m/sec.) and their Maxim machine guns.

The prototype was finished on March 1, 1938 and by March 15 had already covered 470 km in tests. By June it had been shipped to Switzerland for testing by the Swiss army. It came back on July 9 with the Saurer Diesel engine installed. By July 26 the driving

The Swiss army ordered 24 tanks of the LTH type in April 1936. The prototype was finished in March 1938 and was tested first at ČKD, later in Switzerland, where it had the Saurer-Arbon Diesel engine and Swiss armament installed.

The LTH was armed with a 2.4 cm Oerlikon gun and two Maxim M.38 machine guns. It carried a slightly modified cupola and had its radio aerial mounted on the turret.

Wading test of the LTH at ČKD's testing track. It could ford water up to 80 cm deep.

LTH during country maneuvers in Switzerland, in the typical three-tone camouflage paint scheme.

tests in the presence of Swiss engineers had been successfully completed. The engine was shipped back to Switzerland and the prototype was disassembled for measurements, as the Swiss had also bought a license for this vehicle. The tanks were sold for 608,330 Kč per vehicle, while for the license for their manufacture the Swiss paid an additional 180,000 S.F.

The production of the whole series started on August 6, 1938. By September 13 the drawings were mostly finished, the prototype was put back together and the first armored body was obtained from Poldi. By October 8, the company had eleven bodies, which were fully assembled by November 3. At the end of November, the first six vehicles were supposed to be shipped to Switzerland, but by January 1939 only two tanks were shipped as ČKD encountered problems with the gun mounts. The whole series was fully shipped only after the German occupation, in April 1939. The Swiss named the tank Panzerwagen 39 and equipped three armored companies of their light brigades with them. The tanks were used till 1950, when they were withdrawn from combat units.

During the war in 1941 the Berna A.G. Olten company developed a prototype of an assault gun, named Nahkampfkanone I, on the lengthened chassis of the LTH tank. It carried a 7.5 cm antitank gun in a lightly armored superstructure, open from the top and from

LTH tank in the Swiss army service and in Swiss markings. Named Panzerwagen 39, they equipped the armored companies of the Swiss army's light brigades.

LTH with special markings.

Front view of the LTH, showing the armored cowls protecting the water jackets of the Maxim machine guns, the rotating periscope in the cupola and the driver's visor.

Swiss LTH with the light antiaircraft machine gun fitted on the turret. First twelve vehicles were supplied by ČKD complete with Scania-Vabis engines, but without armaments. The last twelve were shipped disassembled and were fitted with the Saurer-Arbon Diesel engine.

the rear. Its weight was 10 tons. The second prototype, Nahkampfkanone II was built by using the spare parts for the prototype LTH (which remained in Czechoslovakia) in 1944 by the army workshops in Thun. It carried its 7.5 cm gun in a fully enclosed superstructure with an armor thickness up to 70 mm, and its weight was 24 tons. This vehicle had a 12 cylinder Diesel engine. Neither of these prototypes attained production status.

The last customer for the ČKD TNH tanks before the war was **Latvia**. In December 1935 ČKD obtained a letter from Krašto Apsanges Ministerija, or the Latvian Ministry of Defense. The Latvians asked for a proposal on a small series of light tanks. The Latvian army knew the Czechoslovak weapons: ZB had supplied it with 15,000 rifles and 3,138 ZB vz.26 light machine guns. In the past their tank suppliers were the traditional ones, Renault with twelve FT machine gun tanks in 1923 and Vickers with 16 machine gun Mark IV tanks in 1934. At the same time the Latvians bought six L-181 armored cars from Sweden's Landsverk. The army had enough money left for a purchase of an additional company of tanks, and so it asked for proposals from Vickers and Landsverk. Simultaneously it contacted ČKD. Their specifications were: maximum weight of 5 tons, armor between 6-13 mm, maximum speed 50 km/hour and armament of one 2.0 cm Oerlikon gun (12 vehicles) or a Vickers-Maxim machine gun (four vehicles). The Latvians asked for an answer by January 15, 1936.

ČKD was caught unprepared, as it did not have anything comparable even on its design boards. The AH-IV and TNH tanks were either too light or too heavy. ČKD's design bureau speedily put together a design of a heavier version of the AH-IV tankette, designated as the AH-IV-C. After obtaining an approval from the Ministry of Defense, the offer was sent on January 8, 1936 to Latvia.

The problem was that the Latvian commission arrived in Prague in the spring of 1936 to view the offered tanks. ČKD could have shown them only the two types being manufactured for the Iranians, but was prevented from doing so by the secrecy clause in its contract with Iran. Despite this, ČKD showed the vehicles to the Latvians. Naturally, the Iranians got wind of this breach of contract and it took ČKD much effort to placate them.

The remaining LTH in the Swiss Military Museum. Behind it is the G-13 and the Nahkampfkanone I.

The front view of the museum's LTH shows how the turret was offset to the left.

ČKD did not get this contract despite its best efforts, as in May 1936 the Latvians ordered another sixteen Patrol Mk.1937 machine gun tanks from Vickers. ČKD learned about the contract with Vickers two days after it was signed. This development caused a great disappointment to ČKD, but the company did not plan to lose another opportunity. ČKD was informed not only about its competition's proposals, but also that the Latvian army had in its 1937-1940 budget 3,520,000 Litas (15,241,600 Kč or $ 610,000) for purchase of heavier tanks to replace the aged Renaults. The company submitted through its representative in Kaunas, Aldirgas Sliesoraitis, a proposal for a new tank TNH-L. At a weight of between 7.2 and 8 tons and with an 110 HP(81.3 kW) engine, it was to have a high speed. The armament was proposed to be a gun between 2.0 and 3.7 cm and one or two machine guns. In November 1936 ČKD sent to Kaunas its chief tank designer, Alexander Surin, to support Mr. Sliesoraitis in dealings with the Latvian army.

The Nahkampfkanone I carried a 7.5 cm antitank gun in an almost completely enclosed superstructure of light armor plate. The chassis was lengthened by one additional running wheel. It was developed by Berna A.G. Olten company, but was never introduced into service.

NK I in the museum, showing the superstructure and the modified engine deck. In 1944, the original LTH prototype was rebuilt as a prototype of NK II, but that also was not introduced and was later scrapped.

The lengthened chassis was tested similarly as a carrier for an infantry howitzer in an open superstructure.

The LTL prototype was the only one of the TNH series to have a rear drive. It also used a new Praga F-4 four cylinder engine and was armed with a 2 cm Oerlikon gun and two Maxim machine guns. It was built only in one prototype.

On December 5 the Latvian army commission, led by Colonel Aleksandravičius, arrived in Prague to see the P-II and P-II-a prototypes and to discuss the new offers and proposals. ČKD's design bureau had to modify the TNH-L prototype, because its eight-ton weight was too high for standard Latvian bridges. In February 1937 ČKD offered a new type, the LTL, with a new air-cooled F-IV engine. The tank, with an armament of one 2.0 cm Oerlikon gun and two machine guns and armor 8-25 mm thick, had a maximum weight of 5.6 tons and a maximum speed of 54 km/hour with a three-man crew. ČKD's representative in Latvia had to fight off simultaneous offers from Sweden's Landsverk, which was offering its L-100 and L-120 types. He succeeded by showing the Latvians that even the Swedish army was buying its tanks in Prague.

The Latvian Ministry of Defense finally decided to buy its tanks from Czechoslovakia and after two months of correspondence the order was signed by Colonel Aleksandravičius on May 27, 1937. ČKD was contracted to deliver 21 vehicles of the LTL type for a total amount (with spare parts) of 12,900,000 Kč. The price per vehicle was 574,000 Kč. ČKD knew about the bids of its competitors and had thus to keep its prices low. Nevertheless, the Latvian vehicles were the most expensive of ČKD's export submissions up to that time.

Customer country	Vehicle Cost (Kč/kg)
Iran	76.50
Romania	91.60
Peru	97.60
Sweden	82.90
Switzerland	85.72
Latvia	106.30
TNHSP (for Czechoslovak army)	79.00

ČKD had to present a prototype seven months after signing the contract. Luckily, it was also stipulated that the customer must supply the armaments two months before the deadline, which the Latvians did not. ČKD needed this delay, as it was having problems with the F-IV engine. The weapons arrived in Prague on February 14, 1938 and two months later the prototype was ready for testing. The planned evaluation trials started in May. They were overseen by Latvian Lt.Colonel Masiulis and Lieutenant Dipl. Ing. Tumosa.

On May 28 the Latvians, led by General Popelinčkis, met with the executives of ČKD. They expressed their satisfaction with the trials' results, and did not even object to the increase of the maximum weight from 5.45 tons to 7.2 tons. Their only concern was insufficient engine power, which affected the tank's performance in hilly terrain. It was decided to change the gearing and thus improve the cross-country properties by lowering the maximum speed. The parties also agreed to move the tank to Latvia after covering one third of the prescribed distance, and finish the trials there.

In June 1938 the LTL prototype was returned to the factory for an engine and gearbox change. Afterwards it passed the armor test and shooting trials on a firing range. The tank was achieving the specified performance, but was plagued by problems like track shedding, bearings seizing and breaking of teeth on the driving sprockets. The company was simultaneously testing the LTH prototype, which was much more reliable, owing to the excellent Swedish engine and the well-tested Praga-Wilson gearbox and front drive. ČKD offered this prototype for testing as well, not only for its greater reliability, but because these vehicles were already being manufactured for Peru and for Switzerland and thus making the same type for Latvia would cut tooling expenses.

The Latvians agreed with ČKD's offer and thus both prototypes were sent to Latvia for testing on January 28, 1939. In the following three weeks both prototypes covered more than 1,500 km each without any problems. On February 21, 1939 the army's commission decided that both prototypes met Latvia's needs, and recommended ordering the LTL prototype because of its roomier fighting compartment, easier steering and the possibility of moving even on half its engine. The final decision was made by the Latvian War Council on March 10. The Council surprisingly chose the LTH type, because it felt it to be too risky to order the tanks based on one prototype with a new and unproven engine. Both prototypes were also supposed to be shown in Riga (Lithuania) and Tallin (Estonia), but instead returned to Prague shortly after the German occupation.

ČKD decided to start the production of the 21 vehicles during an executive meeting on April 25, 1939, as the German authorities did not object. The whole series was built in ČKD's satellite factory in Slaný, and delivery was planned for January 20, 1940. This date had to be moved, as certain changes caused delays. For example, the Maxim machine guns were replaced by domestic ZB vz.37 machine guns, the commander's cupola was moved from the right side to the left etc. Thus, the first vehicle was finished on April 15, 1940, the completion of the whole series was planned between July 15 and August 19, 1940.

Meanwhile, the days of independent Latvia were numbered. The Soviet Union forced it to accept on October 10, 1939 a treaty of mutual assistance, and in March 1940 the Red Army marched into this unfortunate country. The democratically elected government was deposed by the "masses" and in July Latvia was incorporated into the Soviet Union for the next fifty years.

ČKD thus lost its customer for the completed 21 tanks. The company immediately found new customers in Sweden and in the newly formed Slovak state. Already on August 3, 1940 the Slovak army representatives came to Prague and after viewing the tanks, decided to buy the whole lot. For this occasion ČKD raised the price per tank from the original 574,000 Kč to 800,000 Kč! The Slovaks accepted and the order was signed in Bratislava on August 26 with the stipulation that the tanks would be armed with the 3.7 cm Škoda A7 gun. The contracted cost covered the tanks as they were, i.e., without guns, machine guns, optical and radio equipment. Obtaining these parts took a long time and cost the Slovaks additional sums of money. The tanks were accepted by the Slovak army commission in November 1940 and were transported to Slovakia.

LT-40 on parade. Lighter and smaller than the LT vz.38, they carried the same armament.

LT-40 tanks of the Slovak army during an inspection parade in Turčianský sv.Martin. The Slovak army got a total of 21 of these tanks.

TECHNICAL DESCRIPTION:

The TNH series vehicles were the forerunner of the highly successful LT vz.38, and shared with it the bolted construction, rugged chassis with four large wheels on each side. Praga-Wilson gearbox and a good engine. While the original TNH (Iran) had a Praga engine of 100 HP(74 kW), the following models used a Scania Vabis 1664 engine of 125 HP(92.4 kW), for LTP and LTH tanks bought from Sweden and for the LT-40 already built by ČKD in license as Praga TNHPS.

Various modifications were made according to customers' wishes, sometimes (LTH) the customer used his own engine and main gun. Detailed description of the design is in Chapter 3, under LT vz.38. The various models differed in overall weight, armor thickness and dimensions, as shown in the following TABLE 2

TABLE 2
Comparison of Various ČKD Export Models

MODEL	TNH	LTP	LTH	LT-40[1]	TNHPS[2]
weight(tons)	8.2	7.3	7.7	7.5	9.2
length(cm)	451	410	426	420	454
width(cm)	208	195	200	198	214
height(cm)	230	216	210	216	220
armor(mm)	8-15	8-25	8-30	8-25	8-25
main gun(mm)	37A3	37A3	24Oer	37A7	37A7
machine guns	ZB-53	ZB-53/ZB-30	Maxim	ZB-53,m. 37	ZB-53,m.37
engine	TN100	S-V	S-V/Saurer	TNHPS	TNHPS
output(HP)	100	125	125	125	125
max.speed(km/hr)	38	40	45	47	42
range(km)	200	187	200	200	210
crew	4	3	3	3	3-4

[1]Originally LTL, upgunned to 3.7 cm Škoda A7
[2]LT vz.38, later PzKpfw 38(t)

Škoda

Škoda's biggest export success before the war was its contract with **Romania** for 126 R-2 tanks. Though Škoda had already tried in 1929 to sell to this Czechoslovakia's ally the PA-III armored cars, the contract was never signed. The second opportunity came during the visit of Chiefs of Staffs of the Romanian and the Yugoslav armies in 1934. Among other armaments, the Š-I, Š-II, P-I and P-II tanks were shown. During the summer both Škoda and ČKD negotiated the possibility of supplying tanks to both armies. As at this time the companies had already signed their cartel agreement, they agreed to enlarge its scope to encompass the states of the "Little Entente", with Škoda getting 60% and ČKD 40% of the orders.

The Romanian purchasing commission visited Prague again in November 1935. As it was already described, the companies placed their bids in collusion as to the pricing. ČKD got the order for the AH-IV (R-1) tankettes, but Škoda at the end landed the contract for the R-2 light tanks that originally was ČKD's. The contract, signed on August 14, 1936, stipulated supplying the prototype for testing in two months. Following the trials and the acceptance of the prototype, the company contracted to begin the deliveries of production vehicles, with the complete order delivered in ten months. Because of the size of the contract, over 200 million Kč ($ 8,000,000), Czech banks granted Romania a loan, which it was supposed to repay both in oil and in cash. The payments were scheduled up to 1947.

Though Škoda presented its prototype in time and the trials began in January 1937, the constantly changing demands of the Romanian commission caused delays. As the production was starting at the same time, these changes caused problems and delays also. Moreover, Škoda already had problems with filling the contracted deliveries for the Czechoslovak army on time, and ČKD was not eager to manufacture its part (41 tanks) of the contract, as it had its production lines filled with its own designs.

Romania asked Škoda to deliver fifteen production vehicles as early as April 1937 so that they could participate in a grand military parade in Bucharest. Škoda sent eleven vehicles in April and another four in May, but had to "borrow" them from the lot manufactured for the Czechoslovak army. The tanks remained in Romania until the end of July 1938 and were used for drivers' training. Both the inexperience of the Romanian drivers and the haste with

Romanian R-2 tanks on parade show the black royal crest on the turret, black chassis number and white St. Michael's cross on the side of the hull, and the large color cross on the engine's deck. On the rear hull's plate it carries the black "combat" registration number.

A group of Romanian military cameramen discussing the filming of the R-2 "in action".

A cameraman being "run over" by the tank during the filming. Note the unusual wooden grate on the front horizontal plate.

which these vehicles were finished caused many defects. The resident team of Škoda mechanics had its hands full with the repairs, and Škoda spent an inordinate amount of money for fast shipments of spare parts. The R-2 tanks also participated in the autumn 1937 maneuvers. Though their properties were impressive, serious defects eliminated one vehicle after another.

Meanwhile, back in Czechoslovakia the Romanian commission was not happy with the prototype it was testing, objecting especially to its cooling system. Further shipments of the production vehicles were halted until the cooling problem could be solved. The prototype was approved as late as May 8, 1938, but only conditionally: it still had to pass trials in Romania. In the meantime the Romanian army came to the decision that these tanks were no longer acceptable. It was not clear if this decision was caused by the bad experience with the prototype and the first series of vehicles, or if ČKD helped to influence it. While originally in 1936 the Romanians talked about increasing the original order by another 63 tanks, now they wanted to cut the order in half, or even cancel it completely. Officially this decision was justified by the tank development in the past two years, with which the Škoda tank did not keep pace.

Instead, the Romanians became interested in medium tanks, and sent a delegation of the Romanian Ministry of Defense, led by its secretary General Negrei at the end of May 1938 to Czechoslovakia to see what Škoda and ČKD could offer. The delegation was shown ČKD's V-8-H and Škoda's Š-II-c medium tanks. Subsequent negotiations at the Czechoslovak Ministry of Defense had shown that the Romanians were interested mainly in the AH-IV tankettes (additional 300 vehicles) and medium tanks (about 100 vehicles). The light tanks of the Romanian army were to be represented by the Renaults R-35. The negotiations did save the situation for Škoda. It is not known if the pressure of the Czechoslovak army was decisive in persuading the Romanians, or if Škoda managed to influence General Negrei.

On July 12 three R-2 tanks (Sr.17, 18 and 19) were shipped to Romania for the decisive trials. One vehicle (Sr.19) was chosen to run in the trials. Škoda knew which vehicle would be chosen and prepared it well. It passed all the tests during a 2,500 km long trial run, and was returned to Škoda for final evaluation on August 18, 1938. On August 23, following the final disassembly and checking of the vehicle, the Romanian commission approved the design and allowed shipments of the production vehicles.

Meanwhile, on July 28 Škoda got back the first fifteen R-2 tanks (Sr.1-15) after fourteen months, to be brought up to the standard of the now approved production vehicles. Simultaneously, the shipments of the production vehicles started on September 1, when tanks Sr.20-31 were shipped, followed by Sr.32-41 one week later. Another five were sent on September 15 (Sr.42-46), but further shipments were stopped by the Czechoslovak army's mobilization. The Czechoslovak army confiscated five finished tanks and sent another six, which were almost finished, to Slovakia. Škoda obtained them back immediately after the Munich agreement and shipped Sr.47-51, 58 and 60 on October 15. Further shipments were

A brand new R-2 during the filming. It carries white plates with a black number 010.015 front and back (see previous photographs). For combat, these numbers were changed to black numerals, painted directly on the hull.

hampered by the strained relations with Hungary, as the railroad to Romania ran parallel to the Slovakia-Hungary border.

At the end of 1938 Škoda gained the approval of the Polish authorities to ship the tanks across Polish territory. Twenty tanks (Sr.52-57, 59, 61-73) left on December 22, 1938. The second twenty (Sr.73-93) went on January 6, 1939 and a third twenty (Sr.94-113) on January 27. The last shipment of thirty vehicles (Sr.1-15, 16, 19, 114-126) was shipped on February 22, 1939. The prototype remained as Škoda property and was used for further tests and modifications.

Another Škoda tank export was a sale of a small series of gun tankettes to **Yugoslavia**. Škoda showed its Š-I tankette in Yugoslavia in 1933-1934, but did not obtain any orders for this type. The Yugoslav army did express interest in a heavier vehicle with better armor and armed with an antitank gun.

Škoda developed its Š-I-d prototype in 1935. With an armor between 5-20 mm and a weight of 4.55 tons, it attained a maximum speed of 41 km/hour with an 60 HP(44.3 kW) engine. It was armed with a Škoda A3 3.7 cm gun and one ZB vz.26 light machine gun. This prototype was used for tests and remained as Škoda's property till 1940, when Škoda sold it to the Waffen SS.

The final type approved by the Yugoslav army had armor up to 22 mm and a correspondingly higher weight of 4.8 tons. The maximum speed remained at 41 km/hour. Designated as the T32 in the Yugoslav army, eight vehicles were exported in 1937. The Škoda A3 gun and the ZB vz.30 machine gun remained as their armament.

In 1938 a heavier model, designated as the Š-I-j (from February 1941 as the T-3-D) had a Diesel engine, the Škoda 4.7 cm gun and armor up to 30 mm. Manufactured only as a prototype, it was similarly sold to the Waffen SS in 1943.

Wartime Export of Czech Armored Fighting Vehicles

ČKD

Following the successful delivery of the AH-IV Sv tankettes to Sweden, ČKD offered to the Swedish army its TNH tank, modified to meet Sweden's requirements, under the designation of TNH-Sv. The outbreak of the war forced the Swedish army to speed up the reorganization and expansion of its armored units. AB Landsverk obtained orders for 120 tanks of its improved Strv m/38 model, designated as the m/39 and m/40. Simultaneously the Swedish army ordered 90 tanks of the TNH-Sv type in the autumn of 1939.

ČKD began tooling for this order, but Wehrmacht orders had higher priority and thus the vehicles for the Swedish order were not built until 1941. Designated as the PzKpfw 38(t) Ausführung S, the ninety tanks were built between May and September 1941, chassis numbers 1001-1090. Though manufactured side-by-side with the Ausf.F, they were similar to the old Ausf.C. The German army decided to keep these vehicles for their own use but, as goodwill of Sweden was important to the German war effort, ČKD was allowed to initiate licensing talks with the Swedes.

In early 1941, Sweden ordered one mild steel prototype with no armaments, engine or optics as a basis for the manufacturing license. The prototype was delivered in June 1941 to Stockholm, and after its testing with a Scania Vabis six-cylinder engine type 1664-13, 116 tanks were ordered under the designation Stvr m/41 from Scania-Vabis. The tanks were armed with a Bofors 3.7 cm gun and Swedish machine guns.

In June 1942 another 122 tanks were ordered, though only 104 chassis were completed as tanks. This improved model was designated as the Stvr m/41 S-II. It had a stronger engine of 160 HP(118.3 kW), which improved the power-to-weight ratio and performance. This series also had sloping sides on the turret. The vehicles were heavier (11 tons vs. 10.5 tons) and slightly longer.

A group of Swedish Stvr m/41 I tanks in Sweden. Originally Sweden ordered 90 tanks of the TNH-Sv type, but only one prototype was delivered in 1941. The ordered tanks were manufactured by BMM, but were confiscated by the Germans and Sweden obtained the licensing rights instead.

The original order was for 116 tanks of the Stvr m/41 I type. Part of the first series during Swedish army acceptance trials.

Armed with a Swedish 3.7 cm Bofors gun and KsP m/39 machine guns, the Stvr m/41 had a flat turret roof with two independent periscopes.

The Swedish army used several different camouflage schemes. Here it is a two-tone paint of light and dark greens. The aerial was carried on the turret's side.

Some of the tanks carried the summer camouflage even in winter, as this Stvr m/41 II during the maneuvers in 1948.

During the winter months the Strv m/41 were overpainted in white, as these vehicles during exercises in March 1945 show. Note the winter uniforms of the crews.

The Stvr m/41 I had an improved Scania-Vabis 1664/13 engine with its output increased to 145 HP.

The Strv m/41 II was introduced in June 1942. It was slightly larger and heavier and had a stronger engine with 160 HP output. The sides of its turret were sloped. This vehicle from the Swedish Military museum carried the three-tone camouflage of light and dark blue-green and medium brown.

This Stvr m/41 II, photographed in 1950, has both machine guns removed.

The museum's Sav m/43. It had armor up to 30 mm and weight of 12.4 tons.

In February 1943 Scania-Vabis got an order for an assault gun based on the Stvr m/41 chassis. The prototype was built using the mild steel ČKD prototype and was armed with a Bofors 10.5 cm m/02 L/27 howitzer. Designated as the Stormartillerivagen m/43 or Sav m/43, 18 vehicles were built, armed with the new 10.5 cm Sak m/44 howitzer in a totally enclosed superstructure. Another 18 vehicles were built on the 18 chassis of the original Stvr m/41 S-II order, for a total of 36 vehicles. While the original gun had the recoil cylinder above the barrel, it was later replaced with an improved version with its recoil cylinder under the barrel. The Sav m/43 soldiered till 1970.

In 1945, a Bofors fm 43-45 recoilless 15 cm gun was also fitted to this chassis, but this combination never attained production.

The Swedish Stvr m/41 tanks had a long life. Phased out of active service in 1957, their chassis were used for the Pvb 301 armored personnel carriers, fitted with new air-cooled Diesel engines and manufactured by Hägglunds. The turrets of the old tanks were used as fixed fortifications, guarding Swedish military airfields and other installations.

Small numbers of the chassis were modified during the Korean war as self-propelled guns. The PvKv 3 carried a 5.7 cm antitank gun and the PvKv 4 a 7.5 cm L/60 antiaircraft gun in lightly armored superstuctures.

An assault gun on the Stvr m/41 chassis. Designated Sav M/43 (Stormartillerivagen), 36 vehicles were built, 18 new and 18 on Stvr m/41 II chassis. They carried the 10.5 cm Bofors howitzer in a totally enclosed superstructure.

A prototype, carrying a 15 cm Bofors recoilless rifle fm/43-45 on a modified Stvr m/41 chassis. Built in 1945, it was never produced.

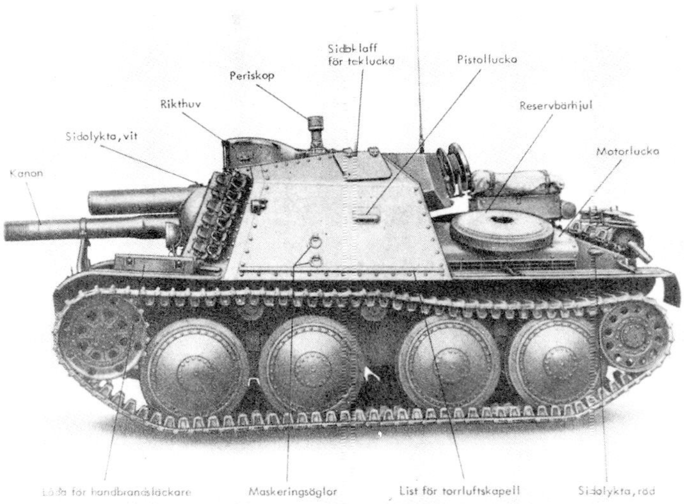

Bild 3. Vagnens vänstra sida

Bild 4. Vagnens högra sida

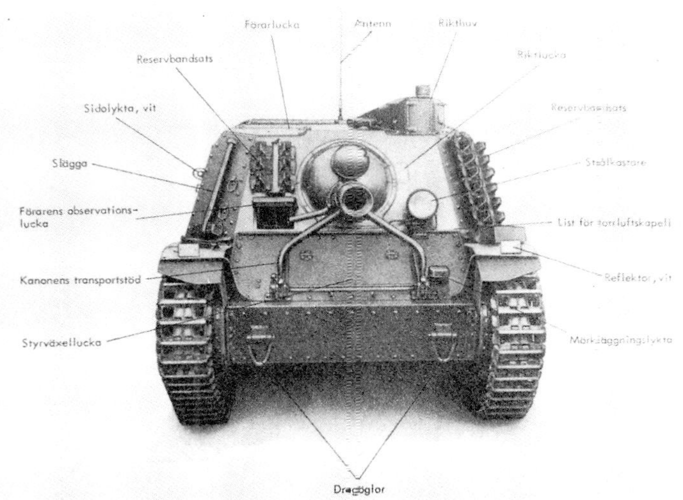

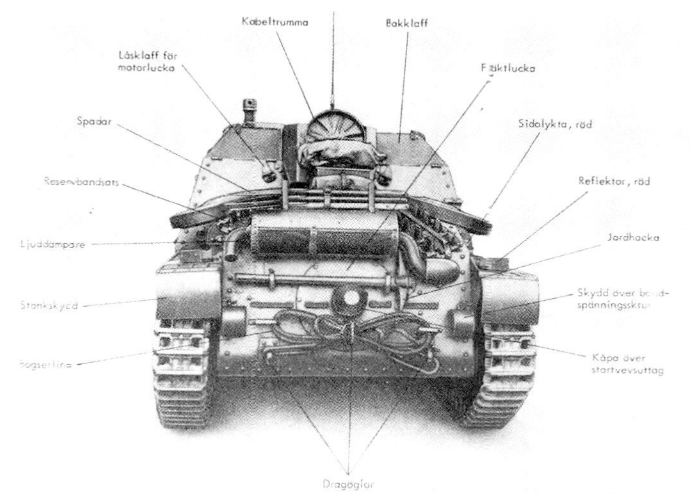

Bild 5. Vagnen sedd bakifrån

Four views of the Sav m/43, showing its clean lines and all exterior fittings.

TABLE 3
Prewar Export of Czech Tanks

MANUFACTURER	TYPE	NUMBER ORDERED	BUYER COUNTRY	BUYER'S DESIGNATION	YEAR DELIVERED
ČKD	AH-IV	50+1	Iran	AH-IV	1936-1937
	AH-IV-R	35	Romania	R-1	1937-1938
	AH-IV-Sv[1]	48	Sweden	Stvr m/37	1938
	TNH	50+1	Iran	TNH	1936-1937
	LTP	24	Peru	Tanque 38/39	1938-1939
	LTH	24	Switzerland	Panzerwagen 39	1938-1939
	LLT[2]	1	Latvia	prototype LTL	1940
	LTS	21	Slovakia	LT-40	1940
	TNH-Sv[3]	1	Sweden(license)	Stvr m/41	1941
Škoda	Š-II-aR[4]	126	Romania	R-2	1938-1939
	Š-I-d	8	Yugoslavia	T 32	1937
TOTAL		389			

[1]Prototype designated AH-IV-S
[2]Series LLT with experimental prototype LTL, LTS production batch
[3]Project designated TNH-S in 1937
[4]Original manufacturer's designation, later changed to R-2

The rear of the PvKv 4 superstructure.

The Pvb 301 carried an automatic remotely controlled 2 cm Bofors canon. The chassis remained unchanged, quite a compliment for a thirty year old design.

The PzKpfw 38(t), though not actually exported by ČKD, was used widely by Germany's allies. Slovakia was the only one of them who bought these tanks directly from ČKD. 37 tanks were acquired between 1940 and 1942. An additional 37 tanks were bought from German stock. Hungary bought 111 PzKpfw 38(t) tanks from Germany between November 1941 and November 1942 (105 tanks and 6 PzBef 38(t)). Bulgaria bought ten tanks in May 1943 and probably inherited additional vehicles from the German units fighting in Yugoslavia. The Romanians planned to order 395 ČKD tanks in January 1941, but the Germans could not spare the company's manufacturing capacity and the deal was refused. Instead, the Romanians obtained in March 1943 50 PzKpfw 38(t) from German depots, to partially offset their losses during the Stalingrad disaster.

Right: Interior view of the Pvb 301, showing the seats for the six infantrymen, the engine compartment on the left up front and driver's and commander's positions on the right.

Though the Stvr m/41 tanks were phased out of service in 1957, their chassis were used for the Pvb 301 armored personnel carriers. The prototype was built by Hägglunds in 1958, and the remaining chassis were converted between 1962-1963. The Pvb 301 soldiered until 1972, when it began to be replaced by the Pvø 302.

Fitted with a new air-cooled Diesel engine, the Pvb 301 was quite fast.

TABLE 4
Wartime Deliveries to Germany's Allies

TYPE	NUMBER	COUNTRY	YEAR
PzKpfw 35(t)	26 old	Bulgaria	1940
Škoda T-11[1]	10 new	Bulgaria	1940-1941
PzKpfw 35(t)	26 old	Romania	1942
LT-38	37 new	Slovakia	1940-1942
PzKpfw 38(t)	37 old	Slovakia	1943-1944
	111 old	Hungary	1941-1942
	10 old	Bulgaria	1943
	50 old	Romania	1943
SdKfz 138	18 old	Slovakia	1944
Hetzer	75 new	Hungary	1944-1945
TOTAL	400		

[1]Original manufacturer's designation Š-II-aB, later T-11.

Škoda

Romania planned to greatly expand its armored units. For this purpose, the Romanian army ordered 280 additional R-2 tanks in August 1938, with the stipulation that 75% of the order would be manufactured by the Romanian company Malaxa. Škoda already had bad experience with Malaxa's owner, who sold plans for some Škoda guns to Germany, and declined.

Shortly after this business deal fell through, Škoda got an order for an uparmored R-2 prototype. In the first half of 1939 it modified the original prototype S-II-aR and submitted it under the designation R-2-a. Simultaneously, both Škoda and ČKD organized comparative trials in Romania not only for the R-2-a prototype, but also for the T-21 Škoda medium tank and the V-8-H ČKD medium tank for October 1939. OKH did not show much enthusiasm for

Pvb 301s during a combined winter exercise.

Two of the first LT-38 tanks, bought by the new Slovak army in 1940 directly from BMM. In all, 37 tanks were acquired from the factory between 1940-1942. In the middle of the group stands Dipl. Ing. Surin, the designer of the 38 family.

Loath to waste anything, the Swedish army utilized the removed turrets from its Strv m/41 tanks and is using them to this day as fixed fortifications for airfield perimeter defense.

First two LT-38 tanks manufactured against an order from the Slovak army. They were basically Ausf.A. At this stage, they have not their armaments fitted.

During the Korean war, the Stvr m/41 chassis was used as a basis for two self-propelled guns. The PvKv 3 (in the middle) carried the 5.7 cm antitank gun, PvKv 4 (on the right) the 7.5 cm antiaircraft gun, both in an partially open lightly armored superstructure.

The L/60 gun of the PvKv 4 was more powerful than the 5.7 cm gun of the PvKv 3, but even it in the fifties was becoming inadequate as an antitank weapon.

this plan, as it wanted to test the Czech tanks first, but finally gave its approval and the three prototypes were sent to Romania on September 25, 1939. The final protocol was signed on November 15, 1939 and showed that all three types withstood the challenging tests successfully.

The Romanian army took some time deciding which tank it really wanted. First it favored the R-2-a. In October 1940 the V-8-H was a clear favorite and in January 1941 they finally ordered 216 T-21 tanks from Škoda and 395 TNH light tanks from ČKD. Although both companies lobbied hard for these orders, and even the Germans were interested in influencing the Balkan countries to join them in their fight against Bolshevism, the lack of manufacturing capacity in both companies finally decided against it.

The Romanians made a last effort to obtain a manufacturing license in May 1942, when both Škoda and ČKD were visited by Colonel Guicelai and the directors of the Resita company. They wanted to obtain licensing rights for the Škoda T-23 medium tank and the Praga TNH light tank. The Czech companies were more than willing to sell the licensing rights, but at the end everybody realized that the Romanian industry was not capable of manufacturing such complicated vehicles. Any further deliveries of Czech tanks to Romania were subsequently only from German depots.

In February 1939 a Bulgarian army commission, led by General Rusev, visited Škoda. The Bulgarians were interested in buying 34-50 Š-I tankettes and 24-40 Š-II-a tanks. Škoda submitted an offer, but the German occupation stopped this promising deal. Bulgaria obtained its Škoda tanks from the Germans, who hoped to influence it to enter an alliance with Germany. In August 1939 a Bulgarian purchasing commission visited Paderborn, whose 11th Panzer Regiment was equipped with the LT vz.35 Škoda tanks. The Germans even arranged a technical presentation by Škoda personnel.

The Bulgarians liked the Škoda tank when it was presented to them in February, and decided to buy 26 of them immediately. The

Comparison of PvKv 3 with PvKv 2, armed also with the 5.7 cm antitank gun. The PvKv was high and conspicuous, resembling the German Marder III, built ten years earlier with a much more effective gun.

The prototype of the PvKv 4 was built in 1954.

tanks were shipped to Škoda for warranty repairs. Škoda was at the same time flooded with similar repairs for the Wehrmacht tanks, which had priority. Thus it took almost six months before the Bulgarians got their tanks back. Škoda charged 4,938,530 Kč for the repairs. The tanks, renamed T-11, were shipped in five transports between February 21 and April 5, 1940.

Bulgaria obtained another ten brand new T-11 tanks shortly after that. These vehicles were originally manufactured for Afghanistan. They carried the improved Škoda A8 gun. The tanks were finished at the beginning of 1940 and were accepted by the Afghan commission on March 12, 1940. Though the tanks were partially paid for, Afghanistan never got them, as the war situation prevented their shipment. The situation was solved at the end by OKH, which on May 14, 1940 confiscated the tanks, but allowed Škoda to sell them to Bulgaria. The ten tanks and 1,000 AP and 4,000 HE rounds were sold for 17,368,844 Kč ($ 695,000) and were shipped to Bulgaria between October 1940 and January 1941.

Bulgaria liked the Škoda tanks and ordered an additional 45 tanks of the T-11 type in January 1941. OKH originally approved the sale and Škoda began ordering armor plate for the order, but in the end the Germans decided to sell the Bulgarians Renault R-35 tanks, as they had hundreds of surplus ones in their depots. Both the Bulgarian army and Škoda protested, but without success.

Post-War Exports of Czechoslovak Armored Fighting Vehicles

ČKD

In 1947 **Ethiopia** was looking for a light tank, armed with machine guns only, and rugged enough to withstand the rock and desert terrain of that country. The ČKD representative in Ethiopia Čermakian persuaded the Emperor that the ČKD tankettes would be ideal. The purchase agreement for 20 vehicles was signed on June 24, 1948 in Adis Abeba by the War Minister Ras Abbeke. The price was $26,750 per vehicle and delivery was promised in 20 months. The Ethiopians asked the retired Swedish Colonel Niels Sahlin, who was then acting as a military advisor to the Emperor, to approve the prototype. He was familiar with the ČKD tankettes, because he was accepting the AH-IV Sv tankettes for the Swedish army in 1937.

The prototype of the AH-IV Hb (The Czech name for Ethiopia is Habeš) was finished by June 29, 1949. It was the riveted prototype of the Romanian R-1, equipped with the new Tatra Diesel engine. Sahlin viewed the prototype in September 1949 and approved it.

Excellent close-up of the R-1 prototype, modified as AH-IV Hb, showing detail of the turret, driver's hatch and visor, and the main armament's mount. On the left is the tank designer Alexander Surin, on the right the retired Swedish Colonel Salin.

One of the A-IV-Hb, produced for Ethiopia ("Habeš" in Czech), being tested in 1949.

Running tests of one of the production AH-IV Hb tankettes.

Three views of the production AH-IV Hb, showing the heightened engine deck, stowage box on the left and aerial on the turret. In front of the drive's visor is the sight for his fixed light machine gun.

The manufactured vehicles were welded. The Tatra 114 air-cooled Diesel engine had an output of 65 HP(48 kW)/2,200 rpm. The tankette, with armor between 6 and 12 mm thick, weighed 3.93 tons and had a maximum speed of 43 km/hour and a range of 200 km. It was armed with one ZB vz.37 and one ZB vz.26 machine gun.

The twenty vehicles were finished in January-February 1950. On March 14, 1950 they were shipped by rail to Gdynia. Two Danish freighters took them to Malmö, where they were loaded on MS Svea, which left on March 29 for Djibuti, arriving on May 9. From Djibuti the tankettes were shipped by rail to Addis Abeba. The Ethiopeans used them till the eighties, when they participated in the fighting with Somalia.

Škoda

During the war Škoda manufactured the Jagdpanzer 38 Hetzer and after the war was repairing both the captured Wehrmacht vehicles and manufacturing new ones for the Czechoslovak army.

On August 15, 1946 **Switzerland** ordered eight G-13 tank hunters for 421,806 S.F. (4,904,363 Kčs - the official designation of the Czechoslovak Crown changed after the war to Kčs), followed by an order for 100 vehicles on November 23, 1946 for 5,704,099 S.F. (66,323,150 Kčs). In 1947 an additional fifty vehicles and spare

First ten tankettes of the Ethiopian order during running trials in the country. As opposed to the original AH-IVs, these vehicles were welded.

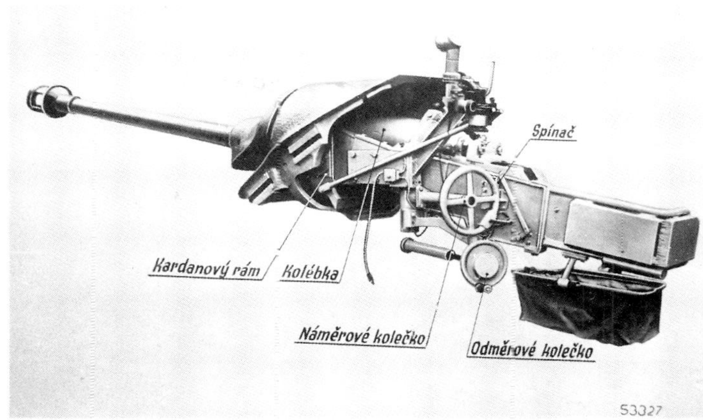

Škoda factory photograph showing the StuK 40 and its mount in the G-13.

parts were ordered for 4,502,024 S.F. (51,932,485 Kčs). The price for one vehicle was 51,650 S.F. (600,585 Kčs). The G-13 was specified with the Sturmkanone 40, as used in the Sturmgeschütz III. The use of the StuK 40 on the Hetzer was not new, as ČKD made a wooden mock-up with this gun at the early stages of Hetzer's development, before the PAK 39 was specified. Škoda obtained an order to modify one Hetzer in 1944 under OKH D3-322. It modified the vehicle # 323815 and retained it until 1946, when it was bought by the Czechoslovak army, who had it back-fitted with PAK 39. Moreover, Škoda manufactured the StuK 40 during the war.

The first eight vehicles were made from the last Hetzer series manufactured for the Germans in April 1945, but never delivered to the Wehrmacht. They carried numbers 323804, 323807 323809, 323810, 323823, 323832, 323861 and 323862. Designated G-13 in the Swiss service, the vehicles retained the ČKD engine, though later 86 vehicles were modified by installing a Saurer-Arbon Diesel engine of 148 HP(109.4 kW)/2,000 rpm. The commander's hatch was moved from the right to the left and was provided with a small rotating cupola with a periscope. The remote machine gun mount was replaced with an antiaircraft mount and Swiss radios with twin aerials were fitted.

The first eight vehicles were delivered on October 12, 1946. The remaining 150 vehicles were manufactured as new by Škoda, and had hull numbers 001 to 100 and 121 to 170. They were delivered in lots of 25, numbers 1 to 25 on June 6, 1947; numbers 26 to 50 on July 28, 1947; numbers 51 to 74 on October 31, 1947; numbers 75 to 100 on December 20, 1947; numbers 121 to 132 on September 30, 1948; numbers 133 to 150 on November 30, 1948 and the final twenty, numbers 151 to 170 on February 16, 1950.

Switzerland paid more than ten million Swiss Francs for the order, a sum badly needed by Czechoslovakia, plundered during the war.

The new state of **Israel** was supported by armaments and aircraft shipments by Czechoslovakia even after the Communist coup in February 1948. The Jewish Agency, led by Mr. Uberall, asked the Ministry of Defense on February 6, 1948 for the possibility of supplying Israel with heavy weapons and with tanks.

A mock-up of the StuK 40 installation in the Hetzer, tested during the war by both Škoda and BMM. The experience gained with these was used by Škoda when designing their G-13 tank hunters for Switzerland in 1946.

Hetzer no.323815 with StuK 40, manufactured during the war, being evaluated by members of the Czechoslovak army armored corps in July 1945 for a possible introduction by the army. Note the Notek lamp and the makeshift driver's visor.

A G-13 in the Swiss service has already the standard driver's visor and commander's hatch with the small cupola on the left side, the Nahkampf machine gun being deleted by the Swiss.

A rear view of the G-13, showing the double antenna of the command vehicle, rear-facing periscope on the right rear plate, machine gun mount above the exhaust, and the external telephone with its cable reel on top.

The Israeli army wanted the following armored vehicles:

1. Fifty light infantry tanks, weighing between 9 and 15 tons, with one 3.7 cm gun (or larger) and two heavy machine guns in a fully rotating turret.

2. Fifty infantry tanks, 15-30 tons, armed with one heavy gun and two heavy machine guns in a fully rotating turret.

3. Fifty tank hunters, 15 tons or heavier, with a 7.5 cm gun (or larger).

For every gun, 500 rounds were to be supplied, divided as follows: (1) 60% AP and 40% HE, (2) 40% AP and 60% HE and (3) 75% AP and 25% HE. The planned supply for each machine gun was 15,000 rounds.

The Ministry of Defense freed for export to Israel at this time only:

- Ten tanks LT vz.38 with 3,000 AP and 2,000 HE rounds (later increased to 4,000 AP and 3,000 HE rounds) and 300,000 rounds of machine gun ammunition.
- 65 tank hunters ST-1 (former Jagdpanzer 38[t]) with 6,000 7.5 cm gun rounds.

Mr. Uberall met with ČKD representatives in July 1948, who offered him both the approved ten LT vz.38 and 12 Stuart tanks, formerly from the roster of the Czechoslovak Armored Brigade in

Nice view of the Swiss G -13, showing the holder of the spare running wheel on the right side of the hull, commander's rotating periscope under the armored cowl, antenna holder on the right rear side and the telephone in the rear. This vehicle has the side skirst removed.

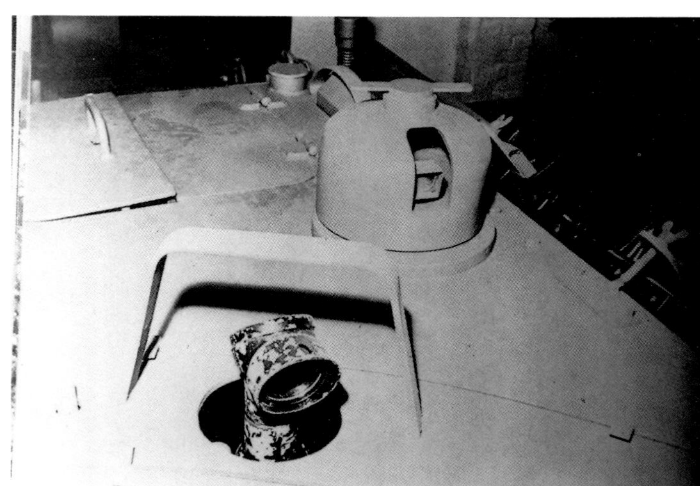

Roof detail of the G-13 in the Munster museum shows the gun spotting scope with its protective guard and the commander's rotating periscope under its armored cupola. In the G-13, the commander sat on the left rear of the vehicle.

A Swiss G-13 at speed. The wheel on the right and the spare track links on the left increased the protection of the thin side armor plates. Some of the Swiss vehicles carried the Notek light, but the driving light (shown turned backwards) was more common.

England. ČKD asked 2,358,650 Kčs for each Stuart tank and 3,250,000 Kčs for each LT vz.38 The Israeli delegation found these prices about double of the current prices for comparable surplus vehicles, and did not close any deal.

The Czechoslovak army offered its vehicles cheaper 1,907,000 Kčs for each ST-1 and 1,228,000 Kčs for each tank. Israel was interested in the vehicles, but found the quoted prices unacceptably high, as surplus Sherman tanks were being sold for approximately half. The contacts were maintained up to 1950, but in the end no sales were consummated and no armored vehicles were shipped to Israel.

5

WEAPONS USED IN CZECHOSLOVAK ARMORED FIGHTING VEHICLES

Škoda Guns

Small caliber infantry guns for direct fire on small targets like individual machine gun positions were developed during the first World War. Škoda designed the 3.7 cm L/27 infantry gun with 450 m/sec muzzle velocity, firing a shell weighing 0.825 kg. This gun was used in one of the first Czech AFV domestic constructions, the Praga L armored car. Such guns were not designed to fight armored vehicles, as their performance was not sufficient for this task.

The first Škoda guns designed for antitank use appeared in 1933. It was the 4.7 cm A2 L/25 gun with 560 m/sec muzzle velocity and a 1.65 kg projectile. This gun was used in the prototypes MU-6 and SU.

The Czechoslovak army did not have any gun that could fight contemporary tanks and the situation in Germany made this shortcoming more dangerous. Škoda started testing its prototype 3.7 cm A3 antitank gun in June 1934. The army's specification, penetration of a 30 mm armor plate at a distance of 1,000 m, was met by this gun with a muzzle velocity of 675 m/sec and a projectile weight of 0.85 kg. The gun had a semiautomatic breech, which allowed a high rate of fire: up to 23 rounds/min., and up to 12 rounds/min. of aimed fire. The new gun could track targets moving at a speed of up to 40 km/hour at distances between 500 and 2,000 m. The gun was also capable of firing at soft targets, using high-explosive ammunition, up to a distance of 4,000 m. The A3 gun was introduced as the 3.7 cm antitank gun vz.34.

Already in 1935 the army found that the A3 gun could not penetrate the new, improved 30 mm armor plates at distances over

The first modern Škoda A3 antitank gun, Czechoslovak army designation 3.7 cm KPÚV vz.34. This is the infantry version, captured by the US Army in Bavaria in 1945.

Škoda's A4 gun, introduced in 1937 as 3.7 cm KPÚV vz.37, retained the 3.7 cm caliber, but had higher muzzle velocity and improved penetration. It was manufactured in three versions, for the infantry (I), hipo traction (J) and moto traction (M), seen here.

Škoda tank gun, developed for tank use from the vz.34 antitank gun. Its designation was 3.7 cm ÚV vz.34. This photographs shows the gun's long recoil, one of its disadvantages. Another was the placement of the recoil cylinder outside the turret, where it was vulnerable to enemy fire. The gun also had the inferior penetration of its infantry sibling.

550 m, and demanded a gun with higher performance. Škoda submitted the improved A4 gun, with a 750 m/sec muzzle velocity. It was introduced as the 3.7 cm antitank gun vz.37. The new gun used the same ammunition as the older vz.34, but with a higher propellant charge. The vz.37 guns could also use the older vz.34 ammunition.

Between 1936 and 1938 the army obtained over 1,100 vz.34 and vz.37 antitank guns. The vz.37 gun had a better performance than the German 3.7 cm antitank gun Mk. 35/36, and could penetrate the armor of all contemporary German tanks. The guns were light, with a low silhouette, easily serviced and with a high rate of fire and very effective ammunition.

The demands on an infantry antitank gun and a tank gun were similar: combat against adversary's tanks. Thus it was only natural that the Škoda antitank guns were used in the Czech armored fighting vehicles. The first Czech tanks, the LT vz.34 and LT vz.35, were armed with the Škoda ÚVvz.34 tank gun, adapted from the KPÚV vz.34 antitank gun. The adaptation of this gun for tank use was not without problems: the gun's recoil was too long, the recoil cylinder was outside the turret and was insufficiently protected, the muzzle brake was not completely satisfactory, and the removal of the spent cases was not fully solved. On top of that, the gun had the inferior performance of its infantry sibling.

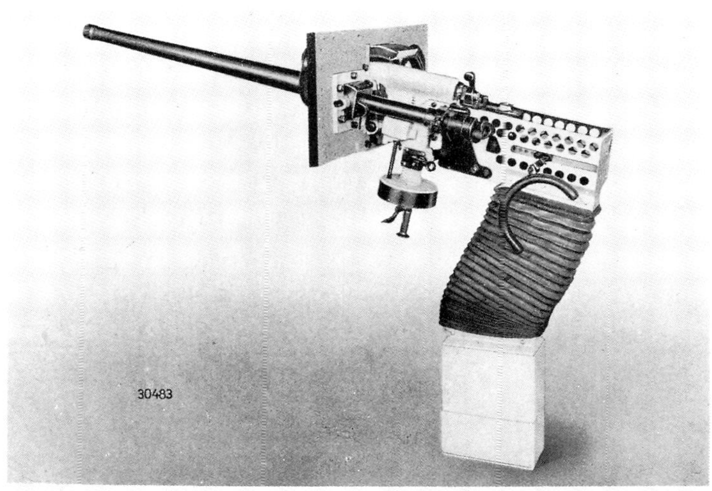

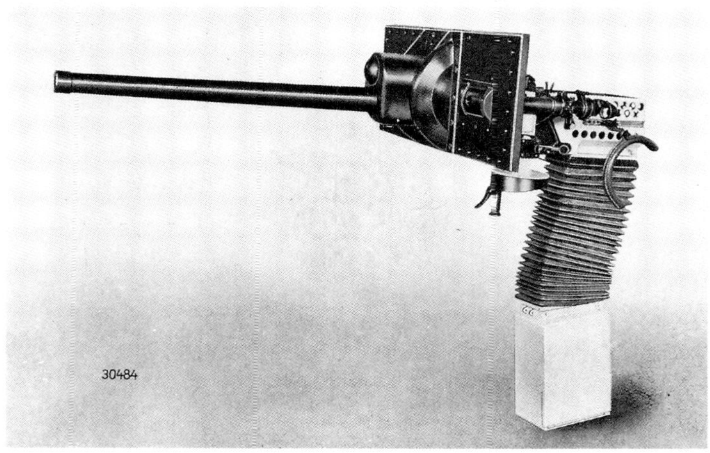

The new tank gun, Škoda A7, had the high muzzle velocity and good penetration properties of the vz.37 antitank gun. It had its recoil cylinder repositioned inside the turret, had an improved semiautomatic breech and shorter recoil. It was used in the LT vz.38 tanks. Its official designation was 3.7 cm ÚV vz.38.

Mounting of the ÚV vz.34 gun in the LT vz.35 tank.

Mounting of the Škoda 3.7 cm ÚV vz.38 gun in the LT vz.38 tank.

The infantry version of the 4.7 cm Škoda A5 antitank gun (official designation 4.7 cm KPÚV vz.38) was introduced in 1938, and after the German occupation was used by the Wehrmacht as a self-propelled gun on the PzKpfw I chassis.

For the new LT vz.38 tanks, Škoda designed two guns in 1937, specifically designed for use in tanks. They were based on the Škoda A4 BETA tank gun, developed for the Iranian TNH tanks. The A7 was based on the 3.7 cm KPÚV vz.37 antitank gun with its higher performance, while the A8 retained the lower performance of the ÚV vz.34 tank gun. On both guns the recoil cylinder was repositioned inside the turret and the removal of spent rounds was improved, as was the recoil and the semiautomatic breech. The army naturally preferred the A7 type with its higher performance and chose it as the standard gun for the LT vz.38 tank. For the Yugoslav T-32 assault guns, Škoda manufactured eight 3.7 cm A3ÚVJ guns, which were modified ÚV vz.34 guns.

The weight of the A7 gun was 275 kg. The barrel was of a monoblock type, L/50, 1,858 mm long. The breech was of a wedge type. During the forward movement of the barrel following its recoil, the breech opened and ejected the spent round. Once a new round was inserted, the breech closed automatically and the gun was ready for firing.

The gun fired two types of ammunition: the antitank armor-piercing round, and a high-explosive round. The AP round had a weight of 1.47 kg, of which 0.85 kg was the actual projectile. Its muzzle velocity was 750 m/sec and the muzzle energy was 24.4 mt. It had a range of 1,500 m. The HE round was lighter at 1.42 kg, with a projectile weighing 0.825 kg. Its muzzle velocity was 730 m/sec, and its range was 4,000 m at 5° elevation. The A7 gun was manufactured widely for the PzKpfw 38(t).

The improving quality and armor of potential adversaries' tanks led to a demand for more effective antitank and tank guns. Škoda started developing 4.7 cm antitank gun simultaneously with the 3.7 cm model. The A5 model was introduced as the 4.7 cm KPÚV vz.38 antitank gun in small quantities. It had a similar construction as the vz.34 and vz.37 antitank guns, with a monoblock barrel and a semiautomatic breech. With a muzzle velocity of 775 m/sec and a projectile of 1.65 kg, it penetrated a 40 mm armor plate at 1,500 m. These guns were later used by the Wehrmacht in the 4.7 cm PAK (t) (Sfl) auf PzKpfw IB (SdKfz 101).

For the medium tanks Š-III and T-III, Škoda manufactured four 4.7 cm Š-III guns with muzzle velocity of 600 m/sec and projectile weight of 1.65 kg. From these, the more modern 4.7 cm Škoda A9 type was developed. It was designed for the ŠP-II-b tank.

For the Škoda T-21 and ČKD V-8-H medium tanks the gun was further improved. Designated as the A11, it followed the design of the A7 gun: the recoil cylinder was repositioned inside the turret for protection, the firing and recoil mechanisms were adapted for turret use and the removal of spent casings was introduced. The muzzle velocity was increased to 782 m/sec for the AP round and 660 m/sec for the HE round. The weight of the complete AP round was 2.79 kg, the weight of the projectile alone was 1.65 kg. The HE

Škoda A11 4.7 cm tank gun was an improved A9 model, which had as its predecessor the A5 antitank gun. Its construction was similar to the smaller A7 gun, with an automatic breach and the recoil cylinder inside the turret. It was used in the T-21 and V-8-H tanks.

The A11 gun in the V-8-H prototype.

round weighed 2.60 kg and the projectile 1.5 kg. The range was 1,500 m for the AP and 4,000 m for the HE round. The weight of the gun was 395 kg and the barrel was L/43.4, or 2,040 mm long. The gun penetrated 35 mm of homogeneous armor plate at 30° from the vertical at 1,500 m, 41 mm at 1,000 m and 48 mm at 500 m.

All the tank and antitank guns developed and manufactured by Škoda are listed in TABLE 5.

TABLE 5
ŠKODA TANK AND ANTITANK GUNS

ŠKODA DESIGNATION	CALIBER (mm)	CZ. ARMY DESIGNATION	USED IN	WEHRMACHT DESIGNATION
AB1/BA1	37	37/70		
A2	47		MU-6, SU	
A3	37	3.7 cm KPÚV vz.34, ÚV vz.34	LT vz.34, LT vz.35, LTP	
A4	37	3.7 cm KPÚV vz.37		
A4Beta	37		TNH	
A5	47	4.7 cm KPÚV vz.38		4.7cm PaK(t) L/43.4
Š-III	47	Š-III	Š-III, T-III	
A6	47	4 cm kanón vz.36	fortifications	
A7	37	3.7 cm ÚV vz.38	LT vz.38, LT-40	3.7cm KwK(t) L/47.8
A8	37		T-11	3.7cm KwK(t) L/40
A9	47		ŠP-II-b	
A10	37	prototype only	fortifications	
A11	47	4.7 cm ÚV vz.38	V-8-H, T-21	KwK41(t)
A17	40		Turán I	
A19	37		TNHnA,T=15	

ZB Machine Guns

The newborn Czechoslovak state in 1918 inherited about 1,000 Austro-Hungarian heavy machine guns of the Schwarzlose model 7/12. These guns had a caliber of 8 mm and had a complicated construction, which required oiling the rounds during firing. By 1922, the army had many different machine guns in its inventory, but the Schwarzlose guns were predominant, with 4,773 pieces on hand.

In 1922, the Czechoslovak army decided to introduce the Mauser system rifle with its 7.92 mm caliber. As it was imperative to have rifles and machine guns of the same caliber, it became necessary to adapt the Schwarzlose machine guns to this caliber. In a heated competition of the Czech gun manufacturers the Janeček Armament factory in Prague finally prevailed and was authorized to adapt the available machine guns under the designation of vz.7/24, and to manufacture new ones as the vz.24.

The Schwarzlose vz.7/24 and vz.24 machine guns were used in the armored trains and in the OA vz.27 armored cars, while the armored cars Škoda Fiat-Torino, PA-I and PA-II used the German Maxim 08 machine guns. Neither of these machine guns was suitable for use in armored vehicles, as they were water-cooled. Any penetration of the cooling jacket meant elimination of the weapon. Moreover, they used cloth ammunition belts, which were flimsy and were adversely affected by moisture and freezing temperatures.

For the newer armored fighting vehicles two types of new machine guns were adopted. Both of them were of a very advanced construction, designed by a very gifted arms designer and manufactured by the Československá Zbrojovka Brno (ZB). Both machine guns were widely exported and used by many armies of the world. In the Second World War they fought on both sides of the conflict.

The first became one of the most famous and most widely used light machine guns. It was a brain child of designer Václav Holek. The Czechoslovak army started exhaustive testing of various light machine guns in March 1923 with the goal of choosing a standard light machine gun for the army. The Zbrojovka Praga gun factory submitted the first of Holek's designs, the Praga II. This machine gun already had the basic concept of a fixed barrel and a gas-oper-

The light machine gun ZB vz.26 (later the improved model vz.30) was used in the tankettes and in the OA vz.30 armored car. It had a magazine with 20 rounds and was not capable of sustained fire as a heavy machine gun would. In its time, it was probably the best light machine gun in the world.

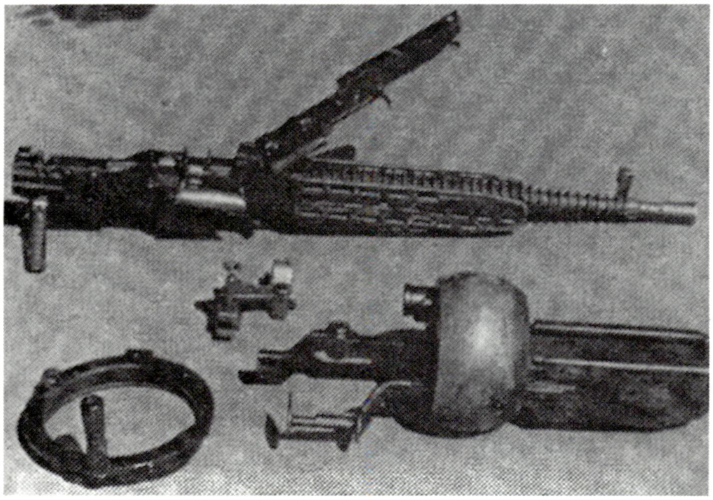

The ZB vz.37 was an excellent air-cooled heavy machine gun. Fed by metal links of 100 or 200 rounds, it was capable of sustained fire. Its license was sold to England. The British army used it during the war in all its armored vehicles under the name BESA. The Germans sustained its production during the war and used it operationally, especially in the Waffen SS.

ZB vz.26 light machine guns in the OA vz.30 light armored car.

ated bolt. Though it suffered many teething problems, it proved to be the best of all the tested machine guns of various reputable manufacturers, except for the Danish Madsen. For follow-up trials a new model, the Praga I-23, was submitted. It used a drum magazine with a cloth belt. Holek opposed this arrangement, as he was aware of its shortcomings, but the company prevailed.

The result of the testing was a demand to order one thousand Hotchkiss and one thousand Praga light machine guns for training purposes as quickly as possible. Meanwhile, Zbrojovka Praga got into serious financial troubles, and the Ministry of Defense tried to persuade the company to sell its patents to the state-owned Zbrojovka Brno. At the end of 1923 Zbrojovka Praga did sell its manufacturing rights for the Praga machine guns to Brno.

The Ministry of Defense ordered a new comprehensive trial for the spring of 1924. From the world's manufacturers Darne, Hotchkiss, Vickers, Lewis and Belgian Browning participated. The I-23 still used the drum magazines. The Browning machine gun surprisingly emerged victorious from these tests. This caused panic in Brno, and Holek finally obtained approval to modify his machine gun for a box magazine. He also heavily modified the machine gun itself, and it was presented to the army's commission in November 1924 as a new model Praga vz.24. The new machine gun performed flawlessly and won easily a new trial against the Browning model. At the end of 1924 it was accepted as the standard light machine gun of the army.

Two of the ZB vz.26 machine guns in the MU-4 Škoda tankette, showing their ball mounts and their characteristic barrels with their gas feeding tubes below them.

Production lines had to be set up for the new machine guns and the design had to be modified for mass production. This took some time and only in the spring of 1927 did the new machine guns start to leave the assembly lines and reach the units. The factory designation of this gun was light machine gun ZB-26, Czechoslovak army's designation was "7.92 mm kulomet vz.26" (kulomet = machine gun). The designation used through this book is light machine gun ZB vz.26.

The ZB vz.26 used the Mauser 7.92 mm cartridge, uniform with the vz.24 infantry rifle and the Schwarzlose vz.7/24 heavy machine gun. Its loaded weight was 9.66 kg. Its barrel was 602 mm long, and its muzzle velocity was 750 m/sec. The cyclic rate was 550 rpm and the range was 3,500 m. It used a twenty-round box magazine. It had an easily exchangeable barrel and iron sights.

This gun was used first in the Škoda tankettes and in the Tančík vz.33, later in the OA vz.30 armored cars. It was also used for export in ČKD tankettes AH-IV (R-1) and originally in the P-II (LT vz.34) tanks. Its use in armored vehicles was not optimal, as the gun was not designed for sustained fire like a heavy machine gun.

The ZB vz.26 was widely used by the Czechoslovak army and, starting in 1927, was extensively exported to 24 countries. The gun was continuously improved, which gave rise to models ZB vz.27, ZB vz.30 and finally the ZGB 33 that became the basis for its most famous offspring - the BREN gun. Zbrojovka Brno sold a manufacturing license to the British War Office in May 1935, following several years of trials and improvements. The British, and later the Canadians and the Australians, manufactured large series of the Bren guns during the war. Both the ZB vz.26 and the Bren guns are used in many armies up to this day.

The machine gun armament of the Czechoslovak tanks was another of the ZB successful designs, the ZB vz.35 and vz.37 heavy machine guns (factory designation heavy machine gun ZB-53 model 35 or 37, Czechoslovak army's designation "7.92 mm kulomet vz.35 or vz.37"). In the Wehrmacht they were designated MG 37[t]). Their designer was the same man who designed the ZB vz.26, Václav Holek. He joined the Zbrojovka Brno in 1928 and started working there on designs of large caliber machine guns and simultaneously on a new, air-cooled heavy machine gun for the Mauser 7.92 mm ammunition.

While the Zbrojovka Brno company worked on a new heavy machine gun since 1930, its first models were not very successful. The ZB-50 looked like the ZB-53, but had problems with cooling and with rate and accuracy of its fire, due to the high weight of its moving parts. The ZB-51 returned to water cooling with complicated water circulation. ZB-52 was again air-cooled and used the same principle of gas operation as the ZGB-33 light machine gun, with the gases taken from the middle of the barrel. By its continuous development, in September 1933 the ZB-53 was born. It became the first model manufactured for the army, the ZB vz.35. By its further development, based on the army trials and use, the final ZB vz.37 model was born.

The gun was gas operated like the ZB vz.26. The gases were bled from the middle of the barrel via a regulated opening, and acted on a piston, connected with the bolt. The barrel was equipped with a finned cooling jacket, and was easily removable without any tools. On the bolt side it rested on springs that absorbed the vibrations caused by the firing and thus increased the accuracy of the gun. Because the gun was also planned for antiaircraft use, it had two rates of fire: 550 rpm for use against infantry and 750 rpm in the antiaircraft mode.

The gun lacked the usual cocking lever. The gunner just pushed the two handles forward until they engaged the bolt. By pulling them back he cocked the gun. He did not have to take his hands from the firing handles and from the firing buttons, a significant advantage. The iron sights were set at 200 m, after raising the distance frame the sights could be set from 200 to 2,500 m. The sights had two scales, for the light and for the heavy round. On the right side of the bolt casing were grooves for attaching a shoulder rest and an antiaircraft sight, on the left side similar grooves were for attaching a spotting scope for use in tanks and in fixed fortifications.

The gun could be set for single rounds or for sustained fire. It was fed by metal link belts with 100 or 200 rounds. For mounting into armored vehicles special mounts for these guns were developed. The gun was fixed in a ball mount (identical for mounting in the front wall of the hull or in the turret); the protruding barrel was protected by a massive armored trough. For aiming a 2.6x spotting scope was used. The gun was equipped with a cloth sack for catch-

Front view of the second modification of the Škoda Š-I-P tankette with its mounts for both the ZB vz.26 and ZB vz.37 machine guns.

The ball mount of the ZB vz.37 in the front turret plate of a tank. It was used in LT vz.35 and LT vz.38 tanks, as well as in the ŠP-II-b, V-8-H and T-21 prototypes.

ing the spent cartridges, and had a different muzzle from the infantry version. The tank barrel was also lighter than the infantry one, and lacked the barrel handle.

The gun was 1,095 mm long, with a 733 mm long barrel. The weight of the gun was between 18.88 and 22.05 kg, depending on the barrel and other equipment. The muzzle velocity was 880 m/sec for the light and 780 m/sec for the heavy round.

In 1934 the army started building its armored units, which badly needed a new air-cooled heavy machine gun. The planned fixed fortifications needed a similar weapon, and Zbrojovka Brno's heavy machine guns were suddenly in the center of the army's interest.

By the beginning of 1935 the company manufactured 17 prototype guns for the army evaluation trials. An order for 500 machine guns was placed shortly after the trial started. This put the company in a difficult situation, as it was manufacturing the prototypes in its prototype workshop and was not ready for large scale production. Because the army insisted on delivery before the end of 1935, it was willing to help the company through financing the necessary new machinery by paying a higher price for these initial guns. As soon as the production line was set up, Zbrojovka Brno immediately started on a second series of 500 guns, anticipating further army orders and also export sales.

The experience gained with the new gun led to 27 modifications in 1936. The modified gun was designated as the ZB vz.37 and was officially accepted by the army on January 19, 1937. For the following twelve years, the gun was manufactured without any further modifications. Its production ended in 1951.

Before September 1938 the army obtained approximately 700 guns of this type for its armored vehicles, 1,464 guns for the fixed fortifications and another 1,300 infantry guns, although it had ordered a total of 9,334 guns (1,536 ÚV - for the AFVs, 3,300 O for the fortifications and 4,398 of the infantry model).

After March 1939 the Germans kept the production lines running and used the gun under the designation MG-37(t) for their second-line units and especially for the Waffen SS.

The gun was also extensively exported from 1936 up to 1948. By that time over 14,000 guns were exported to Romania, Yugoslavia, Iran, China, Spain, England, Turkey, Slovakia, Peru and Chile. In 1948, Israel got 900 of these excellent guns. In 1936, the manufacturing license for the ZB vz.37 was sold to England, which manufactured it under the name BESA (Brno Enfield Small Arms) through the war and equipped with it all its armored vehicles. It was used in this role well into the fifties.

6

CAMOUFLAGE, MARKINGS, AND NUMBERING

The first armored vehicles of the Czechoslovak army, the two Lancia armored cars, were originally painted in Italian army dark green. In the early twenties the upper part of the lower turret was painted white and the cars may have been repainted in the standard khaki color of the Czechoslovak army.

The next armored cars, the Škoda Fiat-Torinos, were painted khaki overall, as were the various Škoda tankette prototypes, the first ČKD built Carden-Loyd tankettes and the Renault FT tanks. This practice was abandoned with the first Škoda armored car, the PA-I. It carried a five-color, almost lozenge type, camouflage. The colors were probably dark green, khaki, reddish brown, light gray and ochre.

The next Škoda armored car, the PA-II Turtle, carried the same five-color scheme but the colored areas were rounded and the various colors were divided with a thin line, probably dark brown. It is interesting that on these vehicles the camouflage was never restored and in later years they had a quite shabby paint.

The official camouflage scheme was introduced in 1930 and was carried by the OA vz.30, tančík vz.33, LT vz.34, LT vz.35 and the prototype of OA vz.27. The remaining Renault tanks were also repainted in this scheme in the thirties. All the outside surfaces were painted in three matte colors: dark green, yellow and dark brown. The green was considered the base color, and the other colors formed rounded color spots roughly 25 - 100 cm long and 5 - 40 cm wide. The border between the colors was sharp and the spots had to disrupt the shape of the vehicle. The paints were manufactured by the Josef Palfy company in Smolnice, and were referenced as yellow no.125, green no.169 and brown no.141.

The inside of the engine hatches were camouflaged the same way, the insides of the crew hatches were upholstered with dark brown leather. The whole inside of the fighting compartment was painted in an ivory color.

The only exceptions from the standard vehicles were the OA vz.27 armored cars. These vehicles were painted overall gray. The reason was that they were confined to roads, and it was found that the three-tone camouflage scheme was very conspicuous on the gray asphalt surfaces. While some tracked artillery tractors were painted in the three-tone camouflage scheme, all the soft skin vehicles of the army were finished in khaki.

The decree of the Ministry of Defense no.15669 Taj.I/7 odd.1937 introduced tactical signs for all tanks for wartime use.

The Lancia armored car after its repainting in khaki color and introduction of the white band on its lower turret.

Škoda's PA-II armored car was painted in the experimental scheme of the late twenties, consisting of dark green, khaki, brown, yellow and gray irregular splotches.

The OA vz.30 light armored cars were the first to carry the three-tone camouflage which became the standard for the Czechoslovak army AFVs in 1930. The colors were dark green, dark brown and yellow.

The signs were carried on the sides and the rear of the turret, and were:

1st platoon - circle;
2nd platoon - triangle;
3rd platoon - square;
4th platoon - lozenge.

The signs were 20 cm in diameter, were made from airplane cloth and were glued to the armor plates. Individual tanks in the platoon were not designated. The companies were assigned the following colors:

1st company - white;
2nd company - sulfur yellow;
3rd company - brick red.

The tank of the company commander carried on its turret an inverted T with a 20 cm base and 5 cm wide arms, in the color of its company. The battalion commander's vehicle and the reserve vehicles carried no signs.

The armored trains used a completely different camouflage pattern. They were painted in irregular sharp-edged fields of light green and light gray, disrupted with wide (25-40 cm) black dividing lines.

The manufacturers were assigned identifying letters, -Š- for Škoda, -P- for ČKD and -T- for Tatra. Tankettes were assigned number I, light tanks II and medium tanks III. A suffix -a- denoted a cavalry tank, -b- an infantry version. For the armored cars the manufacturers used their own identification system, for example Škoda used PA (Pancéřový automobil = armored car) plus the number, while Tatra used their standard chassis/engine number, like T-26/30.

This system was not always followed. For example, Škoda designated its tankettes MU (malý útočný = small attack vehicle) plus a number, or when it used the Š-I designation, it added untypical suffixes, like -d- for "dělový"(gun) etc. For light tanks it originally used SU (střední útočný = medium attack vehicle). Its medium tank Š-II-c should have been actually Š-III, but that designation was already taken. In May 1939. Škoda renumbered its vehicles, using the T-(number) designation, where a tankette (weight under 10 tons) carried a single-digit number, light tanks (weight under 20 tons) having numbers 11-15 and medium tanks (weight under 30 tons) having numbers T-21 - T-25, like T-11, T-21, T-25 etc. ČKD, with its export vehicles, abandoned this system completely and used its own designations like AH-IV. For its tanks, it used a three-letter designation, consisting of letters LT (lehký tank = light tank) and a letter designating the customer country (for example LTP - Peru, LTH - Switzerland [Helvetia]).

Once the vehicle was accepted by the army, it was assigned a two-letter code and a two-digit number showing the year of introduction. Armored cars were OA (obrněný automobil), light tanks LT and medium tanks ST (střední tank). The number was preceded by -vz.- (mk.). Thus we have OA vz.30, LT vz.35, ST vz.39 etc. An exception was the Tančík vz.33.

The numbering system of the armored vehicles changed several times. The first armored cars carried only white numbers, about

Tančík vz.33 was the next type to be painted in the standard camouflage.

The OA vz.27 armored cars were painted medium gray overall, to better blend into the gray asphalt roads they were confined to.

Four views of the LT vz.34, showing how the standard camouflage was applied. It also shows the placement and size of the registration number plates.

The Czechoslovak armored trains used a camouflage scheme of their own, unrelated to the armored vehicles. It consisted of sharply angled fields of very light and medium grays and dark green, divided by wide black lines.

The makeshift armored trains of the Czechoslovak army during the Slovak uprising in autumn 1944 carried a camouflage similar to the standard prewar AFV scheme.

A four-view color plate, showing the LT vz.35 in the standard three-tone camouflage. Note how the colors change depending on the lighting, shadows and reflections.

15 cm high. On the Lancias they were bordered in white and were carried on the side of the hull. the Fiat-Torinos carried them on the side doors. The Škoda armored cars PA-I to PA-III carried larger serial numbers, about 25 cm high. The numerals were red, with a white border (PA-II) and were carried on the side doors.

In July 1921 all army vehicles were assigned police registration numbers. They were white on a black license plate, carried on the front and rear armor plates. These first police numbers were a combination of letters and both Roman and Arabic numerals, for example NVII751 (Lancia) or NIX58 (Škoda PA-II). The police numbers were painted directly on the armor, instead of being carried on separate plates. Up to 1933 the Renault tanks carried only white serial numbers on the sides of their engine covers.

In December 1932 new police registration numbers were introduced. They consisted of five Arabic numerals, white on black plate, carried again on the front and rear of the vehicle. The license plates were 340 x 140 mm, black, with a 3 mm wide white border. The armored fighting vehicles and the tracked artillery tractors were assigned a block of numbers starting with "13...". In the case of armored vehicles the registration numbers were usually painted directly on the armor plates. This numbering system was used till 1939.

TABLE 6 lists all police registration numbers of the Czechoslovak army's armored vehicles from 1918 to 1939, their numbers, dates of introduction and dates of withdrawal from service.

TABLE 6
Registration Numbers of Czechoslovak Armored Vehicles

TYPE	NUMBER MANUF.	REGISTRATION OLD	NUMBERS NEW	INTRODUCED INTO SERVICE	WITHDRAWN FROM SERVICE
ARMORED CARS					
Lancia	2	NVII751, 752	13004, 13005	12. 1918	1936
Fiat-Torino	12	NVII753-764		5.-9.1920	1925-1929
Praga L	1	NVII969		8.1922	1925
Škoda PA-I	2	NIX9, 10	13239, 13240	8.1923	
Škoda PA-II	12	NIX58-69	13267-13275	12.1924-1.1925	3 in 1927, 1937
PA-II trainer	1	NIX70	13276	10.1925	1937
PA-II gun	1	NIX222	13358	11.1927	1937
PA-III prototype	1	NIX216	13353	6.1927	
OA vz.27	15	NIX201-215	13338-13352	5.-10.1929	
Tatra T-26	2	NII674, 678	13321, 13322	7.1929	
Tatra T26/30	8	NIV601-608		1928	1932
OA vz.30 prot.	1	NIV609	13323	1928	
Tatra T17/31	1	NIX257	13354	8.1929	1938
OA vz.30	51		13324-13331, 13376-13418	1934	
TANKETTES					
Carden-Loyd	3	NIX219-221	13355-13357	7.1930	
P-1 prototype	3	NIX223-225	13359-13361	10.1933	
Tančík vz.33	70		13420-13489	2.-10.1934	
TANKS					
Renault FT	7	51 - 57	13006-13012	1.1922-6.1924	1933-1936
KH-60	1		13362	5.1930	1935
P-II prototype	1		13363	12.1932	P-II-R in 1937
LT vz.34	50		13490-13539	4.1934-8.1936	
P-II-a prototype	1		19003	1935	1936
Š-II-a prototype	1		13620	3.1935	
LT vz.35(Škoda)	149		13666-13720, 13818-13860, 13864-13914	12.1936-4.1938	
LT vz.35(ČKD)	149		13721-13817, 13915-13966	1937	
P-II-b prototype	1		13636	7.1936	
Š-II-b prototype	1		13637	4.1936	
ŠP-II-b prototype	1		14120	2.1939	
Š-III-6 prototype	1		13638	4.1939	1939
Š-III-8 prototype	1		13639	1.1940	Wehrmacht
T-III prototype	2		13640, 13641	11.1938	
ČKD LKMVP	1		14124	8.1938	

Škoda's Fiat-Torino armored car in basic khaki and the small white number on its doors.

The ČKD tankette with the old army registration number, used up to December 1932.

In the **Wehrmacht's** service all tanks were oversprayed with the standard dark gray (Feldgrau RAL 7021) paint. On vehicles repaired by Škoda, paints manufactured by the Tebas company from Prague were used (RAL 46-P24 and RAL 7021). The registration number plates were removed. On some tanks 50 mm high white numbers were carried next to the driver's visor and on the left fender. These numbers corresponded to the manufacturer's chassis numbers. Unit signs were carried on small rhomboid plates attached to the hull's sides and on the rear plate.

For the Polish campaign large white crosses were painted on all surfaces. For the French campaign the large white crosses were replaced by smaller black crosses with double white borders (Balkenkreuz), carried on sides of the hull under the turret and on the rear plate. For easier identification by the Luftwaffe, large red German flags with the swastika were draped over the engine cover.

One year later in Russia the vehicles remained in their gray paint scheme, but on the sides and the rear of the turret large (275

The artillery tractors of the Czechoslovak army were also painted in three-tone camouflage, as this BD 25 shows.

The civilian registration plate, used by Škoda for internal testing of its P-II armored car. The manufacturers used their "dealer's plates" for such tests, as any vehicle on a public road had to carry the police registration plate.

The new registration number, white on black with a white border, on the LT vz.34 tank.

Another lot of BD 25 tractors and the Škoda-Martin gun-carrying trucks in the camouflage scheme applied by the manufacturer.

Tractors built for export had the customer's camouflage applied, as this Turkish T-6 in green, brown, yellow and black.

The tractors manufactured for Turkey were painted in a special camouflage of green, brown and yellow. Its effectiveness can be judged by the excellent blending of this T-8 into the surrounding countryside.

PzKpfw 38(t) in Wehrmacht's field gray paint, with the Balkenkreuz and large call number on its turret.

mm) three-digit white call-numbers appeared, designating the unit and the tank's place in it. Starting in February 1943, all German armored vehicles were factory finished in dark sand yellow. The crews were issued color pastes in dark olive drab and reddish brown to camouflage their vehicles depending on the time of the year and the area of operation. The pastes were soluble in gasoline, petrol and water, though water was not recommended. They were applied by spraying, where availability of equipment and time allowed, or by brushing. The variety of the paint schemes was practically infinite, because it depended on so many factors. For winter use, the vehicles were white-washed. In 1944, a new so called "ambush style" was introduced. It consisted of wide stripes of the two camouflage colors, with the bands speckled with small dots of the dark yellow. This new style was also more often applied by the manufacturers during the production. The style of the Balkenkreuzes also varied widely, from the original black with white borders to the final white outline only.

The three color pictures of PzKpfw 38(t)s on the Eastern front in the summer of 1941 show how effectively the road dust can cover the field gray paint and render it inconspicuous.

Some German AFVs, manufactured by BMM, were painted in a camouflage scheme already in the factory, as this GRILLE SdKfz 138/1 shows.

A GRILLE Ausf.M, armed with a 3.7 cm FLAK during the Prague uprising in May 1945, had also its camouflage scheme applied in the factory.

The **Bulgarian** tanks were originally painted in the German gray, but later were oversprayed with a khaki color. On both the front and the rear plates had large plates with their ID number. On the sides of their turrets they had fairly large white two-digit numbers. The old PzKpfw 35(t) carried numbers 25 - 50, the new T-11 had numbers 51 - 60.

The LT-35 tanks of the **Slovak** army carried the original Czechoslovak army camouflage and identification numbers during the war. The vehicles assigned for the invasion of the Soviet Union in 1941 had large red three-digit numbers with white outlines painted on both the sides and the rear of their turrets, designating their units, and Slovak crosses in white on the sides of the turrets. Judging by the available photographs, these tanks belonged to the second platoons of the 1st (121-125), 2nd (221-225) and 3rd (321-325) tank

All the Jagdpanzer 38s had their camouflage paint applied by the manufacturers. This BMM vehicle is in the typical "ambush" paint scheme.

Another Hetzer paint job, probably green over the base ochre.

A group of Slovak tanks showing different camouflage and markings. The two LT vz.35 tanks carry the three-tone camouflage and white three-digit numbers on their turrets, but only no.323 carries also the white cross. The olive-drab LTS-40 in the left background carries the white cross, but no number.

companies. Also known is a tank with a 099 sign, clearly belonging to the battalion headquarters. In later years the call numbers disappeared. The Slovak LT-38 tanks were originally in the old Czechoslovak three-tone camouflage (first five tanks), but later vehicles were delivered first in khaki, and later in the German dark yellow. The LT-40 tanks were painted khaki, while the OA vz.30 armored cars, LT-34 tanks and vz.33 tankettes retained their prewar three-tone camouflage scheme.

By a decree of the Ministry of Defense from May 21, 1942, all Slovak tanks had to carry a vertical white-blue-red tricolor on a shield 15 cm wide and 20 cm high on the sides of the turret in place of the white Slovak cross.

The **Romanian** tanks were painted in a green-gray color overall. Originally they carried the royal crest in black on the sides of the turret, and a black chassis number on the sides of the hull. During the Russian campaign those were removed and the tanks carried, similarly to the Slovak tanks, call numbers of the same type and size on the turret. In place of the German crosses they carried St. Michael crosses in white on the sides of the hull. A large yellow St. Michael cross, outlined in blue and white, had in the center a

An unusual camouflage of a Škoda-made Hetzer.

Romanian R-2 tank in the military museum in Bucharest in the green-gray color of the Romanian armor of the Second World War. The royal crest in the turret and the chassis number on the side were originally in black, and were removed with the introduction of the call number on the turret. The St.Michael's cross in correctly in white. Behind the tank on the right is Renault R-35, on the left TACAM R-2 and behind it PzKpfw IV.

LT vz.35 of the Bulgarian army in the military museum in Sofia in the greenish olive drab color.

roundel blue-yellow-red tricolor. It was painted over the whole width of the engine hatch.

In the home garrisons, the tanks carried front and rear white rectangular plates with black, six digit numbers. Those numbers were changed to all black numerals before the vehicles were committed to combat.

From the end of the war there are pictures of Romanian tanks fighting side by side with the Soviet army against the Germans. They carried tricolor blue-yellow-red roundels, sometimes combined with large red stars on white circular bases.

The **Hungarian** AFVs were painted dark olive green, over which irregular patches of reddish brown and light ochre were applied. After 1944, some vehicles were left in the dark green. Up to 1944, the national insignia consisted of a cross similar to the German Balkenkreuz, but in green with a white border, and having a red triangle in the middle. From 1944, the white cross in a black rectangle was carried on the sides of the hull or the turret, and white recognition numbers on the turret in the German fashion.

TURAN I medium tank of Honvéd in its three-tone camouflage paint, and with the white cross in a black rectangle.

7

ORGANIZATION OF THE ARMORED UNITS OF THE CZECHOSLOVAK ARMY

History and Development of the Armored Formations

After the end of the first World War the new Czechoslovak army had two armored cars, brought by the Czech Legions, and one Austro-Hungarian armored train. In a short time several other armored trains were assembled, and in 1920 Škoda converted twelve Fiat-Torino truck chassis into armored cars.

With the growing number of armored vehicles, it was imperative to subjugate them to a special unit, as they belonged to various headquarters, and their training, supply and combat use could not be coordinated. In October 1920, under the auspices of the V. Department of the Ministry of Defense (MNO - Ministerstvo Národní Obrany), the 3rd Section of Special Units was formed. The 3rd Section was responsible for setting up on October 29, 1920 (by the MNO decree čj.385210-V) a Headquarters of Special Fighting Forces (VZBÚ - Velitelství Zvláštních Bojových Útvarů) in Milovice. This unit was responsible for the training of the crews and the commanders, for the proper coordination of the armored units with other army units and for their proper use. It became responsible for the existing six armored trains and fourteen armored cars, for setting up a training school for new crews and for the maintenance workshops.

VZBÚ began taking inventory of its equipment, but its demand for stationing all the armored units in Milovice was denied by the General Staff, as the situation in Slovakia was far from safe. Meanwhile, the unit was assigned two Fiat-Torino armored cars (nos.13 and 14) from Prague, and began building garages, workshops, setting up warehouses and building a rail line for the expected armored trains. The unit also started obtaining cars, trucks and motorcycles on a regular basis.

On July 7, 1922 the VZBÚ was changed by a MNO decree čj.557467 into an armored battalion. The somewhat improvised structure of the former VZBÚ was thus changed into the standard battalion scheme with headquarters with technical and quartermasters units, a training company, three groups of armored trains, six companies of armored cars and a replacement company. Territorially the new Armored Battalion was subjugated to the 3.Infantry Division in Litoměřice.

The armored battalion had much lower manpower than its infantry counterparts: about 20 officers, the same number of NCOs and between 150-250 men. Service with the armored units was highly selective, and most of the men were Czech nationals.

Between 1922 and 1924 the Czechoslovak army bought seven Renault FT tanks from France. In 1923 it was finally possible to concentrate all the armored units in Milovice. The old armored cars were gradually replaced by new constructions from Škoda (PA-I and PA-II) between 1924-1925. The latest Škoda armored car PA-III was accepted as the OA vz.27, and fifteen of them came to the battalion between May and October of 1929.

In the same year the army ordered the new OA vz.30 light armored cars from Tatra, and in 1933 bought seventy vz.33 tankettes and 51 OA vz.30 light armored cars. The armored cars were placed into cavalry squadrons and some of them were also earmarked with the tankettes for the border areas as supporting units. The border areas were formed during the mobilization and were responsible for initial border defense.

In 1932 ČKD offered its P-II light tank with a Vickers 4.7 cm gun and two light vz.26 machine guns. The army eventually bought fifty of these LT vz.34 tanks, but with a Škoda 3.7 cm gun and ZB vz.35 heavy machine guns.

Organization, Armored Regiments, Mobile Divisions

Colonel Pavlík, the commanding officer of the 1st Armored Regiment (PÚV-1) accepting the regimental standard on May 27,1934 in Český Brod. Note the French style helmets vz.28, which were still worn at this time.

All this new equipment required organizational changes. The original single armored company had already split into two in 1930 (one with Škoda heavy armored cars and one with the light Tatras and the Renault tanks), but in 1933 the armored battalion was upgraded to an armored regiment (PÚV - Pluk Útočné Vozby) with an attached armored trains company, replacement company and an armor training school. The armored regiment consisted of a tank battalion with the 1st and 2nd companies with tankettes, and a 3rd company with LT vz.34 tanks. The armored cars were concentrated in a cavalry battalion with two squadrons.

Hitler's ascension to power in Germany led to complete re-evaluation of the army's plans, which up to that point were oriented mainly against the less dangerous Hungary. Planned armored units comprised fifteen platoons for the border areas, 23 reconnaissance groups for the infantry divisions, four tank and four armored car battalions for cavalry brigades, seven tank companies for reconnaissance corps' groups and fourteen tank battalions for armored reserves of the army headquarters. The smallest tank unit was a platoon with three tanks. A company had four platoons, a three-tank reserve and a commander's tank for a total of sixteen tanks. The battalion had three companies and 49 tanks. The material situation in 1934 was far from the planned one. The General Staff planned a total of 373 cavalry tanks, 336 infantry tanks and 336 medium tanks. To incorporate the planned vehicle strength, it was necessary to change the organization of the armored units. In August 1935, the Ministry of Defense ordered the formation of an armored brigade with three armored regiments and an Armored Training Center. The 1st Armored Regiment remained in Milovice, the 2nd was planned in Vyškov in Moravia and the 3rd in Turčianský sv.Martin in Slovakia. A typical organization scheme of the armored regiment is presented in TABLE 7.

The obverse side of the regimental standard bears the Czech lion with the Slovak shield and the inscription "To us - a fortress, to the enemy - a bulwark".

The reverse side of the regimental standard shows the insignia of the armored corps (an arrow in a circle) interwoven with stylized linden branches (the linden tree is considered to be the sacred tree of the ancient Slavonic tribes). The inscription reads: "The Czechoslovak National Committee in Prague to the 1st Armored Regiment".

TABLE 7
Peacetime Organization of PÚV 1 (September 15, 1938)

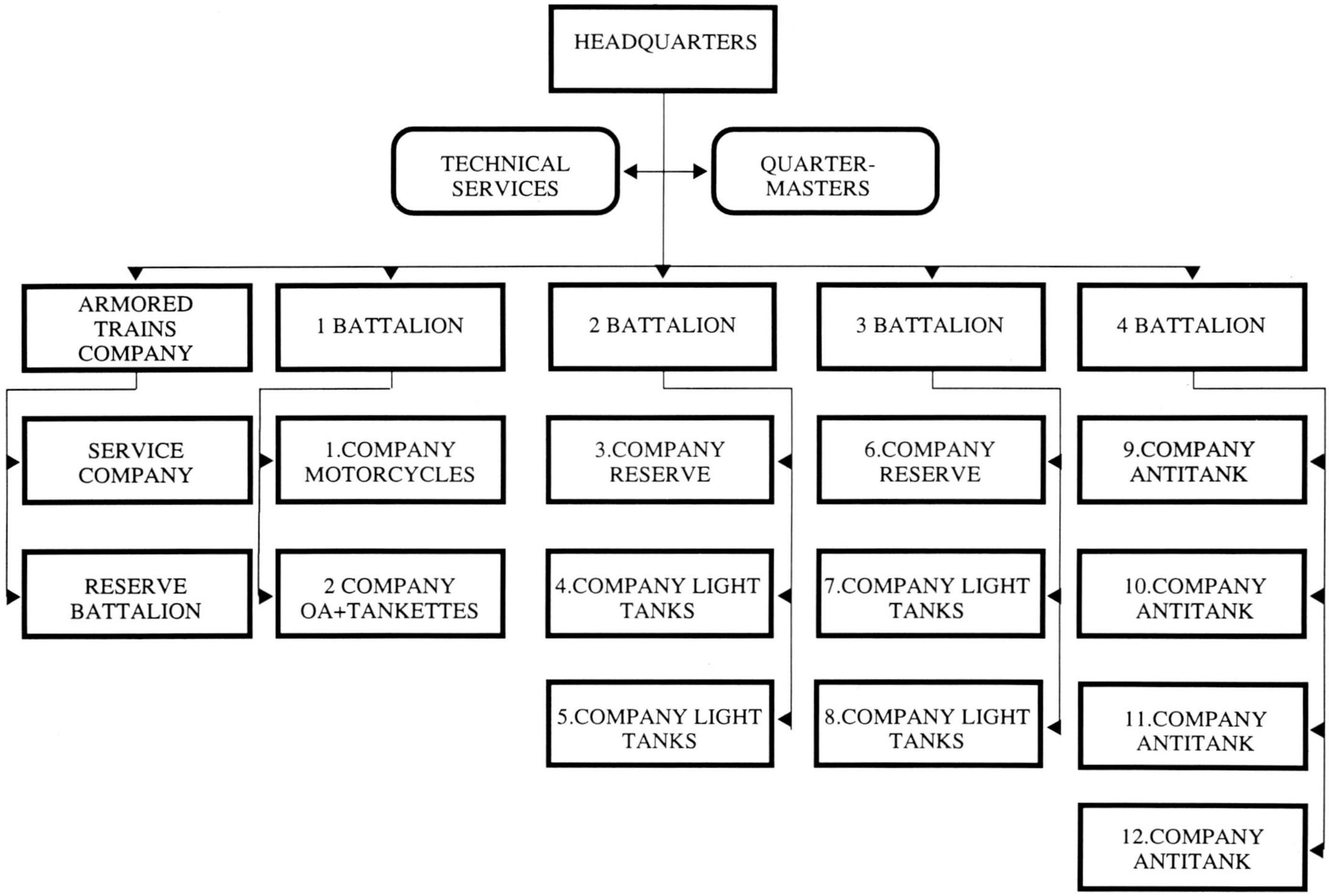

The chosen cavalry tank was the Škoda Š-II-a tank, which became the LT vz.35. For the infantry tank, the Army wanted both Škoda and ČKD to cooperate on the design of ŠP-II-b, but the companies preferred to work on their own prototypes and the ŠP-II-b languished until 1939, when it was scrapped. The medium tanks developed by TATRA as the T-III and by Škoda as the Š-III were not successful either. Thus, the Army did not have any infantry or medium tanks for their planned numbers in 1938.

October 1, 1937 the Mobile Divisions (RD - Rychlá Divize. "Rychlá" literally means "Rapid", but in this work it is translated as "Mobile") were officially formed. They were designed with both French and German experiences in mind. These divisions combined tank and artillery units with cavalry and mechanized infantry. Each was planned to have one brigade of cavalry and one moto-mechanized brigade. The cavalry brigade consisted of two dragoon regiments, a bicycle battalion and an artillery group (a unit smaller than a battalion). The moto-mechanized brigade consisted of two regiments of motorized infantry on trucks and an artillery group. Two armored battalions formed its heart, each with three companies of light tanks. To the headquarters of the division were directly subordinated the reconnaissance battalion, consisting of a company of motorcyclists and a company of armored cars (plus a planned company of light tanks), two companies each of 2 cm antiaircraft Oerlikon guns and of 3.7 cm antitank guns, plus supporting services. TABLE 8 presents the planned organization. Their headquarters were formed on January 1, 1938. RD-1 was stationed in Prague, RD-2 in Brno, RD-3 in Bratislava and RD-4 in Pardubice. The Mobile Divisions had a mobilization strength of 11,000 men, 2,832 horses, 298 motorcycles, 1,009 trucks and cars, 98 tanks, 12 armored cars and 68 guns (antitank, antiaircraft and field artillery). The cavalry of the Mobile Divisions was trained to fight like dragoons, dismounted, and were equipped like infantry with machine guns and mortars. Thus, the horse was seen only as a means of transport with unlimited cross-country capability. The utilization of the RD's cavalry brigades and motorized regiments was planned for various combat situations, best suited to each of them, and close combat cooperation between them was not even envisaged. True to this concept, the various units trained separately, and the whole division was assembled only during the autumn maneuvers. This happened only in 1937; the combat value of these divisions in 1938 is thus open to discussion.

TABLE 8
Organization of the Mobile Division

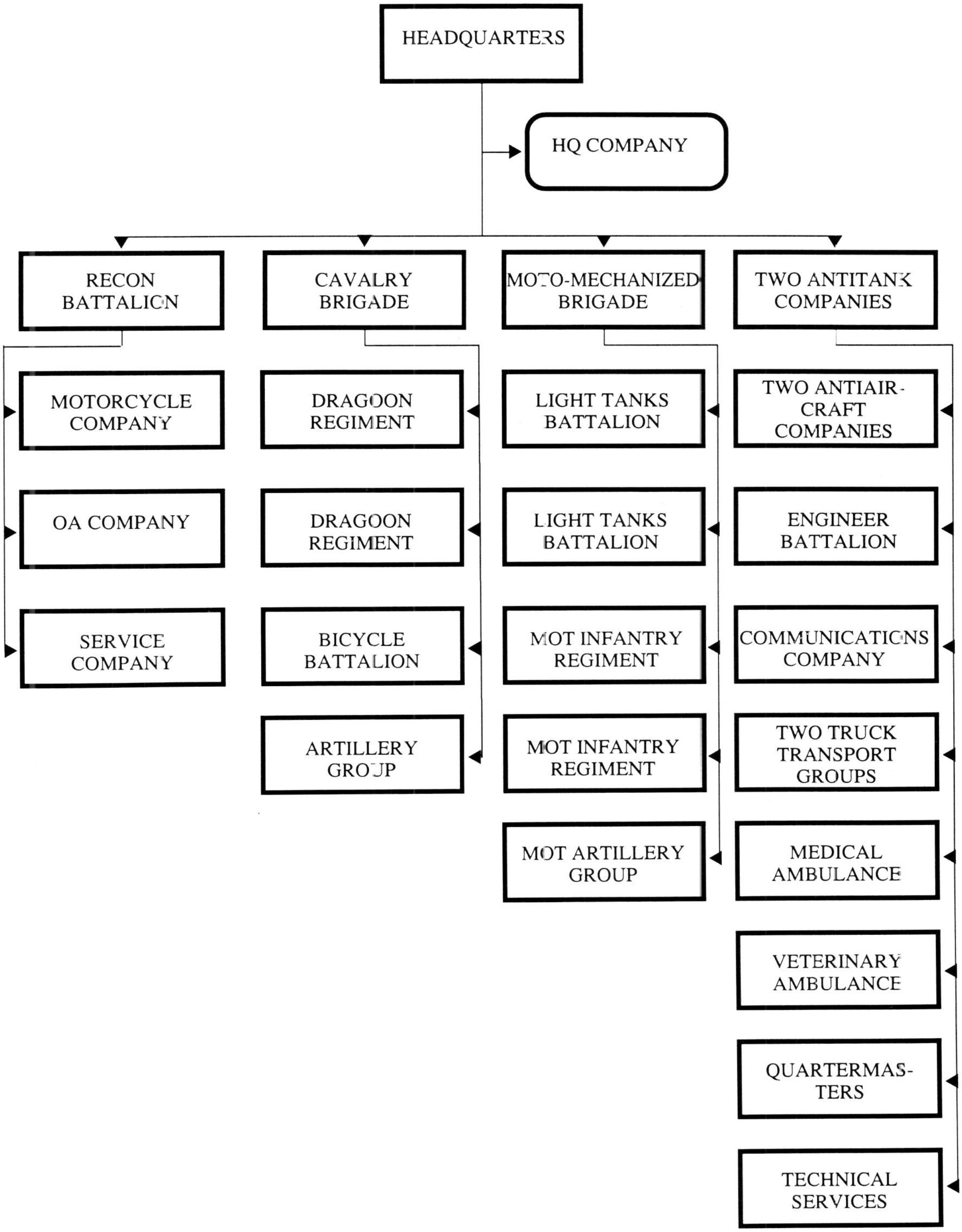

The LT vz.35 tanks were widely used for demonstrating the armored might of the army and to popularize it during the late thirties, to counter any misgiving about the cost of the rearmament. These pictures are from the combined maneuvers, conducted several times each year.

Another propaganda picture from the army maneuvers, showing a LT vz.35 tank with its supporting infantry.

The army planned that the Mobile Divisions would get eight tank battalions, two for each mechanized brigade. The Armored Regiments had to scrap some of their old vehicles, but in December 1936 the first fifteen LT vz.35 tanks arrived at the 1st Armored Regiment in Milovice. The other two regiments started getting their vehicles shortly after that. Of the 298 new LT vz.35s, the PÚV-1 obtained 197 (Škoda made 13666-13720, 13864-13893 and 13903-13914, ČKD made 13721-13784 and 13915-13950), PÚV-2 49 (ČKD made 13785-13817 and 13951-13966) and PÚV-3 52 (Škoda made 13818-13860 and 13894-13902). All regiments were supposed to fill the needs of the four Mobile Divisions with men and material, as each Mobile Division was planned to have 98 light tanks, three OA vz.27 and 9 OA vz.30 armored cars. Besides that, the regiments had to supply 34 independent three-vehicle tank platoons for infantry divisions and border areas, and 23 tankette and six armored car platoons for the border areas.

Starting in 1935, a grandiose build-up of garages, workshops and barracks was started by all three armored regiments, as all the new equipment and manpower had to be quickly housed. Each regiment had more than 1,000 men on its roster. While the officers and NCOs were supplied by the 1st Regiment from Milovice, the crews, transferred from cavalry, bicycle and border units, had to be trained fresh. On October 15, 1935 an armored brigade was formed in Milovice, which acted as headquarters for all the armored regiments, responsible for their organizational, personnel and training matters.

During the reorganization in March 1937, the armored brigade was abolished and in its place the 7th Department of Armored Units was formed at the Ministry of Defense. This provided the armored formations with a voice in the highest places

PÚV-1 in Milovice in 1936 had two battalions. The first concentrated a company of motorcyclist and two companies of tankettes and armored cars, the second four tank companies. It also had a company of armored trains and two new companies of antitank guns. In 1937 PÚV-1 already had four battalions, the first as in 1936, the second and third each with three tank companies, and the fourth with four antitank gun companies.

PÚV-2 in Vyškov also had four battalions: the first with motorcycles and armored cars, the second and third with light tanks and the fourth with medium tanks (planned). In 1937 the first battalion had five companies: two of motorcyclists, one of armored cars and tankettes and two of light tanks. The second battalion had three companies of light tanks, the third battalion three companies of medium tanks [planned) and the fourth battalion three companies of antitank guns.

PÚV-3 in Slovakia had its first battalion with one company of armored cars and tankettes and three companies of light tanks, second and third battalions each had three companies of light tanks, and two companies of antitank guns were subjugated directly to the regimental headquarters. In 1937, a fourth battalion with four companies of antitank guns was formed.

In September 1938 a newly formed PÚV-4 in Kolín was planned to take over part of the PÚV-1's duties, but due to the Munich dictate, it existed only for a short time.

In its final development stage the Czechoslovak armored formations had planned personnel roster of 6,6_8 men. Of this number, PÚV-1 had 1,971, PÚV-2 2,165, PÚV-3 930, PÚV-4 1,405 and UÚV (Učiliště Útočné Vozby, or AFV Training Center) 127 men.

Combined companies of LT vz.35 light tanks, OA vz.30 armored cars and motorized infantry from the mechanized brigades of the mobile divisions were used to quell the uprising of the Sudeten Germans in September 1938.

During the mobilization, PÚV-1 and PÚV-2 were entrusted with an additional duty, namely to field two two-company battalions of tanks each for the border regiments. These were planned to quickly plug any penetrations in the line of fixed fortifications. This idea originated with the ŘOP (Ředitelství Opevňovacích Prací, or Directory of Fortification's Construction), which even allocated 170 million Kč from its budget to form, equip and train special armored formations for this use. The fast pace of events prevented formation of such units.

Armored Training Centers and Armor School

The first Czech officers were sent to study in French armored schools in the early twenties. These officers acted as instructors and trained additional officers and NCOs for this role after their return.

An AFV School was established in the twenties with an armored battalion. Its main role was to train NCOs and the crews of the armored vehicles. It ran courses for drivers, mechanics, armorers and radio operators, but also provided training for officers transferred from other units. As the service with the armored units was considered quite selective and exclusive, many officers served with AFVs all their professional career and some returned to the AFVs even after the war.

In 1935 the AFV School was changed into UÚV, or AFV Training Center. It consisted of a headquarters, a training company and a testing unit. The training company was responsible for training various specialists and commanders, and was staffed by experienced officers and NCOs as instructors. For training, the company had allocated 3-4 vehicles of each type of armored vehicles that the army was using. The testing unit collaborated closely with the Military Technical and Aeronautical Institute (VTLÚ) in Prague in evaluating new constructions and by testing already introduced types.

While the UÚV transferred to Vyškov in September 1937, the testing units remained in Milovice, which was much closer to Prague and thus to the VTLÚ and the manufacturers.

Use of the AFVs during the 1938 Mobilization

The first real test for the new armored formations came on the night of May 20, 1938 when, during a partial mobilization, the Mobile Divisions moved into their designated areas, where they remained until June 8.

Those three weeks in the field showed many important shortcomings. First, both the crews and the commanders were not fully trained, especially in the practical use of their vehicles. Some officers were transferred from infantry and cavalry units and graduated after only four months of armored school. The new soldiers were trained solely at the platoon level and their technical skills were low.

There were also grave deficiencies in the armament of the tanks. Due to the approved exchange of the ZB vz.35 machine guns for the ZB vz.37 ones, almost half the tanks went into the field with no machine guns at all, as the old mounts could not accept the new machine guns. The empty mounts had to be covered with circular plates. This situation was partially alleviated by sending factory specialists to the field units to mount the new machine guns.

There was a general shortage of armor piercing ammunition for the main guns, which was not solved until September 1938. Some tanks lacked the spotting scopes, bulletproof glass blocks for the visors and radio sets.

There was also a shortage of certain more mundane supplies, like towing cables, filling machines for machine gun belts etc. The main problem was a total lack of spare parts, which required withdrawal of defective vehicles to the factories for repairs. The Army lacked the field workshops and retrieval units. Some of these defects were rectified during the next four months, but the technical service remained an Achilles heel of the Czechoslovak armored formations.

To be fair, it must be pointed out that the German Panzers were at this time in a similar situation, as proved by their massive failures during the occupation of Austria.

At the beginning of 1938 the army was aware that the situation in the Sudeten border areas was getting more dangerous, and that army troops would have to be ready to support the border guards and the local police units to maintain peace and to prevent sabotage and provocative actions.

Though the main forces were formed by infantry and cavalry units, armored vehicles were envisioned as very important means of not only stiffening the former, but also as a demonstration of the might of the army and as a psychological deterrent. The Ministry of Defense ordered the formation of ready armored units on July 25, 1938, as the situation was rapidly deteriorating. In all, 41 ready units were formed. Their armored formations consisted of three platoons of tankettes, six platoons of light tanks, eight platoons of armored cars and four platoons of motorcyclists. These units were stationed throughout the border areas, so that they could act quickly and decisively.

By the end of August 1938, 29 new ready groups were formed and each was supported by one armored car. These ready units played a decisive role in suppressing the open insurgency of the

LT vz.35 light tanks during the September 1938 mobilization in Teplice nad Metují. Note the two policemen in black uniforms and English-style police helmets.

Sudeten Nazis. On the other hand, the armored vehicles taken from front-line units of the Mobile Divisions weakened those important formations considerably.

During the night of September 12, 1938, the Sudeten Germans organized marches and demonstrations meant to support their demands for the annexation of the Sudeten areas by the Third Reich. On September 13, martial law was declared in eleven border counties, but the police and army units were not able to restore order completely. The army ordered the motorized brigades of the Mobile Divisions into the threatened areas. Their strong mechanized infantry units, with artillery and tank support, quickly quelled the insurgency and restored order.

Due to a perceived threat from the Wehrmacht, Czechoslovakia fully mobilized its army on September 23, 1938. The Mobile Divisions had several of their units in the border areas, and thus the 1st and 2nd Mobile Divisions had about 40 tanks each, the 3rd only 16 tanks and the 4th 76 tanks. One full armored regiment of about 40 tanks was kept as a reserve of the army headquarters. The remaining tanks were either in the ready units in the border areas or in the factories for the planned warranty modifications. Thus, during the mobilization the army had only 16 tank companies.

In the period between September 12 and October 4, 1938 there were 69 fighting encounters with the Freikorps units (paramilitary units of the Sudeten Germans, armed and controlled by Hitler's Germany), in which armored units (light tanks, tankettes and armored cars) were used. The LT vz.35 tanks and the tankettes were usually used in three-vehicle platoons.

The first skirmishes, in which the armored units participated, took place during the night of September 12 in Stříbro, Planá u Mariánských Lázní and Jáchymov. Heavy fighting took place on September 22 in the Cheb area. A whole motorized brigade counterattacked the Freikorps units that penetrated Czechoslovak territory from Germany. The tanks, in cooperation with the infantry, routed the insurgents.

Heavy fighting was also reported from Kraslice and by September 15 from Varnsdorf and the surrounding area. Tanks were used similarly in Southern Bohemia, especially during the fight for Český Krumlov starting on October 2, 1938. During all this fighting, the tanks provided invaluable assistance to the infantry and police units, as they breached and destroyed the barricades and liquidated the insurgents' machine gun positions with machine gun and gun fire. As the insurgents lacked antitank weapons (besides hand grenades), the tanks' task was easier than it would have been had they been fighting a real army. On the other hand, the small tank groups fought under field conditions and were isolated from their main units and their technical support for prolonged periods. All the armored vehicles, except for the tankettes, were highly praised not only by their personnel, but by the Army's Staff as well.

A LT vz.35 tank company in Varnsdorf in September 1938, with accompanying infantry.

Fighting in Slovakia and Transcarpathian Ruthenia

Following the Munich dictate and the ceding of the border areas to Germany, most of the Czechoslovak army units returned to their peace-time garrisons. They did not stay there long, though, as in October 1938 it was necessary to strengthen the army units in Slovakia and in Transcarpathian Ruthenia to protect these areas against a Hungarian attack.

Units of the 3rd Mobile Division had been reinforced by a battalion of light tanks (Lt-2) from the 2nd Mobile Division plus by two antitank companies. In the second half of October an additional battalion of light tanks (Lt-3) was added, so that the 3rd Mobile Division had seven tank companies. The tanks were used during a Hungarian attack in the area of Feledinec where, in cooperation with infantry, they repulsed a regular Honvéd battalion. The rest of the division did not participate in any fighting. After ceding Southern Slovakia to Hungary, the units returned to their garrisons in December 1938.

A different situation had arisen in Transcarpathian Ruthenia, where heavy fighting raged during October and November 1938. The Hungarians were sending in "Szabadcsapatok" terrorist groups, which ranged in size from platoon to a full battalion. This area was originally considered fairly safe and the army units located there had minimal armored units at their disposal. The 6th Corps reinforced the area by sending in the units of the 17th, 21st and 22nd Infantry Divisions with small supporting armor units.

The first fight took place on October 10 when an infantry unit, reinforced by two tankettes, encircled and liquidated a group of the Hungarian terrorists. In the second half of October two infantry battalions with supporting platoons of tankettes and light tanks isolated a Szabadcsapatok battalion in the woods near Salanek. The tanks and tankettes penetrated the dense woods and surprised the Hungarians who did not expect them to get through. The battalion was defeated after heavy fighting and more than 300 Hungarians were taken as prisoners.

One of the LT vz.35 tanks in the barracks in Humenné, following the defeat of the Hungarian aggressors in March 1939.

OA vz.30 armored cars of the 2. reconnaissance unit in Poljana in Transcarpathian Ruthenia in the winter 1938-1939.

The success of the tanks and the heightened danger of a full-scale Hungarian invasion led to a transfer of a tank company to Mukačevo and Užhorod. The company fought a night battle in Kosiná, but had to evacuate with the other units following the Vienna arbitration of November 2, 1938. During the retreat from Southern Slovakia, the tanks shielded the infantry units against attacks.

The armored units also fought in November 1938 against Beck's Poland, which tried to provoke a border incident, and was sending small terrorists units to the northern borders of Ruthenia. At the end of November the Poles attacked across the border in the Čadca area, but units of the 16th Infantry Division stopped them and the mobilized armored units of the 3rd Mobile Division from Turčianský sv.Martin did not have to take part.

In November 1938 the Army sent further reinforcements to Transcarpathian Ruthenia - three motorized infantry battalions and a combined armored battalion with two companies of LT vz.35 tanks and one company of armored cars. These units stiffened the positions of the 12th Infantry Division in the border areas.

During the hard winter of 1938-1939, one serious drawback of the LT vz.35 tanks became apparent: due to the severe frosts, they were extremely difficult to start. Their oil literally stiffened, water vapor in the pneumatic system froze, and the tanks did not have antifreeze in their radiators, which had to be emptied every night. It took many hours to start the vehicles.

On February 15, 1939 the defense of the borders was called off. The 12th Infantry Division in Transcarpathian Ruthenia was supposed to return all its armored units, but in the end it kept a company of LT vz.35 tanks in Michalovce and a combined company of LT vz.35 tanks and armored cars in Chust and Sevljuš.

All these units participated in the heavy fighting that took place between March 14 and March 17, 1939. The first attack of the Honvéd units was directed against Svalava, with the aim of dividing the units of the 12th Infantry Division and forcing it to capitu-

One of the two LT vz.35 tanks, captured by the Hungarians in early 1939, guarded by a Hungarian gendarme.

late. When stopped, the Hungarians started another attack in the west, in Uhu River valley. The 3rd Battalion of the 36th Infantry Regiment was supported at Onokovce by six LT vz.35 tanks from Michalovce. The tanks were used mainly in leading the counterattacks, but they were also very successful in defense.

On March 14, two LT vz.35 tanks (Škoda prototype number 13620 and one army tank number 13903), returning from the Soviet Union through Romania and manned by Škoda mechanics, arrived into the barracks of the combined company in Sevljuš. The officers of the company confiscated both tanks on the spot, installed machine guns in them and inducted them into their company's roster. The Škoda mechanics volunteered to stay with the tanks in combat as drivers.

Both tanks were used during a counterattack at Fančíkovo, but one of them (13903) was hit by a Hungarian antitank gun and was captured. Its Škoda driver perished with the crew. Another LT vz.35 (13673) was captured by the Hungarians later from the Slovak Army in March 24, 1939. Both tanks made quite a good impression in Hungary. Following the demise of Czechoslovakia, and the incorporation of the Czech lands into Germany as a protectorate, the Hungarians asked Škoda to repair them. Škoda originally asked 645,000 Kč ($ 26,000) for the repairs but, after signing the licensing agreement for the TURÁN tanks, repaired both tanks free. The Honvéd assigned them the numbers 1H-406 and 1H-407 and used them for training up to the end of 1943.

During the defensive battles, the armored units managed to hold back the Honvéd formations and thus allowed the rest of the Czechoslovak army units to retreat into Slovakia. The army units from the Eastern part (from Chust and Sevljuš) had to retreat to Romania, which they did in good order through Tjačevo by March 17. This group had only armored cars (9 OA vz.30, 3 OA vz.27), but a part of the 2nd Armored Regiment surrendered nine LT vz.35 tanks (13792, 13802, 13806, 13810, 13954, 13955, 13956, 13959, 13964) to the Slovak Army on March 18.

This was the last unit of the Czechoslovak army's armored formations to surrender. The rest of the army surrendered on March 15, 1939, following the German occupation of the Czech Lands and the forming of the Protectorate of Bohemia and Moravia.

TABLE 9 lists all armored fighting vehicles on the Czechoslovak army's roster at the end of 1938, and their subsequent fate after March 15, 1939.

TABLE 9
Armored Fighting Vehicles of the Czechoslovak Army

ARMY'S LIST IN 1938		AFTER OCCUPATION	
TYPE OF VEHICLE	NUMBER	NUMBER	USER
Tančík vz.33	70	40	Germany
		30	Slovakia
Renault FT	3	3	Germany
LT vz.34	51	24	Germany
		27	Slovakia
LT vz.35 prototype	1	1	Škoda, Waffen SS
LT vz.35	298	244	Germany
		52	Slovakia
		2	Hungary
Praga P-II-b prototype	1	1	Germany
Škoda Š-II-b prototype	1	1	Germany
ŠP-II-b prototype	1	1	Germany
Škoda Š-III	2	1	Germany
Tatra T-III	2	2	Germany
Praga LKMVP prototype	1	1	Germany
OA vz.27	15	9	Germany
		3	Slovakia
		3	Romania
OA vz.30	51	23	Germany
		18	Slovakia
		9	Romania
		1	Hungary
Tatra T26/30 prototype	1	1	Germany

8

CZECHOSLOVAK ARMY UNIFORMS AND INSIGNIA

The cut of the postwar uniforms of the Czechoslovak army was based on US Army uniforms of First World War vintage. The Czechoslovak army ordered and used in the early twenties 20,000 US Army uniforms.

The Czechoslovak army uniforms were of khaki color, blue for the Air Force. The rank and file blouse had a closed collar with seven front buttons and two breast and two side buttoned pockets. The trousers were full-length and were covered with puttees up to the knees. Black ankle-high boots were standard issue. A simple brown belt had a frame buckle with two tongues. The army originally used old Austro-Hungarian helmets. Those were changed for French helmets in the late twenties. The modern helmets of domestic design were introduced in the thirties. They were round, with straight sides and with a divided chin strap. Their color was khaki overall.

The officers wore a blouse with a closed collar, with seven front buttons and four pockets. For office work or ceremonial occasions, a blouse with a closed collar, long trousers and black shoes were used, otherwise riding breeches and black riding boots were worn. The ceremonial belt was gold braid with a golden circular buckle, for field use a Sam Browne belt was used. Shirts were white or khaki, ties black.

Tank crews in exercise overalls and leather helmets.

Ceremonial headgear for officers was a service cap with cloth covered visors, piping in the arms' color and for generals golden braid across the base of the visor. The senior NCOs wore officer's caps, while junior NCOs and the men wore garrison caps, again with piping in their arms' color.

Both the rank and file and the officers wore their rank on shoulder boards and on the left side of their caps. Collar patches were in the color of their arms.

The colors of the arms were:

infantry	purple
artillery	bright red
cavalry	yellow
engineers	dark brown
air force	light blue
communications	cinnamon brown
quartermasters	dark blue
medical corps	black

Buttons were round, with four fields of parallel lines in the background. On their face the buttons carried crossed swords in raised relief (for combat personnel only). The men's buttons were in gunmetal, NCO's in silver and officers' in gold.

The cap insignia carried the Czech lion on a shield in gunmetal for the men. The same shield in silver, superimposed on a diagonally placed square, was worn by the NCOs. Officers had theirs in gold, with crossed swords placed between the shield and the background square.

Besides the arms' color collar patches, metal signs denoting special units were worn on the collar patches. Regimental numbers were worn on the shoulder tabs, gold for officers, silver for NCOs and gunmetal for the men.

As the armored units were not considered a separate arm, their personnel carried the color patches in the color of their original units, i.e., purple for infantry or yellow for cavalry. Their only badge of recognition was an arrow inside a circle (60 mm OD, 8 mm wide). This was originally carried on the sleeve, made from brown

A closer look on the tankers' helmets. They were quite similar in shape to the steel helmets vz.32, though made of hardened leather instead of steel.

A tank commander in leather coat, breeches, helmet and cavalry gloves.

cloth. Starting from 1930, the insignia were carried in a smaller (25 mm OD) metal version on the shoulder tabs, golden for the officers, silver for NCOs and in gunmetal for the men. In 1935 the insignia was moved to the collar patches and a metal regimental number was carried on the collar opposite the shoulder boards. Members of the Armor School carried a metal "ÚV" in the same position.

The armored troops wore the same uniforms as the rest of the army, but had some special outfits of their own. For the armored vehicle crews, short brown leather coats with suede collars were worn over the normal uniform jacket. Rank insignia were on a cloth rectangle carried on right front. Leather breeches were worn with standard ankle-high boots and leather puttees that covered the whole calf. Special helmets, pressed from thick leather, were also worn. They were similarly of brown color and had a chin strap. They were made in three sizes.

For daily wear during training, repairs etc., light color cotton overalls were issued from 1932. They consisted of a simple jacket with no pockets and trousers with two side pockets and a narrow belt. Over this the normal uniform belt was worn. The rank insignia were again carried on the rectangular cloth on the left side of the breast.

The badge for outstanding drivers was introduced in 1936. It was in gold with a silver wreath for the officers and senior NCOs, gunmetal for NCOs and men. It was awarded following the recommendation of the Armored Brigade (one year after passing the driving test for the officers, five months for the men and NCOs). The badge was carried on the left breast pocket of the blouse. When leaving the army, the men had to turn the badge in and were issued its miniature.

COMPARISON OF RANKS

CZECHOSLOVAK ARMY RANK	WEHRMACHT EQUIVALENT	US ARMY EQUIVALENT
1. Vojín	Schütze	Private
2. Svobodník	Oberschütze	Private 1st Class
3. Desátník	Obergefreiter	Corporal
4. Četař	Unteroffizier	Sergeant
5. Rotný	Unterfeldwebel	Technical Sergeant
6. Rotmistr	Feldwebel	Staff Sergeant
7. Štábní rotmistr	Oberfeldwebel	Sergeant Major
8. Praporčík	Fähnrich	Warrant Officer
9. Podporučík		Second Lieutenant
10. Poručík	Leutnant	Lieutenant
11. Nadporučík	Oberleutnant	Lieutenant 1st Class
12. Kapitán	Hauptmann	Captain
13. Štábní kapitán		
14. Major	Major	Major
15. Podplukovník	Oberstleutnant	Lieutenant Colonel
16. Plukovník	Oberst	Colonel
17. Brigádní generál	Generalmajor	Major General
18. Divizní generál	Generalleutnant	Lieutenant General
19. Armádní generál	General	General

The Slovak army used ex-Czechoslovak army equipment and uniforms. Close-up of the leather helmet with its protecting ear flaps and the leather coat with its suede collar. The side arm is the pistol vz.24.

A couple of Slovak officers, wearing the long leather coats, which the armored units adopted from the air force.

An officer of the armored units in a long leather coat. On the blouse's collar patches he carries the insignia of the armored corps, the color shows that his original arm was infantry. The arm color is repeated on the piping of the cap.

A crew member of an armored fighting vehicle in a standard uniform with black ankle boots and puttees, leather helmet and a belt with a side-arm.

A tank crew member in leather breeches and coat, helmet and hard leather puttees. A standard uniform blouse was worn under the leather coat.

A corporal crew member in working cotton overall and the leather helmet. He wears the normal belt and a side-arm.

A motorcyclist in the leather outfit with long cavalry leather gloves, the steel helmet vz.32 and goggles.

A cavalry officer of an armored car squadron in a ceremonial uniform with red riding breeches and the ceremonial belt.

Cap insignia of the enlisted men, NCO's and officers.

Badges for outstanding drivers, gunmetal for men and NCO's, silver and gold for officers and senior NCO's.

Insignia of the armored corps. The brown cloth one was worn on the left sleeve and was used until 1930. Since then, a small metal insignia was worn on the collar, behind the arm color patch, or, later, on it, when the metal unit sign was moved to the collar as well. The sign was in gunmetal for men, golden for the officers.

A collar of an NCO of the 3rd PÚV, a soldier assigned to the Armor School, and armored corps and unit insignia for men, NCOs and officers.

Shoulder boards: vojín, svobodník, desátník.

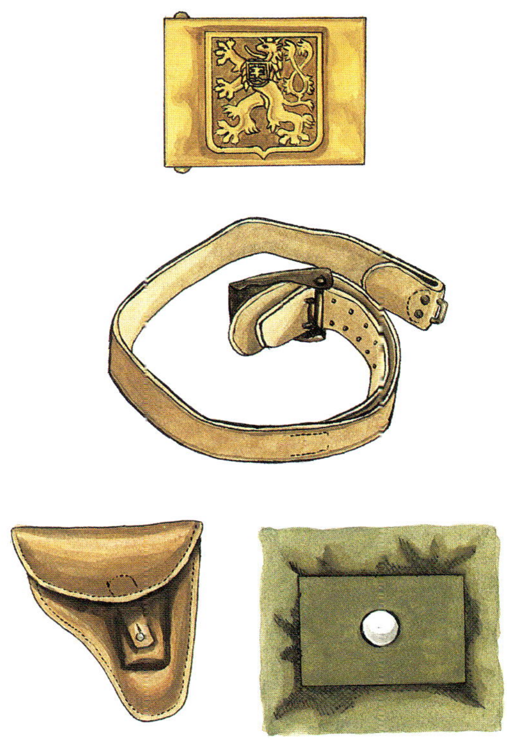

A regulation belt with a brass buckle with the state crest, the belt from inside, leather holster for the side-arm and the cloth with rank insignia, worn on the breast's right side.

Shoulder boards: četař, rotný, četař délesloužící (literally long serving, designation for professional soldiers, who signed up for extended periods).

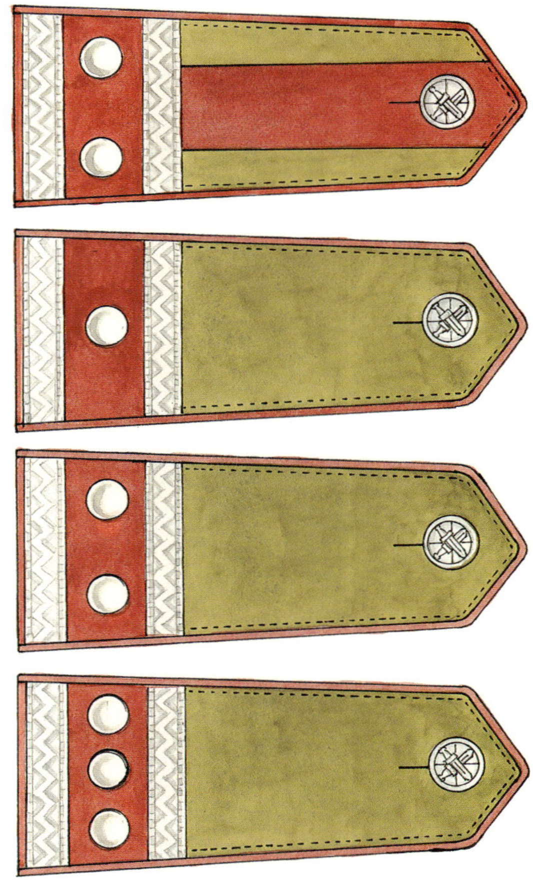

Shoulder boards: desátník aspirant délesloužící (aspirants were NCOs with at least a high-school diploma, who were slated for a school for reserve officers), svobodník aspirant, desátník aspirant, četař aspirant.

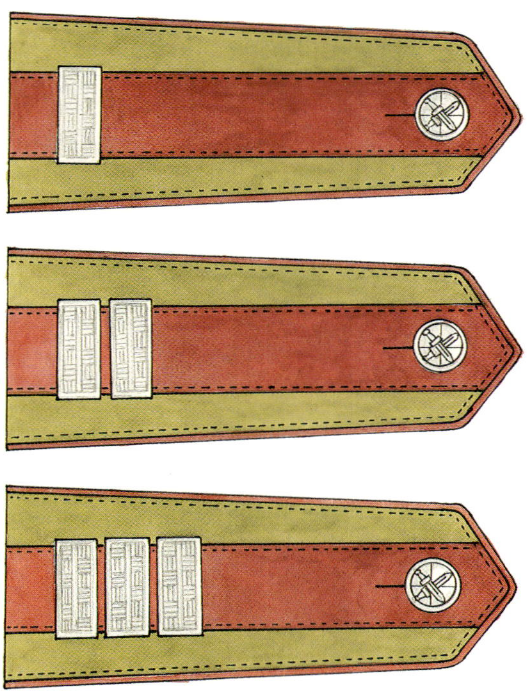

Shoulder boards: rotmistr, štábní rotmistr, praporčík (these senior NCOs were always professionals), bar insignia.

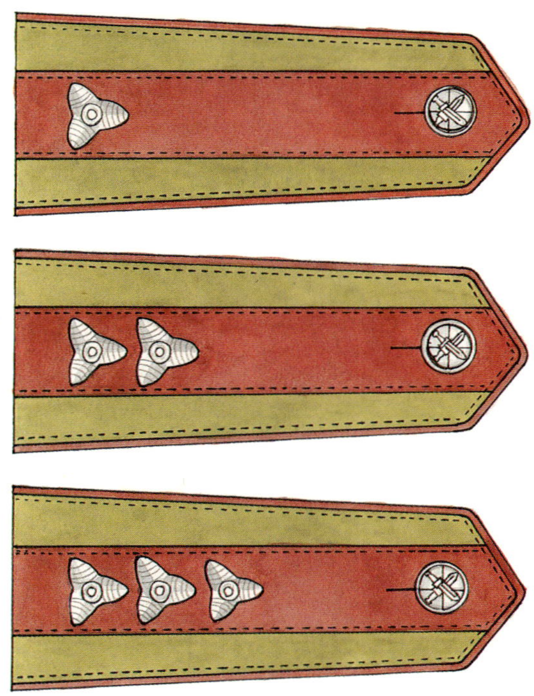

Shoulder boards: as above, but silver stars.

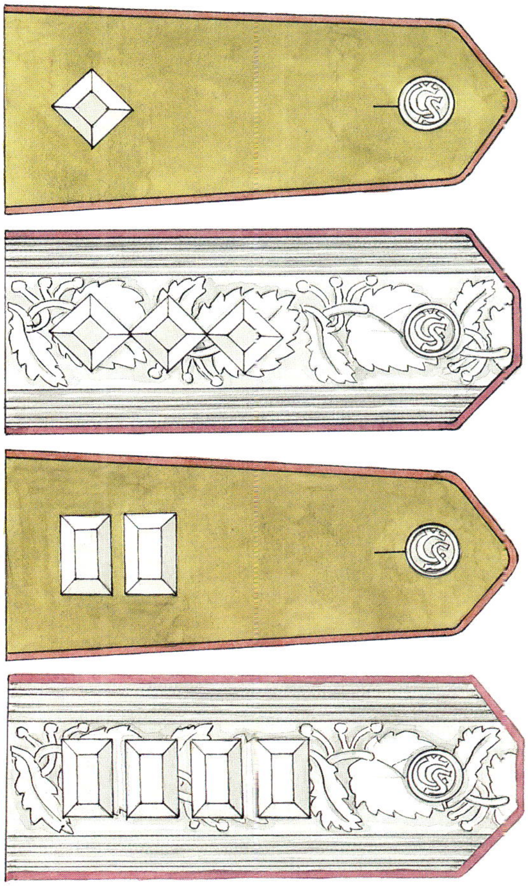

Old field and ceremonial officers' shoulder boards with bar and rectangle insignia. Note also the old style of buttons.

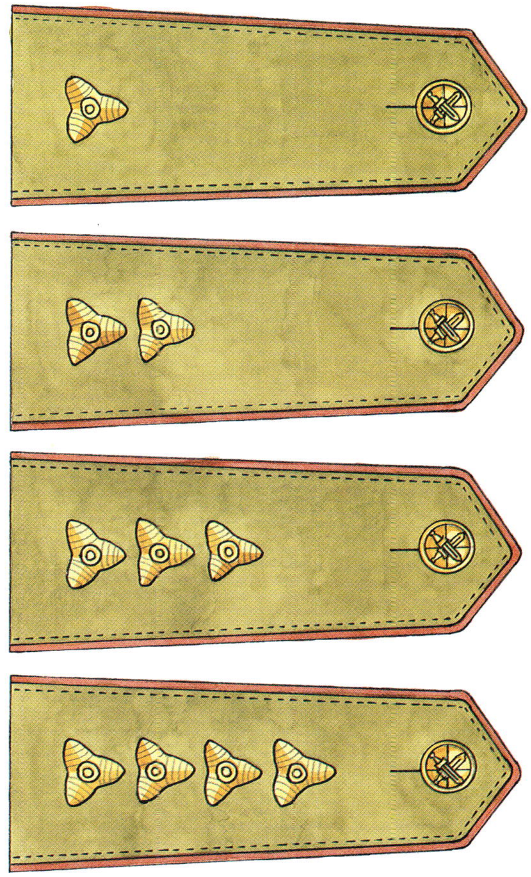

Officers' shoulder boards: podporučík, poručík, nadporučík, kapitán.

General's shoulder board.

Left: Officers' shoulder boards: štábní kapitán, major, podplukovník, plukovník.

Old Austro-Hungarian helmet vz.20.

French style helmet vz.28.

New Czechoslovak helmet vz.32.

Tanker's leather helmet.

9

WARTIME USE AND DEVELOPMENT

WEHRMACHT

Cars with German officers appeared in Milovice on the morning of March 15, 1939. The LT vz.35 tanks were prepared for transport to Germany during the following month. In all, the Wehrmacht confiscated 244 LT vz.35 tanks, which represented an important improvement in their tank strength. These tanks were roughly comparable to PzKpfw III tanks, of which type the German armored formations had 98 in September 1939. Thus, their number of available "mediums" more than tripled.

Though the Germans immediately accepted the LT vz.35, renamed as the PzKpfw 35(t), into their armored formations, they did not order their renewed production, as they viewed the pneumatic installation as too complicated. The Germans obtained the LT vz.35 tanks in various condition, from brand new vehicles from army depots and vehicles after warranty repairs up to veterans of the fights in the Sudeten and Eastern areas. Several tanks were sent to the tank testing center in Kummersdorf. Some of them were stored, but most of the tanks went to the 11th Panzer Regiment in Paderborn and the 65th Panzer Abteilung in Sennelagen.

The tanks were not specially adapted for the service with the Wehrmacht; they were painted over in German standard dark gray camouflage paint, and had an UKW Fu5 phonic radio set, an intercom, the Notek light and rear lights installed. The Scintilla magnetos were changed for Bosch ones, and holders for extra jerrycans were installed on the rear fender. Because the Wehrmacht added a fourth crew member, the loader, it was necessary to lower the ammunition supply. They also had to translate into German all the handbooks and directions for the crews. Some tanks were modified as Panzerbefehlswagen 35(t), or command tanks. Those of company headquarters carried both the Fu5 and Fu7 and two rod aerials, and also had the front machine gun eliminated. PzBefWg of battalion and regimental headquarters carried the Fu5 and Fu8 radios and large frame aerial. Those vehicles had the gun removed and replaced by a wooden replica, and retained only the turret machine gun. All PzBefWg had gyrocompasses installed.

The crews trained hard in the spring of 1939 with their new tanks to be combat ready for the planned Polish campaign. The rosters were filled gradually by vehicles coming from the former

LT vz.35 being delivered to the Wehrmacht. Note the Czech soldier in the turret, but German cars in the background.

Czech LT vz.35s ready for delivery in March 1939 to the Panzertruppe.

Czech crews with their LT vz.35 tanks for the last time - next crews will be German! March 26, 1939.

German officers on one of the LT vz.35 tanks in Milovice, March 1939.

Czechoslovak depots and from the factories following the warranty repairs. By the end of the summer both the 11th Panzer Regiment and the 65 Panzer Abteilung had their companies fully equipped, and additional tanks in reserve and with the staffs.

They both were a part of the 1st Leichte Division. For the Polish campaign (Fall Weiss) they together fielded 112 PzKpfw 35(t) and eight Panzerbefehlswagen 35(t), aside from 65 PzKpfw II and 41 PzKpfw IV. The Czech tanks formed only a small part of all the used German tanks, but more than a third of Germany's gun equipped tanks (PzKpfw III and IV). The Division was part of von Rundstedt's Army Group South and XIV Panzer Corps of the Tenth Army, commanded by General Hoepner.

The tanks covered more than 600 km on very bad roads with no major breakdowns, and participated in fierce fights at Wielun (September 3), Widawa, Radom and Demblin (September 9) and ended their Polish adventure between September 17 and 24 North of Warsaw at Mandlin.

They easily withstood artillery splinters, antitank rifles and 2 cm antitank gun fire. 3.7 cm antitank guns penetrated the 25 mm armor, and seven tanks were heavily damaged. Only one (manufacturer's number 50323) had to be scrapped, the other ten were easily repaired by Škoda.

Meanwhile, ČKD was busily manufacturing the new PzKpfw 38(t) for the Wehrmacht, delivering 78 by August 1939. Panzer Abteilung 67 of the 3rd Leichte Division obtained 57 of these tanks in time for the Polish campaign. The 3rd Division was also part of Army Group South and its Tenth Army's XV Panzer Corps. During this campaign, the Division lost seven of its PzKpfw 38(t), but all were repaired.

German soldiers on a captured LT vz.35 in the Vyškov, garrison of the 2. Armored Regiment.

Czech LT vz.35 tanks being loaded on flatbed cars for transport to Paderborn.

PzKpfw 35(t) of the 11th Panzer Regiment in Paderborn, already in Feldgrau (dark gray) camouflage.

Staff tanks of the 1st Unit of the 11th Panzer Regiment on march into Poland, September 1939. The 1. Leichte Division was one of the best armed of the German armored formations, because all of its tanks were armed with guns. The German-equipped divisions had a mixture of PzKpfw I, II, III and IV tanks, of which only the PzKpfw III had a comparable gun to the PzKpfw 35(t).

Five-tank companies of the 1. Leichte Division prior to the Polish campaign in 1939, marked with the characteristic white crosses.

Following the defeat of Poland, most of the Wehrmacht units returned to their peacetime garrisons. The 1st Leichte Division was renamed as the 6th Panzer Division. Its main force remained the 11th Panzer Regiment and the 65 Panzer Abteilung. The 3rd Leichte Division became the 8th Panzer Division. On top of its Panzer Abteilung 67 it obtained the newly formed 10th Panzer Regiment, both equipped with the PzKpfw 38(t)s. Another Panzer Division obtained these tanks in time for the French campaign; the 7th, (formerly the 2nd Leichte Division) with 25th Panzer Regiment and Panzer Abteilung 66.

For the French campaign in May 1940 (Fall Gelb), the PzKpfw 35(t) tanks were completely repaired by Škoda. They carried more spare track links and rubber tires for their running wheels, which wore out quickly. The 6th Panzer Division, in cooperation with the 8th Panzer Division penetrated the Ardennes, up to that time considered completely impassable for armored units. They were part of von Kleist's Panzer Army of the Army Group A, and specifi-

German crews training with their new PzKpfw 35(t).

Ausf.A of the 3rd Leichte Division with the white cross on the front of the turret.

Tanks of the 1st Unit marching past its standard in Poland.

One of the few PzKpfw 35(t) lost in Poland, hit by artillery fire.

cally of its XLI Panzer Corps. From June 5, the XLI Panzer Corps became part of Panzer Gruppe Guderian.

The divisions crossed the Meuse River already on May 13 and advanced westward to Montcornet. French counterattacks at Donchery and Stonne were unsuccessful. The German advance was slowed slightly by the French army on the Oise and Guise Rivers, but the French commanders of the Second and Ninth Armies decided to start their withdrawal on May 14. Simultaneously, General Guderian moved the direction of his attack more to the West. Thus, when his tanks renewed their attack, they found a gap almost fifty miles wide between the two French armies, and open terrain behind. By the evening of May 15, the German penetration was already 62 miles wide and steadily increasing in depth. French counterattacks by hastily summoned reserves were unsuccessful, and their 1st DCR (Division Cuirassée or armored division) was destroyed by Rommel's 7th Panzer Division when refueling near Flavion on May 15. Rommel's PzKpfw 38(t)s were able to defeat the much heavier Char B tanks by superior command and control methods and their mobility. The 2nd DCR was destroyed the same day by Reinhard's Panzers while moving to support the Ninth army between St. Quentin and Hirson.

Guderian's advance was so fast and so far-reaching that the OKW (Oberkommando der Wehrmacht, the headquarters of the German army) became alarmed that he may be cut off and ordered him to halt on May 17. After furious protests, he was allowed "reconnaissance in force" and finally on May 19 he was freed to move forward again. His corps, followed by the motorized infantry corps of the Kleist group, raced along the Somme toward Abbeville, which fell on May 20. The corridor to the sea was thus established and the BEF (British Expeditionary Force) was cut off from its base, Cherbourg, having to concentrate at Dunkirque.

Meanwhile to the North, Rommel's 7th Panzer Division spearheaded the advance of Hoth's corps and seized Cambrai. He was shortly halted to wait for the following infantry, but advanced the next day to Arras. There he was met by a British armor counterattack and his nose was bloodied, but not enough to stop his advance. Hoth moved up his other divisions and the British had to retreat to Arras on May 22.

From the Channel the 6th and 8th Panzer Divisions turned South again. On June 10 they started a new offensive by crossing the Aisne River at Rethal. Through Suippes, St. Dizier, Chaumont and Langres, the tanks advanced along the Marne River. Finally, they

A weary and very dusty crew of one of the PzKpfw 35(t) in Poland.

PzKpfw 35(t)s of the now 6. Panzer Division getting ready for rail transport.

A lone PzKpfw I leading a column of the 7th Panzer Division's PzKpfw 38(t)s in France in 1940.

turned East to the Meuse River and their last fight was the capture of the fortified town of Epinal, which surrendered on June 21. Four days later the Armistice was signed.

Both the 6th and the 8th Panzer Divisions advanced at an unbelievable pace and were able to penetrate and destroy all the French defensive lines and forces they had encountered with very low losses. The 6th Panzer Division had 62 of its tanks damaged, but only eleven were a total loss and had to be scrapped. Of the 229 PzKpfw 38(t)s participating in the 7th and 8th Panzer Divisions, 54 were damaged and six were subsequently scrapped.

The 7th Panzer Division, as a part of General Bock's Army Group, attacked on June 5 West of Paris. By June 9 the Panzers and General von Manstein's Corps had reached the Seine River. The armor was directed to the West to cut off the French IX Corps, which was slow to retreat from the Abeville area. General Rommel accepted their surrender on June 12 at St. Valery-en-Caux. The 7th Division ended its French campaign at Cherbourg on June 18 after

PzKpfw 35(t) tanks in their jump-off lager before the invasion of France. Note the Panzer Division pennant.

This PzKpfw 35(t) during winter 1939-1940 training carries the rhomboidal plate with call numbers, standard Balkenkreuz and the sign of the 6. Panzer Division, an inverted Y with two dots.

PzKpfw 35(t) during the French campaign carried already the standard Balkenkreuzen in white and lots of exterior stowage.

A company of PzKpfw 35(t) tanks of the 11. Panzer Regiment camouflaged in the woods near Mayen in April 1940.

A column of PzKpfw 35(t) tanks resting during a march.

Tanks of the 6th Panzer Division collecting French prisoners in Brunehamel.

PzKpfw 35(t) tanks advancing across open fields in France, summer 1940.

One of the PzKpfw 35(t) of the 6th Panzer Division after the break through the Weygand line south of Rethel. It carries extra jerry cans and other stores and a German flag over the engine deck for aerial recognition. Note how the aerial bends out of the way to allow full traverse of the gun.

The commander of the 1st Company of PzAbteilung 65 receiving orders to advance on Hauteville on the Oise. France, summer 1940.

PzKpfw 38(t) of the 8th Panzer Division on country maneuvers.

a spirited encounter with the British, who were evacuating their troops.

In 1941, the PzKpfw 38(t) took part in operation Marita, the attack on Greece through Yugoslavia, in the ranks of the 8th Panzer Division. This Division was part of the XLVI Panzer Corps of the 2nd Army of General von Weichs and attacked from Austria and Hungary in early April with 113 PzKpfw 38(t)s and 7 PzBefWg 38(t)s. They quickly overran Northern Yugoslavia because the Croatians welcomed them as liberators. The division got as far as Užice south of Sarajevo when the campaign ended in Greece's capitulation on April 27.

The division lost seven of its tanks during the campaign.

At the beginning of 1941, the PzKpfw 35(t)s were officially retired as first-line equipment, but the 6th Panzer Division used 155 PzKpfw 35(t)s and 5 PzBef 35(t)s for its part of the invasion of

One of the damaged PzKpfw 35(t) in France.

Two factory photographs showing the installation of a smoke generator on the rear wall of the PzKpfw 38(t).

One of the propaganda photographs of the PzKpfw 38(t) during a cross-country run, showing the crosses and the turret call number in red, outlined in white.

Two of the PzBefWg 38(t) with the large frame aerials. This version of the command tank had only the turret machine gun for armament.

the Soviet Union on June 22, 1941. Their tanks had racks fitted for an additional five jerrycans, and usually carried a host of spare parts, with masking nets and recovery equipment.

An additional fifty PzKpfw 35(t) tanks were stored and did not participate in the fighting. Another six of them were sent in December 1939 to the SS Totenkopf Division and were assigned to its reconnaissance group in place of SdKfz 222 armored cars. This division already participated in the French campaign, where it lost one of its PzKpfw 35(t). The Totenkopf Division was in the Russian campaign from the beginning, but it is not known if it used the remaining PzKpfw 35(t) tanks in any fighting.

Of the seventeen Panzer Divisions participating in the invasion of the Soviet Union, six were equipped with Czech tanks. Besides the 6th, 7th and 8th, the 12th, 19th and 20th Panzer Divisions had between them 660 PzKpfw 38(t)s. With the PzKpfw 35(t), this represented more than one quarter of the German tank strength.

The 6th Panzer Division first attacked from Tilsit on the Latvia border. It was, with the 8th Panzer Division, a part of General Hoepner's 4th Panzer Group. Its task was to advance through the Baltic republics toward Leningrad. Already on the second day the Division encountered the Soviet 2nd Tank Division, which had, besides light tanks, about 20 KV I and KV II tanks in its ranks.

Another well-known photograph of an Ausf.A PzKpfw 38(t) on the French Atlantic coast.

One of the knocked-out PzKpfw 38(t) in France.

The lightly damaged tanks were repaired in the field, but the more heavily hit had to be sent back to BMM. While awaiting repairs, this one was snowed-in in the factory collecting area.

An Ausf.E PzKpfw 38(t) of the 8th Panzer Division during the Balkan campaign in summer 1941.

When the 6th Panzer Division tried to cross the Dubisa River by Rasejnija village, it was subjected to fire from the 152 mm howitzers of the KV II tanks. The 3.7 cm guns of the PzKpfw 35(t) tanks were completely ineffective against the 75-110 mm armor of the Soviet tanks. Only the hastily fetched "eighty-eights" were able to destroy the unwieldy behemoths. The recalled 1st Panzer Division with its PzKpfw IIIs and IVs enveloped the flank of the Soviet division and thus sealed its fate. The first tank battle of the Eastern campaign ended.

After penetrating the Stalin line on the Dvina River, the 6th Panzer Division advanced and after fierce fighting at Ostrov, Strugi and the Luž River it finally reached the suburbs of Leningrad on August 20. The long siege started but the division was recalled South - to Moscow. It was transported by train through Pskov and Vitebsk and on October 2, as part of the 3rd Tank Army, started its attack toward Vjazma and Kalinin. From there, it wheeled South and some of its units reached Moscow's suburbs on December 5, 1941.

Tanks of the 6. Panzer Division before the invasion of the Soviet Union in the Memel area. Though these PzKpfw 35(t)s were not first-line equipment at this time, they still provided valuable service and went all the way to Moscow suburbs.

A victory parade of the PzAbteilung 65 in Bielefeld after capitulation of France in 1940.

A quiet moment at the beginning of the Russian campaign in 1941. Note the Notek light, firewood on the left fender and extra jerrycans on the engine deck.

Although the Škoda tanks encountered the new (and much more powerful) T-34 and KV-I tanks, they managed to keep their losses low, and only seven tanks had to be written off in the first four months of fighting. The demise of the PzKpfw 35(t) on the Eastern front in the end was not caused by its opponents, but by the weather. Heavy frosts during the winter of 1941-42 immobilized all the tanks, and the whole regiment had to be pulled from the front and re-armed. As the light tanks lost their luster in Russia, all Panzer Divisions were gradually equipped with medium tanks.

The remaining four Panzer Divisions using the PzKpfw 38(t) were all part of General Hoth's 3rd Panzer Group with XXXIX and LVII Panzer Corps. Bypassing Bialystok, Minsk and Smolensk, they took part in the encirclement battle at Vyasma. From there they advanced North-East to Rshev, Kalinin and Klin in the last desperate attempt to seize Moscow from the North at the beginning of December 1941. The 7th Panzer Division forced the Moscow-Volga canal at Dimitrov, but was repulsed by the fresh Siberian divisions. The Moscow offensive was officially abandoned on December 8, 1941. By that time, the divisions had between them 84 operational PzKpfw 38(t) tanks, with another 202 deemed repairable.

Both Czech tanks had proven their worth in these campaigns. They were well designed, rugged and dependable. Their armor and gun were excellent for a light tank, and it was not the fault of their designers that they were not able to combat more modern medium tanks with superior armor and armament. Though slightly cramped due to their small size, they were well liked by their crews, as their dependability and high speed often got them out of dangerous situations.

Though outgunned already in 1941, the basic PzKpfw 38(t) was manufactured till July 1942, when the production was switched to self-propelled guns and tank hunters. The tanks returning from the front were either refurbished and passed on to Germany's allies, or were converted to self-propelled guns.

The remaining PzKpfw 35(t)s, after being pulled from front-line service, were concentrated in the Vienna Arsenal, from where they were issued to various police and anti-partisan units. Two of the PzKpfw 38(t)s served also on most of the German armored trains. The Wehrmacht had 229 tanks of this type on its roster as late as May 1945. TABLE 10 lists the units and campaigns where both the PzKpfw 35(t) and PzKpfw 38(t) were used.

PzKpfw 35(t) in Russia in summer 1941. On the bad Russian roads, the tanks often had to act as recovery vehicles.

A 5 cm antitank gun PAK 38 with its tractor in the Northern sector of the Russian front, with an PzKpfw 35(t) in the background.

A fully loaded PzKpfw 35(t) in Russia in the summer of 1941. This shows clearly the amount of extra fuel and personal equipment the tanks carried on the long marches.

A PzKpfw 35(t) and an SdKfz 251 died together on this lonely Russian road near Leningrad in the fall of 1941.

The last winter of front-line service for the PzKpfw 35(t). Before Moscow, 1941.

A column of Ausf.B PzKpfw 38(t) tanks at the beginning of the Russian campaign in the summer of 1941. Note the copious exterior stowage, the unditching beam on the left fender and the unusual placement of the Abstand Rücklicht behind the muffler.

A different kind of smoke candles on the rear plate of this Ausf.B.

A nice detail shot of an Ausf.C PzKpfw 38(t), showing the front part of the turret and the driver's visors.

A ditched Ausf.D. Luckily it carries the unditching beam. When tied across both tracks, it would help the tank to climb out of situations like this.

TABLE 10
WEHRMACHT UNITS EQUIPPED WITH CZECH TANKS

Unit	Equipment
Fall Weiss (Poland 1939)	
1st Leichte Division Panzer Regiment 11	75 PzKpfw 35(t), 6 PzBef 35(t)
Panzer Abteilung 65	37 PzKpfw 35(t), 2 PzBef 35(t)
3rd Leichte Division Panzer Abteilung 67	55 PzKpfw 38(t), 2 PzBef 38(t)
Fall Gelb (France 1940)	
6th Panzer Division Panzer Regiment 11 + Pz.Abt.65	118 PzKpfw 35(t), 14 PzBef 35(t)
7th Panzer Division Panzer Regiment 25 + Pz.Abt.66	91 PzKpfw 38(t), 8 PzBef 38(t)
8th Panzer Division Panzer Regiment 10 + Pz.Abt.67	116 PzKpfw 38(t), 15 PzBef 38(t)
Weisung 25 (Yugoslavia 1940)	
8th Panzer Division Panzer Regiment 10	118 PzKpfw 38(t), 7 PzBef 38(t)
Unternehmen Barbarossa (Soviet Union 1941)	
6th Panzer Division Panzer Regiment 11 + Pz.Abt.65	155 PzKpfw 35(t), 5 PzBef 35(t)
7th Panzer Division Panzer Regiment 25	167 PzKpfw 38(t), 7 PzBef 38(t)
8th Panzer Division Panzer Regiment 10	118 PzKpfw 38(t), 7 PzBef 38(t)
12th Panzer Division Panzer Regiment 29	109 PzKpfw 38(t), 8 PzBef 38(t)
19th Panzer Division Panzer Regiment 27	110 PzKpfw 38(t), 11 PzBef 38(t)
20th Panzer Division Panzer Regiment 21	121 PzKpfw 38(t), 2 PzBef 38(t)
From February 1942:	
22nd Panzer Division	114 PzKpfw 38(t)

(All divisions also had PzKpfw II and PzKpfw IV on strength)

In 1942 the production of the PzKpfw 38(t) was switched from the basic tank to various tank hunters and self-propelled guns. These were not used en masse, like the tanks in the Panzer Divisions, but were assigned to tank hunting groups (PJA or Panzer Jäger Abteilung), which were independent army (Heeres) formations, or to tank hunting companies of various Panzer or infantry divisions.

The first such tank hunter was the Panzerjäger 38(t) für 7.62 cm PaK 36(r). It mounted the captured Soviet antitank gun in a simple superstructure. These vehicles were issued to the 5th (8), 6th (6), 7th (18), 8th (6), 15th (4), 19th (12) and 20th (18) Panzer Divisions; the SS division Das Reich got twelve, the 20th Panzegrenadier Division six and PJA 616 four. A large group of 33 vehicles was sent to North Africa and fought with the Afrika Korps there.

The next development was the 7.5 cm PaK 40/3 auf PzKpfw 38(t), which used the German antitank gun in an improved superstructure. The first series were made on the Ausführung H chassis, the later ones on Ausf.M with the engine moved forward and the

PzKpfw 38(t) Ausf.D of the 7th Panzer Division in Russia in 1941.

These PzKpfw 38(t)s are crossing the Drina River on a railway bridge in July 1941. They tow two-wheel trailers with extra gasoline drums to allow them to go long distances without depending on the divisional supply train.

Another PzKpfw 38(t) of the 7th Panzer Division driving into Minsk in July 1941. It similarly tows the gasoline trailer, and is equipped with smoke dischargers on its fenders.

Mud like this could not stop the Panzers, but surely slowed everything else. Summer 1941 offensive in Southern Russia.

fighting compartment to the rear of the vehicle. The bulk of these vehicles went to four PJAs, PJA 559 getting twenty, PJA 616 thirty six, PJA 731 seventy one and PJA 744 thirty eight. Other large recipients were some infantry division (34. ID - twelve, 349. ID - fourteen, 15. ID - twelve), Panzergrenadier Divisions (10. PzGr - twenty-five, 20. PzGr - thirty-one) and some Panzer Divisions (1st - forty-eight, 5th - eighteen, 8th - sixteen, 11th - eleven, 19th - fourteen). The SS Leibstandarte Adolf Hitler obtained twenty and the 1st Ski Jäger Division eighteen. Several other infantry and Panzer divisions were assigned platoon-size units, usually between three

Two PzKpfw 38(t)s with their supporting infantry getting ready for attack against the Red army positions, summer 1941.

PzKpfw 38(t) of the 22nd Panzer Division in Russia in early 1942. It has a welded container on the rear of its turret, a field modification.

and six vehicles. Both of these tank hunters were widely used mainly on the Eastern front, but later in France as well.

Another modification built in quantity was the self-propelled 15 cm howitzer. Under the designation 15 cm sIG 33(SfL) auf PzKpfw 38(t), it was again manufactured in two versions as Ausf.H and Ausf.M. These were assigned mostly to Panzer Divisions, both Wehrmacht and Waffen SS, and to some Panzergrenadier Divisions, usually twelve vehicles per division. The units that used them were the 1st, 2nd, 4th, 5th, 16th, 17th, 24th, 26th Panzer Divisions, the Waffen SS Divisions Liebstandarte Adolf Hitler, Totenkopf and Das Reich, and Hermann Göring Division. Besides the 3rd and 29th Panzergrenadier Divisions, Panzergrenadier Division "Grossdeutschland" had sixteen of these vehicles on its roster.

The other modifications were not concentrated in any units, except for the Flakpanzer 38(t) auf Selbstfahrlafette 38(t), of which the 9th SS Division got ten vehicles in 1944.

In April 1944, the Jagdpanzer 38, better known as the Hetzer, started coming off the production lines. These were planned to equip the Panzer Jäger companies of the infantry divisions. In May, the first twenty manufactured vehicles were delivered to various test-

A PzKpfw 38(t) following a column of PzKpfw IIIs during the attack on the Kertch peninsula in 1942. It again carries a lot of exterior stowage, including bundles of fire-wood. During the lightning advances the field kitchens could not always keep with the Panzers and the crews had to do their own cooking.

Captured PzKpfw 38(t)s being repaired by their Russian captors. The layout of the engine compartment is well visible.

A PzKpfw 38(t) that came to harm in Russia, summer 1941.

An unknown unit of PzKpfw 38(t) surrendering to Soviet soldiers.

An PzKpfw 38(t) being loaded into the Messerschmitt Me-323 Gigant transport plane.

Many of the PzKpfw 38(t) ended their carrier as parts of the armored trains, where there were used to support the trains infantry in counter-attacks. Even the Czechoslovak army used them in this capacity after the war up to 1954.

ing and school units. In July 1944 the first combat unit, Heeres Panzer Jäger Abteilung 731, was issued 45 Hetzers and was sent to Army Group North at the Eastern front. The second unit, PJA 743 got its 45 Hetzers late in July and was assigned to Army Group Center. Each of these two units had 14 Hetzers in each of their three companies and an additional three vehicles in the headquarters' section. One Jagdpanzer 38 in each company and two of the headquarters vehicles had the longer range Fu8 radios for command and control. PJA 731 was also issued four BergeHetzers for recovery of damaged vehicles.

Only three additional HPJA were issued the Hetzers: PJA 741 in September, PJA 561 in February 1945 and PJA 744 in March 1945, as the main purpose for the Jagdpanzer 38 was not to equip these independent units, but to provide each infantry division with its own mobile tank destroyer force. Thus most of the Hetzers were issued to organic Panzer Jäger companies of infantry, Jäger, Panzergrenadier, Kavallerie and Volksgrenadier divisions, 14 vehicles per division. From February 1945, in order to equip more units, only ten Hetzers were issued per division.

By the start of the Ardennes offensive, 18 Panzer Jäger companies plus the PJA 741 had been sent to the Western front with a total of 295 Hetzers. On December 30, 1944 sixty-seven percent of these vehicles were still operational, with only 38 written off as total losses. This was considered exceptional, especially under severe combat conditions and given the Allied supremacy in armor and its mastery of the skies.

The same results were obtained on the Eastern front, where in March 1945 51 Panzer Jäger companies reported 359 operational Hetzers out of 529 (68%), on April 10 there were 489 operational Hetzers out of 661 (74%). The same situation was on the Western front, where 79 out of 101 (79%) were operational, and in Italy, where 64 out of 76 (84%) were operational. These numbers testify both to the mechanical reliability and the excellent serviceability of the design.

Panzerjäger 38(t) für 7.62 cm PaK 36(r) SdKfz 139 was the long name for the first modification on the 38 chassis. This is one of the first prototypes with the sides of the gun cover taken all the way back. The production vehicles had only the short sides.

SdKfz 138 tank hunters on the BMM production line. A total of 275 vehicles were built new and another 336 were converted from PzKpfw 38(t)s.

SdKfz 138 Ausf.M tank hunters in France at the time of the Allied invasion in summer 1944.

The Hetzer was well liked by its crews and trusted by the infantry it supported. It proved to be an excellent tank destroyer and infantry support vehicle, with good armament and armor. Its mechanical reliability allowed it to perform long marches. These were necessary, as the armored units were constantly moved along the front to cover enemy penetrations.

The Hetzer also had its shortcomings. The gun was situated on the right side of the compartment, though it was designed for right-side loading. The commander sat directly behind the gun, so that at the time of firing his view was obscured by the flame and smoke of the discharge. The remotely controlled machine gun was very effective in close combat, but to change the ammunition drum, the loader had to swing it to the side and open its hatch and expose himself to enemy fire. The flame damper on the exhaust proved also to be unsuitable as it increased the engine noise. While the front armor was well sloped and of sufficient thickness (60 mm), the side armor was only 20 mm and was very vulnerable. Thus, the Hetzer could not show its sides to the enemy.

The complete issue of the Jagdpanzer 38 to units is summarized in TABLE 11.

TABLE 11
Issue of Jagdpanzer 38(t) to Units

DATE	NUMBER	UNIT(S)	FRONT
July 1944	45	H.PJA 731	East
	45	H.PJA 743	East
Aug.1944	14	each to 15., 20.SS, 76. and 335 Inf.Div.	East
	14	each to 79. and 257. Inf.Div.	West
	29	8.SS Kav.Div.	East
	14	97. Jg.Div.	East
Sep.1944	14	each to 306. and 376.Inf.Div.	East
	14	each to 183., 246. and 363.Volks Gren.Div.	West
	14	1.Kp./H.PJA 741	East
	31	H.PJA 741	West
	10	16.SS Pz.Gren.Div.	S.West
Oct.1944	14	each to 15.SS, 181. and 304.Inf.Div.	East
	14	349. Volks Gren.Div.	East
	14	each to 18., 272., 277. and 708.Volks Gren.Div.	West
	21	22.SS Kav.Div.	East
	14	each to 44. Gren.Div. and 4. Gebirgs.Div.	East
Nov.1944	14	each to 344. and 19.SS Inf.Div,	East
	14	337.Volks Gren.Div.	East
	14	each to 243., 346., 711. and 716. Inf.Div.	West
	14	each to 9., 26., 47., 62., 167., 326., 340. and 352 Volks Gren.Div.	West
	14	each to Pz.Jäg.Kp. Bock, Lang and Pankow	West
	10	replacements for H.PJA 731	East
	12	replacements for H.PJA 741	West
Dec.1944	14	each for 31.SS and 68.Inf.Div.	East
	14	245.Inf.Div.	West
	7	94.Inf.Div.	S.West
	14	each to 16. and 79. Volks Gren.Div.	West
	14	each to 252., 271. and 320. Volks Gren.Div.	East
	4	each to 128. and 246. Volks Gren.Div.	West
	4	44. Gren.Div.	East
	25	16.SS Pz.Gren.Div.	S.West
	14	Personal Einheit 2a	East
	14	Personal Einheit 33a	West
	55	replacements, various units	East
	50	Hungary	East
	20	rebuilt as Flamm-Panzer	West
Jan.1945	14	each to 14.SS, 21., 73., 83.,129., 203., 211., 271., 359. and 384. Inf.Div.	East
	14	each to 65., 278. and 334. Inf.Div.	S.West
	14	257. Inf.Div.	West

DATE	NUMBER	UNIT(S)	FRONT
	10	181. Inf.Div.	S.East
	4	716. Inf.Div.	West
	14	each to 542., 547. and 551. Volks Gren.Div.	East
	4	16.SS Pz.Gren.Div.	S.West
	14	Personal Einheit 7c	West
	10	replacements, various units	West
	26	replacements, various units	East
	14	Pz.Jg.Kp.z.b.V. Pz.AOK1East	East
	14	each of 2.and 3.Kp./PJA 510	East
	25	Hungary	East
Feb.1945	10	each to 20.SS, 275. and 600. Inf.Div.	East
	14	each to 356.Inf.Div. and SS Pz.Kp. Sarow	East
	10	Polizei Brigade Wirth	East
	14	9. Fallschirm Jg.Div.	East
	10	Begleit Kp. Reichsführer SS	West
	14	each to Personal Einheit 6a, 6b, 9a, 9b, 13a and 43b	East
	20	H.PJA 561	East
	31	H.PJA 743	East
	21	each to PJA Jüteborg and Schlesien	East
	8	replacements, various units	East
March 1945	10	each to 17., 71., 106., 169., 251., 281., 304., 305. and 362. Inf.Div.	East
	10	163. Inf.Div.	Danemark
	10	each to 189, and 716. Volks Gren.Div.,	West
	10	each to 6. and 553. Volks Gren.Div.	East
	10	1. Gebirgs.Div.	S.East
	6	31.SS Inf.Div.	East
	10	Begleit Btl. Reichsführer SS	West
	102	replacements, various units	West
	60	replacements, various units	East
	10	each to Personal Einheit Milowitz F and G	East
	21	Pz.Gren.Div. Feldherrnhalle	East
	20	Pz.Div. Feldherrnhalle	East
	31	each to H.PJA 744 and StuG Brig.236	East
Apr.1945	10	85. Inf.Div.	West
	10	715. Inf.Div.	East
	4	212. Inf.Div.	West
	10	38.SS Niebelungen	West
	20	replacements, various units	East
	10	each to Inf.Div. Scharnhorst and Ullr.chv.Hutten	West
	21	PJA 3	West
	10	each to Jagd Pz.Kp. 1235, 1245 and 1257	West
	10	each to R.A.D. Div. z.b.V. 1, 2 and 3	West
	10	each to 1. and 2. Marine Div.	West
		1,466 vehicles issued to units on the Eastern front	
		896 vehicles issued to units on the Western front	
	TOTAL	2,362	

Germany's Allies

A Slovak LT vz.35 with Slovak army soldiers and its crew in Poland in 1939. The Slovak state was the first of Germany's allies to join the Wehrmacht in military operations.

Slovak LT vz.35s undergoing field repairs. The three-tone camouflage is well visible, as are the white call numbers used during the invasion of the Soviet Union. The tank on the right carries the number 099.

SLOVAKIA

On March 15, 1939 the new Slovak Army inherited a total of 52 LT vz.35 tanks of the 3rd Mobile Division in Turčianský sv.Martin. Nine tanks of its original roster were undergoing warranty repairs at Škoda, and after March 15 were confiscated by the Germans, but the Slovaks inherited another nine tanks from the 2nd Armored Regiment after it retreated from Transcarpathian Ruthenia into Slovakia. Three of these tanks were pressed into service against the Honvéd units in March 1939, but never participated in the fighting due to the armistice. For the Polish campaign, the Slovaks had a company with 13 tanks (cover name Havran) in readiness as a part of their Army Group "Bernolák", but did not use any due to the light resistance of the Poles.

All the Slovak LT vz.35s were repaired by mechanics sent by Škoda in the autumn of 1939. The Slovak Army wanted to buy more tanks of this type, but Škoda had already closed down the production lines and was not able to restart them, due to its German commitments.

At the time of the attack on the Soviet Union in the summer of 1941, the Slovak Army had two companies of LT vz.35s with its Mobile Group (later Mobile Brigade), a total of 30 tanks. Another fifteen tanks were in the tank company assigned to the Slovak Army Corps.

The Slovak anti-fascist officers were striving to conserve as many tanks as possible for the planned uprising against their own fascist government, and thus the tanks of these units suffered many "defects", which required their return to the home garrison.

Nevertheless, the LT vz.35s took part in the heaviest fighting the Mobile Brigade went through at Lipovec and gave a good account of themselves, though three tanks (13838, 13846 and 13857) were destroyed and subsequently scrapped.

Two Slovak LT vz.35s in Poland. Though taking part in the invasion, they were not used due to weak Polish resistance in the Slovak sector.

A Slovak LT vz.35 in faded three-tone camouflage, ex-Czechoslovak registration number plate in the rear and the white call number on the turret. July 1941, Vinnica in Western Ukraine.

This LT vz.35 fell off the bridge is being retrieved by another. Note the removed machine guns and the broken-off cupola's hatch.

Another of the destroyed LT vz.35 at Lipovec. Standing on the tank is Major Dobrotka, the commander of the Armored Regiment.

After all the tank units were returned to Slovakia at the end of 1941, the LT vz.35s were not deemed suitable for first-line front service any longer and were used for training only. This did not prevent them from participating in the Slovak National Uprising in August 1944, when quite a few of them fought bravely against the German units, either as free moving tanks, or as parts of the armored trains or dug-in fortifications. Most of these tanks were lost to German antitank fire. The Germans removed the captured vehicles from the Slovak soil and their further fate is unknown.

Slovakia started ordering the LT-38 tanks from ČKD in early 1940. The first order for ten vehicles was increased by another 20 in August 1940 and an additional seven at the beginning of 1941. In August 1940, Slovakia also bought from ČKD their LTL vehicles, built for Latvia but never delivered. These were upgunned by the Škoda 3.7 cm A7 gun and were named LT-40 in Slovak service.

Both these tanks were used by the Mobile Group during the invasion of the Soviet Union. Ten LT-38s and seven LT-40s participated. One LT-38 was lost during the fighting against the bun-

Slovak LT-38 tanks in front of their garages in Turčianský Sv. Martin, the home of the Armored Regiment. The Slovak army used four-men crews for these tanks like the Germans.

One of the LT vz.35, destroyed by the Red Army during the battle for Lipovec. The Slovak Mobile Brigade lost three LT vz.35s and had several others damaged.

LT vz.35 tanks fording a river in Russia in summer 1941. In the foreground is the LT-40, with only machine gun armament.

One of the Slovak LT-38 tanks supplied by BMM (V-3053) during 1940-1942, direct delivery from Prague, third lot. It carries the tricolor shield on the turret, introduced in 1942.

Slovak LT-38s during training in Slovakia.

A Slovak LT-38 with its crew in working overalls.

kers at Sanok (V-3006), the rest of the tanks were assigned to the Mobile Brigade and fought with it during the battle for Lipovec. There an additional LT-38 (V-3000) and one LT-40 (V-3037) were destroyed and several others were damaged. Following this battle, all the tanks returned to Slovakia.

The Security Division, fighting partisans in the Ukraine, was assigned a company of seven LT-40s in August 1942. These tanks returned back to Slovakia in April 1943 and were replaced by a company of five LT-38s. None of these vehicles participated in any fighting and were used mostly for guarding the divisional headquarters.

Another company with six LT-38s and six LT-40s was sent to the Mobile Division in the Caucasus in October 1942. It arrived safely, but during the Soviet offensive in the spring of 1943 and the subsequent retreat to the Crimea, all the tanks but one (V-3015) were lost and abandoned.

The Slovak army ordered 58 of the LT-38 tanks from the German depots in June 1943. Only 37 tanks were delivered in batches,

Slovak LT-38 during the uprising in 1944, near Telgart.

Slovak tank crews with one of theirs LT-38 during winter exercise in Slovakia.

One of the Slovak LT-38 during winter maneuvers.

A Slovak LT-38 Ausf.E, destroyed during the Slovak uprising in autumn 1944. The insurgents had about twenty of their LT-38s available and used them until there were destroyed by the Germans.

the last delivery being in July 1943. They were of mixed Ausführungs (A-H). These tanks never participated in any action until the Slovak National Uprising in August 1944. In early 1944, 20 Marder III, Ausführung H were also ordered from BMM, but only 18 were delivered. Some of these vehicles were confiscated by the Germans during the disarming of the two Slovak divisions of the Eastern Army in August 1944, some fought and were destroyed during the uprising.

ROMANIA

Romania was Czechoslovakia's ally before the war in the so called "Little Entente (Alliance)". It was a good customer for various Czechoslovak armaments. Thus it was only natural that it turned to Škoda when it needed tanks for its armored units in August 1936. The Romanians ordered 126 tanks, which for that time was a sizable order.

The Romanians wanted to see a prototype in three months, and in the summer of 1937 asked for an immediate delivery of fifteen vehicles. Škoda had to borrow tanks from the lots made for the Czechoslovak Army, but because these were still suffering various problems, the Romanians began having second thoughts.

The prototype was finally approved in August 1938, and Škoda manufactured the R-2 designated tanks between September 1, 1938 and February 22, 1939. The original fifteen vehicles were upgraded to the prototype standard.

Škoda tried to sell a manufacturing license for this tank to the Romanians, but was not successful, though it had shown its improved S-II-aR prototype in the fall of 1939 in Romania.

Romania took part in the invasion of the Soviet Union and used all of its armored formations in the fighting. The R-1 tankettes were allocated to the Cavalry Divisions and Brigades as reconnaissance vehicles. The only lightly motorized 1st, 7th and 9th Cavalry

One of the Romanian R-2 tanks during the fighting in Bessarabia in the fall of 1941. It shows the small Romanian cross on the hull and the large one on the open engine hatch, and the call number on the turret. The Romanian 1st Armored Division had 108 tanks in 1942, 98 of those the R-2s

The Romanian PzKpfw 38(t)s during the advance to the Kuban front in August 1943. The Romanians obtained fifty of these tanks from the Germans in order to bolster their armored formations, depleted during the fighting in 1942.

Romanian army during the evacuation of Crimea in 1944 with their remaining PzKpfw 38(t)s.

The R-2 tanks of the Romanian 1st Armored Regiment of the 1st Armored division on parade in Tirgoviste before the attack on the Soviet Union in 1941.

Divisions had four each in their reconnaissance squadrons, the motorized 5th, 6th and 8th Cavalry Brigades had six each.

The latter three units took part in liberating the Northern Bucovina as part of the Romanian 3rd Army against the Soviet 12th Army. In cooperation with the German 11th Army, the Romanians crossed the River Dniester between July 17-19, 1941 and breached the heavily fortified Stalin line. On July 19, both the 3rd and the 11th Armies were made part of the Army Group South.

General Racovita's Cavalry Corps joined the German XI Corps, and once the Stalin line was breached, formed the Korne Mechanized Detachment to exploit the opportunity. The detachment consisted of the 6th Mechanized Infantry Regiment, 2nd, 3rd and 5th Mechanized Squadrons with 18 R-1 tankettes, a mechanized pioneer platoon and a section of truck-borne 7.5 cm mountain guns. Korne's unit joined with the Lindemann armored detachment. Colonel Korne distinguished himself in the following battles to such an extent that even Hitler himself mentioned his activities.

The 3rd Army fought between German 11th and 17th Armies. It cleared the Uman pocket in late July, destroying the Soviet 12th Army, and proceeded to Krivoi Rog. On September 19, it crossed the River Dnieper at Berislav and at a personal request of General von Manstein, a new commander of the 11th Army, took defensive positions in the Nogai Steppe.

Men of one of the Romanian Cavalry brigade with their R-1 tankette, mustered in their home garrison in 1940.

On September 26, the Soviet 9th and 18th Armies attacked the 3rd Army with twelve rifle divisions. The situation became quite critical both for the lightly equipped Romanians and for the German formations. The Cavalry Corps was attacked between September 26 and October 3 by at least four Soviet rifle divisions with tank, artillery and aerial support, but held. The front of the 5th Cavalry Brigade at Akimovka was breached on September 26, but Colonel Korne counterattacked with his 2nd Mechanized Squadron and 6th Mechanized Rosiori and closed the breach.

The situation stabilized only after the arrival of the SS 1st Motorized Division in early October. During this battle the Cavalry Corps lost 32% of its strength and all of its R-1 tankettes. Most of these were recovered and repaired, and in the summer of 1942 the Cavalry divisions still had 29 of them. The 5th, 6th and 9th Cavalry Divisions formed General Racovita's Cavalry Corps, which fought as part of the Romanian 3rd Army, commanded by General Dumitrescu, during the conquest of Crimea and the advance into the Caucacus between August and October 1942. The end of the R-1 tankettes came during the Soviet offensive in November 1942, which fell most heavily on the front held by the Romanian army. The Cavalry divisions had to destroy their remaining tankettes, due to the lack of fuel. Nevertheless, eleven of these brave little vehicles survived to the end of the war and took part in the liberation of Czechoslovakia in April 1945.

The mainstay of the Romanian armored formations were the R-2 tanks, which were formed into the 1st Armored Regiment, stationed at Tirgoviste. The 2nd Armored Regiment had 75 Renault R-35 tanks. Both regiments were joined to form the 1st Armored Division. The division was not fully formed by 1941, and was split up before the invasion of the Soviet Union, because the slow and underpowered R-35 tanks could not keep pace with the fast Škoda R-2s.

For the liberation of Northern Bukovina, the Romanian 3rd Army was assigned the 1st Armored Division, but without its 2nd

The Romanian R-2 tanks crossing the River Prut on July 3, 1941 in preparation for the liberation of Bessarabia.

Regiment, which was assigned to the 4th Army's III Corps. They were part of the Army Group Antonescu, formed for this operation, and comprising also the German 11th Army.

The 1st Armored Division crossed the River Prut on July 3, 1941 and thrust toward Mogilev on the River Dniester. The retreating Soviets, supported by elements of the 2nd Mechanized Corps, made a stand at Brinzeni, where the first tank versus tank engagement took place. The Romanians destroyed two T-28 tanks for the loss of one of their R-2s. Due to fierce Soviet resistance in the southern sector, the 1st Armored Division was turned south and used to envelop the Soviet defenses at the Cornesti Massif from the North.

This the division achieved on July 14, with a loss of only two R-2s. Repulsing the Soviet counterattack the next day, the division on the 16th took Chisinau, where it lost one R-2 destroyed and five damaged. It wiped out the Soviet rearguard and chased its remnants over the Dniester on July 19, loosing another 3 R-2s while overrunning the Soviet artillery positions.

With the liberation of Besarabia complete, the Army Group Antonescu was dissolved. The 4th Army was reorganized for the invasion of Soviet Union proper, and on August 3 started crossing the River Dniester. The 1st Armored Division crossed on August 5 and was subordinated to V Corps. Its objective was to sweep behind Odessa and cut it off from the main Soviet forces. The drive from Bujalik to the coast took from August 11 to August 14, and was very costly. The opposing Soviet troops were of high quality, and the Romanian infantry was not trained for cooperation with and protection of its tanks. The division lost five tanks on the 11th, eight on the 12th, nine on the 13th and 25 on the 14th!

The 1st Armored Regiment was now shifted west to support III Corps. It attacked on August 18 and broke through the Soviet line at Karpovo, but its supporting infantry was not able to follow the tanks, which were caught in the open. Soviet antitank guns destroyed eleven tanks and damaged twenty four.

On August 20, the 1st Armored Regiment had only twenty R-2s left, while 46 were sent back for repairs. The 1st Armored Division supported the I Corps, but due to the weakened state of the division, it could not be shifted to the 3rd Army, as requested by the Germans.

The 2nd Armored Regiment lost half its R-35 to mechanical breakdowns, but found that the heavily armored Renaults were well suited to support infantry attacks. They were used to support the attacks of the I Corps on the western flank.

Following the Soviet army evacuation of Odessa by October 16, the damaged and destroyed tanks were shipped back to Romania for repairs. In June-July 1942, the Romanians obtained additional 26 PzKpfw 35(t) from the Germans to replace battle losses.

The fully refurbished and retrained 1st Armored Division with 109 R-2 tanks arrived at Stalino on August 29, 1942 under the command of General Gherghe. It was to act as a mobile reserve of the Romanian 3rd Army, which was guarding the left flank of the German 6th Army at Stalingrad.

During the training, the R-2s were firing against several captured T-34 tanks. The crews have found to their dismay that the 3.7 cm gun has no effect on the T-34's armor. The test had also persuaded the Germans that the division needed new equipment. The division got on October 17 eleven PzKpfw IVGs and eleven PzKpfw IIINs to form medium tank companies in each R-2 battalion.

The Soviet counteroffensive started on November 19, 1942. The Romanian infantry lines were punctured in several places by the sheer weight of tanks and attacking infantry, despite their stubborn resistance. Army Group B ordered its armored reserve, the XLVIII Panzer Corps, to counterattack with its 22nd and 14th Panzer Divisions and the Romanian 1st Armored Division. The counterattack was disorganized from the start, as the 22nd Panzer Division was redirected from the original attack axis. Moreover, the headquarters of the 1st Armored Division was attacked during the night by a spearhead of the Soviet 26th Tank Corps. The attack was beaten back, but during it the German liaison detachment's radio was destroyed and the division thus for two days lost contact with the XLVIII Panzer Corps. The 14th Panzer Division was too weak to mount a counterattack by itself.

On November 20, the 1st Armored Division counterattacked with the reserves of the 5th Infantry Division and was soon en-

A Romanian crewman with its R-2 tank on the River Don in November 1942, shortly before the beginning of the Soviet counter-offensive.

One of the few remaining R-2 tanks of the Romanian 1st Armored Division, following the Soviet breakthrough in November 1942 and encirclement of the German 6th Army in Stalingrad.

TACAM R-2 from a different view. The vehicles had the opening for the hull machine gun covered with a circular plate.

gaged in heavy fighting between Sredne-Zarinski and Zhirkovski with the Soviet 19th and 216th Tank Brigades with their supporting infantry and a 7.62 cm antitank regiment. The division lost 25 tanks, 19 of these the R-2s.

The division tied down the Soviets, but failed to join with the 22nd Panzer Division, and the Soviet 157th Tank Brigade with supporting mechanized infantry penetrated the resulting gap and captured Perelazovskie with V Corps headquarters and the rear echelons of the 1st Armored Division.

The 1st Armored Division lost additional 20 tanks during the heavy fighting the following day. The situation was deteriorating fast, as the Soviet motorized formations were dividing and bypassing the weakened Romanians. General Dumitrescu wanted to retreat and save what remained from his army, but was ordered to hold by the Germans.

The Romanian self-propelled gun TACAM R-2, build on the chassis of their R-2 tanks. It carried the Soviet ZIS-3 7.62 cm 1941 L/46 antitank gun in a partially open superstructure. Twenty R-2s were thus modified and the Romanians used them up to the end of the war.

The 1st Armored Division tried to break through to the 22nd Panzer Division on November 22, and fought the Soviet 8th Tank Brigade, loosing ten more tanks. It also lost the greater part of its antitank units and fuel trucks. Following the collapse of the overtaxed Romanian infantry divisions at Golovski, the 1st Armored Division tried to break through to its depots at Cernishevskaia. At this time, it was already down to 50% of its original strength and very low on fuel. The Soviets blocked its way and the division was forced to leave 21 R-2s behind, due to lack of fuel. The division finally was able to regroup at Oserski with eleven PzKpfw IIIs and IVs and nineteen R-2s.

The division got some fuel during the night of November 23/24, and more was airlifted the following day. The division was ordered to attack to help the 22nd Panzer Division to break its encirclement, but was too weak to penetrate the Soviet front and was itself heavily attacked. The situation was saved by German Stukas and the division was able to retreat behind the River Chir.

The division participated in further heavy fighting and by December 2 had only three serviceable tanks and 944 men. It lost over 5,000 men, 129 tanks and 457 trucks. It was reinforced by several hastily repaired tanks and took part in the final defensive battles, which led to the total destruction of the 3rd Romanian Army by the end of the year. The 1st Armored Division departed from the operational zone by January 1, 1943. Its survivors reached their base in Romania by March 31, 1943. The division lost 81 R-2s (30 abandoned due to lack of fuel, 24 due to mechanical failure and only 27 destroyed by the enemy), ten PzKpfw IIIs and ten PzKpfw IVs.

During the subsequent rearmament, the Romanians obtained PzKpfw IV and fifty PzKpfw 38(t) tanks from Germany, and the Škoda tanks were relegated to the reserves. As there were about forty of them left, the army headquarters decided to rebuild them into tank hunters. The Leonida company modified between July and September 1943 one R-2 tank by removing its turret and mounting the Soviet ZIS-3 7.62 cm M1936 antitank gun in an open, lightly armored superstructure, constructed from armor plates taken from

Two of the eleven remaining R-1 tankettes with the Regimentul 2 blindat (2nd Armored Regiment), fighting alongside the Soviet army during the liberation of Czechoslovakia and Eastern Austria in March 1945. The vehicles are crossing the River Váh in early April 1945, in support of the Soviet 141st Rifle division, closing on Slovakia's capital, Bratislava. The vehicles carry the blue-yellow-red roundel of the new Romanian army.

captured BT-7 and T-26 Soviet tanks. The gun was modified for Romanian ammunition and Septilici antitank and German panoramic sights were fitted. The resulting tank hunter was called TACAM R-2 (Tun Anticar cu Afet Mobil, or self-propelled antitank gun; TACAM was a generic name of all Romanian tank-hunters).

After performance and firing tests performed at the Suditi proving grounds during late 1943, the Mechanized Troops Command gave its clearance for further conversion to be carried out by Leonida company. The work was delayed until late February 1944, because the German replacements for the R-2 tanks were slow in coming. By this time, the M1936 gun was replaced by the more modern M1941 L/46 gun. By June 1944, twenty vehicles were modified, but then the conversions were stopped, as the 7.62 cm gun was found ineffective against the Soviet heavy IS tanks. Its replacement by the German 8.8 cm gun was planned, but due to the Romanian switching sides on August 23, 1944, it never took place.

The TACAM R-2s were organized into the 63rd Tacam Company, and were used during the liberation of Bucurest, Ploesti and Northern Transylvania. Ten of them were lost. The remainder was issued in November 1944 to the 2nd Armored Regiment, which used them during the liberation of Austria and Moravia in 1945.

Two more conversions were planned on Czech chassis. In November 1943 the fourteen surviving R-1 tankettes were to be armed with the Soviet 4.5 cm antitank gun and used for security duties under the name TACAM R-1. The plan was canceled before any conversions were performed.

TACAM T-38 were meant to use the Soviet 7.62 cm antitank guns on the chassis of PzKpfw 38(t), similarly to the German SdKfz 139 tank hunter. The conversions were never begun for the same reason the TACAM R-2 program was stopped - the inadequacy of the gun.

The last project, using partially Czech chassis components, was the tank destroyer MARESAL. Begun in 1942 on a captured Soviet T-60 chassis, it developed by 1943 to a very modern tank hunter, strongly similar to the Jagdpanzer 38(t). It used the T-38 chassis, Hotchkiss engine and gearbox and the new Resita M1943 7.5 cm antitank gun. The vehicle had armor between 10 and 20 mm only, but was very fast and its testing proceeded well.

The Romanian army ordered 1,000 vehicles, based on the performance of the M-05 prototype, and planned to form 32 antitank battalions, each with 32 vehicles. As the program had Hitler's support, Rogifer company was able to start production in March 1944, but it was heavily disrupted by Allied bombing raids and damage to the railways. The first series was supposed to be finished in November 1944, but due to the Romanian switchover, it was further delayed. The whole program was stopped on October 26 by the Soviets, who took all the plans, photographs, prototypes and produced parts.

BULGARIA

The next user of the Czech tanks was Bulgaria. Because it fought during the first world war on the side of Germany, its army was constrained by the peace treaty limitations. The Bulgarians contacted Škoda already in 1928. They were interested in PA-II armored cars, but due to the treaty limitations, Škoda replied negatively.

The next contacts occurred in 1936, when Bulgaria approached ČKD through intermediaries of Czech origin. These were similarly unsuccessful, and the Bulgarians returned to Škoda in February 1939. This time Škoda was willing to supply both tanks and tankettes, but the German occupation stopped any possible deals.

Finally, the Bulgarian Army obtained its LT vz.35 tanks from Germany. In August 1939, a Bulgarian delegation visited the 11th Panzer Regiment in Paderborn, where it was shown the tanks, complete with a technical presentation by Škoda experts. The tanks made a very good impression and the Bulgarians bought 26 of them on the spot. The tanks were shipped to Pilsen, where Škoda was supposed to bring them to a "like new" status. Because it had its hand full with repairs for the Wehrmacht, the Bulgarians obtained their "new" tanks only between February and April 1940 under the designation T-11.

All of the twenty six Škoda LT vz.35 tanks of the Bulgarian army on parade in Sofia in May 1940. The Bulgarians got another ten T-11 tanks, built originally for Afghanistan with the newer A8 gun, by the end of 1940.

One of the LT vz.35 tanks of the Bulgarian army during trials.

One of the T-11 tanks during the ceremonial transfer of the unit flag.

Both the LT vz.35 and T-11 tanks during a review. They are easily discernible by their guns: the LT vz.35 had the conspicuous recoil cylinder above the gun, while the T-11's A8 gun had it repositioned inside the turret. The first three tanks on the right are the T-11s, the rest the LT vz.35.

Škoda supplied another ten T-11 tanks in 1940. These were the tanks manufactured originally for Afghanistan, but the Germans confiscated them and subsequently freed them for the Bulgarians. All ten vehicles were shipped between October 1940 and January 1941.

The Bulgarian army formed two tank companies, and because its experience with the new tanks was very favorable, ordered additional 45 tanks from Škoda in January 1941. Though Škoda asked for permission to fill this order, the Germans declined and sold to the Bulgarians surplus Renault R-35 tanks, of which they had hundreds in their depots. Both Škoda and the Bulgarians protested, but without success. In May 1943, the Bulgarian army obtained ten PzKpfw 38(t)s from German depots.

The Bulgarians eventually used their T-11s against the Germans in 1944-45 during the fighting in the Yugoslav mountains, where the light and highly mobile tanks were very successful. Their combat losses were low, but most were immobilized by a lack of spare parts.

A couple of T-11 tanks of the Bulgarian army lined up for field exercises. Note the Russian-style of the officers' uniforms and the German helmet.

A T-11 tank during the field exercises. Note the two types of uniforms: the cotton "working" uniform and the "proper" uniform with high boots and cavalry breeches. All crew members wear leather helmets with side flaps, similar to the Italian type. In the background is a PzKpfw 38(t).

Honvéd officers inspecting a freshly delivered PzKpfw 38(t). Germany supplied 111 of these tank to Hungary between November 1941 and June 1942. They equipped the 1st Armored Division, which took part of the invasion of the Soviet Union in 1941.

A Hungarian PzKpfw 38(t) Ausf.G, with a German aerial and a Notek light.

The newly acquired PzKpfw 38(t)s of the Hungarian army on parade of the 1st Armored Division's units.

The remaining tanks were incorporated into the tank brigade of the 1st Bulgarian Army, which participated in the liberation of Austria and ended the war south of Vienna.

Right after the war, the Bulgarian army ordered from Škoda spare parts for both its T-11 tanks, and for the PzKpfw 38(t)s. Škoda shipped the requested parts before 1948. Bulgaria used the remaining Czech tanks up to the beginning of the fifties, when its army began using Soviet equipment.

HUNGARY

Honvéd raised its 1st Armored Division (Tabori Pancéloshadosztaly) under the HUBA I reorganization of October 1, 1941. Its 30. Tank Regiment had two battalions with a total of three light tank companies with 89 PzKpfw 38(t). Hungary bought between November 1941 and November 1942 a total of 111 of these tanks from Germany, 105 combat tanks and six PzBefWg 38(t) (Honvéd numbers 1H-725 - 1H-832 and 1H-876 - 1H-878). The 1st Armored Division was overrun by the Soviet Army during the Stalingrad battle, lost most of its equipment and was subsequently disbanded.

HUBA II was initiated on October 1, 1942. An Armored Corps was raised, consisting of the 1st and the 2nd Armored Division and

A Hungarian PzKpfw 38(t) of the 1st Armored Division crossing the Don River in the fall of 1942.

Hungarian Ausf.G during the winter 1942. During the Soviet Stalingrad counter offensive, the Hungarian 1st Armored Division was practically destroyed and lost most of its equipment.

the 1st Cavalry Division. Each armored division had a reconnaissance battalion with Csaba armored cars and Toldi or PzKpfw 38(t) tanks, a tank regiment with three battalions (Turan I, Turan II and PzKpfw IV tanks), a motorized infantry regiment with three battalions, three artillery battalions and antitank artillery and engineer battalions.

In 1943 eight assault gun battalions (Roto.ö) were raised. Each of them was supposed to have 30 Zrinyi assault guns, but due to the lack of these vehicles, only four were thus equipped. The remaining four battalions (7., 13., 16. and 25.) were equipped with StuG III and with 75 Hetzers. Fifty of these were acquired in December 1944 and 25 in January 1945.

Even when the Germans occupied Hungary in March 1944, Honvéd units continued fighting side-by-side with German formations against the Soviet army. The 2nd Armored Division was sent as part of the 1st Army to Galicia in April. On April 17 it counterattacked from Solotvina to Kolomija, but was repulsed with heavy losses. In July, it had to cover the retreat of the 1st Army to the defensive line "Hunyadi" in the Carpathian mountains. It took part in the fierce battle of Torda from September 13, but its battered units had to be withdrawn on September 23.

The 1st Cavalry Division joined the 2nd Reserve Corps in the Pripet area on June 10, 1944. When the front of the German Army Group "Center" collapsed, the division found itself in the center of the Soviet offensive. It had to perform a fighting withdrawal to Brest-Litovsk, which it reached on July 15. During the month of heavy fighting, it lost all of its tanks.

After the turn-about of Romania, Hungary raised the 2nd Army from training depots and stiffened it with units of the 1st Army, including the 2nd Armored Division. This army defended Transsylvania. It was joined there by the 3rd Army with the 1st Armored Division. Both divisions suffered heavy losses in defensive battles against the Soviet Army.

From October they fought in the puszta in the vicinity of Debrecen and Nuiregyhazi. In cooperation with German armored units, they managed to stabilize the front on the Tisza River by October 29, 1944.

On October 30, the bloody fighting for Budapest started. The siege lasted for four months. In the city the remnants of the 2nd Armored Division were trapped with the Billnitzer csoport (group), named after its commander and consisting of the 6. Assault Gun Battalion and remnants of three other assault gun battalions with a mixture of Zrinyis, StuG III and Hetzers. These units surrendered with the city.

The 1st Armored and the 1st Cavalry Divisions were stationed North of Budapest on the Danube River, where in heavy fighting most of their units were destroyed. The last remnants retreated into Austria and into Slovakia, where they surrendered at the beginning of May 1945.

Development and Manufacture of the PzKpfw 38(t) Series

PzKpfw 38(t) Ausf.A during trial runs on a forest road. The crewman is dressed in a long winter coat, a sure sign this is a peaceful drive.

Two factory shots of the Ausf.C PzKpfw 38(t).

The Czechoslovak army ordered 150 tanks of the LT vz.38 type on July 22, 1938. ČKD started manufacturing the order, but at the time of the German occupation of the Czech lands on March 15, 1939 did not finish a single tank. The Heereswaffenamt commission in May decided to accept the whole order and to include the tank in the Wehrmacht's armory under the designation PzKpfw 38(t).

The first nine tanks of **Ausführung A** were delivered in May and the last ones in November. Because the tank was very successful in the Polish campaign, another 325 tanks were ordered at the end of 1939. The order was divided into 110 vehicles of Ausf.B, 110 of Ausf.C and 105 of Ausf.D The last vehicles of the Ausf.B were shipped in May 1940, the Ausf.C was finished in August and the Ausf.D by November 1940.

The Ausf.A was practically identical to the LT vz.38 as manufactured for the Czechoslovak army. The tanks had German Fu5 radio sets installed and the usual German stowage was provided.

Ausf.B PzKpfw 38(t) tanks of the 7th Panzer Division refueling in the French countryside during the 1940 campaign. The division was commanded by General Rommel.

Circular bolted splash guards around the machine gun mounts were fitted. The **Ausf.B** had some small changes in external stowage. Notek lights were installed, as were smoke generators on the rear plate. The gun sight cover was slightly modified. The **Ausf.C** introduced a splash protector for the turret ring and a German aerial. The engine's muffler was moved to the top of the rear plate. Ausf.C and D had the hull front armor increased to 40 mm, while the driver's front plate and the front of the turret remained at 25 mm.

A larger change was introduced on the 275 vehicles of the **Ausf.E**, manufactured from November 1940 to May 1941. The frontal armor of both front plates and the turret was increased to 50 mm and both the upper side of the hull's side armor and the sides of the turret to 30 mm. This increased the weight of the tank from 9,150 kg to 10,140 kg and required the beefing up of the front spring clusters from 14 to 15 springs, as the tanks became nose-heavy. The other properties were not adversely affected. This and the following **Ausf.F**, whose 250 vehicles were manufactured from May to October 1941, is recognizable by the straight driver's plate, bolted armor on the turret front, and additional jerrycan holders.

An Ausf.G with the straight front plate and a large stowage box on the left fender.

Another Ausf.G in Russia several months later. Note the smaller number of rivets on the front plate and the German aerial.

Two factory shots of the Ausf.G, showing the clean front plate. The driver's outside aiming device for the hull machine gun is clearly visible in the front view. If you compare the previous photographs of the PzKpfw 38(t), in almost all instances this device was either broken off or removed by the crew. The rear view shows the proper position for the Abstand Rücklicht. This is probably the last PzKpfw 38(t) manufactured.

Concurrently with the Ausf.F was manufactured the **Ausf.S.** These tanks were originally ordered by Sweden and their manufacture was supposed to start in 1940. The Germans eventually confiscated the whole series of 90 vehicles for their own use. These tanks were started as Ausf.A-C, but had their frontal armor increased to 50 mm, while the side armor remained 15 mm.

After the invasion of the Soviet Union, an additional 1,000 tanks were ordered, split into two series, 500 of Ausf.G and 500 of Ausf.H. Of the 500 chassis of Ausf.G, only 306 were finished as PzKpfw 38(t) between October 1941 and October 1942, the remaining chassis being converted to tank hunters. The whole Ausf.H series was built as tank hunters and self-propelled artillery.

The **Ausf.G** had a simplified construction of the hull and the turret that needed fewer bolts while maintaining the armor thickness. The cost of each tank without its armament was 56,000 Deutsche Marks.

BMM also manufactured side-by-side with the Wehrmacht orders 37 tanks for the Slovak state, basically the Ausf.A, between 1940 and 1942. Similarly as with the PzKpfw 35(t), two types of Panzerbefehlswagen or command tanks were modified from the normal tanks. Company headquarters tanks had the Fu5 and Fu6 radio sets, two rod aerials and the front machine gun deleted, while battalion and regimental headquarter vehicles carried the Fu5 and Fu8 radios and the large frame aerial. Those tanks had the main gun removed and replaced by a wooden replica, retaining only the turret machine gun. Both types of PzBefWg had gyrocompasses installed.

The identifying features of the various Ausführungen are not always a sure way to identify them. Tanks coming back to the factory for repairs had additional equipment fitted and replacement parts usually were not of the same Ausführung. Cases are known when an Ausf.A tank was fitted with an Ausf.G turret. The tank in the museum in Banská Bystrica in Slovakia is an Ausf.A, but has an engine cover from an Ausf G. Similarly, various pieces of equipment were installed in the field (large storage boxes, jerrycan holders). The only safe identifying feature is the thickness of the armor and the placement and number of the bolts.*

Ausf.A-D had six bolts vertically on both sides of the front plate of the turret, and six bolts on the straight sides of the turret front. **Ausf.E-F** had four bolts on the front sides and the sides, while Ausf.S had five on the sides and four on the front. **Ausf.G** had three bolts on the right front and one on the left, and four bolts on the side panels. Starting from Ausf.E, the circular guard around the turret machine gun disappeared and the ball mount was flush with the front plate of the turret.

Ausf.A-D had the staggered front plate before the driver, while **Ausf.E-F** had a straight plate with 13 bolts. **Ausf.G** had the same plate, but only with six bolts.

The hull's front plate on **Ausf.A-D** had 12 bolts on its upper edge and three pairs of bolts in the middle. **Ausf.E-G** had only 11 bolts on the upper edge and no bolts in the middle. The connections of the front hull plate to the side plate also varied (see illustrations). Finally, the rounded sides of the engine covers had on **Ausf.A-E** 14 bolts in two rows, while **Ausf.G** had only four bolts in the corners.

The original engine used in the 38 series was the Scania-Vabis 1664, built under license by BMM and designated as the **Praga TNHPS**. Its output was 126 HP(93.1 kW)/2,200 rpm. Starting with the Aus.H, this engine got a second carburetor and its rpm were increased. Its new designation was the **Praga AC**. In this form its output increased to 150 HP(110.9 kW)/2,500 rpm. The engine was first tested on tank chassis no.1200, whose cross-country performance improved by 20% and its maximum speed increased to 49.5 km/hour with lower fuel consumption. The last variant, developed for the Jagdpanzer 38, was the **Praga AE**. Its output was 160 HP(118.3 kW)/2,600 rpm and 180 HP(133 kW)/2,800 rpm. Because the rpm regulators were set between 2,500 - 2,700 rpm, the production vehicles usually did not reach the maximum output.

In May 1942 vehicle no.1481 was tested in Kummersdorf with tropical filters and an improved cooling system. These improvements were later used in tropicalization of the SdKfz 139 for the Afrika Korps. Another interesting testing program was the flotation device tested in February 1941. It consisted of a large, boat-like float AP-1, fitted around the tank. Two propellers in the rear were connected to the tank's engine. In calm water the prototype attained speeds up to 8 km/hour. The adaptation was rugged enough for ocean use, but it is not known for what operation it was considered.

*(Refer to Chapter 14: Plans for bolt diagrams, pgs 315-16)

TABLE 12
Monthly Production of PzKpfw 38(t) at BMM

YEAR/MONTH	1	2	3	4	5	6	7	8	9	10	11	12	TOTAL
1939						21	39	18	34	30	11		153
1940	10	24	31	30	30	30	38	24	35	44	27	44	367
1941	44	50	53	49	68	57	65	64	76	53	50	49	678
1942	59	62	28	1	21	26				1			198
1939-1942									TOTAL PRODUCTION				1396

TABLE 13
Chassis numbers of the PzKpfw 38(t) series

AUSFÜHRUNG	NUMBER MANUFACTURED	CHASSIS NUMBERS
A	150	0001 - 0150
B	110	0151 - 0260
C	110	0261 - 0370
D	105	0371 - 0475
E	275	0476 - 0750
F	250	0750 - 1000
S	90	1001 - 1090
G	259	1101 - 1359
	47	1480 - 1526

Modifications on the Kpfw 38(t) Chassis

Once the standard tank became unsuitable for front-line combat, the excellent chassis was used for tank hunters, self-propelled artillery and other uses. The **Panzerjäger 38(t) für 7.62 cm PaK 36(r) (SdKfz 139)** was the first of these modifications. It was a simple conversion. The turret and the top plate of the fighting compartment were removed and a captured 7.62 cm Russian antitank gun was mounted on a cross, whose members were welded to the hull sides and the front and rear plates. A crudely constructed gun shield from 10 mm armor plate provided only a rudimentary protection for the crew. The gun was equipped with a straight sight. It was rechambered for German ammunition that gave it a muzzle velocity of 960 m/sec. It fired a 4.15 kg shell that could penetrate 94 mm armor at 1,000 m. Thirty rounds were carried in the former fighting compartment. Though poorly protected, this modification combined a proven chassis with an effective gun and provided antitank capabilities to the hard pressed infantry and Panzer Grena-

Canvas covered SdKfz 139 in BMM's factory yard. The used Russian gun was very effective, in some respects better than the German PAK 40.

dier units. From April to October 1942, 344 SdKfz 139 were built, 194 on the Ausf.G chassis, the rest on that of the Ausf.H, which had a more powerful engine of 150 HP. At least 39 further vehicles were converted from PzKpfw 38(t) tanks, returned to BMM during 1943.

The 7.5 cm **PaK 40/3 auf PzKpfw 38(t) Ausf.H (SdKfz 138)** was a similar adaptation, only this time using the German PaK 40, which became available in May 1942. The first 42 vehicles were manufactured in November 1942. A total of 275 vehicles of the Ausf.H was built, while another 336 were converted from the basic tank during 1943.

The gun was mounted in a way similar to the SdKfz 139, though its shield was of a better construction and provided more protection for the crew. The gun had a muzzle velocity of 930 m/sec and with a 4.1 kg shell could penetrate 90 mm armor at 1,000 m. On both models the hull machine gun was retained for close protection.

Front view of the SdKfz 139. The hull machine gun was retained for close defense.

Panzerjägers 38 being loaded on a train. These already have the short sides of the gun shield, which was made from 10 mm armor plate.

The gun was protected against the elements with a canvas cover, stretched over a frame in the rear. It was provided with celluloid windows.

A SdKfz 139 captured in 1942 in Libya. This vehicle was evaluated and tested by the British School of Tank Technology (Report STT 2469). Note the two seats in the rear for the gun crew.

A well masked SdKfz 139. Considering its poor armor protection, it certainly was a wise precaution, as its goal was to strike first and disappear quickly. Russian front, 1942.

The Panzerjäger 38(t) mit 7.5 cm PaK 40/3 Ausf.M (SdKfz 138) was the final version of this series. The Ausf.M chassis was developed for the Panzerjäger to lower the silhouette and improve the layout of the fighting compartment. By moving the engine to the front part of the hull the fighting compartment in the back became larger, lower and more easily accessible. The front part was redesigned with a single glacis plate sloped at 67°. The driver sat at the right side under a cast armored hood with a hinged visor. The gun was mounted low in the rear and was protected by a 10 mm thick four-sided superstructure. The rest of the armor was only 15 mm. The crew consisted of four men, but three of them rode in the fighting compartment, as the hull machine gun was deleted. 27 rounds for the gun were normally carried. BMM manufactured 942 vehicles of this type between May 1943 and June 1944. BMM shipped only 941 of them, vehicle no.2321 was retained for testing by the factory.

The **15 cm sIG 33(Sfl) auf PzKpfw 38(t) Ausf.H "Grille" (SdKfz 138/1)** was a self-propelled Rheinmetall-Borsig howitzer.

A group of SdKfz 139s serving with Afrika Korps. A total of 33 vehicles of this type were shipped to Africa.

Another destroyed SdKfz 139 in North Africa. In the background is a disabled Italian tank M-14/41 of the Ariete Division.

A prototype of a Sturmgeschütz (assault gun) on the 38 chassis. Though never introduced, the gun shield was used for the next modification, carrying the 7.5 cm PaK 40/3 on an Ausf.H chassis.

The weak armor protection is apparent on this destroyed Slovak SdKfz 138. Called also Marder III, the Slovak army bought 18 of them in 1944, and used two of them during the Uprising in 1944. This is one of them.

The prototype was developed by Alkett on the Ausf.H chassis. The gun was again placed on a cross-member bolted to the sides of the hull. The armor shield was 25 mm thick on the front and 15 mm on the sides, and covered almost the whole length of the vehicle. These vehicles were meant as fully tracked supporting artillery for armored formations. BMM manufactured 90 of them starting in February 1943. Another 110 vehicles of the Ausf.K were built by June 1943, before the production was switched to the Ausf.M chassis.

The **15 cm sIG 33(Sfl) auf PzKpfw 38(t) Ausf.M (SdKfz 138/1)** was the final version of the Grille. The prototype was built as Ausf.K. 118 vehicles on the Ausf.M chassis were built from December 1943 to April 1944, and another 74 by May 1945 as part of series 11. Both versions of the Grille carried a very limited supply of ammunition - 18 rounds. To rectify this situation, simultaneously with the Grille production, the

Munitionspanzer 38(t) (Sf) Ausf.M (SdKfz 138/1) was built, the first ten vehicles in November 1943 with the engine in the back,

SdKfz 138 Ausf.H in France in 1944.

A pair of SdKfz 138s on the Russian front in 1943. The gun shield had a better shape, but the vehicle was still too high and poorly protected.

A wooden mock-up of the last of the series, the Panzerjäger 38(t) mit 7.5 cm PaK Ausf.M. This model had the engine moved forward and the fighting compartment to the rear. This allowed for a lower and much roomier gun compartment. The front plate was sloped.

This front view of the production SdKfz 138 Ausf.M shows the driver's cast hood and the rear gun placement. The front plate was only 15 mm thick, but was well sloped.

Rear view shows the roominess of the fighting compartment, and additional traveling lock on the gun's breech. 942 vehicles of this type were manufactured.

The same vehicle from the other side. Note the engine's air intake in the rear.

another 93 vehicles of the Ausf.M standard were built between January and May of 1944 for a total of 103 vehicles (in TABLES 12 and 13 they are designated SdKfz 138/1M). They carried 40 rounds for the 15 cm howitzer. These vehicles were identical to the original Grille, but the gun was not mounted. Its aperture in the front plate was plated over and the fighting compartment was filled with ammunition racks. It was possible to re-equip these vehicles with the howitzers in the field, if necessary.

The **Flakpanzer 38(t) auf Selbstfahrlafette 38(t) Ausf.M (SdKfz 140)** carried the 2 cm FLAK 38 (L/55) enclosed in an armored superstructure, whose upper part could be opened to ease the work of the crew and to allow greater depression of the gun. With a crew of 4-5 men the vehicle carried 1,040 rounds of three types of the 2 cm ammunition. Manufactured as a stop-gap before the antiaircraft tanks based on PzKpfw IV chassis became available, it was used mainly in the West. The vehicles had low firepower and routinely became themselves a target of the Allied fighter bombers. 141 vehicles were built between November 1943 and February 1944.

Front view, showing the clean lines, spare track for added protection, and the gun's traveling lock.

Abandoned well-camouflaged SdKfz 138 Ausf.M after the Allied outbreak in Normandy in summer 1944.

BMM's production line for the Grille, or 15 cm sIG 33(Sfl) auf PzKpfw 38(t), Ausf.H, how it was named officially. Its armor shield was heavier at 25 mm, side aprons were 15 mm thick.

The **Auklärer auf PzKpfw 38(t) mit 2 cm KwK 38 (SdKfz 140/1)** was developed to fill the gap after the termination of the production of the "Luchs" reconnaissance tank in 1944. In February and March 1944, four old PzKpfw 38(t) chassis were used for this conversion, one of them with a Tatra Diesel engine. On a modified upper part of the hull was mounted the 2 cm Hängelafette 38 open-top turret, as used for example on the SdKfz 234/1. Another modification was planned for the 7.5 cm KwK38 L/24. BMM modified two chassis by placing the gun with a limited traverse in a heightened superstructure. As far as it is known, the 7.5 cm gun modification existed only as wooden mock-ups and did not reach production status. 70 production vehicles were built between February and March 1944 as part of the Ausf.M series. They had the Hetzer Praga AE engines and ZF gearboxes installed and attained speeds up to 58 km/hour on roads. They fought both on the Eastern and the Western fronts in armored reconnaissance companies.

The howitzer at full elevation. Note how the sliding armor shield underneath the barrel closed the opening in the front wall. The front plate was an extension of the original driver's front plate, and his position in the hull was the same as in the original tank.

A total of 200 of these vehicles was manufactured, 90 on Ausf.H chassis, 110 on Ausf.K. The howitzers were supplied by Rheinmetall-Borsig.

A captured Grille in an interesting camouflage scheme.

(Clockwise from left) Three inside views of the fighting compartment of the Grille, Ausf.H, showing the howitzer with its breech and scope, the radio set, various fittings and holders for the sixteen rounds carried. In the rear view, the driver's seat low in the right front side of the hull can be seen.

The **Munitionsschlepper auf Fahrgestell PzKpfw 38(t)** was a field modification. Old PzKpfw 38(t) tanks had their turrets removed and were used as munitions carriers for supplying self-propelled gun and tank formations.

The **Schulfahrerwanne PzKpfw 38(t)** were PzKpfw 38(t) chassis with turrets and armaments removed. They were used for driver training. Toward the end of the war, some of them were equipped with wood burning gas generators to save precious gasoline. Such generators were quite common on civilian trucks from 1943 on.

The **Mörserträger auf Fahrgestell PzKpfw 38(t)** was a prototype of a mortar carrier for the armored formations. It was never introduced.

The **Armored personnel carrier on SdKfz 138, Ausf.M** existed in only one prototype. The gun was removed, the front plate was solid and the rear armor was brought to full height and had a double door, opening to the sides. Inside were benches for eight soldiers.

The **PzKpfw 38(t) with PzKpfw IV** turret was proposed by Krupp in 1944 to make it powerful enough to serve as a first-line combat tank. The front plate was angled and its thickness was increased to 50 mm. It was to be fitted with a lightened BW-turret with either the 7.5 cm KwK 43 L/48 or a recoilless 8 cm antitank gun PAW 600 and 50 mm armor. The commander's cupola was eliminated. This vehicle was never built.

A Grille with its crew. Aside from the driver, there were four men to service the howitzer.

Two Grilles Ausf.H and supporting Kradschützen in the country. They had the stronger Praga AC engine and a maximum speed of 47 km/hour.

The business end of the howitzer with the traveling lock, shield details and the driver's visors.

Stocking the ammunition.

The later Grille Ausf.M had the gun moved to the back, while the engine and the driver were moved to the front. This version was built up to May 1945, with a total of 183 vehicles manufactured. This factory photograph shows the howitzer in a traveling position and the canvas top extended.

The same vehicle with the gun at maximum elevation. The front opening is again covered by an armor shield, and the frame for the canvas top is split and turned to the back so as not to interfere with the crew's servicing the gun.

Rear view. On the left are steps for the crew. The muffler was covered with a perforated shield to protect the crew from burns.

Front view, showing the sloping front plate and the driver's armored hood with a new type of visor.

The fighting compartment of the Grille Ausf.M was still quite cramped. The tubular holders are for the shells, while the little boxes are for the powder charges, as the 15 cm howitzer used two-part ammunition.

TABLE 14
Production on PzKpfw 38(t) Chassis

BMM SERIES	AUS- FÜHRUNG	VEHICLE TYPE PzKpfw 38	SdKfz 139	SkKfz 138	SdKfz 138/1	SdKfz 140	SdKfz 140/1
1	A	150					
2	B	110					
3	C	110					
4	D	105					
5	E	275					
6	F	250					
	S	90					
7	G	306	194				
8	H		150	260	90		
9	K			389[1]	111[2]		
10	M			568	118+103[3]	141	70[4]
11					74		
TOTAL		1,396	344	1,217	393+103	141	70

TOTAL PRODUCED ON THE PzKpfw 38 CHASSIS: 3,664

[1] 15 vehicles with engine in the back, 374 vehicles with engine in the middle
[2] 110 vehicles with the engine in the back, one vehicle with the engine in the middle
[3] 118 howitzer vehicles and 103 munitions carriers (10 with the engine in the back, rest with the engine in the middle)
[4] All with the engine in the back.

Series 7, 8 and 9 (Ausf. G, H and K) each had 500 chassis, while series 10 (Ausf. M) had 1,000 chassis. Series 11 comprised only 74 chassis before the production was switched to series 12 and Jagdpanzer 38. Chassis numbers went from 0001 to 3674 (there was a gap in the numbers between 1090 and 1101).

This Grille Ausf.M resides in the Aberdeen Proving Grounds Armor Museum. The engine intake was on the right rear side. The exhaust pipe was led out from the same location. The driver had a small visor on the right side, but could not observe to the left.

The driver's hood was welded and had a split two-part hatch in its top. On this picture one half of the hatch is missing and the opening is welded shut with a metal plate. The protective armor shield under the gun was not sliding, as on Ausf.H, but was hinged and spring-loaded.

Left: An American soldier rides a captured Grille in Italy, 1944.

Same vehicle from the rear, with the rear door open. It had holders for three ready shells. The insulated exhaust pipe ran around the back to the muffler.

Two views of the captured Grille, which was evaluated by the English School of Tank Technology. It has a sprayed camouflage and carries the wires for affixing branches and foliage for improved camouflage on its sides.

Three inside views of the Aberdeen Grille show the shell holders and the two massive recoil cylinders of the gun.

A battery of Grille's in firing position. The front vehicle is Ausf.M, the other two are Ausf.H.

Abandoned Grille Ausf.M. Note the open driver's visor and the Notek lamp on the front edge of the hull.

Two BMM factory photographs of the Munitionspanzer 38(t) Ausf.M. 93 vehicles were built (plus ten on Ausf.H chassis) to supply the Grille formations with ammunition. They carried 40 rounds. It was possible to retrofit them under field conditions with the howitzer. Note they carry the traveling lock for the gun. Note also the split two-part driver's hatch.

A rear view of the Munitionspanzer.

A Munitionspanzer modified by installing the 3.7 cm FLAK gun during the Prague uprising in May 5-9, 1945.

The Flakpanzer 38(t) SdKfz 140 carried one 2 cm FLAK 38 in a lightly armored superstructure with collapsible walls. 141 vehicles were built and were used mainly on the Western front, where the fighter bombers were more numerous.

Another Flakpanzer before installation of its gun. The driver had a cast hood, not welded as on the Grille.

Rear view of the Flakpanzer 38(t). The hinges between the lower and upper plates are well visible.

A well camouflaged Flakpanzer 38(t) with its side walls lowered, ready for combat.

A destroyed SdKfz 140 in Normandy in 1944. The hatch of the driver's hood is open, the cover plate over the front clutches is missing, and the sides of the fighting compartment are in the folded-down position.

The prototype of the Aufklärer auf PzKpfw 38(t) SdKfz 140/1 at BMM. It carries the Hängelafette turret with the 2 cm KwK 38 L/55 gun and one machine gun. It has also the smoke dischargers fitted, which were not usual on the production vehicles.

A production SdKfz 140/1. A total of 70 vehicles was produced, with Praga AE engines as used on the Hetzer. They attained a maximum speed of 58 km/hour.

TABLE 15
Monthly Shipments of PzKpfw 38(t) Modifications from BMM

YEAR/MONTH VEHICLE	1	2	3	4	5	6	7	8	9	10	11	12	TOTAL
1942 SdKfz 139				38	82	23	50	51	50	50			344
SdKfz 138											42	68	110
1943 SdKfz 138	60	35	30	34	26	36	99	55	107	140	91	70	618
SdKfz 138/1		25	40	52	52	31					1	14	215
SdKfz 138/1M												10	10
SdKfz 140											50	51	101
1944 SdKfz 138	74	53	79	47	31	39							323
SdKfz 138/1	20	18	30	15	21	27	14		9				154
SdKfz 138/1M 5	10	20	18	40									93
SdKfz 140	27	13											40
SdKfz 140/1		37	33										70

Two views of a captured Aufklärer 38(t) on the Western front.

The Aufklärer 38(t) had the 50 mm armor of Ausf.H, and carried four men.

Rear top view, showing the widened hull and the low turret.

Front view of the SdKfz 140/1. The hull machine gun was eliminated. The vehicle was very low, 28 cm lower than the PzKpfw 38(t).

A mock-up of the Auklärer 38(t) with the 7.5 cm KwK 38 L/24. This was the older design which retained the tank's front vertical plate.

A newer version already had a sloped, one-piece front plate, and the gun in a much lower superstructure.

Another view of the second version with the 7.5 cm gun. Both versions were built only as wooden mock-ups and were not accepted for production.

The Munitionsschlepper 38(t) was a simple field modification: the turret was removed and the opening was covered with a tarpaulin on a simple frame. These vehicles were used as munitions carriers for the motorized artillery formations.

TABLE 16
Total Production of PzKpfw 38(t) and its Modifications

TYPE	NUMBER PRODUCED	AUSFÜHRUNG
PzKpfw 38(t)	1396	150 A, 110 B, 110 C, 105 D, 275 E 250 F, 90 S, 306 G
SdFkz 139	344	194 G, 150 H
SdKfz 138	1217	275 H, 389 K, 568 M
SdKfz 138/1	393	90 H, 111 K, 118 M, 74 series 11
SdKfz 140	141	141 M
SdKfz 138/1M	103	103 M
SdKfz 140/1	70	70 M

There was one interesting development on the PzKpfw 38(t) chassis, namely the **Praga TNHnA** (neue Ausführung). It was a fast reconnaissance tank, developed as BMM's entry into Wa.Prüf-6 competition for a new reconnaissance tank for the Wehrmacht. At the beginning of the war the Germans did not have a suitable fast fully tracked vehicle for their reconnaissance companies. On September 15, 1939 the tank testing and development center of the army's armament office (Wa.Prüf-6) was asked to develop a suitable design. Both the Polish and the French campaigns had shown the need for such a vehicle, and thus in the summer of 1940 Wa.Prüf-6 officially asked three companies to submit their prototypes. The companies were BMM, Škoda and MAN. The new tank had to have a maximum speed of 50 km/hour and a weight between 12-13 tons. Front armor was planned to be 30 mm, side armor 20 mm. Armament was planned as one gun between 2.0 and 3.7 cm and one ma-

The surplus PzKpfw 38(t) turrets were used in the fixed fortifications. Hundreds of them were placed on the coasts of Europe, this one is on Corsica.

Unarmed PzKpfw 38(t)s of the RMS were used for drivers training. The RMS was a paramilitary organization connected with the German auto club.

The Schulfahrerwanne 38(t) was the hull of the PzKpfw 38(t) with the turret removed, used for drivers training. These vehicles are fitted with the wood burning gas generators, widely used to save gasoline on civilian trucks and buses. They were too unwieldy and large for smaller vehicles.

One of the TNHnA reconnaissance tanks, with its larger road wheels, new hull and turret and heavier armor.

The prototype of the Mörserträger (mortar carrier) on the 38 chassis Ausf.M was planned as a heavy mortar self-propelled carrier, but was never introduced.

chine gun in a fully rotating turret. Ground pressure was specified at a maximum of 0.8 kg/cm2.

BMM used its well proven design of the PzKpfw 38(t) for the new tank. It had to slightly increase the size of the hull due to the need for a much stronger engine. The turret was completely redesigned, with sloped sides and an observation cupola for the commander. The chassis remained the same, only the diameter of the running wheels increased from 775 to 810 mm. BMM developed a new eight-cylinder gasoline engine of 248 HP(183.3 kW) and a new Wilson gearbox for the tank.

Škoda developed its prototype T-15 at the same time, while MAN developed its prototype based on the PzKpfw II. The final VK 1303 prototype was changed so much that it did not resemble the original PzKpfw II. While the MAN prototype retained the 2 cm KwK of the PzKpfw II, both the Škoda and BMM designs used

The armored personnel carrier on Ausf.M chassis prototype.

The new Praga V-8 engine of the TNHnA (PzKpfw 38(t)nA) tank.

Rear view of the TNHnA with its new engine and double mufflers. The turret with its fixed cupola and large vision devices is well visible.

the Škoda 3.7 cm A22 tank gun. Wa.Prüf-6 ordered five prototypes: the first to be made from mild steel plate and riveted, the second from mild steel and welded, the third from proper armor riveted and the last two from proper armor, welded. As the manufacturers finished their designs by the end of 1940, full-size wooden mock ups were ordered first.

The companies obtained the final order for the five prototypes in the summer of 1941. The tanks were supposed to be delivered between November 1941 and April 1942. The testing of the prototypes went on at the Kummersdorf testing center until autumn of 1942. During comparative tests of the prototypes, the TNHnA had shown the best results and also its superlative dependability. The testing center ran the final tests between October 6-8, 1942. The tested tanks covered 338 km in nine hours, and reached maximum speeds of up to 75 km/hour. The testing center recommended accepting the BMM design, but the connections of the MAN company prevailed and it got the order for 800 of their "Luchs" tanks. In the end, it made only 131 of them, as in May 1943 the manufacture of all light tanks was stopped.

BMM obtained the approval to finish all its prototypes from mild steel, because it did not obtain the armor plate from its suppli-

Driving levers and steering column of the TNHnA tank.

Steering clutch with the cooling ring of the TNHnA tank.

The sole TNHnA prototype with the Tatra Diesel engine during trials with its civilian crew.

T-15 during the trials at Kummersdorf testing center.

ers. In one of these vehicles (and in one Luchs tank) the new Tatra 103 air-cooled Diesel engine was tested in 1943.

One of the prototypes of the TNHnA remained after the war in ČKD and was used as a test-bed for the new semi-automatic Škoda 4.7 and 5.7 cm tank guns, but was finally scrapped in the fifties. Škoda retained one of the T-15 prototypes and after the war fitted it with a LT vz.35 turret.

The Vollkettenaufklärer 38(t) "Kätzchen"

In late 1943, Heereswaffenamt Wa.Prüf-6 asked Auto Union to develop a light, fully tracked reconnaissance vehicle, capable of carrying 6-8 men in an open-top superstructure. The vehicle was designed to attain speeds in excess of 50 km/hour and was to be lightly armored.

Auto Union first built a wooden mock-up, and after the layout was approved, in early 1944 constructed two prototypes for evaluation. The vehicle had an open top, with the engine in the back and the powered front sprockets. The driver sat on the left, and next to

A prototype of the Luchs reconnaissance tank with the Tatra Diesel engine.

One of the Škoda T-15 reconnaisance tanks, developed in competition with the BMM's TNHnA and MAN's Luchs. This vehicle is welded.

One of the prototypes of the Vollkettenaufklärer 38(t) Kätzchen (little cat). This was more of an armored personnel carrier than a reconnaissance vehicle. Well armored and fast, it could carry up to 8 men.

Side view of the Kätzchen.

him was a machine gun in the usual "Kugelblende". In the vehicle were two long benches for the rest of the crew.

The engine used was the Maybach HL 50Z of 5,000 cc displacement and 200 HP(147.8 kW) output. It was squeezed into the left rear of the vehicle, to make room for the crew door, which was on the right side of the rear plate. The armor was fairly light, 30 mm front and 14.5 mm sides and rear.

The carriage consisted of five overlapping wheels on each side with a torsion bar suspension, and the tracks from PzKpfw IV. The gear-box was hydraulic. The prototypes were tested in summer 1944 on the testing track and were well liked for both their layout and their mobility. Problems were encountered with the gear-box. Therefore, and also because of the decision of September 1944 to limit all new constructions to two chassis only, namely the Panther and 38(t), it was eventually decided to order a prototype from BMM in Prague, maker of the Jagdpanzer 38 Hetzer.

The WaPrüf-6 Pz.Ia ordered two prototypes from BMM on September 6, 1943. They were supposed to be based on the PzKpfw 38(t)nA. One was planned with the Tatra 103 Diesel engine, one with the Praga NR engine with an output of 280 HP. The prototypes were built in 1944. They were wider than the Auto Union model and heavier, being much better armored. Their front plate was 50 mm, sides 30 mm and the rear plate 20 mm thick. They retained the general layout with the open top and the engine in the rear, but disposed with the Kugelblende for the front machine gun, which was instead mounted behind an armored shield as carried by the SdKfz 250 and 251 halftracks. A rear mount for another machine gun was also provided.

The new Tatra 103 twelve cylinder air-cooled Diesel put out 220 HP(162.6 kW) at 2600 rpm, giving the vehicle a maximum speed of 64 km/hour on roads. Enough fuel was carried for endurance up to 600 km. The suspension used the well-tested layout of the PzKpfw 38(t), and the Praga-Wilson gear-box was used.

The BMM "Kätzchen" was clearly a better design than the Auto-Union one, being better armored and faster. The use of the Diesel engine made it probably also safer for its users. If manufactured in quantities, it would have proven to be not only a suitable reconnaissance vehicle, but also a good armored personnel carrier as well. The fate of the two prototypes after the end of the war is not known, but the Czech army clearly was not interested in their further development.

KÄTZCHEN COMPARISON

	AUTO-UNION	BMM
Weight	8.0 t	10.5 t
Length	5.12 m	5.10 m
Width	2.36 m	2.50 m
Height	1.50 m	1.50 m
Engine	Maybach	Tatra 103/Praga NR
Output	200 HP	220 HP/280 HP
Max. Speed(road)	55 km/hr	64 km/hr
Endurance		600 km
Armor front	30 mm	50 mm
sides	14.5 mm	30 mm
rear	14.5 mm	20 mm
Crew	6-8	6-8
Armament	1x MG	2x MG

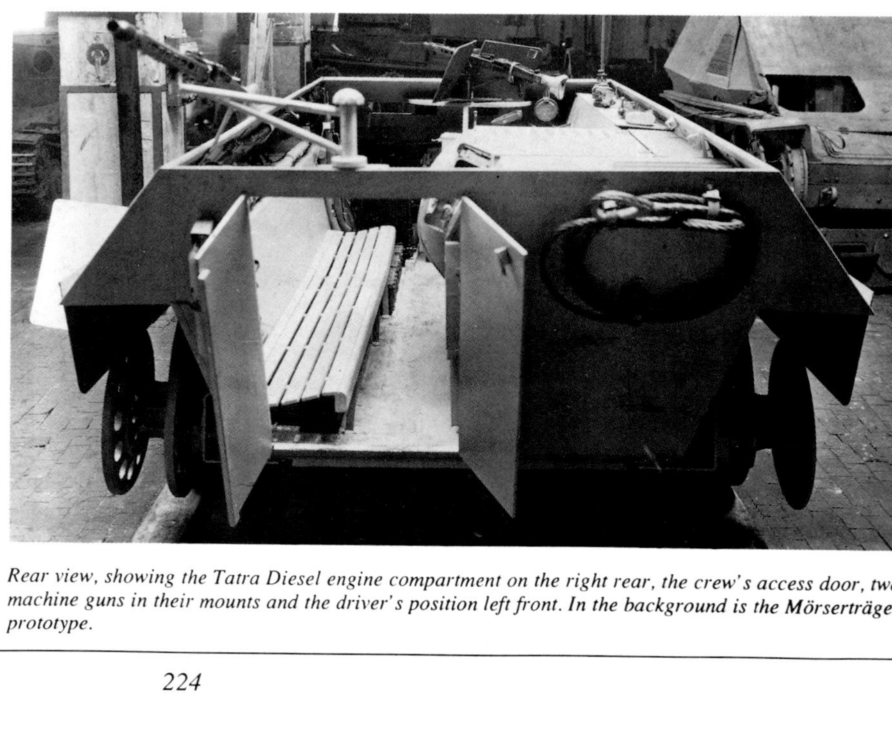

Rear view, showing the Tatra Diesel engine compartment on the right rear, the crew's access door, two machine guns in their mounts and the driver's position left front. In the background is the Mörserträger prototype.

Jagdpanzer 38 - Development

A front view comparison of SdKfz 138 AusfM and the prototype of the Jagdpanzer 38(t), showing the wider and much lower profile of the latter.

A brand new Hetzer leaves the factory. A "Werkschutz", or a factory guard, is looking on. These guards were in all factories to watch for pilfering or sabotage.

In November 1943 the Allies heavily bombed the Alkett factory in Berlin and thus disrupted the production of Sturmgeschütz III. OKH investigated the possibility of transferring the production to BMM, but found that the factory was not capable of manufacturing the 24 ton vehicle. Adolf Hitler then agreed to the production capacity of the BMM plant being totally utilized for the production of a "leichten Panzerjäger" (light tank hunter). This vehicle was planned to have a maximum weight of 13 tons and a high speed of up to 60 km/hour to make up for its thinner armor.

On December 17, 1943 the design drawings were presented for the vehicle to be constructed from components of the PzKpfw 38(t) alter (original) and neuer Art (the new design for a reconnaissance vehicle). It was planned that the final version of the Jagdpanzer would mount a recoilless gun but, as such a gun was not ready in time, designs were completed for mounting the available 7.5 cm Panzerjägerkanone.

A Hetzer production line at BMM factory in Prague. On the right are the brand new 7.5 cm PaK 39s with Saukopfblenden, ready for mounting. Once the production got underway, BMM was manufacturing around 150 vehicles per month, with an all-time high of 298 Hetzers in November 1944. This photograph was taken in June 1944.

The design advanced with great speed and by January 24, 1944 a wooden mock-up was completed. It was presented to Heeres Waffenamt two days later. The gun chosen was the Panzejägerkanone 39, used already in the Jagdpanzer IV. Three vehicles were ordered immediately to be completed in March 1944 for troop trials.

The vehicle was officially named by the WaffenAmt as the "Sturmgeschütz neuer Art mit 7.5 cm PaK 39 L/40 auf Fahrgestell PzKpfw 38(t)". This was abbreviated to "Stu.Gesch.38(t)". The official name used by the Panzertruppe was "Leichte Panzerjäger 38(t)". All these organizations recognized the official name change to "Jagdpanzer 38 (SdKfz 138/2)" in November 1944. The name "Hetzer" was never officially adopted and originated from the troops as their nickname for the Jagdpanzer 38, as General Guderian explained to Adolf Hitler in his briefing papers from December 4, 1944.

TECHNICAL DESCRIPTION:

Though the Jagdpanzer 38 was planned to use 80% of PzKpfw 38(t) components, its hull was totally new. It was low and balistically well shaped. The upper front plate was 60 mm thick and angled at 60°, the lower plate was of the same thickness and inclined 40°. The thinner (20 mm) upper and lower side plates were inclined by 40° and 15°, respectively. The 7.5 cm PaK 39 was mounted on the right side of the front plate. This resulted in a very limited traverse of only 5° to the left and 10° to the right instead of the 15° + 15° called for in the original specification. The offset gun mount also resulted

Hetzer's cross-country performance being evaluated at BMM test track, in comparison with the Ausf.M chassis.

A top view of a production Hetzer. In the front part is the gun's spotting scope under its protective guard. Behind it on the left is the Rundumfeur machine gun mount; behind it is the two-part gunner's hatch. The commander's hatch is on the right.

in overloading the right side suspension by an additional 850 kg. The vehicle was also nose-heavy and its front sat lower by 10 cm.

The driver sat on the left side for the first time in a Czech-designed vehicle (before the war, in Czechoslovakia driving was done on the left side, thus all designs placed the driver on the right). The gunner and loader were in the hull and had a common hatch with the driver in the left rear top plate. The commander sat directly behind the gun on the right side and had his own two-part hatch. Vision devices were very limited: the driver had a twin periscope to the front, with no provision to ride head-up. The gunner had the main gun periscope sight "Sfl.ZFla". The "Rundumfeuer"(all-round fire) machine gun on the top of the vehicle had its own periscope sight. There was a fixed periscope at 9 o'clock for the loader, and the commander had a scissors periscope "SF14Z". With the hatches closed the Jagdpanzer 38 was virtually blind on the right side.

The Hetzer was the first welded armored vehicle manufactured by BMM. The armored plate was again provided by Poldi or VHHT, as for all the other Czech-made AFVs.

The chassis followed the original PzKpfw 38(t) layout. The driving sprockets and the idlers were used as they were, but the

A BMM Hetzer in the "ambush" camouflage scheme. The colors are the basic sand yellow with dark green and reddish brown fields, and sand yellow spots in the darker fields.

road wheels were of the larger diameter as the wheels of the TNHnA, and only one return roller was used. The road wheels and the return roller were provided with rubber tires. It proved necessary to use thicker leaf springs to achieve balance and to accommodate the larger weight of 16 tons. The width increased from 2.14 m of the PzKpfw 38(t) to 2.63 m.

The power was provided by a Praga AE six-cylinder in-line gasoline engine with an output of 160 HP/2,600 rpm. BMM tried to increase the output and at the beginning of 1945 had an improved version of the engine with Bosch magnetos and rpms up to 3,200, but this engine was never used in the production vehicles. The top speed was only 40 km/hour. The engine exhaust was very hot and thus it was necessary to lead it outside by the shortest way, and to provide the muffler with a flame-damper.

The cooling system of the engine consisted of a radiator, a ventilator, an oil cooler for both the engine and the gearbox and a water pump. The vehicles were also equipped with an engine water heater that used a blow-torch for winter starting. This arrangement was standard on German-designed tanks, but was a first for a Czech-

Size comparison between a Hetzer and the Jagdpanther. These were the only two chassis that have been approved for continuous production from September 1944 on. The Jagdpanther carried the 8.8 cm PaK 43/3, and though heavier by 30 tons, had a comparable speed with the Hetzer.

A front view of a Hetzer in a different paint scheme. The hull was welded and had very clean lines with well sloped armor.

A top view of the Hetzer, showing the layout of the hatches.

An ex-Swiss G-13, acquired by Mr. Terry Johns of Florissant, MO, and restored as an German vehicle. The following photographs are of this vehicle.

A Hetzer with the top plates removed, showing the gun on the right front with the commander's area behind it; the driver on the left. The engine is in the middle of the engine compartment with the radiator behind it and the air filters on the rear right. The gasoline tanks are on both sides in the rear.

View from the engine compartment to the driver's station through the door in the fire-wall. The radio set had been removed.

The rear wall with the starting handle. The small step on the right is where the blowtorch for warming the engine's water in cold weather would be attached.

An "opened" Hetzer showing the periscope and the handles for the Rundumfeuer machine gun mount.

The detailed view of the gun's spotting scope and the machine gun mount. Its armored shield has been removed.

The Notek light and its cable on the front wall. It provided diffused soft light which was sufficient to illuminate the road in front of the vehicle, but could not be seen from the air.

The Abstand Rücklicht with the upper "distance" four rectangles showing.

The same light with the lower standard red and orange rear lights unmasked.

The spotting scope from the gunner's side. In the rear the driver's episcopes.

The radio set on the left wall. The yellow stripe denotes the Panzer frequencies.

designed vehicle (it was experimentally tested on the Mörserzugmittel 35(t), but was not officially introduced).

In the engine compartment there were two fuel tanks, connected by hoses. The main left tank was equipped with the fueling neck and held 220 liters, the right one had a capacity of 100 liters, for a range of approximately 185 km. During driving, the gasoline from the right tank flowed into the left one as this was emptied, except for a reserve of 50 liters.

The well-proven Praga-Wilson gearbox was used again, but the clutches had to be strengthened and a new drivetrain had to be developed to accommodate the higher strains caused by the increased weight.

The installation of the fairly large gun in a small fighting compartment was made possible by a new mounting, invented by Dipl.Ing. K. Stollberg and used for the first time in the Jagdpanzer IV. The gun was fixed in a Cardan frame, fastened to the front wall. This mounting eliminated the old mountings that used the lower and the upper lafette. From outside, the gun was protected by a cast "Saukopf" ("swine's head") armor mantlet.

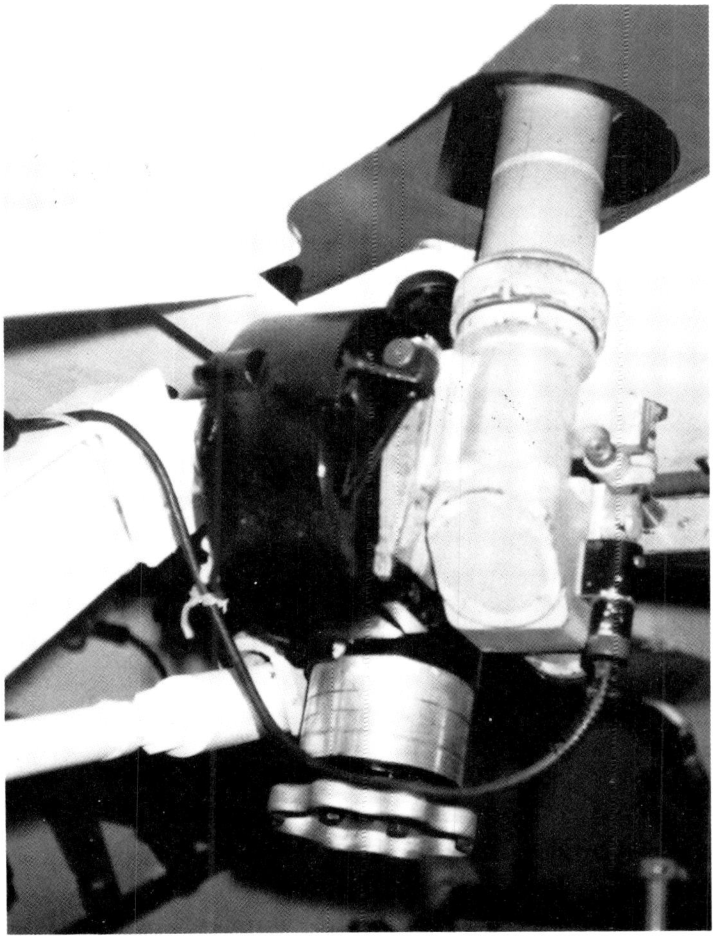

The spotting scope from the front, showing the Cardan joint connecting it to the gun.

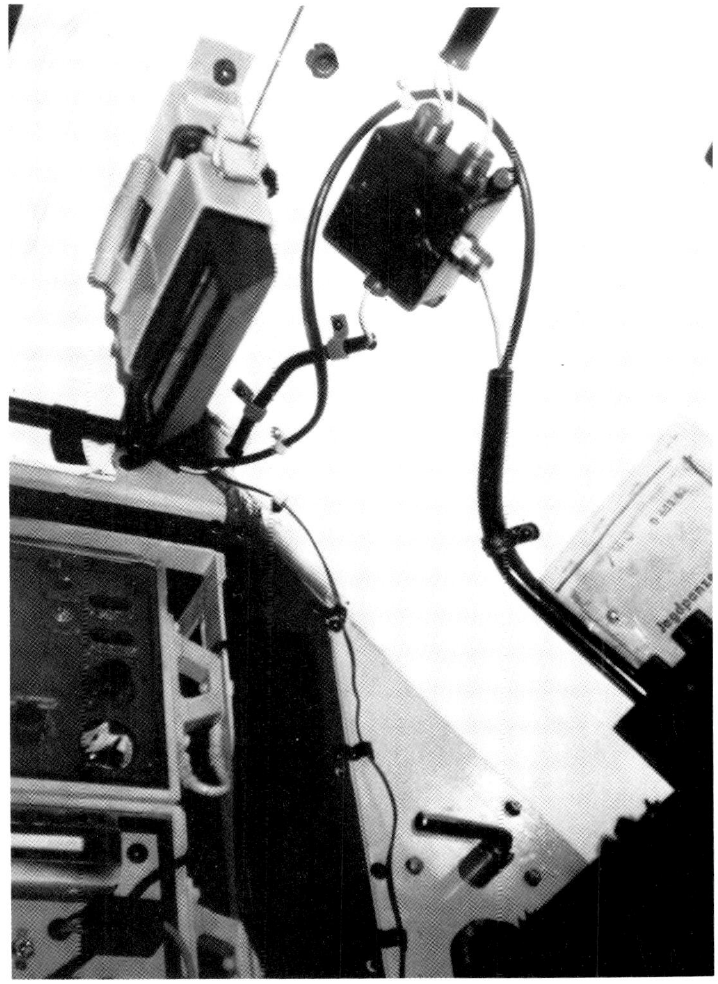

The loader's fixed episcope at 9 o'clock.

The 50-round drums of the machine gun ammunition.

A view of the gun's breech and the elevating and traversing wheels.

One of the drums fitted on the machine gun.

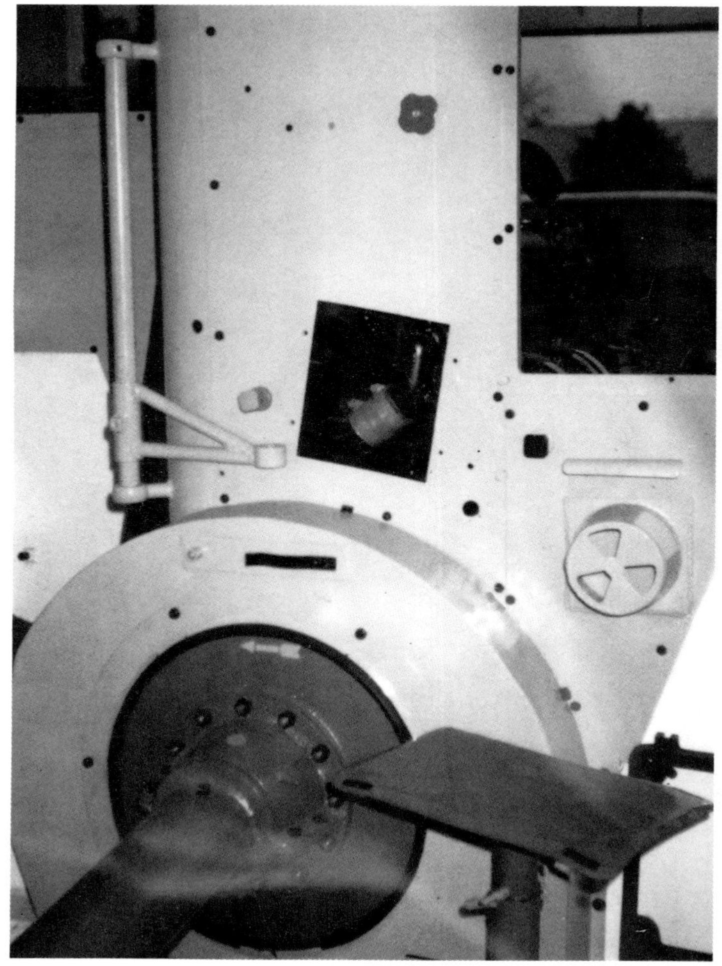

The main shaft coming from the engine compartment forward. On the left, the commander's area. Above the shaft is the sump pump. Below the open firewall door is the adjustable outlet for the fighting compartment heating air.

The gun was semi-automatic and fired AP (Panzergranate 39 or 40) and HE (Sprenggranate 34) rounds at muzzle velocities between 550 m/sec (HE) up to 930 m/sec (AP). The range was between 2,000 and 3,600 m. The gun could also fire shaped charge rounds (Holladungsgranate 38[c]) and smoke-screen rounds (Nebelgranate). A total of 41 rounds for the main gun were carried, 1,200 rounds for the machine gun.

The machine gun was fixed on a fully rotating mount on the top plate of the fighting compartment, and was protected by an angled armor shield. It was fed from a 50-round drum magazine. The loader could fire it from inside the fighting compartment and observe via a periscope sight with 3x enlargement and an observation field of 8°.

Since the design was rushed into production in a record time of less than four months from conception to the initial vehicles being completed, it is remarkable how few problems were encountered. Some production changes were:

April 1944: the outside towing brackets were dropped and were replaced by extending a section of the side armor plate and drilling holes in it to form a bracket.

The weight of the gun mantlet was decreased by decreasing its size.

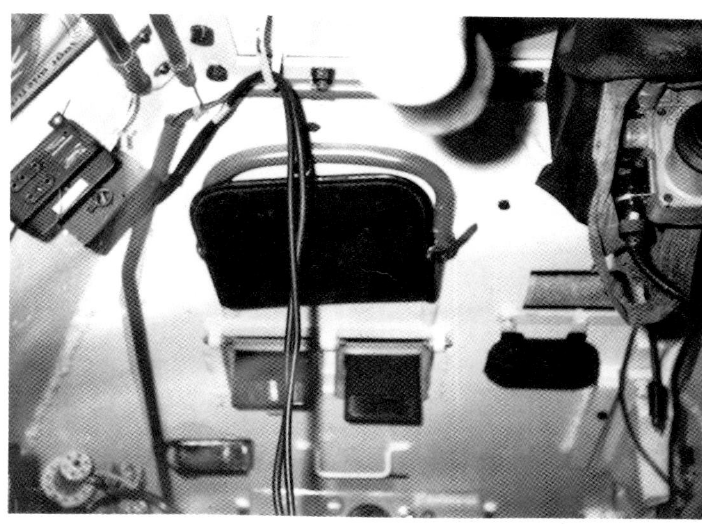

The top of the driver's compartment, showing his head-pad, the two episcopes and the intercom box on the left. One of the escape handles is seen below the episcopes.

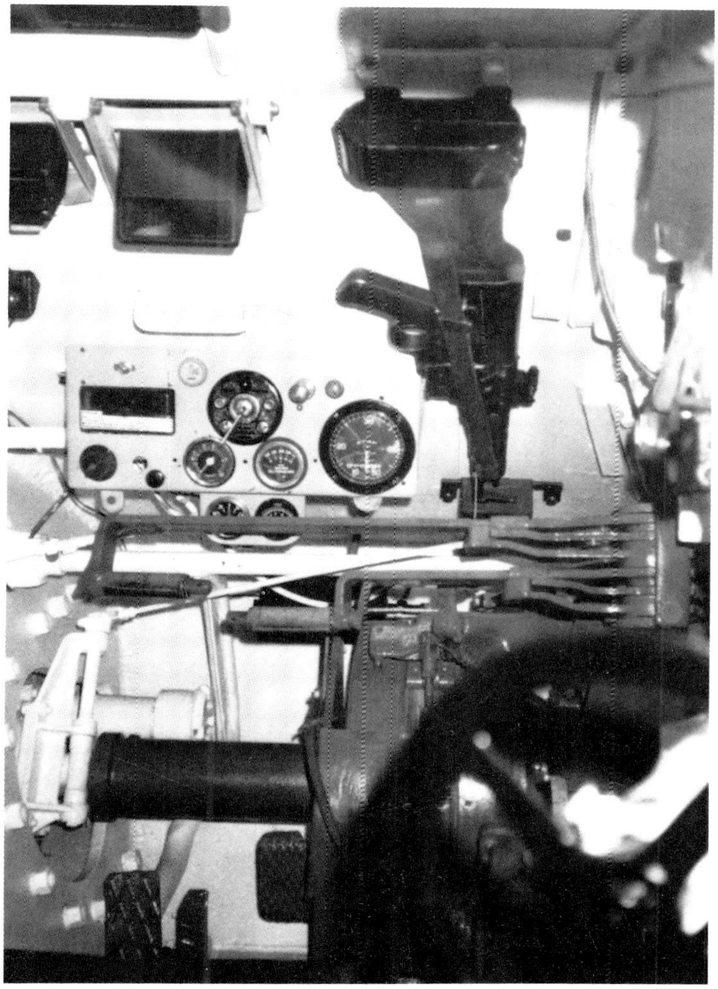

The driver's area. On lower left, the edge of his seat can be seen. On the right is the gear box. Up left are the episcopes and below them, the instrument panel. The left driving shaft is seen below the steering levers.

The main shaft and driver's pedals.

A Hetzer driver in his seat.

The instrument panel and the steering levers. On the panel, from right to left, are the speedometer, oil pressure warning light, water temperature gauge (missing), ignition switch, oil pressure gauge, fuse box and switch for the outside lights.

The commander in his area behind the gun. Gun rounds are stored on the right wall.

Two photographs of well camouflaged Hetzers of Waffen SS on the Western front in 1944.

A destroyed Hetzer on the Western front in 1944. The side armor was only 20 mm thick and was easily penetrated.

Holes were no longer drilled in the outer ring of the drive sprocket wheel.

The armor guard of the machine gun was cut shorter to prevent the fouling of the main gun sight guard.

May through July 1944: three smaller hatches were installed: a commander's hatch that opened to the rear, a hatch to fill the radiator on the lower right and a hatch to fill the fuel tanks on the left of the engine deck.

The heat guard of the muffler was deleted.

Three short threaded cylinders were welded to the roof of the fighting compartment as base mounts for a two-ton crane. This jib crane was used for lifting heavy components during maintenance of the gun, engine or drive train.

August 1944: a lighter inner and outer gun mantlet was introduced, reducing the weight by another 200 kg.

A burning Hetzer and his destroyer.

This Hetzer was destroyed by an American M 10 tank destroyer in November 1944. It carries a hand-painted ambush scheme.

One of the Hetzers from Škoda production line in Prague was taken over by the insurgents during the Prague uprising in May 1945. The opening for tae gun was hastily plated over and the vehicle was armed with machine guns. Note the late model of the idler wheel - flat dish with four holes.

Road wheels were introduced with a larger diameter center disc and a smaller rim. The new rims were drilled for 16 holes instead 32 for the old.

A whole series of changes to the idler wheels was introduced to save machining time during manufacturing:

- six holes on the original style flat plate;
- welded spokes with eight holes on a flat plate;
- eight holes in a smooth dish;
- stamped ribs in a dished plate with six holes;
- six holes in a smooth dish;
- four holes in a smooth dish.

Two handles were welded inside above the driver's seat to aid him in quick exit.

September 1944: the ends of the "Schürzen" side plates were bent inward to prevent them from being torn off when snagging on trees or other obstacles.

A Berge Hetzer with the insurgent crew during the uprising.

Hetzers of an unidentified Waffen SS unit in the last days of the war, May 1945, near Náchcd in Northern Bohemia.

To prevent breaking of the leaf springs, the front sets were increased to 9 mm thickness, while the rear ones remained at 7 mm.

October 1944: the armored housing above the driver's periscopes was removed. It was found that several times it caught shells that hit lower on the front plate and skidded upwards, and caused them to penetrate. The periscopes were mounted flush with the front plate and above them a thin metal guard was attached to prevent rain or sun interfering with the driver's vision.

Bolts holding the rims of the road wheels were working loose. New were riveted instead of bolted.

To mask the glowing exhaust at night, a "Flamm-Vernichter"(flame-damper) exhaust replaced the cylindrical muffler.

A spring compensator for the breech-heavy main gun was installed to aid in its elevation.

A large nozzle with an overflow pan was fitted to allow rapid filling of the fuel tanks. A Solex "Handpumpe" replaced the unreliable electric fuel pump.

A head cushion was attached to the inside of the commander's hatch.

November 1944: to increase the number of rounds carried, the location of the sight bracket storage box was moved to the right side of the commander, thus gaining storage space for an additional five rounds of the 7.5 cm PaK ammunition.

A new, more durable water pump was installed.

A better designed distribution vent in the firewall was installed for improved heating of the fighting compartment.

A heating plate was installed for the battery to prevent it from freezing.

A graveyard of the Hetzers in Southern Moravia, following the last large tank battle of the Second World War in April 1945. General Schörner's Army Group Center fought the Soviet Army to prevent its encirclement, as the Germans were desperately trying to reach the American lines to surrender. Before the battle, it still had 246 operational Hetzers.

The last war action of the Hetzers was the fighting during the Prague uprising between May 5 and May 9, 1945. This Sturmgeschütz III and Hetzer fought their way into the Old-town Square on May 8, and were destroyed there by Czech soldiers, using captured Panzerfausts, but not before they destroyed the old town-hall and several historical houses.

January 1945: a new Model 6.75 final drive with a stronger 10 : 80 gear ratio replaced the older Model 6 with its 12 : 88 gear ratio. This change was necessitated by failures of the final drives during frequent turns of the vehicles when engaging targets (due to the limited main gun traverse).

Rings were welded to the upper hull front and sides for holding branches used for camouflage.

On March 19, 1945 General Guderian ordered the immediate change to Diesel power, but his order could not have been carried out. Studies had shown that a switch to Diesel engines would have changed the vehicle profoundly and would have totally disrupted its production.

The Hetzers coming from BMM and Škoda assembly lines were in their majority painted in the new "ambush" scheme. While the BMM vehicles were spray-painted completely, the Škoda vehicles had the small spots applied by a brush.

Jagdpanzer 38 Variations

The **Panzerbefehlswagen 38** carried, in addition to the standard Fu5 radio set, the Fu8 radio and a second aerial.

The **Jagdpanzer 38 Starr** was meant to carry a gun in a "Starr" configuration, i.e., a normal gun mounted rigidly without a recoil cylinder in the front plate. The recoil of the gun was dissipated through the whole vehicle. This arrangement allowed the use of a smaller and lighter mount, provided additional space inside the vehicle and an increased traverse of the gun. Because the construction of such a gun mount was not yet ready, the final configuration of the Jagdpanzer 38 carried the standard 7.5 cm Panzerjägerkanone 39 in a normal mount.

The use of the 7.5 cm Panzerjägerkanone 39 in a normal mount had its shortcomings. The gun was well offset to the right, overloading the right suspension. It had a limited traverse and it was bulky for the small fighting compartment.

All these disadvantages would have been solved by using the rigid mounted gun, and so its development was carried on, though the production used the regular mount. Both Krupp and Rheinmetall-Borsig had been assigned the development of the rigid mounts by

A wooden mock-up of the Starr mount for the Hetzer at BMM.

A rear view of a late Hetzer with the standard Praga AE gasoline engine. Compare with the view of the Starr Hetzer.

A front view of a Hetzer Starr. The much smaller gun mantle is evident. The driver's episcopes are protected only by a metal cover against rain, but this cover was not strong enough to deflect antitank rounds inside like the original armored casting. On the right front fender the wooden block to support the jack is mounted.

The rear view of the Hetzer Starr with the Tatra Diesel engine. The difference between the standard engine are the raised air intake on the rear deck and the cover over the former radiator opening in the rear plate.

One of the Hetzers used by the Czechoslovak fighters during the Prague uprising in May 1945. This vehicle has the gun mantlet, but no gun.

Speer's Reichsministerium für Rüstung und Kriegsproduction in early 1943. The original tests, conducted on the PzKpfw II chassis with a 12 cm mortar in April 1943 at the Rheinmetall testing range had shown that the concept was valid. When firing the mortar, the unbraked vehicle rolled only about 19 cm, and the suspension compression was a mere 20-25 mm.

Further tests were conducted with the 7.5 cm KwK L/48 gun, mounted rigidly in the turret of a PzKpfw IV in a reinforced 100 mm thick front plate. The forces generated by the firing were measured to be around 130 tons, which moved the heavier PzKpfw IV only about 5 cm backwards during the firing of the gun.

Once the decision was made to install the rigid mount into the new Jagdpanzer 38, Alkett was authorized to carry on the development in cooperation with Krupp. They tested the rigid mount in March 1944 on a Sturmgeschütz III (L/48, L/60 and L/70 guns were planned, though only the L/48 was tested at this time). BMM delivered to Alkett one converted Jagdpanzer 38 in May 1944, and three more incomplete vehicles were shipped in September, to be completed by Krupp/Alkett.

The first tests had been conducted in Hillersleben side by side on the Jagdpanzer 38 and Jagdpanzer IV. Test firings had shown the feasibility of the project, but also several complications with the laying equipment and optics. The "O" series of ten vehicles was completed in December 1944 and January 1945 by BMM, side-by-side with the normal production. None of these were issued to the troops. The order for the first production series of 100 vehicles was issued in February 1945 to Škoda, but none of these vehicles were built before the end of the war.

After the war, the Czechoslovak Army inherited a sizable number of Hetzers. Out of these, nine were Hetzers with the Starr gun mount. The German numbers of the Starr Hetzers were 321679, 321681, 321682, 321683, 322370, 322372, 322373, 322374 and 322971. All the Starr Hetzers were eventually converted to normal Hetzers with the regular gun mount.

The air-cooled Tatra Diesel engine with its air-filters in the engine compartment of Hetzer Starr. Only 14 vehicles were built.

A complete Hetzer of the Czech insurgents. Behind it is another gun Hetzer. These vehicles were probably captured from the Germans after their retreat from Prague on May 8, 1945.

A frontal view of the Bergepanzer 38(t). BMM built 181 of these recovery vehicles, while Škoda built none. The Bergepanzer had a lowered open top superstructure, a spade in the rear, and a five-ton winch in the right side of the crew compartment. It also carried a disassembled two-ton jib crane on the left hull side plate.

A rear view of the spade. It was anchored in massive joints welded to the lower part of the rear hull plate.

Bergepanzer 38

The recovery vehicle Bergepanzer 38 was built concurrently with the Jagdpanzer 38. It had a weight of 14,5 tons and a crew of four. It carried a lower, open-top superstructure and no gun. It was equipped with a five-ton winch, a rear spade and a collapsible two-ton crane. It was not very successful, as the engine was weak for recovery purposes.

Flammpanzer 38

In December 1944 twenty production Hetzers were modified as flame-throwing tanks by having their gun removed and replaced with the 14 mm Flammenwerfer 41 flame-thrower. A simulated barrel was fitted over the flame-thrower to disguise the special purpose of the vehicle. 700 liters of the fuel for the flame-thrower were carried internally. With a range of 50-60 m, the fuel was enough for 87.5 seconds of fire. The weight was 15.5 tons and the crew was again four men. These vehicles were made specifically for the Ardennes offensive, but most of them were actually used as part of the XIII SS Corps of the Army Group G during the "Nordwind" offensive in the Low Vosges in January 1945.

15 cm sIG 33/2 (Sfl) auf Jagdpanzer 38

Since the production of the self-propelled howitzer on the PzKpfw 38(t) chassis had been terminated early in 1944, and since the front units demanded these support vehicles, it was decided to build the self-propelled howitzer on the Bergepanzer 38 chassis starting from

The same vehicle from the left. The winch cable opening in the rear plate is well visible, as is the spade. Note the rear idlers: on the left side, the vehicle has the stamped dish with six holes, and on the right a flat dish with six holes.

The spade in the lowered position. It was raised and lowered by the winch.

A Flammpanzer 38 was a conversion from a Hetzer. The gun was replaced with the Flammenwerfer 41 and 700 liters of fuel were carried internally. Twenty were converted for the Ardennes offensive in December 1944.

15 cm sIG 33/2 auf Jagdpanzer 38 was a conversion from the Bergepanzer. The howitzer was carried in a heightened superstructure. Thirty were converted.

November 1944. The gun was carried in a heightened superstructure, which otherwise followed the clean lines of the Hetzer design. Various sources claim that a total of 30 vehicles were converted, but according to available documents neither BMM nor Škoda did these conversions. They must have been performed by a German company, probably Alkett.

Aufklärungspanzer 38

With the phasing out of most German tank chassis in late 1944, only the 38(t) and 38(d) were to remain in the light class. The Jagdpanzer 38 was to be a basis for a new reconnaissance vehicle, armed with the short 7.5 cm K51 gun in a sloped, open top superstructure (Gerät 564), with a crew of three. There were three other versions of the Aufklärungspanzer 38 planned, namely with the 2

The fake gun barrel is well visible on this picture of a captured Flammpanzer 38 near Bastogne.

Two photographs of the self-propelled howitzer at a minimum and a maximum elevation of the gun. A spring-loaded hinged protective plate under the gun was used similar to the sIG Ausf.M.

cm FLAK 38 (Gerät 563), with the 2 cm KwK Zwilling (Gerät 585) and finally a version armed with the 12 cm mortar GraW42 (Gerät 586). Only prototypes were built by the end of the war.

Jagdpanzer 38d

Originally long-term plans for tank production specified that the PzKpfw IV chassis would be replaced by the Pz III/IV chassis by mid 1945. However, these plans were canceled in autumn 1944 when Adolf Hitler decided that henceforward all light and medium construction would be based on 38(t) and 38(d) chassis only. The 38(t) was to continue in production at BMM and Škoda as Hetzer, Hetzer Starr, sIG (Sfl) and the Aufklärungspanzer 38.

The 38(d) was a larger, redesigned version of the 38(t). It used the new Tatra twelve cylinder air-cooled Diesel engine developing 220 HP, a new drive train and new drive and sprocket wheels. The redesigned vehicle was large enough to accommodate the 7.5 cm PaK 42 L/70, and thus could replace the Pz IV/70. Alternative weapons were the PaK 39 L/48 and StuH 42, so that the vehicle could replace the StuG III as well. Only prototypes had been completed, but it was planned from mid 1945 that Alkett, Krupp-Gruson, MIAG and Ni-Werke would be producing between them 1,250 units per month.The Jagdpanzer 38(d) was supposed to weigh 16 tons with 80 mm frontal armor. The new engine gave it a top speed of 42 km/hour and it had a range of 220 km on roads.

In late 1944 a specification was issued for a fully tracked personnel carrier based on a lengthened 38(d) chassis. By adding a fifth road wheel, the length was increased to 6.2 m. The armor was 30 mm at the front and 20 mm on the sides. The vehicle was designed to carry a hemispherical turret with a dual purpose 2.0 cm gun and had a crew of four. It could carry eight men in its rear section. Its weight was planned to be 12 tons and the maximum speed of 30 km/hour with a range of 200 km. Only a mock-up was built of this vehicle.

Flakpanzer 38(d) "Kugelblitz"

Besides the Jagdpanzer vehicles, the 38(d) was intended to replace the Flakpanzer Kugelblitz, once the production of the Pz IV chassis was ended. The vehicle was designed with a small, one-man turret with the formidable armament of two 2 cm MK 151 and two 3 cm MK 103 cannons. The hydraulic traverse and elevation permitted 45°/sec movement. The ammunition supply was planned as 1,200 3 cm and 1,000 2 cm rounds. There were two versions planned, the Ausf. Protektorat and the Ausf. Reich, the difference between them being in the hull configuration. Again, the vehicles existed only as wooden mock ups.

A rear view of the self-propelled howitzer.

The only prototype of the Aufklärungspanzer 38 built before the end of the war. It carried the short 7.5 cm K51 gun in an open top superstructure, though other armament versions were on the drawing board.

Other vehicles planned on the Jagdpanzer 38(d) chassis were:

Jagdpanzer 38(d) 638/28 - 10.5 cm StuH (Gerät 547);
Jagdpanzer 38(d) 638/29 - 7.5 cm PaK 42/1 (Gerät 548);
Jagdpanzer 38(d) für PWK 10H73 (Gerät 543);
Aufklärungspanzer 38(d) - four versions of armaments were planned, namely the 7.5 cm KwK L/48, 7.5 cm K51, 2 cm KwK Zwilling and the 12 cm GraW42. One prototype with the Tatra Diesel engine and armed with the 7.5 cm K51 L/24 was tested by late 1944 in Kummersdorf.
28 cm Sturmmörser 38(d) - a carrier for the 28 cm mortar (Gerät 589);
Bergepanzer 38(d);
Schützenpanzerwagen auf 38(d) - with a lengthened chassis and a weight of 12 tons, its planned armor was 20-30 mm, armed with a 20 mm dual purpose cannon in a spherical turret, designed to carry four-men crew and a PanzerGrenadier section of eight men. Mock up only.

Leichter Einheitswaffenträger

10.5 cm lFH 18/40/5-GW 638/26 (Gerät 587)
15 cm sIG 33/2-GW 638/27 (Gerät 588)
8.8 cm PaK 43/1 L/71 (GW 638/18 Sf)

The initial designs for the gun carrier (Waffenträger) were based on the Pz III/IV chassis being developed in 1943. The Wa.Prüf-4 decided that these were too heavy and too costly for the purposes of the artillery. In February 1944 new specifications were issued for a Waffenträger to replace the towed artillery weapons. The gun was to be dismountable from a low rear platform without any special equipment. When on the platform, it had to have a 360° traverse and an elevation -8° +45°. Other requirements were a machine gun

Ardelt prototype of the 8.8 cm PaK 43/3 Waffenträger vehicle with Krupp-Steyer running gear.

In the rear is the Rheinmetall-Borsig prototype of the le.Einheitswaffenträger with the 8.8 cm PaK 43.

for close defense, a radio set, a maximum speed of 35km/hour, a range of between 100 and 150 km, and a minimum of 50 rounds for the gun carried on the vehicle. All the guns were also to be capable of direct fire against tanks. Krupp was given the overall responsibility for the project. Adler and Steyer were to develop the chassis, using Pz 38(t) components, while Rheinmetall cooperated on the gun development.

For the Waffenträgers a front engine layout was proposed, as it allowed a lower and better accessible gun platform in the rear. The engine was on the right front, the driver sat on the left alongside it. The driver's compartment was collapsible to allow a greater depression of the gun. Steyer proposed a vehicle based on the RSO running gear, but Ardelt's design based on the regular Pz 38(t) chassis was accepted for production.

Prototypes were built in late 1944. In this version, the vehicle with the 10.5 cm gun had a weight of 13.5 tons, length 6.35 m, width 3.16 m and armor between 10 and 20 mm. There was again a four-men crew, and the standard Praga engine gave the vehicle top speed of 35 km/hour.

Production was planned for spring 1945 with 350 units per month being produced by September 1945. Production vehicles were planned on the larger chassis of the 38(d) with its more powerful engine. A prototype of a Waffenträger based on the 38(d) and mounting the 8.8 cm PaK 43 was built and successfully tested at Hillersleben as late as April 27, 1945.

The Leichter Einheitswaffenträger was also called the Krupp II.

Mittlerer Einheitswaffenträger
10.5 cl lFH 18/40/5-GW 638/21 (Gerät 578)
12.8 cm K81/3-GW 638/22 (Gerät 579)
15 cm sIG 33/2-GW 638/20 (Gerät 577)
15 cm sFH 18/6-GW 638/23 (Gerät 580)
Known as Krupp I, these vehicles were developed simultaneously

A production version of the Ardelt vehicle.

Krupp-Steyr prototype of the le.Einheitswaffenträger for 8.8 cm PaK 43/3 L/71 with the RSO running gear.

with the Krup II to have more possibilities for the types of guns mounted. They were longer, with six road wheels per side. This caused problems with the width to length ratio, and the design was not ready for production before the end of the war.

Starting again on the 38(t) chassis, production vehicles would have used the 38(d) chassis, with armor between 10 and 20 mm. The weight depended on the gun used: with the 10.5 cm gun it was planned to be 13 tons, with the 12.8 cm gun 15.8 tons. Again, the mounting of the 8.8 cm PaK 43 was planned.

TABLE 17
Production of Jagdpanzer 38 and its variants

DATE	PLANNED (WafAmt)	SHIPPED TO UNITS	PRODUCED BY BMM JgPz 38	Berge	Staar	PRODUCED BY ŠKODA JgPz 38
1944						
March			3			
April	20		20			
May	50		50	8	1	
June	100		100	2		
July	175	90	100			10
Aug.	175	127	150	8		20
Sep.	250	125	190	14	3	30
Oct.	330	161	133	50		57
Nov.	350	274	298	19		89
Dec.	380	309	223		5	104
1945						
Jan.	430	373	289	39	5	145
Feb.	350	277	273	19		125
March	350	451	148	19		153
April	250	175	70	3		47
TOTAL	3210	2362[1]	2047	181	14	780

[1]Includes 75 vehicles shipped to Hungary and 20 rebuilt as Flammpanzers.

All Jagdpanzer 38 chassis numbers were six-digit. BMM was assigned series 321001-323000 and 325001-327000 while Škoda was assigned numbers 323001-325000 and 327001-332000, as the Wehrmacht had ordered a total of 11,000 Jagdpanzer 38 vehicles in four orders (late 1943 for 2,000, February 14, 1944 for 4,000, June 17, 1944 for 2,000 and finally 3,000 on October 19, 1944).

TABLE 18
Production and Shipments of Jagdpanzer 38
(Cumulative Data)

DATE	PRODUCTION BMM[1]	SHIPPED FROM BMM	TOTAL PRODUCTION[2]	SHIPPED TO UNITS[3]
1944				
APRIL	23	23	23	
MAY	73	69	82	
JUNE	173	132	184	
JULY	273	218	294	90
AUG.	423	368	472	217
SEP.	613		709	342
OCT.	748		949	503
NOV.	1,046		1,355	777
DEC.	1,274	1,207	1,687	1,086
1945				
JAN.	1,568	1,555	2,165	1,459
FEB.	1,841	1,828	2,582	1,736
MAR.	1,989	1,976	2,902	2,187
APRIL+MAY	2,242	2,060	3,022	2,362

[1] Includes 14 Starr Hetzers and 181 Berge Hetzers.
[2] Combined production of BMM and Škoda.
[3] OKW data (see TABLE 11). Includes 20 vehicles rebuilt as Flammpanzers.

A Mittlerer Einheitswaffenträger with the 10.5 cm leFH 18/40 howitzer.

Škoda Wartime Developments

Following the German occupation, the Škoda works in Pilsen were integrated into the German armaments program as a part of the Hermann Göring Werke. While before the war Škoda was a major tanks manufacturer, after 1939 it became only a repair shop first for its own PzKpfw 35(t) tanks, later for the PzKpfw I and II. Škoda also manufactured various sub-assemblies for tank production of both German and Austrian companies.

Another situation was in the gun manufacturing area. Škoda was first supplying the 3.7 cm KwK for the BMM PzKpfw 38(t) tanks, but in 1942 it switched to producing the 7.5 cm StuK 40, used in the StuG III. Up to the end of the war, Škoda manufactured 3,750 of these guns, which represented 40% of this type made. Another successful program was the manufacture of 15 cm StuH 43 howitzers for the Brummbär self-propelled gun. Škoda made 356 of these, supplying 100% of the Brummbärs. Škoda also made the 7.5 cm KwK 42/1 for the Panther Schmall Turm and developed an autoloader for this application.

Another Škoda gun, the 4.7 cm A5 antitank gun, was used in one of the first German Panzerjäger vehicles, built on the PzKpfw I chassis. Alkett modified 202 of them in time for the French campaign, and after their success, another 174 were built on the chassis of the captured Renault 35R tanks.

Škoda tried to further develop its Š-II-a tank. It had available the LT vz.35 prototype and the Š-II-aR prototype, developed for Romania. These two vehicles were used for various experiments. They were originally designated as the T-11 in 1939. The T-12 was a version with the 4.7 cm gun. The T-12D had a Diesel engine, required by the Yugoslav army. The T-13 had heavier armor and its weight raised to 13 tons. In 1941 a new prototype designated T-13M had mechanical steering, but otherwise was identical to the T-

Škoda during the first war years was repairing aside from its own PzKpfw 35(t) also certain German equipment, like this PzKpfw I.

Škoda's 4.7 cm A5 antitank gun was widely used on the PzKpfw I chassis. The combination was very successful in France, and was utilized also at the beginning of the Russian campaign in 1941. Here it is accompanied by the SdKfz 251/10 halftrack with the 3.7 cm PaK 35/36.

The wooden mock-up of the le.F.H.43(Sf.) Škoda, the self-propelled 10.5 cm howitzer on the T-25 chassis.

Škoda's ŠK-13 Dampfschlepper, or steam tractor from 1945. Based on a 38(d) chassis lengthened by two more road wheels, it could pull 9.2 tons at 15 km/hour.

11 tank. The Germans were not interested in any of those developments and the prototypes remained Škoda's property. So did the T-21 and T-23 (T-21 with mechanical steering) prototypes, and the T-22, ordered and tested by the Wehrmacht in 1941, but not accepted for production.

Škoda tried to get into tank manufacturing in 1941, when the experience from the Russian front led to demands for more powerful tanks and tank hunters. In the latter category, Škoda offered a tank hunter based on its Š-II-c medium tank, armed with the 7.5 cm Škoda A13 antitank gun in a low, well-armored superstructure. The vehicle was offered to the representatives of Wa.Prüf-6, but they were not interested, even when the vehicle was recommended by the president of Hermann Göring Werke Voss.

Almost simultaneously, Škoda offered its prototype of the medium tank T-25. It was clearly influenced by the T-34 design, as it had well-sloped armor and a turret well forward. Škoda planned to use a new eight cylinder engine with 450 HP output, which would have given the vehicle a very favorable power/weight ratio of 22 HP/ton and a high speed of 60 km/hour. The vehicle was planned to be 6.04 m long and 2.75 m wide, with 460 mm wide tracks and 0.68 kg/cm^2 ground pressure. The vehicle was designed to cross a ditch 265 cm wide, wade in water 120 cm deep and negotiate a 40° gradient. Škoda also developed a new 7.5 cm A18 KwK tank gun, semiautomatic and provided with a drum auto-loader. The gun's barrel was cleaned with compressed air after firing, and the traverse of the turret was hydraulically operated. Though very advanced, this design also did not elicit any interest from Wa.Prüf-6 and did not get past the mock up form.

In January 1943, Škoda offered a self-propelled 10.5 cm howitzer on the T-25 chassis, under the designation le.F.H.43(Sfl) Škoda. The howitzer was in a fully rotating turret and, as the competing designs from that time, was removable from the vehicle. With the armor between 16 and 30 mm, the weight of the vehicle was calculated at 24.2 tons. The gun could fire a 14.8 kg shell at 610 m/sec. up to a distance of 13 km. This vehicle was built only as a wooden mock-up and was not accepted for production.

Škoda also participated in the already mentioned competition for a fast light tank for the reconnaissance units of the Wehrmacht together with BMM and MAN. Škoda completely changed its Š-II-a design to meet the specifications. The hull and the turret were based on the Š-II-a, but those were the only parts not changed. The engine was new - a V-8 engine with an output of 215 HP(159 kW); so was a new epicyclical gearbox with six gears, rear drive and a completely new running gear, using four large (720 mm OD) wheels on each side, sprung with half-elliptical springs. The steering and gear changing was hydraulic-mechanical, as such a system was proven to be much more dependable than the standard Škoda pneumatic steering.

Škoda finished the first of the five ordered prototypes on October 16, 1941 and on December 2 submitted the second prototype,

A finished lot of 8-ton artillery tractors SdKfz 10, manufactured by Škoda, which built 2,000 of them during the war.

Tatra's schweres Wehrmachtschlepper was based on their heavy truck Tatra 111 with an air-cooled Diesel engine. Prototypes were built and tested, but it did not attain full-scale production due to the war's end. The vehicle was further developed by Tatra after the war as Type 809, but did not attain production.

Tatra's sWS during the Ardennes offensive in December 1944, being passed by a Panther tank.

which was already welded. After two months of testing at Škoda both tanks were sent to Kummersdorf, where they were thoroughly tested in competition with the BMM and MAN entries. Though the testing commission recommended the BMM entry, MAN was given the order. Škoda was left with finishing the remaining three prototypes. The third and fourth tanks without the turret were shipped in August and October to Alkett's research institute in Berlin-Borsigwalde, the fifth one remained in Pilsen. Škoda put it into running condition in 1947, equipped it with an LT vz.35 turret and tried to use it as a demonstrator for foreign customers.

During the war, Škoda experimented with the gasoline-electric drive units, based on its ŠET design, and cooperated with several German companies on the development of such drives for extra-heavy tanks.

SWS during the cross-country trials.

In January 1945 Škoda obtained an order from OKH to develop a steam driven tracked tractor and recovery vehicle, based on the Pz 38(d) chassis. Škoda finished a prototype of the "Dampfschlepper" under its designation ŠK-13. It was powered by two 112 HP(82.8 kW) steam engines from the "Sentinel" trucks Škoda was building under a license before the war. The engines were fed from a central boiler, operating at 25 atm. and 320°C. The vehicle had a weight of 20 tons, attained speeds up to 15 km/hour and had a range of 150 km. Its pulling strength was 9.2 tons. A second prototype (ŠK-23) remained unfinished by the war's end.

Also in January 1945, Škoda started the development of a 30.5 cm Granatwerfer (mortar) which was to be mounted on the Selbsfahrlafette GW 609/9 (Gerät 817), based on the Tiger B chassis. The prototype was ready in three months, but was never mounted in the actual vehicle, due to the end of the war. On the same chassis was planned a smoothbore 42 cm mortar, also designed by Škoda.

From July 1944, Škoda started tank manufacturing by participating in the Jagdpanzer 38 program. By the end of the war, 780 of these vehicles were manufactured by Škoda in several factories (Plzeň, Radčice, Praha). Škoda also participated in the development of a gun for the Starr mount under the coding D3-287, and mounted successfully into one Jagdpanzer 38 (no. 323815) the 7.5 cm StuK 40 antitank gun.

10

POST-WAR DEVELOPMENTS

The Jagdpanzer 38 Hetzer was developed by ČKD (BMM) in Prague and was manufactured by both ČKD and Škoda, over 2,800 having been delivered in the last year of the war. It was also widely used by the Wehrmacht anti-tank units which surrendered in May 1945 inside the borders of the newly formed Czechoslovak Republic. It is therefore not surprising that the Czechoslovak army decided to utilize it as its main armored vehicle.

On November 27, 1945 the Headquarters of the Armored Corps instituted new designations for the ex-German vehicles. The Hetzer became the ST-I (Stihač Tanků = Tank Hunter or Jagdpanzer), the Marder was designated as the ST-II (the army had only 12 of them and used them only for training; all were scrapped in late 1948) and ST-III was reserved for a driver's training vehicle based on the Hetzer chassis.

There were more than 300 Hetzers left by the various German units available to the Czechoslovak army, which placed orders with both ČKD and Škoda for their repair and refurbishing. Moreover,

An ST-I in the Military Museum in Prage, Kbely. The ST-Is had the side aprons usually removed.

The LT vz.38 tank finally serving with the army it was designed for. After the war, the Czechoslovak army got a total of 38 of them and used them under the designation LT vz.38/37 for driver training. They were part of the 21st and 22nd Tank Brigades. After 1949 the remaining 17 LT vz.38/37 were used as parts of armored trains and remained with them until 1955, when both the trains and the tanks were scrapped.

ST-I, the new designation for the Hetzer, during a parade in Prague. In Czechoslovak army's service the Rundumfeur machine gun was deleted, the exterior stowage was modified and a normal driving lamp was fitted instead of the Notek lamp. The crew is wearing the Russian padded tanker's helmets.

Rear view of the Kbely ST-I, showing the muffler arrangement, rear towing hooks and right side body fittings.

A front view of a camouflaged ST-III, showing the untypical driver's visor and the superstructure with its viewing ports.

An ST-III trainer with the superstructure adapted for drivers training.

A detail of the "pulpit" of the ST-III fitted into the former gun opening.

Rear view of the ST-III showing the boxy addition with its two-part hatch.

Driver's position in the ST-III. The instrument panel and the steering levers were not changed from the original Hetzer, but the visor is new.

Right front seat for the instructor. The gun cut-out in the front plate is well visible. The angular box had a large opening in the front wall and its own hatch.

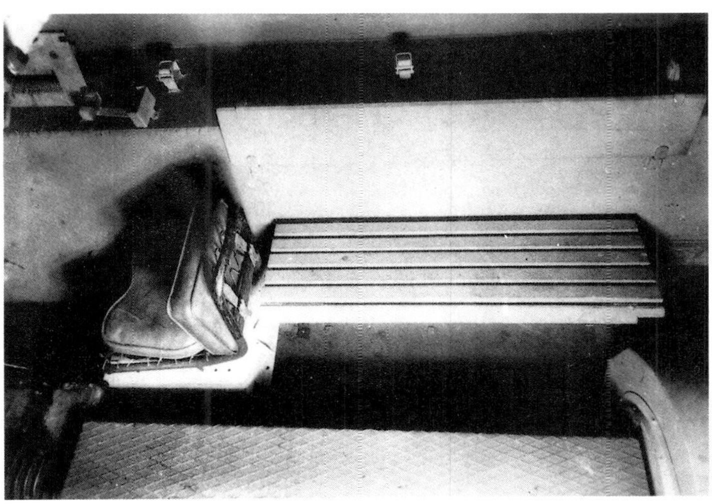

Right and left benches for the pupils inside the hull of the ST-III.

the factories had many vehicles in various stages of production on their production lines, and the army decided to finish them and have them delivered. The first order went to ČKD in February 1946 and was for fifty standard gun ST-I vehicles and fifty ST-III trainers, whose prototype was approved by the army shortly before that. ČKD delivered them during 1946 and 1947. The ST-III used the standard chassis, engine and slightly modified superstructure. Though the armor thickness was maintained, a fixed box was placed on top of the original hull. The gun was deleted and in its place a "pulpit" for the instructor was added. The front plate before the driver was also modified.

In February 1947 the army ordered another 20 vehicles from Škoda, and followed it by an order for an additional 30 in early 1950. Thus the army obtained 100 new ST-I and 50 ST-III vehicles on top of the repaired ones.

By January 1, 1946 the army had on its list 18 ST-I vehicles; by January 1, 1949 already 249, 246 gun vehicles and 3 Berge Hetzers. Another three Berges were sent to Škoda for refurbishing and an additional 14 were stored at Milovice (armored corps training center), but it is not known if they were ever transferred to the army.

Based on the new organization, the ST-Is were concentrated in the 21st and 22nd Tank Brigades, planned as armored units of the newly-formed motorized divisions. In 1948, they were all transferred to Assault Gun Regiments nos. 351 and 352, where they soldiered with the remaining StuG IIIs (Czech designation ShPTK 40/75) until the early fifties. Once the Czechoslovak army converted completely to Soviet armaments and equipment, all ex-German vehicles were transferred into the army's reserve, without being allocated to specific units. They were scrapped between the late fifties and early sixties

The MP-1 prototype. The gun opening was plated over. It already carries the cylindrical turret with the Flammenwerfer 41 and the Degtarev machine gun (not fitted in this photograph).

Front view of the MP-1. Compared with the previous photograph, the right side of the hull was again modified.

By June 1948, there were about 90 Hetzers stored in Milovice. Of this number, 8 were total wrecks, 65 were the basic gun models, 14 Berge Hetzers, 2 flame-throwing modifications on low body (Berge?) vehicles and one gun vehicle (15 cm sIG). The army, based on combat experience of both the German and Allied armies, planned the introduction of flame-throwing tanks. Originally the army wanted to adapt fifteen PzKpfw IIIs from its depots for this role, but the tanks were both antiquated and mechanically in bad condition. The second possibility was to procure OT-034 Soviet flame-throwing tanks. The Soviets had no objections, but pointed out that the production of both the OT-034 and OT-034/85 tanks had been terminated because of their obsolescence, and proposed to supply the new flame-throwing tanks based on the T-54 instead. Because these were planned for production at the beginning of the fifties, the army decided to convert 75 of the stored Hetzers to flame-throwing tanks as a stop-gap measure.

In February 1949 the army contracted ČKD to develop a prototype. ČKD modified the body by plating over the gun opening. It fitted the vehicle first with a turret from the PzKpfw 38(t), but in the final version used a cylindrical turret with the ex-German 1.4 cm Flammenwerfer 41 and a Dektarev DT-28 machine gun with its armored shield as used on the T-34/85 tanks. The operator sat in between the weapons. Three fuel tanks with a total volume of 1,000 liters were installed inside the hull, two large ones on the right side and one smaller on the left. Seven cylinders with pressurized air were carried in a special box, manufactured from 8 mm armor plate and fixed on the rear plate of the vehicle.

The prototype was finished in February 1951. Firing tests with the German fuel Np showed insufficient range (only 60 m) and excessive dispersion of the flame. Konstrukta in Prague was assigned to develop a new flame-thrower. A new domestic fuel (Sh) was also developed. At the same time, ČKD was asked to modify

Right side with the extension for the compressed cylinders storage.

The rear view of the MP-1.

Detail of the flame-thrower Flammenwerfer 41.

the fuel tanks by splitting the two large ones into three smaller ones and the small one into two, to assure gradual emptying of them during firing. At the same time, other modifications were carried out (like exchanging old German radio sets for Soviet types, used in the T-34/85 tanks).

The prototype was ready for testing in June 1953. When using the Sh fuel, a range between 90 and 140 m with acceptable dispersion was achieved. At the same time, problems with valves and fuel leaks were encountered, and ČKD kept modifying the prototype further. Additional tests were conducted in July 1954 and a range of between 140 and 150 m was achieved. The internal arrangement was also improved. Driving tests showed that the vehicle was not adversely affected by the increased weight (17 tons) and changed weight distribution, caused by adding the air cylinders box in the rear. The design was finalized in 1955, but at that time the vehicle was obsolete and the army lost interest.

Inside of the original MP-1 turret. As it was adapted from the PzKpfw 38(t) turret, it maintained its original layout of the machine gun on the right and the main armament on the left, here the DT-28 machine gun and the flame thrower with its fuel line. The gunner's episcope is in the center. The final round turret had the layout reversed, with the flame-thrower on the right and the machine gun on the left.

Four views of the Praga DT III tractor and recovery vehicle, developed for Switzerland after the war.

Two views of the OT-810 (Obrněný transportér, or APC). It had the chassis and a drive-train from SdKfz 251 Ausf.D, but had a new Tatra V-8 Diesel engine of 9,848 cc displacement with an output of 130 HP(96 kW). The body was totally enclosed and was sealed against chemical weapons and radiation fallout. The commander had a circular hatch, the crew two oblong hatches in the top plate. Firing ports were also reintroduced.

The Czechoslovak army had also a small number of the PzKpfw 38(t) in its light tank companies. Though these were used mostly for training, they participated in their last combat mission between August and September 1947, together with Stuart light tanks, brought back by the Czechoslovak Armored Brigade from England.

Since late 1945, bands of nationalist Ukrainians, who collaborated with the Germans during the war, operated in Eastern Poland in a partisan fashion. The Ukrainians were joined by stray SS men, left behind the front. Though pursued by both the Polish and the Soviet army units, they managed to survive in the mountains for two years. When their murdering and pillaging of remote villages became unbearable, the Polish army initiated a large-scale offensive in the spring of 1947 and managed to annihilate and disperse most of the "Bandera" units (these bands were called "Bandera bands" after a famous Ukrainian nationalist, Stefan Bandera). The survivors reformed and retreated into Czechoslovakia, with the aim to escape to West Germany.

The Czechoslovak army was initially ill prepared to fight these bands in the mountains, but in the summer of 1947 finally assembled sufficient well-trained units for an offensive action. They were supported by a combined company code-named "Wolf", consisting of light tanks from three tank brigades. The antiquated light tanks were chosen because of the bad roads and inaccessibility of the mountain areas, impassable for normal battle tanks like the T-34/85.

The light tanks reached the mountains and helped to liquidate the famous band "Burlak" in the Low Fatra mountains in Slovakia.

11

FULLY TRACKED ARTILLERY TRACTORS

Development, Manufacture, Technical Description

The Czechoslovak army's heavy artillery formations were originally equipped with artillery tractors with large diameter wheels, dating from the First World War (Graf, Stift and Daimler). Domestic constructions were the Śkoda Z and the Škoda U, designed by Praga but manufactured by Škoda. A total of 106 vehicles of the Z and 30 vehicles of the U type was purchased between 1921-1923. The army also had 32 Daimler BE "trains" (gasoline-electric units for transporting very heavy guns and mortars).

The first fully tracked tractor was made by ČKD under the designation MT. Two vehicles were bought in 1925, but were scrapped in 1932, as they were not very successful and were used only for driver training. The same fate befell the Vollmer design of the wheel-cum-track vehicles, which were also originally built as artillery tractors. In 1923, Hanomag tractors WD 25 and WD 50 were purchased in small quantities and the BD 25 and later the BD 30 were built under a licensing agreement with Hanomag by Breitfeld-Daněk between 1925-1927.

Starting in 1930, Škoda attempted to provide fully tracked artillery tractors of all sizes both for the Czechoslovak army and for export. Its most successful model was the MTH (Malý Traktor Housenkový, or Small Tracked Tractor). The army bought a total of 55 vehicles of the I, II and III variants between 1935-1939. The MTH had a running gear based on the MU tankette and 36 HP(26.6 kW) engine driving the rear sprockets. For the medium category, Škoda offered its STH (Střední Traktor Housenkový, or medium tracked tractor) model, designed to tow the 15 cm guns. The tractor was under-powered and slow (maximum speed 14 km/hour) and the army was not interested. Škoda improved it by installing a more powerful engine of 64 HP(47.3 kW). The speed increased to 21 km/hour, but the army bought just one prototype of each model. The heavy tractor VTH (Velký Traktor Housenkový, or large tracked tractor) was similarly unsuccessful and was bought also in one prototype only.

Praga MT tractor was built in two prototypes in 1925. Though offered as an artillery tractor, Praga hoped to develop it into a light tank, as its designation implied (MT - malý tank, or small tank). The engine on the rear spade is a winch.

MT in cross-country tests. It was not very successful and Praga and later ČKD soon came with better designs.

BD-25, Breitfeld-Daněk license of the Hanomag WD 25 tractor.

Škoda's most successful artillery tractor, the MTH (Malý traktor housenkový, or small tracked tractor). The Czechoslovak army bought 55 of them.

BD-25 were the light tractors, again under Hanomag license.

Before the war Škoda exported to Yugoslavia twelve VD-50 tractors (Hanomag WD-50 license) and Škoda vz.28 wheeled artillery tractors (Latil TR-4 license) at the end of the twenties.

Tatra supplied the army in 1930 with a wheel-cum-track artillery tractor KTT, but it remained only as a prototype. In 1937 Tatra submitted its medium tractor V-740 with 65 HP(48 kW) engine, which was competing with the Praga IV model. As the army accepted the Praga IV, the V-740 remained similarly in one prototype.

Praga (ČKD) was more successful with its designs. In the category of light tractors it sold 32 vehicles of its Praga III type to the army in 1935. The Praga T-III/3 was ordered by the Dutch East Indies in 1939. It had the running gear of the AH-IV tankette and a truck cab. With 78 HP(57.6 kW) engine, its maximum speed was 30 km/hour. The Dutch obtained one prototype, but the remaining

The Hanomag WD 50 tractors were used to tow heavy guns and mortars, but the army had only six of them.

The STH, or medium tractor, was not accepted by the army, as it was too slow. Only two prototypes were manufactured.

The sole prototype of the VTH, or heavy tractor.

The other Tatra heavy tractor V-740 lost to Praga IV and was not built either.

40 vehicles of the order were confiscated and used by the Wehrmacht.

The design most widely used before the war was Praga IV, of which type the army purchased 115 units by 1939. With an engine of 57 HP(42 kW) it could tow 4.5 tons and carry over one ton.

By far the most successful of all the Praga artillery tractors was the T 6 (the vehicles designated by the Roman numerals had low-rpm engines, the vehicles designated by Arabic numerals had high-rpm engines). The Czechoslovak army did not get any by 1939, but the tractor was widely exported before and during the war. Manufactured up to 1944, hundreds were used by the Wehrmacht and Waffen SS. By far the largest customer was Turkey. The Turks bought 434 T 6 tractors between 1937-1939. The Romanian army ordered 221 vehicles in 1941, but got only 130. The rest of the order was confiscated by the Wehrmacht. Portugal ordered 30 vehicles in 1942, but as far as is known, this lot also ended in the German artillery formations. Sweden was also interested in this

Tatra's wheel-cum-track KTT tractor from 1930 had some advanced features, but remained in prototype only.

The 32 vehicle series of Praga III tractors, delivered to the army in 1935.

Praga HT (modernized BD III) developed for Greece.

Prototype of the Praga V, developed for Turkey.

The prototype of the Praga T-III/3, ordered by the Dutch East Indies in 1939. It had the running gear of the AH-IV tankettes and good engine. The rest of the order was confiscated by the Wehrmacht.

Praga IV, the most widely used artillery tracked tractor of the Czechoslovak army before the war.

type and the T 6Sv is mentioned in ŠKD's reports, but they were never ordered. Slovakia ordered 30 tractors of this type, but at the end obtained only eight. The Waffen SS ordered 500 vehicles in 1942, but by November 1943 got only 95 tractors. The whole order was never delivered. The SS vehicles had all-steel wheels, for the first time used on some Romanian vehicles. The T 6 tractors were designed to tow guns weighing up to six tons and to carry one ton. The engine output varied from 75 to 110 HP (55.4 to 81.3 kW), depending on the model, and maximum speed was over 30 km/hour.

The T 7 was a heavier version of the T 6 with 112 HP (82.8 kW) engine and could tow guns weighing up to eight tons. It was exported to Turkey together with the T 8 tractors in 1938-1939 (40 T 7 and 62 T 8). The heaviest of the Praga tractors was the T 9. Powered by 142 HP (105 kW) engine, it could tow guns weighing up to 10 tons at speeds up to 20 km/hour. Its first customer was again Turkey, which ordered 66 vehicles. At the end only 16 were delivered, as the rest was confiscated by the Wehrmacht. Five T 9s from the Turkish order ended in Slovakia, where they were used to tow 8.8 cm FLAK guns. The production of the T 9 ended in 1943 with a total of 76 vehicles produced.

Three views of the final version of Praga V tractor with the shortened chassis.

The most successful overall was the Praga T 6. Widely exported before the war and manufactured for the Wehrmacht, the Waffen SS, Romania and Slovakia, hundreds were manufactured. These photographs are of the Turkish T 6 tractors in very colorful camouflage scheme.

Praga T 6 tractors towing German 10 cm Kan.18 during a parade of the Turkish artillery units.

Praga T 9 was the heaviest of the Praga tractors. Only 76 were built. They were used by the Wehrmacht, the Slovak army and even Turkey got 16 out of its order for 66 vehicles.

Use by the Army, Wartime Use

Though the Czechoslovak army initiated the production and design of fully tracked artillery tractors in the twenties, the rate of motorization of its artillery formations was excruciatingly slow. Up to 1935 the number of motorized artillery formations not only did not increase, but some formations already motorized were converted to horse traction. For example, during the years 1929-1933 the artillery was assigned a total of 22 trucks and two tractors!

The situation was greatly improved during the modernization that started in 1934. Though the artillery had to cede priority to other arms, it nevertheless obtained 410 new traction vehicles of various types between 1934 and 1937. Most of these were special trucks. Besides three heavy artillery regiments, which were motorized already in the twenties, four medium artillery corps regiments were fully motorized. Also fully motorized was the main artillery reserve, consisting of four light, one medium and three heavy artillery regiments.

By September 1938 both the heavy and the antiaircraft artillery were fully motorized, while the field (both light and medium) artillery was 17% motorized, antitank units were 30% motorized and mortar units only 7.5% motorized. Though not satisfactory, such level of motorization was comparable with the contemporary European armies.

During the war, both Škoda and BMM manufactured German tracked tractors. Škoda made 2,000 complete Zugkraftwagen 1t D7 (SdKfz 10) artillery tractors and 800 chassis for the SdKfz 251. Both orders were fully delivered. Škoda also manufactured 206 RSO (Raupen Schlepper Ost) tractors with large wheels. BMM manufactured 600 Zugkraftwagen 5t BN9 (SdKfz 6) half-tracks in the engineer version.

Tatra cooperated with Büssing-NAG on the development of the sWS (schwerer Wehrmacht Schlepper) and built some of these between 1944-1945.

TABLE 19 lists all tracked artillery tractors of the Czechoslovak army and their registration numbers, while TABLE 20 shows the export of these vehicles.

TABLE 19
CZECHOSLOVAK ARMY TRACKED TRACTORS

MANUFACTURER	YEAR INTROD.	NUMBER IN INVENTORY	REGISTRATION NUMBERS OLD	NEW
LIGHT				
Hanomag WD-25	1923	2	NIX104,105	13283,13284
Orion	192?			
Dinos	1924	1	NIX101	13280
Praga MT	1925	2	NIX107,108	scrapped 1932
Hanomag WD-50	1923-27	6	NIX33,46,102,103,131	13281,13288,13419
Breifeld-Daněk BD25	1925	6	NIX132-137	13289-13294
Breifeld-Daněk BD30	1927	12	NIX172-183	13308-13319
Praga III	1935	32		13585-13614
Škoda MTH I	1935	25		13558-13582
Škoda MTH II	1935	13		13621-13633
Škoda MTH III	1939	17	already for Wehrmacht	14125-14141
MEDIUM				
Škoda STH-B	1932	1		13366
Škoda STH	1936	1		13645
Praga IV(NT)	1935	1		13635
Praga IV	1938-39	114		13976-14089
HEAVY				
Škoda VTH	1937	1		13861
Tatra V-740	1937	1		13862
WHEEL-CUM-TRACK				
Tatra KTT	1930	1	NIX907	13337

TABLE 20
EXPORT OF CZECH TRACKED TRACTORS

COUNTRY	TYPE ORDERED	NUMBER SUPPLIED	NUMBER DELIVERED	YEAR	REMARK
Yugoslavia	Škoda VD-50 (license WD-50)	12	12	1930	for Škoda 30.5 cm mortars
Romania	Praga T 6R	221	130	1941-44	91 confiscated by the Wehrmacht
Portugal	Praga T 6	30	?		1944 still at BMM
Turkey	Praga V	13	13	1934-35	
	Praga T 6	434	434	1937-39	
	Praga T 7	40	40	1937-39	
	Praga T 8	62	62	1937-39	
	Praga T 9	66	16	1937-39	50 confiscated by Wehrmacht, five of these in 1941 sold to Slovakia
Slovakia	Škoda MTH	11	11	1939	ex Czechoslovak
	Praga III	3	3	1939	ex Czechoslovak
	Praga IV	38	38	1939	ex Czechoslovak
	Praga T 6	30	8	1943	
	Praga T 9	5	5	1941	

Praga T 8 was an export version, manufactured solely for Turkey. Turkey was by far the best customer for Praga tractors, having bought 565 of various types between 1934 and 1939.

12

ARMORED TRAINS

Trains have been eagerly adopted by the armies of the world not only for transporting men and material, but also as armored systems, armed with guns and machine guns. The first use of armored, gun-armed trains dates to the American Civil War. The armored trains were used mainly in areas where the road system was badly developed and thus precluded the use of armored cars. Such situation existed on the Eastern front during the First World War, and both Russian and Austro-Hungarian armies built and used armored trains extensively.

In the newly formed republic, conditions for their use were favorable. The Czech Lands and even Slovakia had a wide net of railway lines and both the Russian legionnaires and the Austro-Hungarian demobilized soldiers and sailors had experience with their use. Moreover, the industry was fully capable of building them quickly and in quantity. In Prague, immediately after the proclamation of the new state, its representatives were able to acquire an armored train, consisting of cars from Austro-Hungarian armored trains nos. I, II and IV.

In early 1919 intense fighting with both the Poles and the Hungarians started in both Southern Slovakia and in Těšínsko. The Hungarians fielded several former Austro-Hungarian armored trains, and the Czechoslovak army had to build new trains to oppose them. In this year all the permanent and improvised armored trains were built, and in the years following they were only modernized and reorganized.

The first captured Austro-Hungarian train consisted of the complete Panzerzug II with a locomotive MAV 377-116, two machine-gun cars (nos.140-914 and S150-003) and an artillery car (no.7-98499). The machine-gun cars had two heavy Schwarzlose 8 mm M.7/12 machine guns on each side and a fifth in the front wall. The artillery car had its main armament, a Škoda 7 cm naval gun, in the front wall, and a Škoda 4.7 cm naval gun in its left wall. The train also had a reserve locomotive (377-362) from Panzerzug VI and another machine-gun car (no. S4140-972) from Panzerzug I.

The Czechoslovak army headquarters assembled the necessary crew and already on November 18, 1918 sent the train, renamed "Pancéřový vlak II", to Slovakia. On the way, the train acquired another machine gun car (no.S150-271) from Panzerzug VII, which Czech soldiers captured near Trnava. As the train became too long and unwieldy, it was divided into two parts. Part II-a had the original equipment from Panzerzug II and part II-b the rest of the cars with the reserve locomotive.

The armored train IIa moved all over Slovakia between December 1918 and spring 1919 in the role of a firefighter. On April

Armored train no.3 (ex-Hungarian) with artillery car Kn 141.172 and machine gun car 149.902. It was armed with one 7.5 cm gun and eight heavy machine guns.

The artillery car Kn 141.172 (ex Hungarian) of the armored train no.3. It carried a 7.5 cm gun in the rotating turret and a heavy machine gun in the roof cupola.

Inside of the artillery car 7-89499 (ex Hungarian) with the 7.5 cm and 4.7 cm guns. It was part of the armored train no. 1.

A typical Austro-Hungarian machine gun car with an observation cupola.

29 it moved to Lučenec to help secure border areas, assigned by the peace treaties to Czechoslovakia. During the next two months it fought the Hungarians almost daily between Sečany -Lučenec - Filakovo and on several occasions fought artillery duels with a Hungarian armored train. On June 12, with its artillery car under repair, the crew of the armored train IIa used a ramming attack against the Hungarian train in the station of Hronská Breznice. The pusher car, loaded with rails, was sent downhill into the station to ram the Hungarian train. The attack succeeded and the Hungarian train was heavily damaged, but the unprotected train IIa hit a mine the next day. The floor of the machine gun car was torn and one member of the crew was killed and several others were wounded.

On July 21, 1919 this train got a new number - 1. The repaired cars gradually returned and the completed train guarded the border between Lučenec and Filakovo till March 1920, when for the first time the fire under the locomotive's boiler was extinguished.

The armored train IIb was made combat ready on December 15, 1918 in Prague and left to secure the German Sudeten areas first, but at the end of December returned to Slovakia, where it helped during the occupation of Košice. It guarded the area as part of the 6. Division of the Italian Legion till May 1, 1919, when it attacked the Hungarian station of Miškolec, where it secured 18 locomotives and 300 railway cars, which the Hungarians removed from Slovakia. It got its new number - 2 - on June 21, 1919.

The Hungarians lost their train no. IV (former Austro-Hungarian Panzerzug VII), which was blocked in Sečovce and captured by the 36th Infantry Regiment. The train consisted of locomotive 377-455, artillery car no. 141-172 and machine gun car no. S149-902. The train was repaired by Škoda and was drafted on January 1920 as "Pancéřový vlak 3".

The Austro-Hungarian armored trains were all built the same way. The MAV 377 locomotives had an armored cabin for the crew. The boiler was also armored, and armored plates covered the wheels and cylinders. There were ten locomotives adapted in this way. The Czechoslovak army used three of them, while a fourth one was armored the same way in 1919 by the railway workshops in Vrútky.

The inside of the old Austro-Hungarian machine gun car with its heavy machine guns, ladder to the observation cupola and observation/rifle ports.

Škoda artillery car Ke 335.267 of the armored train no.6. It carried two 7.5 cm guns in rotating armored mounts, one at each end.

The machine gun (or infantry) cars were built on the standard two-axle railway cars type 140 with a hand brake, or type S148 - S150 without a brake. The armored body had an outer shell of 12 mm thick armor plate and an inner armor 8 mm thick. Between them was a 45 mm thick layer of hard (oak) wood plates. The side walls each had two larger embrasures for machine guns and between 10-13 small ones for rifles. The front wall had one large machine gun embrasure and 4-7 small ones. The access door was in the side turned toward the engine. In the center of the roof was a small cylindrical observation tower with a searchlight. The second machine gun car in the train always carried between its axles a tank with water for the locomotive. Both the wheels and these water tanks were protected by armored plates. There were three variants of Austro-Hungarian machine gun cars, and all three were used by the Czechoslovak armored trains.

The artillery car no. 7-98499 had a similar construction as the machine gun cars, but the captured artillery car no. 141-172 had its 7 cm gun in a rotating naval turret in its front part. The fixed part of the car had on the roof a box-like structure with a frontal machine gun and commander's observation cupola. In the side walls there were on each side one machine gun and seven rifle embrasures. During the war, a total of six artillery cars was manufactured in Austro-Hungary.

The first domestic armored train was built in three weeks during December 1918 in Brno, the capital of Moravia. It had a locomotive (478-12) and two coal cars (Ik 622.016 and Ik 604.621). The State Armament Works in Brno-Zábrdovice armored the locomotive and both cars. The first car had two Maxim 1910 machine guns in the front wall, and above them a Škoda 7.5 cm mountain gun on a rotating mounting. The infantry car carried two heavy and two light Schwarzlose M.7/12 machine guns.

The train was named "Brno" and already in January 1919 was sent to Těšínsko to fight the Polish army. During a duel with a Polish armored train it was hit on the artillery car and on the locomotive, but it was quickly repaired and soldiered until December 1920, when it was demobilized. The locomotive was returned to

Cleaning the 7.5 cm gun.

the State Railways, and the cars were stored in Milovice till 1925, when they were disassembled and used as flatbed pusher cars in front of the regular armored trains.

The Military Headquarters in Brno decided to put together two more trains, based on the good experience with the "Brno" train. The new trains were named "Bratislava no.3" and "Generál Štefánik no.4". The armor was made by the Královopole Steel Mills. Each train consisted of a pusher car type In, an artillery car type Ik with one 7.5 cm M.15 Škoda mountain gun and two machine gun cars type Ik with Maxim machine guns.

"Bratislava" left for Slovakia in July 1919. Shortly after arrival, it lost its pusher car near Nové Zámky, when the Hungarians dynamited a bridge under it. The train was sent for repairs to Škoda in August, but these were deemed not worthwhile. The train was disassembled, the locomotive and the cars were returned to the State Railways and its no.3 was given to the captured Hungarian train, being currently repaired by Škoda.

Front end of a Škoda artillery car with the front machine guns, the gun rotating turret and the observation cupola, It is painted in the official camouflage scheme of light and medium gray, medium green and black.

A frame for attaching the armor plates to the steam locomotive.

A fully armored locomotive 377-455.

The crew of an armored train ready for inspection.

The second armored train, no.4 from Brno, came late to fight the Hungarians, as an armistice was signed in July 1919. The train had again a pusher car, two artillery cars of the same type as on train no.3 (Iko 168.660 and Iko 171.130), an unarmored locomotive (no.66.01) and a machine gun car (Gruh 114.243). The train got an armored locomotive (no.179.01) the same month, and was stationed with armored train no.1 in Lučenec till 1923, when in the fall they were relocated to Milovice. In 1925, the train was demobilized and its cars were returned to the State Railways.

The last improvised armored train was built in Slovakia in 1919. The railway workshop in Vrútky armored one locomotive no. 377-483 according to old Austro-Hungarian plans. Two flatbed cars were "armored" by using concrete shells, and were armed with Italian heavy machine guns. This train was assigned the no.7 and cooperated with the regular train no.2 in Southern Slovakia. Its locomotive was assigned to the captured Hungarian train and, after the repair of its original locomotive no. 377-455, it was assigned to train no.4, with which it remained till 1923. The concrete shell was too heavy for the used cars, and was removed by 1921.

The engineer in the cab of his armored steam locomotive.

The Škoda works in Pilsen routinely repaired, modified and upgunned both the captured and improvised armored trains, but in the first half of 1919 they started manufacturing their own equipment. First were two artillery cars, In 316.603 and Ke 333.509, each with one 7.5 cm naval gun. They were both assigned to armored train no.2, which up to that time had only machine gun cars. This train thus became the longest, as it had aside from its locomotive and the two new Škoda artillery cars, another improvised one with 8 cm gun vz.5/8 and three machine gun cars, one Austro-Hungarian, one Hungarian and one with concrete armor (the second concrete car had to be scrapped). The train was renumbered as train no.7 and patrolled the railways of Southern Slovakia till spring 1920.

In 1919 Škoda also manufactured two complete armored trains, no.5 "Plzeň" and no.6 "Praha". Both could be divided into two equal parts, if necessary. Each train had two locomotives type 99, armored with 6 mm nickel steel plates, two artillery cars, two machine gun cars, two pusher cars and one ammunition car. All the cars had 8 mm armor.

The artillery cars had two rotating (210°) turrets with 7 cm (later 7.5 cm) guns, in their front plates two machine guns and in the sides rifle embrasures. Each car had an observation tower on the roof.

The machine gun cars had five machine gun and 10-12 rifle embrasures in their sides and two machine guns in both the front and rear walls. Access was through armored doors in the sides, in the front walls, on top of the observation cupola and in the floor. The hatch in the cupola allowed the use of an antiaircraft machine gun or a mortar. Each car had between its axles boxes with 500 kg of coal, every other car carried inside it a tank with 4.5 m^3 water for the locomotives, which could be supplied by built-in pipes even while under way.

The first (command) machine gun car carried also an 8 kW gasoline generator, which supplied the train's electrical net with 110 V of electric current. All the cars were connected with signal

The crew mounting the machine gun car. The men wear the new helmets vz.32 and very dirty working overalls.

bells, phones and voice tubes. The train carried four (7.5) cm guns, two 9 cm mortars and twenty Salvátor-Dormus heavy machine guns. All weapons were made by Škoda. The crew was three officers and 88 men, who at this time were mostly recruited from former sailors of the defunct Austro-Hungarian navy.

In Southern Slovakia in the summer of 1919 there were six armored trains, which remained there till 1923. They were divided into three groups of two and were stationed in Košice, Lučenec and Bratislava. The trains were originally subjugated to the commanders of infantry divisions or army groups but, starting in 1920, they were assigned to VZBÚ, which commanded all armored vehicles. On July 7, 1922 this unit was changed into an armored battalion (from 1933 an armored regiment) with its site in Milovice.

The trains, stationed for such a long time in various places in Slovakia, saw their equipment suffer and the discipline of their crew grow lax. The Milovice command tried very hard to have them returned there, but this happened only in 1923. All six trains were transferred to Milovice to rail sidings built for this purpose; in 1926 they were permanently placed under the roof in a newly built depot. Under the new organization of the armored battalion, the trains were organized in an armored trains company of five combat and one training armored train from September 1, 1925.

The army had to pay a rent for its railway equipment to the State Railways. Because it was quite high (in 1921 - 651,345 Kč, about $ 26,000; by 1922 already 811,760 Kč, about $ 32,500), the army in 1925 kept only the locomotives and combat cars, and returned all the other cars to the State Railways. Even the four locomotives from armored trains no. 5 and 6 were returned, while their armor was stored. In the case of a mobilization, the State Railway had to make sure that the locomotives would be fully armored and ready in under 48 hours. The four locomotives were 99-09, no. 320.009; 99-12 no. 320.008; 99-16, no. 320.012 and 99-67, no. 320.032.

In September 1925 the company of armored trains was fixed in its final composition, which remained stable till the end of the republic in March 1939. The composition of the six armored trains was as follows:

Armored train no.1:
Pusher car In 707.016; artillery car 7-89499; machine gun car Kn 140.914; locomotive 377-116, no. 310.412; machine gun car Kn 150.003.
Armament: one 7.5 cm gun, one 4.7 cm gun (till 1929), nine (from 1929 11) heavy and two light machine guns.
Crew two officers, one NCO, 80 men.

Armored train no.2:
Pusher car In 700.820; artillery car Ik 315.784 (Škoda); machine gun car Ke 140.972 (Austro-Hungarian); locomotive 377-362, no. 310.440; machine gun car Ke 150.271 (Hungarian).
Armament: two 7.5 cm guns, 11 heavy and two light machine guns.
Crew two officers, one NCO and 82 men.

Armored train no.3:
Pusher car In 707.126; artillery car Kn 141.172; locomotive 377-455, no. 310.450; machine gun car Kn 149.902 (all Hungarian).
Armament: one 7.5 cm gun, eight heavy and two light machine guns.
Crew two officers, one NCO and 74 men.

Armored train no.4:
Pusher car In 707.691; artillery car Ke 306.809; machine gun car Ke 302.591; locomotive to be supplied during mobilization; machine gun car Ke 62.339 (all Škoda).
Armament: two 7.5 cm guns, 20 (later 12) heavy and two light machine guns.
Crew two officers, one NCO and 91 men.

Armored train no.5:
Pusher car In 707.626; artillery car Ik 307.901; machine gun car Ik 334.623; locomotive to be supplied during mobilization; machine gun car Ik 309.364 (all Škoda).
Armament: two 7.5 cm guns, 20 (later 12) heavy and two light machine guns.
Crew two officers, one NCO and 91 men.

Armored train no.6 (training):
Pusher car Ik 622.616; artillery car Ke 335.267; machine gun car Ke 309.218; locomotive 377-483, no. 310453, machine gun car Ik 314.850 (all Škoda).
Armament: two 7.5 cm guns, 20 (later 12) heavy and two light machine guns.
Crew two officers, one NCO and 91 men.

The company also had two armored ammunition cars Gg 28.922 and Gg 143.314, which were built by Škoda in 1919 and were originally parts of armored trains no.5 "Plzeň" and no.6 "Praha". All these armored cars - four locomotives, six pusher cars, six artillery cars, eleven machine gun cars and two ammunition cars, were bought by the army from the State Railways in February 8, 1926.

The crew of the Tatra reconnaissance rail car. The commander carries his rank on a patch on the right side of his breast.

The company got its only addition in August 1927, when it obtained an armored reconnaissance car Tatra type 18. It had a fully rotating turret with two Schwarzlose vz.7/24 heavy machine guns, was powered by a gasoline engine, had armor 5-8 mm thick and a crew of five men.

Though the cars of the armored trains were now standardized, their armament changed quite often. The originally mounted Škoda 7 cm L/30 naval guns were rebored to 7.5 cm during the years 1919-1920 . The sole 4.7 cm gun from armored train no.1 was removed in 1929 and was replaced by two heavy machine guns. The mortars were eliminated, and the five types of heavy machine guns originally used (Russian, German, Italian and two Austrian types) were replaced by German 7.92 mm Maxim 08s in the beginning of the twenties.

In 1925 the Maxims were replaced by French 8 mm Hotchkiss machine guns and finally in 1929 all were replaced by 7.92 mm

Three views of the Tatra reconnaissance rail car. It carried two machine guns in a fully rotating turret and had a gasoline engine. Only one was built for the Czechoslovak army, though Poland bought six of them.

Three of the Polish Tatra reconnaissance rail cars during evaluation trials.

The armored train no.4 with one artillery car and two machine gun cars under way.

One of the Škoda-built armored trains (nos.4, 5 or 6) in various training settings.

Schwarzlose vz.7/24 or vz.24. ZB vz.26 light machine guns were used as antiaircraft guns. The combat supply was 300 rounds for a gun and between 6,000 - 9,000 rounds for each machine gun.

The trains themselves were gradually improved and modified. All got the automatic Knorr braking system, individual cars were connected by armored bridges and, in the command cars, radio sets for contact with the higher command centers were installed. All the locomotives and cars were subjected to regular inspections by the railway workshops of the State Railways, but these could not change the age of all the vehicles.

In the early thirties it became more and more obvious that the armored trains would have to be modernized. The army asked both Škoda and ČKD to submit projects for armored motorized rail vehicles. About the size of a standard express car, they weighed between 54-72 tons, had armor up to 32 mm thick and carried three 6.6 and 8 cm guns in two fully rotating turrets and several heavy and large caliber machine guns. The Škoda project finally won, but was built only as a wooden mockup before the German occupation intervened.

In 1934, the Ministry of Defense simultaneously planned the building of improvised armored trains from standard railway stock in the case of mobilization. The trains were supposed to be built by the railway workshops, which were provided for this purpose with the necessary materials. In all, twelve trains were planned for use with first-line troops in the border areas. Their crews were recruited from the local infantry regiments, augmented by several artillery men and railway men.

For these trains, the locomotives type 310.0, 311.4, 314.0, 422.0 or 423.0 were envisaged. Their only modification was the added protection for the crew against splinters and small caliber infantry rounds, usually by boiler plate or by hanging chains. Pusher cars of the P or N type were not modified at all. For the combat cars, tenders type U with mid-high side walls were used. Into each, a box from wooden plates 5 cm thick was built, and the 15 cm wide gap between this box and the sides of the car was filled with compacted gravel.

The command machine gun car of the armored train no.4, showing the roof aerial for its radio set.

The end of the Czechoslovak armored trains. A German officer in the observation cupola of the Škoda artillery car.

The cars were equipped with embrasures, in the artillery car front wall for the 8 cm vz.5/8 or vz.17 gun and two machine guns in the sides, in the machine gun car for four machine guns in the sides and one to the rear. All machine guns were of the vz.7/24 or vz.24 Schwarzlose type. In September 1938 these improvised armored trains were duly built and some of them participated in the fighting against the Freikorps insurgents in the Sudeten border areas.

One of these improvised armored trains, no.40, was built for the infantry regiment in Lučenec in Slovakia in 1938. It was subjugated to the 40. Border area and was stationed in Zvolen. The locomotive 310.422 was fully armored with armor plate, as were the cars (U-7.76290 and 7.17369). The train was armed with one 8 cm vz.17 gun, seven vz.24 heavy machine guns and one ZB vz.26 light machine gun. Its crew was one officer and 42 men. Following the formation of the Slovak state on March 14, 1939, this train was taken over by the Slovak army. It was used during the Hungarian invasion of eastern Slovakia on March 23-26, 1939, and later even during the war with Poland in September of the same year.

A low view of the armored train no.4, showing the armor protection of the running gear.

During the September 1938 mobilization all the permanent armored trains were activated. Between September 23 and 27, 1938, four trains moved out from Milovice into their assigned areas. Armored train no.1 left on September 26 for Plzeň, on October 9 it moved to Rokycany and after 14 days returned to Milovice. Armored train no.2 was sent first to Jihlava, where it remained for one full month; from there it went to Trnava and it returned to Milovice only on December 9. Armored train no.3 went to Slovakia, first to Levice, followed by Nové Zámky, Surany and Nitra and returned on November 20. Armored train no.4 was also sent to Slovakia. It was in Zvolen, Lučenec, Lovinobaňa and again in Zvolen, and returned to its home base on December 5. This train had assigned the armored reconnaissance Tatra car, which collided on November 22 with a shunting engine near Zvolen and was totally destroyed, while three members of its crew were wounded. None of the armored trains participated in any fighting, and armored train no.5 did not even leave its home depot.

The German occupation on March 15, 1939 found all the armored trains in their home depot in Milovice. Though all the rolling stock was quite ancient, it was confiscated by the Wehrmacht except for the locomotives, which were too weak. The combat cars were incorporated into Panzerzüge nos. 23, 24 and 25, activated in March 1940. Trains no.23 and 24 took part in the occupation of Denmark in April 1940 and remained there. Train no.25 passed through Luxembourg and performed securing services in the French-Belgian border areas. All three trains were taken out of service in autumn 1940. Trains no.23 and 24 were reactivated in the spring of 1941 and were sent to Serbia. Train no.25 was reactivated in December 1941. It was first sent to the rear areas of the central Eastern front, where for some time it cooperated with the Slovak army's

The German gun car BP 42 of the Czechoslovak armored train "Sokol" in late May 1945 before moving to support army units during the liberation of the former Sudetenland.

Security Division in anti-partisan duties. In October 1942 it returned to France. In mid-November 1942, train no.24 was still in the Balkans and train no.25 in France. Train no.23 was transferred home for rebuilding.

In December 1943 train no.23 was back in the Balkans, train no.25 in France and train no.24 was pulled back for rebuilding. It was sent to Italy in the spring of 1944, France in summer 1944 and Eastern front in the Fall of 1944.

In the summer of 1944, the Wehrmacht's armored trains training and replacement unit was transferred from Rembertow in Poland to Milovice, where it remained until the end of the war. After the Allied invasion in France, trains no.24 and 25 were withdrawn from Southern France and sent to Slovakia and Eastern Poland and were with Army Group A at the beginning of 1945. At this time, train no.23 was still with Army Group F in the Balkans. The armored trains of Army Group A (Center) were lost during the Soviet offensive in late January 1945, while train no.23 was captured in May 1945 by the Tito partisans in Slovenia.

Thus ended the long operational life of the Czechoslovak armored trains, none of which returned to their longtime base, the Milovice depot.

In May 1945, the reborn Czechoslovak army found on the Czechoslovak soil a large amount of German armored railway stock. There were several reasons for this abundant bounty: the Wehrmacht's training center for armored train crews was moved with its equipment from Rembertow in Poland to Milovice in 1944. In Česká Lípa armored railway cars were built for the Germans by the railway car manufacturer Bohemia. Moreover, several German armored trains retreated to Czechoslovakia at the end of the war. The total comprised probably armored trains nos. 27, 80 and 81, Streckenschutzzug Moritz, Panzertriebwagen no.36 (Littorio) and Schwere Spähzüge nos.205 and 206. On top of those, there was a large number of improvised Flakzüge (with flatbed cars, concrete armor and 2 cm and 3.7 cm antiaircraft guns).

According to the first official report from May 18, 1945, the army had 12 improvised trains (Flakzüge), one armored train with a steam engine and five cars in Prague, another armored train with a steam engine and seven cars in Milovice. In Milovice were also two gasoline powered armored trains (Schweres Spähzug no.206) with a total of nine cars. All the armored trains were used during the liberation of the Sudetenland in June-July 1945, where they found additional four BP 44 armored cars in Česká Lípa.

The first postwar organization of the Czechoslovak army included a company of armored trains, formed officially in Nymburk on October 1, 1945. The company was commanded by the 1. Army District headquarters, and technically was subjugated to the 11. Tank Brigade. It consisted of a platoon of steam driven armored trains with one train, consisting of a locomotive, a pusher car, one artillery car, two machine gun cars, two tank carrying cars and a gasoline powered draisine. The second platoon of heavy scout cars consisted of a pusher car, light scout car Littorio, two artillery cars and three machine gun cars. An improvised training train consisted of a steam locomotive, a pusher car, an artillery car, three machine gun cars, and six reserve machine gun and three artillery cars and a training draisine. The company also had support units and a garrison train.

Because the armored train company gradually obtained additional equipment, by September 1946 it was upgraded to an armored train battalion, with 37 officers, 39 NCOs and 622 men. The

Czech crews in an ex-German heavy scout car armored train (Schweres Spähzug). The first car is the command car with the frame aerial. Two such trains, nos. 205 and 206, were captured from the Wehrmacht at the end of the war.

Ex-German Panzejägerwagen with PzKpfw IV turret and its 7.5 cm KwK L/48. These cars were introduced in 1944 on the BP 44 trains to provide an anti-tank capability. The Czechoslovak army had five of these cars after the war.

battalion was organized into a headquarters with a technical and quartermaster's units; a company of steam driven armored trains with trains the "Dr.Beneš", "Masaryk", "Štefánik" and "Svoboda"; a company with the gasoline driven trains "Pavlík", "Stalin" and "Hurban" and a light motor car; and a reserve company with the training armored train "Orlík". The trains generally had 6 -9 cars (pusher car, 1-2 artillery cars, 2-3 machine gun cars, 2 tank carrying cars and one mortar car). The carried tanks were LT vz.38s. The five available artillery cars carried, besides a 2 cm Flakvierling, a 10.5 Le.F.H.18 (one), PzKpfw III turret with the short 7.5 cm gun (two), or PzKpfw IV turret with the 7.5 cm KwK L-48 (two).

The Czechoslovak army was reorganized on April 1, 1949. The armored train battalion was reorganized in the fall of 1949. Its company of gasoline driven trains was split as a separate unit and was stationed in Sopot near Chotěboř. At this time it had three trains with 5-7 cars each and the motor draisine. The company of five steam driven armored trains remained in Nymburk. Each train had nine cars and a motor draisine. The battalion was subjugated directly to the headquarters of the armored units. The names of the armored trains were abolished and they got new numbers. The eight available garrison trains were concentrated into only two, one in Nymburk and one in Sopot.

The whole battalion was finally abolished between 1954-1955. Most of the armored cars were scrapped. Some machine gun cars were used by the Czechoslovak air force as armored protected sites for directing traffic at its field airfields. Two of them survive to this day, one in the Prague Military Museum, one in Bratislava, slated for the planned railway museum.

13

VEHICLE SPECIFICATION SHEETS

Vehicle Type: armored car
Manufacturer: Lancia-Ansaldo
Manufacturer's Designation: Lancia
Years of Production: 1914-1918
Number of Vehicles Produced:
Czechoslovak Army Designation: Lancia
Registration Numbers: NVII751, 752
Wehrmacht Designation: N/A
Export: none

Weight: 3.9 t
Length: 5.60 m
Width: 1.82 m
Height: 2.75 m
Ground Pressure: N/A

Armor: 6-9 mm
Armament: 3 heavy MG Vickers-Terni
Ammunition Carried: 15,000
Crew: 6

Engine Type: Lancia 1Z
Displacement: 5,000 cc
Horse Power: 36 HP(26.6 kW)/1,200 rpm
Maximum Speed: 60 km/hour
Range: 330 km

Obstacles - step: 35 cm
ditch: 80 cm
ford: 80 cm

Special Features: two turrets one above the other
by 1929 rearmed with Schwarzlose vz.24 machine guns

Vehicle Type:	armored car
Manufacturer:	Škoda, on Praga chassis
Manufacturer's Designation:	Praga L
Years of Production:	1922
Number of Vehicles Produced:	1 prototype
Czechoslovak Army Designation:	Praga L
Registration Numbers:	NVII969
Wehrmacht Designation:	N/A
Export:	none
Weight:	2.5 t + the chassis
Length:	5.10 m
Width:	1.94 m
Height:	2.55 m
Ground Pressure:	N/A
Armor:	6 mm
Armament:	3.7 cm Škoda L27, 1 MG Maxim 08
Ammunition Carried:	100 gun, 5,000 MG
Crew:	3
Engine Type:	Praga
Displacement:	
Horse Power:	44 HP(32,5 kW)
Maximum Speed:	40 km/hour
Range:	
Obstacles - step:	
ditch:	
ford:	
Special Features:	

Vehicle Type:	armored car
Manufacturer:	Škoda, Plzeň
Manufacturer's Designation:	Škoda Fiat-Torino
Years of Production:	1920
Number of Vehicles Produced:	12
Czechoslovak Army Designation:	Fiat-Torino
Registration Numbers:	NVII753-764
Wehrmacht Designation:	N/A
Export:	none
Weight:	6.9 t
Length:	5.44 m
Width:	2.00 m
Height:	2.65 m
Ground Pressure:	N/A
Armor:	5-6 mm
Armament:	2 MG Maxim 08
Ammunition Carried:	18,000
Crew:	5
Engine Type:	Fiat
Displacement:	
Horse Power:	35 HP(25.9 kW)
Maximum Speed:	15 km/hour
Range:	
Obstacles - step:	
ditch:	
ford:	
Special Features:	two independent turrets

Vehicle Type:	armored car
Manufacturer:	Škoda, Plzeň
Manufacturer's Designation:	PA-I
Years of Production:	1923
Number of Vehicles Produced:	2
Czechoslovak Army Designation:	PA-I
Registration Numbers:	NIX9-10, new 13239,13240
Wehrmacht Designation:	N/A
Export:	none
Weight:	7.6 t
Length:	6.60 m
Width:	2.26 m
Height:	2.74 m
Ground Pressure:	N/A
Armor:	3-5.5 mm
Armament:	2 MG Maxim 08
Ammunition Carried:	
Crew:	4
Engine Type:	Škoda, 4 cylinder
Displacement:	9,730 cc
Horse Power:	70 HP(51.7 kW)/1,500 rpm
Maximum Speed:	80 km/hour
Range:	200 km
Obstacles - step:	
ditch:	
ford:	
Special Features:	first of the "symmetrical" Škoda designs, driveable in both directions, both axles driven and steerable, two drivers, in 1929 rearmed with vz.24 machine guns

Vehicle Type:	armored car
Manufacturer:	Škoda, Plzeň
Manufacturer's Designation:	PA-II
Years of Production:	1924-1925
Number of Vehicles Produced:	12
Czechoslovak Army Designation:	PA-II "Želva" (Turtle)[OA vz.23 unofficial]
Registration Numbers:	NIX58-69, new 13267-13275
Wehrmacht Designation:	N/A
Export:	3 sold to Vienna police in 1927
Weight:	7.36 t
Length:	6.00 m
Width:	2.16 m
Height:	2.44 m
Ground Pressure:	N/A
Armor:	3-5.5 mm
Armament:	4 MG Maxim 08
Ammunition Carried:	6,250
Crew:	5
Engine Type:	Škoda, 4 cylinder, water cooled
Displacement:	9,730 cc
Horse Power:	70 HP(51.7 kW)/1,500 rpm
Maximum Speed:	70 km/hour
Range:	250 km
Obstacles - step:	30 cm
ditch:	45 cm
ford:	40 cm
Special Features:	rounded body, 4 MG in corners, symmetrical construction

Vehicle Type:	armored car
Manufacturer:	Škoda, Plzeň
Manufacturer's Designation:	PA-II děl.
Years of Production:	1927
Number of Vehicles Produced:	1 prototype
Czechoslovak Army Designation:	PA-II dělový
Registration Numbers:	NIX222, new 13358
Wehrmacht Designation:	N/A
Export:	none
Weight:	9.40 t
Length:	6.06 m
Width:	2.16 m
Height:	2.81 m
Ground Pressure:	N/A
Armor:	3-5.5 mm
Armament:	7.5 cm Škoda L28, 1 MG Maxim 08
Ammunition Carried:	48 gun, 1,500 MG
Crew:	4
Engine Type:	Škoda, 4 cylinder, water cooled
Displacement:	9,730 HP
Horse Power:	70 HP(51.7 kW)/1,500 rpm
Maximum Speed:	45 km/hour
Range:	250 km
Obstacles - step:	25 cm
ditch:	30 cm
ford:	45 cm
Special Features:	designed as a support vehicle, too heavy, not introduced

Vehicle Type:	armored car
Manufacturer:	Škoda, Plzeň
Manufacturer's Designation:	PA-III
Years of Production:	1927 prototype, 1929 production
Number of Vehicles Produced:	15 + one prototype
Czechoslovak Army Designation:	OA vz.27
Registration Numbers:	NIX201-216, new 13338-13353
Wehrmacht Designation:	N/A
Export:	3 captured by Romania in 1939 3 inherited by Slovak State
Weight:	6.6 t
Length:	5.35 m
Width:	1.95 m
Height:	2.66 m
Ground Pressure:	N/A
Armor:	3-5.5 mm
Armament:	2 MG vz.7/24, plus one ZB vz.26 in reserve
Ammunition Carried:	5,750
Crew:	5
Engine Type:	Škoda, 4 cylinder, water cooled
Displacement:	5,700 cc
Horse Power:	60 HP(44.3 kW)/1,600 rpm
Maximum Speed:	35 km/hour
Range:	250 km
Obstacles - step:	20 cm
ditch:	40 cm
ford:	30 cm
Special Features:	one MG in a turret, one in front plate, symmetrical, two drivers

Vehicle Type:	armored car
Manufacturer:	Tatra, Kopřivnice
Manufacturer's Designation:	T-72
Years of Production:	1933-1934
Number of Vehicles Produced:	51
Czechoslovak Army Designation:	OA vz.30
Registration Numbers:	13324-13331, 13376-13418
Wehrmacht Designation:	N/A
Export:	18 with Slovak State after 1939, 9 captured by Romania, 1 by Hungary
Weight:	2,78 t
Length:	4.02 m
Width:	1.52 m
Height:	2.02 m
Ground Pressure:	N/A
Armor:	3-6 mm
Armament:	3 light MG ZB vz.26 (one in reserve)
Ammunition Carried:	3,000
Crew:	3
Engine Type:	Tatra 71, air-cooled 4 cylinder boxer
Displacement:	1,910 cc
Horse Power:	32 HP(23.7 kW)/2,500 rpm
Maximum Speed:	60 km/hour
Range:	300 km
Obstacles - step:	28 cm
ditch:	50 cm
ford:	30 cm
Special Features:	good cross-country performance light armor and armament

Vehicle Type:	armored car
Manufacturer:	ČKD, Praha
Manufacturer's Designation:	Praga TNSPE
Years of Production:	1936-1937
Number of Vehicles Produced:	7
Czechoslovak Army Designation:	not accepted
Registration Numbers:	not assigned
Wehrmacht Designation:	none
Export:	7 to Romania
Weight:	12.0 t
Length:	7.99 m
Width:	2.20 m
Height:	2.65 m
Ground Pressure:	N/A
Armor:	4-8 mm
Armament:	1 MG ZB vz.26, 1 water cannon
Ammunition Carried:	MG 1,000, 5,000 l of water
Crew:	3
Engine Type:	Praga TN, 4 cylinder, water cooled
Displacement:	7,800 cc
Horse Power:	105 HP(77.6 kW)/2,000 rpm
Maximum Speed:	50 km/hour
Range:	250 km
Obstacles - step:	
ditch:	
ford:	60 cm
Special Features:	armored car for riot police

Vehicle Type:	tankette
Manufacturer:	Vickers
Manufacturer's Designation:	Mk.VI
Years of Production:	1930
Number of Vehicles Produced:	3 bought
Czechoslovak Army Designation:	Carden-Loyd Mk.VI
Registration Numbers:	NIX219-221, new 13355-13557
Wehrmacht Designation:	N/A
Export:	none
Weight:	1.4 t
Length:	2.46 m
Width:	1.70 m
Height:	1.22 m
Ground Pressure:	0.27 kg/cm^2
Armor:	6-9 mm
Armament:	1 MG vz.7/24
Ammunition Carried:	
Crew:	2
Engine Type:	Ford T, 4 cylinder, water cooled
Displacement:	
Horse Power:	22.5 HP(16.6 kW)
Maximum Speed:	45 km/hour
Range:	160 km
Obstacles - step:	40 cm
ditch:	120 cm
ford:	66 cm
Special Features:	widely exported to many countries in many different models ČKD built three CL-P (Carden Loyd-Praga) tankettes in license with Praga AH engine and AN gearbox, these were rebuilt as P-1 prototypes later

Vehicle Type:	tankette
Manufacturer:	ČKD, Praha
Manufacturer's Designation:	P-I
Years of Production:	1930-1934
Number of Vehicles Produced:	70 + 4 prototypes
Czechoslovak Army Designation:	Tančík vz.33
Registration Numbers:	NIX223-225 (prototypes), new 13359-13361, 13420-13489
Wehrmacht Designation:	none
Export:	one prototype gift to Iran after 1939, 30 in Slovak army
Weight:	2.3 t
Length:	2.70 m
Width:	1.75 m
Height:	1.45 m
Ground Pressure:	0.41 kg/cm^2
Armor:	4-12 mm
Armament:	2 light MG ZB vz.26
Ammunition Carried:	2,600
Crew:	2
Engine Type:	Praga, 4 cylinder, water cooled
Displacement:	1,950 cc
Horse Power:	30 HP(22.2 kW)
Maximum Speed:	35 km/hour
Range:	100 km
Obstacles - step:	50 cm
ditch:	120 cm
ford:	40 cm
Special Features:	

Vehicle Type:	wheel-cum-track tractor/light tank
Manufacturer:	Breitfeld-Daněk, Praha
Manufacturer's Designation:	KH-50
Years of Production:	1925-1930
Number of Vehicles Produced:	2 prototypes, 1 rebuilt as KH-60, 1 scrapped
Czechoslovak Army Designation:	KH-60
Registration Numbers:	13362
Wehrmacht Designation:	N/A
Export:	2 KH-60 to Soviet Union, 1 KH-70 to Italy
	about 10 t
Weight:	4.50 m
Length:	2.39 m
Width:	2.53 m wheels, 2.38 track
Height:	0.80 kg/cm²
Ground Pressure:	
	6-14 mm
Armor:	4.7 cm Vickers gun, later 2 MG vz.24
Armament:	
Ammunition Carried:	2
Crew:	
	Škoda, 4 cylinder, water cooled
Engine Type:	
Displacement:	60 HP(44.3 kW)
Horse Power:	35 km/hour wheels, 15 km/hour track
Maximum Speed:	6 hours
Range:	
	50 cm
Obstacles - step:	200 cm
ditch:	95/84 cm
ford:	
Special Features:	went through KH-50, KH-60 and KH-70, modified many times. Change from wheels to track took 10 minutes and needed special ramps the vehicle carried with it. Not successful.

Vehicle Type:	tankette
Manufacturer:	Škoda, Plzeň
Manufacturer's Designation:	MU-2
Years of Production:	1931
Number of Vehicles Produced:	1 prototype
Czechoslovak Army Designation:	not accepted
Registration Numbers:	none
Wehrmacht Designation:	none
Export:	none
Weight:	
Length:	3.20 m
Width:	1.70 m
Height:	1.44 m
Ground Pressure:	
Armor:	4-5.5 mm
Armament:	1 MG vz.24
Ammunition Carried:	3,400
Crew:	2
Engine Type:	Škoda, 4 cylinder, water cooled
Displacement:	
Horse Power:	33 HP(24.4 kW)
Maximum Speed:	
Range:	
Obstacles - step:	50 cm
ditch:	100 cm
ford:	50 cm
Special Features:	MG in rotating turret (290°), chassis a loose copy of the Carden-Loyd

Vehicle Type:	tankette
Manufacturer:	Škoda, Plzeň
Manufacturer's Designation:	MU-4, later Š-I and T-1
Years of Production:	1932 -1934
Number of Vehicles Produced:	1 prototype
Czechoslovak Army Designation:	not accepted
Registration Numbers:	not assigned
Wehrmacht Designation:	none
Export:	none
Weight:	2.20 t
Length:	2.98 m
Width:	1.67 m
Height:	1.30 m
Ground Pressure:	0.35 kg/cm^2
Armor:	4-10 mm
Armament:	2 light MG ZB vz.26
Ammunition Carried:	3,600
Crew:	2
Engine Type:	Škoda, 4 cylinder, air-cooled
Displacement:	2,660 cc
Horse Power:	40 HP(29.6 kW)/2,500 rpm
Maximum Speed:	40.5 km/hour
Range:	200 km
Obstacles - step:	50 cm
ditch:	90 cm
ford:	50 cm
Special Features:	survived, now restored in Prague Military Museum

Vehicle Type:	tankette/light tank
Manufacturer:	Škoda, Plzeň
Manufacturer's Designation:	MU-6
Years of Production:	1933
Number of Vehicles Produced:	1 prototype
Czechoslovak Army Designation:	not accepted
Registration Numbers:	not assigned
Wehrmacht Designation:	none
Export:	none
Weight:	3.0 t
Length:	3.84 m
Width:	1.87 m
Height:	1.93 m
Ground Pressure:	0.5 kg/cm^2
Armor:	3-5.5 mm
Armament:	4.7 cm Škoda A2 gun, 3 light MG ZB vz.26
Ammunition Carried:	
Crew:	4
Engine Type:	Škoda, 6 cylinder, air-cooled
Displacement:	3,640 cc
Horse Power:	55 HP(40.5 kW)/2,700 rpm
Maximum Speed:	41.2 km
Range:	150 km
Obstacles - step:	50 cm
ditch:	150 cm
ford:	50 cm
Special Features:	in 1934 rebuilt as a carrier for the 4 cm Z1 dual purpose gun, later scrapped, as the chassis was too light

Vehicle Type:	tankette
Manufacturer:	Škoda, Plzeň
Manufacturer's Designation:	Š-I-P, after 1939 T-2
Years of Production:	1937
Number of Vehicles Produced:	1 prototype
Czechoslovak Army Designation:	not accepted
Registration Numbers:	not assigned
Wehrmacht Designation:	none
Export:	none
Weight:	4.60 t
Length:	3.65 m
Width:	2.03 m
Height:	1.56 m
Ground Pressure:	0.60 kg/cm²
Armor:	8-15 mm
Armament:	1 MG ZB vz.35, 1 light MG ZB vz.26
Ammunition Carried:	4,300
Crew:	2
Engine Type:	Škoda, 6 cylinder, air-cooled
Displacement:	3,990 cc
Horse Power:	60 HP(44.2 kW)/2,500 rpm
Maximum Speed:	45 km/hour
Range:	200 km
Obstacles - step:	50 cm
ditch:	130 cm
ford:	50 cm
Special Features:	originally developed as Škoda's own project of a reconnaissance light tank. In this form it carried a small turret, meant for the ZB-60 15 mm heavy machine gun. In 1939 modified into the above version with one light and one heavy MG. Tested in 1943 with center drive sprocket.

Vehicle Type:	assault gun type, first for Škoda
Manufacturer:	Škoda, Plzeň
Manufacturer's Designation:	Š-I-d
Years of Production:	1935
Number of Vehicles Produced:	1 prototype
Czechoslovak Army Designation:	not accepted
Registration Numbers:	not assigned
Wehrmacht Designation:	none
Export:	bought by Waffen SS in 1940
Weight:	4.55 t
Length:	3.70 m
Width:	2.00 m
Height:	1.68 m
Ground Pressure:	0.48 kg/cm²
Armor:	8-20 mm
Armament:	3.7 cm Škoda A3 gun, one MG ZB vz.26
Ammunition Carried:	25 gun, 2,600 MG
Crew:	2
Engine Type:	Škoda, 6 cylinder, air-cooled
Displacement:	3,770 cc
Horse Power:	60 HP(44.2 kW)/2,500 rpm
Maximum Speed:	41 km/hour
Range:	200 km
Obstacles - step:	50 cm
ditch:	130 cm
ford:	50 cm
Special Features:	commander's cupola

Vehicle Type:	assault gun
Manufacturer:	Škoda, Plzeň
Manufacturer's Designation:	Š-I-d
Years of Production:	1937
Number of Vehicles Produced:	8
Czechoslovak Army Designation:	not accepted
Registration Numbers:	not assigned
Wehrmacht Designation:	PzKpfw 32(j)
Export:	Yugoslavia T-32
Weight:	4.80 t
Length:	3.58 m
Width:	1.95 m
Height:	1.76 m
Ground Pressure:	0.48 kg/cm^2
Armor:	5-22 mm
Armament:	3.7 cm Škoda A3 gun, 1 MG ZB vz.30J
Ammunition Carried:	42 gun, 1,000 MG
Crew:	2
Engine Type:	Škoda, 6 cylinder, air-cooled
Displacement:	3,770 cc
Horse Power:	60 HP(44.2 kW)/2,500 rpm
Maximum Speed:	41 km/hour
Range:	250 km
Obstacles - step:	50 cm
ditch:	130 cm
ford:	50 cm
Special Features:	

Vehicle Type:	assault gun
Manufacturer:	Škoda, Plzeň
Manufacturer's Designation:	Š-I-j (T-3D)
Years of Production:	1938
Number of Vehicles Produced:	1 prototype
Czechoslovak Army Designation:	not accepted
Registration Numbers:	N/K
Wehrmacht Designation:	N/K
Export:	developed for Yugoslavia sold to Waffen SS
Weight:	5.80 t
Length:	3.59 m
Width:	2.05 m
Height:	1.80 m
Ground Pressure:	0.50 kg/cm^2
Armor:	8-30 mm
Armament:	4.7 cm Škoda A9J gun, 1 MG ZB vz.30J
Ammunition Carried:	42 gun, 1,000 MG
Crew:	2
Engine Type:	Škoda Diesel, 4 cylinder, water cooled
Displacement:	3,770 cc
Horse Power:	60 HP(44.2 kW)/2,200 rpm
Maximum Speed:	31 km/hour
Range:	6 hours
Obstacles - step:	50 cm
ditch:	130 cm
ford:	50 cm
Special Features:	last of the Škoda assault gun designs

Vehicle Type:	tankette
Manufacturer:	ČKD, Praha
Manufacturer's Designation:	AH-IV
Years of Production:	1935 prototype, 1936-1937 production
Number of Vehicles Produced:	50 + 1 prototype
Czechoslovak Army Designation:	not accepted
Registration Numbers:	not assigned
Wehrmacht Designation:	none
Export:	Iran 50+1 - AH-IV
Weight:	3.50 t
Length:	3.20 m
Width:	1.79 m
Height:	1.69 m
Ground Pressure:	0.45 kg/cm²
Armor:	6-12 mm
Armament:	1 MG ZB vz.35, 1 light MG ZB vz.26
Ammunition Carried:	3,700
Crew:	2
Engine Type:	Praga, RHP 6 cylinder, water cooled
Displacement:	3,468 cc
Horse Power:	55 HP(40.7 kW)/2,500 rpm
Maximum Speed:	45 km/hour
Range:	150 km
Obstacles - step:	50 cm
ditch:	150 cm
ford:	80 cm
Special Features:	excellent cross-country ride

Vehicle Type:	tankette
Manufacturer:	ČKD, Praha
Manufacturer's Designation:	AH-IV-R, later R-1
Years of Production:	1937-1938
Number of Vehicles Produced:	35 + 1 prototype
Czechoslovak Army Designation:	not accepted
Registration Numbers:	not assigned
Wehrmacht Designation:	none
Export	35 Romania, R-1
Weight:	3.90 t
Length:	3.20 m
Width:	1.73 m
Height	1.67 m
Ground Pressure:	0.50 kg/cm²
Armor:	6-12 mm
Armament:	1 MG ZB vz.35, 1 light MG ZB vz.30
Ammunition Carried:	3,700
Crew:	2
Engine Type:	Praga RHP, 6 cylinder, water cooled
Displacement:	3,468 cc
Horse Power:	55 HP(40.7 kW)/2,500 rpm
Maximum Speed:	45 km/hour
Range:	170 km
Obstacles - step:	60 cm
ditch:	150 cm
ford:	80 cm
Special Features:	advanced chassis, excellent cross-country ride

Vehicle Type:	tankette
Manufacturer:	ČKD, Praha
Manufacturer's Designation:	AH-IV-Sv (prototype AH-IV-S)
Years of Production:	1938
Number of Vehicles Produced:	48 + 1 prototype
Czechoslovak Army Designation:	not accepted
Registration Numbers:	not assigned
Wehrmacht Designation:	none
Export:	48 Sweden Stvr m/37, supplied in parts, assembled by Oskarhams
Weight:	4.68 t
Length:	3.40 m
Width:	1.85 m
Height:	1.96 m
Ground Pressure:	0.54 kg/cm^2
Armor:	6-15 mm
Armament:	2 MG Ksp m/39
Ammunition Carried:	3,960
Crew:	2
Engine Type:	Volvo FC, 6 cylinder, water cooled
Displacement:	4,390 cc
Horse Power:	85 HP(62.8 kW)/2,850 rpm
Maximum Speed:	58-61 km/hour
Range:	200 km
Obstacles - step:	60 cm
ditch:	160 cm
ford:	90 cm
Special Features:	both MG in the turret, observation cupola and radio

Vehicle Type:	tankette
Manufacturer:	ČKD, Praha
Manufacturer's Designation:	AH-IV-Hb
Years of Production:	1949-1950
Number of Vehicles Produced:	20 + 1 prototype(rebuilt from R-1 prototype)
Czechoslovak Army Designation:	N/A
Registration Numbers:	N/K
Wehrmacht Designation:	N/A
Export:	20 Ethiopia
Weight:	3.93 t
Length:	3.20 m
Width:	1.82 m
Height:	1.73 m
Ground Pressure:	0.48 kg/cm^2
Armor:	6-12 mm
Armament:	1 MG ZB vz.37, 1 light MG ZB vz.26
Ammunition Carried:	2,800
Crew:	2
Engine Type:	Tatra 114, air-cooled Diesel
Displacement:	4,940 cc
Horse Power:	65 HP(48 kW)/2,200 rpm
Maximum Speed:	42 km/hour
Range:	200 km
Obstacles - step:	50 cm
ditch:	150 cm
ford:	100 cm
Special Features:	welded construction

Vehicle Type:	light amphibious tank
Manufacturer:	ČKD, Praha
Manufacturer's Designation:	F-IV-H
Years of Production:	1938-1941
Number of Vehicles Produced:	2 prototypes
Czechoslovak Army Designation:	not accepted
Registration Numbers:	not assigned
Wehrmacht Designation:	none
Export:	none
Weight:	6.50 t
Length:	4.85 m
Width:	2.50 m
Height:	2.08 m
Ground Pressure:	0.50 kg/cm^2
Armor:	6-14 mm
Armament:	1 MG ZB vz.37
Ammunition Carried:	3,000
Crew:	3
Engine Type:	Praga F4, 4 cylinder, water cooled
Displacement:	7,180 cc
Horse Power:	120 HP(73.9 kW)/2,200 rpm
Maximum Speed:	45 km/hour land, 7 km/hour in water
Range:	200 km
Obstacles - step:	80 cm
ditch:	220 cm
ford:	swims
Special Features:	pontoons and two screws allowed full unrestricted swimming

Vehicle Type:	light amphibious tank
Manufacturer:	Škoda, Plzeň
Manufacturer's Designation:	ŠOT
Years of Production:	1938-1939
Number of Vehicles Produced:	1 prototype
Czechoslovak Army Designation:	not accepted
Registration Numbers:	not assigned
Wehrmacht Designation:	none
Export:	none
Weight:	7.50 t
Length:	5.25 m
Width:	2.50 m
Height:	2.38 m
Ground Pressure:	0.51 kg/cm^2
Armor:	6-15 mm
Armament:	2 MG ZB vz.37
Ammunition Carried:	4,000
Crew:	3
Engine Type:	Avia TR-12, 7 cylinder air-cooled radial
Displacement:	12,078 cc
Horse Power:	154 HP(113.8 kW)
Maximum Speed:	41.5 km/hour
Range:	7 hours
Obstacles - step:	80 cm
ditch:	215 cm
ford:	designed to swim
Special Features:	electromagnetic clutches Cotal, otherwise not very successful design. Too heavy to swim

Vehicle Type:	light tank
Manufacturer:	Renault
Manufacturer's Designation:	Renault FT
Years of Production:	1917-1925
Number of Vehicles Produced:	7 bought from France
Czechoslovak Army Designation:	Renault FT
Registration Numbers:	13006-13012
Wehrmacht Designation:	none
Export:	none
Weight:	6.50 t/6.70 t
Length:	4.94 m
Width:	1.74 m
Height:	2.14 m
Ground Pressure:	0.47 kg/cm²
Armor:	6-22 mm
Armament:	3.7 cm Puteaux gun/MG vz.24
Ammunition Carried:	237 gun/4,800 MG
Crew:	2
Engine Type:	Renault
Displacement:	
Horse Power:	35 HP(25.9 kW)
Maximum Speed:	7.5 km/hour
Range:	35 km
Obstacles - step:	60 cm
ditch:	180 cm
ford:	70 cm
Special Features:	

Vehicle Type:	light tank
Manufacturer:	Škoda, Plzeň
Manufacturer's Designation:	SU (later Š-II)
Years of Production:	1934
Number of Vehicles Produced:	1 prototype
Czechoslovak Army Designation:	not accepted
Registration Numbers:	not assigned
Wehrmacht Designation:	none
Export:	none
Weight:	8.00 t
Length:	4.50 m
Width:	2.00 m
Height:	2.10 m
Ground Pressure:	0.50 kg/cm²
Armor:	8-15 mm
Armament:	4.7 cm Škoda A2 gun, 2 MG vz.24
Ammunition Carried:	60 gun, 2,500 MG
Crew:	3
Engine Type:	Škoda, 4 cylinder, water cooled
Displacement:	8,013 cc
Horse Power:	110 HP(81.3 kW)/1,800 rpm
Maximum Speed:	31 km/hour
Range:	
Obstacles - step:	80 cm
ditch:	200 cm
ford:	80 cm
Special Features:	predecessor of Š-II-a, introduced the pneumatic steering and gear changing

Vehicle Type:	light tank
Manufacturer:	ČKD, Slaný (first 6), ČKD Praha (remainder)
Manufacturer's Designation:	P-II
Years of Production:	1932 prototype, production 1934-1936
Number of Vehicles Produced:	50 + 1 prototype
Czechoslovak Army Designation:	LT vz.34
Registration Numbers:	13490-13539, prototype13363
Wehrmacht Designation:	none
Export:	none
Weight:	7.50 t
Length:	4.60 m
Width:	2.10 m
Height:	2.22 m
Ground Pressure:	0.50 kg/cm^2
Armor:	8-15 mm
Armament:	3.7 cm Škoda ÚVvz.34 gun, 2 MG ZB vz.35
Ammunition Carried:	60 gun, 2,000 MG
Crew:	3
Engine Type:	Praga, 4 cylinder, water cooled
Displacement:	6,082 cc
Horse Power:	62.5 HP(46.2 kW)/1,350 rpm
Maximum Speed:	30 km/hour
Range:	160 km
Obstacles - step:	80 cm
ditch:	200 cm
ford:	80 cm
Special Features:	

Vehicle Type:	light tank, cavalry version
Manufacturer:	ČKD, Praha
Manufacturer's Designation:	P-II-a
Years of Production:	1935
Number of Vehicles Produced:	1 prototype
Czechoslovak Army Designation:	none
Registration Numbers:	19003
Wehrmacht Designation:	none
Export:	none
Weight:	8.5 t
Length:	4.70 m
Width:	2.10 m
Height:	2.36 m
Ground Pressure:	
Armor:	8-16 mm
Armament:	3.7 cm Škoda ÚVvz.34 gun, 2 ZB vz.35
Ammunition Carried:	
Crew:	3
Engine Type:	Praga SV, 4 cylinder, water cooled
Displacement:	4,800 cc
Horse Power:	115 HP(85 kW)
Maximum Speed:	36 km/hour
Range:	
Obstacles - step:	
ditch:	
ford:	
Special Features:	

Vehicle Type:	light tank - cavalry version
Manufacturer:	Škoda, Plzeň - ČKD, Praha
Manufacturer's Designation:	Š-II-a, T-11 after 1939
Years of Production:	1935-1940
Number of Vehicles Produced:	434 + 2 prototypes
Czechoslovak Army Designation:	LT vz.35
Registration Numbers:	13666-13860,13864-13966, prot.13620
Wehrmacht Designation:	PzKpfw 35(t)
Export:	Romania 126 R-2 in 1937-1939 Bulgaria 10 T-11 in 1941
Weight:	10.50 t
Length:	4.90 m
Width:	2.06 m
Height:	2.37 m
Ground Pressure:	0.51 kg/cm^2
Armor:	8-25 mm
Armament:	3.7 cm Škoda ÚVvz.34, 2 MG ZB vz.37 gun
Ammunition Carried:	78 gun, 2,700 MG
Crew:	3
Engine Type:	Škoda T-11/0, 4 cylinder, water cooled
Displacement:	8,620 cc
Horse Power:	120 HP(88.7 kW)/1,800 rpm
Maximum Speed:	34 km/hour
Range:	120 km
Obstacles - step:	80 cm
ditch:	210 cm
ford:	90 cm
Special Features:	pneumatic steering and gear changing

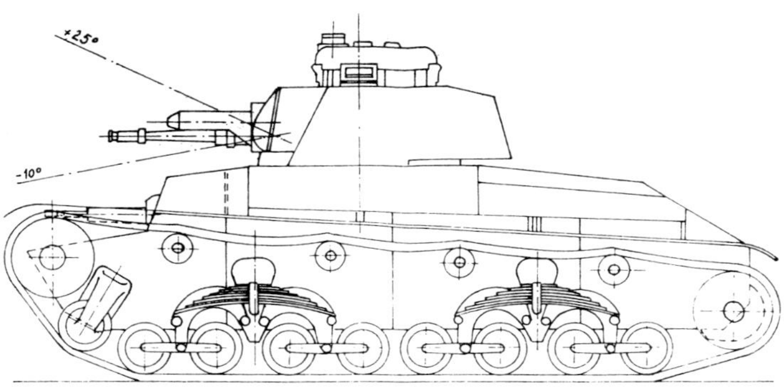

Vehicle Type:	light tank - infantry version
Manufacturer:	Škoda, Plzeň
Manufacturer's Designation:	S-II-b
Years of Production:	1936
Number of Vehicles Produced:	1 prototype
Czechoslovak Army Designation:	none
Registration Numbers:	13637
Wehrmacht Designation:	none
Export:	none
Weight:	13.10 t
Length:	5.14 m
Width:	2.15 m
Height:	2.39 m
Ground Pressure:	0.64 kg/cm^2
Armor:	10-25 mm
Armament:	3.7 cm Škoda ÚVvz.34 gun, 2 MG ZB vz.35
Ammunition Carried:	84 gun, 3,000 MG
Crew:	4
Engine Type:	Škoda T-11/0, 4 cylinder, water cooled
Displacement:	8,013 cc
Horse Power:	105 HP(77.6 kW)/1,800 rpm
Maximum Speed:	26.2 km/hour
Range:	8 hours
Obstacles - step:	80 cm
ditch:	220 cm
ford:	80 cm
Special Features:	

Vehicle Type: light tank - infantry version
Manufacturer: ČKD, Praha
Manufacturer's Designation: P-II-b
Years of Production: 1936
Number of Vehicles Produced: 1 prototype
Czechoslovak Army Designation: none
Registration Numbers: 13638
Wehrmacht Designation: none
Export: none

Weight: 11.0 t
Length: 4.95 m
Width: 2.25 m
Height: 2.40 m
Ground Pressure:

Armor: 10-25 mm
Armament: 3.7 cm Škoda ÚVvz.34 gun, 2 MG ZB vz.35
Ammunition Carried: 90 gun, 3,000 MG
Crew: 4

Engine Type: Praga, 4 cylinder, water cooled
Displacement: 4,800 cc
Horse Power: 120 HP(88.7 kW)
Maximum Speed: 30 km/hour
Range: 7 hours

Obstacles - step: 80 cm
ditch: 220 cm
ford: 100 cm

Special Features:

Vehicle Type: light tank
Manufacturer: Škoda, Plzeň
Manufacturer's Designation: T-13M
Years of Production: 1940
Number of Vehicles Produced: 1 prototype
Czechoslovak Army Designation: N/A
Registration Numbers: N/A
Wehrmacht Designation: none
Export: none

Weight: 12.60 t
Length: 4.90 m
Width: 2.12 m
Height: 2.33 m
Ground Pressure: 0.60 kg/cm^2

Armor: 8-30 mm
Armament: 3.7 cm Škoda A7 gun, 2 MG 37(t)
Ammunition Carried: 78 gun, 3,000 MG
Crew: 4

Engine Type: Škoda, 4 cylinder, water cooled
Displacement: 8,620 cc
Horse Power: 135 HP(99.8 kW)/2,000 rpm
Maximum Speed: 33 km/hour
Range: 6 hours

Obstacles - step: 80 cm
ditch: 200 cm
ford: 80 cm

Special Features: developed from T-11, but with mechanical steering and gear changing

Vehicle Type:	light tank - infantry version
Manufacturer:	Škoda - ČKD
Manufacturer's Designation:	ŠP-II-b
Years of Production:	1938-1939
Number of Vehicles Produced:	1 prototype
Czechoslovak Army Designation:	none
Registration Numbers:	14120
Wehrmacht Designation:	none
Export:	none
Weight:	16.55 t
Length:	5.38 m
Width:	2.44 m
Height:	2.29 m
Ground Pressure:	0.60 kg/cm^2
Armor:	10-30 mm
Armament:	4.7 cm Škoda A9 gun, 2 MG ZB vz.37
Ammunition Carried:	80 gun, 3,000 MG
Crew:	4
Engine Type:	Praga V-8, water cooled
Displacement:	14,000 cc
Horse Power:	250 HP(148.8 kW)
Maximum Speed:	45.8 km/hour
Range:	7 hours
Obstacles - step:	80 cm
ditch:	220 cm
ford:	90 cm
Special Features:	more of a medium tank, it had some advanced features, but the cooperation between Škoda and ČKD never really worked

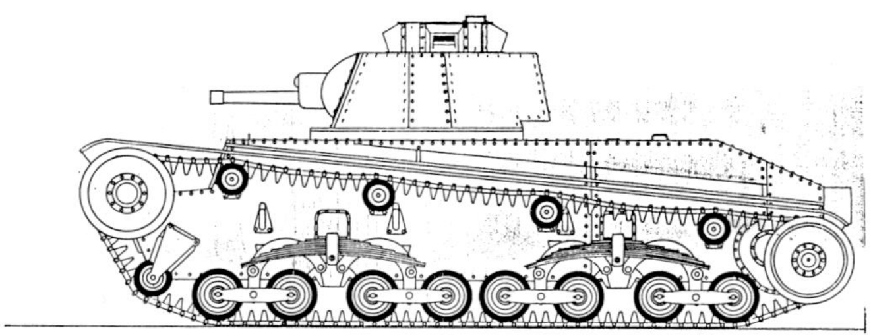

Vehicle Type:	medium tank
Manufacturer:	Škoda, Plzeň
Manufacturer's Designation:	Š-III
Years of Production:	1934-1939
Number of Vehicles Produced:	2 prototypes
Czechoslovak Army Designation:	Š-III
Registration Numbers:	13638, 13639
Wehrmacht Designation:	none
Export:	none
Weight:	18.60 t
Length:	5.83 m
Width:	2.54 m
Height:	2.48 m
Ground Pressure:	0.90 kg/cm^2
Armor:	16-32 mm
Armament:	4.7 cm Škoda Š-III gun, 2 MG ZB vz.37
Ammunition Carried:	80 gun, 4,000 MG
Crew:	4
Engine Type:	Škoda, six or eight cylinder
Displacement:	12,800 cc (six cylinder)
Horse Power:	190 HP(140.4 kW)/1,800 rpm
Maximum Speed:	27.5 km/hour
Range:	8 hours
Obstacles - step:	100 cm
ditch:	250 cm
ford:	100 cm
Special Features:	started as wheel-cum-track, prolonged development, unsuccessful design

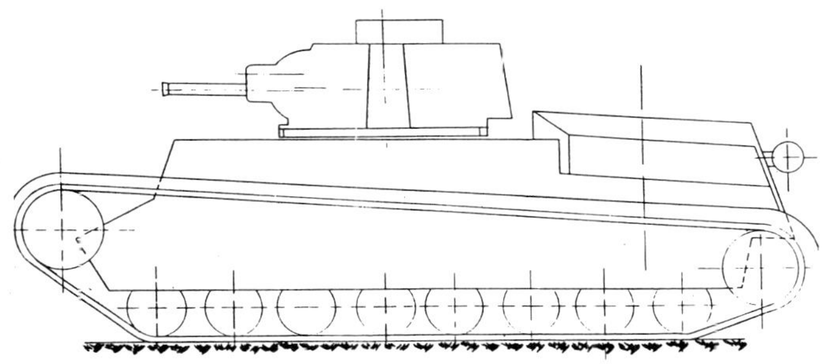

Vehicle Type: medium tank
Manufacturer: Tatra, Kopřivnice
Manufacturer's Designation: T-III
Years of Production: 1934-1939
Number of Vehicles Produced: 2 prototypes
Czechoslovak Army Designation: T-III
Registration Numbers: 13640, 13641
Wehrmacht Designation: none
Export: none

Weight: 16.40 t
Length: 5.85 m
Width: 2.56 m
Height: 2.42 m
Ground Pressure: 0.80 kg/cm²

Armor: 16-32 mm
Armament: 4.7 cm Škoda Š-III gun, 2 MG ZB vz.37
Ammunition Carried: 80 gun, 4,000 MG
Crew: 4

Engine Type: Tatra, 11 cylinder air-cooled radial
Displacement: 18,000 cc
Horse Power: 280 HP(207 kW)/1,800 rpm
Maximum Speed: 35 km/hour
Range: 50 km (!)

Obstacles - step: 100 cm
ditch: 250 cm
ford: 100 cm

Special Features: concurrently developed with Š-III, and as bad. Engine powerful, but overheating constantly and with extremely poor mileage.

Vehicle Type: medium tank
Manufacturer: Škoda, Plzeň
Manufacturer's Designation: Š-II-c, after 1939 T-21
Years of Production: 1938
Number of Vehicles Produced: 1 prototype
Czechoslovak Army Designation: not accepted
Registration Numbers: not assigned
Wehrmacht Designation: none
Export: license sold to Hungary

Weight: 16.50 t
Length: 5.56 m
Width: 2.45 m
Height: 2.37 m
Ground Pressure: 0.58 kg/cm²

Armor: 16-30 mm
Armament: 4.7 cm Škoda A11 gun, 2 MG ZB vz.37
Ammunition Carried: 80 gun, 3,000 MG
Crew: 4

Engine Type: Škoda, V-eight, water cooled
Displacement: 13,800 cc
Horse Power: 240 HP(177.4 kW)/2,200 rpm
Maximum Speed: 50 km/hour
Range: 180 km

Obstacles - step: 80 cm
ditch: 220 cm
ford: 90 cm

Special Features: retained pneumatic steering and gear changing of the Š-II-a. Excellent design

Vehicle Type:	medium tank
Manufacturer:	Škoda, Plzeň
Manufacturer's Designation:	T-22
Years of Production:	1941
Number of Vehicles Produced:	1 prototype
Czechoslovak Army Designation:	N/A
Registration Numbers:	N/A
Wehrmacht Designation:	none
Export:	none
Weight:	18.00 t
Length:	5.56 m
Width:	2.45 m
Height:	2.39 m
Ground Pressure:	0.76 kg/cm^2
Armor:	8-50 mm
Armament:	N/A, no turret
Ammunition Carried:	N/A
Crew:	4
Engine Type:	Škoda, V-eight, water cooled
Displacement:	15,000 cc
Horse Power:	260 HP(192.2 kW)/2,200 rpm
Maximum Speed:	48 km/hour
Range:	160 km
Obstacles - step:	80 cm
ditch:	220 cm
ford:	90 cm
Special Features:	improved T-21 with a stronger engine, prototype ordered and tested by Wehrmacht in 1941

Vehicle Type:	medium tank
Manufacturer:	Škoda, Plzeň
Manufacturer's Designation:	T-23
Years of Production:	1941
Number of Vehicles Produced:	1 prototype
Czechoslovak Army Designation:	N/A
Registration Numbers:	N/A
Wehrmacht Designation:	none
Export:	none
Weight:	18.00 t
Length:	5.56 m
Width:	2.45 m
Height:	2.39 m
Ground Pressure:	0.76 kg/cm^2
Armor:	8-50 mm
Armament:	4.7 cm PaK(t), 2 MG ZB vz.37
Ammunition Carried:	80 gun, 3,000 MG
Crew:	4
Engine Type:	Škoda, V-eight, water cooled
Displacement:	15,000 cc
Horse Power:	260 HP(192.2 kW)/2,200 rpm
Maximum Speed:	45 km/hour
Range:	160 km
Obstacles - step:	80 cm
ditch:	220 cm
ford:	90 cm
Special Features:	identical to T-22, but with a mechanical gearbox. Planned to get Škoda KwK 41(t) gun (A11)

Vehicle Type:	antitank gun carrier
Manufacturer:	ČKD, Praha
Manufacturer's Designation:	Praga LKMVP
Years of Production:	1938
Number of Vehicles Produced:	1 prototype
Czechoslovak Army Designation:	LKMVP
Registration Numbers:	14124
Wehrmacht Designation:	none
Export:	none
Weight:	7.10 t
Length:	4.28 m
Width:	2.15 m
Height:	1.69 m
Ground Pressure:	0.54 kg/cm^2
Armor:	6-12 mm
Armament:	3.7 cm KPÚV vz.37 gun
Ammunition Carried:	90
Crew:	2 + 4
Engine Type:	Praga TN, 4 cylinder
Displacement:	7,800 cc
Horse Power:	92 HP(68 kW)/1,800 rpm
Maximum Speed:	52 km/hour
Range:	8 hours
Obstacles - step:	80 cm
ditch:	180 cm
ford:	50 cm
Special Features:	the gun was carried on the vehicle, but could be also towed. It was possible to fire the gun from the vehicle, if necessary.

Vehicle Type:	antitank gun carrier
Manufacturer:	Škoda, Plzeň
Manufacturer's Designation:	Škoda LKMVP, after 1939 PÚV-6
Years of Production:	1938-1939
Number of Vehicles Produced:	1 prototype
Czechoslovak Army Designation:	not accepted
Registration Numbers:	not assigned
Wehrmacht Designation:	none
Export:	1940 bought by Waffen SS
Weight:	6.80 t
Length:	4.32 m
Width:	2.17 m
Height:	1.69 m
Ground Pressure:	0.63 kg/cm^2
Armor:	6-12 mm
Armament:	3.7 cm KPÚV vz.37 gun
Ammunition Carried:	90
Crew:	2 + 4
Engine Type:	Demark, 6 cylinder
Displacement:	6,174 cc
Horse Power:	76 HP(56.2 kW)/2,600 rpm
Maximum Speed:	40 km/hour
Range:	8 hours
Obstacles - step:	50 cm
ditch:	150 cm
ford:	50 cm
Special Features:	gun carried on the vehicle or towed, could be fired from the vehicle if necessary.

Vehicle Type:	medium tank
Manufacturer:	Weiss, Mavag, Raba, Ganz
Manufacturer's Designation:	TURÁN I
Years of Production:	1941-1944
Number of Vehicles Produced:	285
Hungarian Army Designation:	40.M TURÁN I - közepes harckocsi
Registration Numbers:	H-803 - H-871 (Weiss) 1H-001 - 1H-086 (Raba) 1H201 - 1H-268 (Mavag) 1H-426 - 1H-489 (Ganz)
Weight:	18.20 t
Length:	5.50 m
Width:	2.44 m
Height:	2.39 m
Ground Pressure:	0.78 kg/cm^2
Armor:	8-60 mm
Armament:	4 cm Mavag 41.M gun, 2 MG 34/40 A.M.
Ammunition Carried:	101 gun, 3,000 MG
Crew:	5
Engine Type:	WM Z-Turán, eight cylinder
Displacement:	14,866 cc
Horse Power:	260 HP(192.2 kW)/2,200 rpm
Maximum Speed:	47.2 km/hour
Range:	165 km
Obstacles - step:	80 cm
ditch:	220 cm
ford:	90 cm
Special Features:	from 1944, some vehicles modified by adding perforated side skirts on the hull and the turret

Vehicle Type:	heavy tank
Manufacturer:	Weiss, Raba, Ganz
Manufacturer's Designation:	TURÁN II
Years of Production:	1943-1944
Number of Vehicles Produced:	139
Hungarian Army Designation:	41.M TURÁN nehéz harckocsi or TURÁN 75 rövid csövü
Registration Numbers:	2H-000 - 2H-053 (Weiss) 2H-077 - 2H-086, 2H-213 - 2H-235(Raba) 2H-400 - 2H-435 (Ganz) 2H-054 - 2H-061 and 2H436 - 2H-437 manufacturer unknown
Weight:	19.20 t
Length:	5.50 m
Width:	2.44 m
Height:	2.44 m
Ground Pressure:	10.83 kg/cm^2
Armor:	8-50 mm
Armament:	7.5 cm Mavag 41.M gun, 2 MG 34/40 A.M.
Ammunition Carried:	56 gun, 1,800 MG
Crew:	5
Engine Type:	WM Z-Turán, eight cylinder
Displacement:	14,866 cc
Horse Power:	260 HP(192.2 kW)/2,200 rpm
Maximum Speed:	43 km/hour
Range:	150 km
Obstacles - step:	80 cm
ditch:	220 cm
ford:	90 cm
Special Features:	modified turret to accept the larger gun breach. From 1944, armored perforated skirts mounted on hull and turret

Vehicle Type:	heavy tank
Manufacturer:	Weiss
Manufacturer's Designation:	TURAN III
Years of Production:	1943-1944
Number of Vehicles Produced:	1 prototype
Hungarian Army Designation:	43.M TURÁN nehéz harckocsi or TURÁN 75 hosszú csövü
Registration Numbers:	H-830
Weight:	23.30 t
Length:	6.86 m (with gun)
Width:	2.60 m (with skirts)
Height:	2.65 m
Ground Pressure:	0.88 kg/cm^2
Armor:	35-95 mm
Armament:	7.5 cm Mavag 43,M gun, 2 MG 34/40 A.M.
Ammunition Carried:	32 gun, 1,800 MG
Crew:	5
Engine Type:	WM Z-Turan, eight cylinder
Displacement:	14,866 cc
Horse Power:	260 HP(192.2 kW)/2,200 rpm
Maximum Speed:	40 km/hour
Range:	120 km
Obstacles - step:	80 cm
ditch:	220 cm
ford:	90 cm
Special Features:	effective (long) gun, excellent armor production stopped by German occupation and Allied bombing

Vehicle Type:	assault gun
Manufacturer:	Weiss, Ganz
Manufacturer's Designation:	ZRÍNYI II
Years of Production:	1943-1944
Number of Vehicles Produced:	66 (140 ordered)
Hungarian Army Designation:	40/43.M ZRÍNYI II rolamtarack (Zrínyi 105)
Registration Numbers:	3H-000 - 3H-059 (Weiss) 6 vehicles not known (Ganz)
Weight:	21.50 t
Length:	5.90 m (with gun)
Width:	2.89 m
Height:	1.90 m
Ground Pressure:	0.91 kg/cm^2
Armor:	25-75 mm
Armament:	10.5 cm 40/43.M Mavag howitzer, 1 MG
Ammunition Carried:	52 gun, 500 MG
Crew:	4
Engine Type:	WM Z-Turan, eight cylinder
Displacement:	14,866 cc
Horse Power:	260 HP(192.2 kW)/2,200 rpm
Maximum Speed:	40 km/hour
Range:	220 km
Obstacles - step:	80 cm
ditch:	220 cm
ford:	90 cm
Special Features:	side skirts

Vehicle Type: tank hunter
Manufacturer: Weiss
Manufacturer's Designation: ZRÍNYI I
Years of Production: 1944
Number of Vehicles Produced: 4
Hungarian Army Designation: 44.M ZRÍNYI rohamágyú (or Zrínyi 75)
Registration Numbers: prototype H-801 rest not known

Weight: 22.00 t
Length: 7.60 m (with gun)
Width: 2.89 m
Height: 1.90 m
Ground Pressure: 0.93 kg/cm²

Armor: 25-100 mm
Armament: 7.5 cm 43.M Mavag gun, 1 MG
Ammunition Carried: 70 gun, 500 MG
Crew: 4

Engine Type: WM Z-Turan, eight cylinder
Displacement: 14,866 cc
Horse Power: 260 HP(192.2 kW)/2,200 rpm
Maximum Speed: 40 km/hour
Range: 220 km

Obstacles - step: 80 cm
ditch: 220 cm
ford: 90 cm

Special Features: side skirts, same gun as planned for TURAN III

V-8-H

V-8-H II

Vehicle Type: medium tank
Manufacturer: ČKD, Praha
Manufacturer's Designation: V-8-H
Years of Production: 1938-1939
Number of Vehicles Produced: 2 prototypes
Czechoslovak Army Designation: ST vz.39 (planned)
Registration Numbers: not assigned
Wehrmacht Designation: none
Export: none

Weight: 16.20 t
Length: 5.35 m
Width: 2.27 m
Height: 2.34 m
Ground Pressure: 0.56 kg/cm²

Armor: 12-32 mm
Armament: 4.7 cm Škoda A11 gun, 2 MG ZB vz.37
Ammunition Carried: 80 gun, 3,000 MG
Crew: 4

Engine Type: Praga V-8, water cooled
Displacement: 14,230 cc
Horse Power: 260 HP(192.2 kW)/2,200 rpm
Maximum Speed: 43.5 km/hour
Range: 150 km

Obstacles - step: 100 cm
ditch: 230 cm
ford: 100 cm

Special Features: one prototype tested in 1938-1939. Second prototype manufactured in 1939 and tested by the Germans.

Vehicle Type: light tank
Manufacturer: ČKD, Slaný
Manufacturer's Designation: TNH
Years of Production: 1935-1937
Number of Vehicles Produced: 50 + 1 prototype
Czechoslovak Army Designation: none
Registration Numbers: none
Wehrmacht Designation: none
Export: 50 + 1 to Iran

Weight: 8.20 t
Length: 4.51 m
Width: 2.08 m
Height: 2.30 m
Ground Pressure: 0.52 kg/cm^2

Armor: 8-15 mm
Armament: 3.7 cm Škoda A4 BETA gun, 2 MG ZB vz.35
Ammunition Carried: 60 gun, 3,000 MG
Crew: 4

Engine Type: Praga TN100, 4 cylinder, water cooled
Displacement: 7,940
Horse Power: 100HP(73.9 kW)/2,000 rpm
Maximum Speed: 38 km/hour
Range: 200 km

Obstacles - step: 80 cm
ditch: 180 cm
ford: 90 cm

Special Features: First of the famous TNH series

Vehicle Type: light tank
Manufacturer: ČKD, Praha
Manufacturer's Designation: LTP
Years of Production: 1938-1939
Number of Vehicles Produced: 24
Czechoslovak Army Designation: none
Registration Numbers: none
Wehrmacht Designation: none
Export: 24 to Peru (Tanque 38/39)

Weight: 7.30 t
Length: 4.10 m
Width: 1.95 m
Height: 2.16 m
Ground Pressure: 0.55 kg/cm^2

Armor: 8-25 mm
Armament: 3.7 cm Škoda A3 gun, 1 MG ZB vz.35, 1 light MG ZB vz.30
Ammunition Carried: 54 gun, 2,700 MG
Crew: 3

Engine Type: Scania-Vabis 1664, 6 cylinder, water cooled
Displacement: 7,750 cc
Horse Power: 125 HP(92.4 kW)/2,200 rpm
Maximum Speed: 40 km/hour
Range: 187 km

Obstacles - step: 80 cm
ditch: 200 cm
ford: 90 cm

Special Features: capable of operations up to heights of 4,500 m

Vehicle Type:	light tank
Manufacturer:	ČKD, Praha
Manufacturer's Designation:	LTH
Years of Production:	1938-1939
Number of Vehicles Produced:	24 + 1 prototype
Czechoslovak Army Designation:	none
Registration Numbers:	none
Wehrmacht Designation:	none
Export:	24 to Switzerland (Pzw.39)
Weight:	7.70 t
Length:	4.26 m (4.46 m with the gun)
Width:	2.00 m
Height:	2.10 m
Ground Pressure:	0.60 kg/cm^2
Armor:	8-32 mm
Armament:	2.4 cm Oerlikon M.38, 2 MG Maxim M.38, 1 light MG vz.25
Ammunition Carried:	114 gun, 2,800 MG
	3
Crew:	
	12 tanks Saurer-Arbon Diesel CT1
Engine Type:	12 tanks Scania-Vabis 1664
	7,980 cc/7,750 cc
Displacement:	120 HP(88.7 kW)/125 HP(92.4 kW)
Horse Power:	45 km/hour
Maximum Speed:	200 km
Range:	
	80 cm
Obstacles - step:	180 cm
ditch:	80 cm
ford:	
Special Features:	

Vehicle Type:	light tank
Manufacturer:	ČKD, Praha
Manufacturer's Designation:	LTL
Years of Production:	1938
Number of Vehicles Produced:	1 prototype
Czechoslovak Army Designation:	not accepted
Registration Numbers:	not assigned
Wehrmacht Designation:	none
Export:	developed for Latvia
Weight:	7.20 t
Length:	4.20 m
Width:	1.95 m
Height:	1.80 m
Ground Pressure:	0.50 kg/cm^2
Armor:	8-25 mm
Armament:	20 mm Oerlikon gun, 2 MG Maxim
Ammunition Carried:	255 gun, 3,000 MG
Crew:	3
Engine Type:	Praga F-4, 4 cylinder, water cooled
Displacement:	7,180 cc
Horse Power:	125 HP(92.4 kW)/2,200 rpm
Maximum Speed:	54 km/hour
Range:	300 km
Obstacles - step:	80 cm
ditch:	190 cm
ford:	90 cm
Special Features:	the only ČKD light tank with rear drive

Vehicle Type:	light tank
Manufacturer:	ČKD, Slaný
Manufacturer's Designation:	LLT
Years of Production:	1939-1940
Number of Vehicles Produced:	21
Czechoslovak Army Designation:	none
Registration Numbers:	none
Wehrmacht Designation:	none
Export:	bought by Slovakia as LT-40
Weight:	7.50 t
Length:	4.20 m
Width:	2.15 m
Height:	2.16 m
Ground Pressure:	0.50 kg/cm^2
Armor:	8-25 mm
Armament:	3.7 cm Škoda A7 gun, 2 MG ZB vz.37
Ammunition Carried:	66 gun, 3,000 MG
Crew:	3
Engine Type:	Praga TNHPS, 6 cylinder, water cooled
Displacement:	7,750 cc
Horse Power:	126 HP(93.1 kW)/2,200 rpm
Maximum Speed:	47 km/hour
Range:	200 km
Obstacles - step:	80 cm
ditch:	190 cm
ford:	90 cm
Special Features:	originally built for Latvia, after its occupation by USSR, bought by the army of the new Slovak State, upgunned to 3.7 cm Škoda gun

Vehicle Type:	light tank
Manufacturer:	ČKD, Praha/Scania Vabis
Manufacturer's Designation:	THN-Sv/Stvr m/41 - Stvr m/41 S-II
Years of Production:	1941-1944
Number of Vehicles Produced:	1 prototype by ČKD, 116 + 104
Czechoslovak Army Designation:	none
Registration Numbers:	none
Wehrmacht Designation:	none
Export:	license sold to Sweden in 1941
Weight:	10.50 t/11.00 t
Length:	4.54 m/4.60 m
Width:	2.14 m
Height:	2.35 m
Ground Pressure:	0.57/0.59 kg/cm^2
Armor:	10-50 mm
Armament:	3.7 cm Bofors Stvr-K m/38 gun, 2 MG KsP m/39
Ammunition Carried:	100 gun, 4,000 MG
Crew:	4
Engine Type:	Scania-Vabis 1664-13/603-2, 6 cyl.
Displacement:	7,750 cc/8,470 cc
Horse Power:	145 HP(107.2 kW)/160 HP(118.3 kW)/ 2,300 rpm
Maximum Speed:	43 km/hour
Range:	180/230 km
Obstacles - step:	80 cm
ditch:	180 cm
ford:	80 cm
Special Features:	flat-roof turret, S-II sloped sides of the turret

Vehicle Type: self-propelled gun
Manufacturer: Scania-Vabis
Manufacturer's Designation: Sav m/43
Years of Production: 1943-1944
Number of Vehicles Produced: 36
Czechoslovak Army Designation: none
Registration Numbers: none
Wehrmacht Designation: none
Export: none

Weight: 12.40 t
Length: 4.60 m (5.05 m with gun)
Width: 2.14 m
Height: 2.29 m
Ground Pressure: 0.62 kg/cm²

Armor: 10-30 mm
Armament: 10.5 cm Bofors Sak m/44 howitzer
Ammunition Carried: 43
Crew: 4

Engine Type: Scania-Vabis 1664/13, 6 cylinder
Displacement: 7,750 cc
Horse Power: 140 HP(103.5 kW)/2,300 rpm
Maximum Speed: 43 km/hour
Range: 180 km

Obstacles - step: 80 cm
ditch: 180 cm
ford: 90 cm

Special Features:

Vehicle Type: light tank
Manufacturer: ČKD, Praha
Manufacturer's Designation: THN-S or TNH-P
Years of Production: 1938
Number of Vehicles Produced: 1 prototype
Czechoslovak Army Designation: LT vz.38
Registration Numbers: not assigned
Wehrmacht Designation: none
Export: none

Weight: 8.80 t
Length: 4.51 m
Width: 2.08 m
Height: 2.24 m
Ground Pressure: 0.50 kg/cm²

Armor: 8-25 mm
Armament: 3.7 cm Škoda A7 gun, 2 MG ZB vz.37
Ammunition Carried: 90 gun, 2,700 MG
Crew: 4

Engine Type: Praga TNHPS, 6 cylinder, water cooled
Displacement: 7,754 cc
Horse Power: 126 HP(93.1 kW)/ 2,200 rpm
Maximum Speed: 42 km/hour
Range: 210 km

Obstacles - step: 80 cm
ditch: 210 cm
ford: 90 cm

Special Features:

PzKpfw 38(t)

Vehicle Type:	light tank
Manufacturer:	BMM, Praha
Manufacturer's Designation:	THNPS, TNH-Sv(Ausf. S), TNH-S1(Slovak)
Years of Production:	1939-1942
Number of Vehicles Produced	1396 + 37
Czechoslovak Army Designati	0001-1090, 1101-1359, 1480-1526
Registration Numbers:	PzKpfw 38(t), Ausführung A-G
Wehrmacht Designation:	1396 for Wehrmacht,
Export:	(37 for Slovak State)
	"Ausf.A/Ausf.G"
Weight:	9.15 t/10.14 t
Length:	4.54 m/4.61 m
Width:	2.12 m/2.14 m
Height:	2.23 m/2.23 m
Ground Pressure:	0.50 kg/cm^2/0.53 kg/cm^2
Armor:	8-25 mm/8-50 mm
Armament:	3.7 cm KwK 38(t), 2 MG 37(t)
Ammunition Carried:	72 gun, 2,400 MG
Crew:	4
Engine Type:	Praga TNHPS, 6 cylinder, water cooled
Displacement:	7,754 cc
Horse Power:	126 HP(93.1 kW)/2,200 rpm/130 HP/ 2,500 rpm
Maximum Speed:	42 km/hour
Range:	250 km
Obstacles - step:	80 cm
ditch:	210 cm
ford:	90 cm
Special Features:	radio FuG 5

TNHnA

Vehicle Type:	reconnaissance tank
Manufacturer:	BMM, Praha
Manufacturer's Designation:	TNHnA
Years of Production:	1941-1943
Number of Vehicles Produced:	5
Chassis numbers:	
Wehrmacht Designation:	PzKpfw 38(t) neuer Art
Export:	none
Weight:	11.80 t
Length:	4.62 m
Width:	2.17 m
Height:	2.26 m
Ground Pressure:	0.60 kg/cm^2
Armor:	10-50 mm
Armament:	3.7 cm Škoda A19 gun, 1 MG 34
Ammunition Carried:	90 gun, 700 MG
Crew:	4
Engine Type:	Praga NR, V-8, water cooled
Displacement:	14,230 cc
Horse Power:	248 HP(183.3 kW)/2,500 rpm
Maximum Speed:	64 km/hour
Range:	200 km
Obstacles - step:	70 cm
ditch:	210 cm
ford:	100 cm
Special Features:	2 vehicles had riveted construction, 3 welded; all prototypes made from soft iron plate

Vehicle Type:	reconnaisance tank
Manufacturer:	Škoda, Plzeň
Manufacturer's Designation:	T-15
Years of Production:	1941-1943
Number of Vehicles Produced:	5
Chassis numbers:	
Wehrmacht Designation:	Panzespähwagen T-15
Export:	none
Weight:	10.60 t
Length:	4.58 m
Width:	2.17 m
Height:	2.16 m
Ground Pressure:	0.75 kg/cm^2
Armor:	12-30 mm
Armament:	3.7 cm Škoda A19 gun, 1 MG 34
Ammunition Carried:	78 gun, 2,100 MG
Crew:	4
Engine Type:	Škoda, V-eight, water cooled
Displacement:	10,800 cc
Horse Power:	218 HP(161.1 kW)/2,800 rpm
Maximum Speed:	60 km/hour
Range:	5 hours
Obstacles - step:	75 cm
ditch:	160 cm
ford:	100 cm
Special Features:	welded construction

Vehicle Type:	self-propelled antitank gun
Manufacturer:	BMM, Praha
Manufacturer's Designation:	TNHPS
Years of Production:	1942
Number of Vehicles Produced:	344, 39 converted from PzKpfw 38(t)
Chassis numbers:	1360-1479, 1527-1766
Wehrmacht Designation:	Panzerjäger 38(t) für 7.62 cm PaK 36(r) MARDER III (SdKfz 139)
Export:	"Ausf.G/Ausf.H" none
Weight:	10.67 t
Length:	5.85 m (with gun)
Width:	2.16 m
Height:	2.50 m
Ground Pressure:	0.56 kg/cm^2
Armor:	10-50 mm
Armament:	7.62 cm PaK 36(r), 1 MG37(t)
Ammunition Carried:	30 gun, 1,200 MG
Crew:	4
Engine Type:	Praga TNHPS/Praga AC
Displacement:	7,754 cc
Horse Power:	126 HP(93.1 kW)/150 HP(111 kW)/ 2,500 rpm
Maximum Speed:	47 km/hour
Range:	185 km
Obstacles - step:	80 cm
ditch:	210 cm
ford:	90 cm
Special Features:	first of the self-propelled guns built on the TNH chassis, this one using a captured Russian antitank gun, re-bored for German ammunition

Vehicle Type:	self-propelled antitank gun
Manufacturer:	BMM. Praha
Manufacturer's Designation:	TNHPS
Years of Production:	1942-1943
Number of Vehicles Produced:	275, 336 converted from PzKpfw 38(t)
Chassis numbers:	1768-1949, 1968-1969, 2016-2075
Wehrmacht Designation:	7.5 cm PaK 40/3 auf PzKpfw 38(t), Aush.H MARDER III (SdKfz 138)
Export:	18 to Slovakia in 1944
Weight:	10.80 t
Length:	5.77 m (with gun)
Width:	2.16 m
Height:	2.51 m
Ground Pressure:	0.56 kg/cm^2
Armor:	8-50 mm
Armament:	7.5 cm PaK 40/3, 1 MG37(t)
Ammunition Carried:	38 gun, 600 MG
Crew:	4
Engine Type:	Praga AC
Displacement:	7,754 cc
Horse Power:	150 HP(111 kW)/2,500 rpm
Maximum Speed:	47 km/hour
Range:	240 km
Obstacles - step:	80 cm
ditch:	210 cm
ford:	90 cm
Special Features:	

Vehicle Type:	self-propelled howitzer
Manufacturer:	BMM, Praha
Manufacturer's Designation:	TNHPS
Years of Production:	1942-1943
Number of Vehicles Produced:	200
Chassis numbers:	1767, 1950-1967, 1970-2015, 2076-2100
Wehrmacht Designation:	15 cm Schweres Infanteriegeschütz 33(Sf) auf PzKpfw 38(t), Ausf.H (SdKfz 138/1) GRILLE
Weight:	10.80 t
Length:	4.84 m
Width:	2.26 m
Height:	2.15 m
Ground Pressure:	0.62 kg/cm^2
Armor:	15-50 mm
Armament:	15 cm sIG33/1, 2 MP 40
Ammunition Carried:	16 gun, 384 MP
Crew:	5
Engine Type:	Praga AC
Displacement:	7,754 cc
Horse Power:	150 HP(111 kW)/2,500 rpm
Maximum Speed:	47 km/hour
Range:	200 km
Obstacles - step:	80 cm
ditch:	210 cm
ford:	90 cm
Special Features:	superstructure extended over the engine compartment to accommodate the gun and ammunition

Vehicle Type:	self-propelled antitank gun
Manufacturer:	BMM, Praha
Manufacturer's Designation:	TNHPS
Years of Production:	1943-1944
Number of Vehicles Produced:	942
Chassis numbers:	between 2121 and 3565
Wehrmacht Designation:	Panzerjäger 38(t) mit 7.5 cm PaK 40/3 Ausf.M (SdKfz 138)
Weight:	10.15 t
Length:	5.02 m
Width:	2.15 m
Height:	2.35 m
Ground Pressure:	0.54 kg/cm^2
Armor:	10-15 mm
Armament:	7.5 cm PaK 40/3, 1 MG34, 2 MP 40
Ammunition Carried:	27 gun, 1,500 MG, 384 MP
Crew:	4
Engine Type:	Praga AC. 6 cylinder, water cooled
Displacement:	7,754 cc
Horse Power:	150 HP(111 kW)/2,500 rpm
Maximum Speed:	47 km/hour
Range:	200 km
Obstacles - step:	80 cm
ditch:	210 cm
ford:	90 cm
Special Features:	last version, with the engine in front and the gun in the back. Used till 1945

Vehicle Type:	self-propelled howitzer
Manufacturer:	BMM, Praha
Manufacturer's Designation:	TNHPS
Years of Production:	1943-1944
Number of Vehicles Produced:	193 + 10
Chassis numbers:	between 2101 and 3543
Wehrmacht Designation:	15 cm Schweres Infanteriegeschütz 33/1 auf Selbstfahrlafette 38(t) (Sf) Ausf.M (SdKfz 138/1) GRILLE
Weight:	12.00 t
Length:	4.95 cm
Width:	2.15 cm
Height:	2.47 cm
Ground Pressure:	0.66 kg/cm^2
Armor:	10-15 mm
Armament:	15 cm sIG 33/2, 1 MG34
Ammunition Carried:	18 gun, 500 MG
Crew:	4
Engine Type:	Praga AC
Displacement:	7,754 cc
Horse Power:	150 HP(111 kW)/2,500 rpm
Maximum Speed:	42 km/hour
Range:	190 km
Obstacles - step:	80 cm
ditch:	210 cm
ford:	90 cm
Special Features:	final version with the engine in front and the gun in the back. Manufactured also as munitions carrier, 102 produced in 1944 without a gun, able to carry 40 rounds of sIG ammunition.

Vehicle Type: antiaircraft self-propelled gun
Manufacturer: BMM, Praha
Manufacturer's Designation: TNHPS
Years of Production: 1943-1944
Number of Vehicles Produced: 141
Chassis numbers: between 2893 and 3284
Wehrmacht Designation: Flakpanzer 38(t) auf Selbsfahrlafette 38(t) Ausf.M (SdKfz 140)
Export none

Weight: 9.70 t
Length: 4.61 m
Width: 2.15 m
Height: 2.25 m
Ground Pressure: 0.52 kg/cm²

Armor: 10-15 mm
Armament: 2 cm FlaK38 L/112.5
Ammunition Carried: 1,040
Crew: 4

Engine Type: Praga AC
Displacement: 7,754 cc
Horse Power: 150 HP(111 kW)/2,500 rpm
Maximum Speed: 48 km/hour
Range: 200 km

Obstacles - step: 80 cm
ditch: 210 cm
ford: 90 cm

Special Features: foldable sides of the gun compartment

Vehicle Type: reconnaissance tank
Manufacturer: BMM, Praha
Manufacturer's Designation: TNHPS
Years of Production: 1944
Number of Vehicles Produced: 70
Chassis numbers: N/K
Wehrmacht Designation: Auklärer auf Fahrgestell PzKpfw 38(t) mit 2 cm KwK38(7.5 cm KwK38 L/24)
Export none

Weight: 9.50 t
Length: 4.65 m
Width: 2.25 m
Height: 2.12 m
Ground Pressure: 0.51 kg/cm²

Armor: 8-50 mm
Armament: 2 cm KwK38 L/55, 1 MG42
Ammunition Carried: 300 gun, 1,500 MG
Crew: 4

Engine Type: Praga AE
Displacement: 7,754 cc
Horse Power: 160 HP(118.3 kW)/2,600 rpm
Maximum Speed: 58 km/hour
Range: 250 km

Obstacles - step: 80 cm
ditch: 210 cm
ford: 90 cm

Special Features: the original turret was replaced with the 2 cm Hängelafette 38, as used on the SdKfz 250/9 or 251/23. Two prototypes carried the short 7.5 cm gun in a modified (wooden) superstructure.

Vehicle Type:	tank destroyer
Manufacturer:	BMM, Praha and Škoda, Plzeň
Manufacturer's Designation:	G-13
Years of Production:	1944-1949
Number of Vehicles Produced:	2047 BMM, 780 Škoda till 1945, 258 1946-49
Chassis numbers:	321001-323000 BMM, 323001- Škoda
Wehrmacht Designation:	Jagdpanzer 38(t) für 7.5 cm PaK39 HETZER(SdKfz 138/2)
Export	75 Hungary 1944-1945, 158 Switzerland 1947-1950 100 ST-I for Czechoslovak army
Weight:	15.75 t
Length:	4.87 m (with gun 6.38 m)
Width:	2.63 m
Height:	2.17 m
Ground Pressure:	0.85 kg/cm^2
Armor:	8-60 mm
Armament:	7.5 cm PaK39 L/48, 1 MG34 or 42
Ammunition Carried:	45 gun, 1,200 MG
Crew:	4
Engine Type:	Praga AE, six cylinder, water cooled
Displacement:	7,754 cc
Horse Power:	160 HP(118.3 kW)/2,600 rpm
Maximum Speed:	43 km/hour
Range:	185 km
Obstacles - step:	64 cm
ditch:	180 cm
ford:	80 cm
Special Features:	roof-mounted remotely controlled MG, well sloped armor

Vehicle Type:	flame-thrower on tank destroyer chassis
Manufacturer:	BMM, Praha
Manufacturer's Designation:	N/A
Years of Production:	1944
Number of Vehicles Produced:	20 converted from Hetzers
Chassis numbers:	N/K
Wehrmacht Designation:	Flammpanzer 38(t)
Export	none
Weight:	15.50 t
Length:	4.87 m
Width:	2.63 m
Height:	2.17 m
Ground Pressure:	0.83 kg/cm^2
Armor:	8-60 mm
Armament:	14 mm Flammenwerfer 41, 1 MG34 or 42
Ammunition Carried:	700 liters of fuel, 1,200 MG
Crew:	4
Engine Type:	Praga AE, 6 cylinder, water cooled
Displacement:	7,754 cc
Horse Power:	160 HP(118.3 kW)/2,600 rpm
Maximum Speed:	42 km/hour
Range:	180 km
Obstacles - step:	64 cm
ditch:	180 cm
ford:	80 cm
Special Features:	fake barrel over the flame-thrower to mask the real purpose of the vehicle

Vehicle Type:	armored recovery vehicle
Manufacturer:	BMM, Praha
Manufacturer's Designation:	N/K
Years of Production:	1944-1945
Number of Vehicles Produced:	181
Chassis numbers:	N/K
Wehrmacht Designation:	Bergepanzer 38(t)
Export	none
Weight:	14.50 t
Length:	4.87 m
Width:	2.63 m
Height:	1.71 m
Ground Pressure:	0.78 kg/cm²
Armor:	10-60 mm
Armament:	1 MG34
Ammunition Carried:	500
Crew:	4
Engine Type:	Praga AE, 6 cylinder, water cooled
Displacement:	7,754 cc
Horse Power:	160 HP(118.3 kW)/2,600 rpm
Maximum Speed:	44 km/hour
Range:	180 km
Obstacles - step:	64 cm
ditch:	180 cm
ford:	80 cm
Special Features:	lower, open-top compartment. Fitted with a spade, a winch and a collapsible crane. Basis for several modifications.

Vehicle Type:	self-propelled howitzer
Manufacturer:	unknown
Manufacturer's Designation:	N/K
Years of Production:	1944-1945
Number of Vehicles Produced:	30 converted from Bergepanzer 38(t)
Chassis numbers:	N/K
Wehrmacht Designation:	15 cm Schweres Infanterigeschütz 33/2(Sf)auf Jagdpanzer 38(t)
Export	none
Weight:	16.50 t
Length:	4.87 m
Width:	2.63 cm
Height:	2.40 cm
Ground Pressure:	0.90 kg/cm²
Armor:	10-60 mm
Armament:	15 cm sIG 33/2 L/11, 1 MG34
Ammunition Carried:	15 gun, 600 MG
Crew:	4
Engine Type:	Praga AE, 6 cylinder, water cooled
Displacement:	7,754 cc
Horse Power:	160 HP(118.3 kW)/2,600 rpm
Maximum Speed:	38 km/hour
Range:	130 km
Obstacles - step:	64 cm
ditch:	180 cm
ford:	80 cm
Special Features:	clean lines

Vehicle Type:	tank destroyer
Manufacturer:	BMM, Praha
Manufacturer's Designation:	N/K
Years of Production:	1944-1945
Number of Vehicles Produced:	14
Chassis numbers:	321679,321681-3,322370,322372-322971
Wehrmacht Designation:	Jagdpanzer 38(t) Starr
Export	none
Weight:	14.00 t
Length:	4.87 (6.38 m with gun)
Width:	2.63 cm
Height:	2.17 cm
Ground Pressure:	0.74 kg/cm²
Armor:	10-80 mm
Armament:	7.5 cm PaK 39/1, 1 MG42
Ammunition Carried:	45 gun, 1,200 MG
Crew:	4
Engine Type:	Tatra 103, V-12 air-cooled Diesel
Displacement:	14,800 cc
Horse Power:	220 HP(162.6 kW)/2,000 rpm
Maximum Speed:	46 km/hour
Range:	180 km
Obstacles - step:	80 cm
ditch:	180 cm
ford:	90 cm
Special Features:	gun in a rigid mount

Vehicle Type:	tank destroyer
Manufacturer:	Alkett, Berlin
Manufacturer's Designation:	N/K
Years of Production:	1945
Number of Vehicles Produced:	prototypes only
Chassis numbers:	N/K
Wehrmacht Designation:	Jagdpanzer 38(d)
Export	none
Weight:	16.00 t
Length:	5.27 m
Width:	2.81 m
Height:	1.75 m
Ground Pressure:	0.76 kg/cm²
Armor:	8-80 mm
Armament:	7.5 cm PaK 42/1, 1 MG42
Ammunition Carried:	N/K
Crew:	4
Engine Type:	Tatra 103, 12-V air-cooled Diesel engine
Displacement:	14,800 cc
Horse Power:	220 HP(162.6 kW)/2,000 rpm
Maximum Speed:	N/K
Range:	220 km
Obstacles - step:	80 cm
ditch:	200 cm
ford:	90 cm
Special Features:	planned as a basis for many modifications using so far Pz III or Pz IV chassis

Vehicle Type:	light standardized weapons carriage
Manufacturer:	Ardelt, Rheinmettal, Krupp
Manufacturer's Designation:	Krupp II
Years of Production:	1945
Number of Vehicles Produced:	prototypes only
Chassis numbers:	N/A
Wehrmacht Designation:	Leichter Einheitswaffenträger
Export	none
Weight:	13.50 t
Length:	6.53 m
Width:	3.16 m
Height:	2.25 m
Ground Pressure:	0.40 kg/cm^2
Armor:	8-20 mm
Armament:	8.8 cm, 10.5 cm, 15 cm or 12.8 cm gun
Ammunition Carried:	34-96 (depending on gun)
Crew:	4
Engine Type:	Praga AE, 6 cylinder
Displacement:	7,754 cc
Horse Power:	160 HP(118.3 kW)/2,600 rpm
Maximum Speed:	45 km/hour
Range:	N/K
Obstacles - step:	60 cm
ditch:	180 cm
ford:	80 cm
Special Features:	later versions to be based on Jagdpanzer(d) with the Tatra engine

Vehicle Type:	medium standardized weapons carriage
Manufacturer:	Krupp
Manufacturer's Designation:	Krupp I
Years of Production:	1945
Number of Vehicles Produced:	prototypes only
Chassis numbers:	N/K
Wehrmacht Designation:	Mittlerer Einheitswaffenträger
Export	none
Weight:	14.00 t
Length:	6.75 m
Width:	3.16 m
Height:	2.25 m
Ground Pressure:	0.40 kg/cm^2
Armor:	10-20 mm
Armament:	various guns planned
Ammunition Carried:	20-40, depending on gun
Crew:	4
Engine Type:	Praga AE, 6 cylinder, water cooled
Displacement:	7,754 cc
Horse Power:	160 HP(118.3 kW)/2,600 rpm
Maximum Speed:	35 km/hour
Range:	N/K
Obstacles - step:	60 cm
ditch:	220 cm
ford:	80 cm
Special Features:	production vehicles to be based on the Jagdpanzer 38(d) with Tatra engine

Vehicle Type:	driver training vehicle
Manufacturer:	ČKD, Praha
Manufacturer's Designation:	ST-III
Years of Production:	1946-1947
Number of Vehicles Produced:	50
Czechoslovak Army Designation:	ST-III
Registration Numbers:	N/K
Wehrmacht Designation:	N/A
Export:	none
Weight:	13.50 t
Length:	4.80 m
Width:	2.62 m
Height:	3.06 m
Ground Pressure:	0.40 kg/cm^2
Armor:	10-60 mm
Armament:	none
Ammunition Carried:	none
Crew:	N/A
Engine Type:	Praga AE, 6 cylinder, water cooled
Displacement:	7.754 cc
Horse Power:	160 HP(188.3 kW)/2,600 rpm
Maximum Speed:	47 km/hour
Range:	
Obstacles - step:	64 cm
ditch:	180 cm
ford:	80 cm
Special Features:	fixed superstructure added on top of the fighting compartment, front plate also modified, pulpit for the instructor

Vehicle Type:	flame-throwing tank
Manufacturer:	ČKD, Praha
Manufacturer's Designation:	MP-1
Years of Production:	1950-1954
Number of Vehicles Produced:	1 prototype
Czechoslovak Army Designation:	MP-1
Registration Numbers:	N/A
Wehrmacht Designation:	N/A
Export:	none
Weight:	17.00 t
Length:	5.25 m
Width:	2.53 m
Height:	2.64 m
Ground Pressure:	0.82 kg/cm^2
Armor:	10-60 mm
Armament:	14 mm Flammenwerfer 41, 1 MG DT-28
Ammunition Carried:	1,000 liters of fuel
Crew:	2
Engine Type:	Praga AE, 6 cylinder, water cooled
Displacement:	7,754 cc
Horse Power:	160 HP(118.3 kW)/2,600 rpm
Maximum Speed:	40 km/hour
Range:	180 km
Obstacles - step:	64 cm
ditch:	180 cm
ford:	80 cm
Special Features:	flame thrower in a revolving turret

Vehicle Type:	light artillery tractor
Manufacturer:	ČKD, Praha
Manufacturer's Designation:	Praga MT
Years of Production:	1925
Number of Vehicles Produced:	2
Czechoslovak Army Designation:	Praga MT
Registration Numbers:	NIX107, 108
Wehrmacht Designation:	none
Export:	none
Weight:	N/K
Length:	3.30 m
Width:	1.46 m
Height:	1.55 m
Ground Pressure:	N/K
Armor:	none
Armament:	none
Ammunition Carried:	none
Crew:	1
Engine Type:	Praga, 4 cylinder
Displacement:	2,849 cc
Horse Power:	35 HP(26 kW)
Maximum Speed:	18 km/hour
Range:	N/K
Obstacles - step:	
ditch:	
ford:	
Special Features:	winch on the rear spade, tows 3.5 tons. Plans made to convert it to a tank, but never realized

BD25

BD30

Vehicle Type:	light artillery tractor
Manufacturer:	Breifeld-Daněk, Praha
Manufacturer's Designation:	BD25, BD30
Years of Production:	1925-1926
Number of Vehicles Produced:	6 BD25, 12 BD30
Czechoslovak Army Designation:	Breifeld-Daněk BD25, BD30
Registration Numbers:	BD25: NIX132-137, 13289-13294
Wehrmacht Designation:	BD30: NIX172-183, 13308-13319
Export:	none
	"BD25/BD30"
Weight:	2.40 t/2.80 t
Length:	3.12 m
Width:	1.35 m
Height:	1.39 m
Ground Pressure:	0.40 kg/cm^2
Armor:	none
Armament:	none
Ammunition Carried:	none
Crew:	2
Engine Type:	ČKD/Hanomag, 4 cylinder
Displacement:	4,000 cc
Horse Power:	25 HP(18.5 kW)/950 rpm / 30HP(22.2 kW)/1,260 rpm
Maximum Speed:	8 km/hour
Range:	N/K
Obstacles - step:	
ditch:	
ford:	
Special Features:	Hanomag license tows 3.0 tons

Vehicle Type:	light artillery tractor
Manufacturer:	Škoda, Plzeň
Manufacturer's Designation:	MTH
Years of Production:	1935-1939
Number of Vehicles Produced:	55
Czechoslovak Army Designation:	MTH I, II, III
Registration Numbers:	13558-13582,13621-13633,14125-14141
Wehrmacht Designation:	Leichter Raupenschlepper MTH (MTH III)
Export:	Slovakia 11, ex Czechoslovak army MTH III
Weight:	3.10 t
Length:	3.16 m
Width:	1.67 m
Height:	1.51 m
Ground Pressure:	0.50 kg/cm^2
Armor:	none
Armament:	none
Ammunition Carried:	none
Crew:	2
Engine Type:	Škoda HT18, 2 cylinder
Displacement:	2,760 cc
Horse Power:	32 HP(23.7 kW)/1,600 rpm
Maximum Speed:	10.2 km/hour
Range:	6 hours
Obstacles - step:	
ditch:	
ford:	
Special Features:	tows 2.5 tons, carries 800 kg

Vehicle Type:	medium artillery tractor
Manufacturer:	Škoda, Plzeň
Manufacturer's Designation:	STH
Years of Production:	1932-1936
Number of Vehicles Produced:	2 prototypes
Czechoslovak Army Designation:	STH
Registration Numbers:	13366, 13645
Wehrmacht Designation:	none
Export:	none
Weight:	4.04 t
Length:	4.07 m
Width:	1.70 m
Height:	1.58 m
Ground Pressure:	0.46 kg/cm^2
Armor:	none
Armament:	none
Ammunition Carried:	none
Crew:	2 + 6
Engine Type:	Škoda 304, 4 cylinder
Displacement:	5,520 cc
Horse Power:	64 HP(47.3 kW)/1,600 rpm
Maximum Speed:	21 km/hour
Range:	6 hours
Obstacles - step:	
ditch:	
ford:	
Special Features:	tows 4.4 tons, carries 1 ton

Vehicle Type: light artillery tractor
Manufacturer: ČKD, Praha
Manufacturer's Designation: Praga III
Years of Production: 1935
Number of Vehicles Produced: 32
Czechoslovak Army Designation: Praga III
Registration Numbers: 13585-13614
Wehrmacht Designation: Leichter Raupenschlepper T-III(t)

Export: 3 Slovakia, ex Czechoslovak army

Weight: 3.12 t
Length: 3.95 m
Width: 1.73 m
Height: 2.26 m
Ground Pressure: 0.30 kg/cm^2

Armor: none
Armament: none
Ammunition Carried: none
Crew: 3

Engine Type: Praga, 4 cylinder
Displacement: 3,820 cc
Horse Power: 27 HP(20 kW)/1,300 rpm
Maximum Speed: 10 km/hour
Range: 180 km

Obstacles - step: 30 cm
ditch:
ford: 55 cm

Special Features: tows 1.8 tons, carries 600 kg

Vehicle Type: light artillery tractor
Manufacturer: ČKD, Praha
Manufacturer's Designation: Praga IV
Years of Production: 1935-1939
Number of Vehicles Produced: 114 + 1 prototype
Czechoslovak Army Designation: Praga IV
Registration Numbers: 13635 (P),13976-14089
Wehrmacht Designation: Mittlerer Raupenschlepper T-IV(t)

Export: 38 Slovakia, ex Czechoslovak army

Weight: 4.64 t
Length: 4.07 m
Width: 1.59 m
Height: 1.85 m
Ground Pressure: 0.42 kg/cm^2

Armor: none
Armament: none
Ammunition Carried: none
Crew: 3

Engine Type: Praga N, 4 cylinder
Displacement: 6,082 cc
Horse Power: 57 HP(42.1 kW)/1,200 rpm
Maximum Speed: 21 km/hour
Range: 220 km

Obstacles - step:
ditch:
ford:

Special Features: tows 4.5 tons carries 1.16 tons

Vehicle Type:	medium artillery tractor
Manufacturer:	ČKD, Praha
Manufacturer's Designation:	Praga T III/3
Years of Production:	1939-1941
Number of Vehicles Produced:	40 + 1
Czechoslovak Army Designation:	not accepted
Registration Numbers:	not assigned
Wehrmacht Designation:	Mittlerer Raupenschlepper T III/3(t)
Export:	1 prototype Dutch East India
Weight:	5.40 t
Length:	3.95 m
Width:	1.73 m
Height:	2.26 m
Ground Pressure:	0.30 kg/cm²
Armor:	none
Armament:	none
Ammunition Carried:	none
Crew:	3
Engine Type:	Praga, 6 cylinder
Displacement:	4,387 cc
Horse Power:	78 HP(57.6 kW)/2,300 rpm
Maximum Speed:	30 km/hour
Range:	220 km
Obstacles - step:	
ditch:	
ford:	
Special Features:	ordered by the Dutch East India, but confiscated by the Wehrmacht.

Vehicle Type:	medium artillery tractor
Manufacturer:	ČKD, Praha
Manufacturer's Designation:	Praga TH, later Praga T 6
Years of Production:	1937-1944
Number of Vehicles Produced:	over 900
Czechoslovak Army Designation:	not introduced
Registration Numbers:	not assigned
Wehrmacht Designation:	Mittlerer Raupenschlepper T 6(t)
Export:	434 Turkey, 130 Romania, 8 Slovakia,1 Peru 95 Waffen SS, rest Wehrmacht
Weight:	7.05 t
Length:	4.80 m
Width:	1.80 m
Height:	1.70 m
Ground Pressure:	0.40 kg/cm²
Armor:	none
Armament:	none
Ammunition Carried:	none
Crew:	3
Engine Type:	T 6 SS+Slovak/Turkey,Romania, Peru Praga TNH, 6 cylinder/Praga TN
Displacement:	7,754 cc/7,800 cc
Horse Power:	110 HP(81.3 kW)/1,800 rpm / 75 HP(55.4 kW)/1,300 rpm
Maximum Speed:	31 km/hour / 25 km/hour
Range:	250 km
Obstacles - step:	
ditch:	
ford:	
Special Features:	tows 6 tons, carries 1 ton

Vehicle Type: medium artillery tractor
Manufacturer: ČKD, Praha
Manufacturer's Designation: Praga TH 7, later Praga T 8
Years of Production: 1937-1939
Number of Vehicles Produced: 62
Czechoslovak Army Designation: not accepted
Registration Numbers: not assigned
Wehrmacht Designation: not used

Export: 62 Turkey

Weight: 9.65 t
Length: 5.70 m
Width: 2.06 m
Height: 2.47 m
Ground Pressure: 0.38 kg/cm^2

Armor: none
Armament: none
Ammunition Carried: none
Crew: 2 + 10

Engine Type: Praga TO, 6 cylinder
Displacement: 11,530 cc
Horse Power: 112 HP(82.8 kW)/1,200 rpm
Maximum Speed: 31 km/hour
Range: 200 km

Obstacles - step:
ditch:
ford:

Special Features: tows 8 tons, carries 1 ton

Vehicle Type: medium artillery tractor
Manufacturer: ČKD, Praha
Manufacturer's Designation: Praga TH 6, later Praga T 7
Years of Production: 1937-1939
Number of Vehicles Produced: 40
Czechoslovak Army Designation: not accepted
Registration Numbers: not assigned
Wehrmacht Designation: not used

Export: 40 Turkey

Weight: 8.66 t
Length: 5.83 m
Width: 2.42 m
Height: 2.08 m
Ground Pressure:

Armor: none
Armament: none
Ammunition Carried: none
Crew: 1 + 2

Engine Type: Praga TO, 6 cylinder
Displacement: 11,530 cc
Horse Power: 112 HP(82.8 kW)/1,200 rpm
Maximum Speed: 31 km/hour
Range: 250 km

Obstacles - step:
ditch:
ford:

Special Features: tows 7 tons, carries 1 ton

Vehicle Type:	heavy artillery tractor
Manufacturer:	ČKD, Praha
Manufacturer's Designation:	Praga T 9
Years of Production:	1937-1943
Number of Vehicles Produced:	76
Czechoslovak Army Designation:	not accepted
Registration Numbers:	not assigned
Wehrmacht Designation:	Schwerer Raupenschlepper T 9(t)
Export:	16 Turkey, 5 Slovakia
Weight:	11.60 t
Length:	5.60 m
Width:	2.45 m
Height:	2.54 m
Ground Pressure:	0.43 kg/cm^2
Armor:	none
Armament:	none
Ammunition Carried:	none
Crew:	2 + 6
Engine Type:	Praga, V-eight
Displacement:	14,230 cc
Horse Power:	142 HP(105 kW)/1,500 rpm
Maximum Speed:	20 km/hour
Range:	120 km
Obstacles - step:	
ditch:	
ford:	
Special Features:	tows 10 tons, carries 1 ton

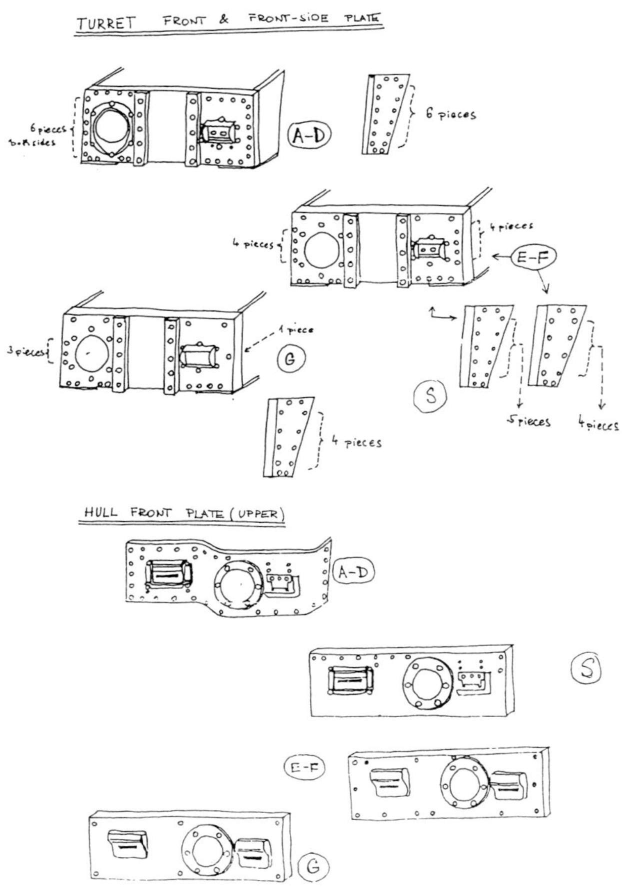

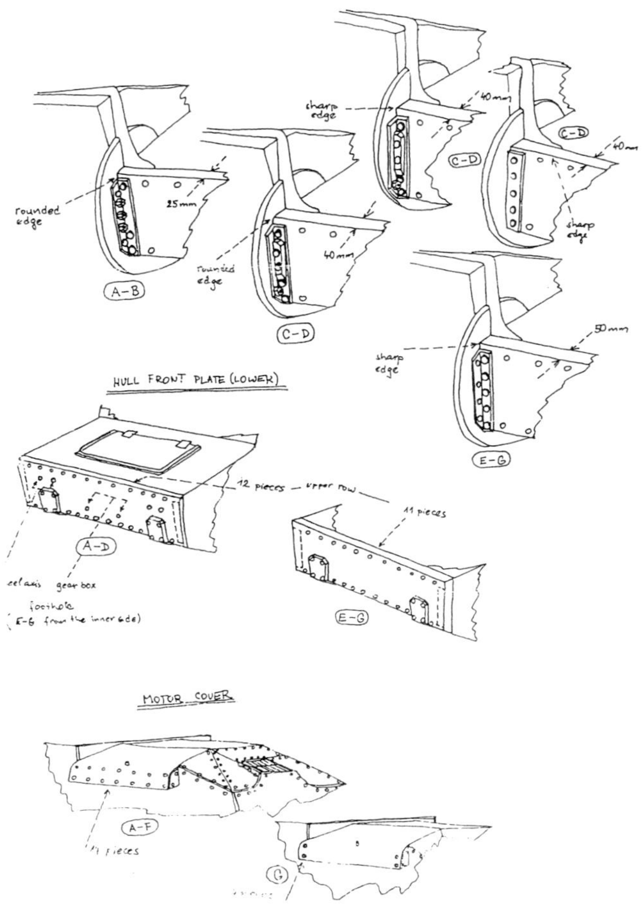

14

PLANS

LIST OF SCHEMATICS

ARMORED CARS

TANKETTES

WHEEL-CUM-TRACK

TANKS

Opposite: Overview of Discerning Features of PzKpfw 38(t) Ausfüngs (Number and Location of Bolts)

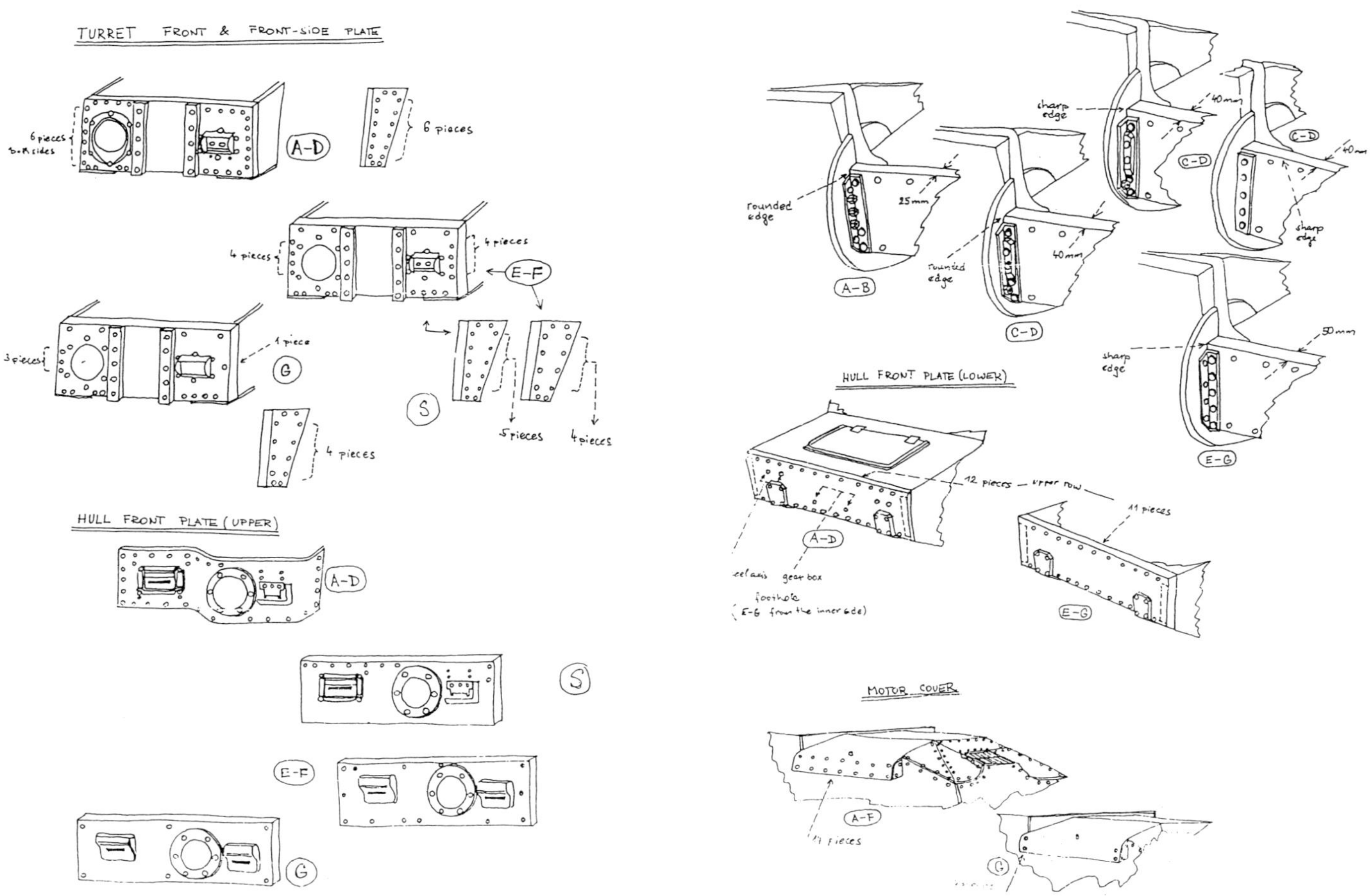

ARMORED CARS

Škoda Armored Car PA-II "TURTLE"

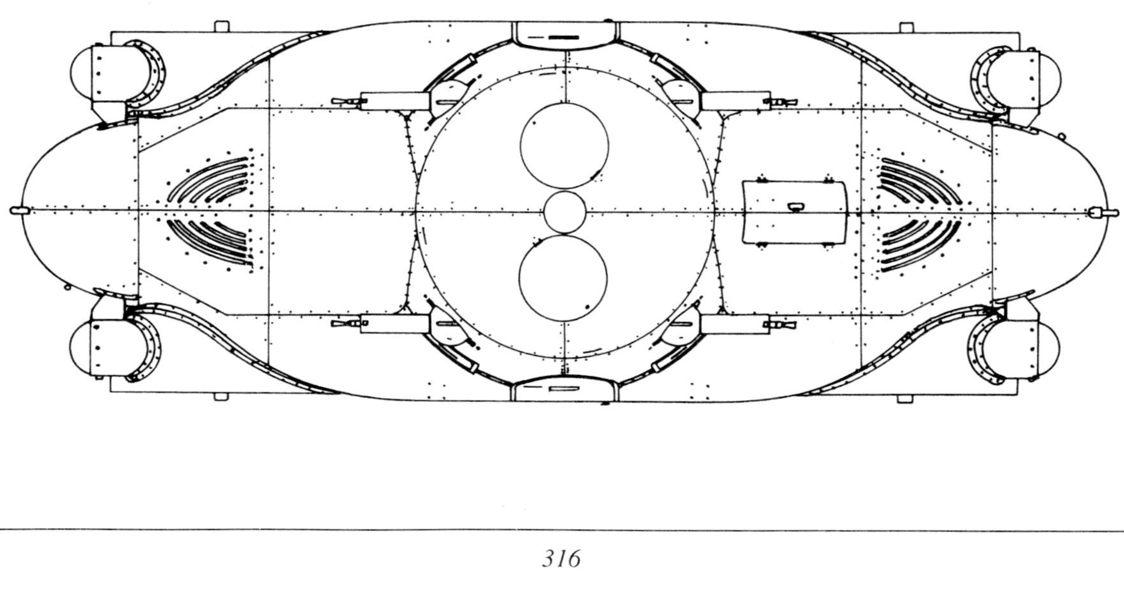

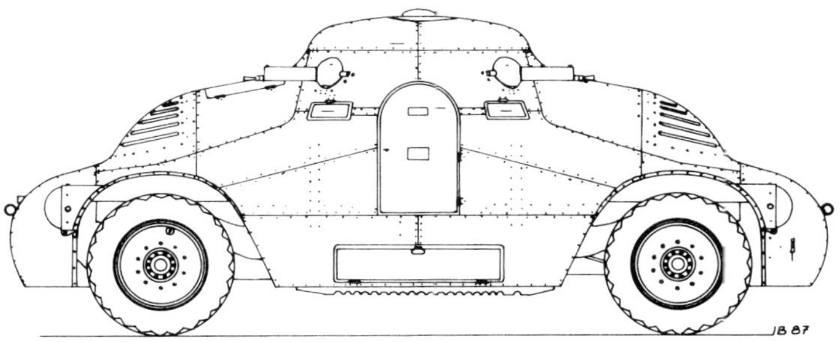

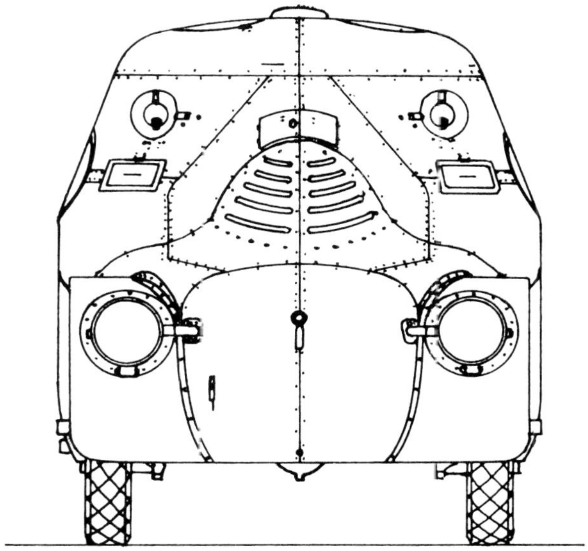

Škoda Armored Car PA-III, OA vz.27

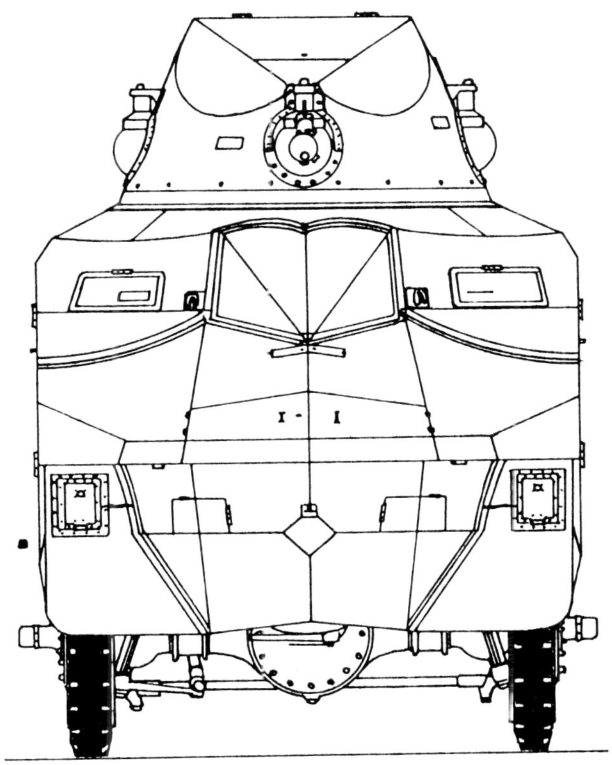

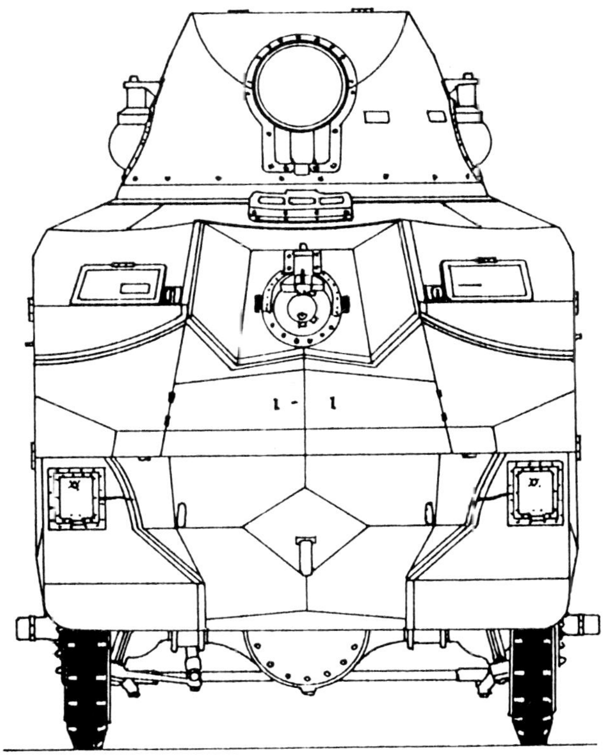

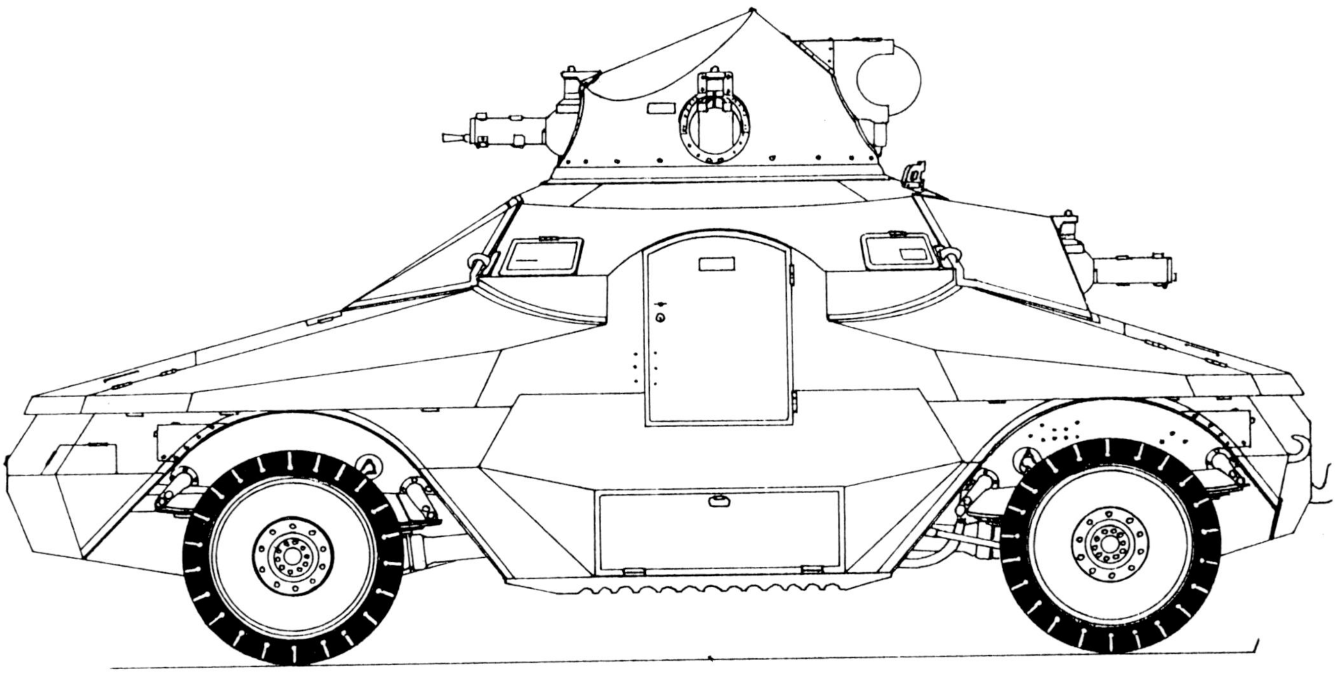

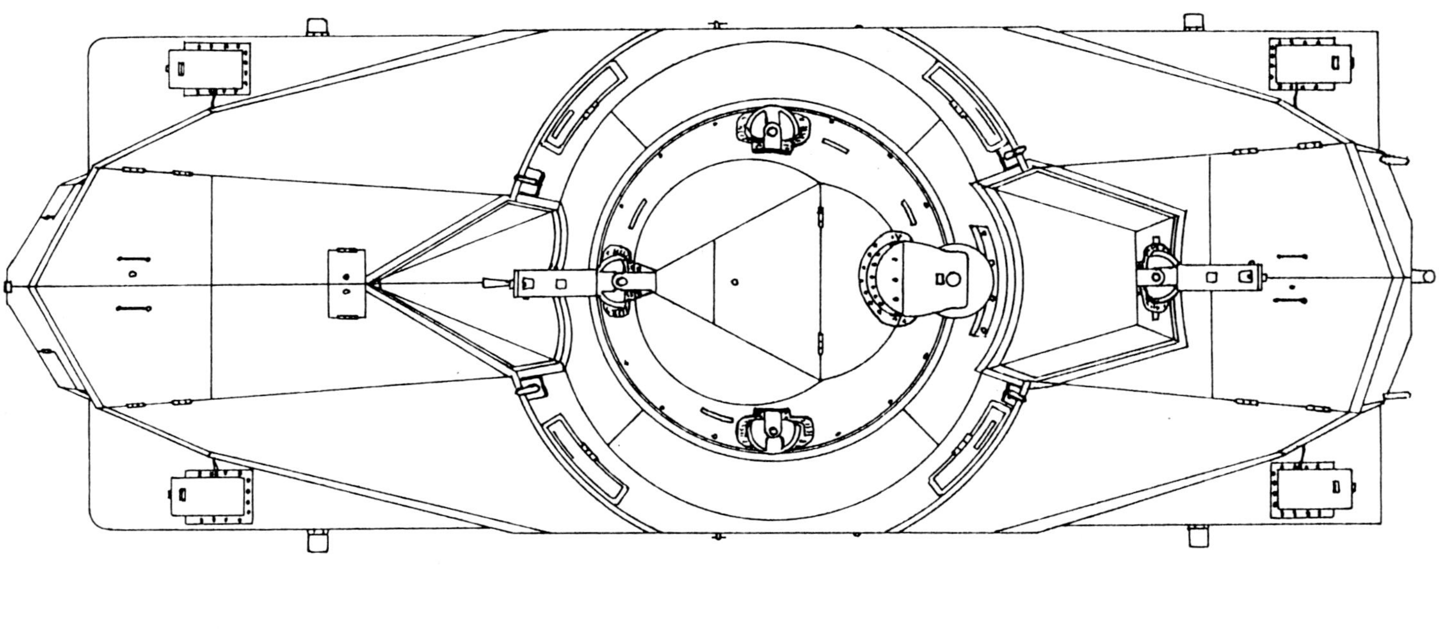

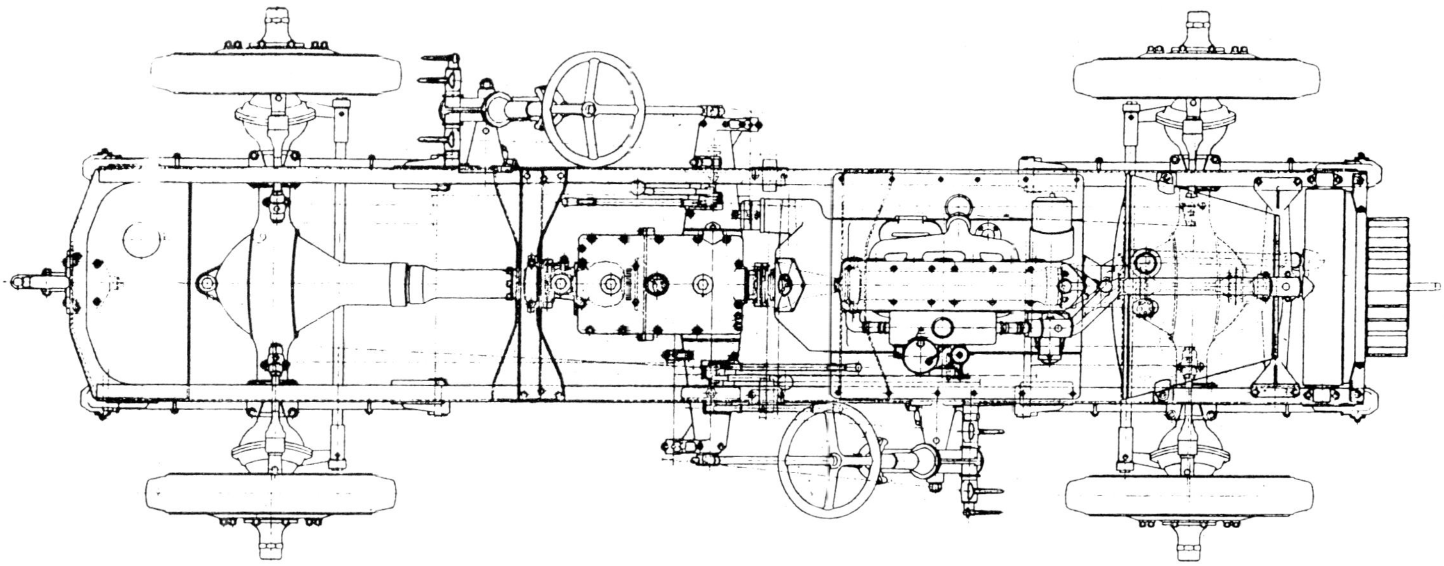

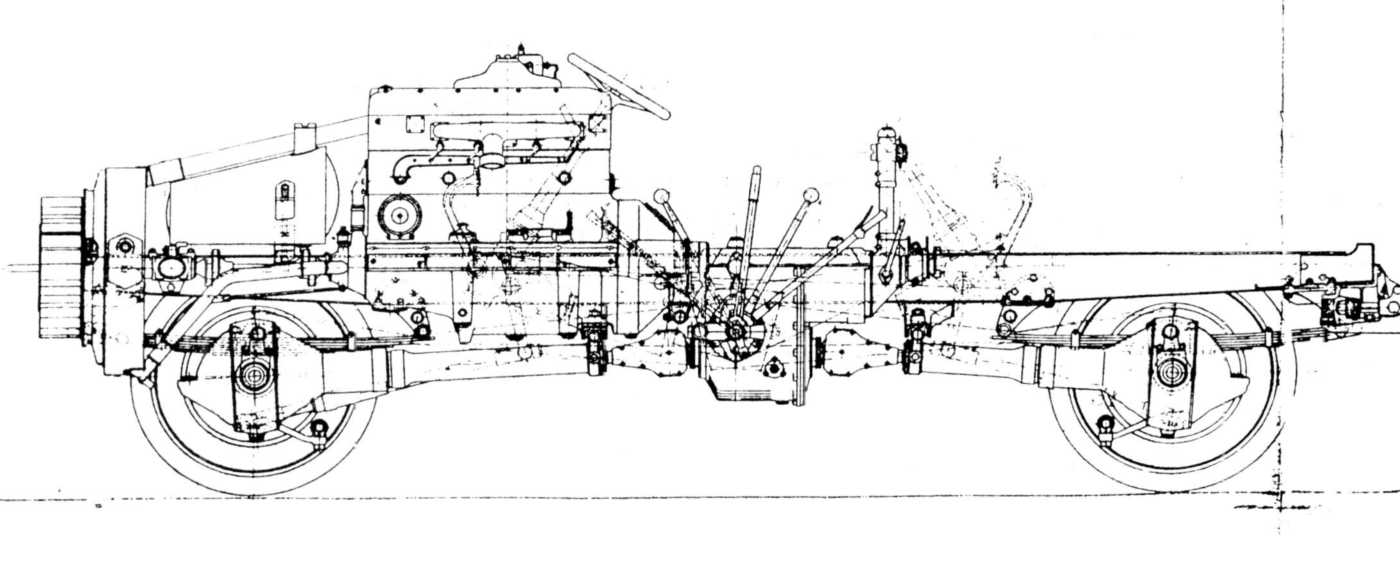

Tatra Armored Car OA vz.30

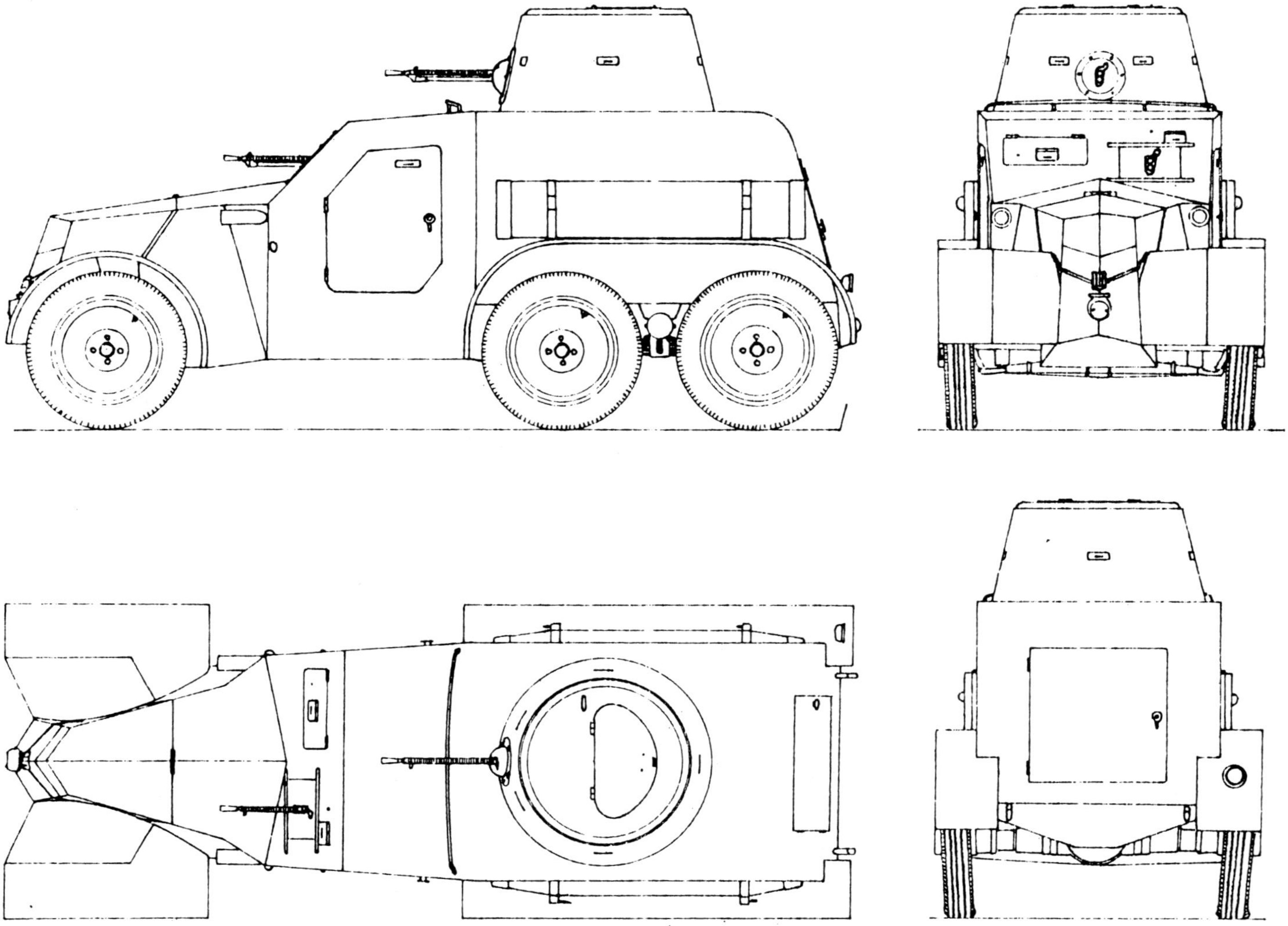

Škoda Project of an Armored Car PAd

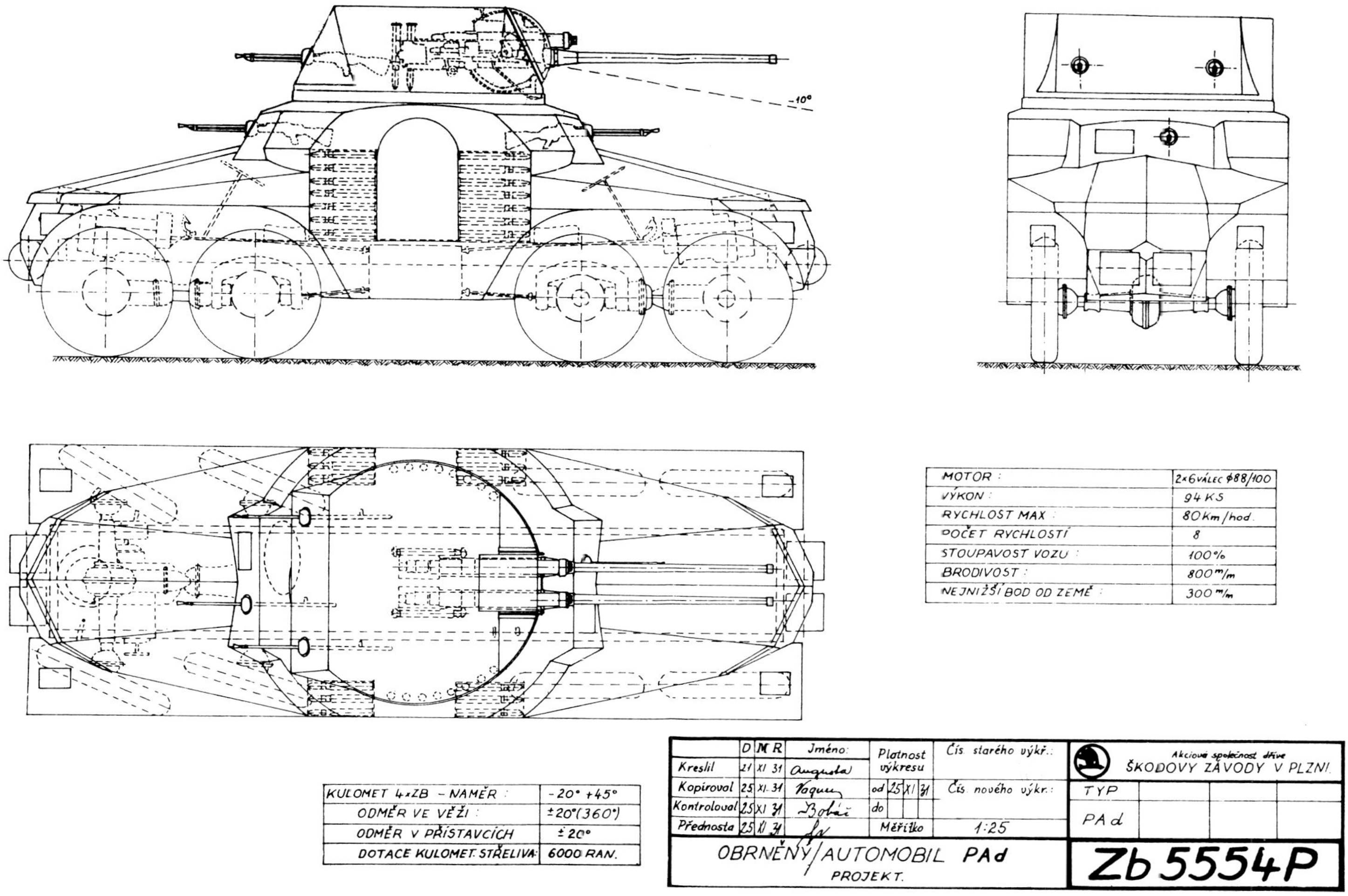

Škoda Project of an Armored Car Zb 5560P

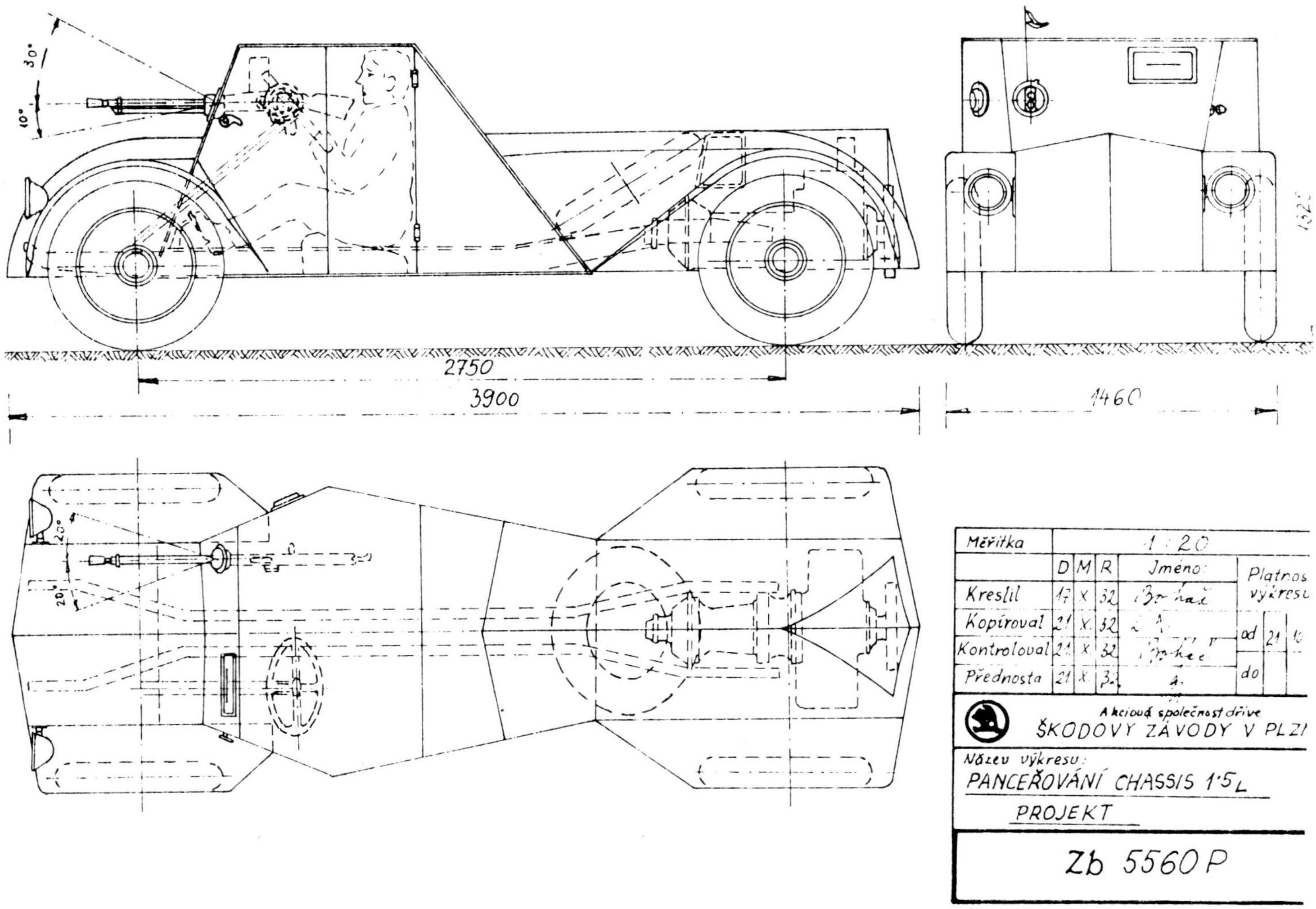

Škoda Project of an Armored Car 6-OAM-6

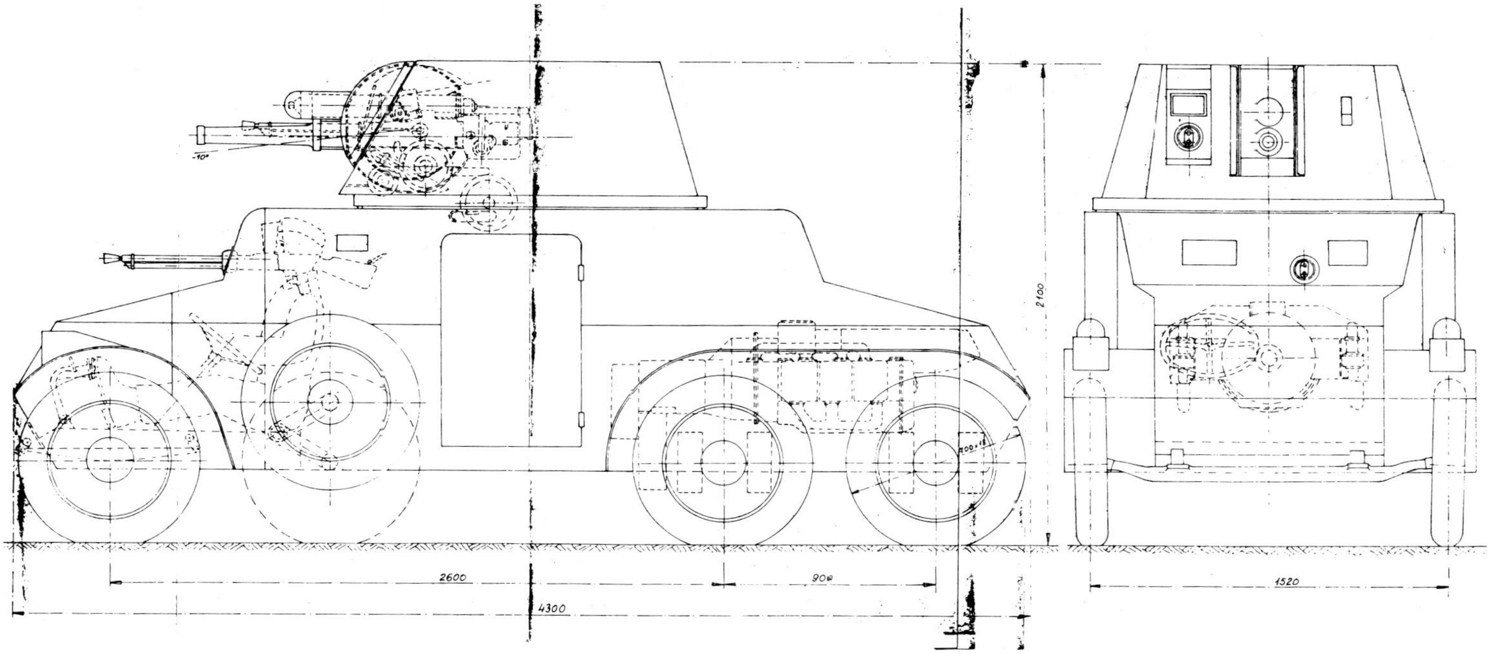

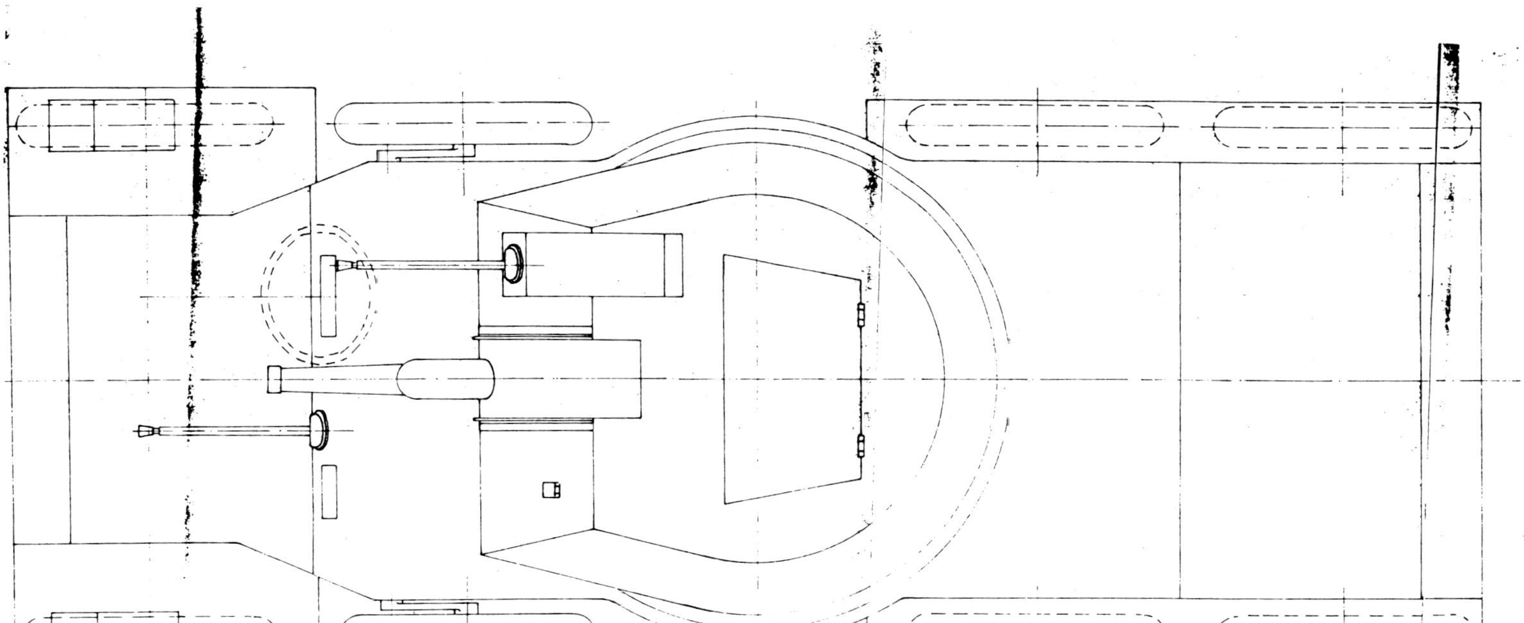

MOTOR	6VALEC ϕ88/100 m/m
VÝKON	49 KS
RYCHLOST, MAX	60 Km
POČET RYCHLOSTÍ	8
DĚLO	47 m/m
NÁMĚR	-10° +85°
ODMĚR	360°
DOTACE DĚL STŘELIVA:	100 RAN
KULOMET 2ZB – NÁMĚR	-20° +40°
ODMĚR VE VĚŽI	±20° (360°)
ODMĚR POD VĚŽÍ	±20°
DOTACE KULOMET STŘELIVA	4000 RAN

	D	M	R	Jméno	Platnost výkresu			Čís. starého výkr.	AKC. SPOLEČNOST DŘÍVE ŠKODOVY ZÁVODY V PLZNI
Kreslil	25	I	32	Boháč					
Kopiroval	1	II	32	Vaqua	od 1	2	32	Čís. nového výkr.	TYP
Kontroloval	1	2	32	Bohač	do				6-OAM-6
Přednosta	1	2	32	[illegible]	Měřítka			1:10	
OBRNĚNÝ AUTOMOBIL PROJEKT									Zb5253P

Škoda Project of an Armored Car 4LT-VI

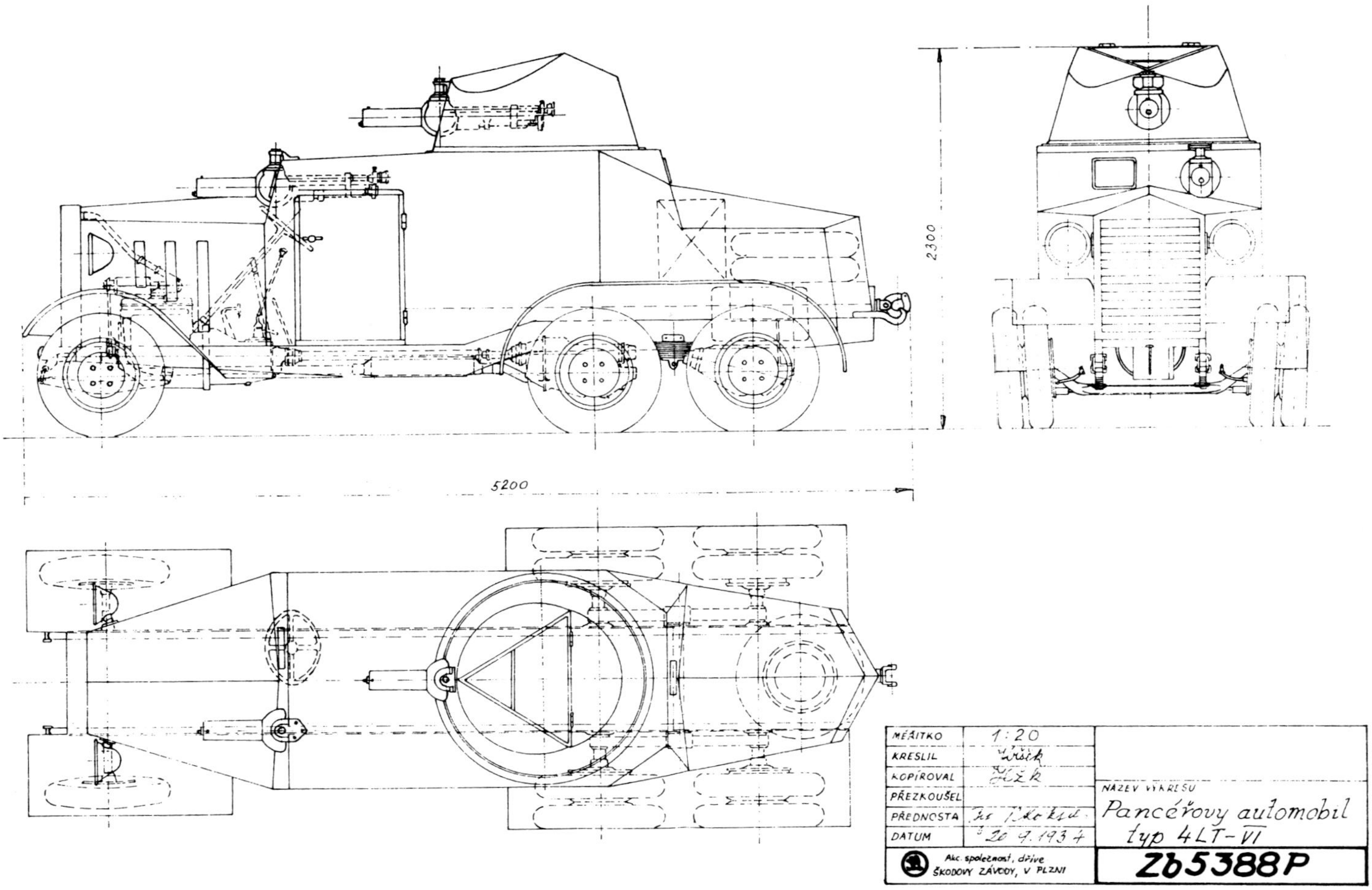

Project of an Armored Attachment for Command Car Type 903

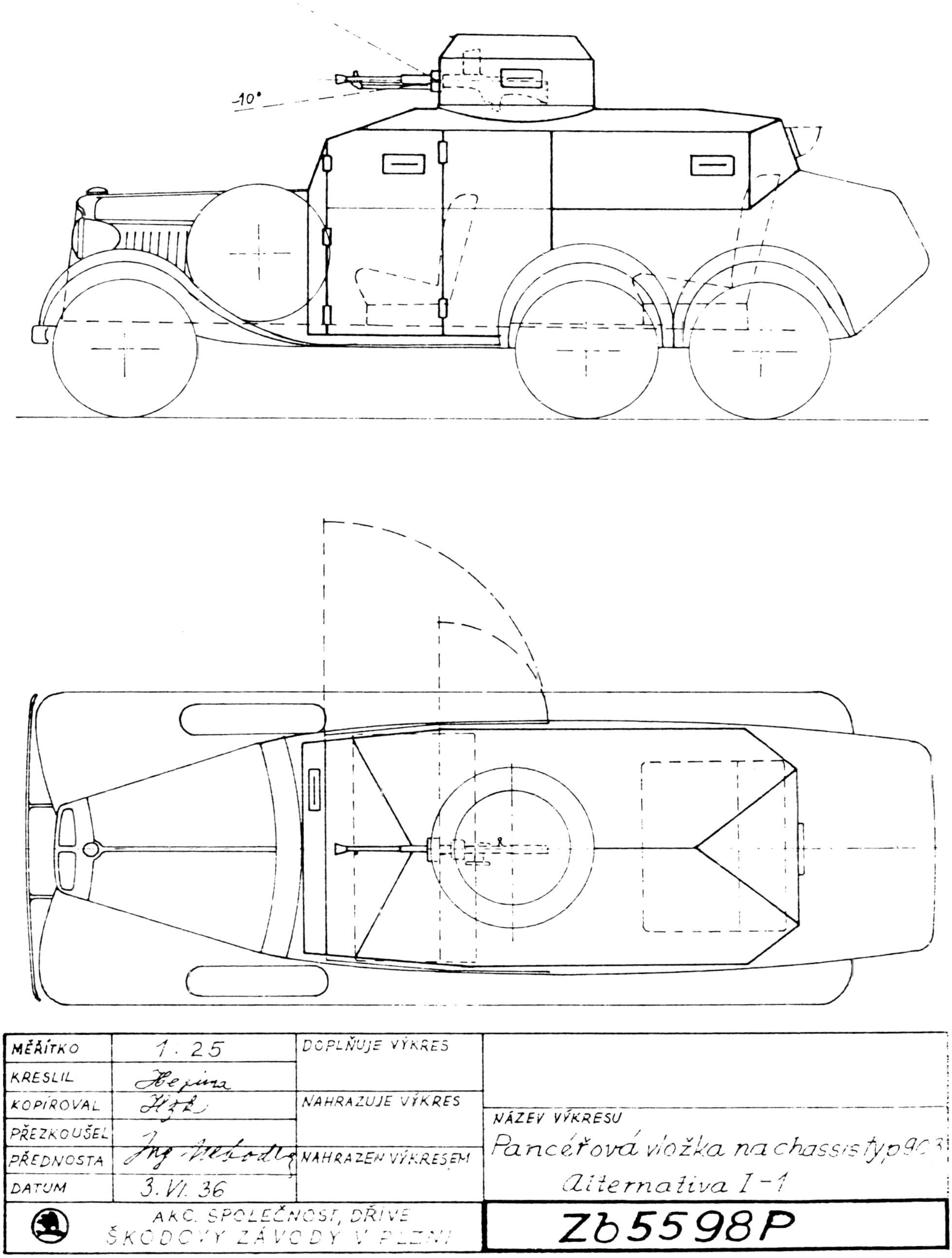

TANKETTES

Škoda Tankette MU-2

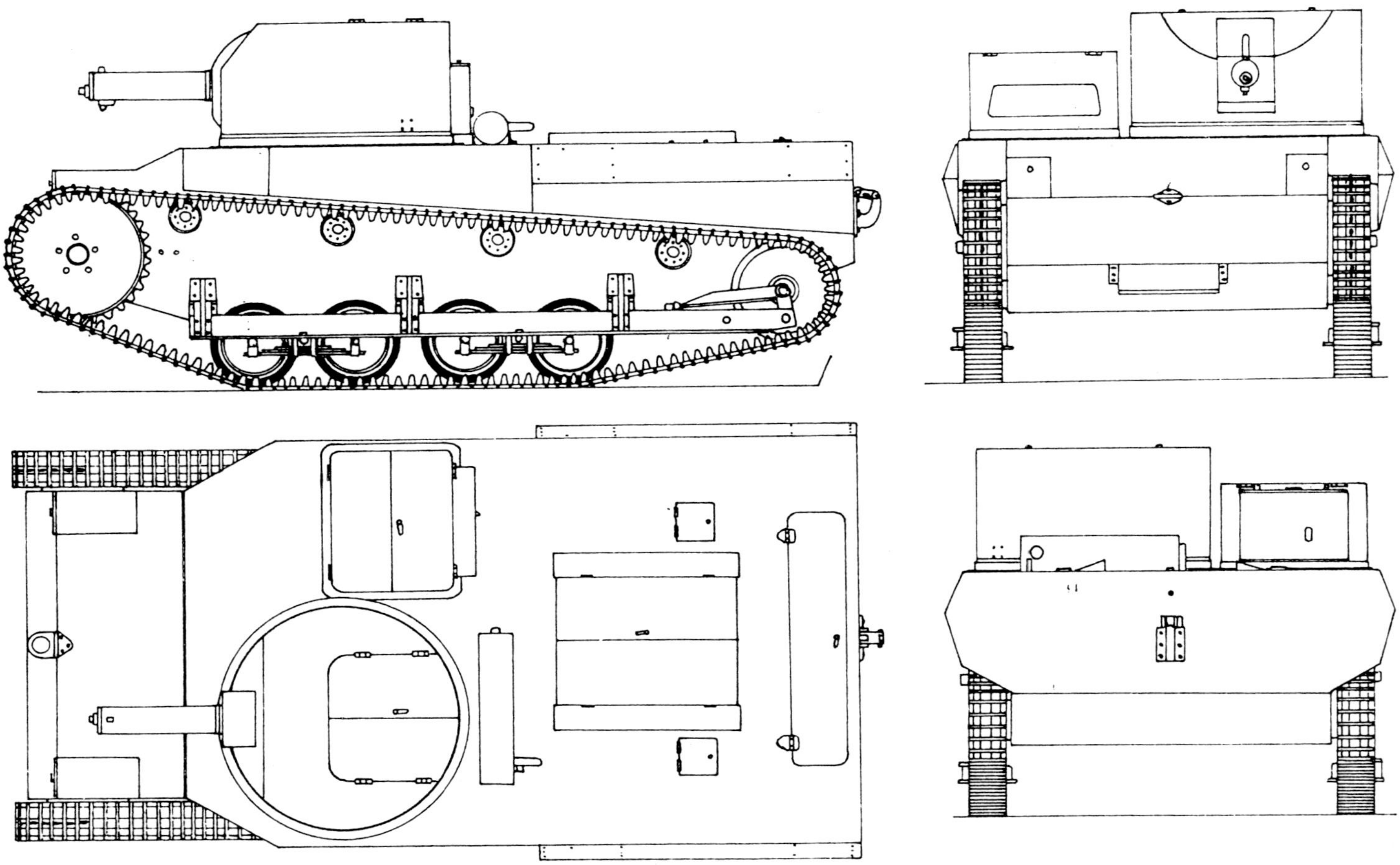

MU-4 Projected as Carrier of 3.7 cm Antitank Gun

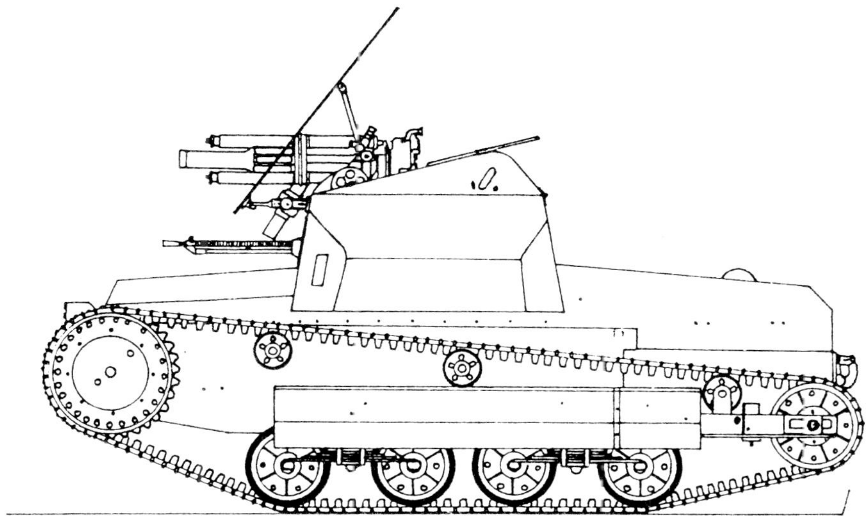

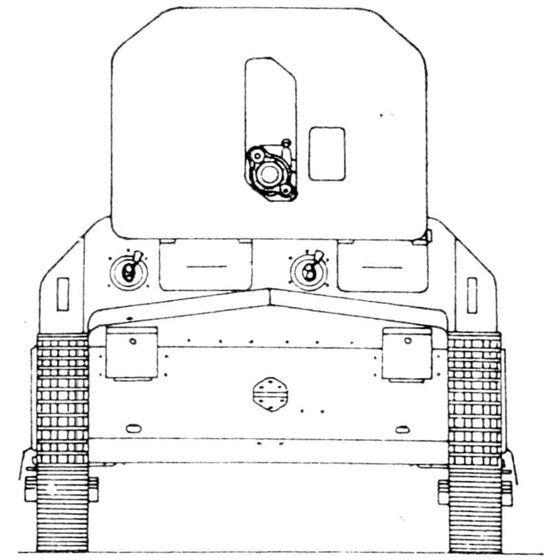

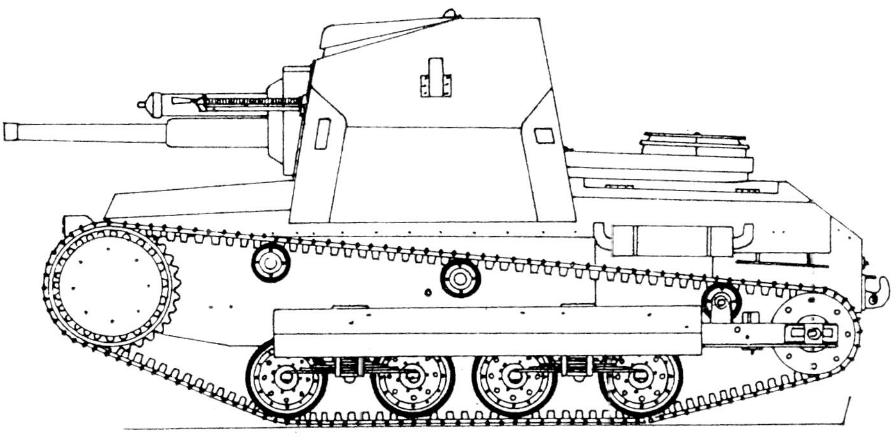

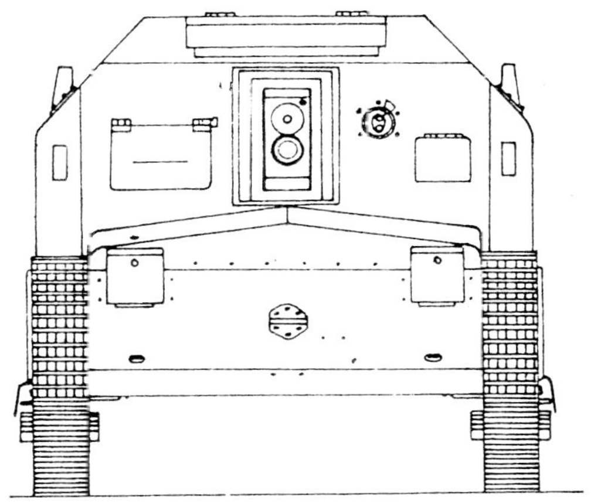

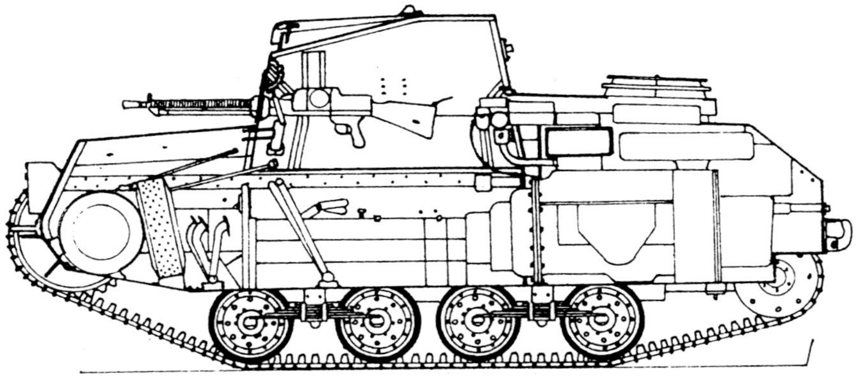

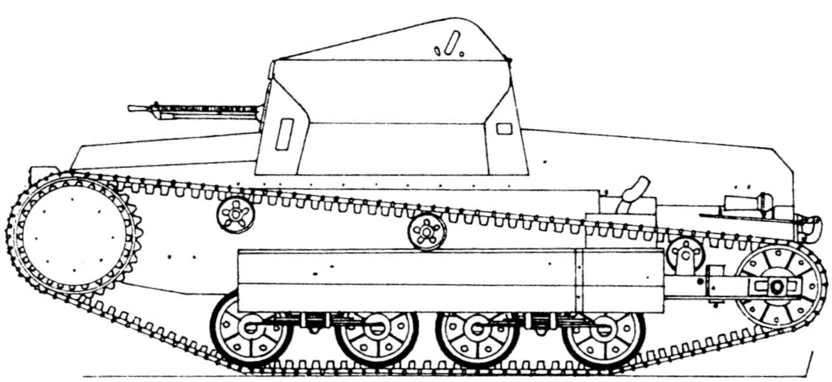

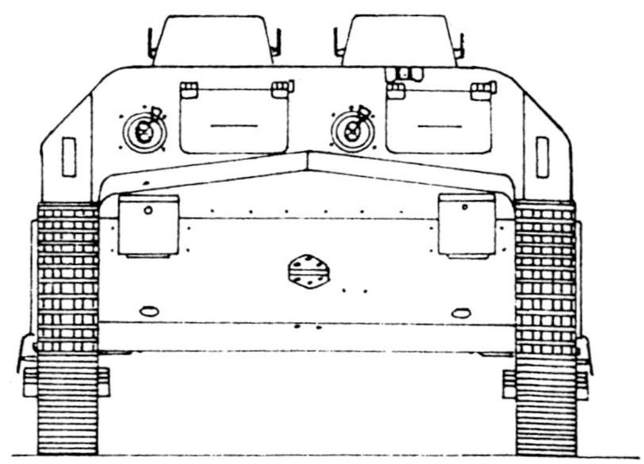

Škoda Tankette MU-4/1(T 1)

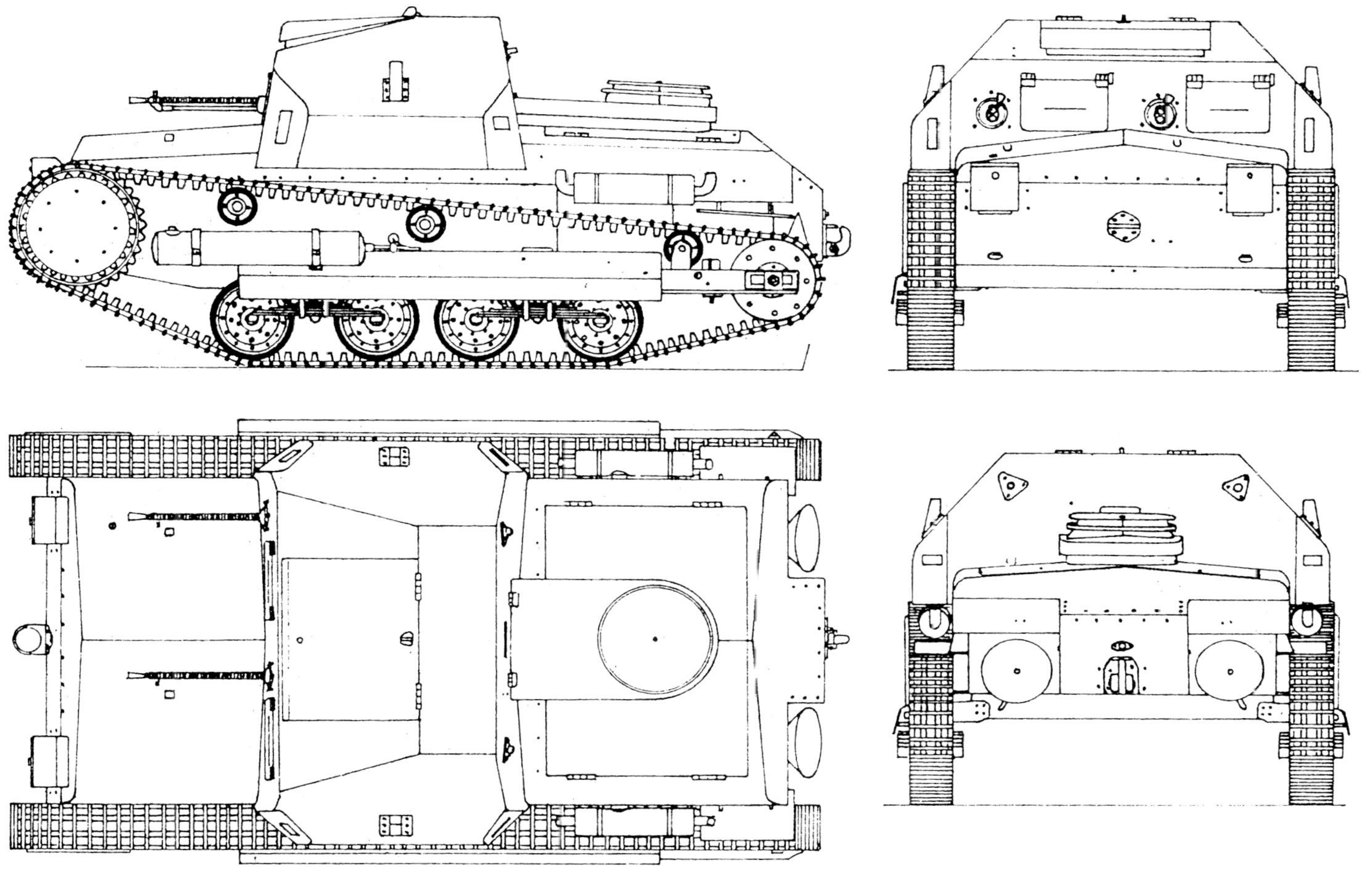

Škoda Tankette MU-6/III

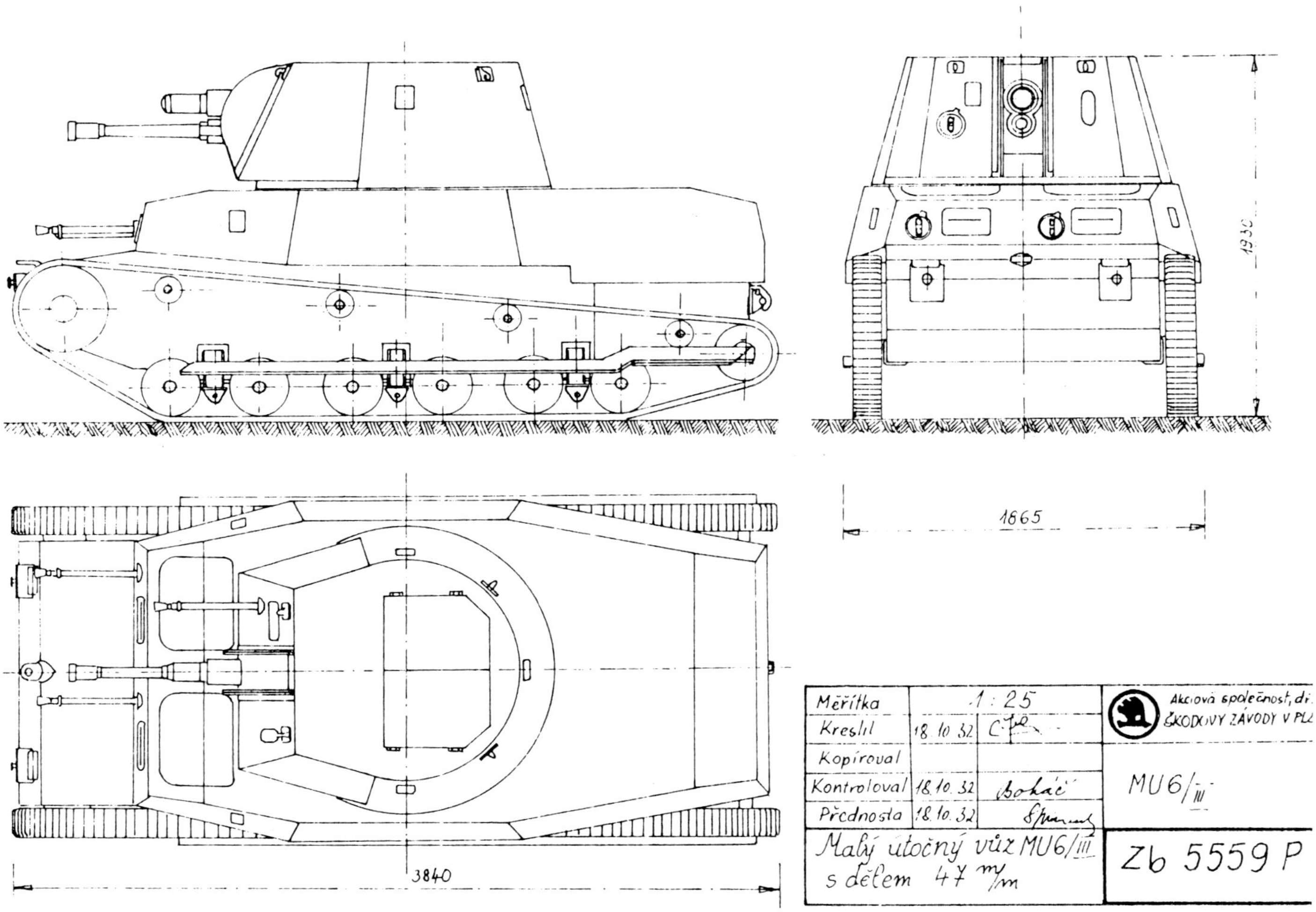

Škoda Tankette MU-6 (4 cm gun carrier)

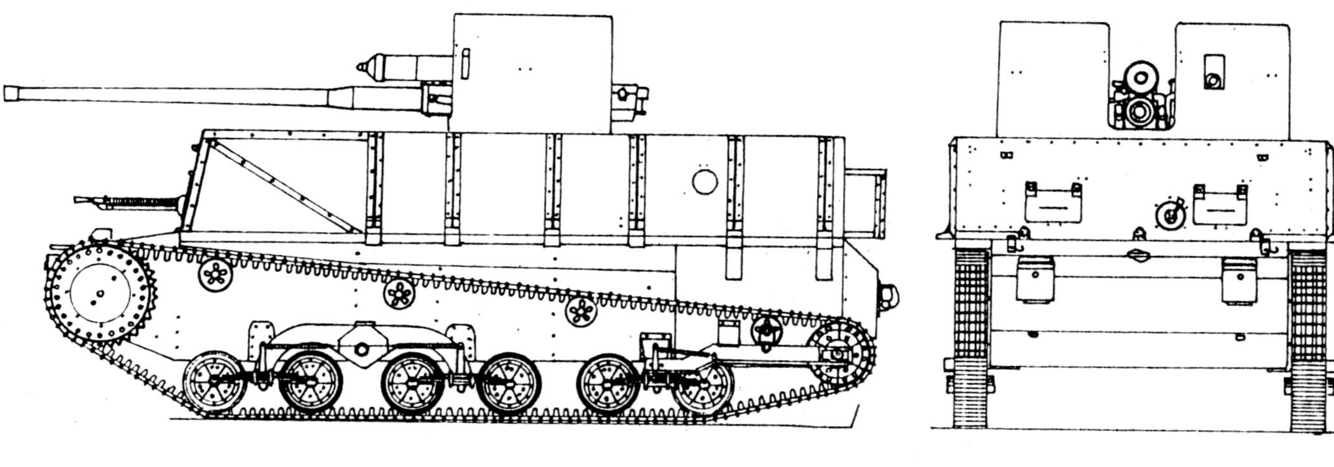

Škoda Tankette Š-I-d (Yugoslav T-32)

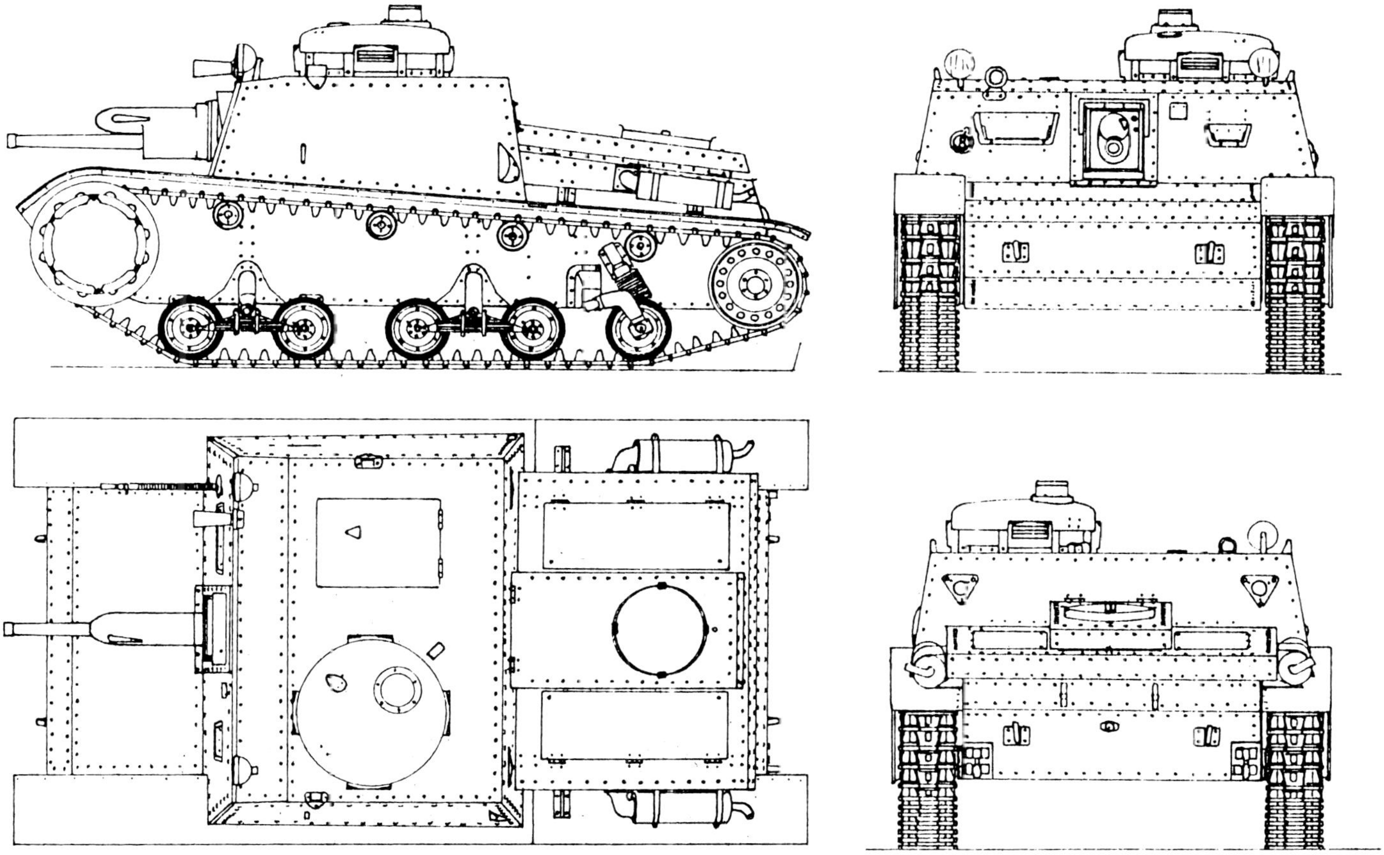

Škoda Tankette Š-I-j

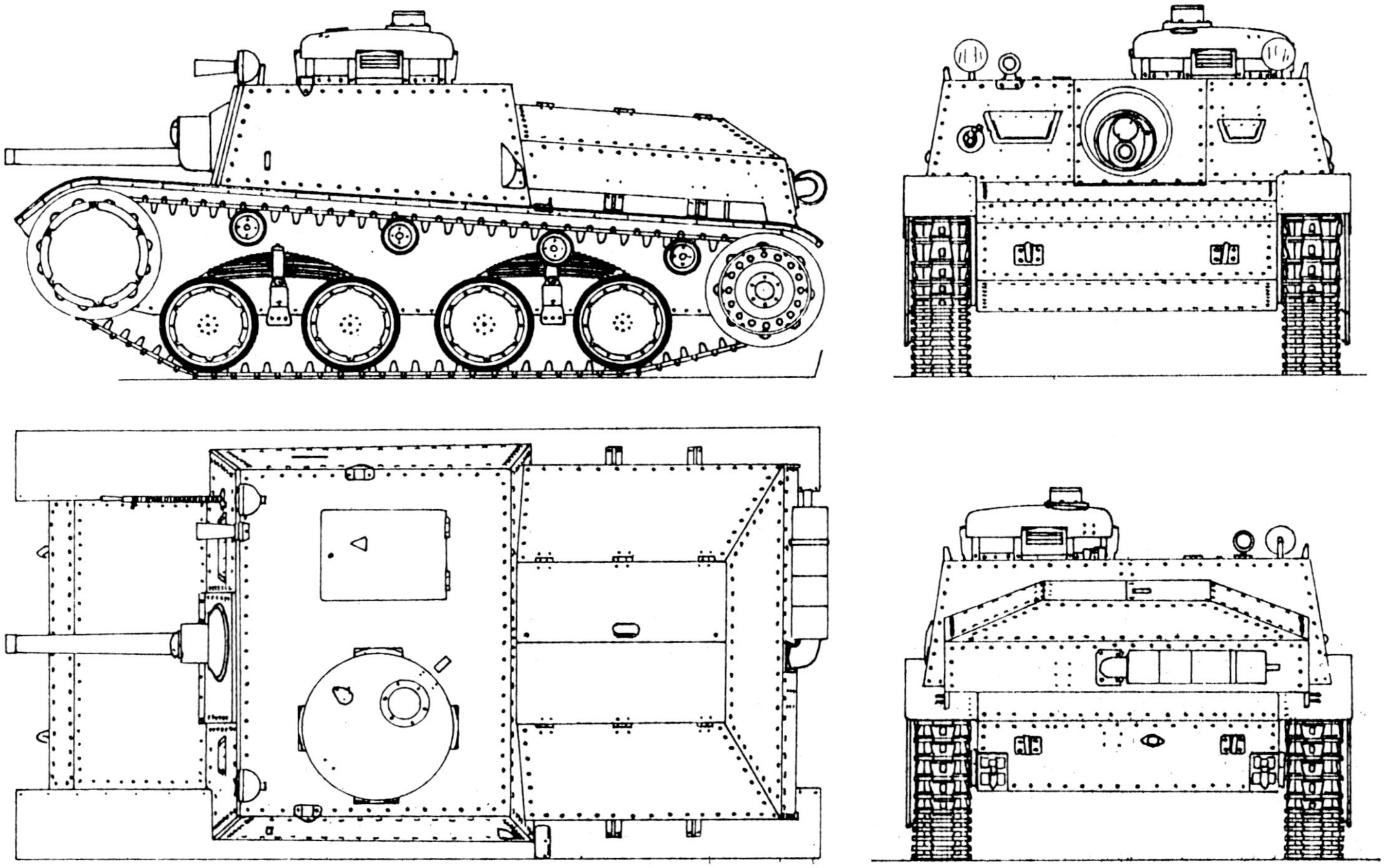

ČKD Tankette Tančik vz.33

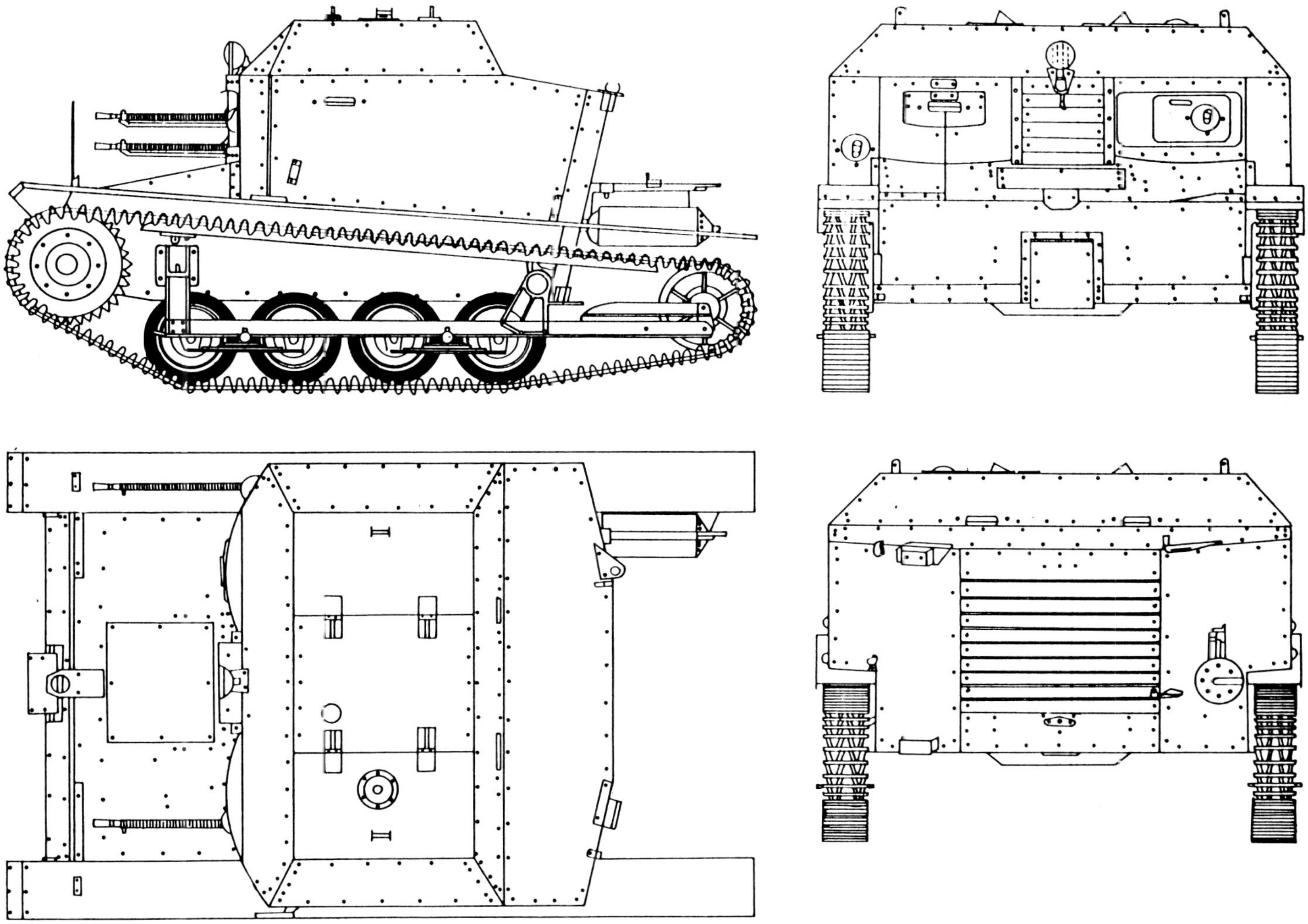

ČKD Tankette AH-IV (Exported to Iran and Romania)

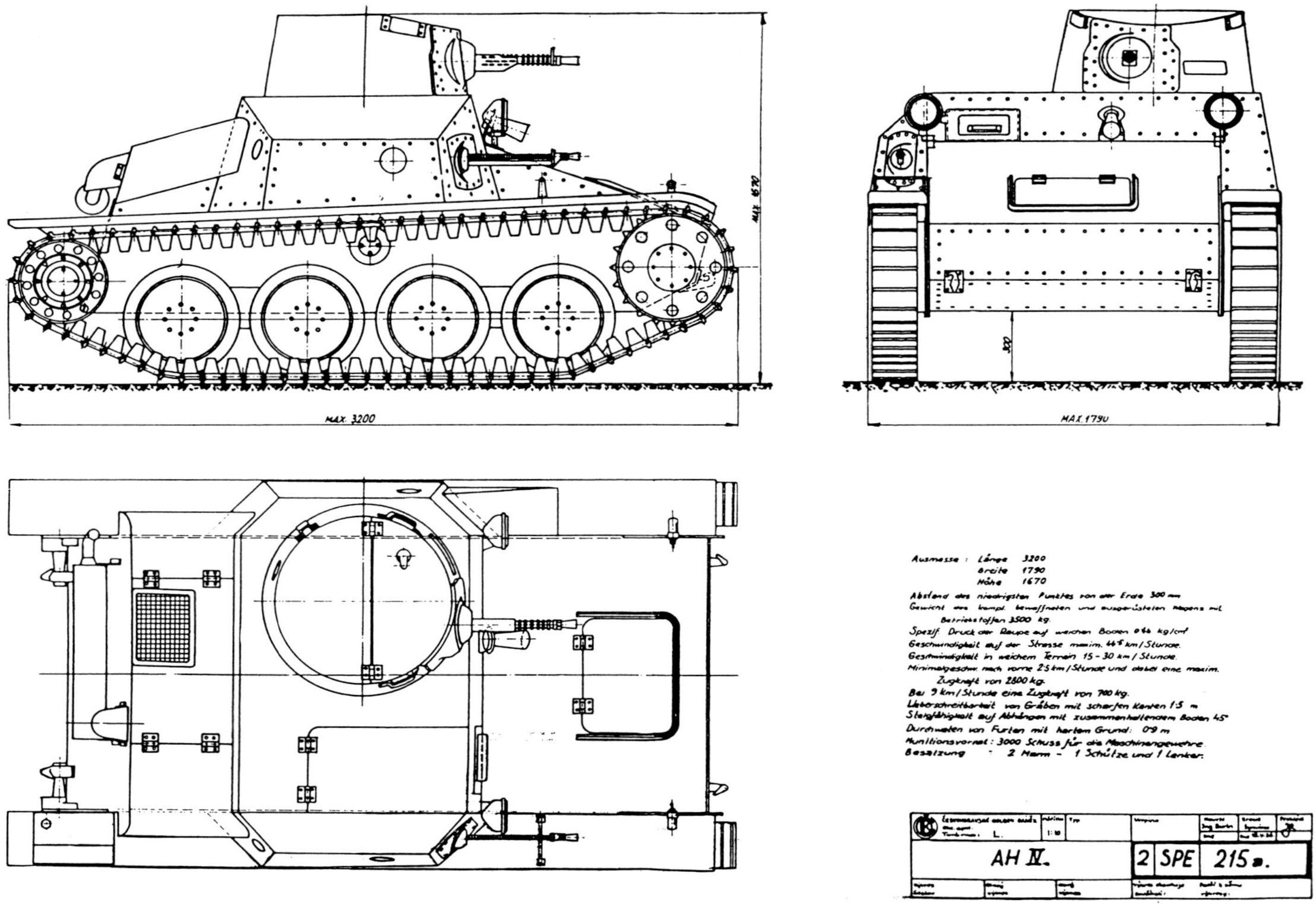

ČKD Tankette AH-IV Sv (Licensed to Sweden)

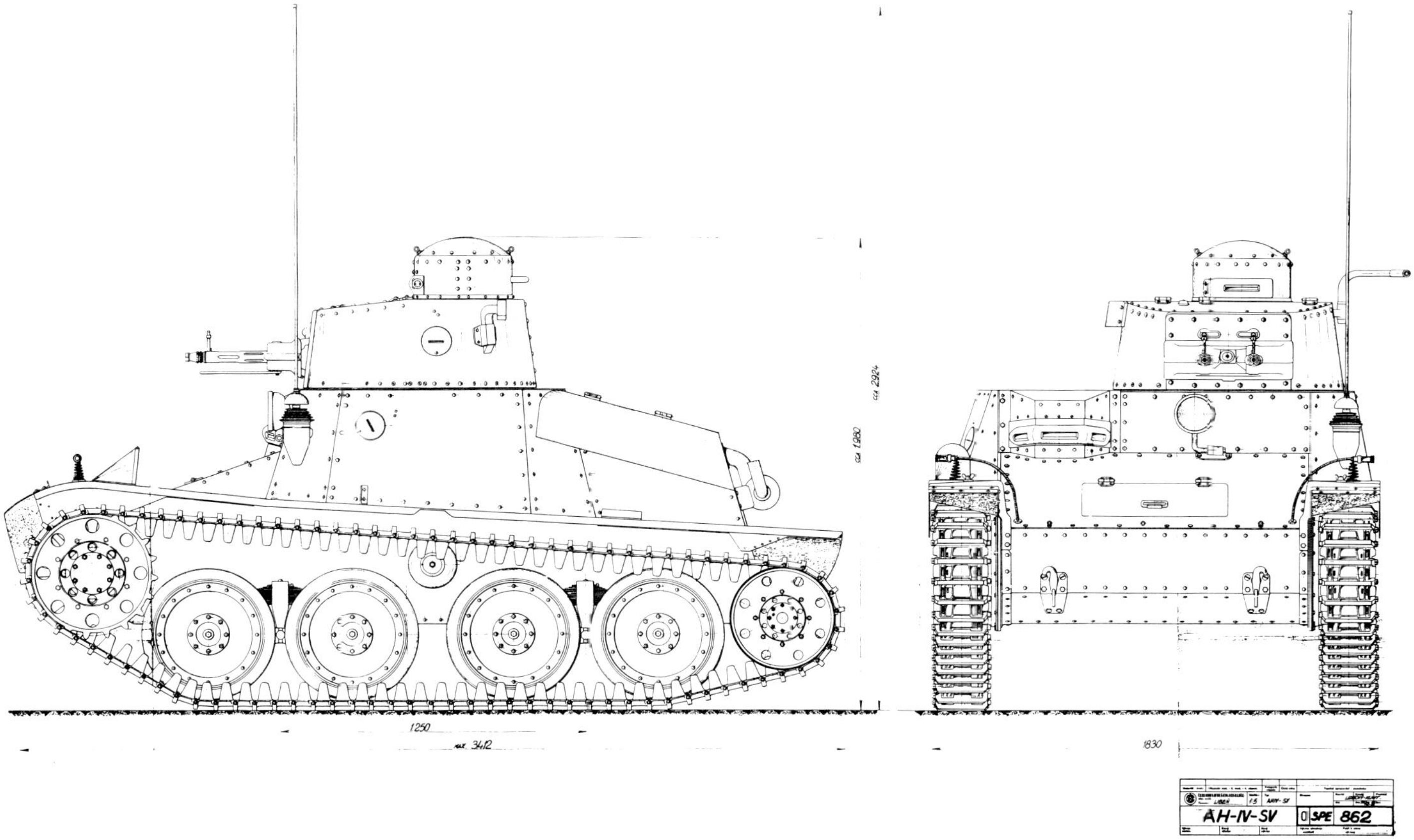

Škoda ŠET Electric Tank

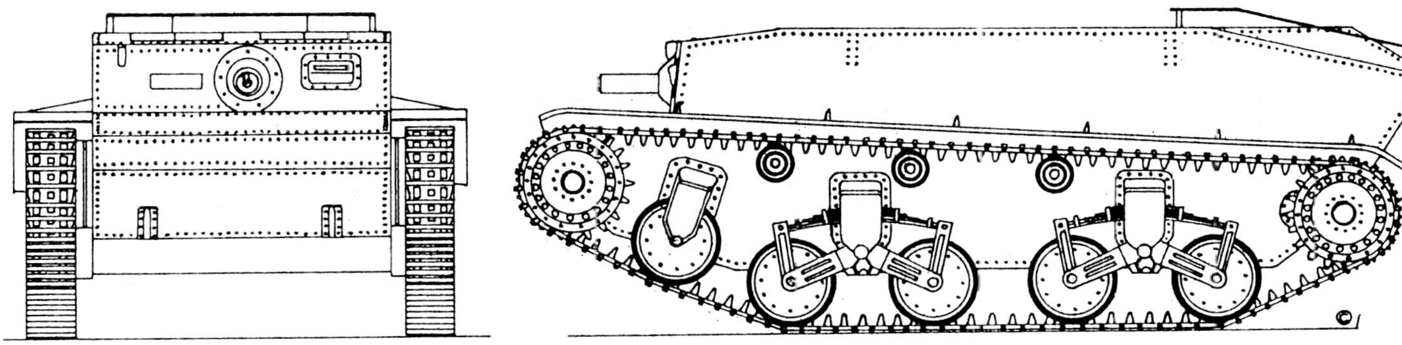

WHEEL-CUM-TRACK

Wheel-cum-Track KH-60 in its "Tank" Form

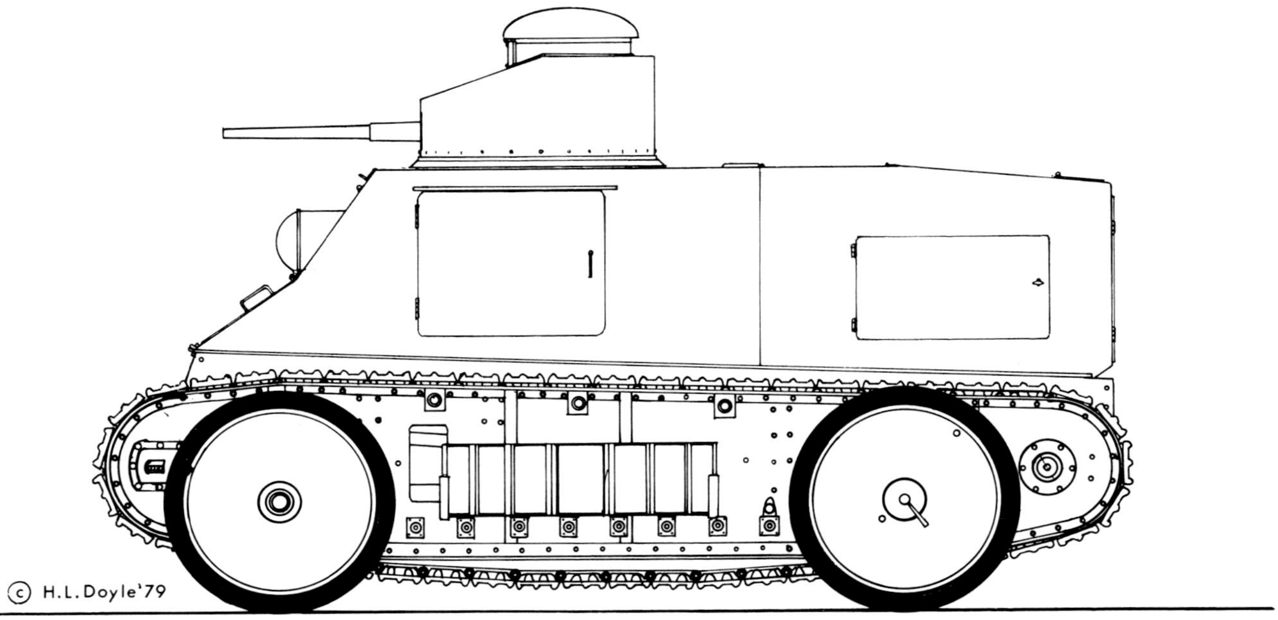

Škoda Project of a Wheel-cum-Track Tank SKU

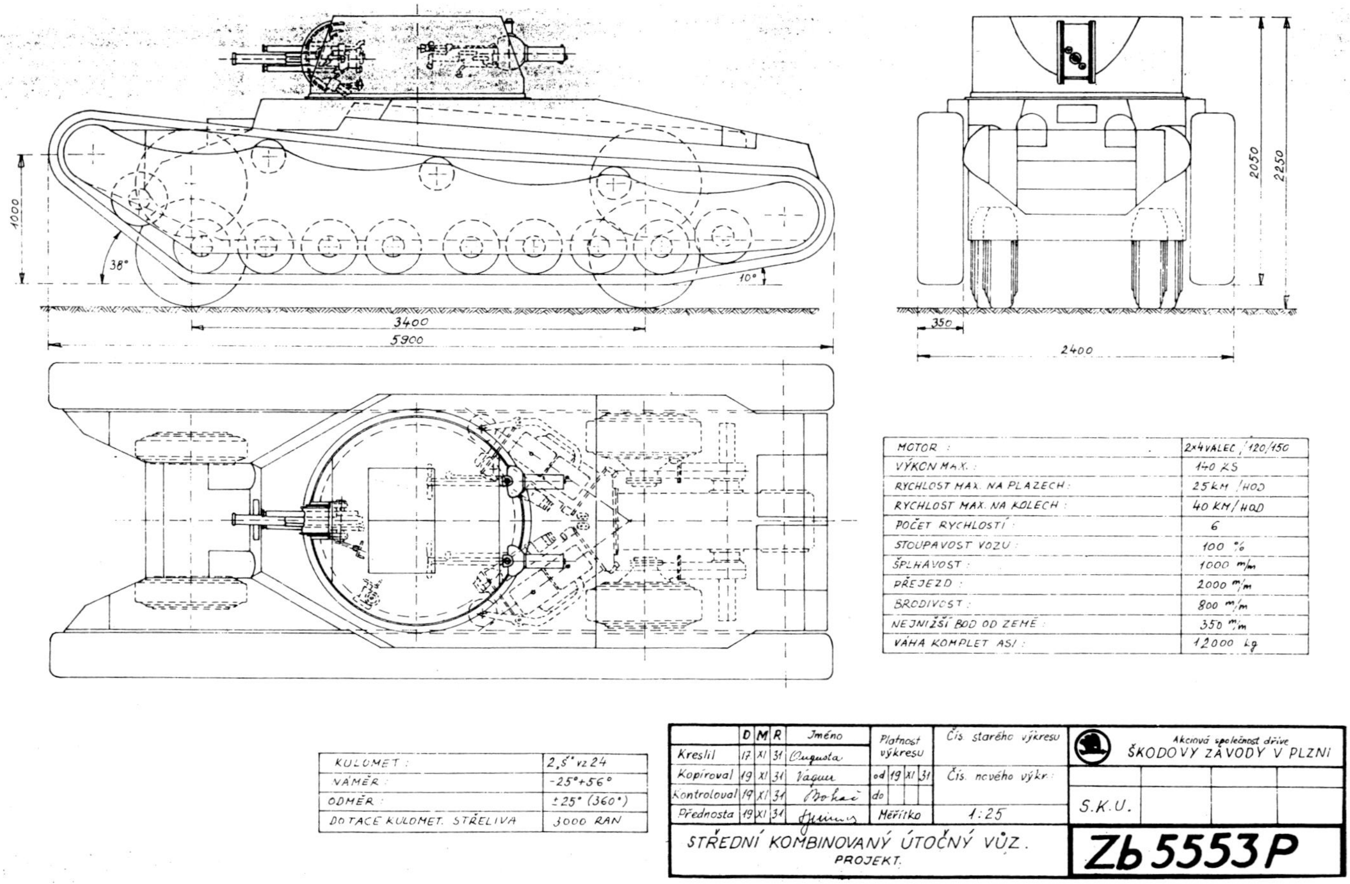

TANKS

Škoda Light Tank SU

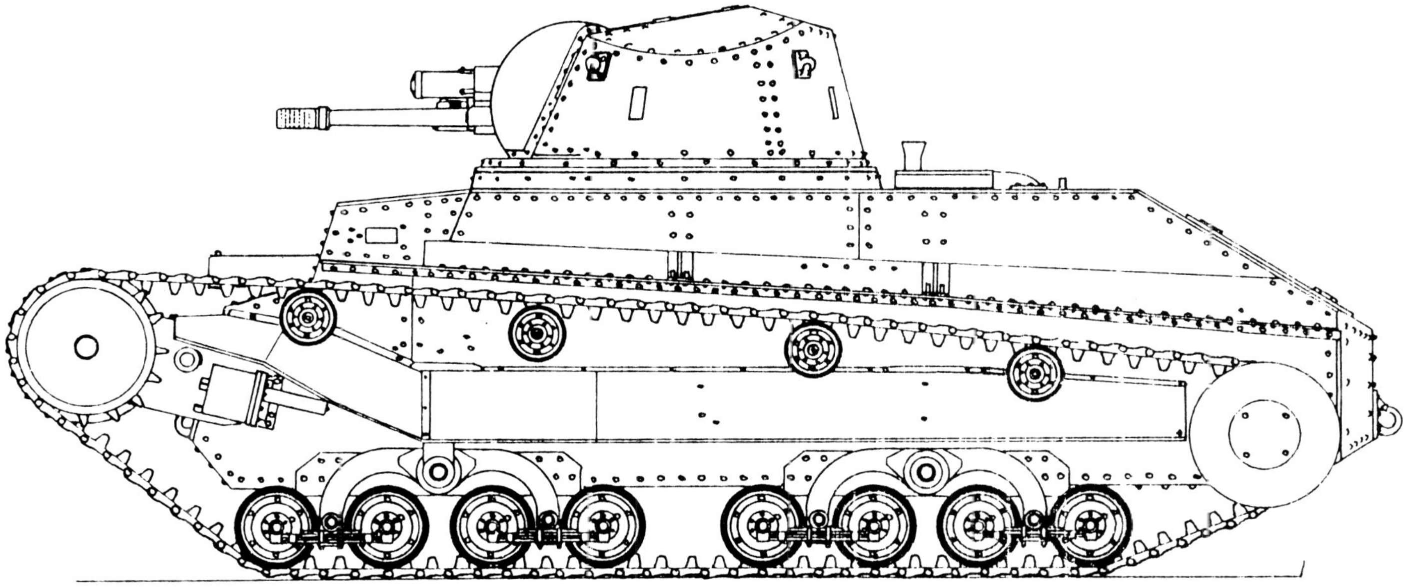

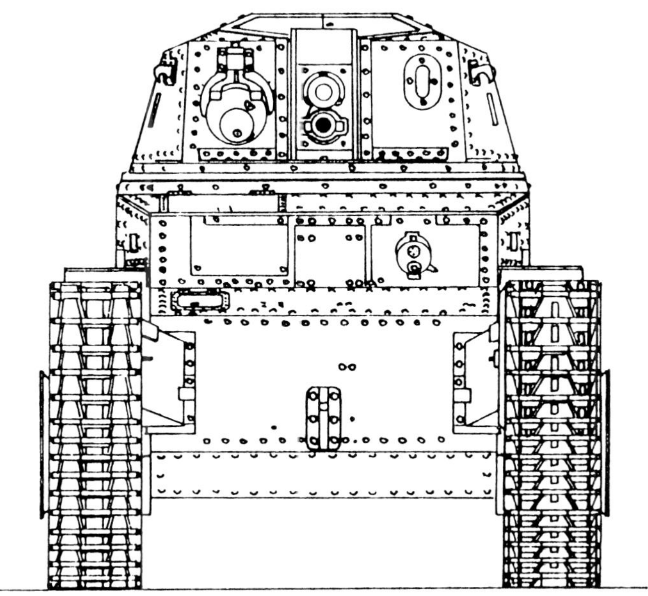

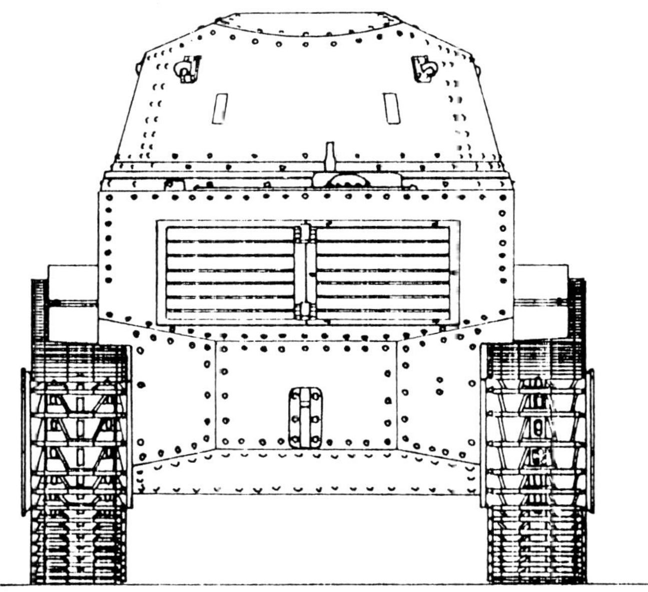

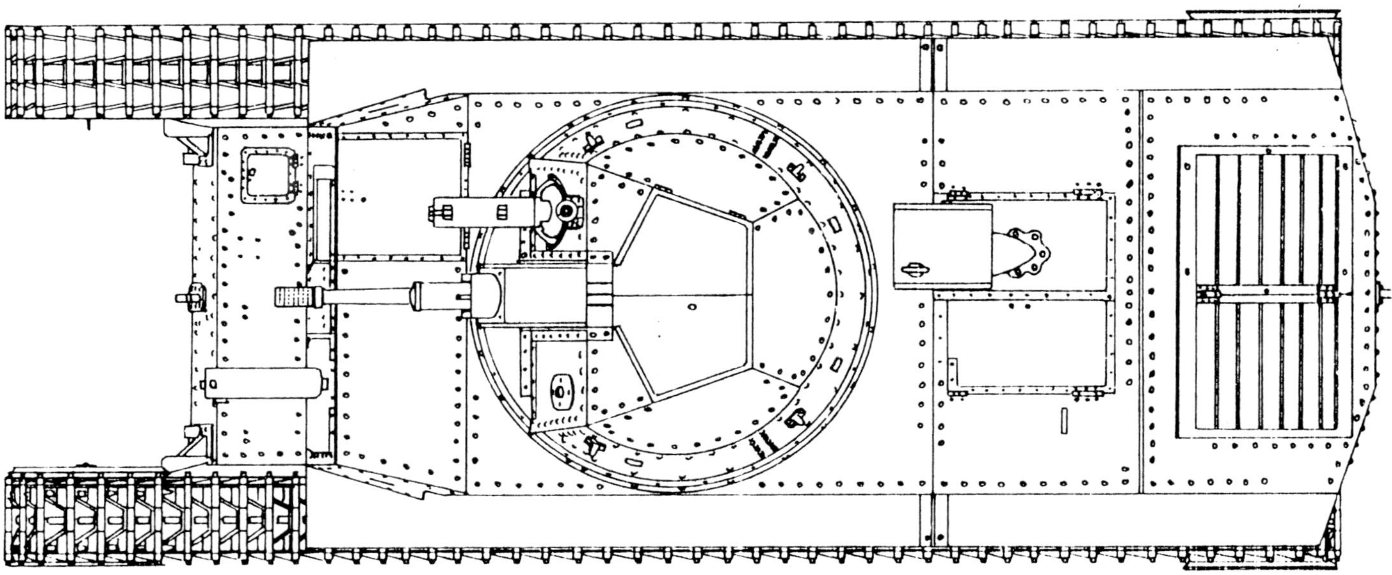

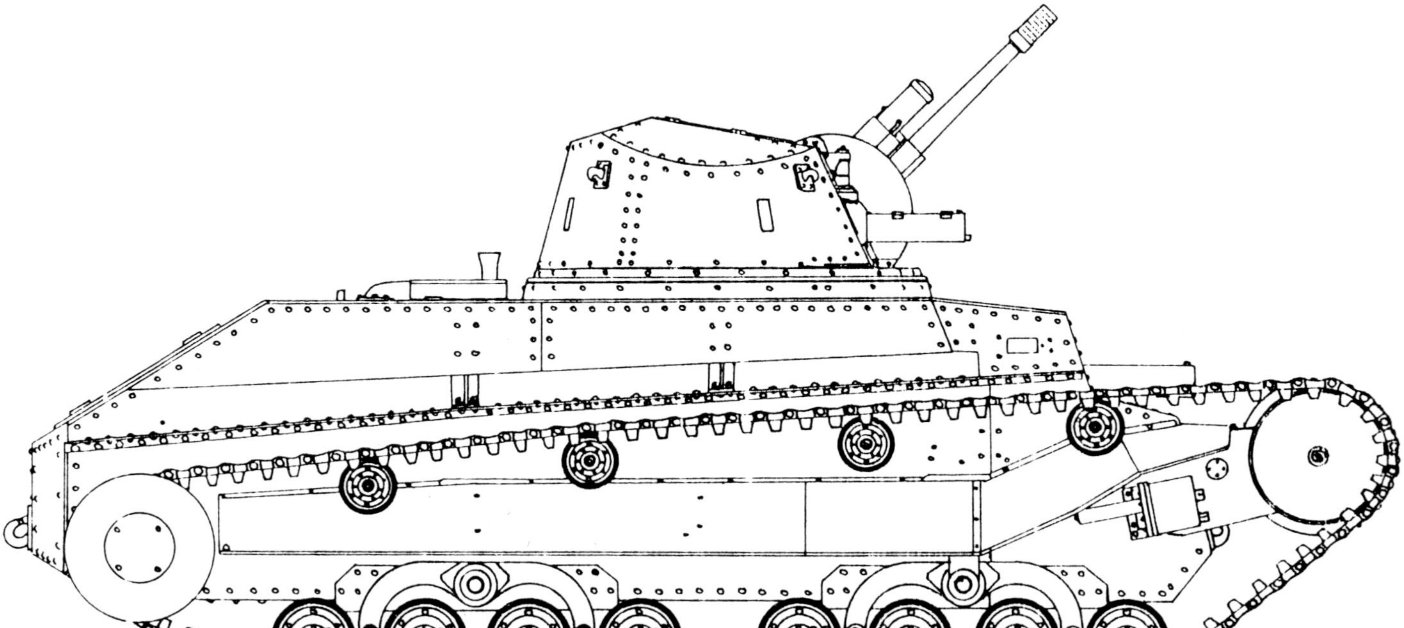

Škoda Light Tank R-2

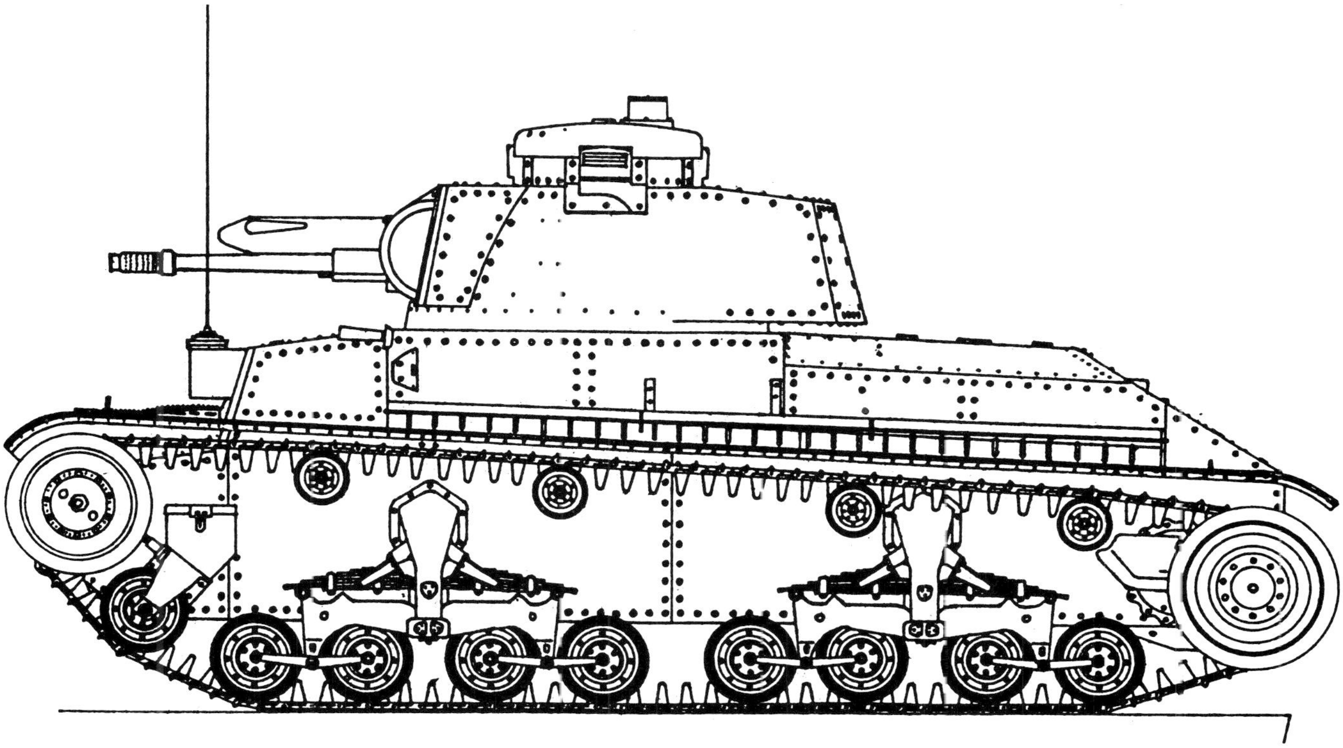

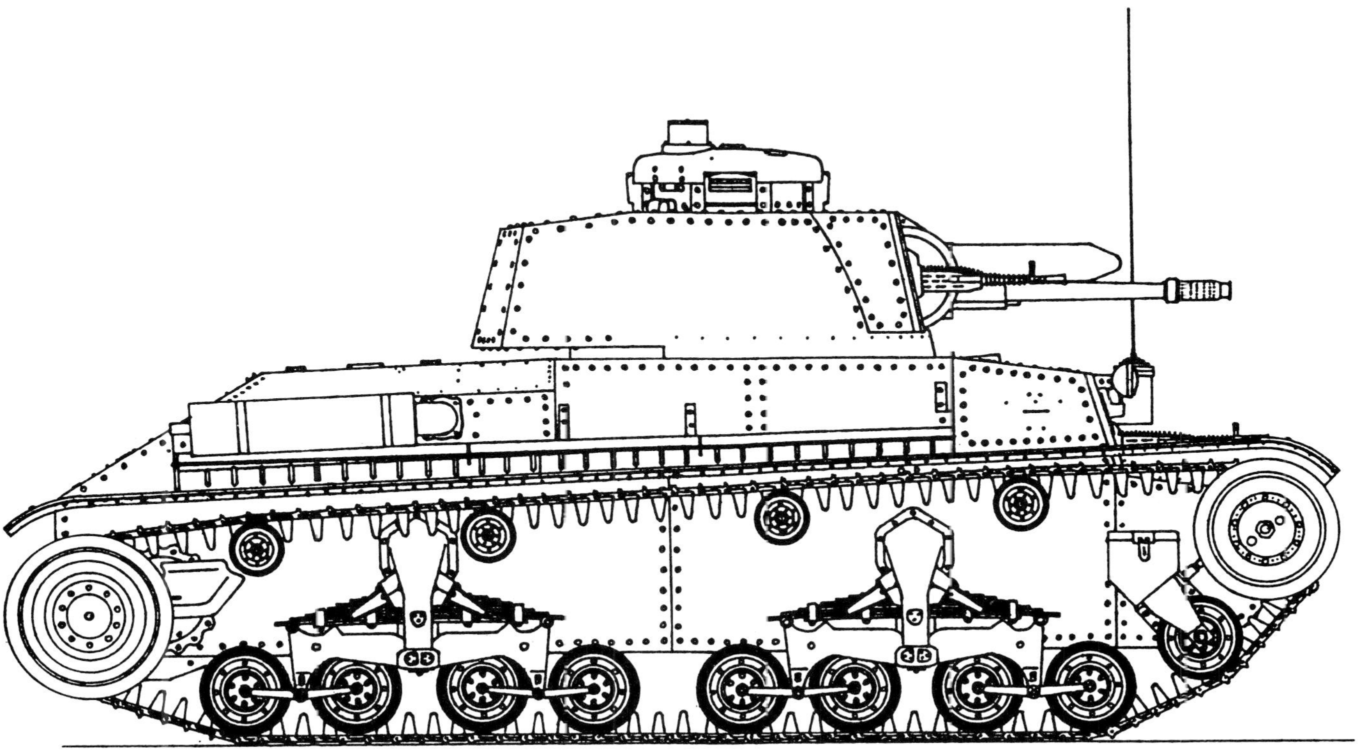

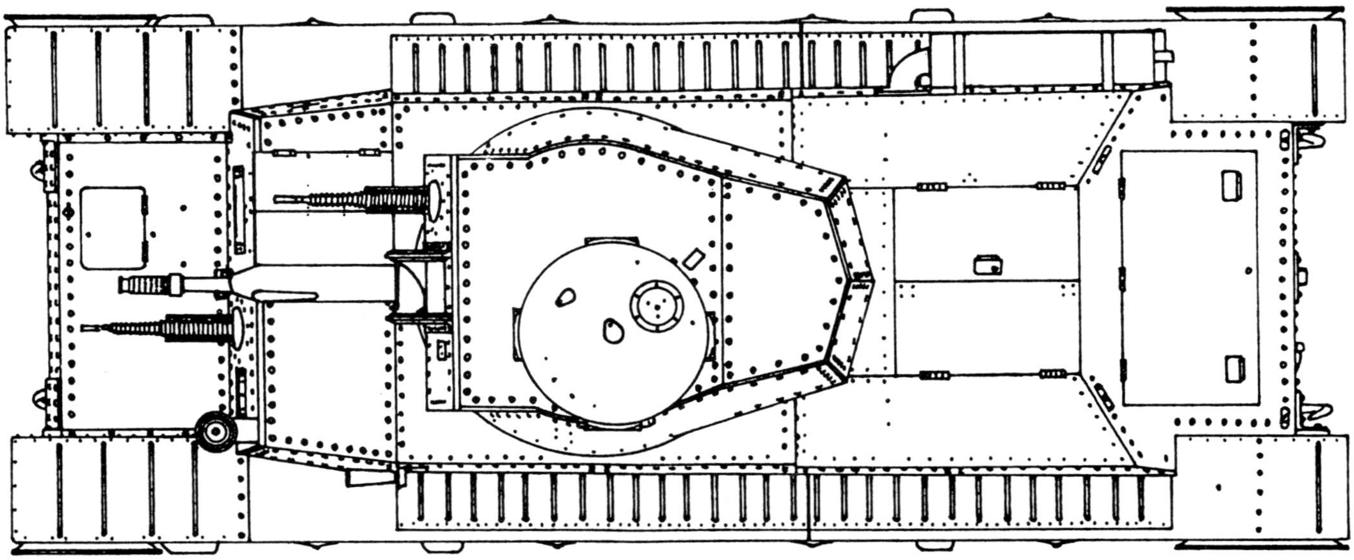

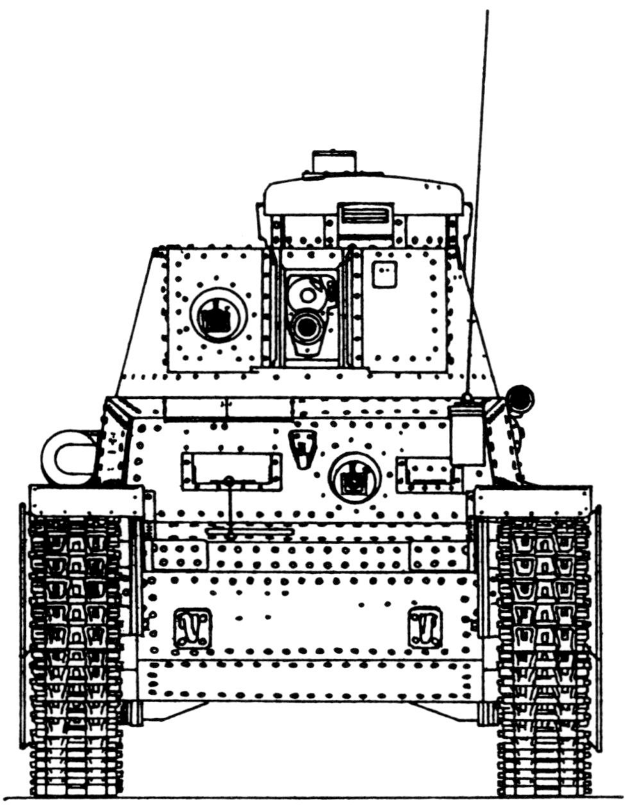

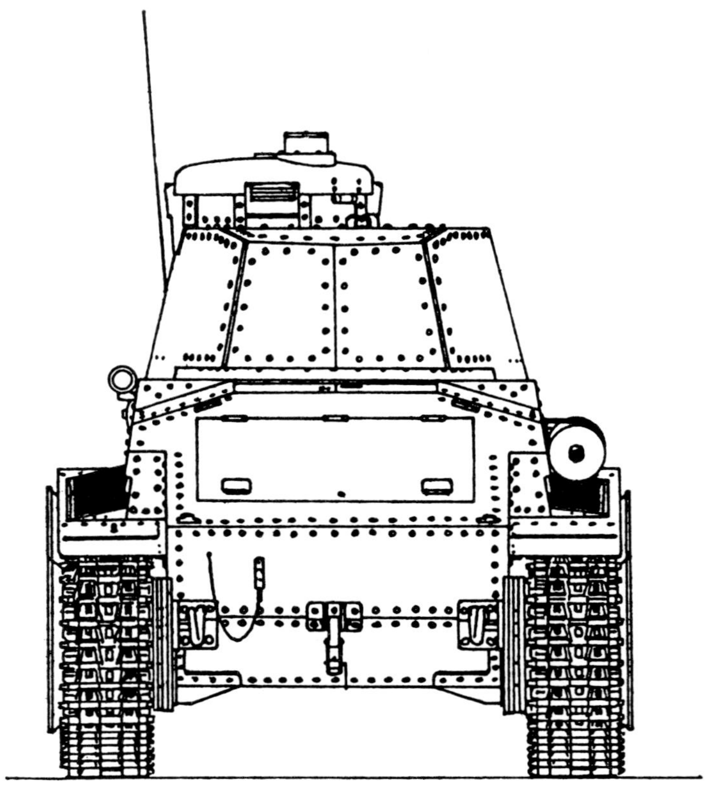

Škoda Light Tank Š-II-c (LT vz.35)

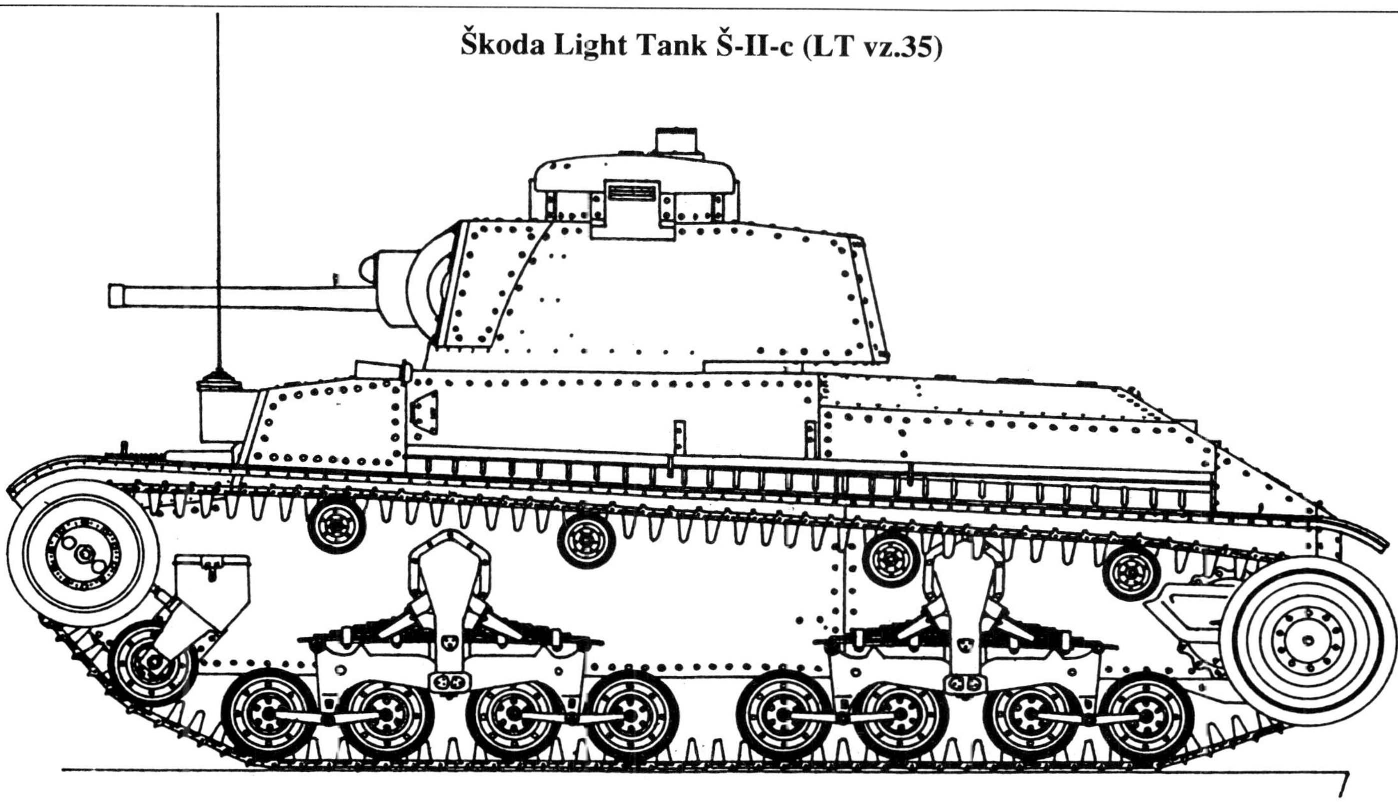

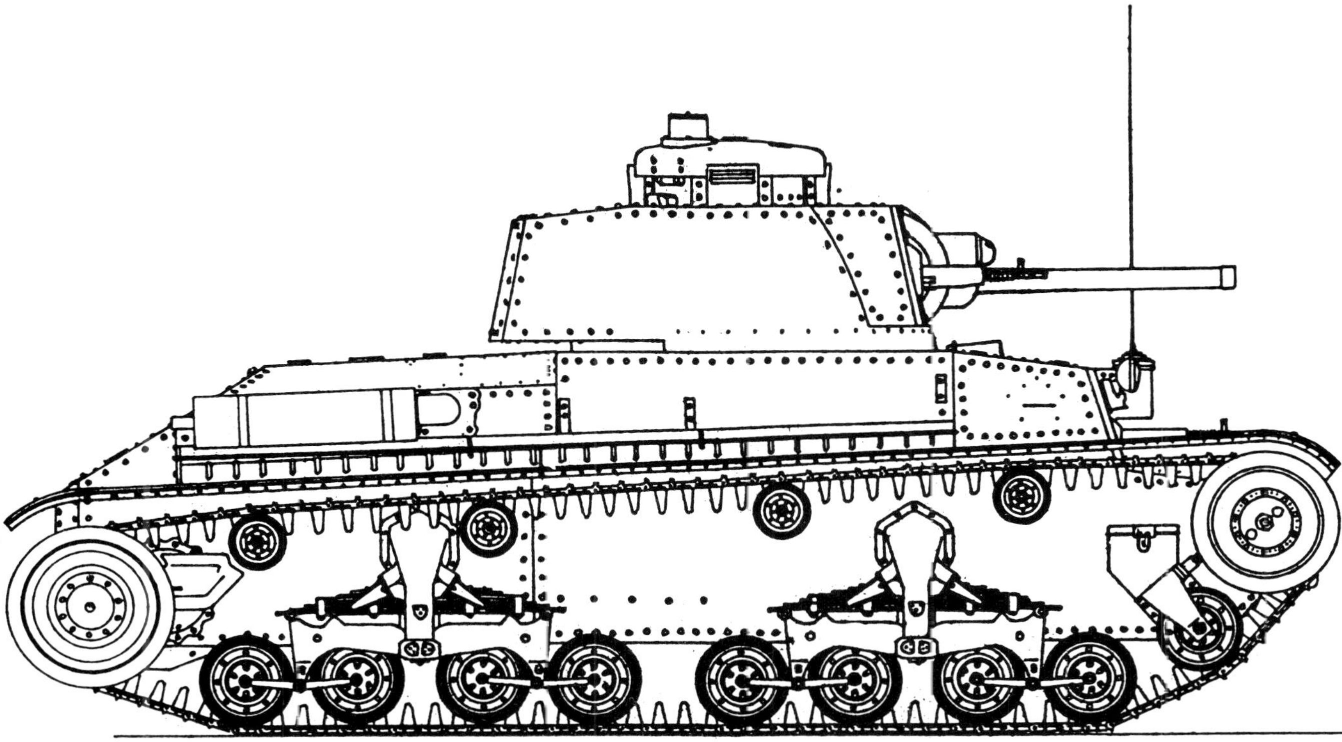

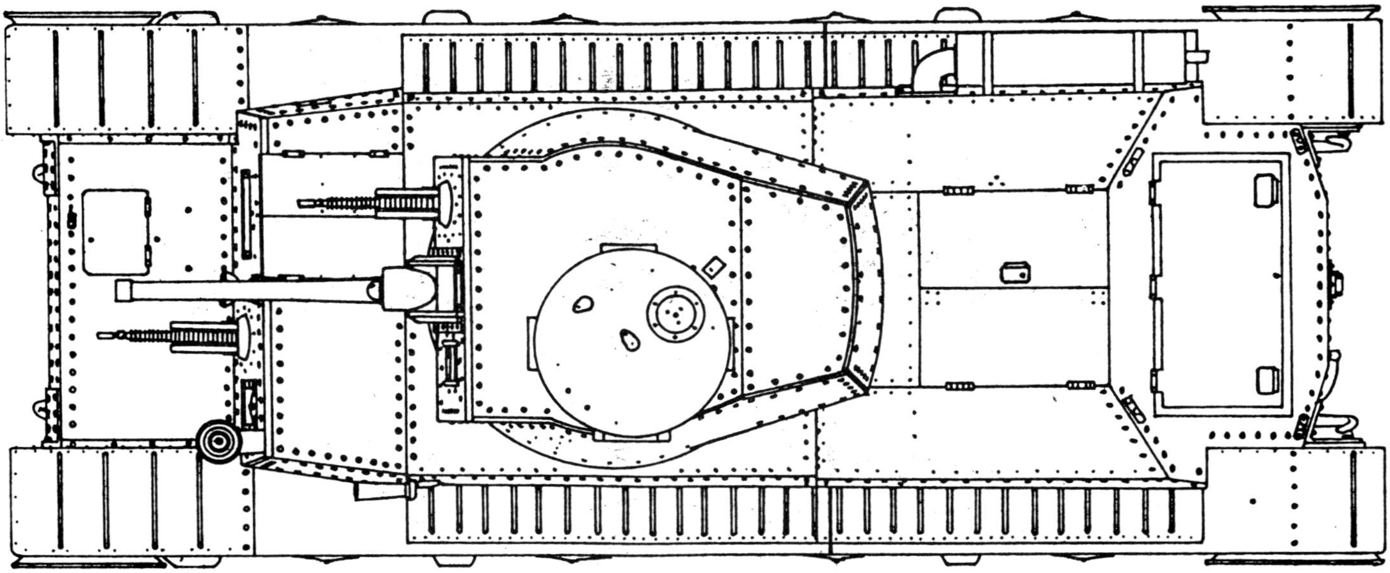

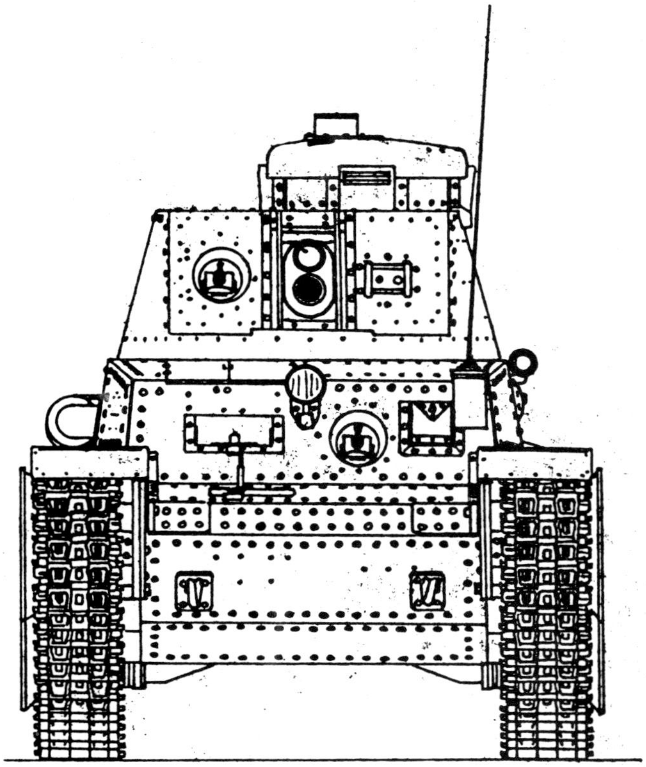

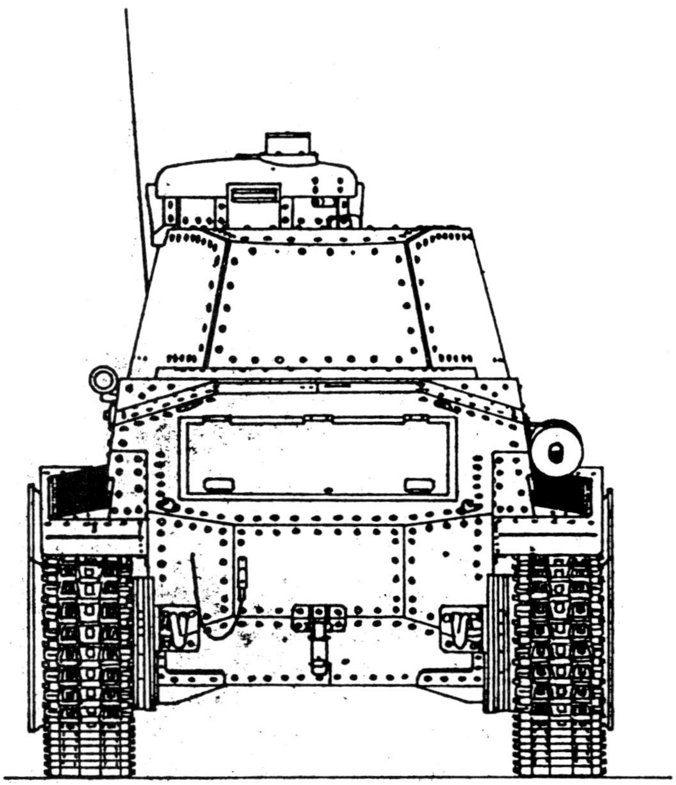

Škoda Light Tank T-11

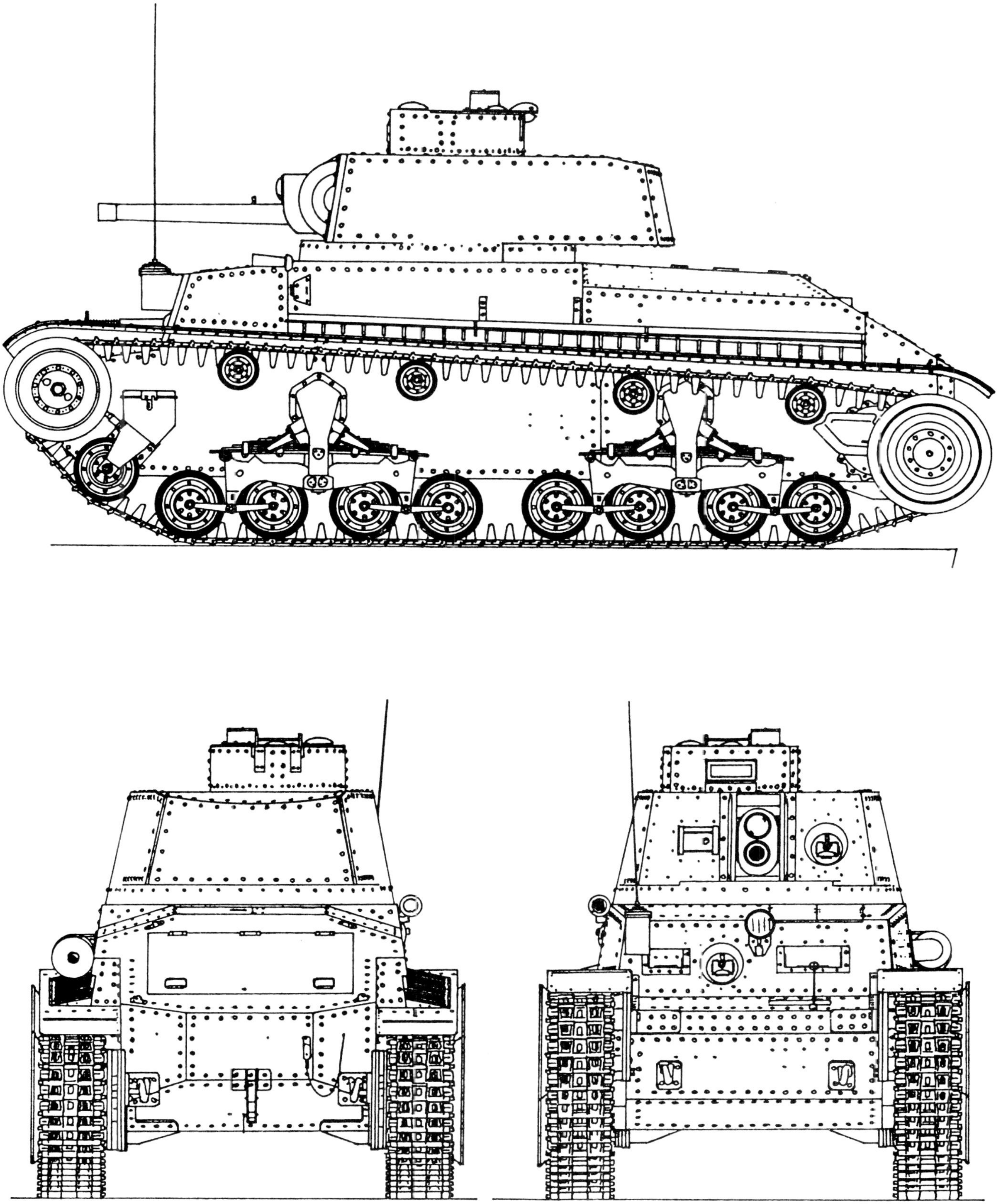

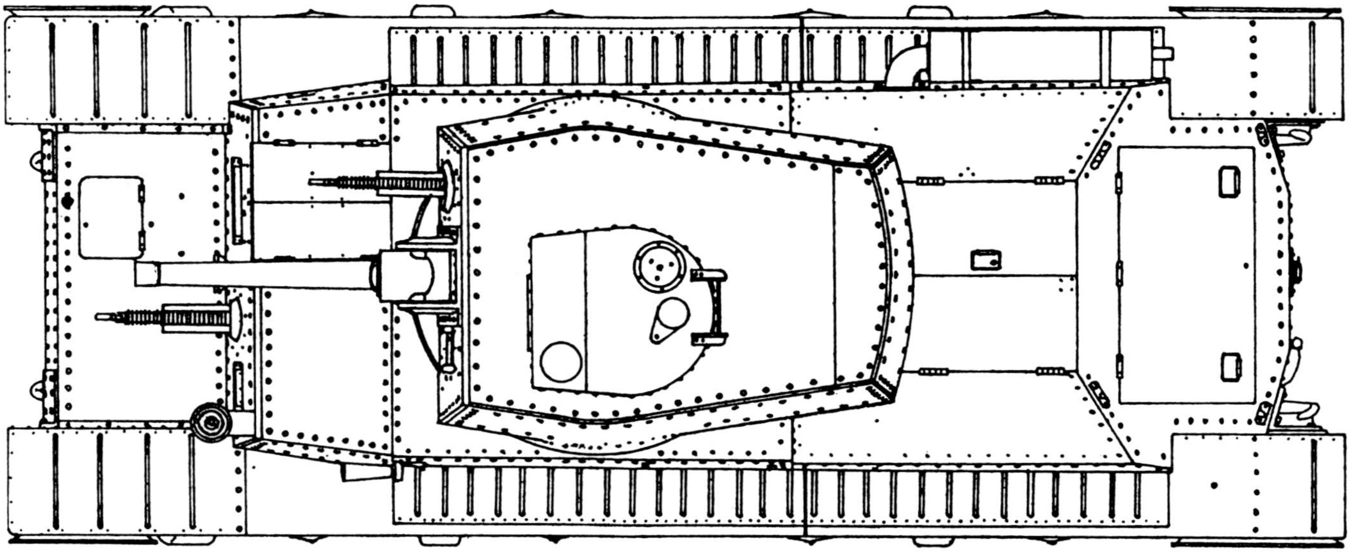

Romanian Tank Hunter Tacam R-2

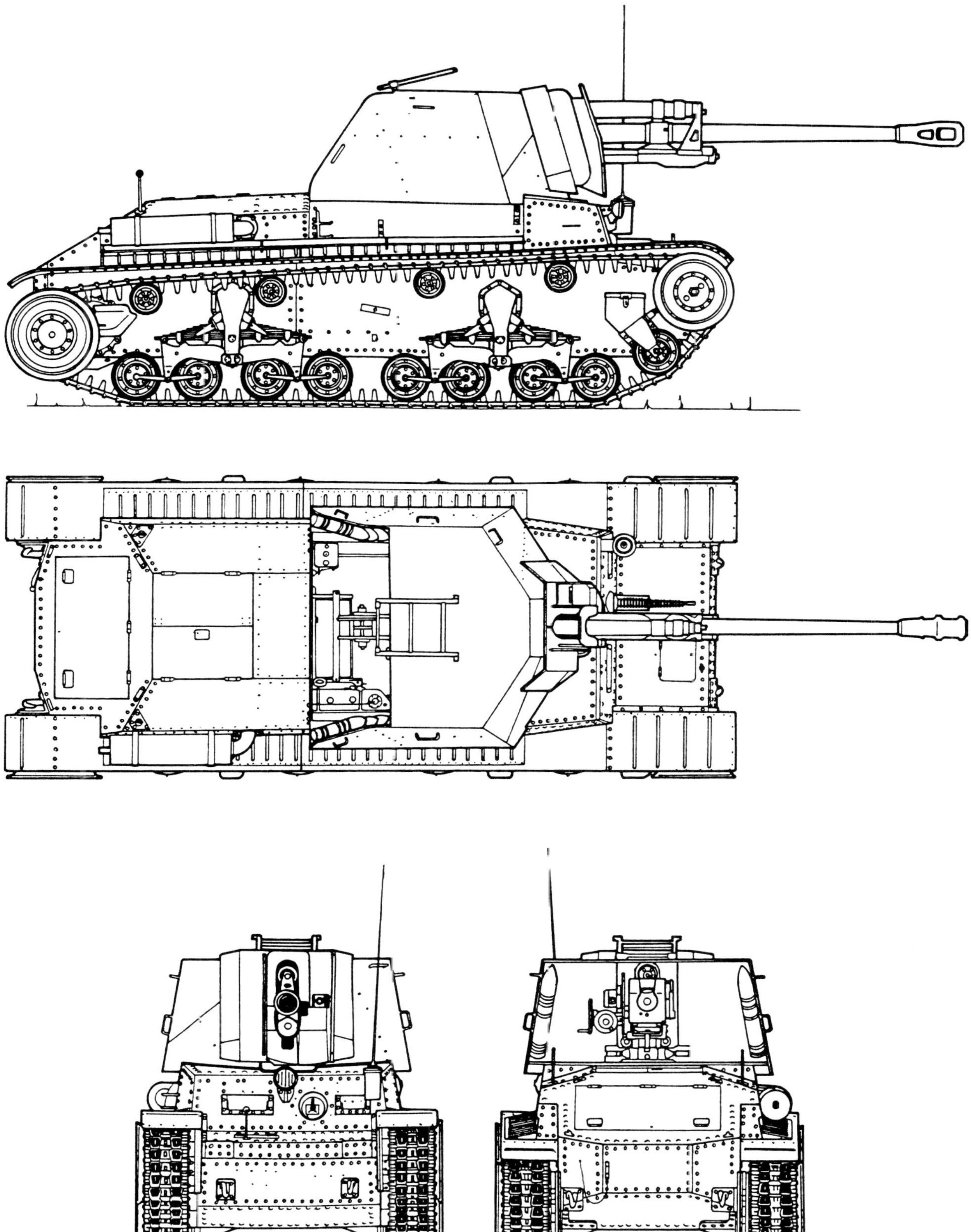

Škoda Medium Tank Š-III

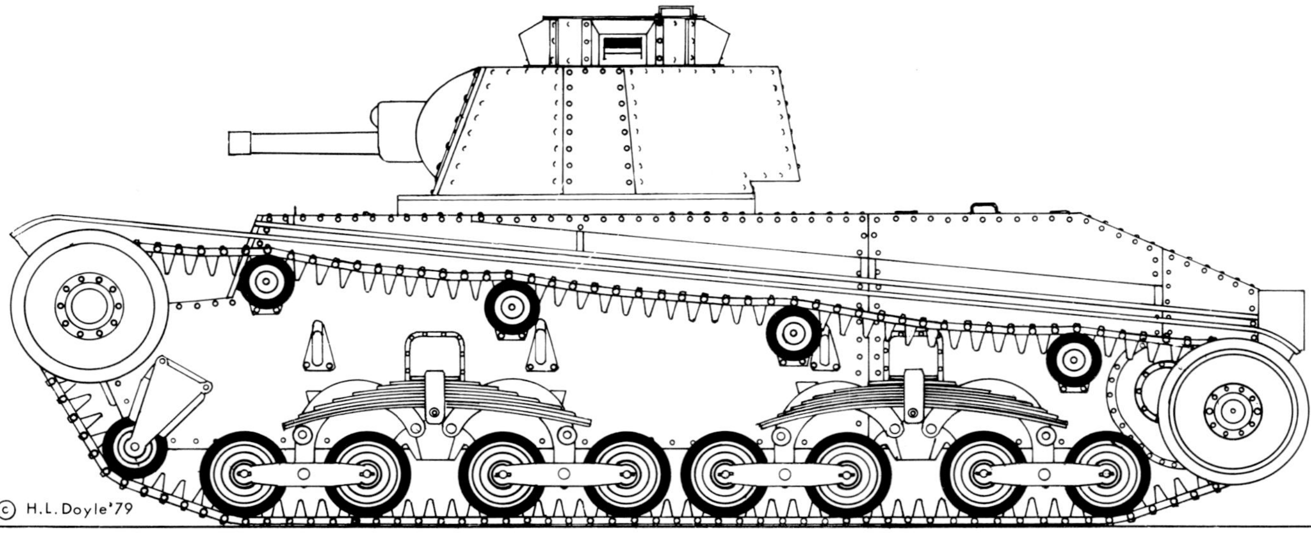

Hungarian Medium Tank Turán I

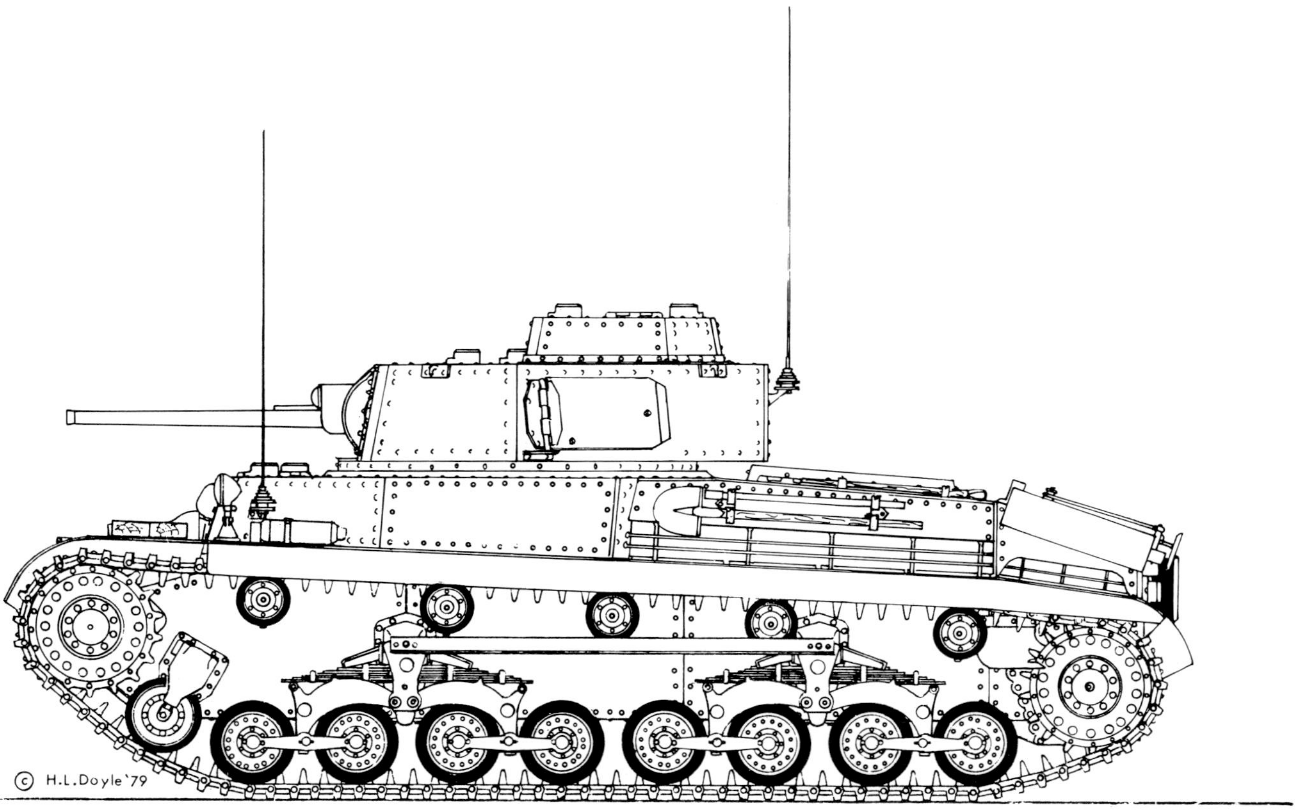

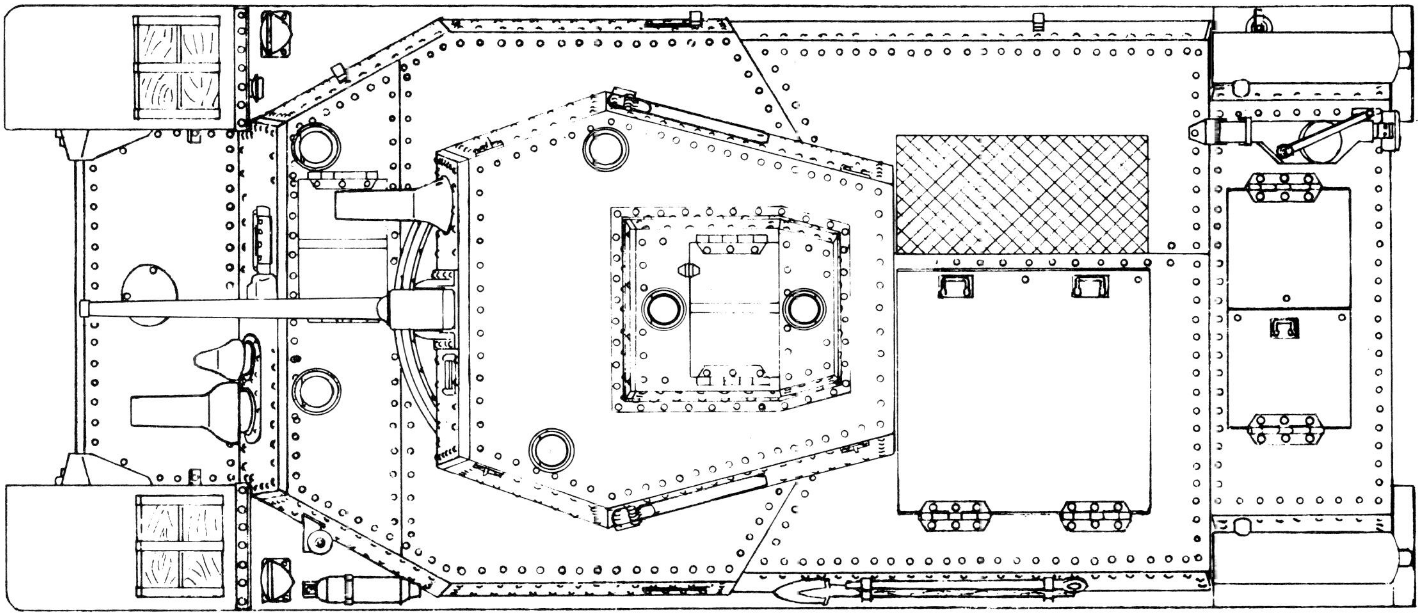

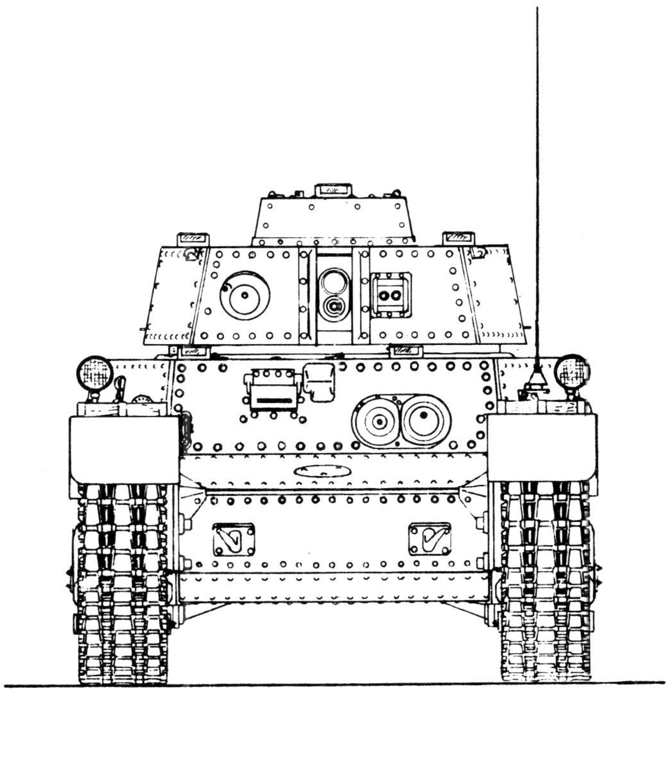

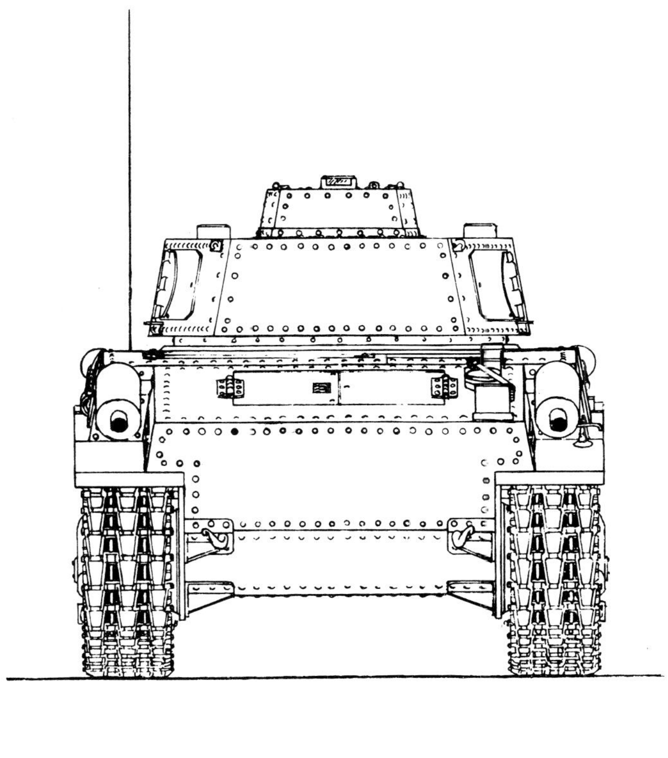

Hungarian Heavy Tank Turán II

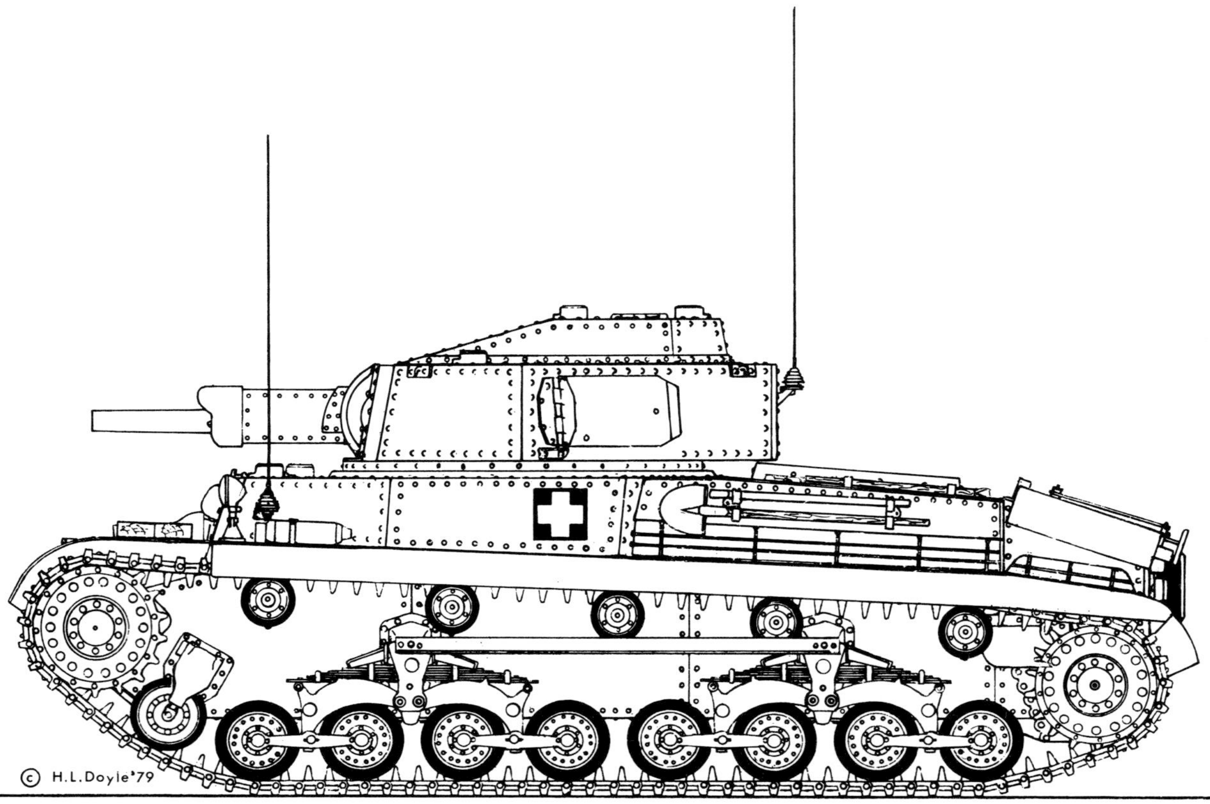

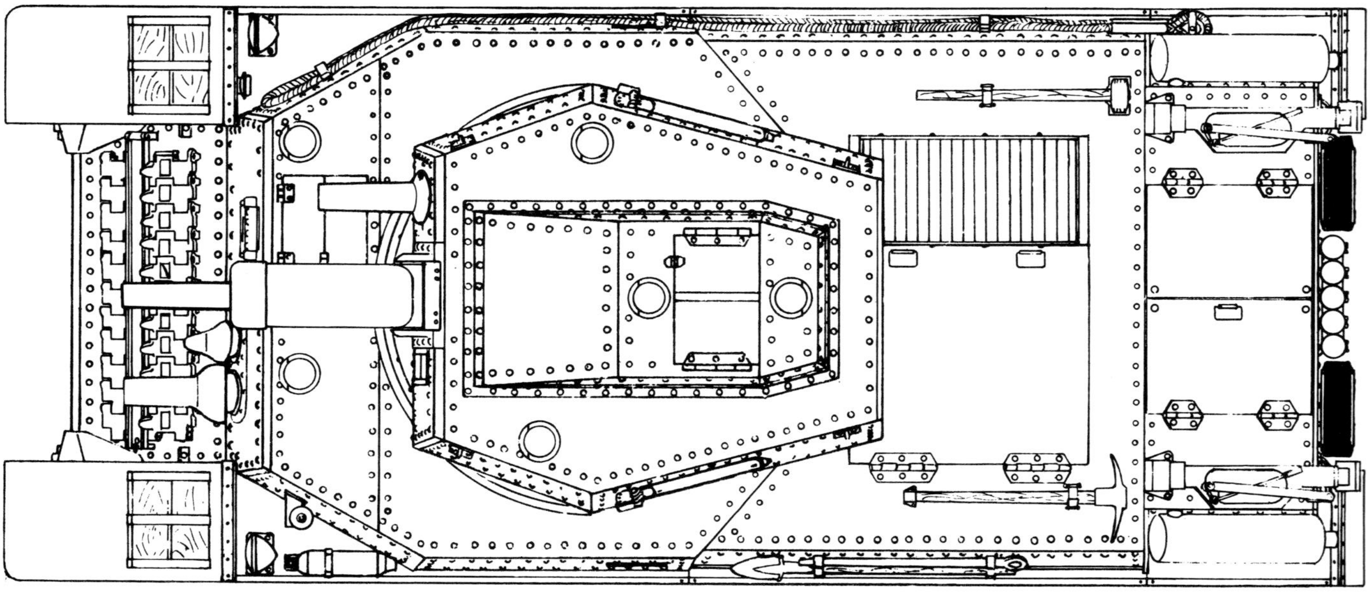

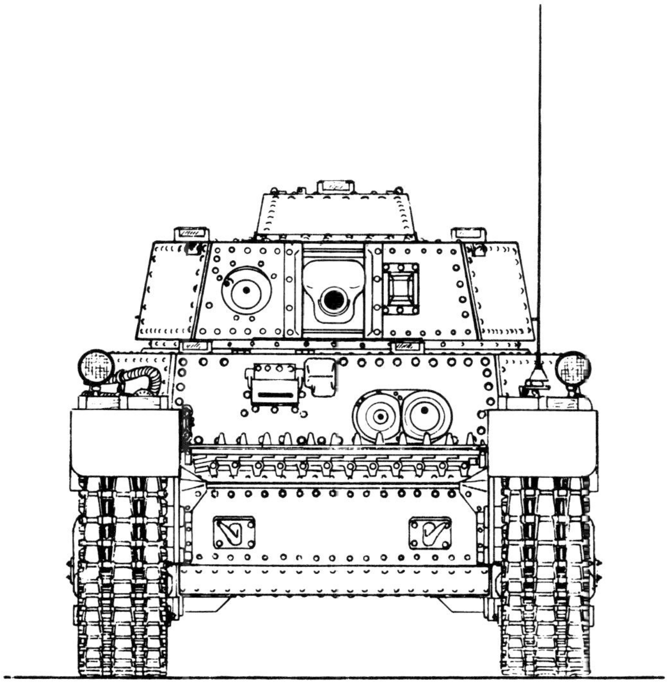

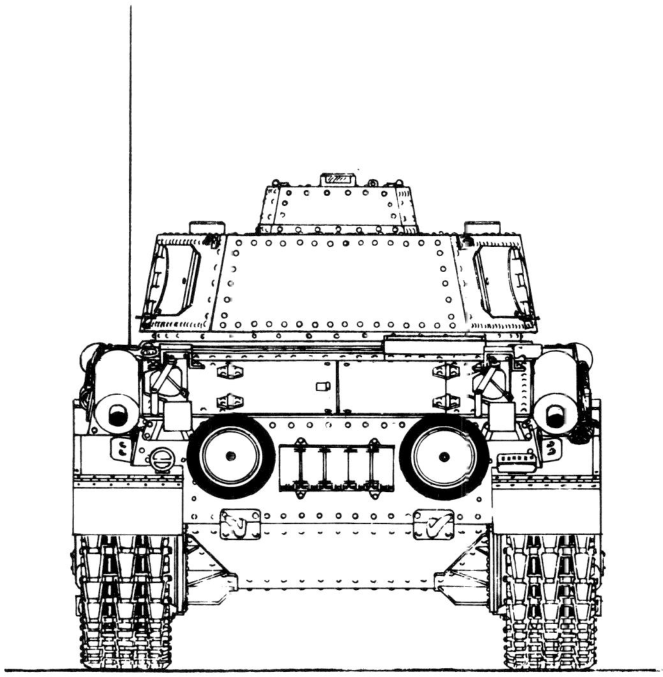

Hungarian Assault Gun Zrínyi II

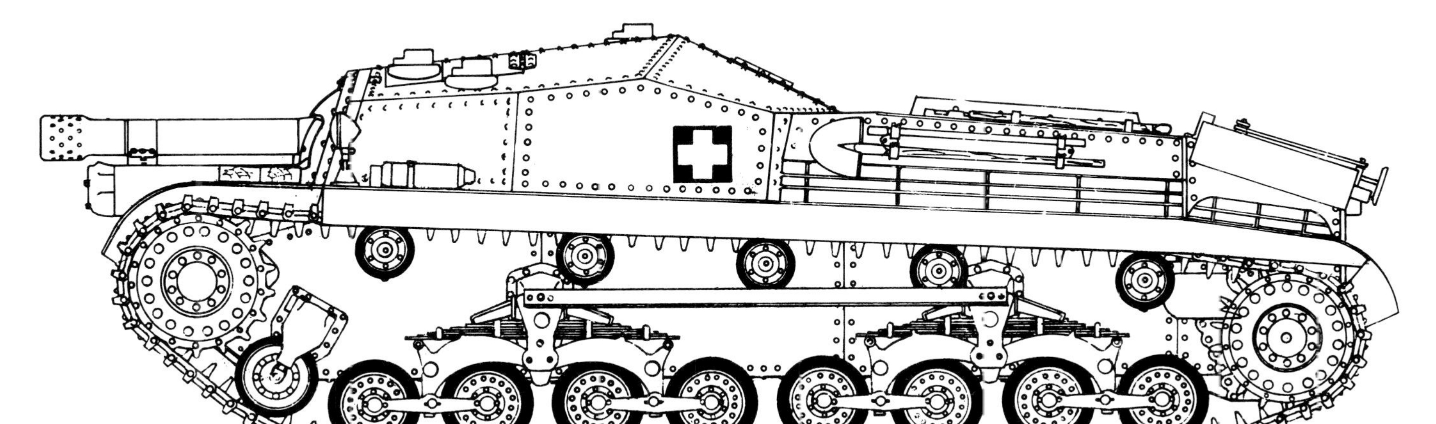

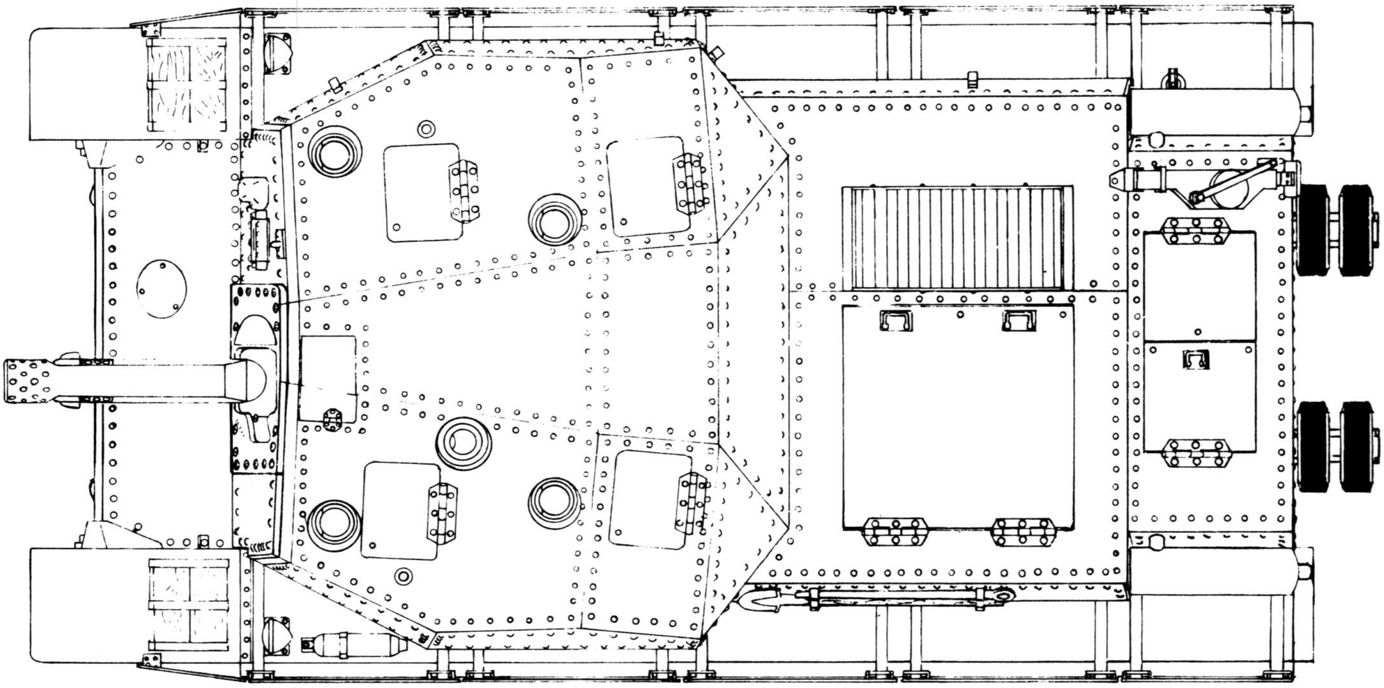

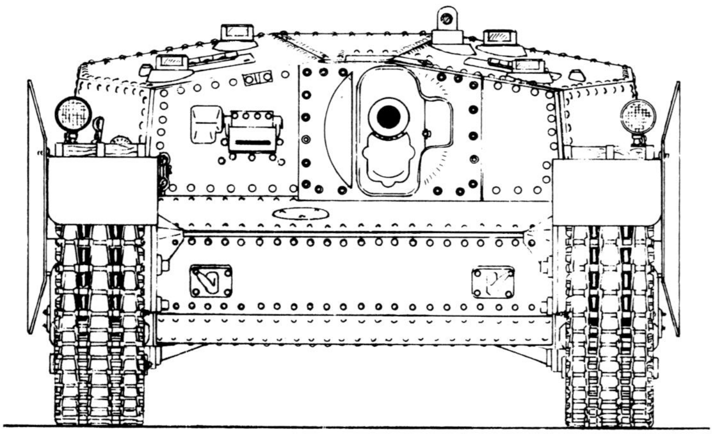

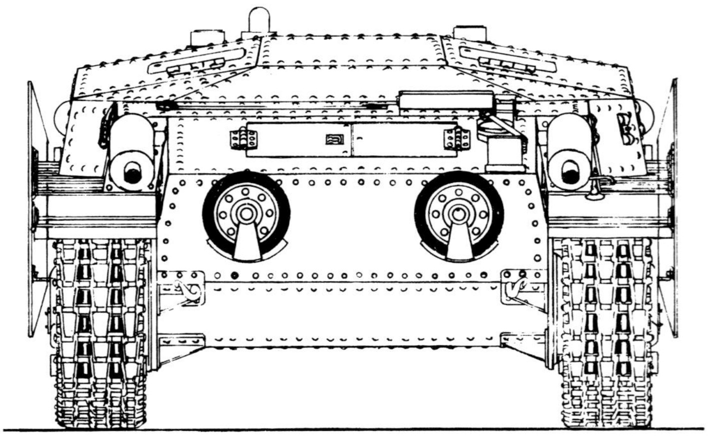

ČKD Light Tank LT vz.34 R

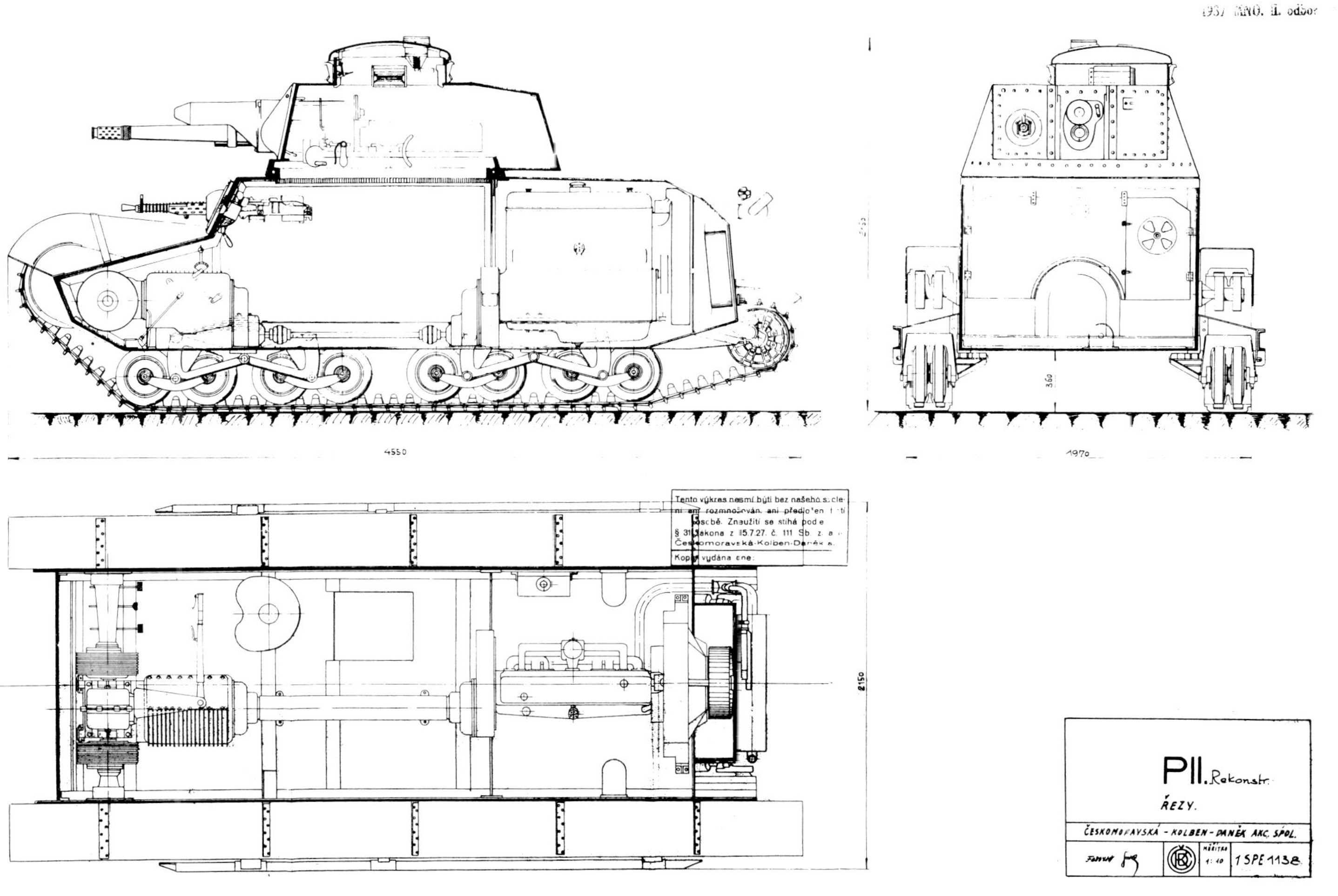

ČKD Light Tank TNH (Exported to Iran)

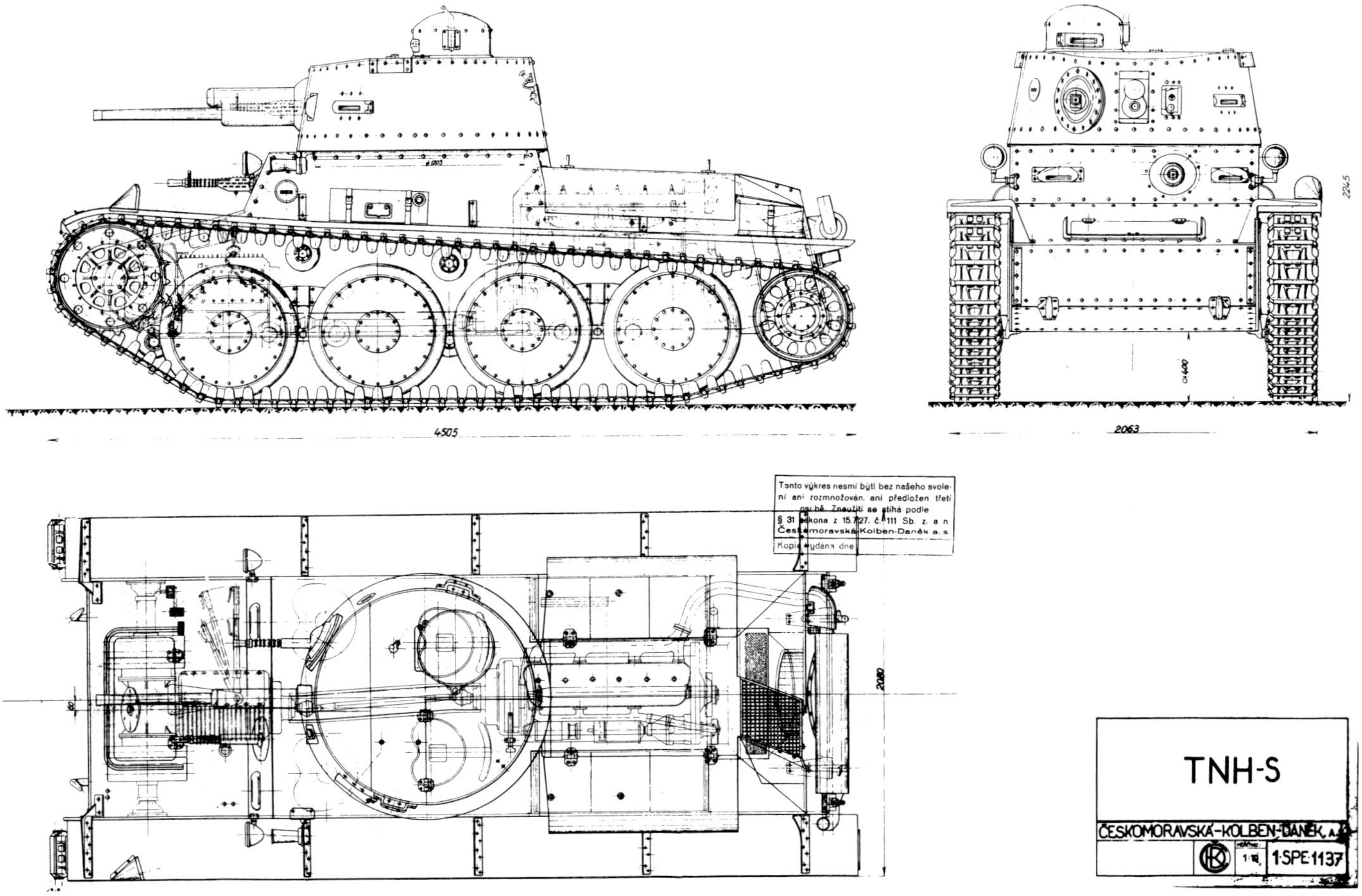

ČKD Light Tank LTP (Exported to Peru)

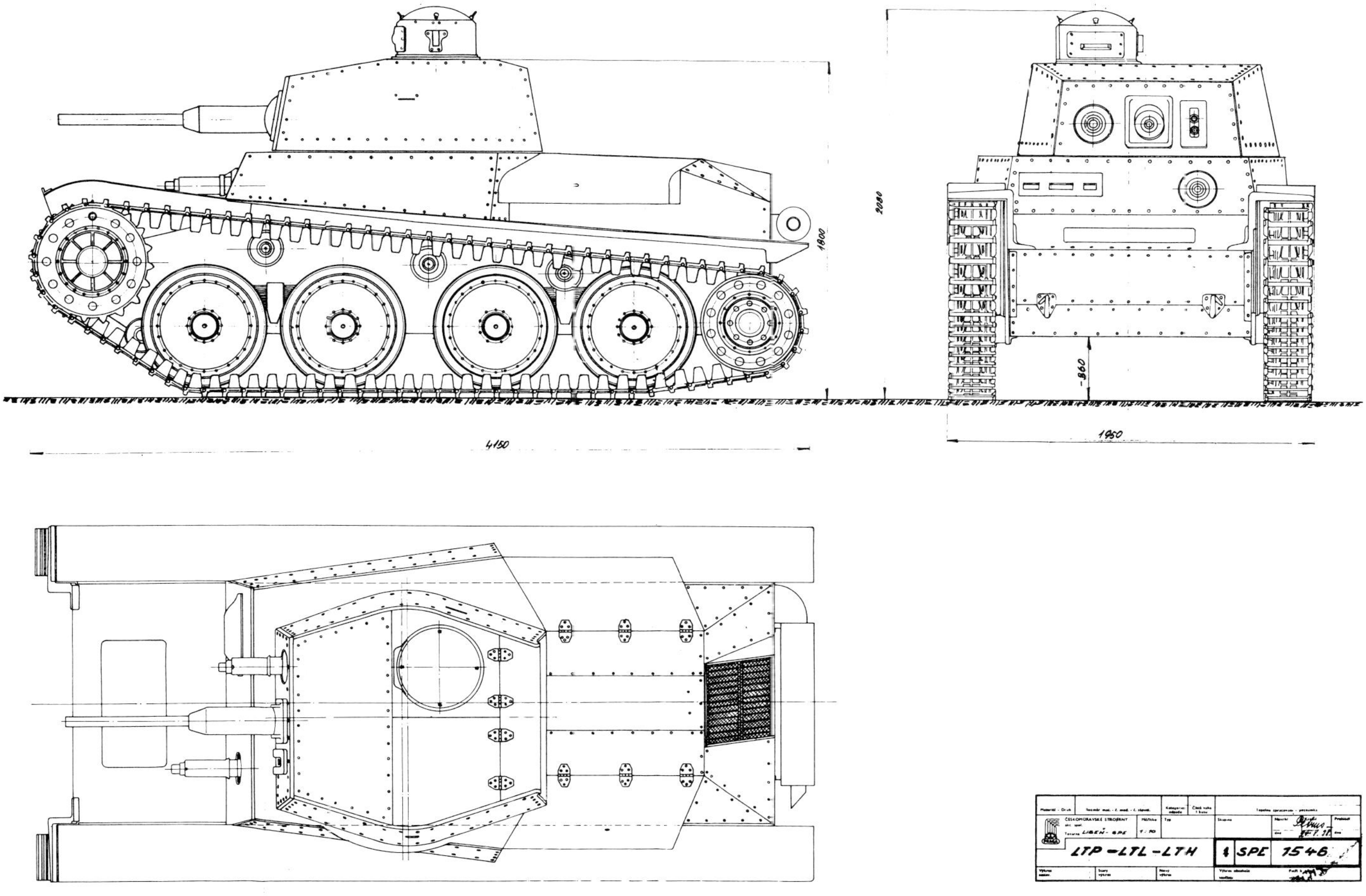

ČKD Light Tank LTH (Exported to Switzerland)

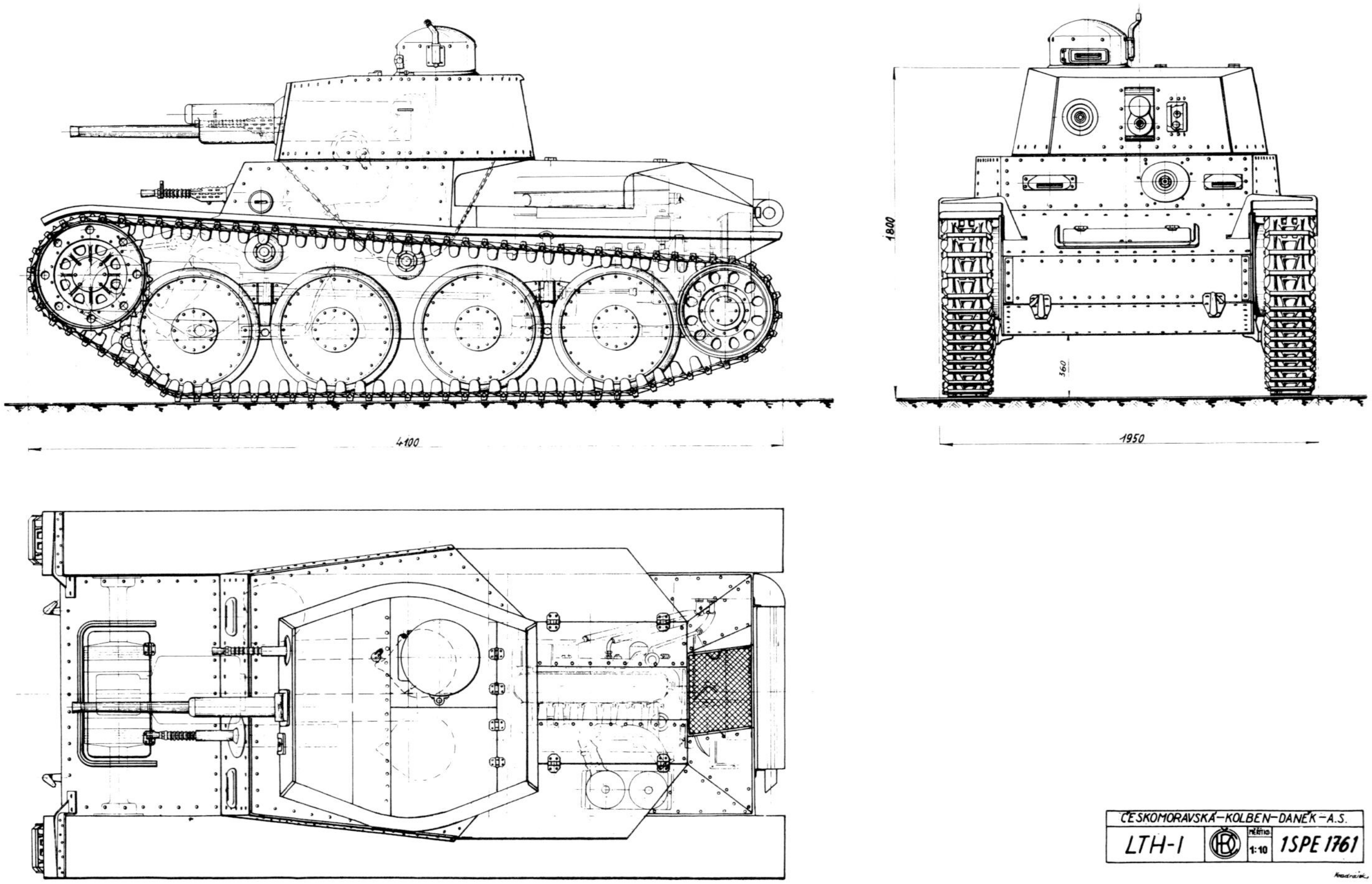

ČKD Light Tank LTL (prototype for Latvia)

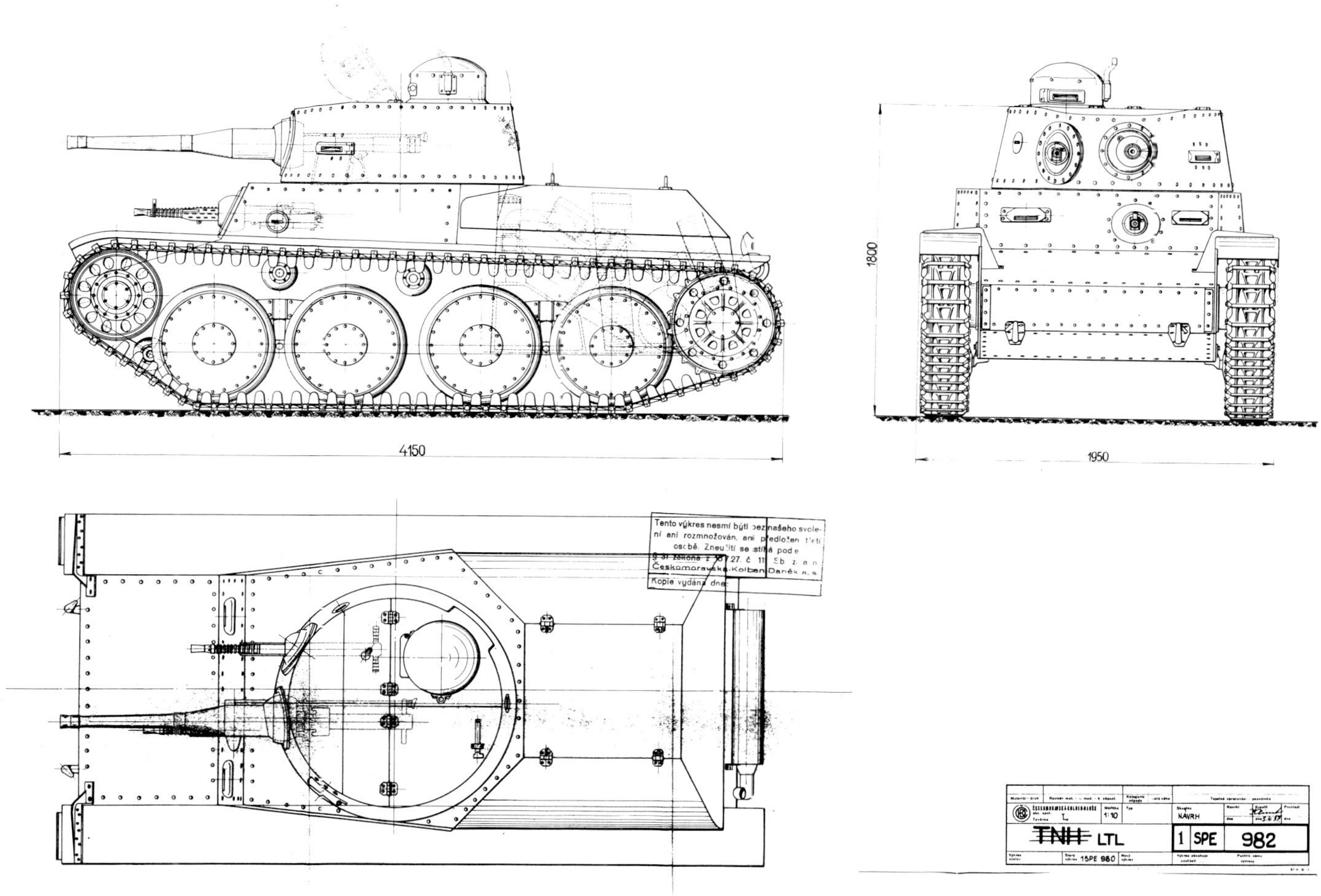

PzKpfw 38(t) Ausf.C

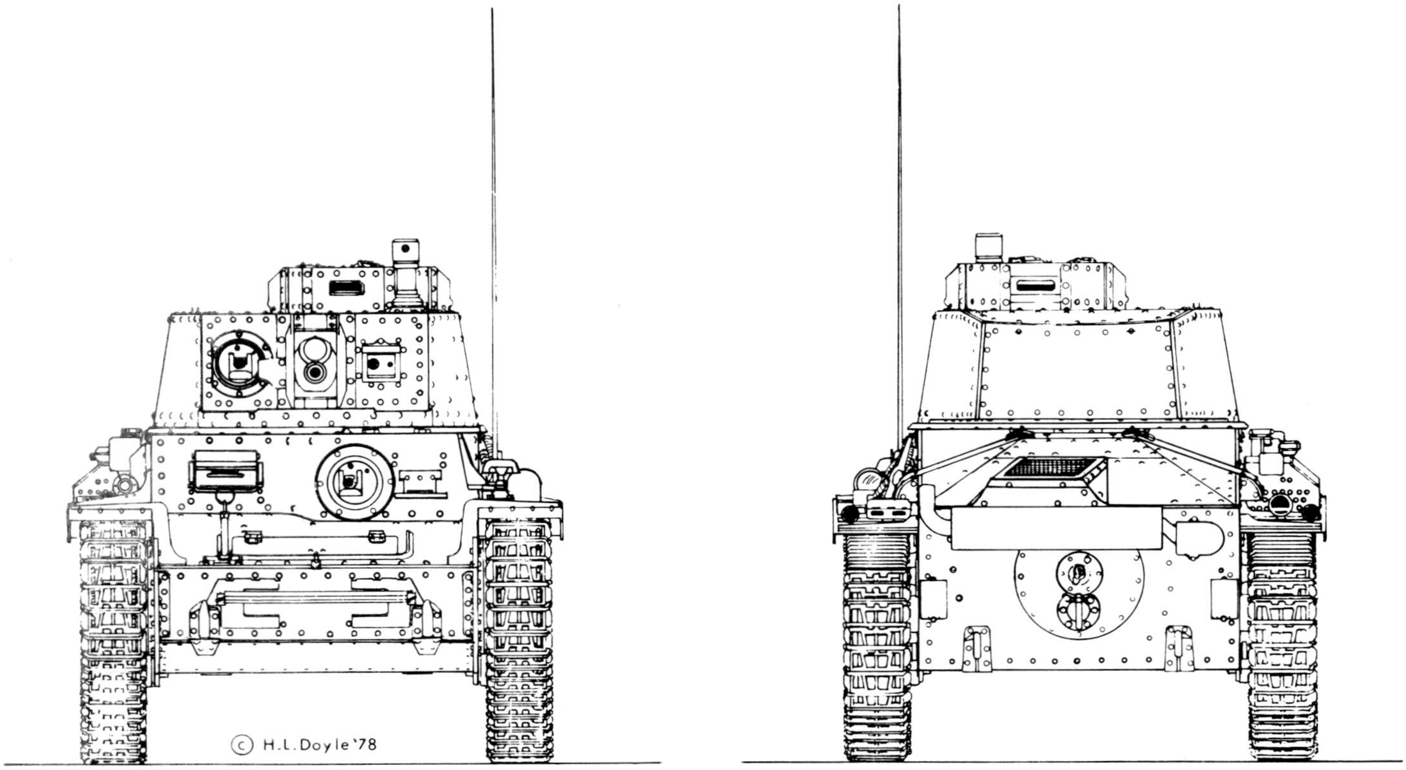

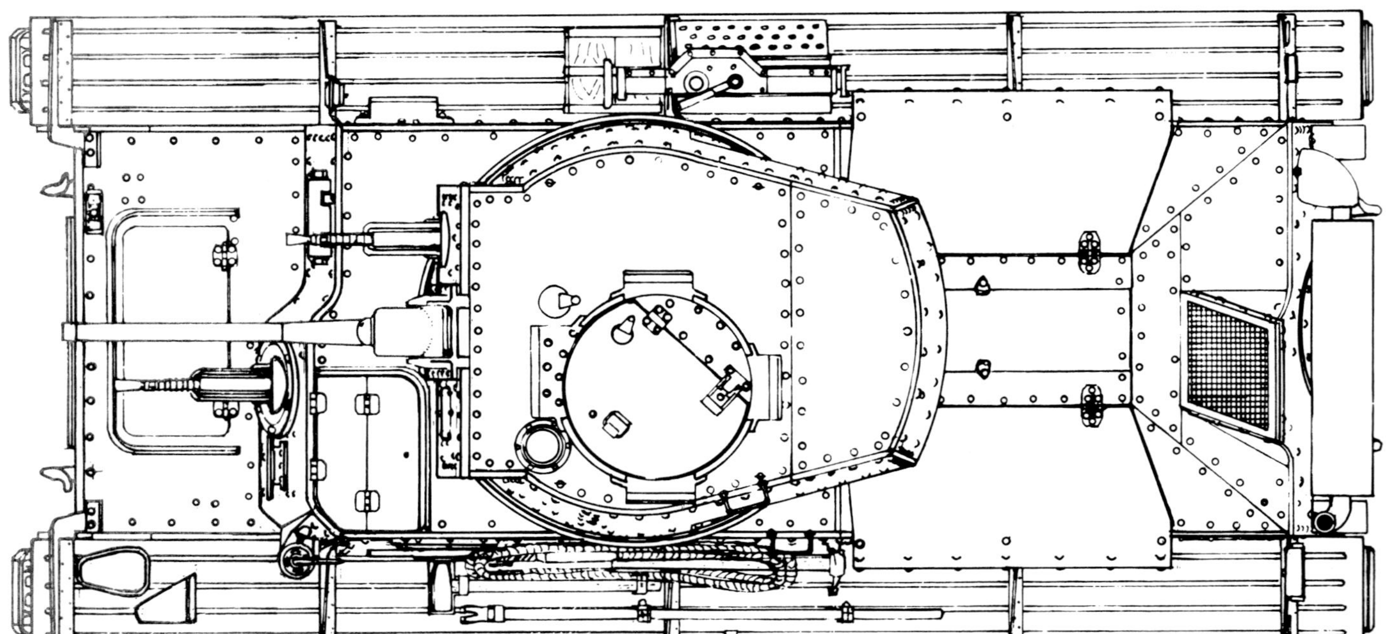

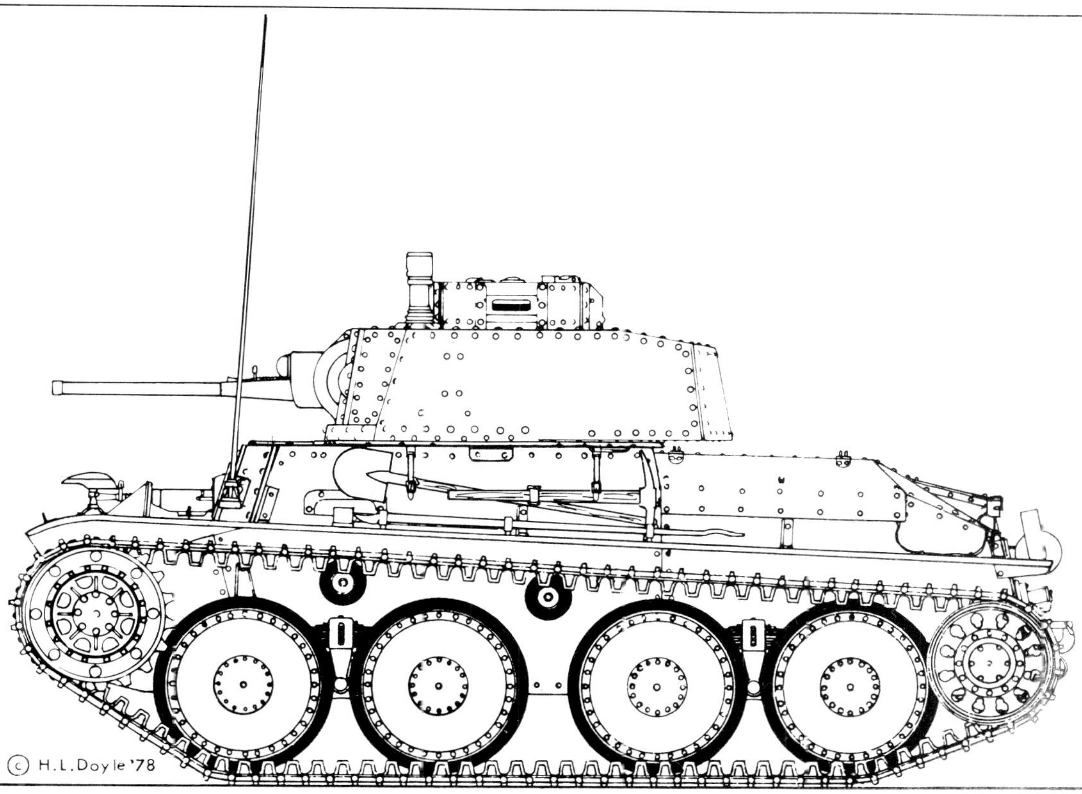

PzKpfw 38(t) Ausf G

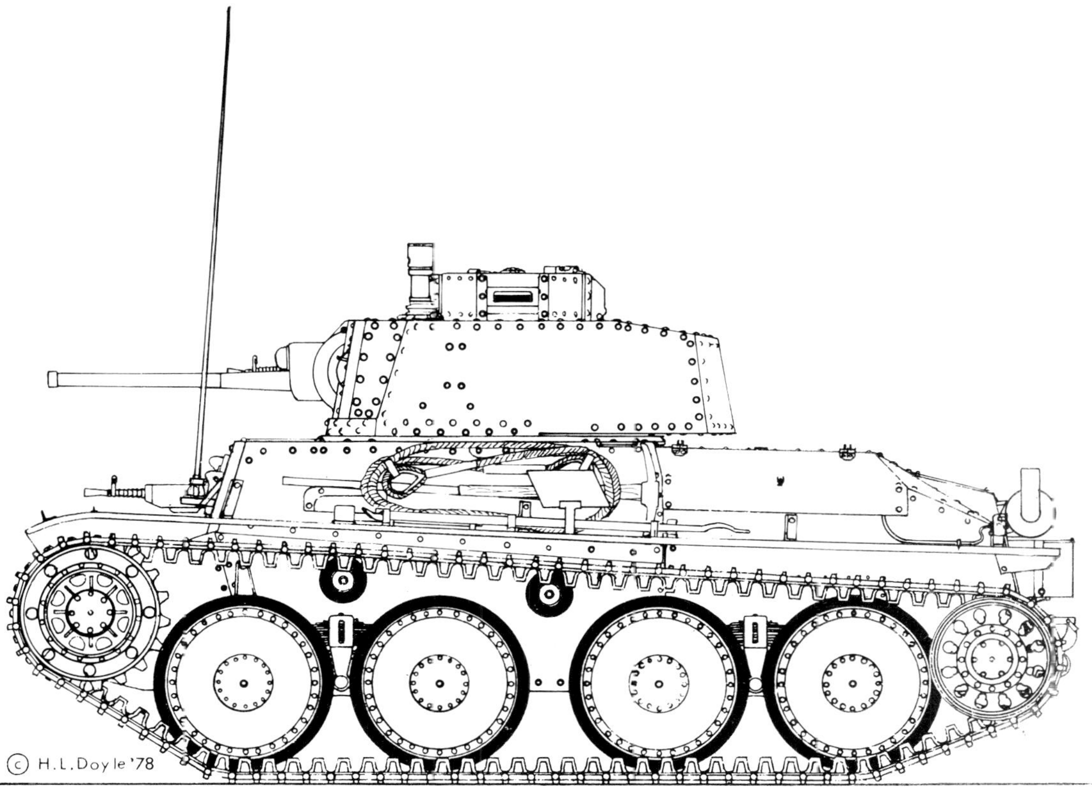

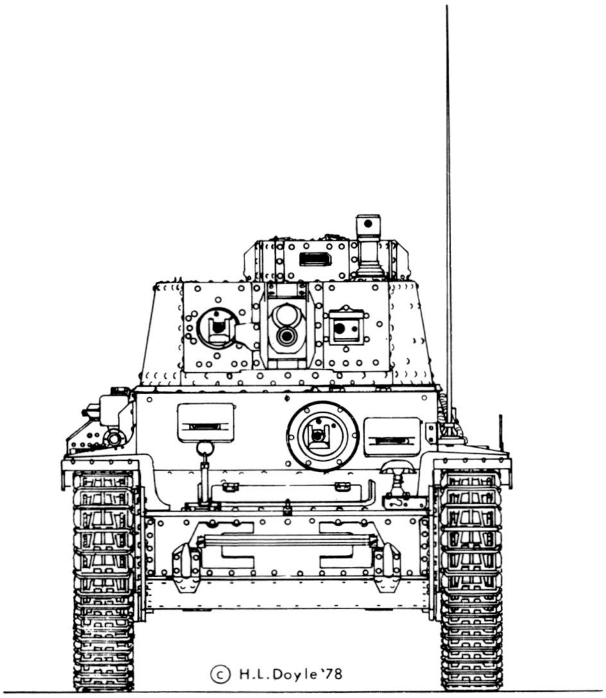
© H.L.Doyle '78

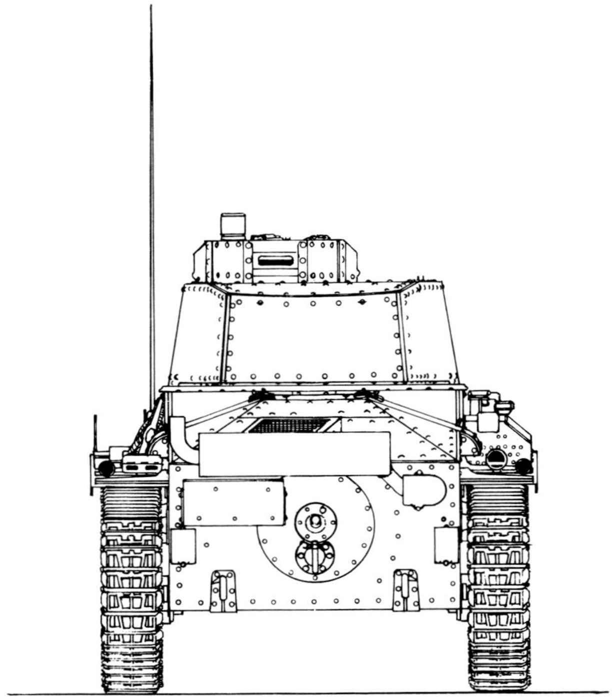

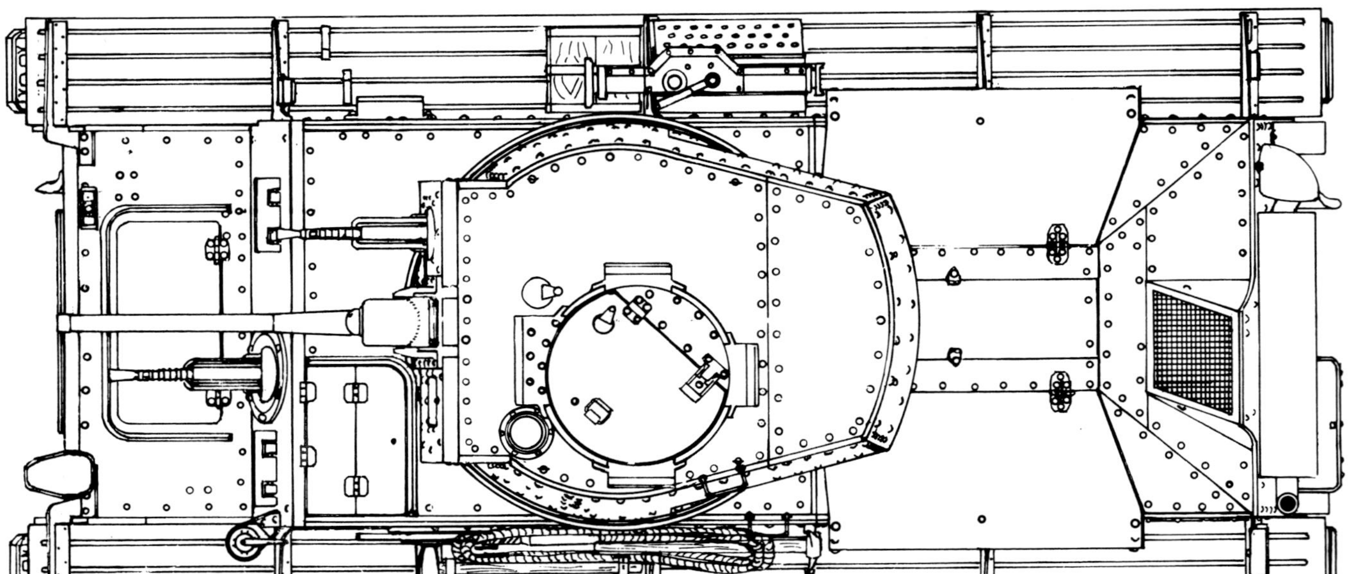

Slovak Light Tank LT-40 (Gun Armed)

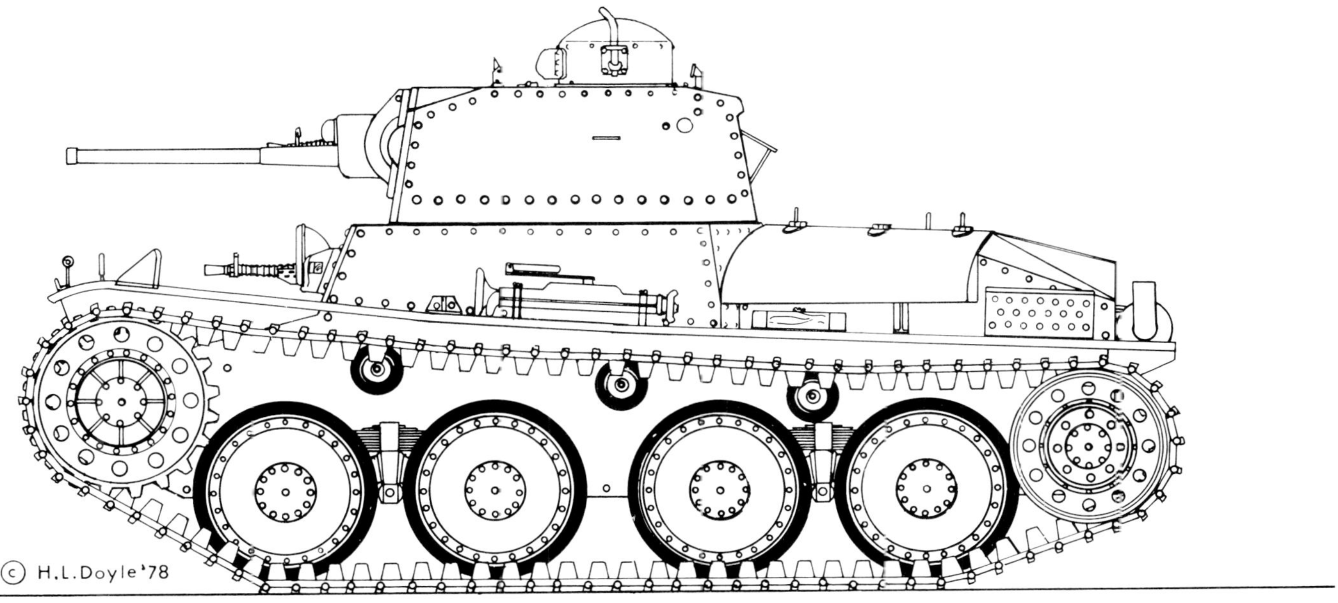

Slovak Light Tank LT-40 (Machine Gun Armed)

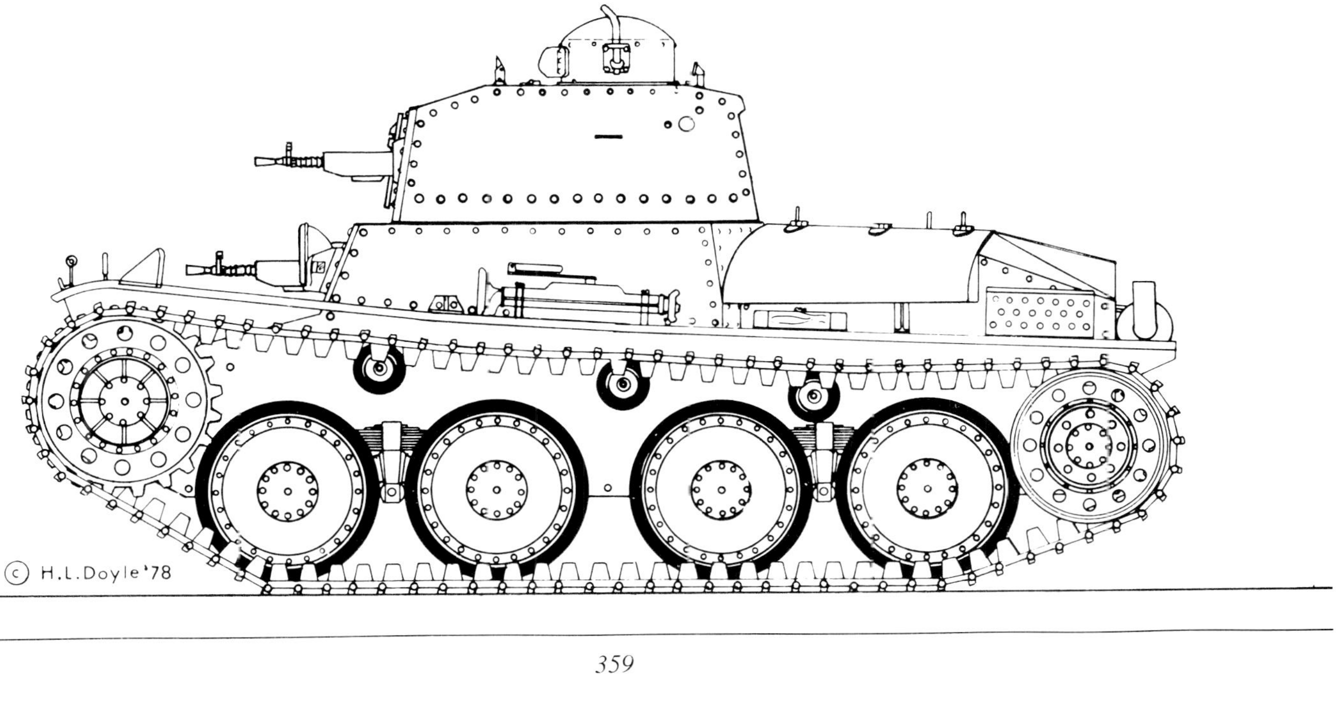

Swedish Light Tank Strv m/41 (ČKD License)

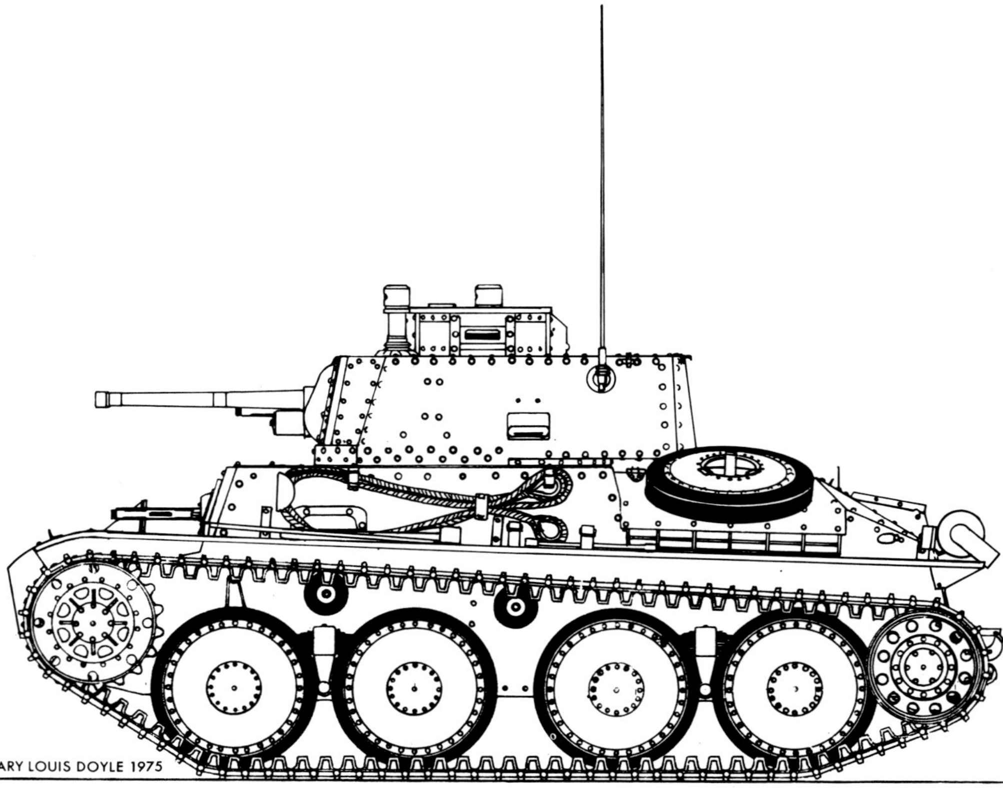

©COPYRIGHT HILARY LOUIS DOYLE 1975

Swedish Light Tank Strv m/41 S II (ČKD License)

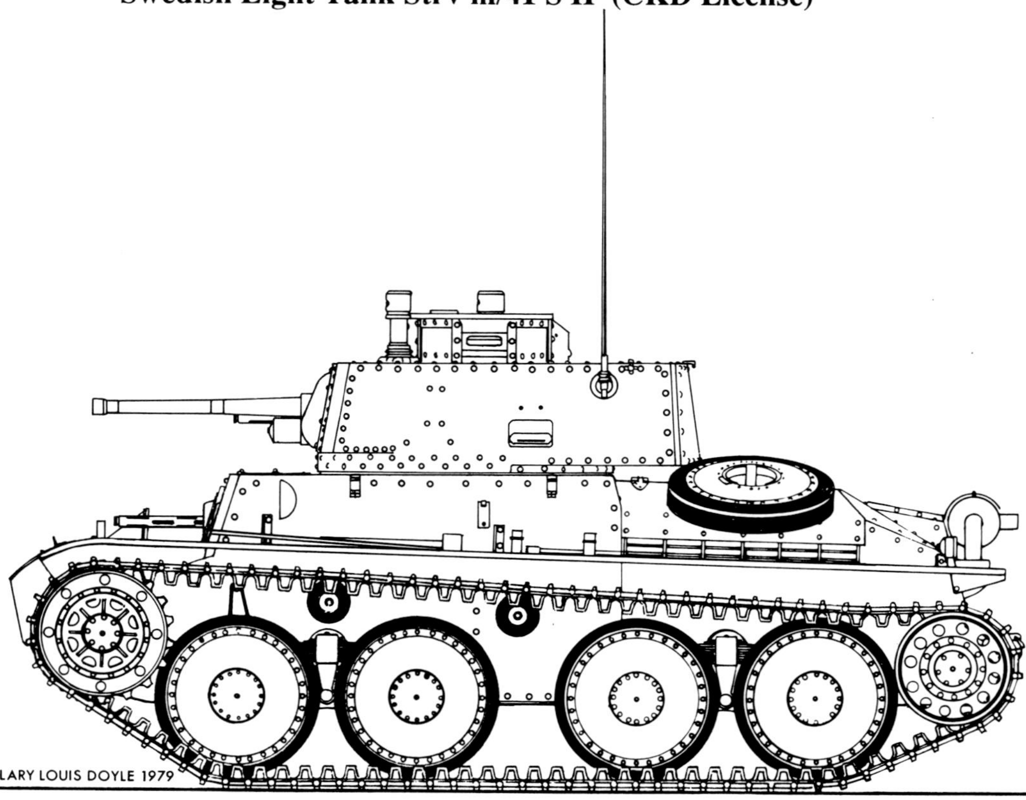

©COPYRIGHT HILARY LOUIS DOYLE 1979

Swedish Assault Gun Sav m/43

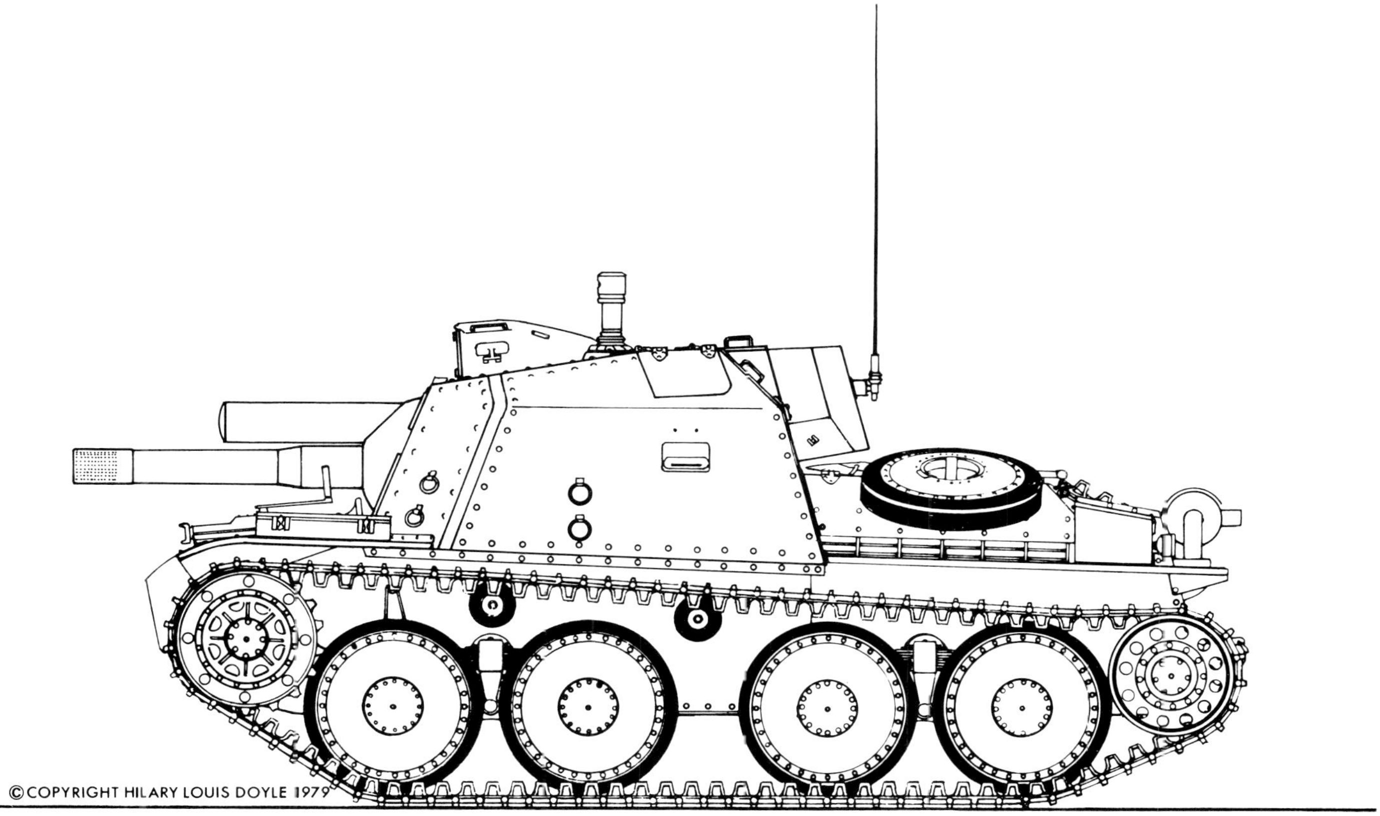

ČKD Medium Tank V-8-H

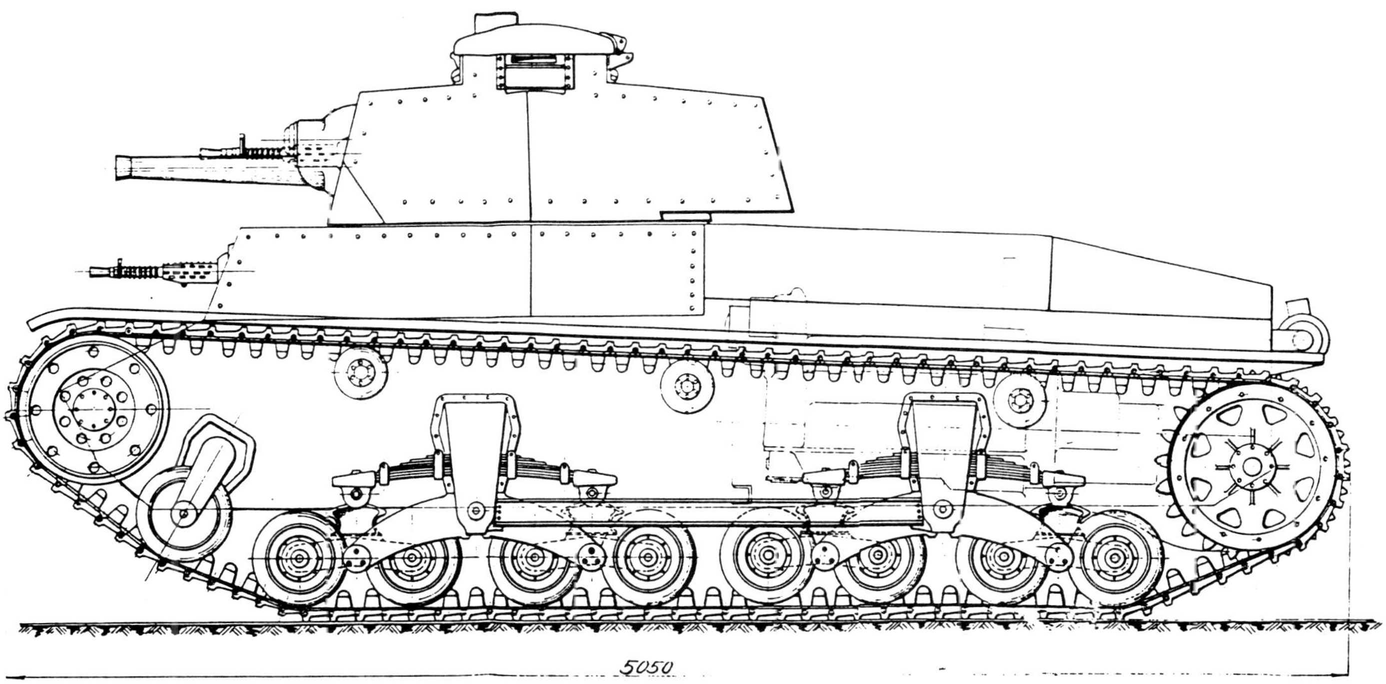

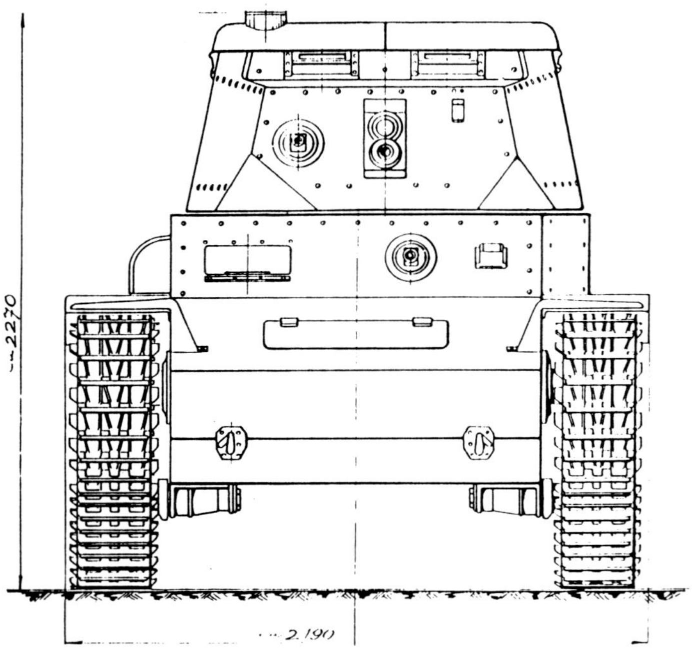
~2270
~2.190

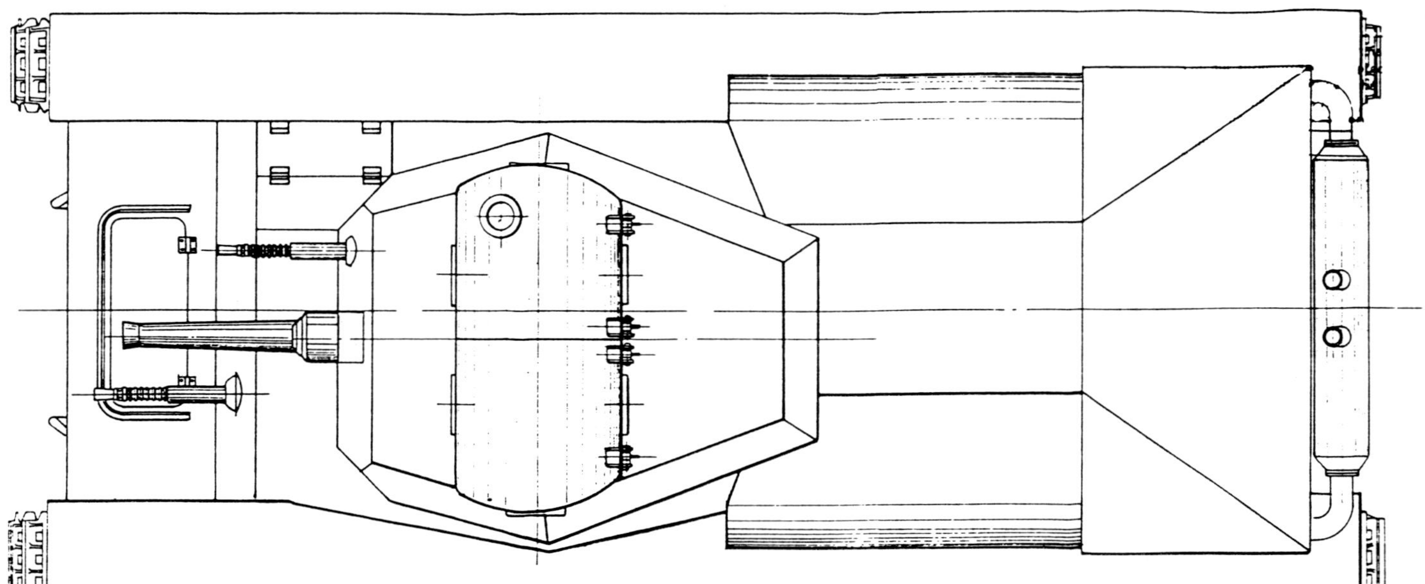

Panzerjäger 38(t) für 7.62 cm PAK 36(r) - SdKfz 139

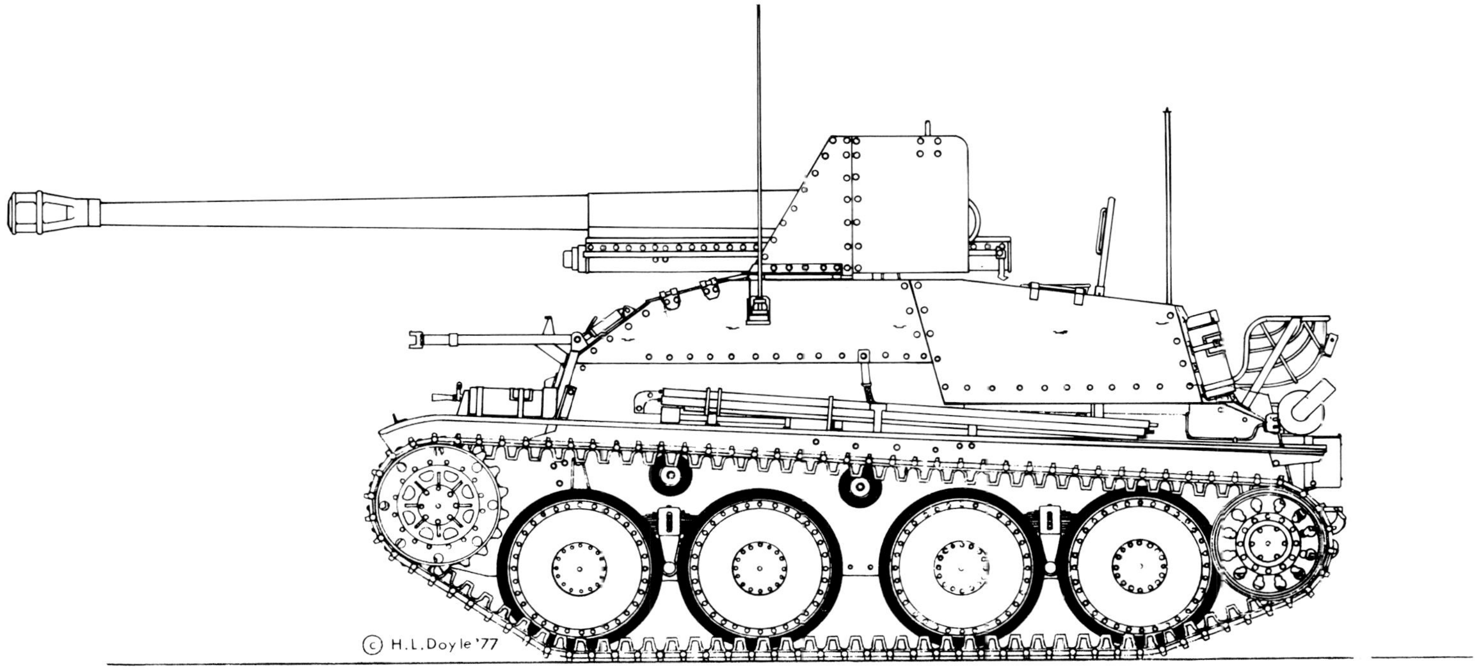

7.5 cm PAK 40/3 auf PzKpfw 38(t) Ausf.H - SdKfz 138

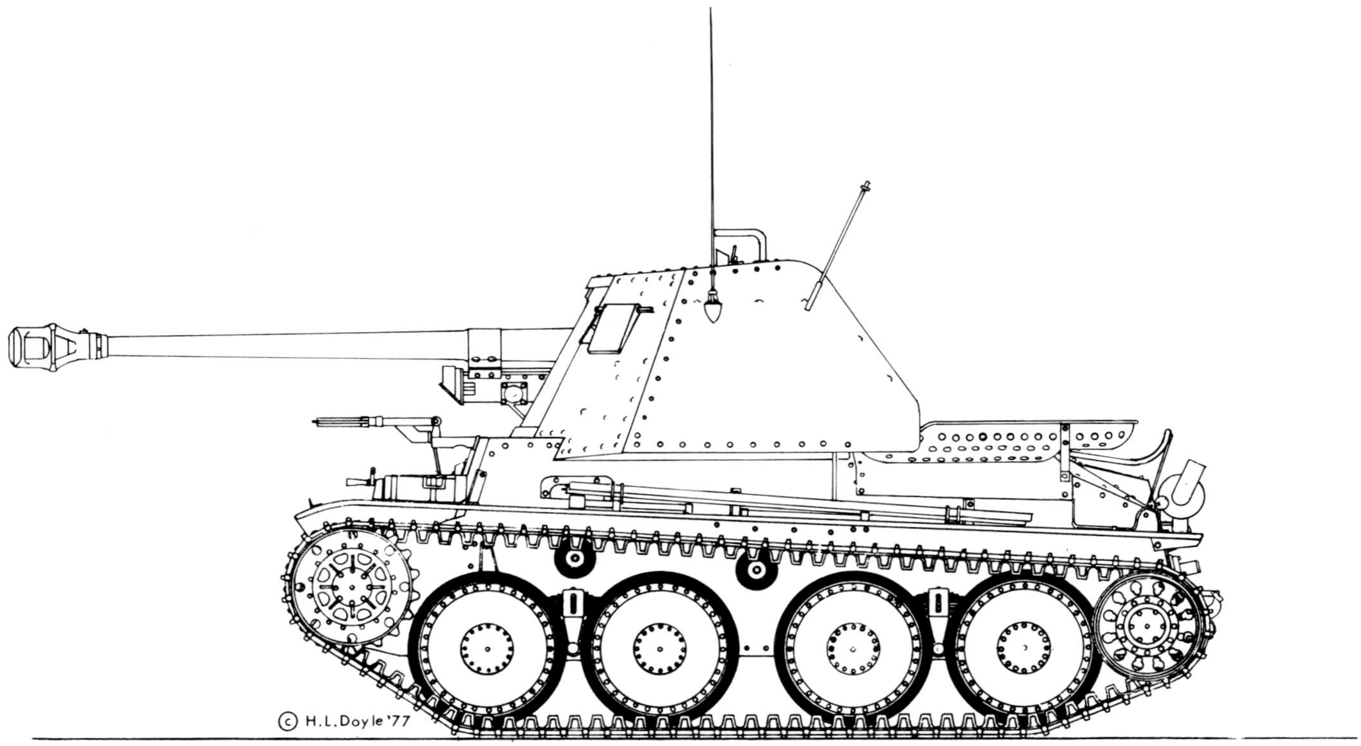

Panzerjäger 38(t) mit 7.5 cm PAK 40/3 Ausf M - SdKfz 138

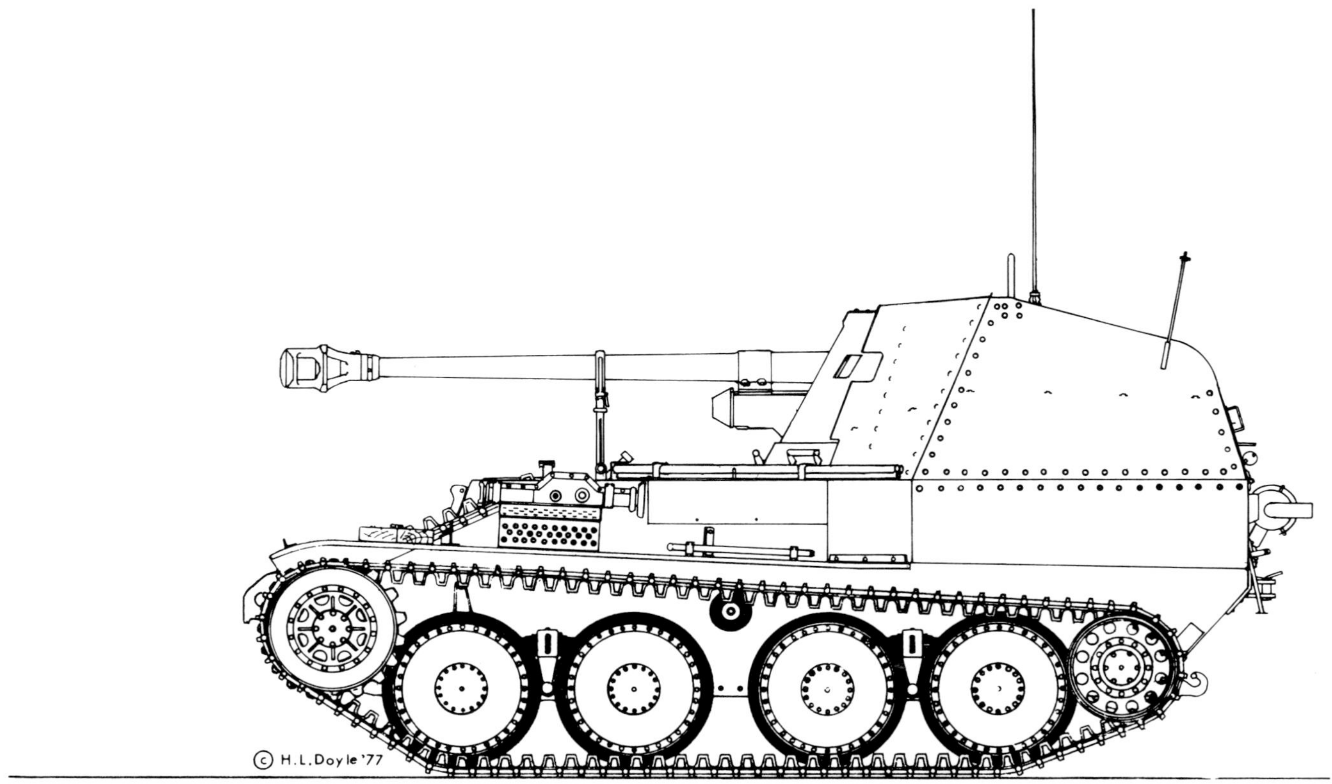

15 cm sIG 33(Sfl) auf PzKpfw 38(t) Ausf H Grille - SdKfz138/1

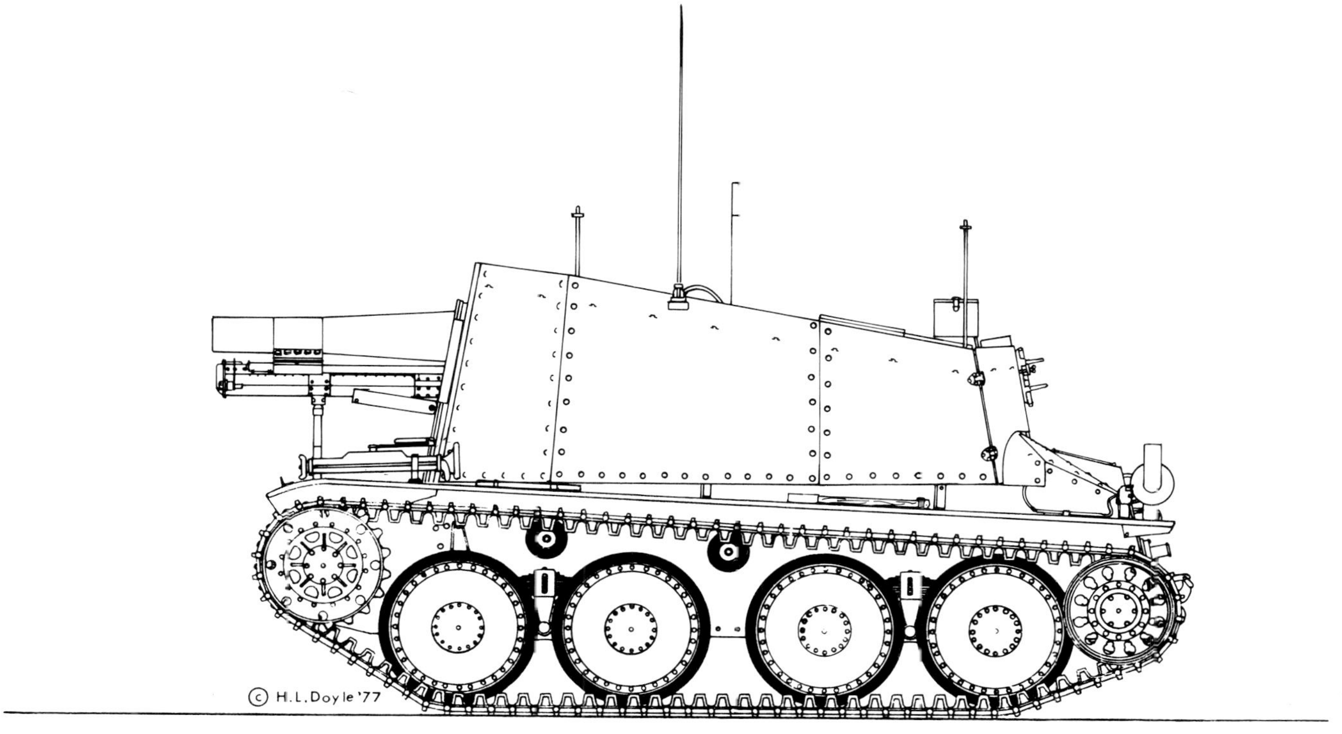

15 cm sIG 33(Sfl) auf PzKpfw 38(t) Ausf M Grille - SdKfz138/1

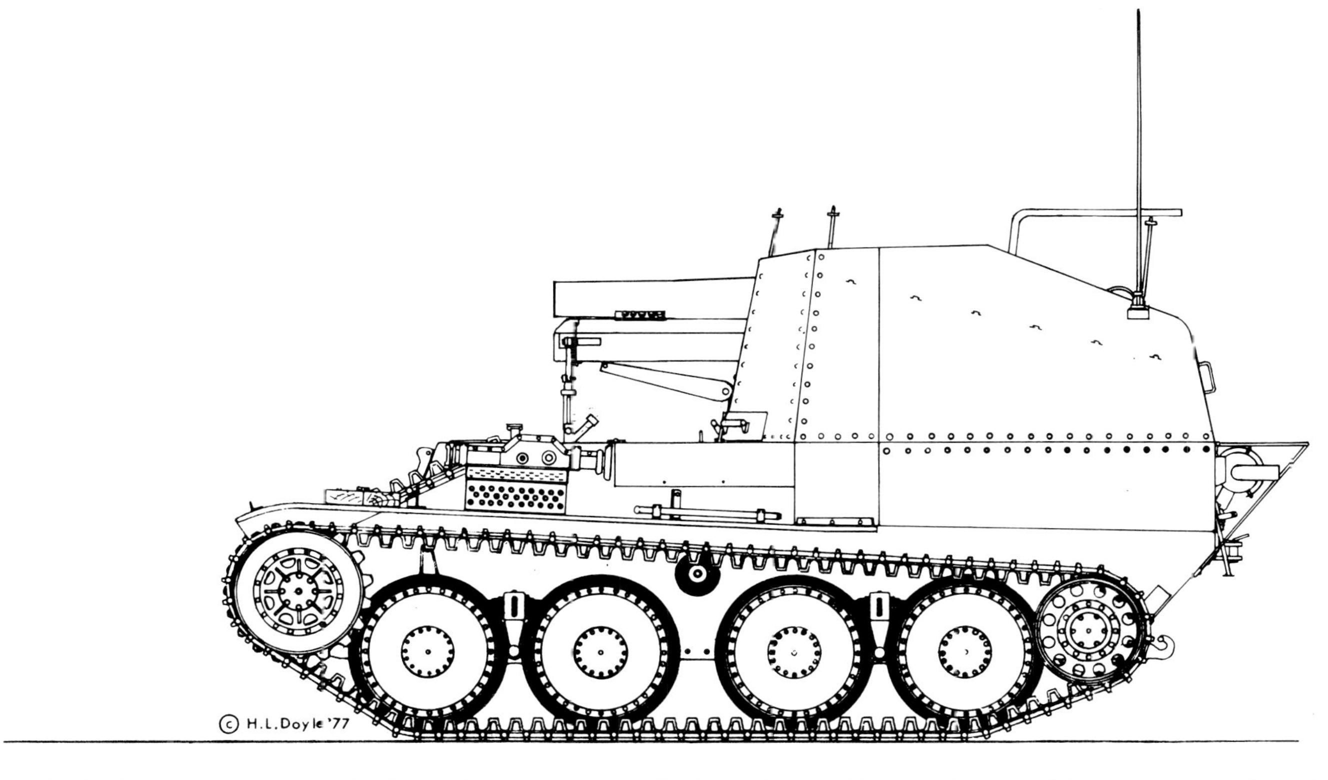

Flakpanzer 38(t) auf Selbsfahrlafette 38(t) Ausf M - SdKfz 140

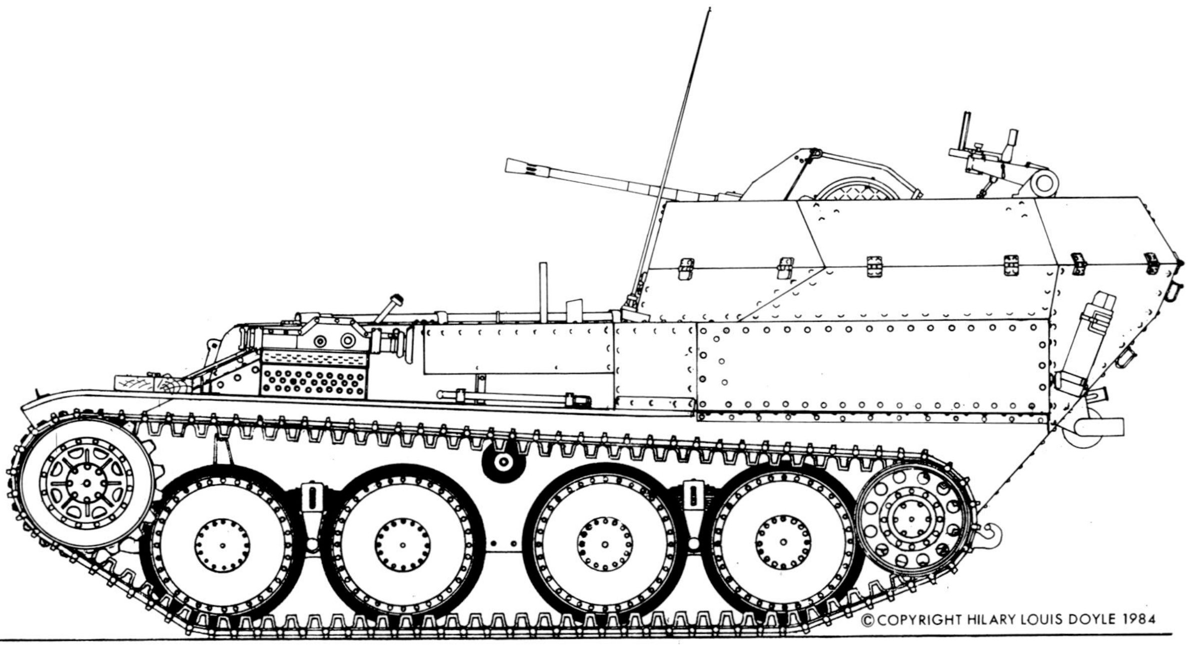

©COPYRIGHT HILARY LOUIS DOYLE 1984

Aufklärer auf PzKpfw 38(t) mit 2 cm KwK 38 - SdKfz 140/1

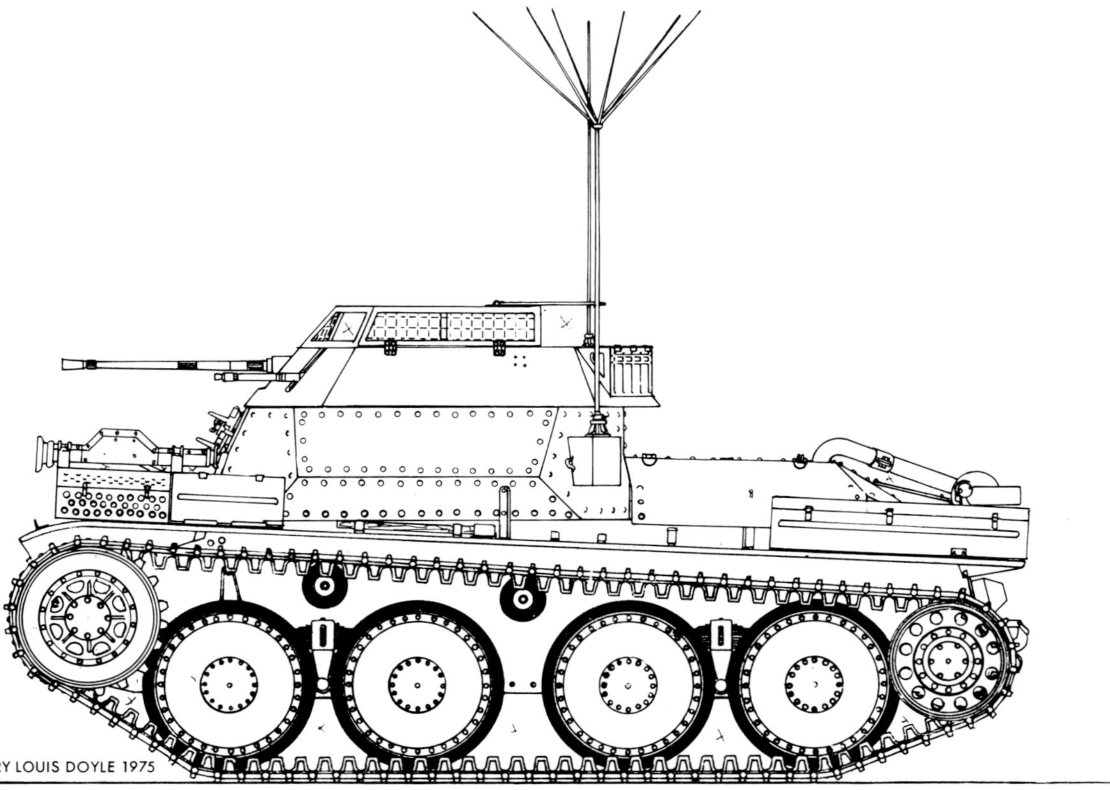

©COPYRIGHT HILARY LOUIS DOYLE 1975

Aufklärer auf PzKpfw 38(t) mit 7.5 cm K51- SdKfz 140/1 - Prototype

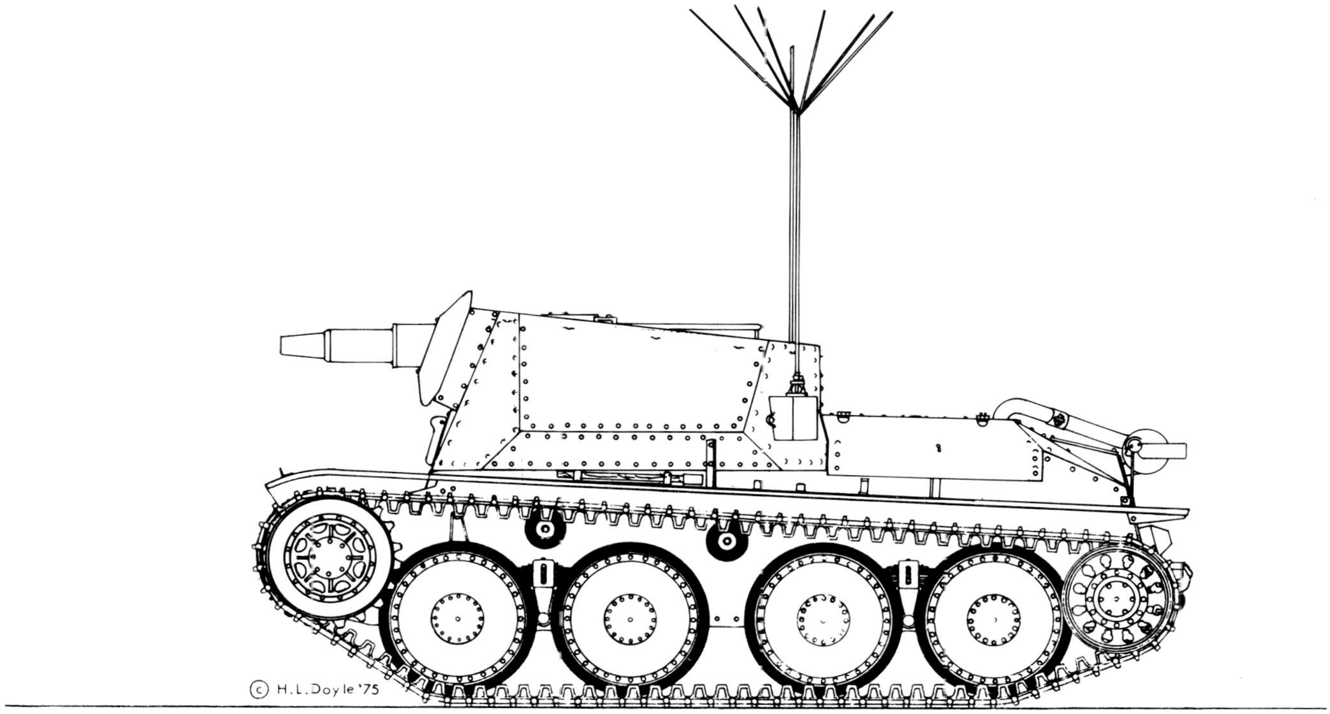

Mörserträger auf Fahrgestell PzKpfw 38(t) - Prototype

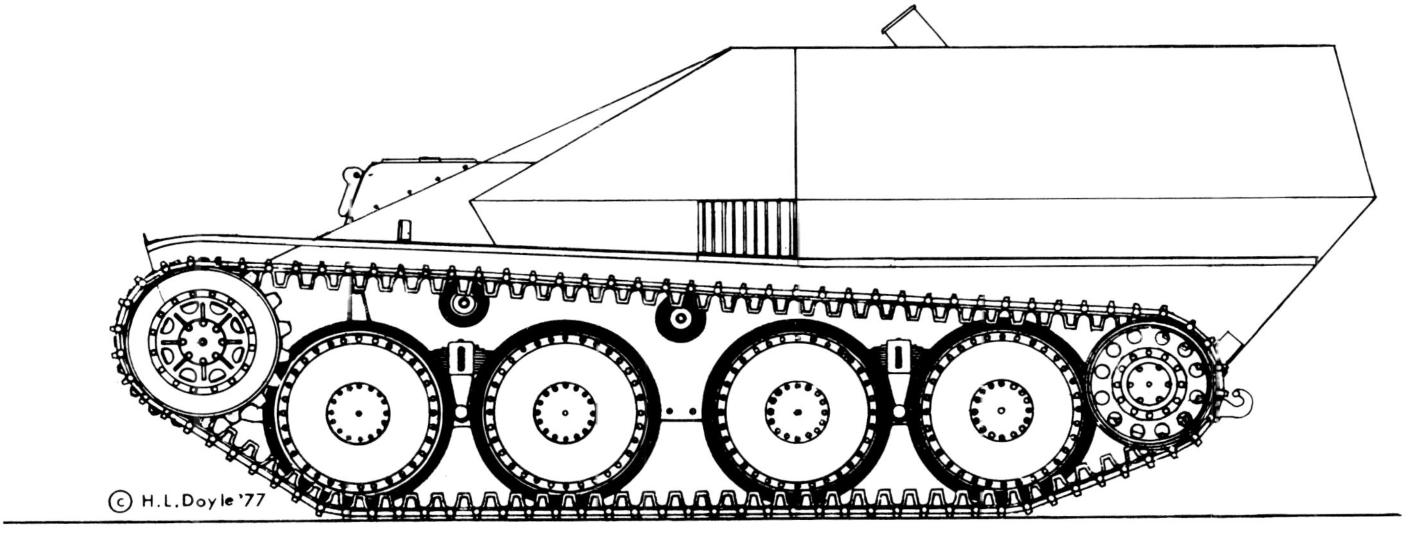

Reconnaissance Tank BMM TNHnA

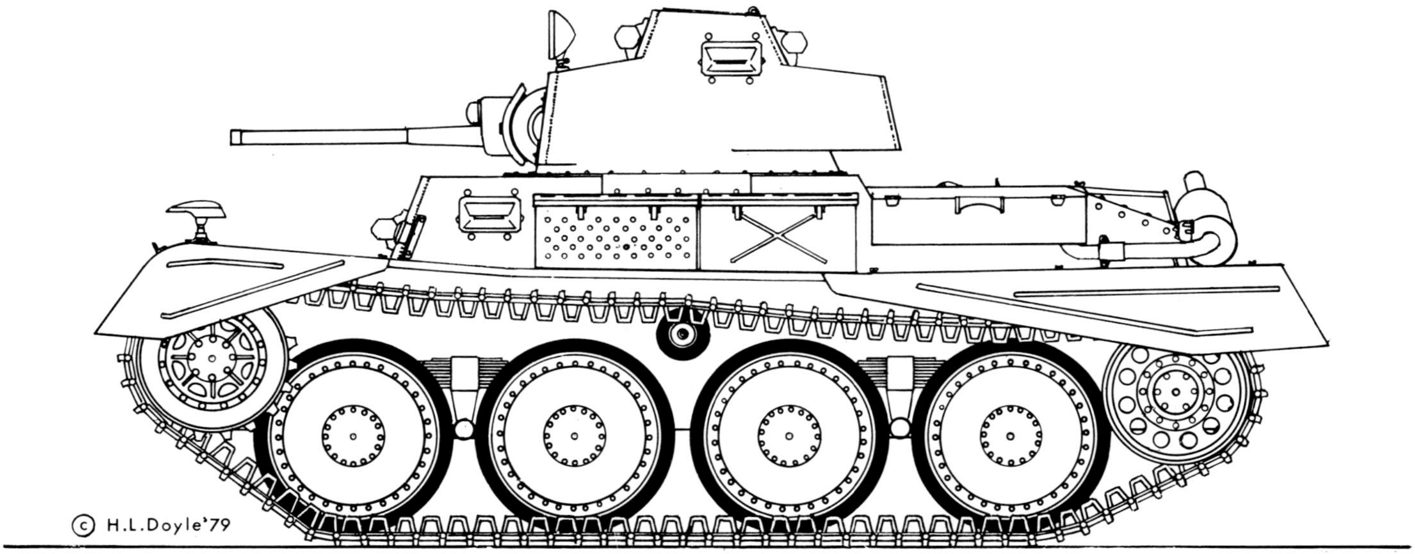

Reconaissance Tank Škoda T-15

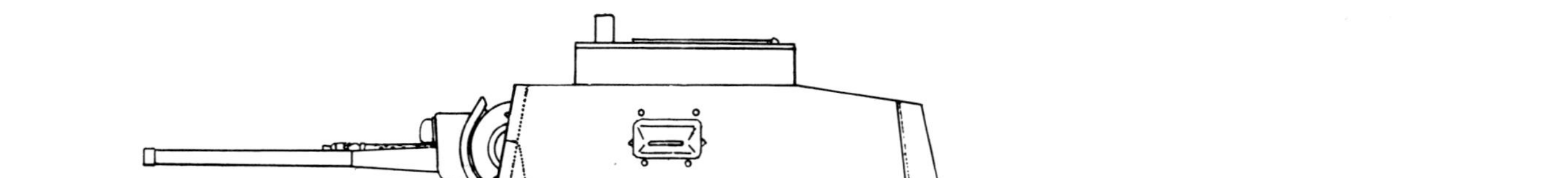

Jagdpanzer 38(t)

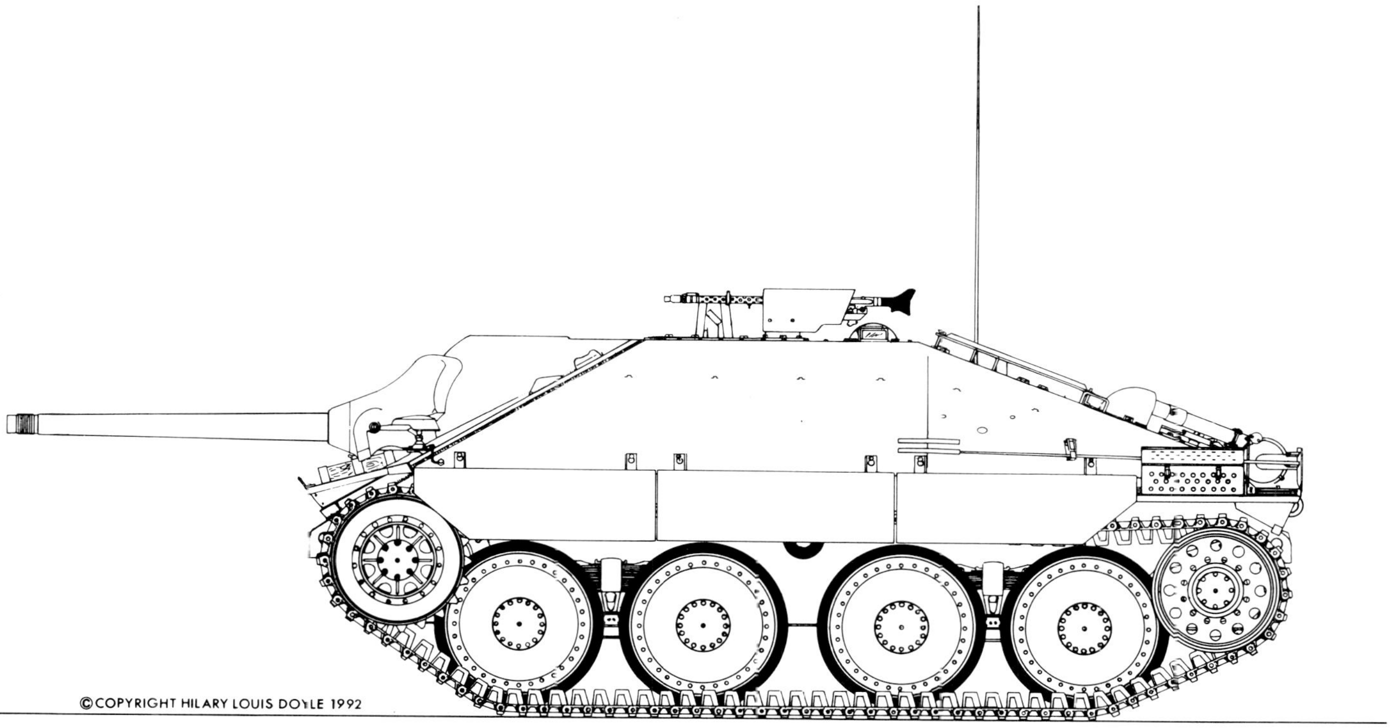

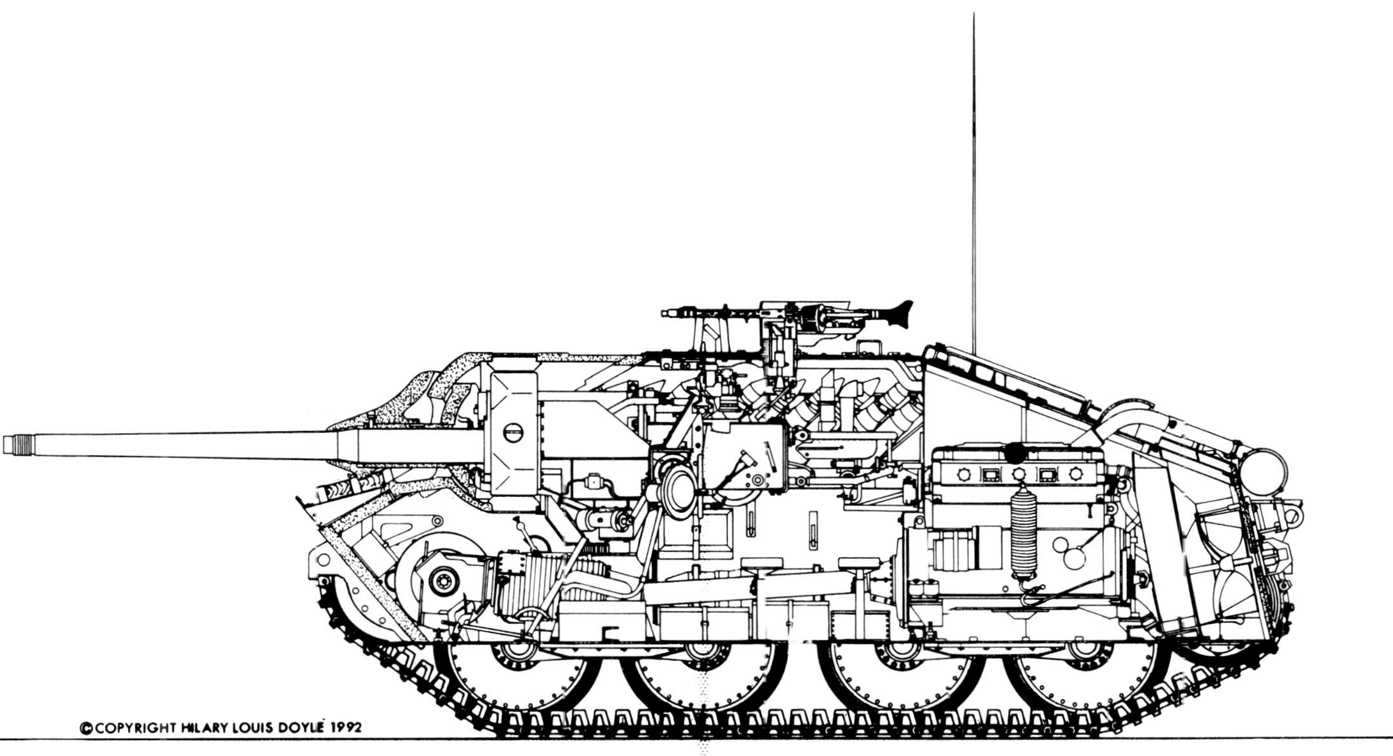

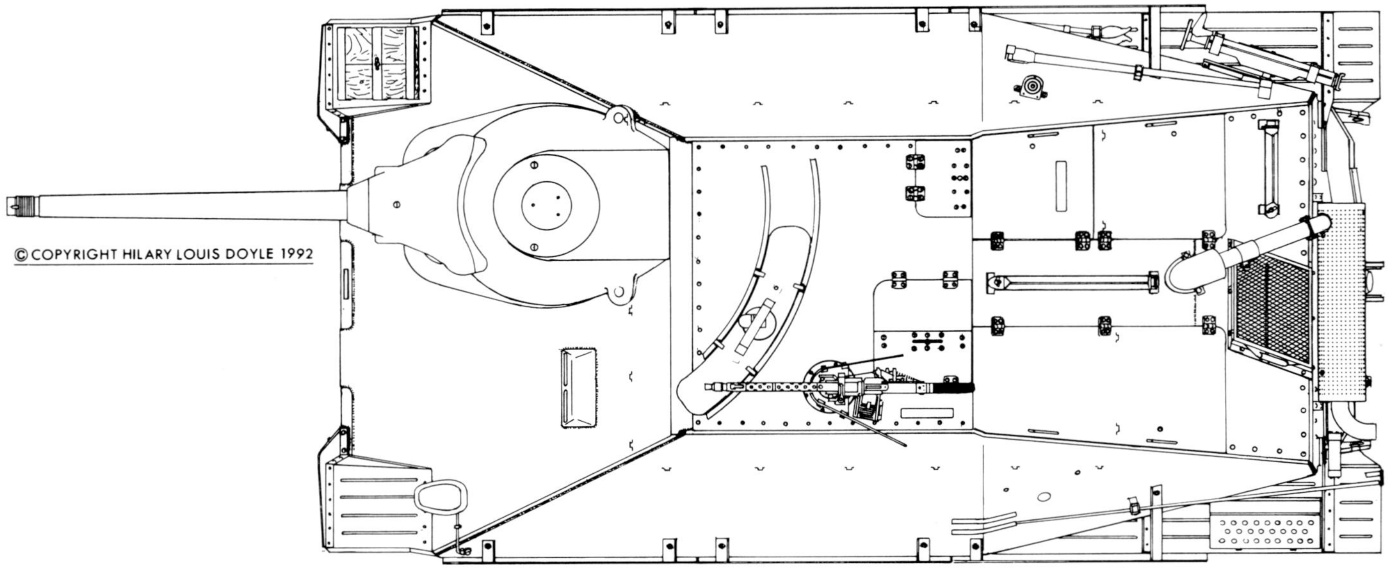
©COPYRIGHT HILARY LOUIS DOYLE 1992

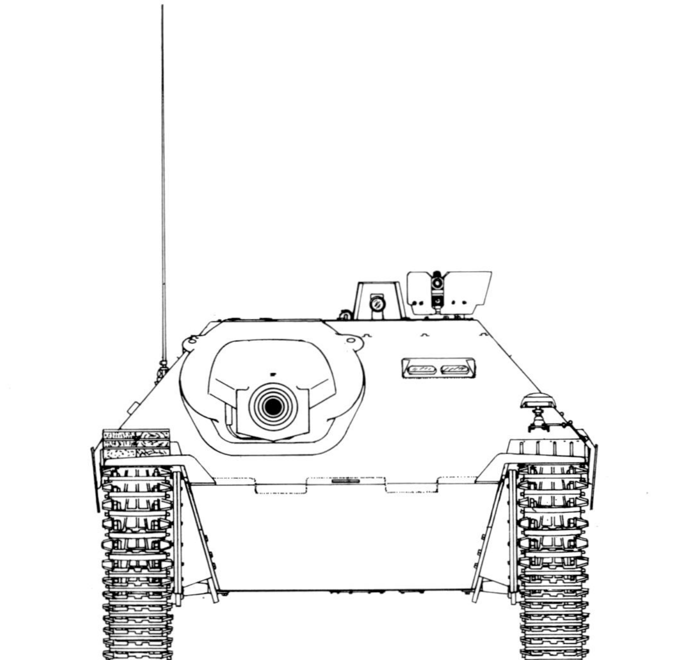
©COPYRIGHT HILARY LOUIS DOYLE 1992

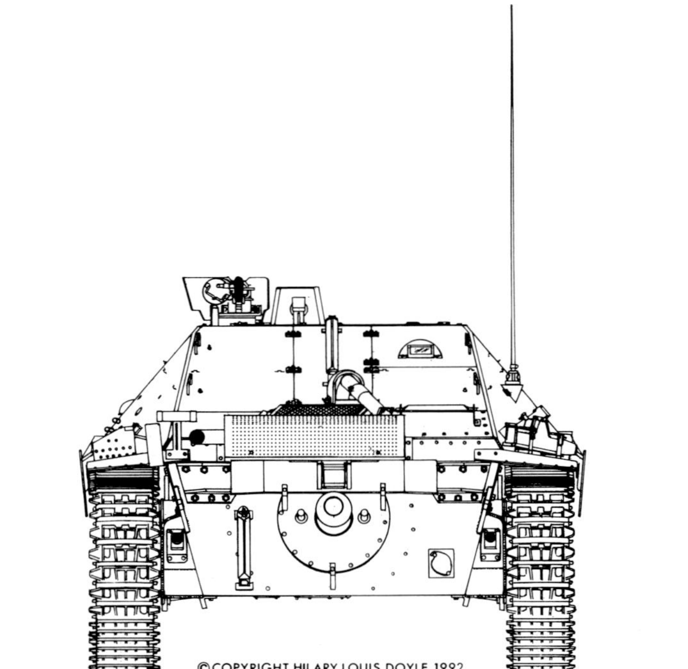
©COPYRIGHT HILARY LOUIS DOYLE 1992

Jagdpanzer 38(t) Staar

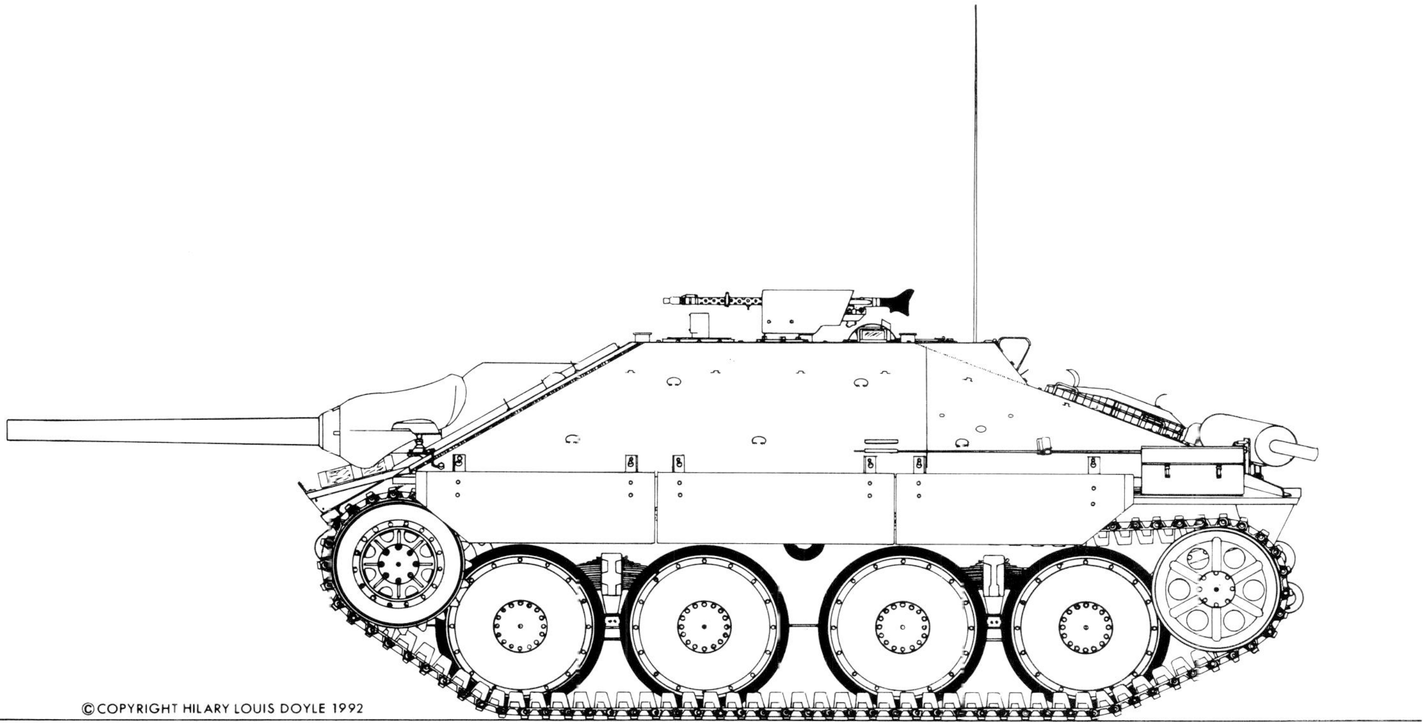

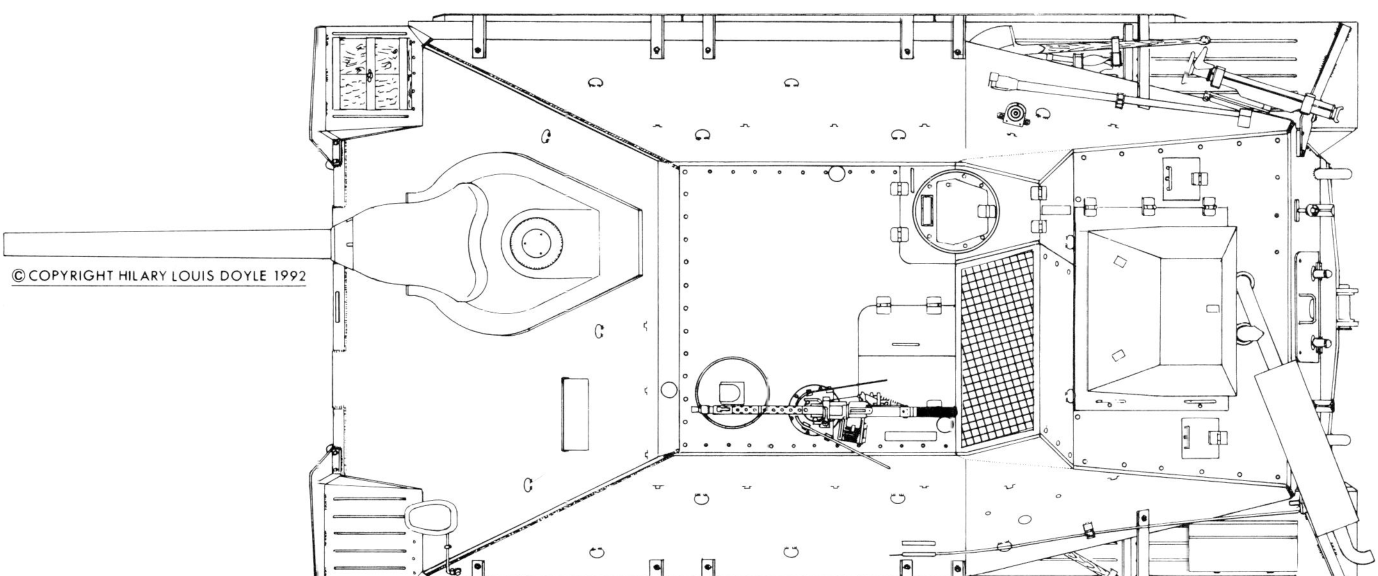

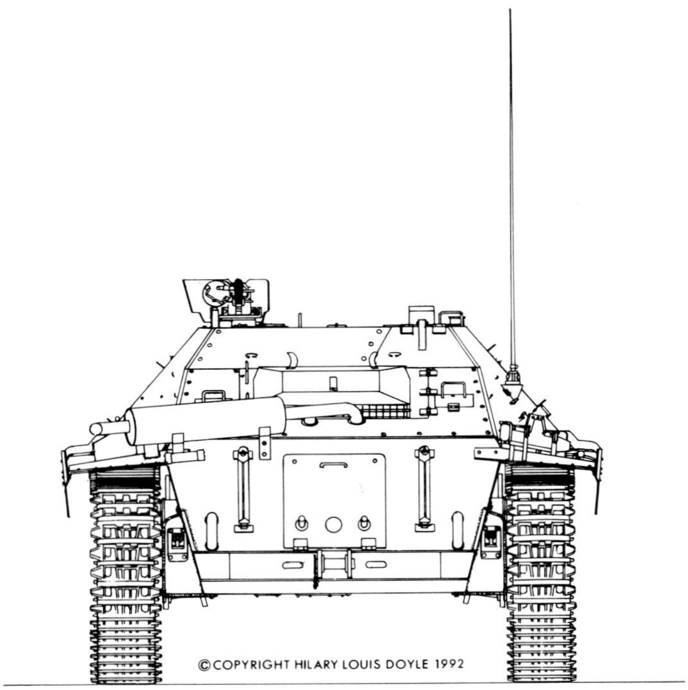

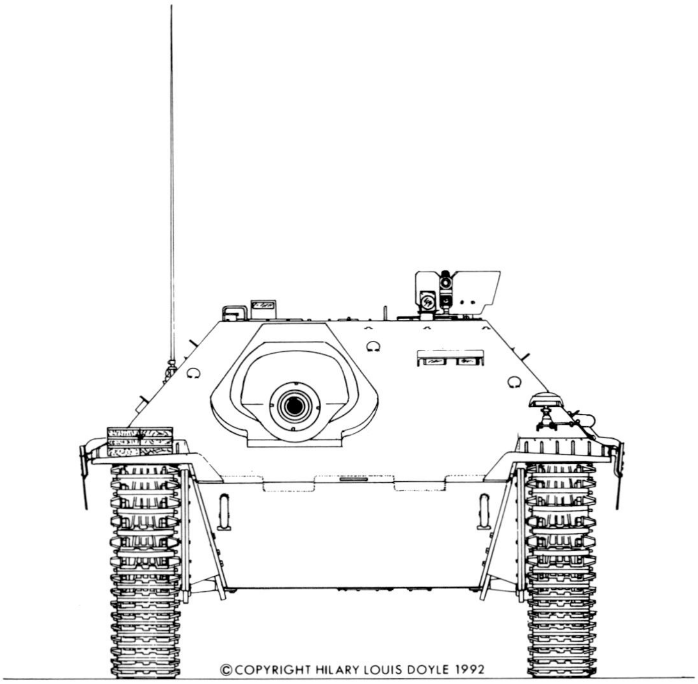

15 cm sIG 33/2 (Sf) auf Jagdpanzer 38(t)

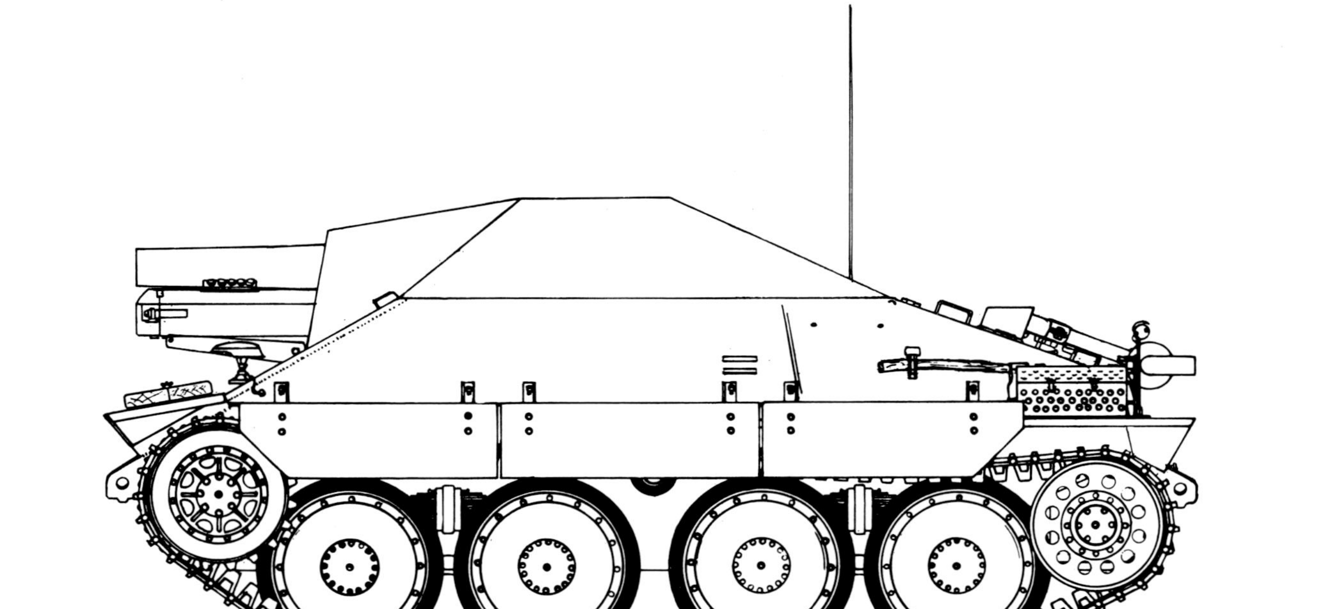

Bergepanzer 38(t)

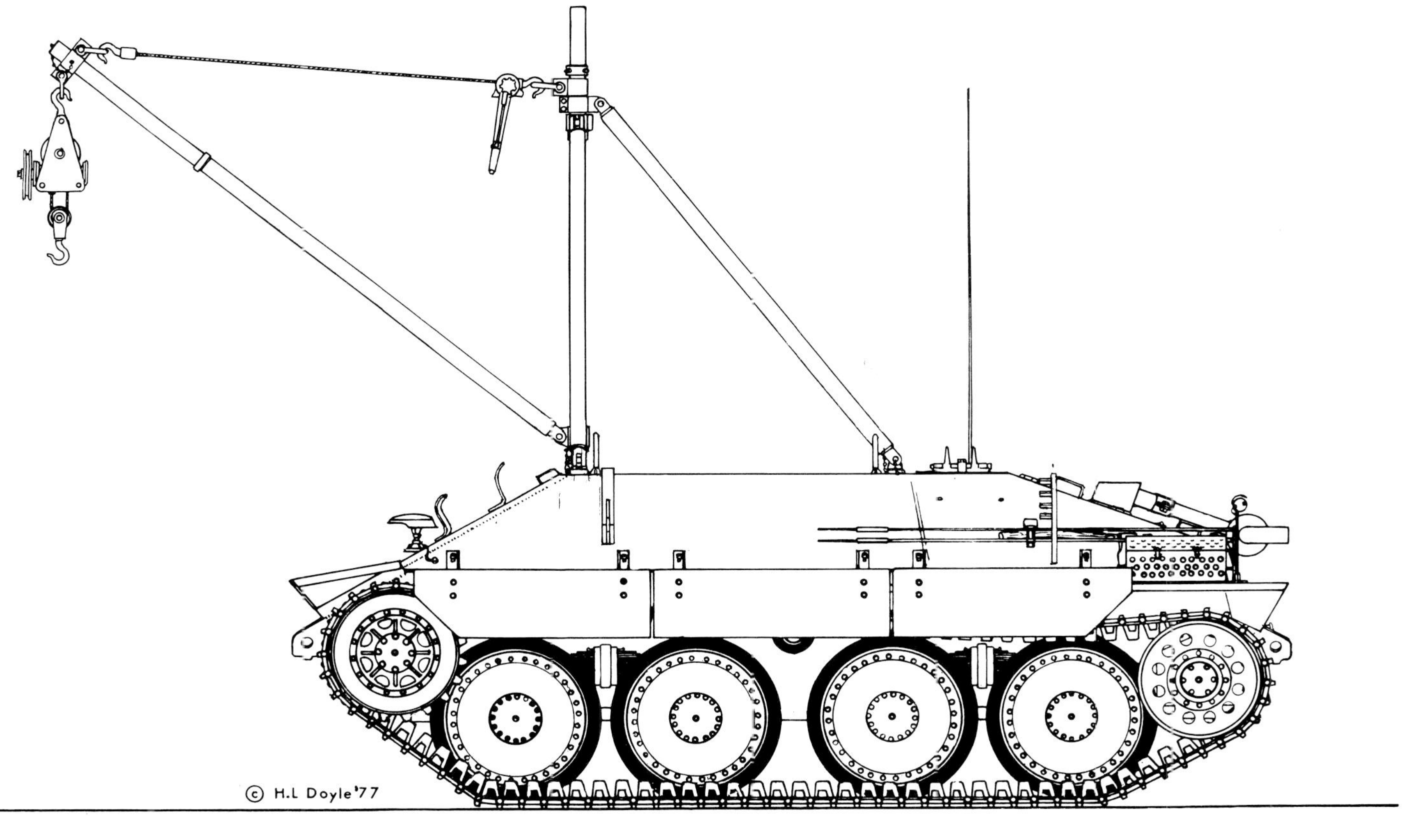

Aufklärungspanzer 38(t) - Prototype

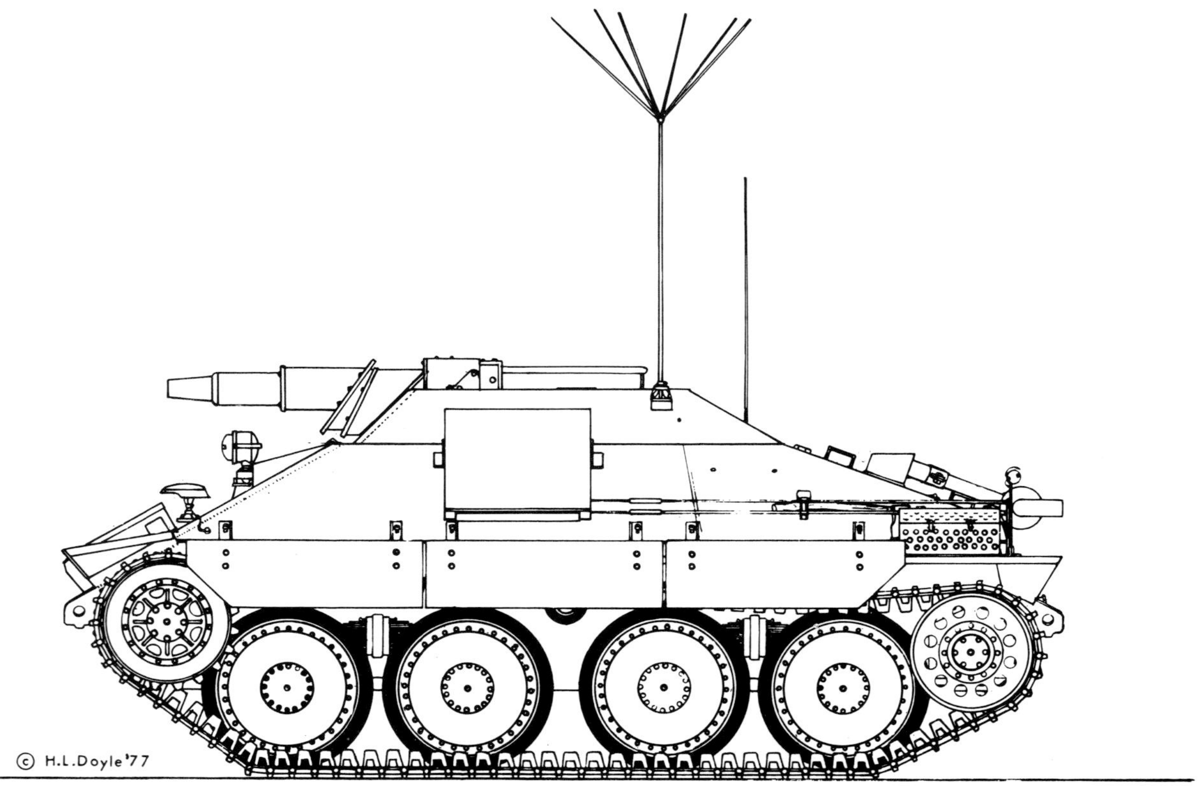

Sturmhaubitze 10.5 cm StuH 42/2 - Prototype

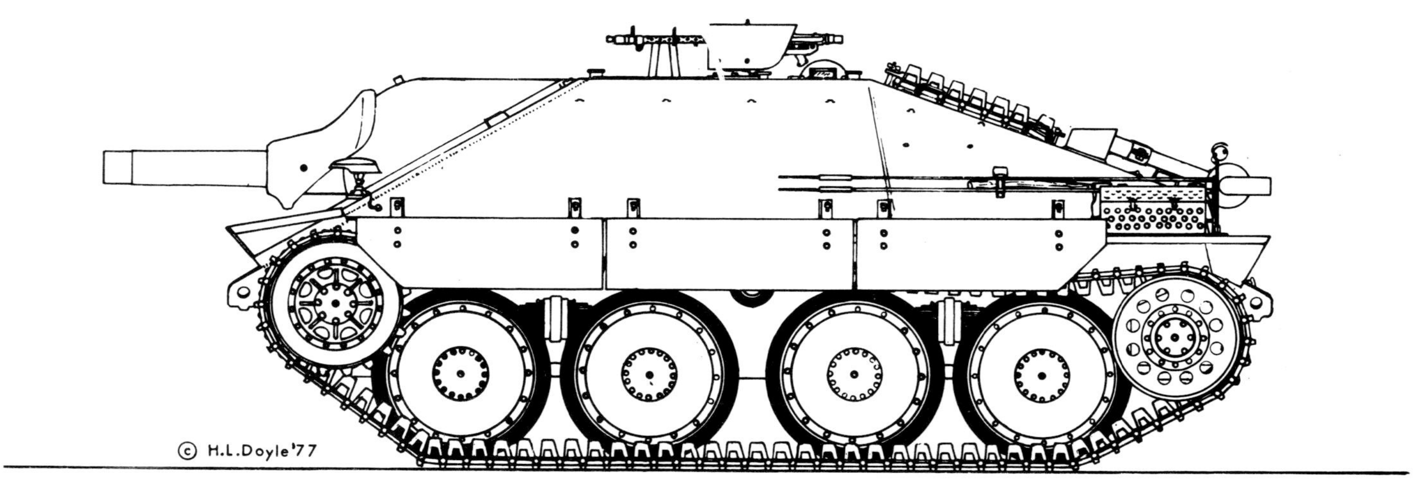

Swiss G-13

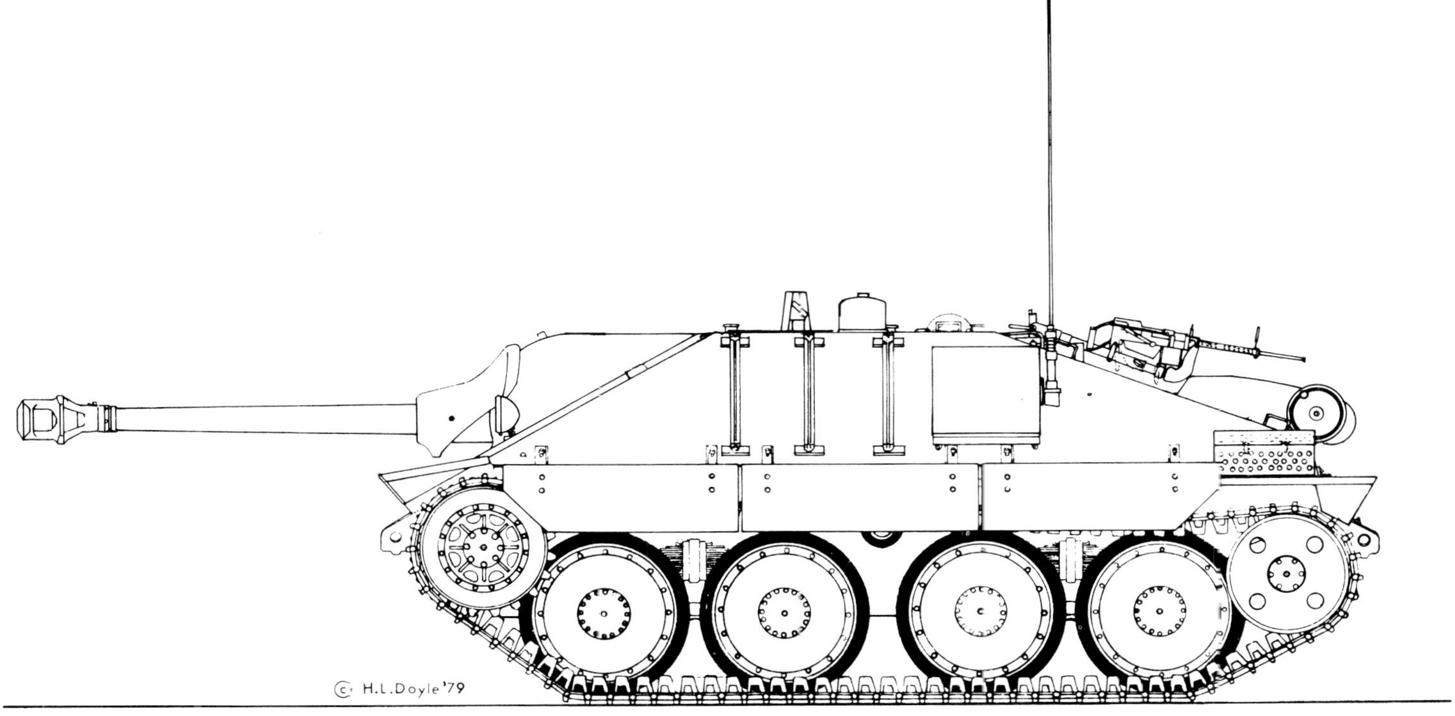

Jagdpanzer 38(d) mit 7.5 cm PAK 42/1 - Project

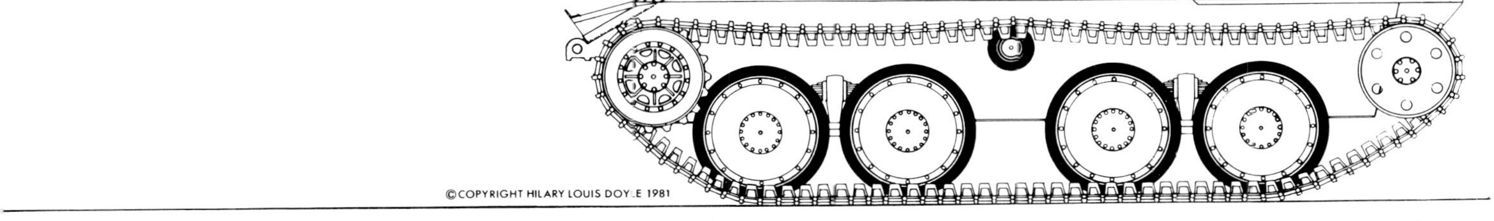

Jagdpanzer 38(d) mit 10.5 cm StuH 42/2 - Project

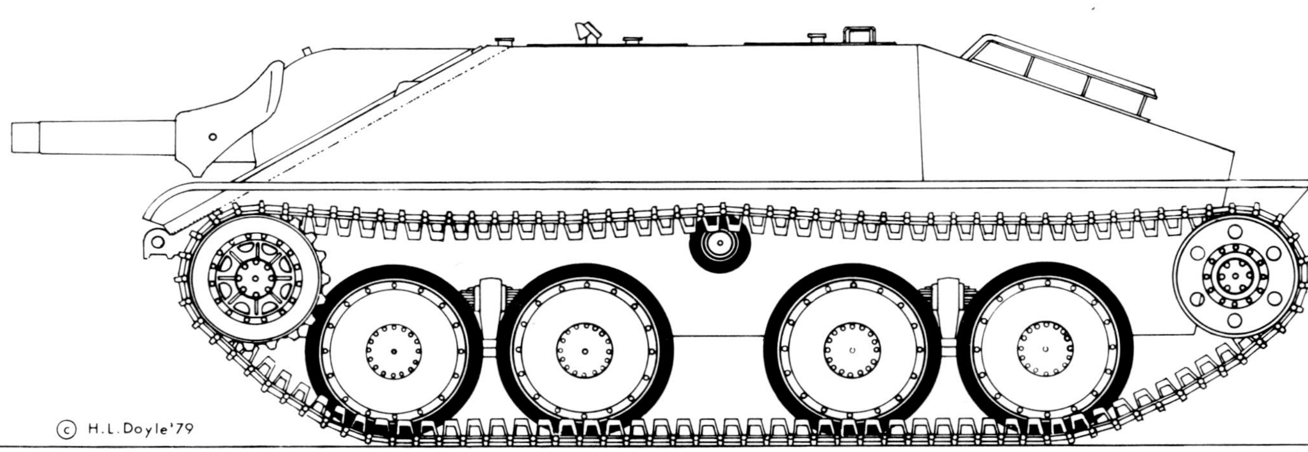

Flakpanzer Kugelblitz - Project

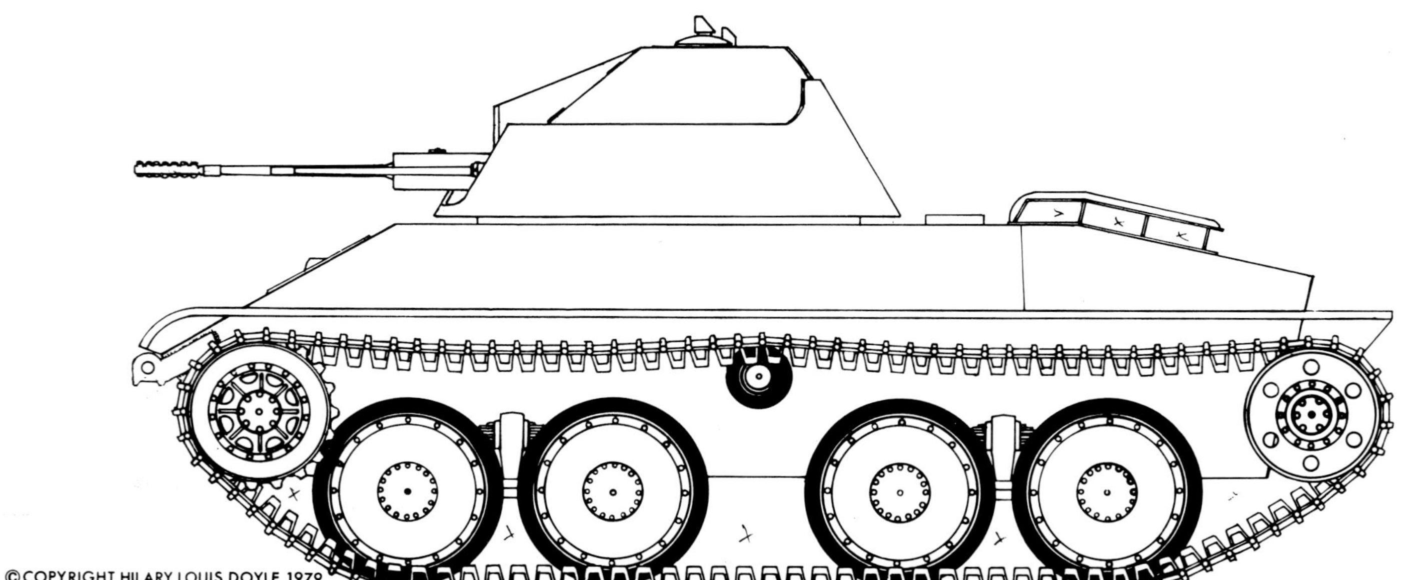

Aufklärung Panzer 38(d) mit 7.5 cm AK7 - Project

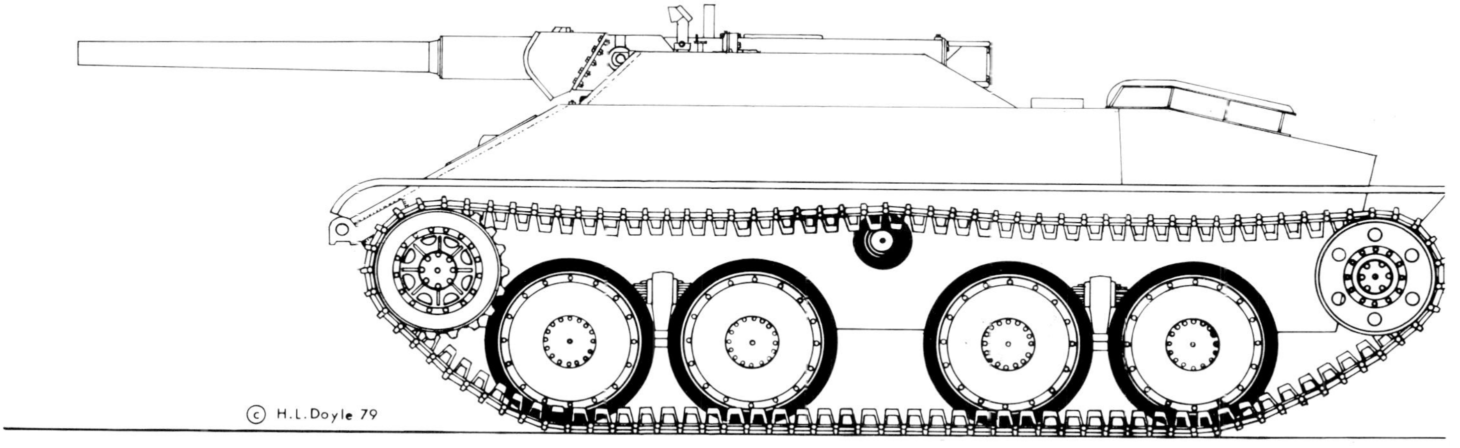

Leichter Einheitswaffenträger 38(t) mit PAK 43 (Wölfert) - Project

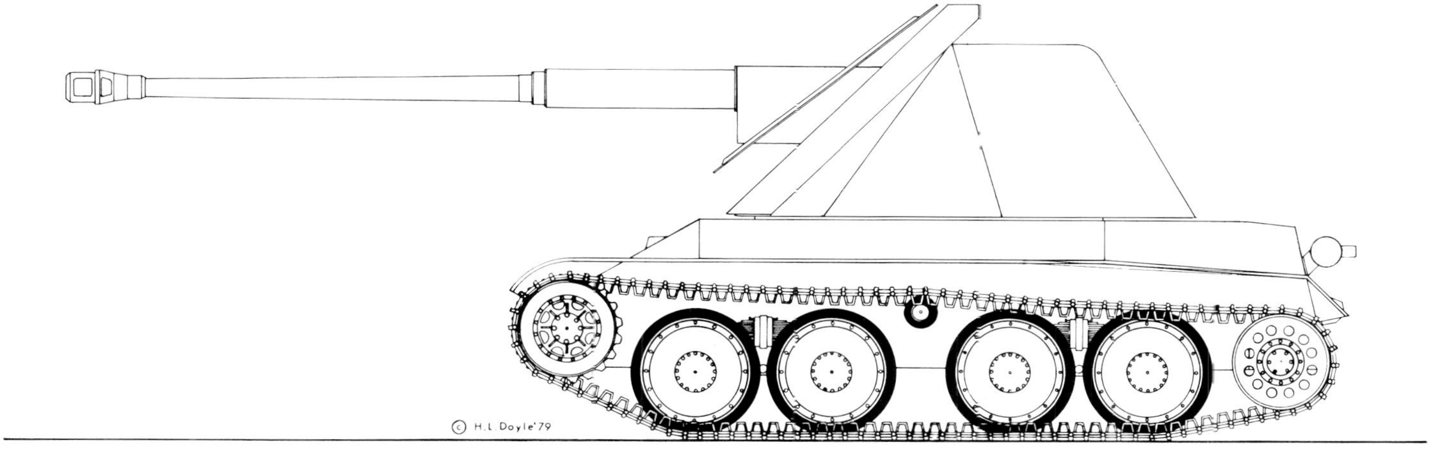

Leichter Einheitswaffenträger 38(t) mit PAK 43(Rheinmetall-Borsig) - Project

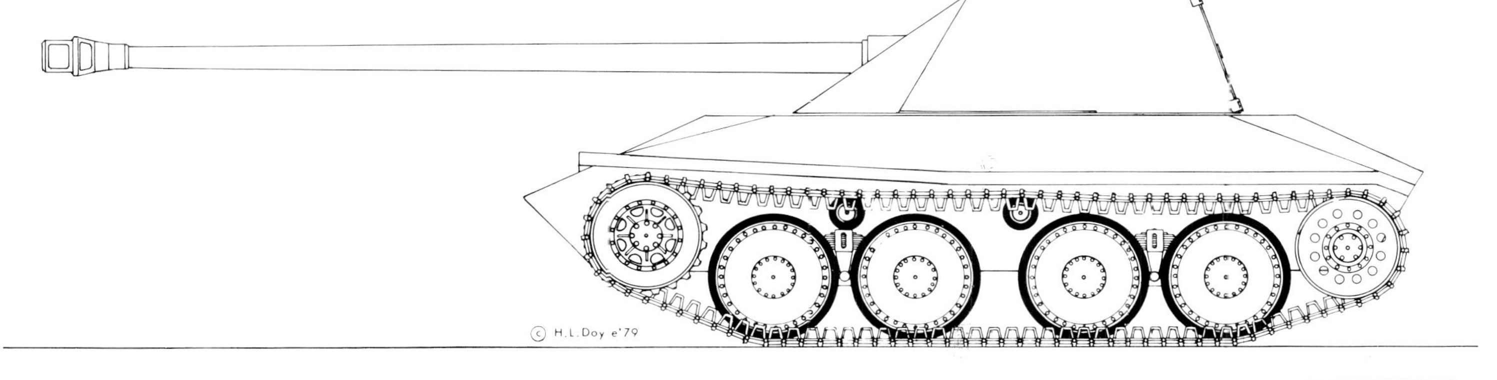

Leichter Einheitswaffenträger 38(t) mit PAK 43 18 Sfl - Project

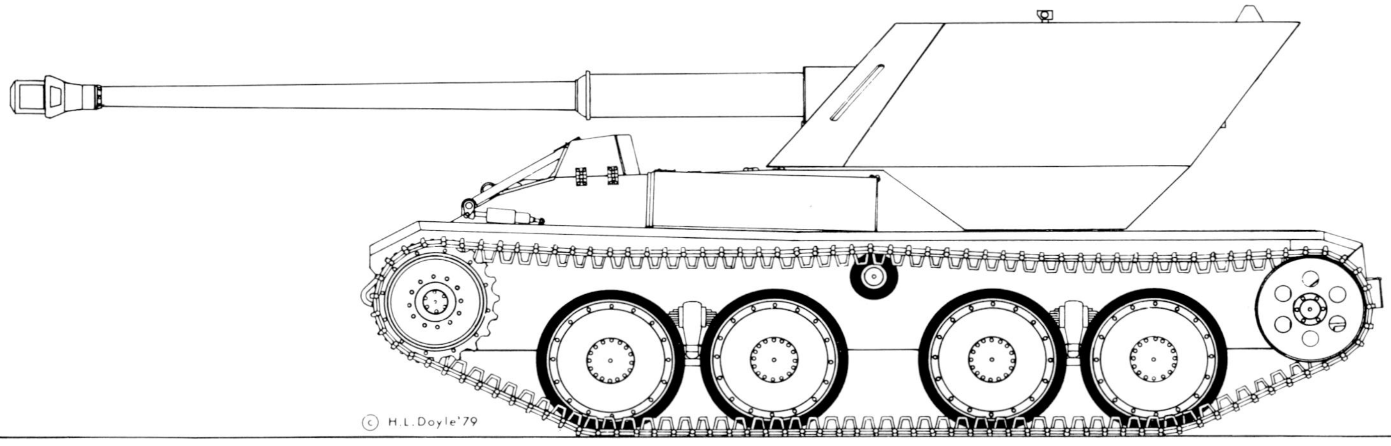

Leichter Einheitswaffenträger 38(t) mit 10.5 cm leFH18 (Wölfert) - Project

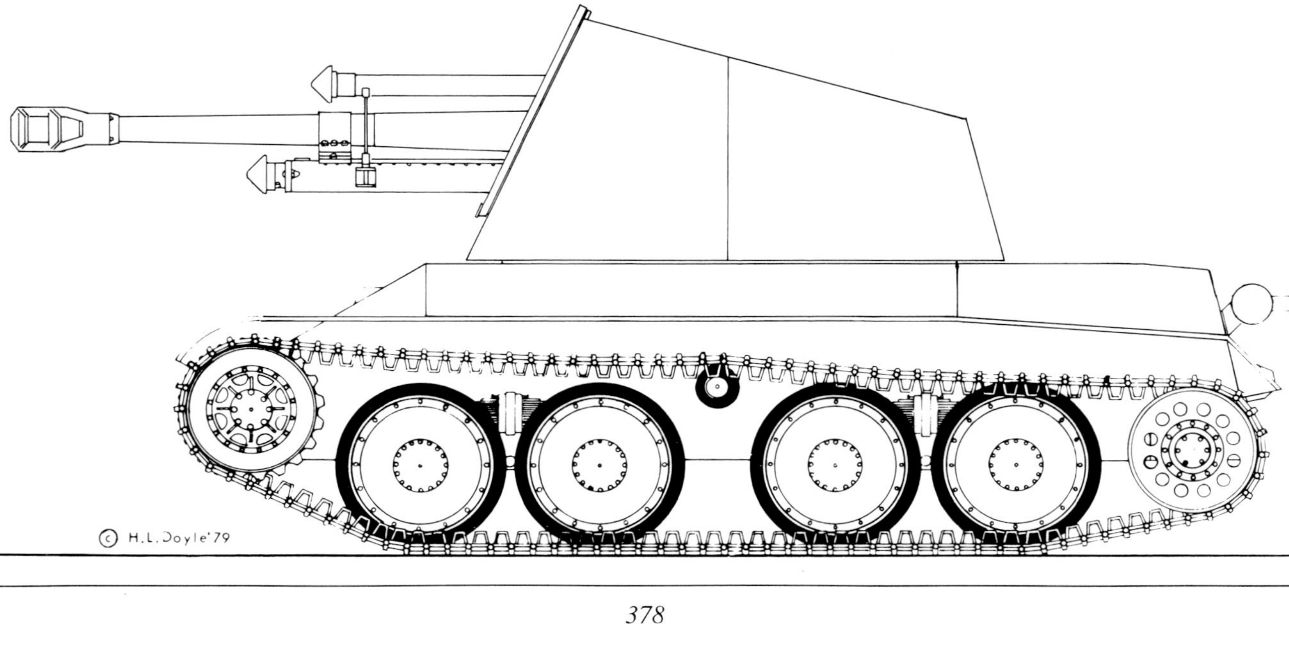

Leichter Einheitswaffenträger 38(t) mit 10.5 cm leFH18 (Rheinmetall-Borsig) - Project

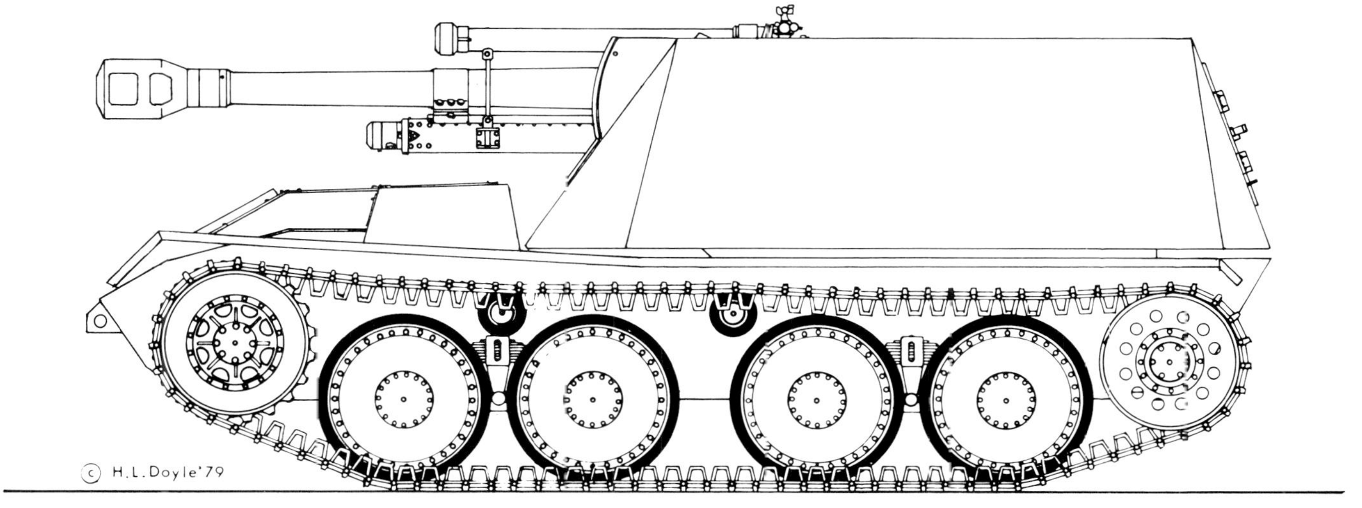

Leichter Einheitswaffenträger 38(t) mit 10.5 cm leFH18 19 Sfl - Project

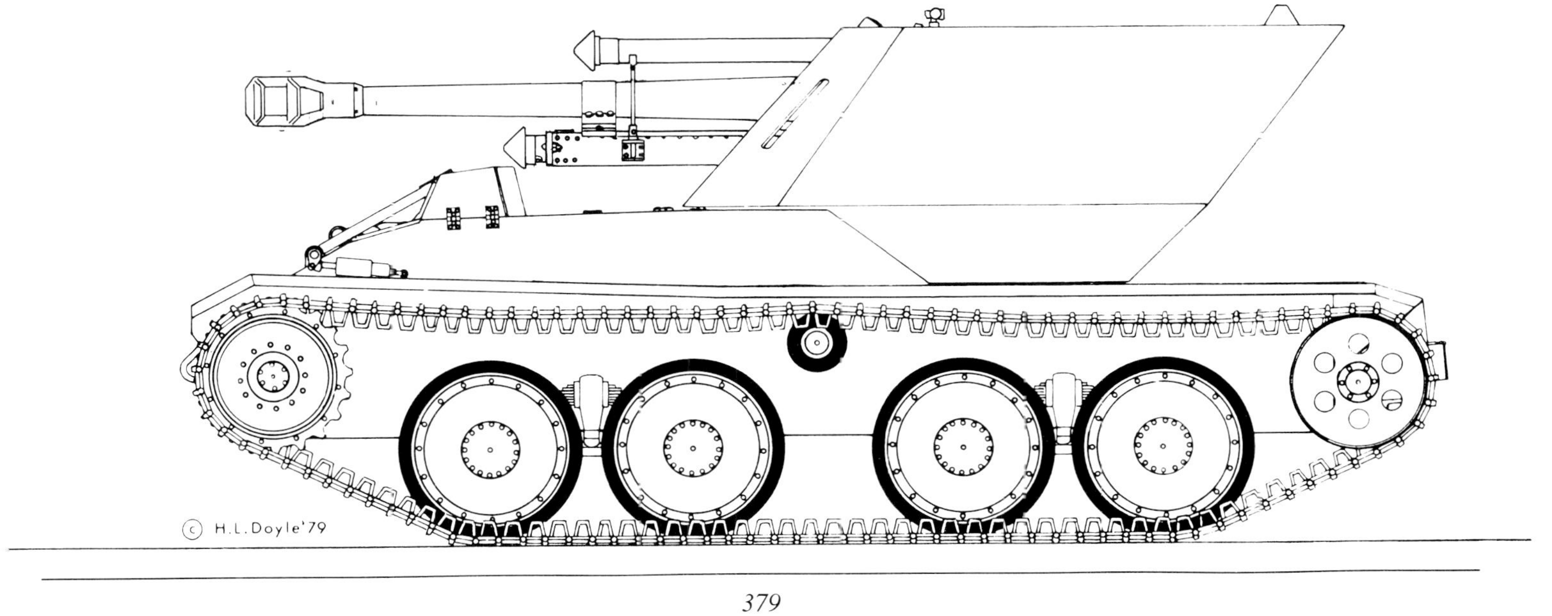

Mittlerer Einheitswaffenträger 38(t) mit 10.5 cm leFH18 (Rheinmetall-Borsig) - Project

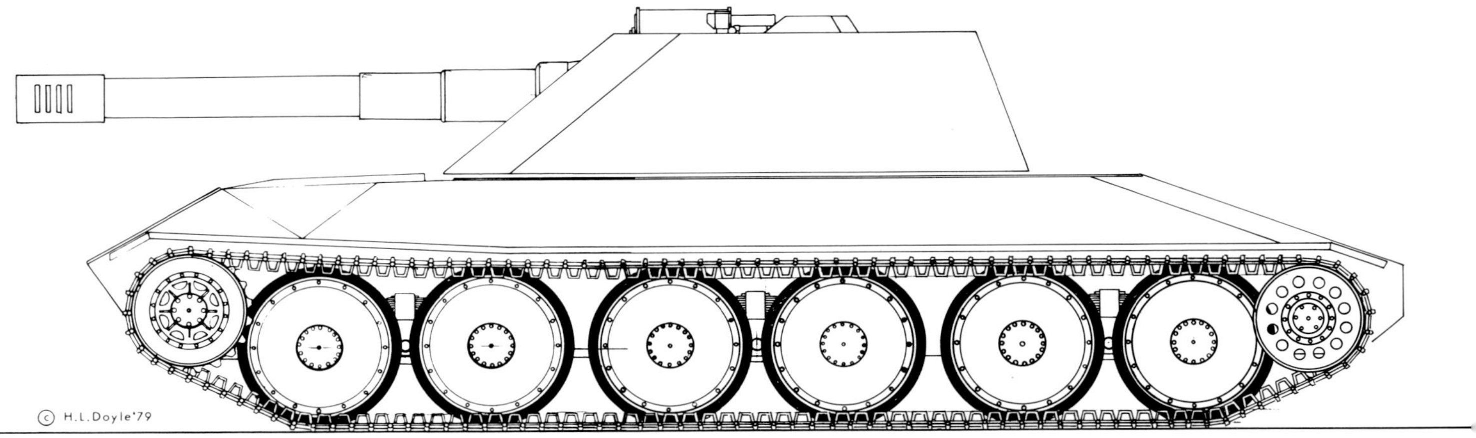

Mittlerer Einheitswaffenträger 38(t) mit 12.8 cm K/81/3 - Project

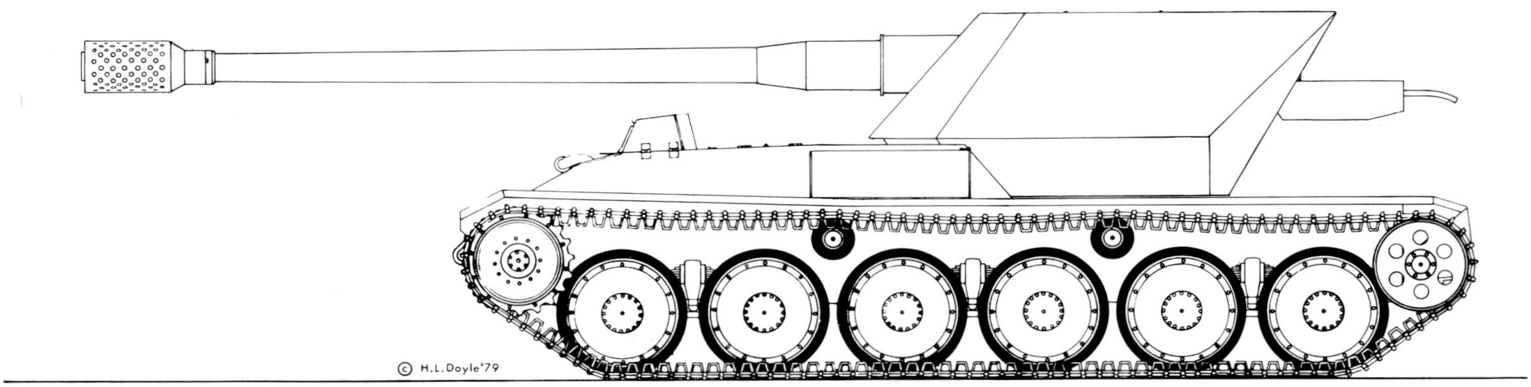

Škoda 105 mm gun carrier - Project

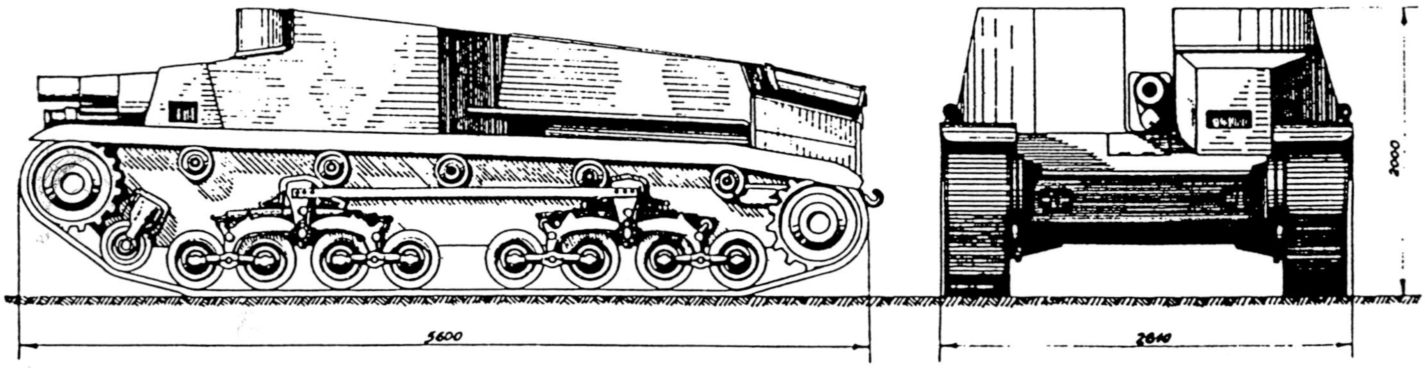

Škoda Medium Tank T-25 - Project

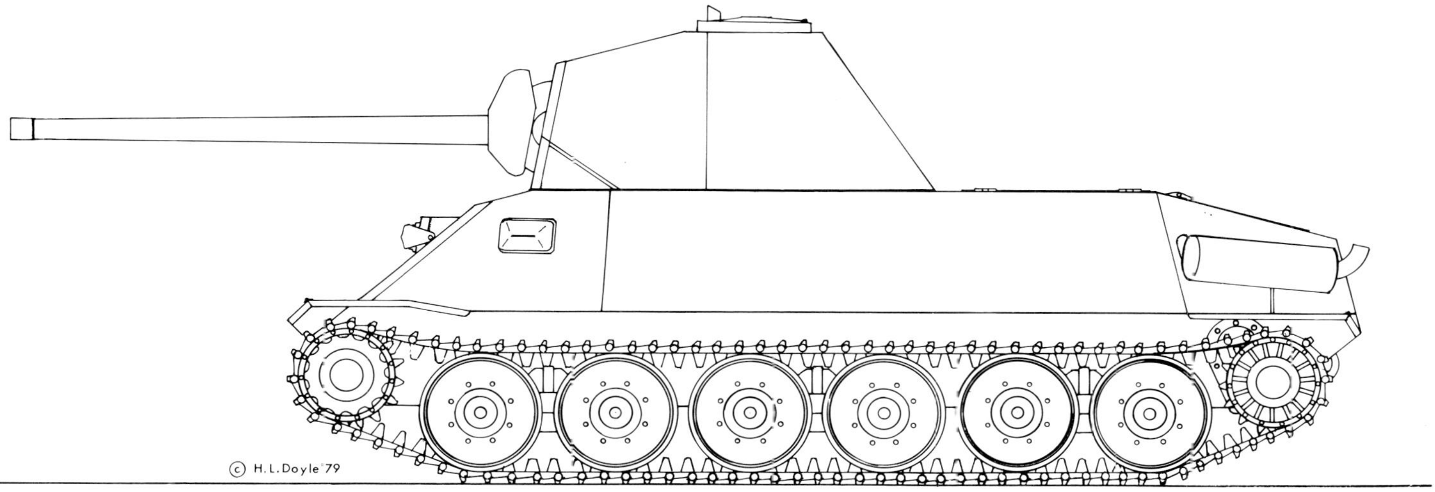

Škoda ŠK-13 Dampfschlepper (Steam Tractor) - Prototype

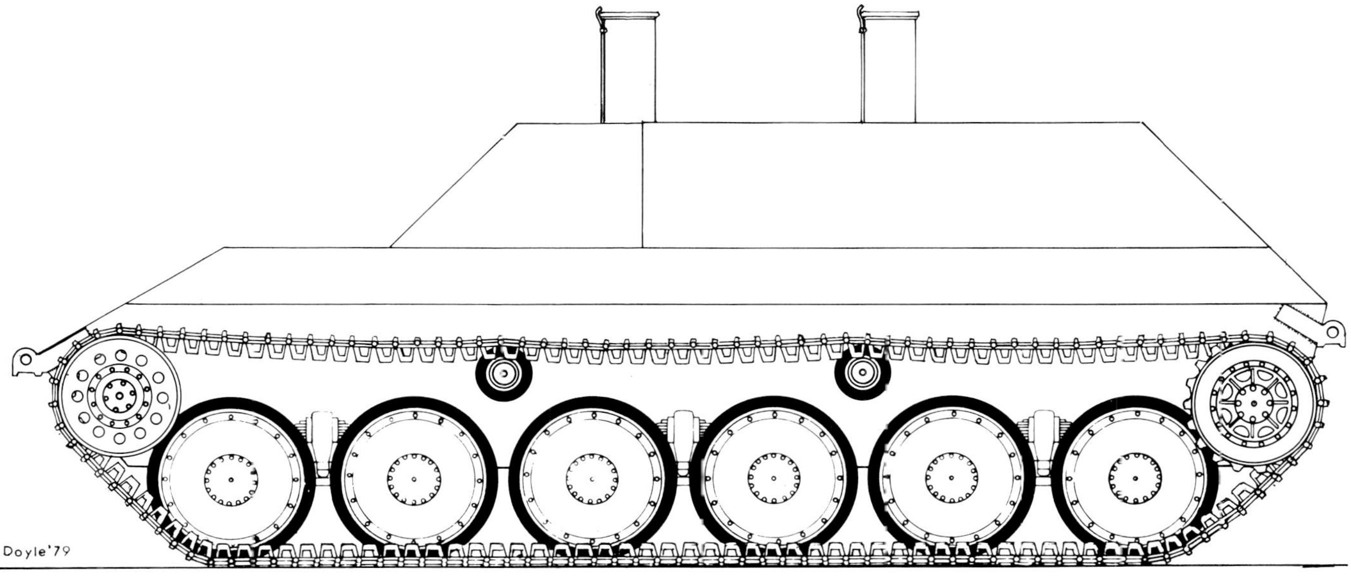

BIBLIOGRAPHY

Axworthy Mark, Scafes Cornel, Craciunoiu Christian"*Third Axis Fourth Ally*" Arms and Armour Press, London 1995

Carell Paul *"Hitler Moves East 1941-1943"* Ballantine Books, New York 1964

Department of History, United States Military Academy West Point *"The Second World War: Europe and the Mediterranean"* Avery Publishing Group, New Jersey 1989

Chamberlain Peter, Doyle Hilary *"Encyclopedia of German Tanks of World War Two"* Arms and Armour Press, London 1978

Doyle L. Hilary, Kliment Charles K. *"Czechoslovak Armoured Fighting Vehicles 1918 - 1945"* Argus Books Ltd., Watford 1979

Edwards Roger *"Panzer, a Revolution in Warfare, 1939-1945"* Arms and Armour Press, London 1989

Francev Vladimír *"Tanky, obrněná auta, obrněné vlaky a drezíny"* (Tanks, Armored Cars, Armored Trains and Draisines) Ars-Arm, Praha 1993

Francev Vladimír, Kliment Charles K. *"Škoda LT vz.35"* MBI, Praha 1996

Handbook on German Military Forces War Department Technical Manual TM-E30-451, 1945

Holub Ota *"Československé tanky a tankisté"* (Czechoslovak Tanks and Tankers) Naše Vojsko, Praha 1980

Jentz Tom *"Panzer Truppen"* (Armored Units) Schiffer Publishing Ltd., Atglen, PA 1996

Karlický Vladimír *"Československé dělostřelecké zbraně"* (Czechoslovak Artillery Weapons) Naše Vojsko, Praha 1975

Klíma Jan et al. *"Československý vojenský atlas"* (Czechoslovak Military Atlas) Naše Vojsko, Praha 1965

Kliment Charles K. *" Armáda Slovenského Státu 1939-1944"* (The Army of the Slovak State 1939-1944) Mustang, Plzeň 1996

Kuba Adolf, Spremo Milan *"Atlas našich automobilů 1929 - 1936"* (The Survey of Our Automobiles 1929-1936) Nakladatelství dopravy a spojů, Praha 1989

Kurowski Franz *"Sturmartillerie"* Maximilian-Verlag, Herford und Bonn, 1965

Macksey Kenneth *"Tank versus Tank"* Salem House Publishers, Topsfield MA 1988

Němec M. *"Návraty ke svobodě"* (Returns to Liberty) Naše Vojsko, Praha 1994

Ogorkiewicz Richard M. *"Armoured Forces"* Arms and Armour Press, London 1970

Order of Battle of the German Army Military Intelligence Division, War Department, Washington DC, March 1945

Pekař J. *"Dějiny Československa"* (History of Czechoslovakia) Akropolis, Praha 1991

Peroutka Ferdinand *"Budování státu"* (Building of the State) Lidové Noviny, Praha 1991

Procházka Zdeněk et al. *"Vojenské dějiny Československa"* (Military History of Czechoslovakia) Díl III (1918-1939), Díl IV (1939-1945), Naše Vojsko, Praha 1988

Rašla Anton *"Neporazená armáda"* (Undefeated Army) Obzor, Bratislava 1969

Rosenkranz Karel *"Osobní a nákladní automobily Tatra 1898-1972"* (Passenger Cars and Trucks of Tatra 1898-1972) Tatra, Kopřivnice 1972

Šáda Miroslav *"Československé ruční palné zbraně a kulomety"* (Czechoslovak Handguns and Machine Guns) Naše Vojsko, Praha 1971

Sander Rudolf *"Organizační a dislokační vývoj Československé armády v letech 1918 - 1939"* (Development of the Organization and Dislocation of the Czechoslovak Army in the Years 1918-1939) Sborník archivních prací, Panorama, Praha 1985

Sawodny Wolfgang *"German Armored Trains in World War II"* Schiffer Publishing Ltd., Chester, PA 1989

Scheibert Horst *"Panzerkampfwagen Škoda 35(t)"* Schiffer Military/Aviation History, Atglen, Pennsylvania 1994

Scheibert Horst, Wagener Carl *"Die Deutsche Panzertruppe"* (German Armored Units) Podzun Verlag, Bad Nauheim 1966

Smith Joseph E. *"Small Arms of the World"* Stackpole Books, Harrisburg, PA 1973

Spielberger Walter J. *"Die Panzewagen 35(t) und 38(t) und Ihre Abarten"* (35[t] and 38[t] Tanks and Their Modifications) Motorbuch Verlag, Stuttgart 1980

Spielberger Walter J., Doyle Hilary L., Jentz Tom *"Kleine Jagdpanzer"* (The Small Tank Hunters) Motorbuch Verlag, Stuttgart 1994

School of Tank Technology, Chertsey, Surrey - Technical Reports
A99 "8-ton Tank (PRAGA - TNH-P)" June 13, 1939
Preliminary no.4 *"Self-Propelled Mounting for 4.7 cm A/Tk.Gun on PzKpfw IB Chassis"* August 28, 1942
Preliminary no.20 *"PzKpfw 38(t) S.P.Mounting for 7.62 cm PAK 36(r) Gun"* November 1943
DTD No.3056 *"7.5 cm PAK 40/3 on Pz.Jäg.38(t) Sd.Kfz.138"* 1943
DTD No.3102 *"Pz.Jäg. 38 für 7.5 cm PAK 39 (L.48)"* April 1945

Tomášek Dušan *"Denik druhé republiky"* (Diary of the Second Republic) Naše Vojsko, Praha 1988

Zorach Jonathan *"The Czechoslovak Army 1918 - 1938"* Faculty of Political Science, Columbia University 1975

Magazines

Atom
AFV News
Historie a Plastikové Modelářství
Historie a Vojenství
Slovenské Vojsko

Archives

ČKD Company Archive, Praha, Czech Republic
Škoda Company Archive, Praha, Czech Republic
Military Museum, Praha, Czech Republic
Military Historical Institute, Praha, Czech Republic
National Archives, Washington, DC, USA
Bundesarchiv, Koblenz, Germany

The Spielberger German Armor & Military Vehicles Series

Four volumes in the classic series by reknowned German panzer historian Walter Spielberger are now available in nev English editions. Known for his emphasis on detail, Spielberger chronicles each production variation and later modifications. Line drawings by Hilary Doyle complement the discussion of each model type.

Size: 8 1/2" x 11" 288 pages hard cover
over 460 photographs
ISBN: 0-88740-397-2 $39.95

Size: 8 1/2" x 11" 256 pages hard cover
over 240 photographs
ISBN: 0-88740-398-0 $39.95

Size: 8 1/2" x 11" 168 pages hard cover
over 200 photographs
ISBN: 0-88740-448-0 $29.95

Size: 8 1/2" x 11" 168 pages hard cover
over 200 photographs
ISBN: 0-88740-515-0 $29.95